MW01503315

The Caring Motivation

An Integrated Theory

OFRA MAYSELESS

OXFORD
UNIVERSITY PRESS

OXFORD
UNIVERSITY PRESS

Oxford University Press is a department of the University of Oxford. It furthers
the University's objective of excellence in research, scholarship, and education
by publishing worldwide.Oxford is a registered trade mark of Oxford University
Press in the UK and certain other countries.

Published in the United States of America by Oxford University Press
198 Madison Avenue, New York, NY 10016, United States of America.

© Oxford University Press 2016

First Edition published in 2016

Library of Congress Cataloging-in-Publication Data
Names: Mayseless, Ofra, 1953– author.
Title: The caring motivation : an integrated theory / Ofra Mayseless.
Description: Oxford ; NewYork : Oxford University Press, [2016] | Includes
bibliographical references and index.
Identifiers: LCCN 2015036627 | ISBN 9780199913619
Subjects: LCSH: Caring. | Motivation (Psychology)
Classification: LCC BJ1475 .M4285 2016 | DDC 177/.7—dc23
LC record available at http://lccn.loc.gov/2015036627

1 3 5 7 9 8 6 4 2

Printed by Sheridan, USA

I would like to dedicate this book to the force of life that pulsates in our world and to our creation and creativity; for me, this has a deep and fresh emerald color, like the budding leaves in spring, which then become lush and plentiful.

May we unleash this capacity in our lives!

CONTENTS

ACKNOWLEDGMENTS

My writing journey was embedded within two parallel landscapes: nature and the sphere of ideas. I started writing this book at the end of the summer of 2009 in a green, lovely rural area in France (Auvergne), with hills and green forests. I continued working on the book the following summer, also in France, in an old but renovated house overlooking a magnificent, awe-inspiring valley with a river. A variety of landscapes followed—a cottage in a mountain overlooking the Sea of Galilee, a New Jersey beach, and finally my own home with a garden on Mount Carmel in Israel, overlooking the Mediterranean Sea. Nature was therefore an indispensable aid to my capacity to breathe and think clearly and be creative, and I feel very thankful for that.

The other sphere in which I lived while writing this book is the sphere of ideas. The Internet—with its infinite options for reaching and learning of ideas, research, thoughts, and the insights of others—was, for my inquisitive spirit, like an infinite, magical candy world, full with intellectual sweets where anything is possible; if you have a question or wonder about something and know how to search for it, you will find it, because people's wisdom, ingenuity, and creativity are extraordinary and abundant. This book covers very broad and different domains of thought and research. For each chapter I needed to acquaint myself with new concepts and distinct research traditions in order to gain the understanding and insights I needed. This was an amazing journey; not easy but stupendous during which I met—intellectually and spiritually—many wise, knowledgeable, creative scholars and found many answers to the riddles that preoccupied me. I feel deeply thankful for their wonderful and remarkable work and talent.

The seeds of this book grew and developed to become the current volume through a large number of conversations, discussions, and exchanges with many people—colleagues, friends, and students—and I would like to thank them here for their support, good advice, and the fruitful dialogues that often helped me to uncover and articulate my insights or sent me on a new search to find answers. These are Anat Scher, Hadas Wiseman, Lily Orland-Barak, Miri Scharf, and Ruth

Sharabany, my close colleagues and friends; Bracha Oren Simon, Amir Freimann, and Iris Wolberg, my friends and companions in my spiritual path; Pninit Russo-Netzer and Sofi Barzilai, former students and spiritual companions; and Osnat Beery Grinspan—my beloved and precious sister whose help and encouragement were always there for me whenever I needed.

Throughout this process I had a special and unique personal connection with Ouri—my deceased son, soul mate, and guide—who was with me to show me the way and encourage me whenever I needed him. I was also warmly supported by my family: my husband, Meir; my son, Oded; his wife, Idit; little Daniel, a new addition to the family who brought us joy and delight; and my daughter, Naama, who also read and commented on the book and gave me great and most valuable advice and help. Their reassurance, interest, encouragement, and support have been very precious and extremely significant to me. My surging love and gratitude are extended to them.

I also want to thank Tamar Garden, a young, talented, and enthusiastic woman who helped me throughout those years by researching and summarizing, reading my drafts, commenting and correcting them, and many other editing needs. Her skilled professional help and amiable personality proved to be a wonderful and indispensable gift. Finally I want to thank Nimrod Chiat, my copy editor, who skillfully helped me convey my ideas and insights in a manner that I hope is precise, faithful to what I wanted to convey, and clear.

I have been studying care and caregiving for a large part of my academic career, first in parenting and then in leadership, teaching, and mentoring. The first insights regarding caring as a broad motivational system evolved some 14 years ago as part of my interest in attachment theory. While staying in beautiful Vancouver on sabbatical at Simon Fraser University, I even wrote a paper summarizing and discussing my thoughts but never published it. In retrospect this paper, in the format of a chapter, included major insights that are articulated in this book; but the paper was also quite basic and its claims were not substantiated by research. This book is therefore a culmination of my long interest in this extraordinary aspect of human experience and reflects my attempts to understand it and conceptualize it. As a person, the need to deeply understand things is a core and defining facet of my spirit, and caring with its multitude emanations has profoundly intrigued me. In going over the final draft of this book I feel very pleased and content that I was able to marshal the vast literature on caring that is discussed here and to arrive at answers that satisfied my curiosity and offer a comprehensive and hopefully clear account of this amazing and very special facet of human experience. So my last thanks are due to the guiding and loving spirits with whom I wrestle, through whose care I flourish, and whom I will join when my time comes.

The Caring Motivation

1

Introduction

The Green Mile, a motion picture adapted by Frank Darabont from the 1996 novel by Stephen King, takes place in 1935 at the Louisiana State Penitentiary's death row. Within this isolated and inhumane setting, Eduard "Del" Delacroix, one of the prisoners, adopts a stray mouse. He tames the animal, names him Mr. Jingles, and teaches him to roll an empty spool across the floor. The love, tenderness, and care he offers to this mouse and the happiness and meaning Mr. Jingles gives to his life are special and remarkable.

Both life and fiction offer many stories of extraordinary feats of love and care as well as outstanding acts of altruism and heroism, but I have chosen to start with what might appear to be an unusual account of caring in order to demonstrate the innate and inexorable human need to care, even under the most extreme circumstances.

Caring as an emotion, a bond, and a behavioral manifestation is all around us. It is observed in mothers playing with their toddlers, fathers tending to their infants, psychotherapists offering their clients understanding and acceptance, mentors empowering their protégées, spouses cheering up their partners, friends consoling one another, drivers stopping to pick up hitchhikers, and teachers encouraging their students.

All these phenomena may be perceived as forms of care, but what are their origins? Are they innate, biologically driven, and natural, or are they learned and mostly governed by social norms and expectations? Are they mostly reactions to the needs of others, or do individuals actively and intrinsically look for opportunities to help others and care for them? Is care an emotion, a cognition, or a form of behavior? This book seeks to answer these questions, among many others, and to discuss and unravel our universal motivation to care, tend, provide, empower, and nurture.

In discussing this book with colleagues and friends, I am often asked "but you actually mean—love, don't you?" Not necessarily. Love is a compound and multifaceted word. It represents very different kinds of strong and positive emotional and motivational relations but, more importantly, it also often indicates the *receiving* end of a close relationship—the need to *receive* care, recognition, acceptance, company, praise, or help. In this book I focus on the *giving* end of such relations and its unique characteristics. Hence the term *love*, with its composite multilayered meanings, does not fit here and can actually lead to confusion and ambiguity.

Caring has been discussed in very diverse domains, most often in regard to its manifestations. For example, the developmental literature discusses the caregiving that parents provide to their children, including their parenting practices, parenting styles, and parenting faults and failures. Gerontologists discuss the caregiving provided by children to their elderly or sick parents; scholars of marital relations study caregiving between spouses in regular times and times of trouble; social psychologists discuss caring in the context of prosocial behavior and altruism, often focusing on understanding the care provided to strangers; while organizational psychologists discuss it in the context of the "helping professions," such as nursing and social work, and as expressed in organizational citizenship behaviors. This book builds on this extant and significant literature and seeks to go beyond it to present a general conceptual model of caring as a fundamental and encompassing human motivation.

Caring as motivation

Specifically I want to present and discuss the *motivation* to care, tend, nurture, and help other entities grow, thrive, heal, and develop. I contend that this motivation is a *fundamental human motivation*. In fact, it is probably a fundamental motivation in other species as well. In stating that it is a *motivation* I mean that people do not just react with empathy and care when the situation demands it but are also intrinsically motivated to actively and purposefully look for opportunities, situations, and relationships in which they can provide care and nurturance and experience the intrinsic satisfaction involved in realizing that another "entity" or "object" has benefited from their care (e.g., they have made someone happy or have managed to make the environment less polluted). The motivation to *give* or provide care is thus distinct from the motivation to *receive* care, although there are cases in which an individual will both receive and give care within the same relational context (e.g., marital relations).

Caring as fundamental

In stating that caring is *fundamental*, I mean to say that it is a core motivation that is universal. It is also fundamental in two other ways. Along with others (e.g., Bowlby, 1969/1982), I contend that our survival as a species would be strongly compromised without it. In that sense, it is as fundamental as hunger or thirst, though less pressing. Without someone to care for us as infants, we would not survive (Bowlby, 1969/1982). But even later, as we grow up and become more self-sufficient, we would probably not last for long—physically, psychologically, or spiritually—if we had no one to rely on. Caring is like the air we breathe—we cannot live and survive without it, but it is often invisible and unacknowledged except when it is lacking. The motivation to care is also fundamental in a third sense: it often provides essential meaning to the lives of individuals. Very few individuals live without a meaningful caring relation toward an "entity," such as person, pet, garden, private collection, or worthy cause. In fact, caring is one of the frequent avenue to find meaning in our lives.

Caring as manifested in diverse domains

I further contend that this is a core motivation with a very diverse set of possible manifestations and targets. These include the caring of parents for their children (which has come to represent the prototypical type of care) (Hrdy, 2009), the caring of children for their parents, the caring and support of romantic partners for each other, caring among friends, prosocial behaviors, kind deeds for strangers, altruism, charity, caring for pets, caring for plants, caring for inanimate objects (such as a stamp collection), as well as caring for the environment. My major claim is that all of these manifestations ensue from and represent this core motivation. All of these expressions are conceived as manifestations of the same overarching caring motivational system.

Individual differences

I am often confronted by people who ask "but what about mean people who don't care about anyone or anything? How come there is so much evil in the world?" It is interesting that such a question normally pops up regarding this "positive" motivation, as if asserting that *having a motivation* to "do good" automatically means that everyone *is* good and is *always* good. However, alongside the fundamental caring motivation we also experience a host of other urges and needs, which interact with caring in affecting our conduct and behavior. Furthermore, as with other human motivations (e.g., hunger or the need to achieve), there are also individual differences in the motivation to care. The antecedents of these individual differences may be diverse and include hereditary as well as environmental and contextual factors. That is, the existence of individual differences means that although all of us have an innate caring motivation, some individuals will have a strong motivation to care; will deliberately, actively, and passionately look for opportunities to care; and will invest substantial effort, time, and resources in caring while others may be reluctant to care even when presented with the opportunity to do so. We can further expect individual differences in this motivation to be reflected in the preferred breadth or scope of caregiving. Specifically, people care in many *different ways* (styles) (i.e., sensitively as opposed to in a domineering way) and show personal preferences to care for *different kinds of recipients* (plants, children, old people, dogs, the environment) and in *different kinds of provisions* (physical care, emotional care, teaching).

Finally, just as other fundamental motivations (e.g., hunger) may go awry (e.g., people starve themselves to death or overeat in a way that jeopardizes their health), individuals may harm and offend instead of caring or care in a way that endangers their own health and well-being.

Why is this book necessary?

The insistence on defining caring as a fundamental motivation may look trivial, but it is not. Indeed, as I demonstrate in this book, it is highly significant that despite being all around us, caring has actually been overlooked and has only recently (e.g., Taylor, 2002) been recognized as a motivation despite being recognized as practice. An illustration of this neglect can be seen in Maslow's (1943, 1970) famous hierarchy of universal human needs. Basing his model on at least three central and pivotal psychological doctrines—psychoanalytic, behavioral, and humanist—Maslow overlooked this motivation almost completely, and his hierarchy offered no room for caring and tending. He did incorporate social aspects related to relationships—such as the need for affection, love, and belongingness (the *receiving* end of relationships), as well as the need for esteem—but nothing about caring as a motivation. Although caring motives might be subsumed under the need for self-actualization, since they are certainly connected to people's sense of life having meaning and of self-fulfillment (Wong & Fry, 1998), Maslow did not accord them a special place or name them as such in his list of self-actualizing endeavors. This neglect is not incidental and reflects the prevailing discounting attitude toward caring as a motivation at the time. Furthermore, because caring has mostly been studied and examined as a practice, its study has been tied to specific manifestations and hence has been dispersed among a very large number of research traditions and domains with little communication among them. Consequently the similarity in core processes at the biological, psychological, and cultural levels has not been recognized enough and the prevalence and pervasiveness of the caring motivation, including interrelations among its multifaceted manifestations, frequently went unnoticed. This book, therefore, is ultimately about rectifying this lacuna and claiming a center-stage role for caring as a fundamental, multifaceted, comprehensive, and encompassing human motivation. Such a view can uncover a large number of insights about human conduct, individual and gender differences, and the organization of society, to name just a few of the ramifications. Furthermore such a view opens up new and exciting domains of research while also highlighting a large number of applied implications.

The organization of this book

This book is organized into four major parts. The first part presents conceptual frameworks and theories that discuss the origin and nature of the motivation to care. In reviewing the extant theoretical models that relate to caring as a motivation, I try to give voice to the scholars who have developed and suggested these models or theories, often using their own words and terms to acquaint the reader with the way in which these scholars have thought about these issues. The second part discusses the scope and content of this motivation—what it includes. Here I present empirical research with a variety of cared-for "entities" (e.g., offspring, romantic partners, friends, strangers, nonhuman entities) as well as review findings from several research traditions—such as altruism, volunteering, and mentoring—and a variety of contexts—such as education, the workplace, and leadership. Together these underscore the diverse ways in which caring is expressed. The third part of the book discusses the development of caring as part of a normative developmental trajectory and the nature and antecedents of individual differences in the motivation to care, as well as gender differences in caring.

The fourth part builds on the evidence presented and discussed in previous sections and presents my own take on the caring motivation as a fundamental, multifaceted, comprehensive, and encompassing human motivation, discussing its implications. In this part a conceptual model of the caring motivation is presented. In it caring is depicted as a caring *motivational system* that is innate, fundamental, and biologically based and is encompassing, sophisticated, complex, and flexible. This part describes what this system includes: its major "components" and ways of operation, its common core, and its diversity; this part also provides a comprehensive description of ultimate causes (the "what for" question) and proximate causes (the "how it operates" question). Finally, I discuss the implications of this model for our view of human nature and present research and applied implications. At the end I also present my personal view (which, unlike the rest of the book, is not scientifically based), whereby I see caring as a central manifestation of our divine and innate spiritual core.

Each of the four parts begins with an introduction and overview and ends with a conclusion. The conclusion summarizes and ties together the different perspectives and literatures discussed in that part, also highlighting central insights extracted from the chapters. In the last part (Part IV), such a conclusion is accorded a separate chapter (titled "Summary and major contributions"), which includes a general summary of the tenets of this book as well as a discussion of its main unique contributions. Similar concluding remarks are also presented at the end of each chapter.

I invite you to enter this volume with an open mind and an inquisitive soul and to judge for yourself how caring vibrates all around us, how vast are its expressions and manifestations, and how central it is in our nature.

CONCEPTUAL FRAMEWORKS REGARDING CARING

Part I Introduction

Several conceptual models have discussed relational constructs closely related to caring, arguing that they occupy a central and significant role in human experience. Most of these are highly inclusive and do not discriminate between diverse forms of connectedness. Specifically, although they often involve caring in some form, they do not discuss it in particular. What follows is a brief overview of these models so that the reader can get a general sense of the sorts of caring-related constructs that have been introduced and discussed as parts of larger constructs such as relatedness, communal sharing, and warmth.

Several scholars have discussed relational constructs along with other aspects as central to human functioning and experience. Bakan (1966), for example, has discussed themes of communion (a focus on others and on forming connections) and agency (a focus on self and on forming separations), which are both seen as necessary for optimal well-being. Similarly, McClelland (1980) has discussed motives for achievement and affiliation and McAdams (1980, 1982) has considered two major motivations: personal power (e.g., achieving impact, fame, or recognition) and interpersonal intimacy. McAdams (e.g., McAdams, Hoffman, Day, & Mansfield, 2006) includes love and friendship, as well as helping others, as part of the intimacy motivation, but does not differentiate between general connectedness and caring. Mills and Clark (1982) refer to two central categories of relationships, communal and exchange, in which the former involves, among other things, both mutual responsiveness and care.

Blatt and others (Blatt, 2008; Guisinger & Blatt, 1994) have suggested a model of human development that includes a transactional and dialectical process in which individuality and relatedness are considered as two central and interconnected components. Relatedness was presumed to comprise a large number of interpersonal motives and experiences, including intimacy, mutuality, cooperation, attachment, and caring for others. Yet as in other conceptions, caring was not considered as a motive in and of itself. Similarly, Fiske (1992) has proposed an elaborate theory arguing that people are fundamentally sociable and organize their social lives in terms of their relations with other people. He postulated four relational models, one of which was communal sharing, which includes being kind and altruistic and caring for significant others. Finally, Baumeister and Leary (1995) postulated a need to form and maintain strong and stable interpersonal relationships, which they termed *the need to belong*. As part of fulfilling this need, people also provide care and comfort to others, but Baumeister and Leary did not address this motivation in specific terms and viewed its enactment and ramifications as part of the general need to belong. Yet as will be discussed in this book, the differentiation between caring and other relational needs or motivations is important.

And indeed a number of scholars have distinguished between different dimensions of relatedness or connectedness and discussed tending, caring, and prosocial behavior as a separate and important category in its own right. These include, for example, Weiss (1974), whose model included the social provision that he termed *opportunity for nurturance*. Similarly, Josselson (1996) suggested an intriguing model of "the space between us"—the space of relatedness—in which she identified eight dimensions, one of which is *tending and care*. Even Erikson's (1963) famous life-span developmental model included a developmental phase in midadulthood that centered on caring and caregiving. The developmental goal of this phase was termed *generativity* and involved motivation, concern, and activities geared for the nurturance, well-being, and empowerment of youth and subsequent generations. Finally, a compelling exposition of the centrality of care in human existence was provided by Shelley Taylor (2002), who built upon her innovative suggestion that women tend and befriend others under stress rather than engaging in a fight-or-flight reaction. These important conceptualizations will be discussed in other sections in the book, but I would first like to focus on six broad conceptual viewpoints/frameworks that have influenced and informed the conceptualization of caring, tending, and caregiving. These include spiritual views, evolutionary theories, empathic processes, biological, neuroscientific and genetic research, attachment theory, and feminist orientations. This choice is not random—it reflects my attempt to examine caring from several different angles and points of view and to adopt a holistic and multifaceted approach.

Spiritual Views of Caring: Caring as Divine

Psalm 86:15 *But You, O Lord, are a God full of compassion, and gracious,*
long suffering and plenteous in mercy and truth.

Jonah 4:2 *... for I knew that thou art a gracious God, and merciful, slow to*
anger, and of great kindness, and repentest thee of the evil. (King James Bible)

Although it cannot be considered a theory in the usual sense, I decided to begin
this theoretical journey with a discussion of various conceptions of caring as
divine. Western individualistic thought was long in accepting the importance
and centrality of connectedness and relatedness in human life and development
(Guisinger & Blatt, 1994; Josselson, 1996; Taylor, 2002; Gilligan, 1982). Even
when these dimensions were accepted as central, they were often conceived as
reflecting the needy side of the relationship. In contrast, the motivation to care
and to nurture was often conceived as somewhat unusual and remarkable (e.g.,
altruistic actions of people enacted on behalf of total strangers) or as something
so natural that it need not be explained (e.g., the love and devotion of mothers
to their children). Interestingly, however, caring, compassion, and kindness were
distinctly present as important possibilities in the spiritual lives of individuals as
part of their faiths and religious belief systems. A discussion of the motivation
to care would therefore be lacking if I did not refer to the spiritual realm and its
relevance to the ethos of care in human history.

Several central spiritual traditions view the divine as epitomizing love, giving, protection, forgiveness, compassion, and caring. Divinity often carries connotations of goodness, beauty, beneficence, justice, and other positive, prosocial
attributes.[1]

Benevolence was not the sole prerogative of the divine, however. Various eso-
teric and mystical schools of thought—such as the Islamic Sufis, the Christian
Gnostics, the Advaitan Hindus, and the Zen Buddhists, as well as a large number

---

[1] Monotheistic faiths also feature an equivalent cohort of negative supernormal beings and
powers, such as demons or devils, which are not conventionally referred to as divine.

of perspectives developed within new religions or contemporary spiritualities mostly as part of the New Age movement (Heelas, 1996; Hanegraaff, 1998)— further hold that all humans are in essence divine. This divine essence, which supposedly involves unconditional love and caring, was expected to be brought to the fore through spiritual practices and was conceived as the ultimate purpose of life on earth.

It could be argued that these faiths consider the motivation to care, tend, provide, and protect as a reflection of the true, authentic, and sacred nature of humans; thus, they argue, all spiritual development involves humans becoming more empathic, caring, compassionate, and giving. The following is a brief overview of these teachings in some of the traditions already mentioned: Christianity, Buddhism, Judaism (Kabbalah), and New Age spiritualities.

Christianity

In Christianity, God and Christ are depicted as offering grace and salvation from a universal condition of sin and death. According to both Catholic and Protestant doctrines, Jesus brought salvation to humankind by dying to atone for mortal sins and in particular for the original sin of Adam and Eve. By atoning and offering divine grace (an "unmerited favor" from God) to humankind, Christ allowed humans to attain salvation and partake of the divinity of God. The life of Christ taught Christians how to behave in their earthly lives—that is, with mercy, love, and compassion for others, and especially those in need.

One of the best-known stories in the New Testament is the parable of the Good Samaritan, which illustrates the exercise of human kindness, help, and caring. All in all, therefore, Christian teachings focus on the giving side of human behavior and advocate a life of love, compassion, sharing, and care: "And now abideth faith, hope, and love, even these three: but the chiefest of these is love" (1 Corinthians 13:13).

Buddhism

Buddhism is traditionally conceived as a path to salvation attained through insight into the ultimate nature of reality. It encompasses a variety of traditions, beliefs, and practices that are largely based on the teachings of Siddhartha Gautama, commonly known as the Buddha, who is assumed to have lived around 400 B.C. Adherents recognize the Buddha as an awakened teacher who shared his insights in order to help people escape from the cycle of suffering and rebirth. The Buddha's teachings provide instructions on how to understand the true nature of phenomena, end suffering, and achieve nirvana. These teachings do not discuss an ultimate entity and hence do not ascribe qualities of care to a godly figure, but they are highly related to special kinds of caring.

Some consider the Four Noble Truths as containing the essence of the Buddha's teachings. The first states that life as we know it leads to suffering (*dukkha*). Second, suffering is caused by attachments to worldly pleasures. Third, suffering ends when one is freed from desire. This is achieved by eliminating all delusion and thereby reaching a liberated state of enlightenment. The fourth truth identifies a path laid out by the Buddha to reach this liberated state (*nirvana*).

This path includes several practices, among which are cultivating the wisdom that purifies the mind, thus offering insight into the true nature of all things. This includes the practice of Buddhist ethics or morality, which comprises ethical conduct, altruism, and abstention from unwholesome deeds, thus calling upon the mental discipline required to develop mastery over one's own mind. This is done through the practice of various contemplative and meditative practices. One who practices this path can become a *bodhisattva*—who has renounced his or her own salvation in order to lead others to nirvana. Mahayana Buddhism encourages anyone who wishes to do so to follow a bodhisattvic path, to take the bodhisattvic vows, and to work toward the enlightenment of all sentient beings.

More specifically, a bodhisattva is expected to practice several perfections, such as the perfection of giving (*dāna*), characterized by unattached and unconditional generosity, giving and letting go, and *mettā*, which has been translated as "loving-kindness, benevolence" (love without attachment). Buddhist meditation practices (the Four Immeasurables) encourage the practitioner to radiate the mental states of (1) loving-kindness or benevolence, (2) compassion, (3) sympathetic joy, and (4) equanimity in all directions. Thus even though the ultimate objective is seen as freeing oneself from the cycle of conditioned existence and suffering (*saṃsāra*), an important purpose of life on earth is to help others to become free also. This is not merely a recommendation but also an intrinsic motivation, because—according to Buddhist teaching—a divine being is filled with perfect love and desires to share this quality because of the joy it brings to each individual soul.

Judaism and Kabbalah

One of the most important spiritual traditions in which human spiritual nature is conceived as giving, providing, and "bestowing," is Kabbalah (or "receiving" in Hebrew). This is a discipline and school of thought concerned with the mystical aspects of Judaism. Kabbalah seeks to define the nature of the universe and humanity as well as the nature and purpose of existence. Originally developed within Jewish thought, Kabbalah is currently also open to non-Jewish individuals who are interested in its teachings (Yehuda Ashlag with commentary by Michael

Laitman, 2005). There are many interpretations of these teachings, but several are currently more prevalent; central among these is Lurianic Kabbalah, which was developed by Rabbi Isaac Luria in the 16th century and later interpreted (among others) by Rabbi Yehuda Ashlag, a 20th-century Kabbalah scholar.

According to Lurianic Kabbalah, which itself relies on earlier Kabbalistic teachings, the essence of God is *light*. In the beginning, there was only light, but its nature was to share, and it had no recipient. The light therefore created a vessel (*Kli*) to be its recipient. Upon receiving this light, the vessel came to inherit some of its properties, particularly its desire to share. To accomplish this, the vessel refused the light, an act called restriction, and broke into two parts so that it could share the light with itself. It is from these two parts that the souls of all males and females are derived. The breaking of the vessel also created 10 unique *Sefirot*, all of which have particular relationships to humans and to the perceivable universe.

Sefirot, meaning "enumerations," are the emanations through which God (who is referred to as The Limitless) reveals himself and continuously creates both our physical realm and the chain of higher metaphysical realms. They channel the divine life force and reveal the unknowable divine essence. Ashlag defines the primary quality of this source as the "will to bestow" (*Ratzon Lehashpia*). By nature each human is a vessel (*Keli*) with a will and desire to receive without limits. But each also has a spiritual light—a soul—and hence an inner spiritual desire to bestow, which mirrors the divine qualities. However, this desire must be developed in order to transform egoistical desire, or the desire to receive, into altruistic desire, or the desire to give. The way to this goal is through the intensive study of Kabbalah. Ashlag's system focuses on the transformation of human consciousness from a state of desiring to receive to desiring to give. Ashlag believed that the coming of the Messiah meant that humans would attain this quality, which would allow them to give up their selfishness and love one another for the sake of life's purpose.

Contemporary spiritualities

Similar views regarding the centrality of love and care as well as the similarity between humans and the divine are expressed in a large number of new religions or contemporary spiritualities often forming part of the New Age movement. The latter is commonly considered as originating at the end of the 19th century and was brought to widespread public attention during the 1970s and 1980s. The movement encompasses a wide range of ideas and practices that are not organized in any formal way (Heelas, 1996). These include such practices as personal spiritual growth, holistic medicine, reincarnation, channeling, ecofeminism, and neopaganism. New Age ideas and practices are often associated with a general belief that a spiritual era is dawning in which individuals and society will be transformed. Indeed, several researchers (e.g., Hanegraaff, 1998) have suggested that some of the New Age practices can also be seen as new religious movements. Although the different beliefs, new religions, or new spiritualities are diverse, a number of researchers (Heelas, 1996; Hanegraaff, 1998; Rose, 2005) have suggested that there are several general beliefs common to their adherents, some of which are closely related to the themes of this book.

One of these central ideas is the belief that everything that exists is a manifestation of a higher, more comprehensive spirit or single source of divine energy. Consequently the divine is viewed as being within each and every one of us and our ultimate purpose in life is seen to reflect this. The purpose of all existence is to imbue the world with love, wisdom, and enlightenment. Some practitioners of contemporary spiritualities believe that this involves transforming one's consciousness and mind to the point where the self is transcended and evolves to become one with the entire universe. It is further believed that the spiritual self does not need to rely on authorities to reveal its true nature and that we as humans are free to choose our path, although coaching and mentoring to this end are deemed important. Finally, a perennial viewpoint is adopted whereby all religions and spiritual traditions are seen as expressions of this general spirituality; this is reflected in the highly eclectic nature of contemporary spiritualities.

Together, these beliefs encompass a view suggesting that all life in all its different forms and states is interconnected. Cultivating one's own spiritual self thus means responsibility not only for oneself but for all existence. The ramifications for caring are clear—tending the spiritual self means caring for all living and nonliving entities. Unsurprisingly, contemporary spiritualities are strongly tied to a large number of political actions to save the planet, "go green," and the like (Heelas, 1996; Hanegraaff, 1998). Though highly divergent, contemporary spiritualities therefore involve a plea for greater compassion, empathy, and care for all beings, suggesting that this progression reflects the core developmental progress of humankind.

Chapter conclusion

This brief overview of spiritual traditions underscores the centrality and elevated level of morality attributed to caring—the giving side of human nature—in human thought. Within these traditions, the qualities of caring, compassion, and bestowing are ascribed to the divine and/or to highly developed human beings and viewed as central qualities that should be nurtured and promoted in human life. Thus the legacy and ethos of care as a quality to aspire to and a godly or supreme attribute appears to be evident. In fact, in a large number of spiritual traditions, it provides a compass for our ultimate destiny. It thus comes at no surprise that religiosity has been associated with benevolence and prosocial responding across cultures and religions (Saroglou, Delpierre, & Dernelle, 2004).

3

Evolutionary Approaches to Caring/Caregiving

Darwin's theory of evolution, as well as, modern (neo-Darwinian) perspectives, which include midlevel evolutionary theories and principles (i.e., conceptions that strived to explain a more limited class of phenomena than general-level theories) offer important insights regarding the motivation to care. Evolutionary theories address caring as part of parenting as well as caring for kin and caregiving for non-kin, including altruistic acts and struggle with the issue of the selfish vs. benevolent view of human nature and human development (Dawkins, 1976/2006). The first and most important contribution of evolutionary theory is related to Darwin's identification of natural selection as a primary mechanism for evolution and for the survival of the fittest. Natural selection identifies general heritable traits that make it more likely for an organism to survive and successfully reproduce, leading them to become more common over successive generations. This is because the offspring of these parents have better chances to survive and hence these heritable traits (genes) have higher chances of being "transferred" to the next generation. The human motivation to care for one's infant is such hereditary trait.

Evolutionary accounts further distinguished between proximate and ultimate causes of behaviors. *Proximate causes* or *goals* refer to the mechanisms that enable the organism to exhibit a specific behavior and explain it in temporal closeness to the act (e.g., helping because of feeling empathy), whereas ultimate causes or goals are construed with regard to evolutionary considerations referring to why a behavior came to be. Evolutionary models regarding caring were mostly concerned with explaining how caring is associated with advantage in the ultimate sense, often termed one's "fitness," including survival in the long run, reproductive success, and the propagation of one's genes to the next generation.

Parental care

Human infants (and, in fact, the young of all mammals) are born helpless. In order to survive, grow up, and reproduce, they need protection and care. This care includes a large number of very diverse behaviors (e.g., feeding, nurturing, keeping the child warm, protecting, soothing, and teaching); it represents a high level of commitment and responsibility and an intricate knowledge of how to provide such care in a way that is sensitive and responsive to the child's changing needs. This reasoning led Bowlby (1969/1982) to postulate the existence of a caregiving behavioral system in adults whose proximate goal was to provide protection for their offspring but whose ultimate evolutionary goal was to increase the fitness of the species.

Natural selection processes, therefore, favored parents that are motivated to care for their newborns and are committed to their long-term care. Said differently, if at any point in our ancestral history there were parents who did not have such heritable traits, their infants had much lower chances of survival and of reaching an age old enough for successful reproduction; hence these somewhat uncaring genes did not pass on to the next generation. In principle, because of such processes, we are all probably descendants of such caring parents and hence carry with us these "caring" genes. This convincing and straightforward reasoning highlights the vital necessity of the motivation to care among parents and underscores its potential as the prototype for the general motivation to care.

This general depiction of the motivation to care does not, however, entail a totality of investment on the parents' part. Two midlevel evolutionary theories discuss conditions that moderate the general evolutionary motivation to care for one's progeny. The *parent-offspring conflict* theory (Trivers, 1974) suggests that although parents maximize their own fitness if they contribute to the fitness of their offspring, parents and offspring do not always face similar stakes. Parents generally wish to allocate their resources equally among their offspring, while each offspring may want a little more for itself. Furthermore, an offspring may want more resources from the parent than the parent is willing to give because parents also have other needs besides caring for that offspring. Thus *parent-offspring conflict* refers to a conflict of "adaptive interests" between parent and offspring. Furthermore, if all things are not equal (as is often the case), a parent may engage in discriminative investment toward one offspring or the other; for example, from an evolutionary point of view, a parent with limited resources would prefer the offspring who was most able to mature successfully.

Another qualification refers to differences between mothering and fathering. Evolutionary theories have mostly focused on mothers and described somewhat different processes of natural selection for fathering. I take up the issue of gender differences in caring and caregiving in greater detail in a later part of this book (see Chapter 15), but will here describe the midlevel evolutionary theory of *parental investment and sexual selection* (Trivers, 1972), which is highly relevant to gender differences in parenting. This theory suggests that there are differences between the sexes in terms of their initial investment in their progeny and that these differences affect sexual selection and parental caregiving. Women invest more time and effort in producing offspring than men, but they can be certain that the child they bore is theirs. Men, on the other hand, can have children without investing much in their creation yet cannot be sure that a certain child is theirs unless they secure the fidelity of the woman with whom they have sexual relations. With regard to sexual differences in parenting, the theory suggests that mothers and fathers experience their motivation to care somewhat differently and exhibit it in different ways. Because of the high investment in each child, women are interested in finding a mate who possesses desirable attributes that can be passed on genetically to offspring (Gangestad & Simpson, 2000) and would most likely be interested in mates who were likely to provide and care for them and their offspring. In contrast, men would prefer to attract as many females as possible and would be less inclined to care for the offspring. According to Trivers (1972), these differences account for various sexual differences, among which are the competition among males for females' consent to have sex and women's careful and selective strategy in choosing their sexual partners.

Caring for nonprogeny

It makes evolutionary sense that parents invest in caring for their children at great cost to themselves. But why would individuals care for others? This issue has puzzled evolutionary researchers for some time because of the general inclination to view individuals as highly selfish (Dawkins, 1976/2006) and because the direct evolutionary benefits of such a strategy were unclear. In contrast, a large number of behavioral observations have demonstrated that such caring is abundant among animals in general and humans in particular. Evolutionary researchers were especially puzzled by the human tendency to provide for and help even total strangers. The following offers descriptions of a number of theories that have attempted to reconcile this apparent paradox.

Inclusive fitness theory, proposed by Hamilton (1964) as a revision to Darwin's evolutionary theory, suggests that because we share genes with other relatives besides our children our fitness is related to the successful survival of our genetic relatives, not just our offspring. He termed this *inclusive fitness*. It therefore makes evolutionary sense to care for our genetic relatives and in some cases to even sacrifice our lives to this end. This mechanism applies to one's family members as well as to members of one's ethnic or national group, who tend to marry within the boundaries of the group and hence to share their genes (Wynne-Edwards, 1962).

But what, then, of caring for total strangers? Trivers (1971) broadened the concept of inclusive fitness and suggested an additional mechanism—*reciprocal altruism*. This concept suggests that altruism, defined as helping an unrelated other despite an associated cost, could have evolved because it could be beneficial to incur this cost if there was a chance that the person whom I helped might at some point return the favor and perform an altruistic act for me. This necessitated the evolution of genes that propagate an altruistic norm or an exchange orientation but also genes that allow the identification and the punishment of those who do not reciprocate so as to create a balance of give and take even among non-kin. Trivers (1971) therefore suggests that the human altruistic system is sensitive, unstable, and regulated by a complex psychology of emotional dispositions that evolved along with the altruistic trait (genes). These include the formation and sustenance of friendships—and thus such behaviors as liking and disliking, gratitude and sympathy—that reinforce the confidence in possible reciprocation. They also include moralistic aggression, which involves educating or even punishing nonreciprocators and free-riders (i.e., cheaters) in order to put them at an evolutionary disadvantage.

But helping others and incurring costs in order to benefit others may also occur when direct reciprocation does not apply, as in large nonintimate groups and even with total strangers whom the person does not expect to meet again, and even in conditions when the benefactor remains anonymous. Donations for a cause represent such a case, as do heroic acts of rescue involving unfamiliar others in an emergency and anonymous kidney donations to strangers. What can account for such behaviors? Such benevolent acts should theoretically be exploited by others in order to gain a fitness advantage and eventually become extinct. One theory that has been offered in order to settle this contradiction is the notion of *strong reciprocity*. This refers to a tendency to voluntarily cooperate in order to reward others for cooperative, norm-abiding behaviors and also a tendency to impose sanctions on noncooperators and punish others for norm violations (Fehr & Fischbacher, 2003).

Unlike reciprocal altruism, which suggests that individuals reward and punish others only if they expect to receive direct benefits (Axelrod & Hamilton, 1981), strong reciprocators incur the costs of rewarding or punishing even when they themselves do not directly gain from their acts; they may even reward or punish based on their partners' reputation and without prior direct contact with them. Consequently strong reciprocation sustains a moral norm of reciprocation and fairness that deters those who try to exploit the situation by punishing noncooperators and rewarding cooperators based on their reputation. The perception of others as fair, decent, and honest or unfair and dishonest may suffice to instigate rewarding or punishing behaviors. One's reputation as a fair and benevolent partner therefore becomes a significant social indicator and can earn an individual a variety of benefits in groups that rely on cooperation to survive, such as the hunter-gatherer tribes in our ancestral history. Strong reciprocity thus constitutes a powerful proximal mechanism for sustaining cooperation within groups, as indeed was demonstrated in studies of the prisoner's dilemma and the dictator game (Fehr & Fischbacher, 2003). These games involve competitive contexts in which players can either trust or not trust others and hence behave cooperatively or noncooperatively and even betray the others. What might be the ultimate mechanisms that provide evolutionary advantage to this predisposition for strong reciprocity? Two evolutionary theories provide a relevant conceptual framework.

Group selection theory (Wilson & Sober, 1994; Sober & Wilson, 1998) suggests that individuals may be altruistic toward others within their in-group (i.e., their tribe) and may opt to risk themselves if this enhances the benefits to their group. If the group as a whole and the altruistic members within it (those with altruistic genes) is more successful than other groups, such altruistic genes would have been evolutionary selected at the group level. Simulations of such possibilities indicate that this mechanism might have worked only in relatively few cases because selection between groups is a much weaker force compared with the advantages for nonaltruists in the groups and especially in light of the possibility of migration between groups (Fehr & Fischbacher, 2003; Simpson & Beckes, 2010). In fact, some researchers have argued that differences among groups are better understood in their cultures rather than in their genetic compositions and that cultural transmission often occurs through social learning (i.e., imitation, teaching) and the establishment of norms and legacies (Fehr & Fischbacher, 2003).

In line with this realization, *Gene-culture coevolutionary models* (also called *multilevel selection models*) (McAndrew, 2002; Gintis, Bowles, Boyd & Fehr, 2003; Richerson & Boyd, 2005) acknowledge the limitations of the gene-centered evolutionary models and attempt to provide comprehensive explanations of the observed pervasiveness of benevolent and prosocial behaviors toward others. These scholars suggest that the emergence of complex cultural structures can affect the inclusive fitness of members in stable, cooperative, productive groups. Both culture and genes were seen as vehicles in processes of natural selection and as affecting each other. Genes that allowed flexibility in the creation of cultural values and norms and compliance with them—as well as genes that promoted cooperation and caring together with high capacities to detect disloyalty, betrayal and cheating—had an evolutionary advantage. Cultures that fostered norms of caring and cooperation along with normative mechanisms for the detection and punishment of nonreciprocators or cheaters probably also had evolutionary advantages. The cultural equivalents of the biologically based genes were described as *memes*. These included the cultural norms, values, and practices that were transferred from generation to generation through socialization (Dawkins, 1976/2006).

Caring for in-group vs. out-group members

The discussion of cultural groups and natural selection based on cultural aspects is closely related to one of the most salient features of human groups—the differentiation between in-groups and out-groups. In this respect, caring and cooperation are often directed more toward in-group members than out-group members. In our evolutionary past, cultural groups such as tribes were often stable; hence the differentiation between in-group and out-group was also stable. However, current research shows that the demarcation between what is considered in-group vs. out-group can be variable and flexible depending on context. Individuals may perceive themselves as belonging to a large number of possible in-groups, and the saliency of such membership is variable between individuals and within the same individual depending on various internal and external cues and needs. The temporary saliency of a certain dimension for comparison with others (i.e., gender, fandom, alma mater, a particular illness) may provide a cue that activates the demarcation into in-group vs. out-group. People respond more favorably to group members who happen to be even superficially more similar to themselves—and thus more kin like in some way (See review in Van Vugt & Schaller, 2008). The immediate context plays a strong role in this perception, as demonstrated by the ease with which in-groups can be created. The tendency to form such divisions is so strong that even trivial insignificant differentiation may yield an in-group–out-group bias. This is known as the *minimal group paradigm* (Tajfel, 1970).

In experiments designed to test this paradigm, strangers are randomly split into groups and provided with an arbitrary and virtually meaningless distinction, such as a preference for certain paintings or the color of their shirts. This triggers a tendency to favor one's own group at the expense of others observed in higher perceptions of attractiveness, a higher allocation of resources, and a stronger willingness to help in-group members regardless of the fact that (1) participants did not know each other previously and could not expect to meet again, (2) their groups were completely meaningless, and (3) none of the participants had any inclination as to which painting or color they liked better before the experiments began (see review in Tajfel, 1978; Tajfel & Turner, 1986).

Studies have shown that any differentiation of "us" and "them" has clear, and at times even significant consequences in terms of in-group favoritism and out-group negativity. In one of the most important experiments on this issue (the Robbers Cave Experiment), Muzafer Sherif divided 11-year-old boys in a summer camp into two equal groups and encouraged each group to bond (Sherif, 1967). Later on, when the two groups played competitive games, hostility and out-group negativity broke out and it proved difficult to contain, despite efforts by the camp directors. Only subsequent interventions where the boys had to cooperate in order to solve a joint crisis overcame this schism. What might be the specific reproductive advantages that were promoted by these tendencies? Van Vugt and Park, for example, discuss an interesting *tribal instinct hypothesis* (Van Vugt & Park, 2008). They suggest that this in-group/out-group bias reflects specific human adaptations for managing intergroup relations that advance their capacity for survival and successful procreation—specifically, evolved tenden cies to form coalitional alliances and to exploit and dominate other individuals or groups. They further suggest that intergroup conflict was common in prehis-toric times. Hence the capacity for cooperation evolved along with the capacity to differentiate between one's in-group (i.e., tribe), where cooperation is expected to take place, and other groups, which could be exploited to ensure the tribe's survival. According to this portrayal, prosocial, benevolent, and cooperative sen-timents and behaviors had to be preferentially exhibited within one's coalition (tribe) in order to advance one's reproductive and inclusive fitness. Yet coalitions and cooperation across various groups also occurred and contributed to the inclu-sive fitness of the members of the cooperating groups. Thus intergroup assistance could be expected to evolve if the different groups considered the possibility of forming a joint coalition in order to serve a common cause. In this sense a per-ception of in-group vs. out-group can be seen as evolutionarily advantageous, as can a certain degree of flexibility in the demarcation between in-groups and out-groups. Hence, although individuals would tend to help similar others more than they helped dissimilar ones, the application of the caring motivation can in principle be wide.

Selective investment theory

Another fairly recent evolutionary theory has been suggested to account for what its creators termed *costly long-term investments*, such as raising offspring, assisting a terminally ill mate, and risking one's life to protect comrades in war (Brown & Brown, 2006a). Keeping with the theme of this book, they too focus on the "giv-ing" side of caring, claiming that it has long been neglected. They suggest that costly long-term investments are evolutionarily beneficial and were selected when individuals attained mutual reproductive dependence, or, in their terms *fitness interdependence*. This refers to the notion suggesting that the survival and reproduction of one individual is enhanced by the survival and reproduction of another. In such cases, helping another individual with whom one shares "fitness interdependence," whether genetically or otherwise, actually leads to a reproduc-tive benefit to oneself and increases one's fitness. In this way selective investment theory explained the evolutionary benefit of investing in the survival of others and caring for them even when the individuals ostensibly do not share genes, as is often the case with romantic partners and close friends. In fact, adopting an

evolutionary point of view, Brown and Brown (2006b) suggest that humans probably started out as altruists and caring rather than as being just selfishly motivated.

Brown and Brown (2006a) further suggest that a proximate motivational
mechanism that evolved to sustain such "costly long-term investments" among
"fitness interdependent" individuals is the social bond, which is described as
involving "a strong and enduring affinity for another" who is marked as irreplace-
able (Brown & Brown, 2006a; p. 8). This bond, which is "a cognitive-affective representational structure with neurohormonal underpinnings" (Brown & Brown,
2006a; p. 21) is conceptualized as an evolved emotional regulatory mechanism
that overrides self-interest and activates emotions associated with concern for
others. such as sympathy and compassion. Such bonding was not indiscriminate
but rather based on joint synchronized interactions involving high emotional
arousal and reflecting "fitness interdependence"—that is, relations describable as
involving strong and stable affectional bonds. Noteworthy in the context of this
book is their argument suggesting that "high-cost altruism was a necessity for
ensuring the survival, growth and reproduction of increasingly interdependent
members of ancestral hunter-gatherer groups" (p. 21). In a more recent publication Brown, Brown, and Preston (2012) expand their initial theory and provide
a preliminary description of a dedicated neurobiological system responsible for
this general caregiving system. In other words, this theory can be seen as suggesting an overarching and evolutionarily selected mechanism for caring in the
context of interdependent relationships or "an evolutionary sound foundation
for understanding high-cost giving to others in close relationships" (Brown &
Brown, 2006b; p. 62).

Reflecting this growing realization of the evolutionary centrality of caring is an evolution-influenced revision of Maslow's famous hierarchy of universal human needs (Kenrick, Griskevicius, Neuberg, & Schaller, 2010). As
mentioned previously (Chapter 1), this hierarchy did not discuss or include
motives for caring and tending. The suggested revision attempts to rem-
edy this shortfall by including various aspects that directly relate to caring.
Specifically, parenting—a central motive in caring—was placed at the top of
the hierarchy and affiliation, mate selection, and mate retention were added as
additional needs in other locations within the hierarchy appearing earlier in
the life cycle. This reflects an ongoing trend in evolutionary psychology that
now recognizes the adaptive functions of social affiliation, including warmth,
closeness, care, social support, and cooperation in dyads and groups. The
accordance of a special privileged place for parenting, a significant manifestation of the caring motivation, reflects the central place that current evolutionary accounts give to these caring and tending capacities and goals and rectifies
the lacunae in Maslow's highly recognized and widespread hierarchy of universal human needs.

Developmental processes related to caring in our evolutionary history

Taken together, these theories suggest that a motivation to care for others—including one's offspring, close kin, others from one's tribe or ethnic group, and even total strangers—is evolutionarily adaptive and has developed through natural selection. Many scholars have posited that parenting, and maternal care in particular, is the origin of all caring relationships and acts of caring (Krebs & Davies, 1991; Hrdy, 1999; Bell & Richard, 2000a,b; Taylor, 2002; Brown & Brown, 2006a). Yet the caring for close group members, the tribe, has also been delineated as central and critical to the evolutionary development of caring (Caporeal, 1997).

The Evolution of parental care

Bell (2001) presents an interesting theory concerning the evolution of mammalian parental caregiving with a specific focus on the evolution of maternal care, suggesting that parental caregiving evolved through a series of changes and adaptations. In this process old structures served as the basis for the development of new systems, which were somewhat differentiated yet also overlapping with each other and with the old ones and thus increased the complexity of the organism. He further proposes that maternal caregiving preceded the development of infant attachment, as an attachment to a mother who does not care does not make any evolutionary sense. According to Bell's suggestions, the first phase of this development began with the evolution of mammal-like reptiles about 240 million years ago (MacLean, 1990). Most reptiles identified their own offspring as strangers and tended to react aggressively, often killing the young if they came too close. Hence the first phase in the development of maternal caregiving involved the development of an inhibition of this rejection behavior when facing their offspring. This allowed for proximity between mothers and their young. Because the same mothers continued to reject and attack strangers, this proximity also provided a certain degree of protection.

The second phase involved the development of a dyadic emotional preference bond of mothers toward their young, which was instigated by the secretion of the neurotransmitter oxytocin. This dyadic bond resulted in mothers' preference for the scent of their young and their choice to stay close to them. Such an emotional bond first evolved in reptiles and preceded the emergence of mammals. At this stage, caregiving behavior included mostly simple, automatic, reactive behaviors. The third phase involved the development of mammary glands and then live births and probably started in the development of sweat glands that included some nutrients besides sweat in premammals who hatched eggs. Following Clutton-Brock

(1991), Bell suggests that mammals could only appear after mothers began feeding their hatched offspring by lactation noting that warm-bloodedness and lactation probably developed before live births. Two very similar major neurotransmitters, oxytocin and vasopressin, were probably involved in the evolution of live births and in the development of this caregiving bond, which includes physical closeness and feeding via lactation.

The fourth and final phase in the development of the caregiving system involved the development of a full-blown behavioral system that comprised a very complex set of proactive and future-oriented behaviors and goals including protection, nurturance, and teaching. This system is much more complex than those described in earlier phases and it might be only partially controlled by oxytocin and vasopressin. Insel (1997), for example, reports that oxytocin promotes the onset of maternal behavior (i.e., the formation of the dyadic bond) but not its maintenance in female rats. Bell (2001), Insel (1997), and others argue that a host of other biological agents and biological processes are implicated in the maintenance and development of a caregiving bond. In humans, according to Bell (2001), this system includes a large variety of goals besides physical closeness and protection, such as caring for the emotional needs and well-being of the children as well as empowering them and teaching them social skills, social norms, and cultural heritage. Bell's (2001) model does not address other types of caring, such as caring for a sexual partner or a tribe member. Yet his description of the phases clearly suggests the historical phylogenetic primacy of *maternal* caring over paternal caring and over caring for group members, because group living probably emerged at a later stage in our ancestral history.

The evolution of cooperation and caring in groups

Another perspective on the evolution of care is offered by Caporeal (1997), who discusses the development of cooperation and caring in groups that relate to caring with friends, romantic partners, familiar others, and even strangers as well as cooperation in child rearing. When evolutionary processes and natural selection are examined, they generally refer to the kind of environment that was prevalent during the past 1.5 million years or so rather than in the more recent history of human civilization. This environment, often referred to as the *environment of evolutionary adaptedness* (EEA) (Bowlby, 1969/1982) roughly coincides with the start of the Pleistocene (1.8 million years ago). Evolutionary psychology thus suggests that most human psychological mechanisms are adapted to reproductive problems frequently encountered in Pleistocene environments. For thousands of generations, this environment was probably made up of small cooperative groups of hunters and gatherers termed *bands* (with an average size of 30 people). These groups (who were mostly genetically related) cooperated in hunting, food gathering, and guarding against predators as well as caring for children.

Coordination, cooperation, and reciprocity were therefore essential and critical attributes of these groups and in fact constituted the evolutionary reason for the natural selection of such a lifestyle. Group living has clear evolutionary benefits for a large number of species (Caporael, 1997). Humans who lived in such closed groups—where they could depend on each other for hunting, defense, and rearing progeny—had much higher chances of survival and reproduction than lone individuals or groups that were not cooperative (Dunbar, 1996; Caporael, 1997). Hence cooperative skills and caring for others besides one's offspring probably evolved as a survival strategy (Dunbar, 1996; Caporael, 1997). This is true also for child care, which in these tribal groups, especially from infancy on, was a common behavior dispersed among members of the tribe with varying degrees of genetic closeness to the child, including older children (Eibl-Eibesfeldt, 1989; Brewer & Caporael, 1990; Simpson & Belsky, 2008). It would thus be possible to argue that parenting, especially after infancy and weaning, may have evolved as a joint group task rather than a specific dyadic relation between a mother and her offspring. Evidence from contemporary hunter-gatherer cultures confirms that infants are indeed cared for by their biological parents but also by a large number of other caregivers including older siblings (Hrdy, 2009).

Both the *group selection theory* and the *gene-culture coevolution model* discuss the evolutionary processes that reflect the importance of groups and their culture for survival. According to their perspectives, cooperative, prosocial, caring behaviors with group members were naturally selected and presumably evolved together with the evolution of parental care extending beyond infancy, when group members appear to occupy central roles in caring and socializing. Furthermore, as suggested by Bell (2001), the evolution of parental care and of care and cooperation within social groups informed and influenced each other.

Individual differences

Evolutionary theories were also suggested to account for individual differences in caregiving. In fact, evolutionary principles suggest that there is a certain degree of flexibility in gene manifestation. Our genetic inheritance allows for individual differences and variant manifestations that may reflect adaptations to different environmental and living conditions.

Another midlevel evolutionary theory, the *life history theory* (Williams, 1966; Stearns, 1976; Clutton-Brock, 1991), is particularly relevant in this respect. According to this perspective, natural selection was seen to favor fitness as including both one's own survival, growth, and reproduction as well as caring for one's progeny across the life span. Depending on their specific living circumstances, individuals had to solve problems related to these sometimes competing goals in a way that would maximize their long-term fitness (Charnov, 2003). These choices resulted in a range of individual differences that reflected the ways in which individuals negotiated various decisions throughout their lives (Belsky, Steinberg, & Draper, 1991). These decisions include how much to invest in mating vs. parenting, when to have children (i.e., early or delayed reproduction), how many children to have, and how much to invest in each child (i.e., adopting a strategy of investing in higher quality or in higher quantity) (Daly & Wilson, 1983). Belsky et al. (1991) as well as others (Chisholm, 1996) suggest that early environmental risk, including parenting risk indicators (inconsistent sensitivity, neglect, abuse) set the stage for a reproductive strategy involving an early onset of mating and parenting, a low investment in mates and offspring, and a strategy of quantity over quality in terms of investment in child rearing. The reverse is true for low-risk or safe and protective environments such as those that enhance the secure attachment of children to parents. As secure children grow up, they tend to postpone becoming sexually active and engaging in parenting; they prefer to invest in monogamous relationships, to choose sexual partners who have desirable attributes, and tend to show a higher degree of investment in their own children. These notions underscore the flexibility with which our evolutionary selected caring systems are displayed in light of environmental cues.

Chapter conclusion

Evolutionary theories contain many interesting discussions and debates that examine and contrast the different explanations for the appearance and survival of human behaviors (see, e.g., Gould, 2002, for a review). What is particularly pertinent to the focus of this book is the growing interest of evolutionary theorists in the overwhelming centrality of caring, giving, providing, and helping that characterizes human experience at various levels and in a diverse range of relationships and situations (Kenrick, Griskevicius, Neuberg, & Schaller, 2010). Together, a variety of models have been proposed to explain the pervasive propensity of humans to help others, kin and nonkin, even those who are total strangers, and also to explain the more infrequent occasions of highly costly altruistic behaviors. What I share with this highly distinguished group of evolutionary researchers is the realization that caring, compassion, or—in evolutionary terms—cooperation and "high-cost giving" are all around us, not only with our offspring or genetic kin but in a range of relationships and situations and that they are fundamental to our human nature.

Taken together, the application of this growing system of evolutionary principles to the understanding of caring, helping, cooperation, and pro-social behavior suggests that caregiving and caring as enacted in different relational contexts—such as parents for their progeny or caring for relatives, friends, or one's own ethnic group, as well as prosocial cooperation with total strangers—were naturally selected throughout our evolutional history and are important, significant, and even vital mechanisms for the sustenance of human life. Such caring, tending, and cooperating are innate and fundamental because they serve to enhance our inclusive fitness and hence our chances to survive, reproduce, and propagate these caring genes to next generations. This amounts to a claim that a hard-wired, biological tendency to care in close relations as well as for strangers exists and is part of our genes as *Homo sapiens* and our memes as cultural groups. It further means that we ought to identify the proximal mechanisms that activate such care and sustain it in daily life. In this respect, empathic processes are of key importance and will be the focus of the next part of our discussion in the chapter that follows.

4

Empathic Processes as Key Experiences in Caring

From an evolutionary perspective, the ultimate reason for the different kinds of care and prosocial behaviors is related to their contribution to the individual's inclusive fitness. But what in the ongoing life and experiences of individuals causes them to provide care? Empathy- related processes within and outside affectional bonds are currently deemed key proximate causes and are possibly the most significant mechanism that motivates a person to care for and help another and affect the quality of such care. Hoffman (2000; p. 3), a pioneering and a central scholar of empathic processes, describes empathy as "the spark of human concern for others, the glue that makes social life possible." Empathic processes work so well because they give individuals an emotional stake in the welfare of others. As such, empathic responses are predominant in a large number of species and are also present in human infants shortly after birth (Preston & de Waal, 2002).

Empathy reflects the ability to discern and experience the emotional and behavioral state of another being vicariously. Such physiologically based affective and motivational states precede and trigger a large range of prosocial and caring acts and provide a central source of internally governed motivation to prosocial behavior (Decety, Norman, Berntson, & Cacioppo, 2012). The study of empathic processes therefore provides a revealing understanding of core processes that are relevant to caring in a large number of domains, such as parenting, romantic relations, generosity, cooperation, and altruism. Furthermore, the study of empathic processes has become a meeting ground for several research paradigms—evolutionary theories, the study of psychosocial mechanisms, and neuroscientific research—which have contributed to an interdisciplinary understanding of the central proximate mechanism for the caring motivation and its enactment. Accordingly, the following chapter weaves together evolutionary, psychological, and neuropsychological points of view and research and discusses the extant knowledge on empathic processes.

Among other methods, psychologists have examined empathic processes through experimental studies geared to arouse empathy by such means as staging distress or pain, recounting stories about people in need, or presenting short videos including empathy-arousing scenes. The participants' reactions, subsequently observed, could include changes in physiological measures, changes in facial expressions, self-assessments in questionnaires, and actual behaviors. For example, while a mother and her preschooler are playing in the lab, the mother ostensibly bumps her knee at the table and shows that she is hurting by her facial expressions, by rubbing her knee, and by saying "Ouch Ouch!" The facial expressions as well as the child's behaviors are coded. Is the child concerned? Does the child start to cry or become distressed? Does the child approach the mother and try to soothe her? In this situation, for example, the large majority (more than 80%) of 3-year-olds show concern and soothe their mothers. In some studies, investigators also asked participants to report their own empathic and prosocial behaviors in general or asked others (friends, teachers, parents, and spouses) to report on these aspects of the participants' behavior. Interestingly, most researchers did not differentiate between various kinds of relations, and—as discussed in the following—uncovered similar core empathic processes of people with their own children, with friends, and with strangers. Thus once empathy was aroused in any of these contexts and if it was not countered by anxiety and overarousal, it elicited the motivation to care in the form of concern for others.

Brain studies have utilized mostly two major methods of uncovering the neural structures and mechanisms involved in human caring—functional magnetic resonance imaging (fMRI) and electroencephalography (EEG). The fMRI method uses an MRI scanner and the presentation of specific auditory, visual, or touch stimuli in order to identify active brain areas. This method allows good spatial resolution since it can identify brain activity with millimeter precision. It is, however, limited in temporal resolution and is thus of little use in diagnosing quick changes in brain activity over time. In contrast, the EEG-based assessment of brain activity and the event-related potentials (ERP) technique in particular provides information on the brain's electrical activity with good temporal but poor spatial resolution. The ERP technique involves the time-locked recording of EEG waveforms across the scalp by using numerous electrodes and indicating the relation of these waveforms to the sensory, emotional, and cognitive processes that occur both as a certain stimulus is presented and after its presentation.

These techniques have been used extensively in the past two decades to examine empathic processes in humans, and provide us with an understanding of the neuronal correlates of caring and caregiving. As we shall see further on, this research has demonstrated impressive similarities in the functioning of empathy across various kinds of caring, corroborating this book's claim of the existence of a generalized motivation to care.

Evolutionary development of empathic processes

Using an evolutionary prism, de Waal and colleagues (Preston & de Waal, 2002; de Waal, 2008) proposed an evolutionary and biologically based account of the development and operation of empathy. According to de Waal (2008), empathic processes developed as part of the parenting system in those species, such as birds and primates, where parental sensitivity to an offspring's emotional cues is critical to the offspring's survival. De Waal (2008) further proposed two major stages in the development of empathy in humans. The first is the development of a basic neural mechanism, which Preston and de Waal (2002) termed the *perception action mechanism*. The second involves the development of *sympathetic concern*.

The *perception action mechanism*, which develops in the first phase automatically and unconsciously activates neural representations of states in the subject that are similar to those perceived in the object. De Waal (2008) reviews animal research demonstrating the existence of such automatic mechanisms in a large number of species. Two such automatic processes that might be part of the perception action mechanism are discussed extensively. *Mimicry* refers to an automatic process whereby an individual copies (i.e., mimics) the motor actions of others, including facial expressions, vocalizations, and gestures (Singer & Lamm, 2009). A similar process that involves the automatic copying of the feelings or emotions of another individual is termed *emotional contagion*. Both processes are present in early human infancy.

The significant discovery of mirror neurons in macaque monkeys and later in humans provides a remarkable and compelling preliminary corroboration of these ideas (see review by Rizzolatti & Craighero, 2004). Mirror neurons fire both when an animal acts and when the same animal observes the same action performed by another, providing preliminary evidence for the existence of neural strata for learning through imitation. In fact, the tendency to emulate others without extrinsic rewards is as prevalent among nonhuman primates as it is among humans (Bonnie & de Waal, 2006). Similarly, mirror neurons fire both when an animal feels an emotion that can be discernible in a certain way and when the same emotion is experienced by another. Thus the neuron "mirrors" the behavior of the other or the emotion experienced by the other as though the observer were acting or experiencing the emotion. In line with this suggestion, recent fMRI studies have reported a neural similarity between self-generated and vicarious emotions, demonstrating the similarity in brain activation when we feel our own pain and when we empathize with and feel the pain of another person (Carr et al., 2003; Singer, Seymour, et al., 2004; Decety & Jackson 2006). Although little is known about how mirror neurons are implicated in empathy and care, this discovery accords with the suggested automatic neural mechanism for emotional contagion.

According to de Waal (2008), *sympathetic concern* evolved at the next evolutionary step and included attempts to understand the other's situation and emotions as well as the inclination to alleviate the other's distress. Such concern also requires a capacity for taking an empathic perspective and a distinction between self and other, which necessitates a more elaborate cognitive mechanism. De Waal (2008) reports that such a capacity probably appears only in humans and apes and not even in monkeys. For example, consolations provided to a distressed other, which are a clear manifestation of this empathic concern, do not appear in macaque mothers (Schino, Geminiani, Rosati, & Aureli, 2004). Current theories suggest that there are several distinctions within this later evolutionary developmental phase (Decety & Jackson, 2004). Researchers tended to differentiate between *empathy*—which includes both emotional and cognitive facets and is different from mimicry or emotional contagion—and the resultant *concern* for the other, which entails the motivation to alleviate the other's distress or pain. I will discuss each of these processes—empathy and concern—separately at length.

Empathy

Empathy is depicted as an affective response similar to the one experienced by the other or expected to be felt by the other but one that also requires the person having the empathic reaction to experience a distinction between self and other (e.g., Singer & Lamm, 2009). Neurological studies have indeed demonstrated that the same brain areas are activated in experiencing one's own physical pain when one is seeing another person in pain, looking at pictures of faces in pain, and even *imagining* another person in pain (Singer, Seymour, et al., 2004; see review in Gonzalez-Liencres, Shamay-Tsoory, & Brüne, 2013).

Contemporary theorists have further differentiated between two somewhat different yet related kinds of empathy, which they refer to as emotional and cognitive empathy (Gonzalez-Liencres, Shamay-Tsoory, & Brüne, 2013). *Emotional empathy* is an embodied and affective representation of the mental state of another individual. *Cognitive empathy* reflects an understanding of what another person knows, intends, feels, or desires and can occur by imagining and by perspective taking. Thinking about how the readers of this part may feel and asking myself "Will they be interested or bored?" is an example of such perspective taking. It is related to one's theory of mind (i.e., the capacity to consider the internal mental world of oneself and others while understanding the self-other distinction). Hence it is often described as reflecting mentalizing processes (i.e., thinking about the mind of the self and others). Current neurological studies demonstrate the commonality as well as the distinctiveness of these two types of empathy in humans. For example, a study of patients with brain lesions revealed distinct brain areas associated with emotional and cognitive empathy (Shamay-Tsoory, Aharon-Peretz, & Perry, 2009).

A recent meta-analysis of neuroimaging studies has also shown a relative distinction between emotionally based empathy vs. cognitive empathy or empathy based on perspective taking (Fan, et al., 2011). The meta-analysis included data from 40 fMRI studies that examined the activation of brain areas during different empathy-inducing tasks and across a variety of feelings such as pain, disgust, and happiness. The findings suggested the existence of a shared network of brain regions across all tasks and stimulus domains, corroborating the neural basis of empathy suggested by earlier descriptive reviews of neuroimaging studies (e.g., Singer & Lamm, 2009). These areas included the dorsal anterior cingulate cortex (dACC), anterior midcingulate cortex (aMCC), and supplementary motor area (SMA), cortical midline structures related to cognitive functions, and the bilateral anterior insula(AI)—a structure that is part of the pain system and is involved in the awareness of body states and social emotions.

In addition—as found in the lesion-based study by Simone Shamay Tsoory and colleagues—Yan Fan and colleagues (2011) provided evidence for some distinctiveness in the brain areas associated with affective-perceptual vs. cognitive-evaluative empathy. Affective-perceptual tasks were distinctly associated with the right AI—a brain area that developed earlier in evolutionary history, while cognitive-evaluative forms of empathy were distinctly associated with the aMCC—a more recently developed brain area. In addition, and showing the commonality between these two types of empathy, the left AI was similarly engaged in both types of tasks. Supporting the association between self reports of empathy and brain activity, individuals who scored higher on standard empathy scales had higher empathy-related brain activity in both the ACC, related to cognitive empathy, and the AI, related to emotional empathy (Singer et al., 2006).

From these and other studies it appears that the affective/emotional empathy facet is less conscious, more directly perceptual and automatic, and less effortful, reflecting bottom-up processes, involving an embodied emotion, and that it developed earlier in the phylogenetic process (i.e., the evolutionary process of the development of organisms). In contrast, the cognitive empathy facet is more conscious, involving a directed cognitive effort of perspective taking, and reflecting top-down processing and a clearer self-other distinction. It would have evolved later, which is why it appears in very few species beside humans (e.g., chimpanzees).

Smith (2006) suggests that the two types of empathy might reflect different evolutionary processes. Emotional empathy ("the vicarious sharing of emotion," as Smith refers to it) could have evolved as part of the close bonds and processes that promote inclusive fitness, or fitness reflecting relations with genetically related kin. Emotional empathy can be seen as reflecting the need to sustain long-term bonding in a cohesive and close-knit tribe. Within such bonds emotional empathy promotes the provision of help and care and is a key mechanism for the inhibition of violence. This is similar to the processes described by Brown and Brown in their selective investment theory (2006a). On the other hand, cognitive empathy ("mental perspective taking" in Smith's terms) enabled the understanding and prediction of behavior based on attributed mental states; as such it facilitated human communication and the building of social expertise. It could have evolved when hominid groups became larger, more sophisticated, and more socially complex. Such complexity entailed the need for more sophisticated forms of reciprocation and cooperation, the formation of alliances, and the detection of deceit; thus it required a more sophisticated cognitive ability to discern and understand the experiences and minds of others. The processes that shaped the formation of such human groups as well as the development and elaboration of the cognitive aspect of empathy probably reflected the coevolution of environments and genes that created social norms, moral laws, and the capacity to orchestrate complex and moderately stable cooperation among human groups. Researchers have noted that despite the moderate distinctiveness of the two types of empathy, they mostly work in concert and complement each other; that when one type is missing or works poorly, this impairs the functioning of the individual as a whole (Smith, 2006; Gonzalez-Liencres, Shamay-Tsoory, & Brüne, 2013). Both emotional and cognitive empathy give individuals a stake in the welfare of others; hence each can provide the proximal bases for the emergence of the motivation to care, which is described in the next section.

Concern, compassion, and sympathy—the motivation to care

The motivation to care emerges through an almost automatic activation of concern for the welfare of the other that emanates from empathy. Researchers have used different terms for that concern (for the purpose of this book, the distinctions among them are not crucial). *Compassion*, for example, has been described as a feeling that arises in witnessing another's suffering, inducing caring or comforting behavior (Singer & Lamm, 2009; Goetz, Keltner, & Simon-Thomas, 2010; Gonzalez-Liencres, Shamay-Tsoory, & Brüne, 2013). Compassion does not necessarily involve a common feeling between the compassionate person and the other. A lonely person might not induce loneliness in the compassionate person but could instead engender pity and potentially caring behavior aimed at reducing his or her distress. *Sympathy* is quite similar to compassion and involves feelings of concern and sorrow for the other person; it may also be based on cognitive processes in which the observed individual's distress is consciously identified through perspective taking and without direct interaction with or observation of the other. As with compassion, it entails a prosocial motivation to ameliorate the distress of an individual in a stressful situation (Eisenberg et al., 1994; Eisenberg, 2010). *Empathic concern* is quite similar to both compassion and sympathy and refers to an other-oriented emotional response elicited by and congruent with the perceived welfare of someone in need. It includes feeling *for* the other—having sympathy, compassion and tenderness, and feeling moved, soft-hearted, and warm (Batson, 2010).

Together, these terms—*compassion, sympathy,* and *empathic concern*—all refer to a general state of concern with the other person's plight and welfare that is based on emotional and/or cognitive empathy and one that motivates a subsequent desire to alleviate the distress, pain, or fear in the other—namely a motivation to care. In line with this depiction, empathy has been shown to lead to prosocial behavior. In an illuminating neuroimaging study, Carrie Masten and her colleagues (Masten, Morelli, & Eisenberger, 2011) examined such processes in a social context. During an fMRI scan, participants watched a situation in which one person was being excluded or included by two others. Afterward participants sent emails to these people and neutral coders rated the extent to which these emails were prosocial. The results indicated that the observation of exclusion served to activate the regions of the brain associated with mentalizing or perspective taking—the cognitive empathy aspect. In highly empathic individuals, it also activated the social pain–related regions—the emotional empathy aspect. These empathy-related activities (in mentalizing as well as in social pain–related areas, i.e., the dorsal medial prefrontal cortex [DMPFC] and the AI respectively) were associated with later prosocial behavior (e.g., comforting) in the emails sent to the victim. These findings suggest that empathy-related neural responses to the exclusion of a stranger promote spontaneous prosocial conduct directed toward this stranger.

Findings at the psychological level were similar in demonstrating the strong association between empathy that leads to empathic concern and prosocial behavior (Eisenberg, Spinrad, & Sadovsky, 2006; Batson, 2010). For example, about three decades ago Daniel Batson (see review in Batson, 1991) put forward the empathy-altruism hypothesis, which claims that empathy evokes a prosocial motivation directed toward the ultimate goal of increasing the welfare of the person in need. In a large number of studies across a variety of situations, Batson and his colleagues provided strong evidence for the link between empathy and altruistic prosocial behavior. In one case, participants watched a seemingly distressed female undergraduate allegedly receiving electric shocks and could volunteer to take the electric shocks in her place. In another, participants read about a single mom who needed help in coping with her assignments and could volunteer to help her. Empathic concern was either aroused by various instructions or occurred naturally and was then assessed. The findings across all these studies showed that between 50% and 90% of the participants volunteered to help once high levels of empathic concern were aroused (naturally or experimentally).

A host of other studies on children and adolescents have demonstrated that they too tend to help a distressed person once empathy is aroused (See review by Eisenberg, Fabes, & Spinrad, 2006). Eisenberg and her colleagues, for example, observed empathic reactions and prosocial activities after exposing children to empathy-inducing film clips, crying babies, or injured adults (see review in Eisenberg, Spinrad, & Sadovsky, 2006). In such cases the majority of children offered help spontaneously. In fact, such prosocial proclivities can be observed even with 10-month-old infants (in, for example, attentive or sad facial expressions) (Davidov, Zahn-Waxler, Roth-Hanania, & Knafo, 2013). In one-year-olds, this proclivity and actual prosocial acts are characteristically expressed toward mothers. During toddlerhood and in the preschool years, they are also extended to siblings, other children, and even adult strangers (Warneken & Tomasello, 2013).

Although empathy appears to work for negative emotions such as pain or distress as well as for positive ones such as happiness, researchers were largely interested in what happens when the other person is in pain or distressed. We thus know much less about empathic processes and their ramifications when we empathize with positive emotional states in the other. Such empathy also leads to a kind of caring that is reflected in joining in and sharing the positive feelings of success, good fortune, enthusiasm, surprise, wonder and happiness in others. The literature on parenting and social support has noted this as part of the motivation to care, as when a parent exerts caring by rejoicing with her child on her achievement or when a friend shares his comrade's happiness in the comrade's graduation ceremony (Vangelisti, 2009).

Modulation of empathic responses

Although very pervasive, such a strong and extensive association between empathy, concern, and prosocial behavior does not involve an automatic human response. The occurrence of empathy and in particular the translation of empathy into the motivation to care and the enactment of such motivation in actual behavior are all modulated by various conditions. Such modulations occur at different points in this process.

Modulation of empathy

For example, although emotional empathy is basic and tends to be quickly and automatically activated in almost all cases, it can be modulated by early experiences with caregivers as well as by previous knowledge (Feldman, 2012). The cognitive and more conscious processes of empathy, which also rely on early experience and knowledge, can also be subject to changes depending on one's state of mind. For example, studies targeting the empathic brain areas that employed the event-related potential (ERP) found indications for a two-stage process, wherein each stage was modulated by different aspects (Fan & Han, 2008). The first stage was an early unconscious component involving emotional sharing and the second was a later component that appears to reflect a cognitive evaluation. The early emotional component correlated with subjective ratings of the pain observed in others and showed a stronger manifestation when real photographs of people in a pain-eliciting situation (e.g., hand trapped in a door or cut by scissors) were presented vs. the presentation of cartoons of exactly the same photos. The cognitive component was modulated by the demands of the task showing stronger manifestation when participants observing these photographs were asked to provide pain judgments vs. when they were asked to count the number of hands (one or two) appearing in those photographs.

Another interesting modulation that demonstrates the power of experience was found in an ERP study on physicians. In general, individuals who are in the helping professions and are constantly faced with others' pain and suffering may be overwhelmed by such experiences if they automatically feel empathy during most of their working time. Indeed, research has identified compassion fatigue and burnout among caregivers in professions involving an intense exposure to others' suffering (Hooper, et al., 2010). Such caregivers would benefit from regulating at least part of their empathic responses. Jean Decety and colleagues (Decety, Yang, & Cheng, 2010) have indeed observed such regulatory processes among physicians. The researchers recorded event-related potentials (ERPs) from physicians and matched controls as they were presented with visual stimuli depicting body parts pricked by a needle (pain) or touched by a cotton swab (no pain). Unlike the controls, the physicians did not display the early or late ERP responses characteristic of the pain vs. no-pain conditions. It appears that emotion regulation in physicians has very early effects that even inhibit the bottom-up (emotional) processing of the perception of pain in others. The authors suggested that the physicians' dampening of their negative arousal in response to the pain of others in this situation may have beneficial consequences, such as freeing up the cognitive resources necessary for being instrumentally helpful.

Modulation of the empathy—prosocial response link

The important role of emotional regulation in the modulation of the empathy–prosocial response has been extensively studied and discussed by a number of researchers. Generally, observing distress, pain, or suffering in others causes distress in the observers along with the almost automatic and immediate processes of empathy. This has often been referred to as *empathic distress* or *personal distress* and may relate to the anxiety and aversive overarousal that individuals may experience when empathizing with a negative and aversive state in another person. At times this distress may be too great and lead to self focus, whereby the observer becomes engaged in relieving his or her own distress rather than helping the other's predicament. In such cases, the observer may opt to disengage physically and psychologically from the distress-provoking situa tion rather than help. Such distress co-occurs and competes with compassion/sympathy in responses to another's suffering (Batson, Fultz, Schoenrade, & Paduano, 1987; Batson, 1991). For example, watching a difficult scene in which someone is in pain, people often feel both empathy and distress and sometimes look away or walk away to alleviate their distress rather offer immediate help. This led Eisenberg and her colleagues (Eisenberg, et al., 1994) to suggest that emotional regulation is a central moderator of the association between empathy and the motivation to care. Compassion, sympathy, and empathic concern can be salient enough to culminate in caring motivation only if individuals are capable of regulating the distress they may feel in being exposed to others' misfortunes. Studies of adults (Batson, 1991) as well as of children (e.g., Eisenberg, Fabes, & Spinrad, 2006) have provided clear support for this process and shown that prosocial and caring behavior was more prevalent as other-oriented empathy increased and self-oriented anxiety decreased (as examined by self-reports as well as by physiological measures and facial indices).

Consequently, individuals capable of modulating their own distress effectively because of genetic or acquired capacities demonstrate clear empathy–prosocial behavior associations whereas, for example, individuals with a genetic background of high negative emotionality—(i.e., the tendency to experience strong negative emotions such as distress or anger) who are easily aroused by the distress of others unless tempered by socialization—demonstrate lower levels of caring and prosocial behavior (See review in Eisenberg, Fabes, & Spinrad, 2006).

Finally, even if a caring motivation is aroused, a person may not always provide such care to the person in need. This may relate to a large number of issues, such as whether the help is deemed appropriate, whether the person feels capable of helping and the general existence of a large number of forces that affect the dynamics of acting upon any human motivation (e.g., costs and benefits of such enactment, relevant alternatives). More specifically, the association between felt empathy, concern for the other, and helping is more controlled and less automatic than the less conscious emotional arousal described earlier, and it is subject to a large variety of socialization processes.

Effects of socialization

Part of the socialization process involves learning to whom we are expected to orient our empathic concern and to provide care and assistance and to whom we are expected to express an opposite attitude. We appear to learn how to

curtail the almost automatic empathic responses and to impose behavioral
(looking aside), cognitive (classifying the other as belonging to an out-group)
and emotional filters for modulating our spontaneous empathic responses (de
Vignemont & Singer 2006). Research has documented several such modulators. One of the central and universal modulators is our tendency to feel empathy and to be motivated to care for family and friends more than for strangers
(Hoffman, 2000). Several recent neuroimaging studies throw light on this
process. An fMRI study showed similar but also distinct patterns of brain activation for empathy with the social suffering of friends and strangers (Meyer
et al., 2013). Specifically observing a friend's exclusion activated the affective
pain regions associated with the direct (i.e., firsthand) experience of exclusion (dorsal anterior cingulate cortex dACC and insula), which correlated with
a self-reported self-other overlap with the friend. The better the relationship
or the closer you are to your friend, the more similar areas associated with
affective empathy are activated when either you or your friend are socially
excluded. In contrast, observing a stranger's exclusion activated regions associated with "mentalizing" and cognitive empathy (DMPFC, precuneus, and
temporal pole). These results suggest the existence of at least two routes to
feeling empathy and concern that can culminate in motivated care. Empathy
for friends' social suffering emanates from emotional sharing and mechanisms
related to self-other connections, whereas empathy for strangers' social suffering may rely more heavily on mentalizing systems, perspective taking, and
possibly beliefs and values.

Empathic neural responses are also modulated by the perceived fairness of
others, at least for males (Singer et al., 2006). In one study, participants played
an economic game with two confederates who played either fairly or unfairly.
While monitored with fMRI imaging, participants then observed the confederates undergoing a painful intervention. Both sexes exhibited empathy-
related activation toward fair players in pain-related brain areas (frontoinsular
and anterior cingulate cortices), the "regular" empathic brain areas. However,
in males these empathy-related responses were significantly reduced when they
observed an unfair person receiving pain. This reduction was notably accompanied by increased activation in reward-related areas and correlated with a
reported desire for revenge. This neuroimaging finding reflects the moderating
role of fairness or trustworthiness in empathic processes in men and perhaps
what has been described by evolutionary researchers as an altruistic punishment, namely the maintenance of cooperation and caring with strangers as an
evolutionary strategy by punishing those who deceive or are unfair. Similar
modulations appear with regard to in-group vs. out-group status in both men
and women (Xu, et al., 2009; Hein, et al., 2010). For example, empathic neural response in the anterior cingulate cortex to the observation of painful

stimulations applied to faces decreased significantly when participants viewed the faces of other races (Xu et al., 2009).

Chapter conclusion

Findings from neuroimaging studies substantiate insights gained from the psychologically oriented research. Together they underscore (1) the pervasiveness of empathic processes; (2) their almost automatic nature; (3) their activation through direct experiences and through imagining, perspective taking, and mentalizing; and (4) the strong association between empathy arousal and the emergence of the motivation to care. Furthermore, these studies expose very similar core processes at the psychological and biological levels across a variety of situations and targets. Together, these attest to the centrality of caring in our functioning, the existence of an innate and inborn mechanism for its arousal, and the similarity in the activation of this central mechanism across a variety of situation and targets.

At the same time the research demonstrated relevant adaptations and modulations whereby such "automatic" processes can nevertheless be modulated by one's upbringing, experiences, and culture and as part of concurrent contextual influences. These modulations regulate empathy and control its culmination in the caring motivation, as with in-groups vs. out-groups and toward fair vs. unfair players. In fact, a comprehensive neural model of empathic processes that captures the core facets of these processes across various relationships with familiar and unfamiliar others has been offered on the basis of the extensive neuropsychological research in this area (Decety, 2012). This model stipulates three major phenomenological and psychological components that incorporate both bottom-up and top-down processes and pinpoints their location in brain areas as well as the neural pathways between them. These include (1) affective arousal and sharing—the emotional aspect, (2) emotional understanding—the mentalizing aspect, and (3) self-regulation. Although most studies describe similar processes for men and women in the core empathic processes, gender variations do appear in certain circumstances, and these issues will be discussed in a special chapter devoted to gender differences (Chapter 15).

Empathy appears to be vital for our evolutionary fitness as a species, whose young need caring and protection for extended periods of time. These are better provided in the context of pair bonds and small groups with biologically related individuals. Our evolutionary fitness as a species also appears to be served by living in complex social groups where sophisticated cooperation and caring for unfamiliar others is needed. Empathy developed as a core biopsychological proximate mechanism that prompts the motivation to care and hence engenders caring in all of these contexts (i.e., parenting, pair bonds, biologically related small groups and complex social groups). Furthermore, empathy allows us to tailor our caring to be adequate and sensitive to the needs of the other. It involves both an almost automatic and rather simple and phylogenetically older mechanism of mimicking and emotional contagion as well as highly sophisticated processes that build upon these core subcortical mechanisms. These advanced and flexible forms of empathic processes in humans involve mentalizing and higher-order processing that allow the identification of nuanced emotions and situations and the voluntary arousal or inhibition of empathy using sophisticated mentalizing processes that involve morality and values.

Most of the studies and theories discussed here have referred to empathic responses to negative affective states in the other, such as physical pain, distress, and exclusion. However, empathy also operates with positive emotions, since we also partake in others' happiness and joy. Either way, empathy is a central biopsychological human mechanism for triggering the caring motivation, which instinctively ties our welfare with the welfare of others around us, those close to us as well as strangers.

5

Biological Bases of Caregiving

The evolutionary perspectives described earlier regarding the emergence and existence of caring and the universal human biopsychological mechanism of empathy mean, among other things, that caring is hard-wired in our genes and is also biologically driven. Recent studies on both animals and humans have identified several biological mechanisms related to the motivation to care and to caregiving actions. For example, several studies addressed and found similarities between mammals and humans in the brain regions associated with maternal caregiving as well as similarities in the neurotransmitters involved in this process, most notably oxytocin (OT), vasopressin, and prolactin as well as similar empathic neurological processes as described in the previous chapter (Gonzalez-Liencres, Shamay-Tsoory, & Brüne, 2013). This chapter will review some of the central findings of studies conducted on the biological, neuroendocrinologial, and genetic bases of caring. It will attempt to demonstrate their similarity across the diverse types and kinds of caregiving—parenting, pair bonds, friends, and strangers—thus supporting the claim of the existence of a hard-wired fundamental and comprehensive caring motivation that relies on similar biological processes within the different domains and manifestations.

Animal studies

Several neuropeptides appear to come up again and again as related to caring behaviors (such as grooming) in animals. Neuropeptides are molecules used by neurons to communicate with each other. Peptides may also occasionally function as hormones. These neuropeptides, and especially OT, which was implicated in the formation of social and pair bonds (sexual/romantic bonds) as well as parental bonds, but also vassopressin, prolactin, and endogenous opioids are selectively released in situations that are relevant to bondings in which caring is implied, such as birth, breast-feeding, and sexual behavior (see review in Insel, 1997, and Carter, 1998, 2007).

Experimental manipulations of these neuropeptides strongly suggest a causal role in caregiving behaviors. OT, for example, induces maternal responsiveness and investment when it is injected into virgin rats; these behaviors can be blocked with OT antagonists, leading to slower pup retrieval and less licking and self-grooming (Pedersen, 1997). In addition, maternal behavior was increased (and infanticide decreased) in wild house mice after peripheral injections (to the blood) of OT (McCarthy, Bare, & vom Saal, 1986), and central treatments with OT (to the brain) increased maternal behavior in multiparous ewes (Kendrick, Keverne, & Baldwin, 1987). Interestingly, OT appears to be mostly associated with the onset but not the maintenance of maternal investment behavior because OT antagonists cannot always block maternal investment once it has started (see review in Insel, 1997). This raises the possibility that the hormones involved in the formation of a social bond lead to long-term changes in neural circuitry, which then acts to promote investment behavior through other biological mechanisms besides those involved in creating the bond.

OT is also involved in other domains besides mothering, such as pair bonds. Prairie voles, for example, are conspicuous in their formation of monogamous pair bonds following mating. The OT and vasopressin secreted during intercourse appear to play a central role in such bonding. For example, central OT treatments induced male partner preferences in female prairie voles. OT antagonists, on the other hand, prevented the development of these preferences. In male prairie voles that had not yet mated, it was arginine vasopressin given centrally that induced an enduring selective preference for a mate (increased affiliation), increased aggression toward other males (mate guarding), and increased paternal care (see review in Insel, 2010). These neuropeptides also appear to inhibit anxiety and fight-or-flight reactions besides facilitating affiliative behaviors and bonding (Carter, 1998). Specifically, OT is known to buffer the stress response, lower the heart rate and blood pressure, and improve the body's ability to store nutrients, repair wounds, and grow (see review in Uvnäs-Moberg, 1998).

The study of these processes in humans has only recently begun to expand with the easier measurement and administration of OT and vasopressin, the advent of new technologies that allow nonintrusive assessments of brain functioning (such as fMRI, EEG, and ERP), and progress in genetic studies. The increasing numbers of recent studies that have examined the neuronal, hormonal, and genetic correlates of caring processes in humans provide us with a growing understanding of the biological correlates of caring and caregiving.

Neurohormonal basis of human caring

During the last decade, growing numbers of studies have provided evidence for processes in humans that are similar to those observed with animals, particularly those relating to OT, which is synthesized in the hypothalamus and has long been known to elicit uterine contraction and milk letdowns in animals and humans. The OT system is reciprocally engaged with the hypothalamic-pituitary-adrenal axis (HPA), which mediates the stress response and has antistress effects that induce a sense of safety and calm. These effects are central for the initiation of breast-feeding and the formation of maternal-infant bonding as well as other bonds (Uvnäs-Moberg, 1998). In line with these effects, recent findings have also linked higher levels of OT to a better-functioning immune system. This connection, along with the stress-reduction effects, may be related to the role of OT and possibly caring in promoting health and psychological and physical well-being (Uvnäs-Moberg, 1998; Feldman, 2012). Furthermore, OT is also connected to the brain's dopaminergic reward system and thus serves to couple processes of bonding and providing care with an experience of reward and intuitive reinforcement; this contributes to the motivation to bond and care by increasing the incentive value of the care receiver for the care giver.

OT acts both as neuropeptide in various brain systems and as a hormone acting peripherally. Its effects in humans are examined by measuring endogenous OT levels in the blood, urine, or saliva as well as by the administration of synthetic OT by nasal sprays. The intranasal administration circumvents the blood-brain barrier and reaches the central nervous system within 30 to 45 minutes (see review in Veening, & Olivier, 2013), thus making it possible to examine the effects of OT interventions on human experience and behavior. These kinds of assessments provide strong evidence of causative processes.

Recent reviews (e.g., MacDonald & MacDonald, 2010; Bartz et al., 2011; Feldmam, 2012; Gonzalez-Liencres, Shamay-Tsoory, & Brüne, 2013) suggest that OT levels interact with other factors in promoting social motivation in a variety of cases implicating caring, such as parenting, romantic bonding, trust, cooperation, generosity, and prosocial behavior. In fact, the similarity across these different domains of caring led Feldman (2012, p. 381) to suggest that "the three prototypes of affiliation in mammals—parental, pair, and filial—share underlying physiological mechanisms and overt behavioral expressions" and that individual differences in these affiliation modes are shaped by experiences in early infancy involving biobehavioral regulators such as touch, body movements, odor, and voice. In the next sections I discuss some of these studies in the various domains.

Oxytocin in human parenting and caring

In a series of intriguing studies, Feldman and her colleagues examined the interplay of OT in human mothering and fathering. These investigators, for example, measured plasma OT in 62 pregnant women in the first and third trimesters of pregnancy and the first postpartum month, when they also observed mother-infant interaction. In these interactions they assessed positive indicators of sensitive and responsive mothering, such as the mother focusing her gaze mostly on the child, the mother's maintenance of an affectionate and stimulating touch and its adaptation to the infant's alertness, and the mother's use of "motherese" (a unique type of speech directed to infants). Higher levels of OT in the first trimester predicted an engagement in more positive and sensitive bonding behaviors after birth. Additionally, higher levels of OT across the pregnancy and the postpartum month were associated with frequent attachment-related thoughts and checking of the infant (Feldman et al., 2007). Furthermore, an increase in plasma OT from the first to the third trimester was associated with maternal bonding to the fetus during the third trimester, reflecting the evolution of a caring bond between mother and infant (Levine et al., 2007). Such OT effects were also demonstrated in foster mothers, whose OT levels were associated with the mothers' expressions of behavioral delight toward their foster infants at two and five months (Bick, et al., 2013). This demonstrates that OT levels are relevant to caring even without the biological and hormonal processes preparing biological mothers for mothering. Demonstrating how the operation of OT in the brain promotes sensitive caring, Riem et al. (2011) found that the administration of OT to mothers increased activation in empathy-related networks. It also reduced the amygdala's activation (a brain area associated with fear, anxiety, and avoidance) in response to the infant's crying, probably reflecting OT's calming and anxiolytic effects in the amygdala and its involvement in furthering empathy.

OT has also been involved in the behavior of fathers, who, like foster mothers, do not undergo the same hormonal changes preparing them for parenting as biological mothers do. As will be discussed in Chapters 8 and 15, maternal involvement in caring is obligatory, but paternal caring is facultative and is observed as an active endeavor in only 3% to 5% of mammalian species (Geary, 2000). In these biparental species, a father's caring shows a number of variations as compared with a mother's caring; these appear to enhance infant survival, growth, and thriving in the context of maternal care by offering caring that complements the care of the mother. Hence, across biparental species, mothers and fathers exhibit a coevolved gender-specific repertoire of parental behavior (Carter et al., 2005). For example, human mothers prefer face-to-face positions and display a maternally affectionate repertoire which involves touch and contact, where parent-infant synchrony is rhythmic and socially focused (Feldman et al., 2007). In contrast, human fathers tend to engage in interactions that induce high positive arousal, exploratory focus, and rough-and-tumble contact, with a synchrony that is outward-oriented and contains quick and unpredictable peaks of positive arousal (Lamb, 2010). It thus appears that mothers' and fathers' styles of caring have evolved to provide distinct parent-child experiences that prepare infants for different challenges. Mothers establish a sense of predictability and safety, while fathers prepare for novelty and excitement; both components are needed for thriving.

Several studies have examined the roles of neuropeptides in human paternal care. For example, in line with the expectation for different maternal and paternal caring, in a study assessing 80 couples and their firstborn children (Gordon et al., 2010a) the plasma OT in mothers and fathers was associated with different kinds of caring behaviors, at least during the first months. The mothers' OT correlated with the *social affective repertoire*, including maternal gaze, affect, vocalizations, and affectionate touches whereas the fathers' OT was associated with *object-oriented stimulatory play*, consisting of positive arousal, object exploration, and stimulatory touch. In another study of 112 mothers and fathers (not couples) and their 4- to 6-month-old infants, mothers who provided high levels of affectionate touch showed an increase in salivary OT from pre- to postinteraction, whereas fathers showed such an increase when they provided high levels of stimulatory contact (Feldman et al., 2010). In the same sample, plasma and saliva OT levels in mothers and fathers were associated with the parent and child's social engagement, affect synchrony, and positive communicative sequences (Feldman, Gordon, & Zagoory-Sharon, 2010, 2011).

In a fine demonstration of the causal role of OT in caring among fathers, the intranasal administration of OT in a double-blind experimental study showed that the subjects' salivary OT increased dramatically, and they showed more frequent touch and longer durations of engagement behavior after inhalation (reviewed in Feldman, 2012). Similar effects were observed in a study by Naber, van IJzendoorn, Deschamps, van Engeland, and Bakermans-Kranenburg (2010), where the intranasal administration of OT in a double-blind within-subject experiment increased fathers' observed responsiveness during play with their children compared with the control fathers who inhaled a placebo. Thus in both mothers and fathers, regular OT levels were associated with sensitive, synchronized care. In addition, in both mothers and fathers, augmented levels of OT through administration contributed to sensitive, synchronized care; additionally, engagement in synchronized care, in turn, also increased OT levels.

Other hormones and neuropeptides are also implicated in parental caring. One study, for example, assessed fathers' levels of OT and prolactin, a peptide hormone often associated with human milk production but also active in a wide range of other roles. The fathers' levels of OT correlated with the fathers' behavior during social play, and their levels of prolactin were associated with play during a session that called for the introduction of specific toys and coordinating explorations with the infant (Gordon et al., 2010b). Another study demonstrated that some of these neuropeptides may have similar effects in mothers and fathers. Although mothers provided more affectionate contact, and fathers provided more stimulatory contact with their 4–6 month-old infants high OT levels were associated with more affectionate contact in both mothers *and* fathers. Additionally, high levels of arginine vasopressin (AVP), a neuropeptide closely related to OT, which is implicated in male bonding and territorial behavior in animals (Wang, Liu, Young, & Insel, 2000) were associated with high object-directed stimulatory engagement in both mothers and fathers (Apter-Levi, Zagoory-Sharon, & Feldman, 2014).

In the studies described earlier as well as others that followed parents for up to 13 years (see review in Feldman 2012), OT levels were comparable for fathers and mothers at different stages of the infants' development and were higher than OT levels in nonattached singles, attesting to the importance of OT in the parental care of men and women and suggesting that OT level may reflect a stable propensity to care. Furthermore, maternal and paternal levels were interrelated at the dyadic level, perhaps demonstrating coregulation of OT levels among dyads of parents or similarity between them in caring that was part of their mating choices (i.e., choosing a partner with a similar caring capacity and motivation). Interestingly, plasma and saliva OT levels in mothers and fathers were also associated with their reports on the quality of their relationship with their own parents and romantic partners, underscoring that a general biologically based propensity to care that implicates OT is anchored in the quality of one's close relations, with parents, romantic partners, and children (Feldman, Gordon, & Zagoory-Sharon, 2010, 2011). Feldman further suggests that this propensity is affected early on by the kind of caring an infant receives from its caregivers (mostly its parents) and even provides evidence that such parental care may exert an effect by modulating the expression of relevant genes (Feldman Gordon, Influs, Gutbir, & Ebstein, 2013).

Taken together, these findings demonstrate that besides birth and breast-feeding, which were identified as key biological conditions that increase OT secretion, other forms of parental caring (e.g., paternal and foster parenting) are also associated with similar levels of OT secretion; dyads appear to be synchronized in this respect. Furthermore, OT levels remained moderately stable across time, demonstrating a stable biological proclivity that probably reflects individual differences in the propensity to care. Other neuropeptides, such as arginine vasopressin are also involved in parenting and mothers and fathers demonstrate similarity as well as distinctiveness in the effects of neuropeptides on their parenting.

Oxytocin and caring in romantic relations

OT is implicated not only in parenting but also in other caring relationships and even in caring for strangers. For example, as regards romantic relations, the administration of OT increased a cohabiting couple's observed positive communication (Ditzen et al., 2009). In addition, greater partner support was linked to higher plasma OT for both men and women in cohabiting couples (Grewen et al., 2005), and salivary OT increased after one week of "warm touch" intervention in both men and women and increased even further after four weeks of practicing warm touch (Holt-Lunstad et al., 2008). Furthermore, fMRI studies showed that the brain regions implicated in mothering were also shown to be active in prolonged romantic relationships (Acevedo et al., 2012) and were correlated with feelings of love and friendship toward the partner in both men and women. These findings and others (see review in Feldman 2012) are very promising in showing a connection between the biological mechanisms involved in parenting and engagement in romantic relations that involve close bonds and care. However, because the romantic bond includes a variety of facets (i.e., attachment, caring, sexual desire), the role of OT as reflecting the caring aspect of these relations is thus far unclear. The research has yet to disentangle the hormonal and neuronal activity profile of the different facets of the romantic bond in order to be able to say a bit more on the role of OT in romantic *caring*. A promising recent study with new lovers specifically examined support provision in a dyadic interaction (Schneiderman, Kanat-Maymon, Ebstein, & Feldman, 2013). The researchers examined the association between genetic variability on the oxytocin receptor gene (*OXTR*) and empathic behavior during the interaction. The researchers found that high cumulative *OXTR* risk that is reflected in the number of allelic variations that had been associated with problems of social functioning was correlated with difficulties in empathic communication among romantic dyads; this was found after controlling for relationship duration, anxiety, and depressive symptoms. This provides direct evidence of the role of OT in modulating *caring* in romantic bonds.

Oxytocin and caring with strangers

In line with the claim of this book for a general hormonal-neuronal network that underpins a variety of caring processes, OT has been implicated in a large number of other caring-related processes with unfamiliar adults apart from close bonds. Specifically in line with the expectation that caring is preceded by the empathic understanding of other people's feelings and experiences, OT has been associated with a more accurate perception of emotional cues in familiar and unfamiliar others (Bartz, Zaki, Bolger, & Ochsner, 2011). For example, in a double-blind placebo-controlled within-subject design, the intranasal administration of OT improved participants' ability to infer the affective mental state of others as assessed by facial expressions around the eyes (the Reading the Mind in the Eyes Test). OT was also found to directly affect empathy. For example, intranasal OT improved empathy-related social but not nonsocial learning (Hurleman et al., 2010).

In the same vein, OT has also been implicated in the generation of higher trust in unfamiliar others. A groundbreaking 2005 paper published in *Nature* demonstrated that the intranasal administration of OT enhanced interpersonal trust in an economic game with strangers (Kosfeld et al., 2005). Kosfeld and his colleagues underscored the importance of trust in friendship, love, families, and organizations and emphasized its key role in economic exchanges and politics. Without trust among trading partners and in a country's institutions and leaders, they argued, economic transactions and political legitimacy would break down. It is interesting to note that they viewed such trust as similar in essence to interpersonal trust in close bonds. They consequently suggested that the same neuropeptide that plays such central role in prosocial exchanges in close relations and bonding will have similar effects in a trust game with strangers. In the trust game, an individual playing the role of investor can anonymously choose a costly trusting option of giving money to the second player in the role of trustee. Whatever amount the investor gives to the trustee is tripled, but the trustee retains it all. Yet the trustee who is informed about the investor's transfer can then honor the investor's trust by anonymously sharing it with the investor. Hence both players can end up with a higher monetary payoff than at the beginning. This game is played only once with the same partner. The dilemma for the investor is whether to trust the trustee. If he or she trusts and the trustee shares, the investor can increase his or her payoff, but the trustee can be selfish and abuse this trust; then the investor is worse off monetarily and psychologically than if he or she had chosen not to transfer money at all. The administration of intranasal OT increased the investors' trust considerably. The investors' average transfer was 17% higher in the OT group than in placebo. Of the 29 participants, 13 (45%) in the OT group chose to transfer all their money—the maximal trust level—compared with only 6 of the 29 participants (21%) in the placebo group. In a follow-up study, such trust-enhancing effects of OT administration were observed even after individuals had been betrayed by another player. This was produced by an OT-mediated reduction of amygdala activation, which probably led to lower levels of anxiety and perceived threats (Baumgartner et al., 2008).

In line with the suggestion that OT enhances trust, the administration of OT to males and females increased the trustworthiness ratings of unfamiliar male and female targets relative to control ratings (Theodoridou, Rowe, Penton-Voak, & Rogers, 2009). An increase in trust was also demonstrated in relation to psychological risks such as providing confidential information to others where participants on OT were 44 times more trusting than participants on placebo (Mikolajczak, Pinon, Lane, de Timary, & Luminet, 2010). These processes were bidirectional, and OT levels were also increased by the experience of interpersonal trust. For example, the perception of another's trust led to higher levels of plasma OT in the observer (Zak, Kurzban, & Matzner, 2005).

Dozens of intranasal OT studies followed the 2005 *Nature* study (Kosfeld et al., 2005), suggesting that this peptide modulates many aspects of caring-related social cognition, particularly those relating to empathy, generosity, and prosocial responding. A recent meta-analysis of more than a dozen experiments involving the intranasal administration of OT provides support for the idea of the prosocial effects of OT (Van IJzendoorn & Bakermans-Kranenburg, 2012). In this meta-analysis and in line with its depiction as enhancing empathy, intranasal OT administration was found to enhance the recognition of facial expressions of emotions (13 effect sizes, N = 408), and to elevate the level of in-group trust (8 effect sizes, N = 317).

With respect to generosity, OT-administered participants were 80% more generous than those given a placebo when they had to make a one-shot decision on how to split a sum of money with an anonymous stranger (Zak, Stanton, & Ahmadi, 2007). This effect was also apparent with donations to charity. Specifically, participants were presented with the opportunity to donate to charity after playing a series of economic games. OT did not affect the decision to donate, just the amount. Among the participants who donated, those given OT donated 48% more money to charity than those given a placebo.

Demonstrating the causal effect of an empathy-based increase in OT on generosity, Barraza and Zak (2009) had participants watch short video clips of emotional and nonemotional scenes and asked them to rate their empathic reactions. They then assessed the participants' OT levels and observed their generosity in an economic game where they could split money that they had received with a stranger. Empathy was associated with a 47% increase in OT from the baseline level, and higher levels of empathy were associated with more generous monetary offers.

Together, these studies demonstrate the clear role of OT in promoting empathy, trust, and generosity toward strangers. Furthermore, results appear to suggest that one way in which OT affects actual caring is through its effects on empathy and trust. In implicating OT in parenting, support in romantic bonds, and empathy, trust, and generosity with strangers, these findings clearly support the view advocated in this book—that caring is a fundamental and comprehensive motivation which relies on a common basis in biological processes.

Modulation of oxytocin's effects on caring processes

Because of OT's positive role in such a wide variety of caring processes and situations, it was dubbed the "love hormone" (see a special issue of *Hormones and Behavior* devoted to OT research, edited by Young & Flanagan-Cato 2012; Van IJzendoorn & Bakermans-Kranenburg, 2012). However, as with empathic responses at the neuronal level, there is increasingly more evidence suggesting that the affiliative-caring and prosocial effects of OT are modulated by a variety of contextual conditions. In my discussion of empathy and evolutionary processes in earlier chapters, I noted the evolutionary "need" to limit the application of empathic and prosocial processes to interactions with partners and groups that would not strongly exploit one's benevolence. In that sense, we would need checks and balances to preserve a fundamental caring motivation so that we would not totally deplete our resources in helping others. In other words, genes that biologically and hormonally trigger an altruistic response that encompasses *limitless* empathy and caring behaviors would probably not have survived in our gene pool for long. As discussed in previous chapters, similarity or in-group vs. out-group status—as well as the perception of someone as dishonest, untrustworthy, or threatening—may have developed as signals to alert us to the potential boundaries of our caring nature. In that sense the caring motivational system should consist of activating mechanisms such as empathy as well as restricting and inhibiting mechanisms for optimal regulation. Interestingly, the study of OT administration in a variety of contexts has uncovered precisely such effects.

For example, a recent meta-analysis suggests that the intranasal administration of oxytocin did not significantly change out-group trust, although it did result in an increase in in-group trust (10 effect sizes; N = 505) (Van IJzendoorn & Bakermans-Kranenburg, 2012). Furthermore, OT was found to increase generosity only in the absence of cues suggesting that a social partner might be insincere (Mikolajczak, Gross et al., 2010).

de Drue and colleagues also found that under high threat conditions, OT is associated with financially "aggressive" behavior toward a competing out-group. A similar finding was described in a dyadic situation that involved a sense of competition (Shamay-Tsoory, Fischer, et al., 2009). The administration of OT increased envy ratings when the participant gained less money than another player and also increased gloating ratings during relative gain conditions (when the participant gained more money than the other player). Shamay-Tsoory and her colleagues have suggested that OT may play a central role in enhancing the salience of social stimuli and is therefore central in affecting social emotions. Accordingly, the specific effects of OT may depend on the social context: OT can increase positive and prosocial responses such as empathy, trustworthiness, generosity, and altruism in positive or neutral social contexts, and it can intensify negative emotions such as envy and gloating and even increase aggressive behaviors in competitive situations.

In line with this suggestion and demonstrating the positive effects of a noncompetitive context, Israel, Weisel, Ebstein, and Bornstein (2012) found that in a context of intergroup *cooperation*, OT not only improves contributions to the in-group but also increases contribution rates in the collective interest of all groups. OT also increased the expectation that others would also contribute and reciprocate the cooperative behavior. These results suggest that the group-oriented prosocial effects of OT may be sensitive to contextual cues, which depend on how the social context is framed. In fact, mutual cooperation is generally a rewarding experience. For example, a neuroimaging study with women demonstrated that a situation of mutual cooperation was associated with the activation of specific reward processing areas that were not activated when the participants received monetary gains in a control condition without a partner (Rilling, Gutman, Zeh, Pagnoni, Berns, & Kilts, 2002).

In a similar vein, Shamay-Tsoory and her colleagues (2013) examined the effects of OT on the empathy of a group of Israeli Jewish participants toward the pain of in-group (Jewish), neutral out-group (European), and adversarial out-group (Palestinian) members. The study was not cast in the context of the intractable Israeli–Palestinian conflict and the empathy-inducing pictures were primed only by names characteristic of members of each of the groups. Hence although cooperation was not primed, conflict and competition were not highly salient. The researchers found that OT remarkably increased empathy for the Palestinians' pain, attenuating the effect of the in-group empathy bias observed under the placebo condition. This remarkable effect demonstrated the powerful function of OT in advancing empathy—even toward out-group members involved in intractable conflicts. Had this study been conducted while priming the conflict and dissimilarity among the groups, OT administration might have had the opposite effects.

Interestingly, OT made the out-group look like the in-group but did not enhance empathic responses toward the in-group members. This suggests that OT may have a saturation point above which OT enhancement will not increase empathy. Indeed, when the level of empathy accords with the relevant and available information, we would not want it to increase beyond what is adaptable. There is an optimal level of empathy and prosocial inclination, though what constitutes an optimal level may change according to circumstances, culture, and individual differences. If this assertion is correct, the administration of OT will tend to enhance sensitivity to emotional cues, empathy, and trust in situations where individuals have diminished sensitivity and caring capacities and when such enhancement accords with contextual and interpersonal conditions (see discussion by Bartz et al., 2011).

Individual differences also emerge between genders (e.g., Fischer-Shofty, Levkovitz, & Hurlemann et al., 2010; Rilling et al., 2012; Shamay-Tsoory, 2013; Rilling et al., 2014). However, research on gender differences is currently sparse; more research is required if we are to understand the bigger picture of gender differences in neuropeptide operations.

Genetics and caring

Like other vital motivations, such as hunger and sleep, caring shows individual differences that are biologically and genetically driven. For example, early studies on adult twins (monozygotic and dyzygotic) have shown that about 50% of the variances on measures of altruism, empathy, and nurturance are genetic in origin (Rushton, et al., 1986). Indications of genetic influence could be identified in demonstrations of empathic concern and in prosocial acts as early as the second year of life (Zahn-Waxler, Robinson, & Emde, 1992). Ebstein, Israel, Chew, Zhong and Knafo (2010) have summarized the current extant research, which demonstrates a greater than 50% hereditability in prosocial behaviors for both boys and girls, and parental warmth showed around 40% genetic effects. Most of the other variance in prosocial and empathic displays was attributed to unshared environment effects.

In a recent review, Knafo and Uzefovsky (2013) examined all the twin studies dealing with the heritability of individual differences in empathy (seven studies, 1,655 subjects; age range 1.2 to 48 years). These studies assessed both emotional and cognitive empathy and used behavioral tests as well as questionnaires. Genetic factors accounted for 35% of the variance in empathy in general (30% for cognitive and 26% for emotional empathy). Genetic effects increased with age and were moderated by socioeconomic and medical risks, with higher risks associated with lower heritability. It appears that a detrimental environment did not allow children to fully develop their genetic potential for empathy.

Another way of examining genetic effects is molecular genetics, which provides a means of studying how naturally occurring variations in human behavior relate to specific genetic variations. In light of the central role of OT in caring and prosocial processes, researchers have thus far mostly examined OT-related genes, most notably the *OXTR* gene that encodes the OT receptor, which is termed OXTR. Genetic variations influencing the number, organization, or functioning of OT receptors would be expected to influence the efficacy of OT signaling in the brain. The extant research has revealed very promising results. Variations in *OXTR* gene were found to relate to susceptibility to mental disorders characterized by social deficits, particularly autistic spectrum disorders but also schizophrenia (see review in Ebstein, Israel, Chew, Zhong & Knafo, 2010). Studies of the *OXTR* (the gene) have targeted specific single-nucleotide polymorphisms (SNPs) of interest. SNPs (pronounced "snips") represent the most common type of genetic variation among people and point to differences in a single DNA building block (a nucleotide). For example, a SNP may replace the nucleotide guanine (G) with the nucleotide adenine (A) in a certain stretch of DNA. Several high-risk variants linked to susceptibility for autistic spectrum disorders were specifically targeted within the *OXTR* gene, such as the rs2254298, rs53576, and rs1042778 SNPs.

Individuals with GG alleles at rs53576 (more than 50% in the European population), for example, performed significantly better than those with other alleles at rs53576 on a test of the ability to read the emotional state of others as well as on self-reported measures of empathy but not on self-reported measures of attachment, demonstrating a possible distinction between providing care and receiving care (Rodrigues et al., 2009). This same GG allele was also associated with higher maternal sensitivity in relation to toddlers (Bakermans-Kranenburg & van IJzendoorn, 2008). Furthermore, it has also been associated with more affiliative displays, increased trust, and lower hormonal and neurocardiac reactivity to social stress (see review in Yamasue et al., 2012; Walter, 2012). Variations in another SNP of the *OXTR* gene at rs2254298 have been associated with prosociality (Israel et al., 2009), trait empathy (Wu et al., 2012), and parental touch during interactions with infants (Feldman et al., 2012). Taken together, these findings clearly accord with an expected connection between several variations in the *OXTR* gene and caring.

In a recent study that examined several variants of the *OXTR* gene and the *CD38* gene, which is needed for the release of OT (all having risk alleles for autistic spectrum disorders), Feldman and colleagues (2012) found that individuals with high-risk alleles in the *OXTR* rs2254298 –or rs1042778 SNPs, or in the rs3796863 SNP of CD38 had lower levels of plasma OT, with similar effects in mothers, fathers, and nonparents. In addition, the risk alleles in the *OXTR* and *CD38* genes were each related to lower frequencies of parental affectionate touch during parent-infant interactions.

Examinations of altruism with unfamiliar adults show that common polymorphisms (e.g., variations in SNPs) in both the OT receptor gene (*OXTR*) and the vasopressin 1a receptor gene (*AVPR1a*) were implicated in human altruistic behavior in economic games similar to the ones that were also used to study empathy and generosity (see review in Ebstein, Israel, Chew, Zhong, & Knafo, 2010).

Reflecting the importance of rewarding experiences in caring, genes involved in the dopaminergic brain reward systems have also been implicated in caring. For example, less efficient alleles of the gene encoding dopamine D4 receptor (*DRD4*) were associated with less sensitive parenting. Conversely, the most efficient allelic combination appeared to buffer the negative effect of daily hassles on maternal sensitivity. In addition, the maternal *DAT1* genotype (another dopaminergic polymorphism in the dopamine transporter) was associated with negative parenting (see review in Ebstein et al., 2010). In sum, research on the genetic underpinnings of caring underscore the key role that genetic variations play, affecting individual differences in this capacity, Research has also begun to map the specific genes that may be involved in caring.

Chapter conclusion

In its entirety, the research on the biological bases of caring demonstrates impressive similarities in the functioning of brain areas, neuropeptides, and genes associated with caring across a variety of situations and relationships such as mothering and fathering, romantic relations, empathy and generosity toward strangers, as well as trust and cooperation in economic games in dyadic and group contexts with unfamiliar others. OT appears to play a central and pivotal role in our motivation and capacity to engage in caring. OT appears to enhance the capacity to correctly identify social cues, to be empathic, to care in a sensitive and appropriate way, to trust others, to cooperate with them, and to be generous and prosocial. Yet it appears also to be implicated in the downregulating empathy and care for others who are perceived as insincere, untrustworthy, and threatening, thus guarding the caring individual from being exploited and in fact contributing to the sustenance of caring across time and generations. Three major processes were suggested as operating to bring about such diverse yet related outcomes of OT: anxiety reduction, an increasing salience of social cues, and the activation of affiliative motivation, which I suggest involves a specific kind of affiliation—that of caring (Bartz et al., 2011).

Research on the heritability of caring processes (e.g., empathy, prosocial responding) has uncovered a substantial 30% to 60% variance in individual differences that is attributed to genetic effects. Furthermore, the early mapping of specific gene variants involved in caring processes using a molecular genetic approach has already made several important contributions. All in all, the expanding research on the biopsychological and hereditary basis of caring demonstrates the clear biological base of a general and encompassing caring motivational system that involves parenting, caring in romantic relations, and empathy and prosocial responding to strangers. The research also demonstrates common core processes and mechanisms (e.g., empathy, trust, sensitive responding) that are similarly manifested in a variety of domains and relations (e.g., involving parents, pair bonds, and unfamiliar others) and a strong hereditary component of individual differences in their manifestations across them. This has led several researchers to propose holistic models for the neural and hormonal basis of the human caregiving system (e.g., Eisler & Levine, 2002; Brown, Brown, & Preston, 2012; Keltner, Kogan, Piff, & Saturn, 2014). These tentative models, as well as the one suggested by Decety (2012) regarding empathic processes, attest to the strong core similarity found across diverse manifestations of caring and illustrate the viability of a common neural and biological stratum being involved in a broad motivational system of caring.

6

Attachment Theory and Caregiving

Attachment theory is one of the most influential theories in psychology and is described as the major contemporary theory in the area of emotional and social development (Cassidy, 2008; Mikulincer & Shaver, 2010). The theory and the vast rigorous research that it has generated are very central in the conceptualizations advanced in this book regarding a comprehensive and fundamental caring motivation. First proposed and discussed by John Bowlby (1969, 1982, 1980) and then elaborated and expanded by Bowlby and many others (see edited handbook by Cassidy & Shaver, 2008, and review book by Mikulincer & Shaver, 2010), it originally set out to explain the bond between parents and children. Building upon concepts from systems theory, ethology, and evolutionary theory, Bowlby suggested that such bonds in humans as well as in mammals are governed by two reciprocal behavioral systems: the attachment behavioral system on the child's part and the caregiving behavioral system on the caregiver's part. The goal of the attachment behavioral system is to receive protection by maintaining proximity to a caregiver in response to perceived stress or danger, while the goal of the caregiving behavioral system is to provide such protection. Two specific functions are relevant to such protection: alleviating distress in stressful circumstances by providing proximity and care (the safe haven function) and providing closeness and availability in safe circumstances to allow exploration, learning, and growth (the secure base function). Both of these functions involve the child's self-protective and affect-regulatory processes. The evolutionary rationale for the adaptive nature of these systems is straightforward. Mammalian infants are not able to survive on their own and need a long period of breast-feeding and growth before they become independent. Thus those born with an attachment behavioral system and whose parents (or at least whose mothers) had the corresponding caregiving behavioral system had much higher chances of surviving to reproduce these "genetic" traits in later generations.

For the most part, attachment researchers have focused on the attachment behavioral system, demonstrating significant advancements in theory, research, and findings (see, for example, the *Handbook of Attachment*, edited by Cassidy

& Shaver, 2008). The study of attachment processes has uncovered individual differences in attachment patterns or orientations that evince wide-ranging consequences in childhood and adulthood as well as in parent-child relations, friendships, romantic bondings, work orientations, psychopathology, affect regulation, and more (Mikulincer & Shaver, 2007a). Three major attachment patterns—secure, ambivalent, and avoidant—were first identified in childhood, followed by a fourth—a disorganized pattern (Ainsworth, Blehar, Waters, & Wall, 1978; Main and Solomon, 1990; see review in Cassidy, 2008). The application of attachment theory to adulthood has revealed two major dimensions that capture individual differences in the enactment of the attachment behavioral system: avoidance, reflecting a deactivation of the system with a tendency to self-reliance at the expense of reliance on others, and anxiety, reflecting a hyper-activation of the system with excessive clinginess on others along with self-doubts and apprehension.

The past two decades have also seen a growing number of studies dealing with the caregiving behavioral system (George & Solomon, 1989, 1996, 1999; Heard & Lake, 1997; Bell & Richard, 2000a; Shaver, Mikulincer, & Shemesh-Iron, 2010). This interest has yielded several insights into the operation of the caregiving system in the parenting role as well as in other realms, such as romantic relations, friendships, and relations with strangers. These insights as well as the innovative and landmark proposal of the existence of a caregiving behavioral system are highly relevant to the thesis advocated in this book and serve an important conceptual and empirical role in its development.

The concept of behavioral systems

One of the most important suggestions by Bowlby (1969/1982) was that the two motivational systems, attachment and caregiving, as well as others such as exploration, affiliation, and sexuality, are not drives as maintained by psychoanalytic theory but function as behavioral systems, which have adaptive functions and were evolutionary chosen via natural selection. Each behavioral system has a set goal. In the attachment behavioral system this set goal involves attaining a sense of safety and security; in the caregiving behavioral system it involves making sure that others' mental and physical welfare and well-being are maintained and promoted.

The operation of behavioral systems is activated and terminated by various internal and external cues. The attachment and caregiving motivational systems are constantly 'working' even when they are not activated because the individual needs to monitor the social and physical environment for relevant activating cues. The systems are activated by cues that signal when a particular set goal becomes salient and are deactivated or terminated by cues that signal the attainment of the desired set goal. For example, distress cues of the care-receiver or the approach of a mean looking person to the care receiver which signal problem or danger activate the caregiving system, and perceived security, well-being and safety of the care receiver de-activate it (Bowlby, 1969/1982). Once activated, a large number of behaviors can be enacted. Attachment behaviors, for example, include expressing distress, seeking proximity and contact with a caregiver, and relaxing once proximity and support have been attained, thus freeing the care receiver for other endeavors, such as exploration. Similarly, caregiving behaviors involve soothing, listening, holding, and protecting the care receiver from predators and other dangers.

Furthermore, behavioral systems are organized as goal-corrected systems with specific set goals rather than a prewired sequence of behaviors. Behaviors are changed and adjusted to serve the different goals, and this adjustment involves a feedback loop. Similar behaviors may reflect the operation of different goals and the same goal may be served by different behaviors in the same individual and across different individuals. The meanings of specific sequences of behaviors derive from the goals that govern them. The behavior of approaching someone, for example, may serve an attachment goal (looking for protection), or a caregiving goal (trying to protect someone). Moreover, different action patterns may serve the same goal. For example, singing, rocking, or nursing are different action patterns whose set goal may be similar—soothing a baby. Thus, in considering the caregiving behavioral system, the functions and goals of the different behaviors should be considered to a greater extent than the specific behaviors enacted; these behaviors may change over time in order to adjust to the changing environments and needs of both the caregiver and the care receiver.

One of the implications of this flexibility is the importance of experience in shaping the way each system is enacted and the development of individual differences in strategies for achieving the set goals. Attachment security, for example, is manifested in being comfortable to depend on others, feeling confident in the availability of support, gaining a sense of security and well-being from others' help, and maintaining a balance between self-reliance and reliance on others. Insecurity is manifested in either tipping this balance toward self-reliance and deactivation of the need for close others or toward reliance on others at the expense of being self-sufficient—the hyperactivation of the attachment behavioral system. As far as the caregiving system is concerned, the extent to which a person is more or less vigilant in the activation of a behavioral system (quick to identify even mild signs of danger vs. brushing aside such signs and reacting only in major crises) may reflect such individual differences.

Bowlby further suggests that because at any point in time several behavioral systems are operating, different behavioral systems need to be coordinated in various ways to allow for the achievement of the distinct goals. Finally, behavioral systems are seen as governed by higher processes of integration and control;

hence they include *internal working models*—namely representations of the world and of ways to achieve the relevant set goals (see discussion by Bretherton, & Munholland, 2008). According to Bowlby (1969/1982, p. 82), working models include a model of the environment (social and nonsocial) as well as a representation of the person's own skills and potentialities; further, they involve conscious as well as less conscious verbal and nonverbal aspects and reflect individual differences in strategies for achieving the behavioral system's set goal (Main, Kaplan, & Cassidy, 1985; Main, 1991).

Caregiving as a behavioral system in parenting

George and Solomon (1989, 1996, 1999, 2008) were the first to take up the challenge of discussing in detail the caregiving system as separate from the attachment system and have provided a comprehensive discussion of its operation from an attachment perspective. Several important features of behavioral systems are relevant to George and Solomon's model. First, the behavioral system operates even if no action is taken; the parent needs to be vigilant so as to be able to perceive cues that may be associated with a separation from the child, a danger or threat to the child, a threat to the parent's capacity to protect the child, or the child's discomfort. Second, the caregiving system interacts with other behavioral systems such as the parents' attachment or exploration systems, which compete for the limited resources of the parent. The final action taken therefore reflects the interaction between the various systems in operation, including possible interactions and competitions between the caregiving system's activation for different children. Third, the "decision" on whether to act and how reveals large individual differences and involves both conscious and unconscious processes. Some parents will quickly intervene when a preschooler is more than 10 meters away from them while others will stay calm. Furthermore, the same parent may react differently to the same cue (e.g., preschooler is distant) depending on other coexisting cues (e.g., the presence of a fence around the yard) and depending on how the parent perceives the child and her or his abilities and personality. Caregiving acts are thus best perceived through the parents' perceptions and internal working models. George and Solomon (2008) and others (see review in Mayseless, 2006b) have suggested various schemes that reflect these individual differences. These schemes also include several broad strategies for providing protection (e.g., flexible protection, close protection, protection from a distance), which are viewed as reflecting the individual differences that tend to emerge in response to specific environmental and cultural contexts. George and Solomon (2008) and others (Crittenden, 2006) have also described situations in which caregivers seem to abdicate their protective role. The study of parents' internal working models of caregiving has led to a new and expanding area of research involving internal representations of parenting (see Mayseless, 2006a).

According to Solomon and George, the caregiving behavioral system develops on the basis of the attachment behavioral system. Infants and children learn about caring as part of their attachment relations, and representations of caring are intertwined with their representations of attachment. For example, the child's understanding of the best way to receive protection informs that child's strategies for how best to provide care. Thus attachment security and insecurity are expected to be associated with the way caring is enacted later in life. (The development of caring is discussed in Chapters 12 and 13.) Additionally, the caregiving system's operation is associated with strong feelings of satisfaction, pleasure, and joy when the child's safety and comfort have been achieved and with heightened anxiety, anger, guilt, frustration, sadness, and despair when the caregiver's ability to comfort the child, maintain proximity, and protect is threatened or unsuccessful.

George and Solomon (2008) have opted for a distinctive and somewhat narrow goal of the caregiving system—parental *protection* of the child. They argue that as a behavioral system that is reciprocal and complementary to the attachment behavioral system, it should be viewed as geared specifically to the satisfaction of attachment needs for protection. According to their suggestion, other infant and child needs, though clearly part of parenting, are not directly governed by the caregiving behavioral system. However, other scholars have discussed the caregiving system as involving a large number of other child care goals, such as promoting competence through efforts to teach and socialize, and have generally embraced a larger scope for this behavioral system (See review in Mayseless, 2006b). Pianta and colleagues (e.g., Steinberg & Pianta, 2006), for example, have assessed the promotion of autonomy as part of the caregiving system, and others as well have examined parenting representations related to this goal (Mayseless & Scharf, 2006).

Attachment theorists claim to discuss parental caregiving in general, but have focused most of their research on maternal caregiving (however, see Paquette, 2004). A significant body of research on paternal caregiving does exist nonetheless and will be discussed later in this book when I turn to examining gender differences in caregiving (Chapter 15).

Caregiving in romantic relations

In earlier discussions of the caregiving behavioral system it was conceived as operating within parent-child relations. However, later on attachment researchers further suggested that in the course of evolution attachment and caregiving came to be implicated also in the formation of romantic relationships (pair bonds) along with the behavioral system governing sexual mating

(Hazan & Shaver, 1987). Thus pair bonds were expected to reflect the operation of three behavioral systems: attachment, caregiving, and sexual mating
(Shaver, Hazan, & Bradshaw, 1988; Hazan & Shaver 1994). The caregiving
system, which might have been evolutionary selected for infant and child care,
came to acquire a double purpose and was also activated in caring for a mate or
romantic partner. This view, which is now common among attachment scholars, underscores the generality of the caregiving behavioral system, which is
viewed as central to at least two domains—parenting and pair bonds. In the
nonreciprocal parent-child relations, the attachment system in the child and
the caregiving system in the parent operate in order to bond the two together.
However, in the moderately reciprocal romantic relationships both partners'
attachment and caregiving systems are activated and partners switch positions
as caregiver and care receiver depending on changing needs and conditions.
Specifically, romantic partners provide the safe haven function, comfort their
companions, and assuage their distress; these partners indeed feel comforted
when their companions are present or anxious and lonely when their partners
are absent. Similarly, just as in parent-child relations, romantic relationships
serve as a secure base that helps partners face the opportunities and challenges
life presents.

These similarities notwithstanding, relationships between adult romantic
partners differ in many respects from relationships between children and caregivers. Yet the core principles of caregiving processes apply to both kinds of
relationships. For example, and as with parent-child relationships, the availability, sensitive responsiveness, and support of a romantic partner in times of
need have significant beneficial outcomes for each of the partners. To the needy
person, receiving optimal care results in feelings of being loved and esteemed,
feelings of gratitude, and feelings of attachment security; to the caregiver, providing optimal care results in feelings of competence and generativity as well
as heightened relationship satisfaction (e.g., Collins & Feeney, 2000; Rholes,
Simpson, Campbell, & Grich, 2001; Feeney & Collins, 2003; Feeney, 2004).
In contrast, a mismatch between the activation of attachment in one partner
and the activation of caregiving in the other, or insensitive responses, often
result in major relational stress and may also lead to negative outcomes for
each of the partners and for the relationship. Unlike the narrow scope of the
caregiving behavioral system that was assumed by some of the scholars who
studied parenting, caregiving in romantic relations is not conceived as limited
to protection or caring reactions to distress and involves a variety of provisions and support, such as sharing the partner's success and happiness and the
provision of warmth and affection (see the discussion of romantic relations in
Chapter 8; also see the description of warmth as a fundamental provision in
the next section).

The importance of warmth and emotional bonding in caregiving

Several researchers provided conceptual refinements and additions to the way in which attachment and caregiving have been depicted thus far. Their goal was to try to account for the formation of bonds of care such as those formed between parents and offspring and between romantic partners, which are distinct from the mere activation of caregiving behaviors. MacDonald (1992) has suggested the existence of a human affectional system that he termed *warmth*. He conceptualized this as distinct from attachment security, although both often overlap in actual relationships. While attachment security was seen as related to the alleviation of fear and the provision of protection and comfort in times of distress and danger, *warmth* refers to positive feelings of affection. It is conceived as a human affectional system meant to enhance cohesive family relationships and *paternal* investment in children. MacDonald (1992) argued that this system evolved separately from the attachment system, and he provided five major arguments to sustain this claim. First, he argued that current psychological and brain research strongly substantiates the existence of two separate biological systems, one governing negative affects such as fear or distress, which are modulated by the attachment behavioral system, and another governing positive affects, such as feelings of affection and warmth, which he assumed to be managed by the warmth system.

Second, he claims that the evolutionary states of attachment and warmth are very different. While the attachment behavioral system appears to operate in a large number of primates and other mammals as well as in birds, the existence of intimate relationships that include pair bonding, affection, and paternal investment is far less common. Pair bonding indicated by monogamy, for example, occurs in only 17% of primates (Hrdy, 1981), and this group does not include some of the most humanlike of primates, such as rhesus monkeys and chimpanzees. Positive affective interchanges thus appear to have developed separately from the attachment system that evolved to protect the young in times of danger. Third, it appears that attachment is formed and activated even when relationships appear to lack warmth and even when they are clearly abusive. Even Ainsworth (1967), a central pioneer in the study of attachment, notes in her Uganda study the interesting combination of low levels of affection (i.e., hugging or kissing), which were apparent, along with high levels of maternal sensitivity and responsiveness. Fourth, MacDonald (1992) notes the different patterns of sex differences in attachment security and in warmth and affection. Whereas girls have clearly been shown to have greater inclinations toward intimate and affectionate relationships than boys, there are no sex differences in attachment security—at least in infancy. Finally, MacDonald (1992) notes the relatively great importance of security in infancy but its lower saliency in later intimate friendships and romantic relations, where greater salience is attached to reciprocated positive social interactions.

Adopting an evolutionary perspective, MacDonald (1992) suggests that the capacity for warmth and intimacy is a basic human biological adaptation that evolved as a proximal mechanism for sustaining high-investment parenting. Following Lovejoy (1981), he sees the prolonged dependence of human children as having evolved because of the benefits of a longer period of relatively high plasticity, which could be utilized for teaching and training high-quality competitive offspring. This reflects what evolutionary researchers have referred to as K-selected species—those that focus their reproductive efforts on a few high-quality offspring rather than many offspring who might not survive or might be less competitive (e.g., Clutton-Brock & Godfray, 1991). Such species require high levels of parental investment, including paternal investment, and result in highly competitive, highly adapted offspring. According to MacDonald (1992), the warmth affectional system evolved to further the bonding between males and females and the bond between fathers (and mothers) and offspring in species such as the human species, in which the prolonged period of the children's dependency on adults necessitated their joint efforts in raising them to maturity. In line with this claim, and as a result of ecological pressures favoring high-investment parenting in certain species, pair bonding and monogamy are common in a wide range of birds and in some species of mammals (e.g., Clutton-Brock & Godfray, 1991). Warmth is thus seen as central in the caregiving bonds between romantic partners and between parents and children and serves to glue and reinforce their relationships. It was nonetheless argued that the flexibility of this affectional system allows for varied levels of operation as adaptations to a diverse range of human ecological conditions (Belsky, Steinberg, & Draper, 1991). When exposed to high levels of warmth, individuals tend to value affective exchanges and look for them in their relationships, with the opposite occurring when children are exposed to cold and nonaffectionate relationships. This process reflects an appetitive, reward-dependent motivational system that adapts to varied environmental conditions. All in all both a caregiving behavioral system and a warmth motivational system were assumed to govern caring motivational processes.

Another conceptual refinement was suggested by Bell and Richard (2000a,b), who advocate what they term a *connection theoretical orientation*. By discussing the caregiving *bond*, Bell and Richard (2000a) attempt to provide an explanation *at the proximate level* of why parents would provide care for their children. Their general argument is that "caring is an enduring dyadic emotion" (2000a, p. 74). This emotion is viewed as the motivation that propels caregiving and is described in a broader sense as an autonomous motivation to see that the needs of the cared for or "dependent" are met. This enduring dyadic emotion explains why parents are attentive to activating cues whereas others in the same vicinity are not. Rather than focusing on "on-off" activating cues, these researchers view the enduring emotion of caring as the proximate overall cause and, in effect, the defining element of the parental bond. Bell and Richard (2000a,b) view the connection orientation as applying also to other caring bonds such as adult romantic relationships. The enduring dyadic emotion they postulate is similar to what other scholars may have referred to as parental love, but Bell and Richard specify what this love, which they term *caring*, means; it reflects a very specific kind of love—the love that propels a person to tend, provide, and nurture another.

Bell and Richard further view the goals of the caregiving system as much broader, because they can, in principle, include all the dependent's needs and thus involve various specialized subsystems such as feeding, clothing, protecting, retrieving, and so on. Hence they significantly broaden the concept of the caregiving behavioral system and underscore the operation of two major overarching intentions: empathy and responsibility. *Empathy* relates to the intention of emotionally knowing the dependents in order to discern their needs. *Responsibility* refers to the committed intention of seeing that these identified needs are met and satisfied. Hence Bell and Richard accord a special place to intentional and conscious decision to be responsible for the other's well-being and thriving. According to Bell and Richard (2000a), empathy and responsibility roughly correspond to sensitivity and responsiveness, although they are more proactive in nature. Both concepts—sensitivity and responsiveness—have been amply discussed and studied within the attachment literature as exemplifying the hallmarks of secure (positive) caregiving (e.g., Mikulincer & Shaver 2007a). Unlike the depiction of the caregiving behavioral system as operating through activations and terminations of caring behaviors governed by internal working models, the connection theoretical orientation tried to explicate the formation and functioning of *enduring bonds* where caring is provided. Like McDonald (1992), who proposes the warmth perspective (1992), Bell and Richard (2000a) underscore the centrality of affection, love, and an emotional bond, which together provide the necessary glue between people and the impetus for the provision of care in this context. Such a depiction accords with the evolution-based selective investment theory advocated by Brown and Brown (2006a,b), which tries to explicate the formation of high-cost giving to others in close relationships and likewise discusses the crucial importance of the formation of an affectionate bond.

A broader view of caregiving

In line with the broad scope of caregiving advocated by Bell and Richard as well as others (Berscheid & Collins, 2000; Reis, 2000), recent theories suggest that the caregiving behavioral system may have evolved to cover other categories of recipients besides children and romantic partners (e.g., siblings and "tribe members" with whom a person shares genes, hence whose survival to reproductive age and success in producing and rearing offspring would contribute to the caregiver's inclusive fitness) (Hamilton, 1964). As discussed in the chapter on evolutionary perspectives, inclusive fitness and evolutionary advantage relate not only to the propagation of one's genes through one's offspring—the parenting role—but also to the extent that those who share copies of one's genes are able to survive and reproduce. This is why caring for and supporting close relatives is also evolutionary advantageous (see review in Simpson & Beckes, 2010).

The operation of the caregiving behavioral system may also have been generalized to one's in-group. This in-group may have included genetically unrelated members but caring for them may still have evolutionary benefit because cooperation and reciprocal support in such groups can be highly beneficial to the fitness of all (see review in Simpson & Beckes, 2010). Furthermore, it has been suggested that the operation of the caregiving behavioral system could have been generalized to anyone in need (Shaver, Mikulincer, & Shemesh-Iron, 2010). This can happen when viewing all humankind and perhaps even other living things as members of a single human and nonhuman family through socialization. Still, because of its origin and possibly because the degree of evolutionary benefit is variable across diverse kinds of relationships, the caregiving behavioral system is more easily activated with other people to whom we are closely related genetically and psychologically, and with others who are similar to us in a variety of dimensions because such similarity probably reflects a proxy indicator for being our in-group—our tribe.

Such a view of the caregiving behavioral system reflects an expansion and redefinition of its scope and aligns with the thesis advocated in this book. In a series of studies conducted in the past decade, Mikulincer and Shaver, along with students and colleagues, have developed a model of prosocial behaviors reflecting the generalized operation of such caregiving behavioral system. They can point to an impressive body of research substantiating this contention, and their studies can be described as following two central lines: one deals with individual differences in caregiving and the other focuses on the interplay of attachment and caregiving in different domains of care. In both, similar processes are observed with regard to a variety of provisions, caring domains, and caring targets. Thus both lines of research substantiate the claim for a general and comprehensive caring motivation and both are presented in more detail in the next sections.

Similar individual differences in caregiving across domains and targets

The first line of research deals with individual differences in caregiving and demonstrates that such differences an be captured by examining the tendencies toward hyperactivating or deactivating the caregiving behavioral system. Hyperactivating involves responses that intensify the system's primary strategy in order to coerce another person to behave in accordance with the system's goals. Hence such caregiving is provided even when it is not needed, and caregiving efforts are intrusive, insensitive, and geared to satisfy the caregivers' needs to feel needed and worthy. This, for example, is reflected in the following: "I sometimes worry that I try to help others more than they want me to," or "I feel bad when others don't want my help." In contrast, deactivation involves responses that reflect disengagement from the system's primary strategy in order to decrease involvement in caregiving. This is reflected, for example, in the following: "I sometimes feel that helping others is a waste of time," or "I feel uncomfortable when I'm required to help others." Thus caregiving cues that might lead to its activation (e.g., the partner's distress) tend to be ignored or dismissed, and when caring is provided it is carried out with insufficient empathy and often in a nonresponsive and insensitive manner that is not truly comforting.

Shaver, Mikulincer, and Shemesh-Iron (2010) have demonstrated the generality of these individual differences by observing their associations with individuals' reported empathy and compassion to strangers and to close others; their general values, such as universalism and communal orientation; and their reported engagement in volunteering (e.g., teaching reading, counseling troubled people, providing care to the sick). As expected, these investigators found that deactivation was associated with less empathic care, compassion, and prosocial actions as well as with a lack of esteem for humanity, as indicated by responses to questionnaires. Furthermore, deactivation was significantly associated with engaging in fewer volunteer activities and less altruistic reasons for volunteering (e.g., other-focused values). Hyperactivation was associated with the importance of interdependence, negative views of oneself as caregiver, and more egoistic reasons for volunteering, such as self-protection and self-enhancement.

In addition, individual differences in caregiving deactivation and hyperactivation were observed in actual behavior—parental caregiving and the provision of support in couple relationships. Specifically, as observed in a videotaped interaction, mothers with greater hyperactivation were more distressed and less helpful when they were interacting with their preschool children. Deactivation was associated with lower warmth and less helpfulness during the interaction. In the romantic relations domain, hyperactivation was associated with reportedly more compulsive (i.e., intrusive) caregiving, less supportive behavior, and more distress during a dyadic interaction whereby one of the partners was asked to disclose a personal problem. Greater deactivation was associated with less responsiveness and a lower sensitivity to the partner's signals and needs, more controlling care, and less supportive behavior toward the partner during the interaction. The generalizability of these individual differences across diverse contexts where caring is enacted provides clear and impressive evidence for the existence of a general motivation to care.

Boosting attachment security shows similar enhancing effects of caregiving in different domains

The second line of research demonstrates that the experimental enhancement of attachment security brings about stronger and better functioning of the caregiving system in a variety of contexts and across diverse kinds of relationships.

The research that examined the effects of boosting attachment security on the caregiving system relates to a core aspect of the interplay between the attachment and caregiving behavioral systems. According to Bowlby (1969/1982), activation of the attachment system tends to take precedence over other behavioral systems such as exploration, affiliation, and caregiving because of the urgent and vital need to protect oneself. When individuals' feelings of security are threatened and they are preoccupied with their own distress or with seeking comfort from others, it will be difficult for them to accurately perceive the needs of others and to address these needs with responsive, sensitive, appropriate support. In contrast, when attachment needs have been met and individuals feel secure, confident, and loved, they can more easily direct their attention to other behavioral systems such as exploration and caregiving (Mikulincer, Shaver, Gilath, & Nitzberg, 2005; Collins & Ford, 2010; Shaver, Mikulincer, & Shemesh-Iron, 2010). A series of studies by Mikulincer and Shaver and their colleagues have elegantly demonstrated this effect by showing that dispositional security (one's attachment style) and the temporary boosting of attachment security by implicit and explicit priming techniques were associated with higher compassion and helping, reflecting the activation of the caregiving system (Mikulincer & Shaver 2001; Mikulincer et al., 2005). Implicit priming involved, for example, exposing study participants to security-related words (*love, hug*) or to the name of their central attachment figure, whereas explicit priming could involve asking them to imagine a scenario with a security-providing attachment figure in which they felt supported and comforted (Mikulincer & Shaver, 2007b; Mikulincer, Shaver, Sahdra, & Bar-On, 2013).

Mikulincer, Shaver, and their colleagues found the benevolent effect of boosting attachment security to be wide-ranging. It was reflected in elevated levels of empathy, compassion, and willingness to help a person in distress, even a stranger (Mikulincer, Shaver, Gilath, & Nitzberg, 2005). For example, subliminal priming with the name of a security-providing attachment figure doubled the number of participants from about a third to two thirds of the participants, who agreed to replace a confederate who had to perform a series of increasingly aversive tasks. Such boosting affected both secure and insecure adults to the same degree, showing that a situational, temporary activation of attachment security leads even chronically insecure persons to feel more secure and to react accordingly. Similarly, even among insecure individuals, priming-induced temporary attachment security was associated with greater responsive care and support provided to a romantic partner who was sharing a personal problem (Mikulincer et al., 2013).

Boosting attachment security also had a positive effect on broader value orientations involving concern for others' welfare, such as benevolence, or concern for people who are close to oneself, and universalism, or concern for all humanity (see Mikulincer et al., 2003). Additionally Mikulincer and Shaver (2001) have shown that the experimental augmentation of attachment security through priming was associated with weaker hostile responses to a variety of out-groups (as defined by secular Israeli Jewish students): Israeli Arabs, ultra-Orthodox Jews, Russian immigrants, and homosexuals.

In sum, boosting attachment security increases empathy, compassion, and the willingness to help strangers in distress (Mikulincer et al., 2005). It also increases the observed sensitive caring and support provided to a needy relationship partner (Mikulincer, Shaver, Sahdra, & Bar-On, 2013) and even generates more universal benevolence, as assessed by the endorsement of humanitarian values and in tolerance toward out-group members (Mikulincer & Shaver, 2001). This effect was generalized and found to be similar in individuals with different attachment styles. The wide-ranging effect of this intervention affects the activation of the caregiving system across diverse contexts and circumstances and accords very nicely with the claim for a general motivation to care.

Both lines of research provide cumulative empirical evidence suggesting that some general processes of caregiving (i.e., the capacity to augment caregiving through boosting attachment security and individual differences in nonoptimal caregiving) play out similarly in very diverse contexts and domains of caregiving: in parenting, romantic relations, toward specific strangers with whom one can empathize, volunteering with strangers, and generally benevolent and humanistic attitudes and values. This striking similarity accords with this book's claim about the existence of a general motivation to care.

Chapter conclusion

Attachment theory and research have provided a viable and comprehensive model for the way caregiving operates as an overarching motivational structure. Based on ethological, evolutionary, and systems theory notions, attachment theory postulates the existence of a *caregiving behavioral system* that is evolutionary chosen and is vital to our existence. It consists of a variety of behavior sequences and acts in a flexible manner governed by internal working models that operate both consciously and unconsciously and reflect different strategies to achieve its goals. Researchers disagree with regards to a narrow (only protection) vs. broad view of the behavioral system's set goal, although current conceptualizations favor a broader perspective that encompasses a variety of provisions, among which protection is just one. Furthermore, researchers underscore the fact that caregiving cannot be viewed only as an "on-off" activated and deactivated behavioral system; instead, it also incorporates the relevant mechanisms of emotional bonding, as reflected in such caregiving bonds as parenting and pair bonds. Although this system was viewed at first as a behavioral system implicated mainly in parenting, researchers later broadened its scope and suggested that it is also involved in other relationships, with close others and with strangers. Specifically researchers have suggested that, throughout our evolutionary history this behavioral system was co-opted to answer new challenges that further our inclusive fitness, such as the bonding between romantic partners, paternal caring, caring and cooperating with group members, and universal caring. Furthermore, research on caregiving from an attachment perspective has uncovered specific individual differences in the way caring is enacted, which appear to involve strategies for providing care and reflect somewhat stable predispositions in adulthood.

In short, attachment theory and research offer a broad conceptual and empirical understanding of caregiving and how it is governed and enacted in diverse domains and relations and with a variety of targets, close and intimate as well as distant and unfamiliar. This fruitful perspective thus provides very sound basis for the claims of this book regarding a universal, general, and comprehensive caring motivation.

7

Feminist Perspectives

Feminist theorists offer a unique and distinct approach to caring and caregiving in society and mothering in particular. These theories reflect a variety of approaches to human society and gender division in general and the role played by caring and motherhood in particular. The historical trajectory of feminist theories also includes various waves or stages that reflect shifts in the concerns and issues addressed. Generally speaking, feminist writers are critical of the contemporaneous structure and organization of human society, particularly insofar as it relates to women and their place and power within society. Their treatment of care and caregiving issues within a society they see as being highly patriarchal, male-oriented, and devaluing is therefore highly colored by these observations and embedded within a general framework of gender inequality. Some of the arguments made several decades ago, which were highly revolutionary at the time, currently form part of the mainstream zeitgeist—at least in the western world.

In this chapter, it is not my intention to review the significant and intriguing work of these spirited writers, nor do I refer to empirical research on gender differences in caring, which will be discussed in Chapter 15; rather, and in line with the book's central focus, I will try to underscore some of the major feminist claims that are relevant to caring and its relation to gender as well as to highlight the feminist accounts that discuss how caring and mothering are culturally construed within patriarchal cultures. To this end, I will summarize my own reading of this literature by using 11 major points or statements.

Caring as the sphere of women

A large number of feminist writers, each using a somewhat unique way of expressing her claim, have noted the strong and universal connection between gender and care (Rich, 1976; Miller, 1976/1982; Gilligan, 1982) and suggested that women are clearly and unequivocally accorded the role of a caregiver, whether as mothers, spouses, daughters, nieces, or friends. Chodorow (1978/1999), for example,

presented a considerable amount of ethnographic and sociological data to substantiate her claim that women are universally largely responsible for early child
care. Others have relied on historical data as well as on other sources in order to
demonstrate the comprehensive, clear, and universal association between women
and caregiving, not just in early child care roles but in other caregiving roles too
(de Beauvoir, 1949/1973; Miller, 1976/1982). Finally, such scholars as Taylor
(2002) have synthesized earlier perspectives and provided a useful summary of
the claims and evidence regarding the universality of the female caregiving role.

Caring and mothering are not freely chosen by women

Another general claim made by feminists is that motherhood and caring roles
were not freely chosen by women but were forced on them through the codes,
socialization practices, and the expectations of patriarchal society, where womanhood and femininity were equated with getting married, taking care of the household and husband, and raising children.

Women and caregiving are devalued and deemed inferior
in patriarchal society

A core feminist observation deals with the writers' patriarchal environment,
although their accounts also referred to other patriarchal societies in history (de
Beauvoir, 1949/1973; Rich, 1976; Miller, 1976/1982). They argue that patriarchal
societies involve a clear division of labor and, more importantly, a clear division
of power between the sexes. This division of power was clear in women's subor-
dinated position in a male-dominated society. Specifically, women were not and
in principle could not be economically independent, were constrained and controlled in decisions regarding their lives and bodies, and had a lower status and less
power than men; they were destined to a life of marriage and child rearing and in
these capacities were expected to tend the house and care for the children and their
husbands. They were denied education and the right to vote even in democratic
societies, and their fate was mostly decided by the men in their lives—their fathers,
brothers, or husbands. In contrast, men had social and economic power and the
freedom to assert this power and to choose their way in life. They were also active
in the workplace, potentially providing them with a sense of achievement and
accomplishment that was denied to women. Furthermore, and owing to the male
dominance within patriarchal culture, accounts of the way males develop (i.e.,
toward autonomy and individuation) were seen as universal and normal, as were
male ways of behaving and thinking (i.e., in a more rational than an emotional

way). In contrast, female development and female ways of behaving and experiencing the world (i.e., by forming relationships and expressing feelings and emotions) were seen as deviant, less developed, and inferior; this was also reflected in the lower status accorded to caregiving and mothering (de Beauvoir, 1949/1973; Rich, 1976; Miller, 1976/1982).

Mothering as a way to subordinate women and relegate them to an inferior status in patriarchal society

Feminist writers insisted on a distinction between being a mother (bearing and giving birth to a child) and mothering (e.g., Rich, 1976; Ruddick, 1989/1995). Mothering was perceived as differentiated from being or becoming a mother in the sense that mothering reflected the caregiving needed for raising children, which can—in principle—be totally separated from childbearing and hence done by anyone including males. They suggested that the subordination of women was partially accomplished by relegating them to the work involved in mothering, which meant that they were not able to freely choose other pursuits that could imbue them with more freedom and a higher status, could better accommodate their talents and desires, and thus could promote their personal growth (Rich, 1976). According to some feminist writers, the enforcement of mothering on women (by equating womanhood with bearing children and with mothering) was not seen as incidental but as a carefully orchestrated though possibly not conscious process meant to induce and enforce women to take that role and thus sustain the division of labor and power in patriarchal culture.

The idealistic and "natural" perception of mothering as another way of subduing women

Feminists have identified several other ways used by patriarchal society to devalue women, such as the idealization of motherhood (Rich, 1976). This idealization included expectations for selfless devotion and perfect attunement and sensitivity accompanied by motherly joy and unconditional love. This constellation of capacities, behaviors, and emotions was viewed as "natural" and "instinctual" and as allegedly reflecting females' motherly nature. A large number of feminist writers (e.g., de Beauvoir, 1949/1973) pointed out that the presentation of mothering as "natural" and "ideal" meant that if mothers were indeed so perfect, this did not count as more than an expression of their true nature and was therefore not highly valued as an accomplishment; yet if they were human and were not always sensitive, patient, and loving and sometimes felt exhausted or mad at their children—their guilt would have to be hidden from others. Such experiences, feminists claimed, served to hamper mothers' self-esteem and their belief in themselves and further helped their subordination and devaluation in patriarchal society.

Mothering as involving ambivalence—love and hate

Those feminist writers who discussed the projected image of an ideal mother uncovered the actual experiences of mothers, often by relating their own experiences (e.g., Rich, 1976; Benjamin, 1988; Ruddick, 1989/1995). These experiences included highly negative feelings, involving boredom, depression, anxiety, fatigue, helplessness, anger and hate as well as highly positive feelings, such as love, tenderness, sensitivity, responsiveness, and joy. Consequently mothering was conceived as involving conflicts, ambivalence, and on occasion a struggle to avoid harming the child as well as love and joy (Rich, 1976; Ruddick, 1989/1995). Accordingly, mothering—and, in fact, any form of caregiving—was seen by these accounts as a setting for both positive and negative emotions, one requiring strong and developed ego defenses that needed to be harnessed in times of depression, anger, or exhaustion, necessarily leading to an abandonment of the romantic view of unconditional, eternal, and natural mother love (Ruddick, 1989/1995).

Mothering as involving thinking and sophistication based on practice

A perspective on mothering complementing the view stressing internal conflict, ambivalence, and struggle was offered by Ruddick (1989/1995). Ruddick represented mothers as reasoners and suggested that mothering involves many informed decisions based on a large foundation of knowledge and expertise acquired through practice, thinking, contemplating, comparing, and reflecting. Mothering was thus depicted as a highly intricate, complex, sophisticated expertise that involved a great deal of thinking based on practice, very much unlike the intuition and natural instincts assumed to govern these caregiving actions. In short, "motherwork" was viewed as a practice or occupation that gave rise to and was informed by "maternal thinking." In this way Ruddick focused on what mothers attempt to do and how they decide to do it and less on what they feel. Ruddick further suggested that mothering (maternal work and practice) begins when a child is perceived as having needs and vulnerabilities and involves a decision to respond to these needs and vulnerabilities by care. Hence the first and most basic aim of maternal practice is protection—preserving the lives of children by caring for them. Ruddick identified two other spheres or tasks that mothers engage in which are more dependent on specific contextual and cultural imperatives. These tasks are nurturance, the fostering of children's emotional and intellectual growth, and training, through which children are taught how to become accepted members of their societies.

How do women become caregivers?

Some of the writers, especially those who adopted a psychoanalytic point of view, claimed that mother-daughter relationships provided the central setting in which mothering and femininity are learned and reproduced as subordinate and caring roles (i.e., Rich, 1976; Chodorow, 1978/1999). These accounts rejected the simplistic view that mothering or caring is instinctual and biological (Rich, 1976) and suggested that "one is not born, but rather becomes, a woman" (Simone de Beauvoir, 1949/1973; p. 301). Furthermore, others suggested that role identification and direct socialization are also insufficient. Chodorow (1978/1999), for example, rejected the notion that biology is responsible for mothering, or that a motherly instinct lies at the roots of motherhood. She similarly rejected the simple model of role identification and socialization for teaching women to mother as well as to uphold other sex-related work divisions in society. Adopting a psychoanalytic feminist orientation, she argued that motherhood (namely parenting exercised by mothers) is socially perpetuated through specific relationships, both conscious and unconscious, actual and fantasized, between mothers and daughters in which an identification based on preoedipal processes as well as the resolution of the oedipal complex through connectedness with the mother served as the bedrocks for the reproduction of mothering.

Why patriarchal society adopted a negative evaluation of women, mothering, and caregiving

Different accounts at different levels of explanation were offered throughout the years in order to explain why patriarchal society adopted a negative evaluation of women, mothering, and caregiving. One of the earliest accounts was offered by Simone de Beauvoir (1949/1973). She suggested that women were oppressed by men through their relegation to being men's "Other" (the capital 'O' indicates the generalized other) and that this existential otherness was fundamental to female oppression. De Beauvoir acknowledged that the self needs otherness in order to define itself as a subject; however the identity of this other is supposed to alternate in that the self is often just as objectified by its other as the self objectifies it. De Beauvoir suggested that in patriarchal societies women were consistently defined as the Other by men who took on the role of the Self; consequently, she asserted, women have historically been considered deviant and abnormal; thus femininity, as well as caring and mothering, were devalued, whereas men were considered to be the ideal to which women should aspire. De Beauvoir claimed that this attitude limited women's success by maintaining the perception that they represented a deviation from the norm and were always outsiders attempting to emulate "normality."

She further suggested that as the ultimate Other, women became a target for idealizations and envy as well as hatred and fear. One example of this is what she referred to as the myth of the "Eternal Feminine." This general myth incorporates multiple myths of women, such as the myth of the mother, the virgin, the mother-land, or nature, and it appears to confine women to an impossible ideal by denying the uniqueness of different kinds of women in different kinds of situations and by set-ting impossible expectations. Indeed, de Beauvoir claimed that the various manifes-tations of the myth of femininity are contradictory and include depictions of females and mothers in particular as angelic guardians of life as well as forerunners of danger and death. She suggested that these attributes reflect men's projection of existential wishes and fears onto women as the generalized Other. According to de Beauvoir, this contradictory projection appears in all feminine myths, forcing women unfairly to assume the burden and blame for existence. She maintained that human existence is an ambiguous interplay between transcendence and immanence, where men have been privileged in expressing transcendence through projects while women have been forced into the repetitive and uncreative life of immanence. Finally, de Beauvoir illustrates how women are forced to relinquish their claims to transcendence and authentic subjectivity through a progressively more stringent acceptance of the "pas-sive" and "alienated" role to men's "active" and "subjective" demands. de Beauvoir viewed the role of a mother (at least as it was expressed in the society she criticized) as reflecting a monotonous existence of immanence as opposed to the transcendence that can be achieve through work and creativity.

Another interesting and somewhat complementary account was offered by Rich (1976). According to her, men are haunted by the idea of "dependence on a woman for life itself" (p. 11), which reflects the fact that they are born of women and cared for by women in the vulnerable early years of their lives. According to her proposition, this dread of being controlled or overwhelmed by women leads them to deny this dependence by degrading and controlling women and conceiving of motherhood as well as caregiving as natural and instinctual and hence unworthy of recognition or appreciation. A similar, sophisticated, and elab-orate account based on a psychoanalytic point of view was offered by Chodorow (1978/1999). According to her, boys, for whom the mother serves as the primary object, need to separate themselves from her so as to be able to adopt a mascu-line identity. The boy's main challenge is therefore to separate, individuate, and become autonomous. This task then becomes a core aspect of his self-definition. It is a major challenge and can be accomplished only by alienating himself from the mother's love and by devaluing her as a possible model for identification. Thus, as Chodorow (1978/1999) and others (e.g., Miller, 1976/1982) have suggested, men who feel a pull back to their dependence on their mothers and on other motherly figures such as their wives need to devalue and derogate them and their mother ing and caregiving in order to free themselves and be separate and autonomous lest they will be tempted to return to these figures' warm yet suffocating embrace. Another, somewhat similar account refers to men's envy of women's unique capacity to give birth and their consequent need to assert themselves as more dominant and establish control over what they are incapable of doing (Miller, 1976/1982).

Masculinity and femininity

Different accounts within the general realm of feminist thought have converged in suggesting that girls and boys, and subsequently men and women, are socialized and raised differently in order to accommodate their specific roles and status in society as well as their specific gender identity—feminine or masculine (e.g., Rich, 1976; Chodorow, 1978/1999). Specifically, masculinity was seen as defined by separation and individuation, stressing autonomy as the desired developmental goal and competition as a central mode of action; in contrast, femininity was seen as defined through connection and intimacy, stressing relatedness as a developmental goal and cooperation as a central mode of action. Defined in this way, both masculinity and femininity were seen as two *modes* reflecting different conceptions of self and morality (Gilligan, 1982) that have important ramifications for caring and caregiving in society, particularly in terms of who does the caring, under which conditions, and to what degree caring and caregiving are esteemed and appreciated.

Masculinity was obviously associated with manhood and femininity with womanhood. However, the nature of the almost universal connection between caring and womanhood or caring and femininity has been approached somewhat differently by different writers. Some, mostly at the earlier waves of feminism, were mainly focused on the idea that caring and mothering were imposed on women in order to sustain a division of power and labor as part of the core characteristics of a patriarchal culture (e.g., de Beauvoir, 1949/1973). Others, who nevertheless agreed with this contention, viewed this connection as reflecting a core characteristic of women or femininity and focused on the strengths that such connection can accrue when the negative values and derisive attitudes were changed (e.g., Miller, 1976/1982) and when women and men were free to choose how and in what capacity they would like to be involved in caring (Ruddick, 1989/1995).

Thus one side of this argument, which I will describe in its extreme and somewhat radical version, involves a suggestion that caring and mothering in particular should not be tied to gender and should not be an exclusively female domain. These writers stressed the distinction between being a mother (giving birth) and mothering; they viewed the societal insistence on women performing the mothering role as a controlling and subjugating process reflecting patriarchal values and culture. There is no reason, they argued, why men should not engage in mothering and caring. According to these accounts, mothering and caring often involved ambivalence and conflict and hampered the woman caregiver's freedom to pursue her authentic self and to grow and develop as an individual (Rich, 1976). In its extreme and most radical form, such an account can be seen as seeking to eradicate gender differences in caring and mothering and as paving the way for an equal share of men and women involved in caring for the young and in caregiving in society (Chodorow, 1978/1999).

The other side of the argument focused on the uniqueness of each gender in terms of caring and mothering and illuminated the positive aspects of women's caring and mothering. Although it admitted the highly negative and repressing outcomes of patriarchal culture for women in general and for women's caregiving in particular, this view sought to change the situation by abolishing suppression and advocating freedom of choice (i.e., the freedom to use contraception, the freedom to have an abortion, the freedom not to have children at all, or the freedom to have or raise children in various familial combinations), along with acknowledging the unique processes that characterize women and their way of being, caring, and mothering. In fact, proponents of this position viewed this feminine uniqueness of caring and mothering as a strength and suggested that humanity can learn from it (Miller, 1976/1982; Gilligan, 1982; Ruddick, 1989/1995). Gender differences in the way of being and acting in the world, the construction of self, and morality were often viewed as different themes rather than as a reflection of a strict gender-based distinction; still, the connection between being a woman and having these "feminine traits" was clearly acknowledged and in some of the accounts traced to social, contextual, as well as biological antecedents (Gilligan, 1982).

Reconciliation and utopian projections into the future

Several of the most prominent feminist writers have suggested various ways of reconciliation between these two modes—femininity and masculinity—and put forward possible "utopian" ramifications. An interesting perspective regarding the reconciliation of feminine and masculine gender identities was offered by Benjamin, a psychoanalyst and feminist. She (1988) discussed issues related to the developmental processes of the two genders. She viewed Freudian theories of development as inevitably reproducing patriarchal gender relationships characterized by domination and submission and most notably reflected in the cultural polarity of male rationality and activity and female emotionality and passivity. Benjamin critically revised parts of this theory and suggested that through intersubjectivity both connectedness (presumably reflecting the feminine side) and autonomy (presumably reflecting the masculine side) could be developed and obtained in children of both genders. In creating intersubjectivity, a special kind of connection and mutual recognition is established between the mother and the child in which each of the partners (mother and child) is acknowledged and validated as different and autonomous yet linked and recognized. If this is done early in life, such intersubjectivity can also be constructed in later life and in other kinds of relationships.

As far as moral judgment is concerned, Gilligan (1982) asserted that the substance of women's moral concerns is their sensitivity to the needs of others and the assumption of responsibility for taking care. These lead women to adopt a specific moral point of view, or an *ethics of care*, which involves hearing voices other than their own and including others' points of view in their judgments as well as looking for solutions that sustain and nurture relationships and cooperation rather than justice and fairness. Specifically, and unlike masculinity and male moral judgments—which tend to focus on fairness, justice, and the letter of the law—women's judgments show an overriding concern with relationships and responsibilities. Women's voices on moral issues thus provide a complementary and much needed point of view. Gilligan (1982) and others (Miller, 1976/1982) have asserted that because male development and male behavior became the norm, female behavior and feminine concerns with caring and relationships, as well as their own kind of moral judgment, were perceived as deviating from the norm and were thus devalued and accorded a lower status. However, both modes—that of justice and that of care—were seen as complementary and necessary for the development of a better society.

A similar contention concerning general modes of acting in the world was raised by Miller (1976/1982). Miller suggested that a core aspect of what women do in life involves "active participation in the development of others" where "others" are both children and adults. Miller argued that professionals used terms such as *mothering, nurturing,* and *caretaking* to describe this endeavor, which is more complex and multifaceted than such all-encompassing terms may imply. She then presented yet another framing of this core characteristic of women (Miller, 1982, p. XX in the foreword to the 2nd edition): "women try to use their powers, that is, their intellectual and emotional abilities, to empower others, to build other people's strength, resources, effectiveness, and well-being." She suggested that understanding and focusing on women's specific psychological development and mode of acting in the world would open up the way for a better understanding of all psychological development, male and female alike, and the delineation of the culturally desired mature person as both autonomous (the expected masculine achievement) and with the ability to engage in "interactions which empower others and, simultaneously, oneself" (Miller, 1982).

Finally, another suggestion that tried to build upon women's strength and caring or caregiving characteristics was presented by Ruddick (1989/1995). Ruddick focuses her discussion on the maternal thinking that ensued from the practice of mothering. This specific way of thinking involved the capacity to hold and experience intense ambivalent feelings, to withstand pressures and to forgo aggressive reactions in serving the goals of preserving the lives of the care receivers, empowering them, and training them to be accepted in their culture and community. Ruddick suggested that applying these outstanding attributes outside of the home environment and in other institutions, politics in particular, could in principle change society and contribute to a politics of peace.

Chapter conclusion

All in all, this highly significant and prolific line of thought and research has exposed some of the most intriguing and central issues in the study of caring as a human motivation. Feminist writers in general have discussed how caring has been construed within culture and within patriarchal culture in particular throughout history; they identified the universal connection between woman-hood and caring, struggled with its origin, and described mothering and what it takes to care for a child; along the way they debunked several alleged truths, such as the myth of the ideal mother or that of the natural mothering instinct. These insights notwithstanding, they still called attention to specific feminine attributes, such as the ethics of care, the capacity to be defined through and within relationships, and the motivation and capacity to care and nurture or to foster the other person's development, which nonetheless appear to character-ize women. Finally, they suggested a reconciliation between the two modes of being and acting in the world—feminine and masculine—without one domi-nating the other.

Part I Conclusion

The six different conceptual paradigms presented and discussed in Part I represent diverse perspectives on caring, tending, and caregiving; together they provide a multilayered view of caring. The spiritual perspective highlights the centrality of care, compassion, and caregiving as qualities of the divine and as a supreme moral quality to aspire to across a variety of spiritual traditions, thus substantiating the universal presence of caring broadly defined in the human legacy and ethos.

The evolutionary perspective provides us with scientific explanations of why caring in a variety of relations—including progeny, romantic partners, friends, tribe members, and even strangers—is evolutionarily worthwhile and contributes to individuals' fitness and the survival of their genes to future generations. Such a contemporary view is not to be taken lightly because of the selfish perspective that characterized evolutionary accounts in the earlier versions of the theory. This perspective is central because it provides ultimate explanations for the existence of caring in a variety of domains and with a variety of targets. It also offers an important insight into the conditions that sustain caring in the long run and make caring an evolutionary asset. The first condition is that caring should not be provided in a limitless manner, and the second is that the giving of care must be embedded within a personal and cultural context that allows for the detection and punishment of those who try to exploit others' generosity and compassion.

The research and study of empathic processes provides us with a perspective on a universal and fundamental proximate mechanism for the activation and sustenance of caring across a wide range of targets and situations. It also underscores the uniqueness of the human experience, which includes evolutionary ancient layers of such processes that we share with other animals—bottom-up emotional and vicarious empathy—and the evolutionary newer and mostly human layers of such processes—top-down mentalizing and perspective taking, which also form the foundations of morality. This perspective also underscores that there are important modulations of empathic processes that reflect adaptations to a variety of conditions and individual differences.

The biological, brain research, and genetic perspectives provide impressive evidence that the caring motivation is rooted in our hormonal and brain functioning and that genetic variations explain a large part of our individual differences in this respect. Furthermore, these perspectives highlight strong similarities in the biological structures, agents, and functioning implicated in caring across a variety of domains, targets, and manifestations from the intimacy and dedication of parenting to generosity toward total strangers.

The perspective of attachment theory provides us with an explication of the psychological structures and mechanisms by which caring and caregiving are experienced and displayed. By postulating the existence of a caregiving behavioral system and elucidating how a behavioral system operates, this perspective provides clear clues as to the psychological organization of the general caring motivation. This perspective also underscores the importance of explaining both caring behaviors and caring bonds, where affection and warmth are central and provides some promising directions. Finally, the rigorous research that characterizes this field also provides clear demonstrations of similar psychological dynamics in caring with different targets and across a variety of manifestations.

Finally, the perspective of feminist scholars provides a crucial cultural context to caring and caregiving and underscores the universal connection between womanhood and caring and the existence of universal cultural processes of devaluating femininity and caring, which can and should be debunked and resolved for a fuller understanding of caring processes and for the well-being of our societies.

Together these perspectives highlight the significance of caring for our survival, the general mechanisms and processes involved in its enactment, and the conceptual foundations whereby we may explore the diverse manifestations of caring presented and discussed in Part II.

MANIFESTATIONS OF CARING AND CAREGIVING IN DIFFERENT DOMAINS AND CONTEXTS

Part II Introduction

The discussion thus far provided a comprehensive conceptual base to the point of view that I present in this book, which considers caring to be a fundamental and encompassing motivation whereby a general motivational system of care is manifested with different adaptations in caring in different domains and with different targets. Most of the discussions thus far have centered on caring for other people close and distant, familiar and unfamiliar. Here I propose an even broader scope. I suggest that dynamics of care ensuing from a similar general caring motivation are also related to caring for pets, plants, and inanimate entities such as the environment. I suggest that one of the reasons scholars and researchers have often missed the similarities across domains and entities is because the study of caring, tending, prosocial behavior, and caregiving as a distinct realm in human experience is dispersed across a variety of traditions and disciplines. The study of parenting, for example, is mostly conducted within developmental psychology; the care provided to elderly or disabled parents is studied by gerontologists who refer to it as *caregiving*; while caring for strangers is usually examined within the realm of social psychology under such rubrics as *prosocial behavior* or *altruism*.

These observations led Berscheid and Collins (2000) to describe the situation as the "balkanization of psychology" (p. 107), whereby research projects on different domains of care developed independently of each other and remained isolated. Berscheid and Collins (2000) further suggest that a theory of caregiving that aspires to account for caregiving behavior in all relationships must integrate these different bodies of knowledge. They highlight the point that people not only reactively engage in caregiving within a caring bond but may actively seek out others to care for and may even care for animals and inanimate objects (i.e., dolls). This view clearly invites and calls for a broad conceptualization of caring such as the one advocated in this book.

The part that follows discusses the different domains or contexts in which caring has been studied and investigated. These domains are seen as different manifestations of the same general motivational system. The kind of care expressed in each domain many not be identical because different manifestations of the general system express variant adaptations and domain-specific processes. Nonetheless, commonalities reflecting their common core are present. For example, sensitivity to the cared for entity and its needs appears to be a central attribute marking a better type of care, and in the diverse manifestations we expect the expression of similar individual differences. Some of these domains or contexts cover a very large and fruitful territory, including thousands of researchers worldwide, such as the study of parenting. Other domains, such as the study of caring for plants, may be the concern of only a few dozen researchers. My discussion of these domains is not intended to be an extensive overview of the relevant research in each but rather to allow the reader to appreciate the prevalent research and theoretical models in each area. In particular, my aim is to expose the richness and the pervasiveness of the caring all around us. Specifically, Chapter 8 focuses on caring in relationships with familiar others. Chapters 9 and 10 focus on caring provided to strangers: Chapter 9 is devoted to conceptual frameworks and Chapter 10 to examples and manifestations. Chapter 11 focuses on caring provided to nonhuman entities, and Chapter 12 focuses on caring in different roles and contexts. Research on the diverse manifestations of the caring motivation can offer us several new insights about this motivation. Specifically, amassing and reviewing the extant research and theoretical models in each chapter has allowed me to extract a variety of insights regarding the caring motivation and its operation.

Caring bonds, a caring state, caring behaviors, caring relationships, and caring dynamics

In discussing the motivation to care and its different and diverse manifestations it is necessary to distinguish between a *caring bond,* a *caring state, caring behavior,* and *caring dynamics.* All of these kinds of care are part of a broad motivational system of caring. A 'caring bond" is an enduring affectional bond between an individual (the caregiver) and an entity or an object in which the caregiver commits to caring for the entity and thus concerns herself or himself with that entity's survival, welfare, and thriving. Such a bond involves an emotional, cognitive, and biological process of connection, and the affectional bond aspect means that the partner in such a relationship is not interchangeable with any other. Often such a bond reflects a conscious and deliberate decision to commit oneself to caring for some person or entity, as is the case with adoption, marital relations, and caring for a pet.

A "caring state" is a state of readiness to care, which includes an assumption of responsibility for the entity being cared for. It may or may not entail a specific observable behavior, although it always involves a cognitive, emotional, and biological investment on the caregiver's part. The mere assumption of responsibility (a caring state) may or may not be associated with a caring bond. Thus a person may assume a temporary responsibility of care, as when babysitting, without having a caring bond with the child. However, a caring bond always entails an assumption of responsibility.

The term *caring behavior* refers to a specific behavior that is directed at the cared-for entity in order to further its survival, well-being, development, and thriving. These behaviors may be enacted toward a person's offspring or toward other people or entities; their provision does not imply the existence of a caring bond between the caregiver and the cared-for entity. A person may, for example, provide care to a total stranger during an emergency situation such as a road accident. Furthermore, a caring bond or the assumption of a caring state does not necessitate the constant enactment of caring behaviors despite the fact that it requires vigilance on the caregiver's part in order to monitor the physical and the psychological well-being of the entity being cared for.

A large number of care situations involve multiple combinations of these aspects and reflect what I refer to as *caring dynamics*. An example of this would be caring for a stranger after a road accident. Although this would include intense care and an assumption of temporary responsibility for the survival of another person, it is not a caring bond and is quite short-term. Another caring dynamic might play out in mentoring a child as part of a practicum in social work. This dynamic reflects continuous but limited caring involving a low-intensity caring bond and the assumption of a limited scope of responsibility. Furthermore, in the first stages of such a connection, the mentor-mentee relation can be described as a *hierarchical caring relationship* where a bond has probably not yet been created (and may never be) because an affectionate bond takes time to be created and the relationship does not require a bond of affection. Similarly an *egalitarian caring relationship* may develop between friends, and this may or may not develop into a caring *bond*. The different domains and contexts of care reflect variant care dynamics as highlighted in the following chapters.

Reactive and proactive caring and their association with life's meaning

Another important distinction is that between *reactive* and *proactive* care. The typical description of caring involves "reactive" caring, meaning that it is activated by a perception of a cue reflecting a need for help and care. For example, a baby is crying, a person asks for directions, or a bookshelf is about to fall on a friend. We often react to such cues with a certain level of empathy or with alarm, and we are motivated to help and provide care. This is the characteristic description provided by attachment researchers regarding the operation of the caregiving behavioral system (see Chapter 6). I contend that such care is only part of the story, depicting us as responders to cues but not as initiators. However, as we will see in this part of the book, people also engage in care proactively.

Proactive care starts as an intrinsic desire to do good, to help others, or to contribute to the well-being of next generation. In such cases we do not react to a perceived need but proactively look for situations or relationships that will enable us to help and provide care. Such a situation may reflect the existence of a need to care, a desire to care, or even a caring drive. Regardless of the term used, it is an intrinsic need or desire often associated with our wish to extend ourselves to others as an expression of self-fulfillment, offering us a strong sense of meaning in life. For example, people proactively decide that they want to be parents and to raise a child; at times they may invest much money and effort toward adopting a child if they cannot conceive one on their own. People also proactively volunteer to help in a variety of settings and organizations, seek to become mentors to youth at risk and proactively donate money to various causes. As we will see in the next chapters, such proactive expressions of our caring motivation, if autonomously enacted, are strongly associated with our search for meaning in our lives and enable us to feel a part of something greater than ourselves. It reflects the inherent association between caring (reactive and proactive) and life meaning and highlights the importance of eudaemonic well-being, the kind of well-being that results from living a meaningful life—a life worth living, in manifestations of care.

8

Caring for Familiar Others

Caring for familiar others has often been differentiated from research on caring for strangers. Unsurprisingly, many of the conceptualizations presented so far discuss close relationships, and particularly parenting and romantic ties involving distinct caring bonds. Close relationships are central arenas for the provision of caring, tending, and nurturing. In fact, parenting in general and mothering in particular is perceived by many scholars as the prototypical and most intensive type of care (Brown, Brown, & Preston, 2012; Hrdy, 1999). The chapter that follows will be concerned with parenting and caring in close relations, as with romantic partners and friends and with care provided to one's own parents as well to familiar others in less intimate and committed relations, such as colleagues, neighbors, and acquaintances.

The first section deals with parent-child relations and addresses the issues most pertinent to the focus of this book. The next three sections refer to three research perspectives implicated in the scholarship on caring for familiar others: research on compassionate love and social support, the study of caregiving through the lens of attachment theory, and investigations of caregiving to the sick and/or elderly.

Caring in parent-child relations

In many respects parental caring is the most central and prototypical case of the motivation to care. Countless papers and books have been published on parenting, and we currently possess much clearer insights and broader and more comprehensive knowledge of this remarkable caring bond. I will not, however, attempt to summarize this extensive literature or to provide a review of the central findings. Readers interested in specific issues can consult the extant and extensive literature on parenting and can also find a good overview in the five volumes of the *Handbook of Parenting* (Bornstein, 2002). Parenting is in fact so central in the motivation to care that it is part and parcel of all the major conceptual paradigms, which is why parent-child relations are considered and discussed in many other sections and chapters in this book. I will here discuss only several selected issues that I deem central to this book's main focus.

Parenting—the most intensive, extensive, and comprehensive caring bond

The first issue that I would like to discuss is the unique nature of parenting in general and mothering in particular. This is by far the most intensive and extensive caring relation in the lives of those who become parents. This is not just caregiving behavior—it is a caring bond. In fact, the parent-child relation may serve as the prototypical caring bond because of its breadth and comprehensiveness in scope and in time. Parents need to ensure the child's physical survival, help the child acquire competence in a variety of domains (i.e., motor, perceptual, cognitive, and emotional), socialize the child as a successful member of society, and contribute to the child's personal happiness, self-actualization, and social embeddedness. This commitment and its enactment involve an unparalleled investment of effort, money, psychological resources, and time, which for most parents outweighs almost any other endeavor in their lives.

Furthermore parenting is often unrestricted in *duration*, namely in how much time is devoted to parenting during a typical day, and in *length*, because most parenting bonds are lifelong. In addition, owing to the prolonged dependence of the human infant on the parent for survival, the parental responsibility is heavy and consequential. Furthermore, as the child grows up and matures, new challenges and needs present themselves and new ways of caring are required. Consequently parenting demands flexibility and the continuing acquisition of new capacities and skills.

Another aspect of the uniqueness of the parenting bond relates to its clear evolutionary adaptiveness. Because the human infant depends on others for survival for an extended period of time, infants whose parents had optimal caring genes and hence tended to assume a wide-ranging responsibility for their survival and for teaching them the skills needed to become autonomous and successful adults had much higher chances of surviving to maturity and having children of their own, thus propagating the caring genes. Consequently parenting was evolutionarily selected and it originates in our humanoid ancestors. Mothering in particular originated even earlier, since mothers among other mammals also show similar caregiving capacities, including caring bonds. Because of its obvious evolutionary inevitability and its relatively early appearance in the phylogenetic process, parenting and in particular mothering is assumed to be the evolutionary precursor of caring in general. Our general empathy, compassion, and teaching skills as well as our capacity to be gentle and nurturing are often ascribed to the genetic infrastructure and cultural context that coevolved to sustain caring for the young. Thus it has been suggested that other well-known adaptations of caring—such as caring for a romantic partner or cooperating with tribe members and even fathering—co-opted existing biological and neurological structures and processes of mothering and built upon them. Yet as the other types of care evolved, this affected also the more evolutionary ancient maternal care and each domain or type of care reciprocally impacted the others, thus creating a multifaceted, complex, comprehensive, and flexible caring motivational system.

Mothering as the epitome of caring

Within parental caring, the mother-child relation often serves as the epitome of caring. Mothering also plays a central role in evolutionary explanations, since it is conceived as obligatory for the survival of the species, unlike fathering which appears to be more facultative (less mandatory) and flexible. Ethnographic research covering more than a thousand different cultures and a variety of historic periods demonstrates that females universally care for their young and that the mother is the predominant caring figure during the first year of the infant's life (See review in Wood & Eagly, 2002). Besides a genetic foundation and biological preparedness, human caring also requires learning and scaffolding. This is also the case with other mammals. Hence this universally pervasive nature of mothering required adaptations in women's psychological makeup and development as well as in women's and men's social roles. Women, for example, are socialized to be caring and empathic, sensitive and responsive, and these skills are then coopted in other close relations (romantic relations, friendships) where nurturance and caring are also necessary, such that women became the ultimate caregivers (Taylor, 2002). Furthermore, because it was obligatory, maternal love was taken for granted, as were other types of nurturance and caring typical of women; accordingly, the caring roles or professions were also taken for granted and accorded low status. During the past several decades, a growing number of scholars have critically discussed these gender issues, also investigated paternal care, and tried to throw light on gender issues related to care (see the elaborate discussion of women's and men's caring in Chapter 15).

Mothering as universal and automatic—or is it?

The obligatory nature of mothering may lead readers to infer that mothering is universal. However, this is not necessarily the case. For instance, historical analyses of marriages and births in England between 1541 and 1871 have identified fluctuations in the percentage of adults 40 to 45 years of age who were never married and did not have children, ranging between 5% to 20% depending on the cohort (Weir, 1984). More recent American estimates from the 1980s report that 10% of women 40 years of age and older had not become mothers (Bloom &

Trussell, 1984). In the year 2000, nearly 19% of women in their early 40s were childless, and similar percentages of childlessness are reported in other western societies (Agrillo & Nelini, 2008). Thus, childbearing, although highly prevalent is clearly not universal, and a nonnegligible minority of woman have been historically and currently childless, whether involuntarily or by choice.

We have almost no information about whether childlessness was voluntary in the past, but current estimates in western industrialized countries such as the United States, Canada, and Italy are that around 4% to 7% of the people are "child-free"—a term referring to having no desire or plans to have children despite having the biological capacity (Agrillo & Nelini, 2008). In most contemporary cultures women are clearly expected to become mothers or at least to express the will to do so; thus decisions to remain child-free were often stigmatized. However, research on child-free couples has demonstrated that their well-being is often better than or at least similar in quality to that of married couples with children (Hansen, 2012). Child-free couples may have other domains and other targets for their caring motivation. For example, there are indications that child-free couples are more likely to have pets (Albert & Bulcroft, 1988). However, it is too early to draw definite conclusions in this regard, since this issue has not been researched extensively.

Another expectation that may be based on the obligatory status of mothering is that the creation and activation of a caring bond reflects a *reaction* to the sight, smell, cuteness, and small size of a baby in light of the hormonal changes of labor and the knowledge that this baby is the mother's baby. Although such responses are common, this is not an automatic reaction and mothers report a variety of experiences: immediate love, affection and connection, difficulty loving the child at first sight and needing a much greater number of mother-baby interactions before a bond is formed, as well as an inability to love the baby and a rejection of a connection with him or her (Badinter, 1981; Parker, 1995).

Furthermore, mothering and maternal care (as well as fathering, for that matter) are not only reactive but also proactive, involving choice that reflects the *proactive nature* of the general caring motivation. This can be observed in two complementary phenomena that characterize human societies. The first is the nonnegligible prevalence of adults choosing not to become parents and thus to remain childless (described earlier); the other is the fervent investment of adults in becoming parents, either by biological means such as in vitro fertilization or by adoption when they have difficulties in conceiving children.

A large proportion of men and women who for some reason cannot conceive go to great lengths and through agonizing and often very costly procedures, risking their health, in order have children. In fact, the agony and anguish of men and particularly women in such a predicament is a prevalent theme in human history and mythology (e.g., in the Bible, Sarah, the wife of Abraham and eventually mother of Isaac, and Hannah, the mother of Samuel, who were both barren and grief-stricken) and in current research on infertility (Greil, 1997; McQuillan et al., 2003; Chachamovich, Chachamovich, Ezer, Fleck, Knauth, & Passos, 2010). The adoption of a child who is not biologically related to the parents presents an evolutionary conundrum because the practice does not contribute to the parents' inclusive fitness, since they do not share the child's genes and often come from different social classes and/or ethnicities. Yet the adoption of biologically unrelated minors is found in all historical eras and in a variety of cultures both contemporary and historical as well as in mythology (Moses in Jewish culture, Oedipus in Greek, Romulus and Remus in Roman).

The strong intrinsic desire to parent among a large number of women who find it difficult to become mothers is urgent and compelling and often associated with a profound sense of ontological and existential life meaning (Wirtberg, Möller, Hogström, Tronstad, & Lalos, 2007; Chachamovich et al., 2010). The desire to parent is obviously also related to social pressures and gender-role expectations, yet the strong intrinsic desire to mother appears to involve much more than "just" obeying cultural mores. The intrinsic and insistent nature of this motivation can be seen in women's willingness to sacrifice a great deal to become mothers (i.e., health, financial security, other pursuits such as career and leisure) as well as in women's efforts to maintain these tedious and costly efforts despite the social pressures of their relatives and friends (Callan, Kloskf, Kashima, & Hennessey, 1988). Furthermore, an indication for the connection of such desires with the intrinsic and general motivation to care is found in the fact that childless women have often coped with their childlessness by caring for others and for pets (Wirtberg et al., 2007). In fact throughout history, unmarried women who had no children of their own were often engaged in other sorts of caring and caregiving, such as taking care of their parents' household and their parents' welfare and health, taking take of relatives' and siblings' children, and being involved in caring professions such as teaching or community service (e.g., among nuns) (Watkins, 1984).

Both choosing to remain childless and exerting oneself in order to have children underscore the same point—that the caring motivation is also *proactive*. This proactivity means that besides responding to an emergent need (i.e., the baby's helplessness), individuals can choose whether or not to form a lifelong parental caring bond.

Parenting, well-being, and hedonic and eudaemonic happiness

Common folk theories about parenting suggest that children make people happier and that having children and raising them is a fundamental mode of fulfillment and delight (see comprehensive review in Hansen, 2012). This notion is reflected in the universal desire to have children. Research shows that 90% to

95% of young adults worldwide plan to have children and that voluntary child-lessness, although increasing, is rare (2% to 6%). In international surveys, a large majority (80% to 90%) agrees that "watching children grow up is life's greatest joy." Nonetheless, there is much cross-cultural variability in many pronatalist beliefs. For example, the proportion of people agreeing with the belief that it is necessary to have children in order to be happy (i.e., "you cannot really be happy without having children") ranges from 5% to 60%. Generally pronatalist attitudes are strongest in eastern Europe, Asia, and Africa and weakest in the richer countries (e.g., members of the Organisation for Economic Co-operation and Development, such as the United States, the Netherlands, and Australia). In addition, pronatalist beliefs are less pervasive among highly educated and younger respondents and in more recent surveys (See a detailed review of these studies in Hansen, 2012).

Scholars who have studied parenting underscore the value of children in offering rewards of love, meaning and fulfillment, excitement and happiness, and companionship and support especially in old age (e.g., Friedman, Hechter, & Kanazawa, 1994). Specifically, scholars have referred to proximal mechanisms, such as the gratification of core psychological needs, that are key to well-being: the needs for companionship, affiliation, meaning, and self-realization as well as the needs for social embeddedness, security, and respect. The latter are associated with the strong social desirability of having children and the universal cultural expectation that adults, and especially women, should bear children, which, when fulfilled, accord parents with respect, a new social role, and integration into social networks and cultural meaning systems (Friedman, Hechter, & Kanazawa, 1994; Stanca, 2012). Finally, scholars have also discussed the developmental psychological task of generativity of midadulthood (first suggested by Erikson, 1963), which involves supporting and caring for future generations and is clearly accomplished by bearing and raising children.

Empirical findings, however, present a more complex picture than that depicted in these prevalent beliefs (Stanca, 2012). These findings are based on cross-sectional studies comparing parents with nonparents and on longitudinal surveys that have studied individuals before and after they became parents. The extant literature includes a large number of studies and surveys conducted on representative samples in a variety of cultures. These include the World Values Survey, which has been administered six times since 1981 and contains representative samples from 97 countries representing 90% of the world's population. Others are the European Barometer offering data from 1975 to 1992; the European Social Survey, which began in 2002 and is held every two years, the US General Social Survey (GSS) of adults (18 years of age and above) of randomly selected households, which has been administered since 1972; the Household, Income and Labour Dynamics in Australia (HILDA) survey, which began in 2001; and more.

As reviewed in Hansen (2012), small but significant *negative* effects of parenting on life satisfaction and happiness were apparent in a variety of cultures, indicating that people are generally happier without biological children and that life satisfaction drops after the birth of the first child for both women and men but recovers to almost preparenthood levels after several years. The effects were generally small in magnitude and moderated by various factors. By and large childbirths' small negative effect on parents' well-being occurs mainly when children live at home and can in fact become positive with nonresident children after the challenges of daily child care subside. Furthermore, people from social groups that generally experience more parenting burdens and challenges and have lower levels of support are more susceptible to negative effects on their well-being. These include women, single parents, parents of lower socioeconomic status, and parents in societies with less pronatalist policies that provide lower levels of state-based supports. When such burdens are lessened through various forms of support—for example, that provided by welfare societies—the impact of resident children on their parents' happiness and life satisfaction can become *positive*.

These findings highlight the often muted reality that parenting is not easy and takes a toll on parents' well-being unless contextual, familial, and cultural supports are provided. In our environment of evolutionary adaptedness when mothering and fathering first evolved, we lived within small groups of interdependent others. In these groups such support was amply available, as indicated by the data regarding sharing in child care in contemporary nonindustrialized cultures. For example, based on ethnographic studies of a large number of nonindustrialized cultures (N = 186), Wood and Eagly (2002) have shown that a large number of people share the burden and responsibility of care for infants and children in these cultures and that this starts early in the infant's life. Specifically, in the majority of the societies studied, children as young as 12 months of age were away from their mothers for half or more of the time and were cared for also by others (i.e., siblings, older women from the family or tribe). Such support lessens the burden and cost of parenting and increases the relative salience of the rewards.

Still, the surveys reported here show that even when such conditions of support prevail, as in the Nordic countries of Europe, where parenting is positively associated with well-being, such effects are small and unsystematic. Umberson and Gove (1989) and Baumeister (1991) suggest that we confuse happiness with meaning and that one of the strongest proximate rewards of parenting is meaning, not pleasure. Meaning is defined as having a sense of purpose and direction in one's activities and efforts, which are seen as part of something larger than oneself (e.g., Steger, Kashdan, & Oishi, 2008). This suggestion is associated with an important distinction between two kinds of well-being—hedonic (related to having a high level of positive emotions and a low level of negative ones) and eudaemonic (related to having meaning and purpose) (Ryan & Deci, 2001; Ryff & Singer, 2006), which will be discussed in the last part of this book. Several strands of research appear to support this suggestion. For example, a national study carried out about three decades ago in the United States showed that parents with resident children (as compared with nonparents) reported lower levels of affective well-being and satisfaction but higher levels of meaning whereas parents with nonresident children over 18 years of age reported higher levels on all indicators of well-being—hedonic and eudaemonic (Umberson & Gove, 1989). In a more recent German study that used retrospective reconstruction of episodes in a day and the feelings and thoughts accompanying these episodes, White and Dolan (2009) found that time spent with children was less pleasurable than other activities, such as watching TV, eating, or reading but was almost the most rewarding (similar to volunteering and work) in terms of feeling competent, focused, engaged, and believing that the activity was worthwhile and meaningful (White & Dolan, 2009). Finally, Nelson and colleagues (Nelson, Kushlev, English, Dunn, & Lyubomirsky, 2013) harnessed three different methodologies: a large representative US survey, an experience-sampling methodology that assesses moment-to-moment feelings and thoughts, and a within-subjects approach to examine whether parents derive more positive feelings from taking care of their children than from their other daily activities. Across all three studies, parents (and especially fathers) reported relatively higher levels of happiness, positive emotions, and meaning in life than nonparents (Nelson et al., 2013). This led Nelson, Kushlev, and Lyubomirsky (2014) to suggest, based on extensive review of the literature, that the association between parenthood and well-being reflects the operation of a large number of moderators. Sleep disturbance, financial problems, and troubled marriages, for example, contribute to unhappiness, while greater meaning in life and the satisfaction of parents' basic needs are associated with happiness and joy.

These interesting results appear to preliminarily affirm the proposal that parenting may be proximally enhanced by its contribution to meaning. Still, even when significant effects of higher or lower levels of meaning and pleasure were found, they tended to be quite small—explaining 1% to 4% in the studied individuals' well-being—and did not reflect the strength of emotions that parents experience and that are often evident in studies that focus on the phenomenology of parenting and give voice to parents' internal world (Benjamin, 1988; Parker, 1995; see review in Mayseless, 2006b). It might be the case that parents experience high levels of both negative (burden, exhaustion, depression, and frustration) and positive emotions (joy, pride, satisfaction, and meaning), both hedonic and eudaemonic, and that these are almost similar in magnitude, such that the net result is only modest either way. I will return to this issue in the last part of the book.

Compassionate love and social support

Besides its role in parenting, caring is also a central part of other close relations—more egalitarian ones, as with romantic partners and friends. In general four distinct motivational systems have been discussed in the study of close relationships: the sexual one—relating to romantic and sexual desire and attraction; attachment—relating to needs for security, protection and the alleviation of distress; companionship/affiliation, relating to sharing affectively positive interchanges; and caregiving—related to the provision of care, nurturance, and support (Furman & Wehner, 1994). This is reflected in recent theorizing suggesting that we have four different kinds of love reflecting each of these domains: romantic love, adult attachment love, companionate love and compassionate love, relating to the sexual, attachment, affiliation and caregiving motivational systems respectively (Berscheid, 2010). Discussions of compassionate love indicate that it involves "attitudes and actions related to giving of self for the good of the other," and some have suggested that it may include both alleviating distress and promoting thriving (Underwood, 2009, p. 4). It has been defined as "containing feelings, cognitions, and behaviors that are focused on caring, concern, tenderness, and an orientation toward supporting, helping, and understanding the other(s), particularly when the other(s) is (are) perceived to be suffering or in need" (Sprecher & Fehr, 2005; p. 630). Furthermore, it may be applied to unfamiliar others and even to all humanity (Sprecher & Fehr, 2005). However, research has mostly focused on romantic relations and found that the enactment of romantic caring is associated with positive outcomes for giver and receiver (e.g., higher self esteem, well-being, relationship satisfaction) (see review in Fehr, Harasymchuk, & Sprecher, 2014).

Researchers have used a variety of other terms besides love to conceptualize and study caring outside of parenting. A fruitful and rich research domain is the study of social support, which relates to caring for familiar others and most notably romantic partners, friends, acquaintances, neighbors, and coworkers. For the most part, social support was assessed as part of adult-adult relations; when studied among children, it was assessed as part of relations among equals—peers or siblings. The term *social support* denotes a large number of social activities that involve supporting and caring for others in various ways. These interpersonal provisions include offering others love, interest, liking, nurturance, advice, and various goods as well as demonstrating a willingness to help if necessary. Thus social support was seen as including instrumental (e.g., showing a person how to solve a problem), tangible (e.g., providing goods), informational (e.g., giving advice), and emotional (e.g., offering validation and reassurance) support.

The study of social support has tended to focus on the receiver of support and examined the kinds of support needed and when they are needed, their effects on the person being supported, and a variety of factors that moderate these effects.

Although the focus of this book is on the giving end, I here provide a very brief delineation of the vast literature on these issues because it can give us clues as to the working of the caring motivation and how prevalent and central is the reliance on its existence and operation.

Within the large body of research on social support and stress buffering, it is common knowledge that people appreciate help when they experience stress or are distressed and that this support serves as a buffer against the negative consequences of stress and adversity (Taylor, 2002). This includes such situations as being sick, having difficulties at work or at school, breaking up with a romantic partner, or experiencing the death of a family member. In such situations individuals often expect someone they care about to offer them support, such as asking how they are, providing them with information and services, and helping them to cope without impinging upon their autonomy and dignity. Hence social support has often been seen as relevant only to assuage people's distress, pain, and anxiety.

However, people often also need support on occasions of positive experiences. They may, for example, want to share their positive experiences with others, and they expect a different kind of support in this case (e.g., Vangelisti, 2009). Individuals expect close others to rejoice in their achievements and encourage them when they play in a championship game, are accepted into medical school, receive an award, or perform in a recital (see Vangelisti, Maguire, Alexander, & Clark, 2007). In such cases the support does not involve help in coping or alleviating stress but rather showing interest in the others' activities by attending the event, giving them encouragement, or demonstrating caring by being supportive. Sometimes people simply want companionship; they want others to share their joy, laugh with them, or take part in their excitement (Rook, 1989; Aron, Norman, Aron, McKenna, & Heyman, 2000). An interesting line of research that examined capitalization (sharing positive events and happenings with others) showed how support on such occasions is associated with a positive spiral process that improves the well-being of both partners as well as their relationship (Gable, Reis, Impett, & Asher, 2004; Reis et al., 2010; Gosnell & Gable, 2013).

The term *social support* often refers not only to actual actions but also to general social integration or embeddedness within a community. Consequently the study of social support has distinguished between received support, the subjective perception of embeddedness. and the perceived availability of help or support. Interestingly, perceived support—namely the general sense that a person can get support if needed—demonstrated a stronger and clearer profile of associations with positive outcomes than received support (Gable, Gosnell, Maisel, & Strachman, 2012). In fact, in general perceived support was viewed as reflecting a dispositional attribute and was closely associated with attachment security (Haber, Cohen, Lucas, Baltes, 2007).

A large body of research has demonstrated the positive outcomes of social support for the support recipient. These positive outcomes include better well-being, greater achievements, and better health (see a review in Taylor, 2002, chapter 5; Uchino, 2009). Social support serves as a powerful buffer in times of stress and appears to counteract the ill effects of various stressors such as depression, anxiety, and illness (Uchino 2009); it even contributed to the relief of posttraumatic stress and to processes of personal growth following trauma (Prati & Pietrantoni, 2009). Support can even affect future adaptations, and its positive effects can transfer to other people associated with the receiver. For example, mothers who perceived stronger social support from their partners during pregnancy experienced less postpartum emotional distress after controlling for their distress in early pregnancy, and their infants were reported to be less distressed in response to novelty (Stapleton et al., 2012).

Biologically social support appears to exert these positive effects on support recipients through the regulation of stress responses, including reduced sympathetic and neuroendocrine activity. Emerging animal and human research suggests that oxytocin and endogenous opioids may be responsible for some of these physiological and health effects (Dickerson & Zoccola, 2009). In fact, a recent meta-analysis conducted on 148 studies and 308,849 participants found that social support significantly affected recipients' potential mortality. Specifically the findings indicated a 50% increased likelihood of survival for participants with stronger social relationships. This finding also remained consistent across ages, sexes, initial health statuses, causes of death, and follow-up periods (Holt-Lunstad, Smith, & Layton, 2010).

Reflecting the importance of the caregiver's motivations and way of providing care, these positive effects were contingent on the identity of the support provider, on the kind of support provided, and especially on the manner of its provision, to name just a few of the relevant factors. Indeed, social support can also be detrimental to support receivers. Received support can potentially incur negative outcomes, such as a reduction in one's sense of independence and competence as well as higher levels of stress, anxiety, and depression (Bolger, Zuckerman, & Kessler, 2000; Vangelisti, 2009).

This is highly relevant to the issue of individual differences in the enactment of the motivation to care. Support is expected to be sensitive to the recipient's needs and goals (e.g., by providing practical suggestions when such advice is requested or offering emotional support when sympathy is needed). Support must also be responsive, such that recipients recognize that their partners understand and validate them (Reis, Clark, & Holmes, 2004). Support that is insensitive, critical, or unwanted has been shown to hamper recipients' confidence in meeting their goals, such as recovering from knee surgery or coping with cancer treatment (Manne & Glassman, 2000; Khan et al., 2009). Additionally, support must reflect caring goals geared to the recipient's rather than the support provider's wishes. Consequently support that is driven by the expectations of the caregiver—for example, that the care recipient lose weight because it is personally important to the caregiver rather than the care receiver—actually contributed to a failure in achieving this goal; in this example, it was associated with weight *increase* rather than weight loss (Kappes & Shrout, 2011).

Receiving support from others can be costly for a number of reasons. For example, it draws attention to the recipient's weakness or vulnerability and may hamper the recipient's self-esteem and confidence. In addition, receiving support may lead the recipient to feel overly indebted and incompetent and may curtail his or her sense of autonomy (Kappes & Shrout, 2011). In fact, support that is not perceived as such—that is, support which the provider reported enacting but the recipient did not report receiving—was associated with the best outcomes (Bolger, Zuckerman, & Kessler, 2000). It might be the case that the recipient felt the support but did not name it in this way and hence accrued the rewards without feeling obliged.

An intriguing research paradigm performed with a group of college freshmen by Crocker and Canevello (2008, 2010) examined the development of relationships among roommates, with a focus on the importance of responsiveness and sensitivity on the part of the support provider. First-semester college students who reported compassionate goals, namely a desire to offer support out of genuine caring for others ("being supportive of my roommate") developed closer relationships, feelings of connection, and trust with others over the course of the semester through processes of projection and reciprocation of responsiveness. However, when students reported holding strong self-image goals, such as offering support in order to be perceived favorably by others, they were lonelier and experienced more conflict with others during the semester (Crocker & Canevello, 2008; Canevello & Crocker, 2010). All in all, it is the responsiveness and sensitivity in the provision of support that appear to be central in moderating its effects (Maisel & Gable, 2009).

The line of research that focused on the support giver's motivations and how such support is provided underscored that other-oriented motivations to care, rather than selfish ones, and responsiveness and sensitivity in providing support in a way that respects the other's needs, autonomy, worth, and competence are central in moderating the outcomes of support for the recipients and the giver-recipient relations. Yet most studies of social support examined the support's recipients and the outcomes of the support and comparatively less research effort focused on the support providers. Such a focus on the care provider was more prevalent within the broad theoretical framework of attachment theory, where an increasing number of studies addressed the caregiving behavioral system and its operation within close and intimate relations and romantic ones in particular. Thus another rich and vast research domain examined caring in close relations by investigating "caregiving in romantic relations." This is discussed in the next section.

Caregiving in romantic
relations—an attachment perspective

According to Bowlby (1969/1982), humans are born with a caregiving behavioral system aimed at providing protection and support to others. Although the care-giving system originally evolved as part of mother-child relations, it has also come to be applied in pair bonds and romantic relations. The application of mutual and reciprocated care in pair bonds reflects the "fitness interdependence" of the partners—their mutual reproductive dependence—whereby helping the other leads to reproductive benefit to oneself (Brown & Brown, 2006a). Although pair bonding may often start based on other motivational systems (e.g., sexual or affiliation motivational systems), attachment and caregiving dynamics follow suit.

In fact, the capacity to engage in the reciprocal dance of intimate emotional bonds with others in both the care-seeking and caregiving roles is a fundamental characteristic of romantic pair bonds. Such bonds embody the second most intense caring relationships (after parenting), and involve establishing caring bonds voluntarily. This bond often comprises a voluntary commitment to protect, take care of, and cherish the other "in sickness and in health." Such a bond is not unique to humans but is not prevalent in the animal kingdom, not even among our closest evolutionary relatives, the primates. And yet such a bond has clear underlying biological and neuroendocrine strata in humans, as described in Chapter 5. In the vast majority of romantic relations, partners are central attachment figures who provide an important (if not the most important) source of support and care, and—once commitments have been made—are often at the top of their mutual attachment hierarchies (Keren & Mayseless, 2013). Reflecting this centrality, research indicates that social care and support are essential to the development and maintenance of thriving and satisfying intimate relationships (e.g., Carnelley, Pietromonaco, & Jaffe, 1996; Collins & Feeney, 2000; Feeney & Collins, 2001).

Within the romantic relations arena, the caregiving system is conceived as involving the provision of the safe haven function—satisfying the partner's needs for protection and support in times of danger or distress as well as the provision of a secure base for exploration, autonomy, and growth (Bowlby, 1969/1982; Collins, Guichard, Ford, & Feeney, 2006). In an optimal state, each partner monitors the needs of the other, appraises his or her needs for assistance or encouragement, and is responsive to direct and indirect requests. The distress or alarm of a close person often activates empathic concern but also distress and anxiety. This requires the caregiver to deal effectively with her or his own emotions, attributions, needs, and dominant behavioral reactions such that the caring provided will suit the care seeker and be adapted to her or his needs. The repertoire of caring behaviors is large and includes showing interest in the other's problems or goals, affirming the other's competence and ability to deal with the situation, expressing love and affection, providing advice and instrumental aid as needed, not interfering with the person's own problem-solving efforts or exploratory activities, and admiring and applauding the person's successes (Feeney, 2004; Feeney & Collins, 2004; Collins et al., 2006). Addressing another person's problems often requires a temporary suspension of one's own goals and plans and the synchronization and/or coordination of one's own actions with those of the care seeker by taking his or her perspective. Consequently good caring is a remarkable achievement that relies on genetic propensities but also on learning and practice, as described in Part III in this book.

Interplay of attachment and caregiving

From an attachment perspective, romantic relations reflect the operation of three behavioral systems: attachment, caregiving, and sexual mating (Hazan & Zeifman, 1994). Some researchers have also discussed another behavioral system "companionship and affiliation," which is highly relevant in friendships and also has a crucial and significant role in the formation of romantic relations (Furman, & Wehner, 1994). In the lives of individuals, the attachment behavioral system is the first to be activated and is vital in the lives and experiences of infants and children. Thus representations and strategies learned as part of its activation also affect individual differences in the others (Collins & Ford, 2010.) Furthermore, because one's own attachment experiences provide a central arena for learning about and experiencing caregiving, beliefs about and strategies for providing care to others draw on one's attachment representations (Main et al., 1985; Kunce & Shaver, 1994). This general contention has been amply demonstrated in parenting, where attachment representations relevant to relations with one's own parents as assessed via the Adult Attachment Interview (AAI) developed by Main and her colleagues (Main et al., 1985) were consistently associated with parental responsiveness and sensitivity to their infants (Van IJzendoorn, 1995). Specifically, secure parents (referred to in the AAI as "autonomous") showed a higher degree of sensitivity and responsiveness in caring for their offspring, both in infancy and later, as opposed to insecure parents, who were dismissive (the avoidant end of "state of mind with respect to attachment" as assessed by the AAI) or preoccupied (the anxious end as assessed by the AAI).

Similar findings relating to the association between attachment representations and caregiving were also demonstrated in romantic relations. For example, the working models of attachment in the context of a person's relations with his or her parents (assessed by the AAI) were associated with spontaneous caregiving in a stressful situation among dating couples. Dating couples were videotaped while the male partner waited to do a stressful task. The recordings showed that women with more secure (autonomous) AAI attachment representations tailored their support to their partner's needs—that is, they provided more support when their partners sought more support (Simpson, Rholes, Oriña, & Grich, 2002). Studies using self-reports of attachment security in adulthood also showed similar associations, indicating that attachment security was associated with higher levels of reported and observed responsiveness in romantic relations (e.g., Kunce & Shaver, 1994; Carnelley, Pietromonaco, & Jaffe, 1996; Feeney, 1996; Rholes, Simpson & Orina, 1999). In one such study, for example, couples were unobtrusively videotaped for five minutes in a waiting room while the woman waited to participate in what was described as a "procedures that arouse considerable anxiety and distress in most people." Independent observers evaluated each partner's behavior, demonstrating that higher levels of women's stress were associated with a greater provision of support by more secure men. Conversely, higher partner stress was associated with lower levels of support among men who scored higher in attachment avoidance (Simpson, Rholes, & Nelligan, 1992). Similar effects were found among dating couples who were videotaped while discussing stressful life events (Collins & Feeney, 2000). In this study, caregivers who reported higher attachment-related anxiety provided less instrumental support, were less responsive, and exhibited more negative caregiving behavior as coded by objective observers.

Attachment may affect the activation of caregiving in yet another way. In Bowlby's (1969/1982) view, the activation of attachment concerns (fear for one's own safety and security), whether due to dispositional insecurity or temporary indications of impeding threats or danger to oneself, decreases the attention that can be allocated to other behavioral systems, such as exploration and caregiving. Because of their urgency, the activation of attachment concerns often takes precedence over other systems. Hence insecure individuals or individuals facing a distressing or alarming situation will find it difficult to focus on another person's plight and activate their caregiving system. In contrast, a person who feels relatively secure is more likely to perceive others' needs and respond to them sensitively by providing adequate support. As described in Chapter 6, Mikulincer, Shaver, and their colleagues (e.g., Mikulincer et al., 2001; Mikulincer et al., 2005), in a series of studies discussed also in Chapter 6, showed that laboratory-induced boosting of a person's sense of attachment security increased empathy, compassion, and the willingness to help strangers as well as romantic partners, even in the case of individuals who were insecure in their attachment styles. The induction of security was achieved by various means, such as the subliminal presentation of pictures that suggested the availability of an attachment figure or by presenting the names of attachment figures. Imagery and the visualization of security- and comfort-arousing scenes with attachment figures or visualizations of attachment figures' faces were also used. In one example, the subliminal priming of attachment security fostered sensitive caregiving behavior toward a romantic partner who disclosed a personal problem (i.e., engaging in listening, understanding, and providing support and solace) and even overcame hindrances to responsiveness induced by attachment insecurity and mental depletion—a procedure that requires moderately high concentration and mental efforts (Mikulincer, Shaver, Sahdra, and Bar-On, 2013).

Although attachment and caregiving behavioral systems tend to work in concert, they are still two differentiated and separate behavioral systems. Feeney (1996), for example, who administered both attachment and caregiving measures to 229 married couples, found that secure attachment and reports of beneficial caregiving provided to the spouse (high responsive and sensitive care) were only modestly associated with each other. Furthermore, the respondents' own security and their spouses' beneficial caregiving contributed independently to marital satisfaction and demonstrated the differentiation of the receiving (i.e., attachment) and giving (i.e., caregiving) systems.

In another study, Crowell et al. (2002) observed 157 engaged couples with an average of 4.25 years dating prior to their engagement and coded their use of a secure base, (i.e., whether a partner conveyed his or her distress or concern clearly and effectively), and secure base support, which reflected the operation of the caregiving behavioral system (i.e., interest in the partner, sensitivity to the partner's distress, willingness and ability to understand the problem, and cooperative responsiveness in a timely fashion). Although the partners were only modestly similar in attachment security in the context of their relations with their parents as assessed by the AAI, the dyads were highly similar in their use of a secure base and in their provision of a secure base. Men and women were equally likely to seek and use support and were similar in the provision of a secure base, demonstrating that both sexes are similar in their potential to be sensitive and responsive providers of a secure base within a committed romantic relationship. In addition, couples were also well coordinated, in that one partner's use of the secure base was strongly associated with the provision of a secure base by the other.

This finding may shed light on a possible developmental process. Although romantic partners may start their relationship with their own notions, skills, and scenarios of caregiving experiences, possibly tied to their attachment representations in the context of their relations with their parents, their romantic experiences and partner inputs become more influential over time. The couples appear to be creating their own scenarios of seeking and providing support and coconstructing and changing their own and their partners' working models of caregiving.

Individual differences in ways or styles of helping

People care and support others in different ways. Some are sensitive and responsive and match the provided support to the needs of the partner. However, others may be too vigilant and anxious to help and smother the partner, or, at the other extreme, may be aloof and detached and let their partners struggle on their own. Yet still others may be cynical and derisive.

Several researchers have set out to assess individual differences in support styles from an attachment point of view. They examined the two major functions discussed by attachment theory: (1) the safe haven function—helping each other cope with stress and anxiety, and (2) the secure base function—being able to support one another's personal growth, exploration, and strivings (Crowell et al., 2002; Feeney & Collins, 2004; Feeney, Collins, Vleet & Tomlinson, 2013). These two functions resemble the categorization within the social support literature into providing support in response to negative (i.e., distress) vs. positive (success) occasions. As with other domains (i.e., parenting), responsiveness and sensitivity were also central dimensions in coding caregiving behavior in the romantic relations domain (Feeney & Collins, 2001; Collins & Ford, 2010). Sensitivity to a romantic partner's cues is reflected by being in tune with the partner and in offering the type and amount of support that is wanted or needed. Responsiveness involves the provision of support in a way that makes partner feel understood, validated, and cared for (Reis & Shaver, 1988). Both were central in the observational codes used in the studies reviewed here.

Using questionnaires to assess helping styles, Kunce and Shaver (1994) identified four relevant dimensions: Proximity vs. distance, reflecting the tendency to approach and contact the care receiver (e.g., "When my partner seems to want or need a hug, I'm glad to provide it"); sensitivity vs. insensitivity (e.g., "I am very attentive to my partner's nonverbal signals for help and support"); cooperation vs. control, measuring the degree to which caregivers are controlling in their attempts to help their partners solve problems. (e.g., "I tend to be too domineering when trying to help my partner"); and compulsive caregiving, measuring the extent to which caregivers get overinvolved in their partners' problems (e.g., "I tend to get overinvolved in my partner's problems and difficulties"). Approaching the partner, sensitive responding and cooperation were deemed to be the optimal forms of helping.

Shaver, Mikulincer, and Shemesh-Iron (2010) approached the issue of individual differences in caring from a different angle. Viewing optimal care as reflecting balanced activation of the caregiving system, they suggested two caregiving dimensions that underlie individual differences in the activation and functioning of caregiving: hyperactivation and deactivation. Hyperactivation involves emotional overinvolvement with others' distress along with doubts about one's capacity as a caregiver. Deactivation involves cognitive and emotional distancing from others' distress or alarm. In a series of studies discussed also in Chapter 6, they demonstrated that the two caregiving dimensions are related to participants' reported measures of empathy, compassion, and altruism. As far as romantic relations are concerned, they found that participants who scored higher on deactivation reported less responsive and more controlling care and were observed as less supportive toward their partner during a dyadic interaction task. Participants who scored higher on hyperactivation, on the other hand, reported more compulsive and overinvolved caregiving and were observed as less supportive and more distressed during the dyadic interaction task.

Collins and her colleagues (Collins et al., 2006, Collins, Ford, Guichard, Kane & Feeney, 2010) have provided a general and very helpful scheme to understand optimal caring within romantic relations. They discussed three broad categories relating to (1) skills and abilities, (2) resources, and (3) motivation. The first category generally involves a large number of social skills, such as the capacity to correctly perceive emotional cues, as well as "general" emotional and behavioral regulation capacities. The second refers to the extent to which individuals have the cognitive, emotional, physical, and material resources to engage in caring. If a person is tired, stressed, sick, or busy, or if her or his psychological resources are depleted—what is often referred to as caregiving burnout or caregiving fatigue—caregiving, if provided at all, will tend to be suboptimal because the caregiver will find it difficult to attend to the needy person's distress empathically. Finally, the quality of care provided will suffer if people lack the motivation to help or act from egoistic reasons. The next section zooms in on the research regarding different motivations to care. This research can offer us valuable insights regarding the caring motivation and how it is best enacted.

Caring motivations

In a series of studies, Brooke Feeney, Collins and colleagues (Feeney & Collins, 2001, 2003; Collins & Ford, 2010; Collins et al., 2010; Feeney & Thrush, 2010; Feeney, Collins, Van Vleet & Tomlinson, 2013) attempted to uncover the motivations behind caring in romantic relations. They assumed that romantic partners have a variety of motivations for helping one another and examined both motivations for the provision of care or the lack thereof and these same motivations in "safe haven" and "secure base" situations. Their findings uncovered two general categories of motivations. The first category comprises other-focused motivations, such as helping a partner because the caregiver loves the partner, wants the partner to feel good and to succeed in his or her personal growth and explorations, and because she or he enjoys helping the partner. The other refers to more self-focused and egoistic motivations—such as supporting a partner in order to avoid negative consequences or to receive a reward (Feeney et al., 2013). Other motivations reported by the participants involved keeping the partner in the relationship and helping her or him because the partner appeared incapable of handling the problems—a situation which, when presented as a motive, was often perceived as obligatory and taxing for the caregiver. The split between other-focused or self-focused motivations, however, is not an all-or-nothing phenomenon. In fact, most individuals tend to possess a mix of different motivations, and this profile may change from one occasion to another and in different phases of the relationship (Collins et al., 2010). Partners in close, intimate, and committed relations may help because of their concern and love but they may also sometimes provide care and support in order to get some type of external or internal reward in return (e.g., to be commended, to receive some benefit, to feel efficacious and in control, to impress others) or in order to fulfill obligations and avoid unpleasant consequences for not helping (e.g., to avoid feeling guilty, to avoid making the partner angry, to make up for a past misbehavior).

Generally speaking other-focused motivations tend to be associated with attachment security, are more prevalent in close, intimate relationships with a high degree of mutual satisfaction, and are associated with more sensitive, responsive, and less controlling or compulsive caregiving (Feeney & Collins, 2003; Feeney et al., 2013). Other-focused motivations were also strongly associated with happiness after a loved one was successfully helped (Feeney & Collins, 2003; Feeney et al., 2013). This connection is not arbitrary, and probably reflects a deep-seated proximal mechanism of joy that sustains caregiving in light of the often arduous "work" of care. It should therefore hardly be surprising that other-focused motivations are also associated with an improved quality of relationship over time (Feeney & Collins, 2003).

The opposite profile of results was found with regard to self-focused motives. Romantic partners who were motivated to help their loved one because they anticipated some benefit for themselves or felt obligated to help were less responsive and more controlling in their support (Feeney & Collins, 2003). The two suboptimal forms of providing support—compulsive and controlling care—were associated with a somewhat different profile of self-focused motivations (Feeney et al., 2013). Specifically, compulsive (overinvolved) caregivers were primarily motivated by self-benefit and feelings of obligation, by perceptions of the partner as needy and incapable, and by the strategic goal of keeping the partner in the relationship. Controlling caregivers, too, reported helping because of obligation or self-benefit motives and perceptions that their partner was incapable of handling problems, but they were also less likely to be motivated by love, concern, and enjoyment. In general what appears to matter is the extent to which caring reflects more autonomous actions associated with love, concern, and enjoyment or the extent to which partners help because they feel obligated and coerced and are concerned with their own needs and anxieties.

In general, the fruitful line of research of romantic caregiving from an attachment perspective provides several insights regarding the motivation to care. The caring motivation appears to be a distinct motivational structure among romantic couples yet it interacts with other behavioral systems and in particular attachment. Through joint interactions, couples develop their own styles and become synchronized and similar in their caregiving. Finally, as was found in the social support research literature, other-oriented caring motivations produce more positive outcomes than egoistic or self-oriented caring motivations or those derived from felt obligation.

"Caregiving"—caring for others with mental or physical health problems

Another area in which motivations of support providers were examined relates to the support and care provided to family members or acquaintances with a disabling mental or physical health condition. This type of care is termed *caregiving* in most of the relevant research literature (Vitaliano, Zhang, & Scanlan, 2003) and was mostly investigated by gerontologists, social workers, and other scholars involved in health research. It includes caring for relatives or friends after heart attacks or heart surgery and for those with cancer, HIV, Alzheimer's disease (to name the most frequent conditions), or other mental and/or physical disabilities. Most of the research in this area has focused on the caregiving provided to spouses and parents, but caring for other kin such as a child suffering from a disability or illness, a parent-in-law, as well as others who are not kin, such as friends or neighbors, was also investigated. Caring for sick or disabled others often reflects the assumption of a responsibility to care and the development of a caring bond. Yet this bond may be less comprehensive than the bond in parenting and even romantic relations because it often involves a narrower scope of provision for a shorter period of time and a shared responsibility with other parties such as siblings or a paid nurse.

The results of studies in this domain revealed a number of findings. First, the research documented a strong gender effect; namely that most caregivers were women, whether spouses, daughters, daughters in law, or sisters (e.g., Dwyer & Coward, 1991; Moen, Robison, & Fields, 1994). In addition, the maintenance of social relations with elderly relatives, even in relatively good health, whether in person or otherwise (e.g. by telephone) was mostly carried out by adult daughters rather than sons (Spitze & Logan, 1990). Second, the caregiving provided is affected by various situational and contextual conditions (i.e., who else could provide help, how far the daughter lived from her mother). Third, most of these situations led to the development of a sense of burden and burnout and a large number of studies documented these deleterious effects (Vitaliano, Zhang, & Scanlan, 2003). For example, in a meta-analysis of 84 studies caregivers mostly of relatives with dementia, were moderately more depressed and stressed and had lower self-efficacy and subjective well-being and slightly more physical health problems than non caregivers (Pinquart & Sörensen, 2003).

Fourth, caregiving often persisted for as long as the recipients needed it despite these negative effects, and caregivers also reported a number of positive gains in personal growth and purpose in life (Marks, Lambert, & Choi, 2002). In fact, a developmental process could be identified in long-term caregiving situations. Caregivers progressed from developing the capacity to care for the care recipient to developing the capacity to also care for themselves within these relations; eventually they went on to transfer this new capacity to less familiar others, expanding their own sense of self and becoming "caregivers for humanity" (Bar-David, 1999). In line with this depiction, a large prospective national study in the United States involving more than 8,000 respondents found that the transition into caregiving was associated with both positive and negative feelings and outcomes on the caregiver's part for both men and women (Marks, Lambert, & Choi, 2002).

In line with the focus of this study, several major sources of motivation for this kind of care were identified (e.g., Cicirelli, 1993; Katz, Gur-Yaish, & Lowenstein, 2010). Chief among these was caring about the care recipients (mother, father, husband, or friend) and loving them. These feelings translated into wanting to alleviate the care recipients' stress or suffering and wanting to fulfill their needs. Another source of motivation relates to a sense of personal (internalized) duty and a commitment to filial obligations. A third motivator was the need to abide by societal expectations even when these were not internalized as a personal duty. One of the most frequent categorizations of motivations in this respect involved a division into obligatory vs. discretionary motives. Obligatory motives involve a sense of obligation to provide the care, whereas discretionary motives involve a desire to provide the care, most often out of love and as an expression of closeness and affection (e.g., Walker, Pratt, Shin, & Jones, 1989, 1990). Interestingly, caring and supporting from obligatory motives was associated with negative feelings in the caregiver, such as a strong sense of burden, while helping as an expression of closeness and affection was not associated with negative feelings in the caregiver despite leading to a greater provision of help (e.g., Cicirelli, 1993). In fact, active helping predicted greater positive affects in spouses in certain situations—and especially for individuals who perceived themselves as interdependent with their spouse (Poulin et al., 2010).

An indication of the importance of loving the care recipient as a central motivation comes from a study by Katz, Gur-Yaish, and Lowenstein (2010). They investigated three random representative samples of urban adults from Norway, Spain, and Israel with at least one living parent aged 65 or older. The sample was not limited to impaired parents, so its results can shed light on the general caregiving provided by adult children to their older parents, possibly reflecting the changes from hierarchical power relations to more mutual ones in response to the parents' growing needs. Indeed, most respondents (around 65% across cultures) reported that their parents needed care and that they engaged in such "role reversals." The authors examined three major motivations—affectual solidarity (the affectionate caring component), filial obligation, and the situational aspect of the parental need for care. In line with the present volume's central concern, affectual solidarity was the strongest motivator in all three countries, reflecting the emotional caring bond between adult children and their parents. Reflecting the centrality of this motivation, affectual solidarity and the perceived need for care were the sole motivational predictors of the amount of help provided in the three countries, while filial norms displayed no such effect.

Within the ebb and flow of caring dynamics in close relations a substantial mixture of motives appears to exist for caring for the elderly and sick. It is clear that this kind of caregiving is motivated by a complex combination of different feelings, attitudes, and desires, some related to various aspects of a sense of duty, commitment, and internalized obligation and some to love, respect, closeness, and empathy, with both interacting and changing at different phases of the caring relation (Callahan, 1985; Walker, Pratt, Shin, & Jones, 1989). Unsurprisingly, this profile is similar to what is known about other caregiving situations and caring relationships, whether in parenting or in regular caregiving interchanges among romantic partners or friends. In all of these, care is provided because of a large variety of changing motives and may induce both positive and negative feelings in the person providing the care. Generally and as with the provision of support in daily normative situations related to romantic partners or friends, caring goals that reflect the other's perspective and are autonomously chosen are associated with higher levels of caregiver well-being as opposed to support provided owing to a perceived obligation or to a need for self-enhancement (Crocker & Canevello, 2008; Feeney & Collins, 2003). Taken together, these findings underscore the prevalence of providing support and care in a variety of relations, the similarity in their dynamics across the variety of targets and despite the distinct characteristics of each domain, and the importance of the reasons for their provision.

Chapter conclusion

This overview of the research on caring for familiar others and close others in particular has highlighted several issues. First, this literature underscores the prevalence of care that emanates from love and concern for the other in the variety of relations addressed in this chapter, such as offspring, biological or adopted, romantic partners, friends, coworkers, kin, roommates, and one's own parents. The research also highlights how much we all rely on such care as recipients and engage in such care as caregivers. Second, the research discussed in this chapter highlights similar care dynamics such as the importance of other-focused and autonomous caring vs. self-focused or obligatory motivations and the complex profile of such caring relations and caring bonds in terms of the combination of motivations. It further exposes the similarity in what constitutes good care and the similarity of individual differences in how people care across the variety of research traditions and despite their disconnection. Third, the chapter exposes a large variety of provisions in situations of both negative and positive affect in the recipient and the complexity and sophistication needed to provide responsive and sensitive care. Fourth, the research uncovers several possible processes that may be implicated in the development of the caring motivational system, such as its connection to attachment and how the capacity to give care develops within close relations such as romantic ones and parenting. Finally, the discussions in this chapter unravels the mixture of positive and negative emotions experienced by the caregiver, suggesting that caring may involve burden, exhaustion, and burnout but also a sense of joy and competence and in particular a sense of meaningfulness.

9

Caring for Strangers: Conceptual Perspectives

The caring offered to strangers provides an interesting arena for examining the interplay of the motivation to care. Caring within close relations is often expected because of the affectionate bond between the individuals involved and is sanctioned by a variety of social norms (Collins, Ford, Guichard, Kane, & Feeney, 2010). Helping a close friend or relative typically results from a prior personal and reciprocal relationship between the helper and the recipient and an implicit or explicit personal obligation to help (Omoto & Snyder, 1995; Dovidio & Penner, 2001). Such caring is often enacted as a reaction to the other person's observed or recounted need; in other words, it is *reactive caring* in the sense that the caregiver is reacting to a situation that demands some sort of care, nurturance, or help. This care appears "natural" and is demanded or driven by the situation. Consequently we find such caring unsurprising. Because of our psychological and sociological expectations for such care, we might "discount" it as a manifestation of a motivation to care: "But, of course a mother would care for her sick daughter," and "a wife would nurse her husband after a heart attack."

Caring for strangers, on the other hand is considered nonobligatory (Omoto & Snyder, 1995). Specifically, caring for strangers is not strongly expected or strongly sanctioned by society; hence we are more surprised by its appearance and wonder why people care about and for total strangers, especially if doing so is costly. Interestingly, besides helping strangers when they exhibit pressing needs, which is reactive caring, some people actively seek occasions for caring for strangers, helping them and nurturing them in a proactive manner and demonstrating *proactive caring*. Both types of care are discussed in the following two chapters.

A considerable and significant body of research has examined caring and caregiving as enacted with strangers. In this chapter I would like to discuss and present three major conceptual and empirical perspectives related to this topic: prosocial behavior, altruism, and generativity. In the next one I present three areas of research that can provide interesting insights into processes of caring for strangers, namely volunteering, monetary donations, and mentoring.

The research dealing with the provision of help and care to strangers was mostly conducted as part of the study of *prosocial behavior*. This research tradition focuses on the *enactment of caring* and studies behaviors that benefit others. By doing so, researchers circumvent the thorny issue of whether prosocial acts are the result of egoistic motives or are other-oriented and possibly reflect altruistic motivations. Studies of altruism have tried to address straightforwardly exactly this thorny issue and examined empirically the *motivation to care* and to provide help and support. Researchers in this area wanted to understand costly prosocial behavior, as when individuals risk their lives to save others who are unrelated to them. Scholars wanted to unravel the motivations underlying caring acts with strangers, and they devised empirical ways to decipher the extent to which such acts are "really" altruistic and not driven by egoistic considerations and needs. Generativity studies view such help as developmentally expected and cast the phenomena of helping strangers within a general *developmental model*.

Studies of prosocial behavior began with a question: "Why do people fail to help others even when help is clearly called for and expected?" The reason for this can be traced to the alarm and apprehension expressed by social psychologists following the case of Katherine Genovese, whose murder was witnessed by a large number of neighbors, none of whom came to her rescue or even called for help. These psychologists tried to comprehend how this could have happened and to explain and understand why and under what conditions individuals will (or will not) provide help and care to strangers. Studies of altruism, on the other hand, began with a complementary enigma: "Why **do** people risk themselves to help others?" Faced with the extraordinary bravery of ordinary people in helping strangers, such as the "righteous among the nations" who saved Jews during the Holocaust, scholars asked what propelled these people to risk themselves and their families in order to save strangers. How does such behavior accord with evolutionary accounts of one's reproductive and inclusive fitness, which appear to favor only help provided to kin? Furthermore, researchers interested in altruism sought to directly answer this question: "Is there really caring that is altruistically motivated, and how can we test this?" Finally, studies of generativity sought to explain individuals' proactive pursuit of opportunities for helping others and even strangers. Unlike the prosocial and the altruism research traditions, which tended to study reactive help—namely help, caring, and support provided following encounter with a need—generativity notions provided answer to yet another question: "How is it that people actively and intrinsically search for occasions where their help is needed?" A concise overview of these three research traditions and their main findings is presented in this chapter, starting with generativity.

Generativity

"I think as you get older, you start thinking, what am I doing for my
community, and you start feeling the need to just do something, to
put something back." (A volunteer at a hospice for terminally ill in the
United States; Oliner, 2002, p. 134.)

Erikson's (1963) famous life-span developmental model included a conceptualization of caring, termed *generativity*, as part of a general view of human nature
and its development. This model includes a stipulation of a developmental phase
in midadulthood that emphasized caring and caregiving. Generally speaking,
Erikson's psychosocial developmental theory posits eight stages in human life.
In each of these a core developmental issue reveals a developmental goal, which
is usually presented as two poles on a continuum, where one pole expresses success in attaining this developmental goal and the other expresses what happens
when individuals fail to attain it. Following early adulthood, in which intimacy
is deemed the central issue, Erikson postulates that the developmental goal of
middle adulthood is *generativity*.

Generativity is expressed in motivation, concern, and activities geared for
the nurturance, well-being, and empowerment of youths and subsequent generations. It can be expressed through parenting, mentoring, taking care of the
environment, and any other activity in which individuals invest in the welfare
of future generations. High levels of generativity reflect the attainment of this
developmental task and are expected to be associated with self-esteem, well-
being, and happiness. Individuals who are unable to express it experience
stagnation, which reflects the lack of psychological thriving and flourishing
in one's life if one does not "pass it forward" to other people—that is, care
about and nurture future generations. Although parenting may be seen as its
prototypical manifestation, any other activity and investment in the community and society may also reflect this general proclivity for generativity
(McAdams, 2001).

In line with Erikson's suggestions, a growing number of studies have demonstrated that generativity may be construed as a personal characteristic by
midadulthood and that individuals indeed differed on this construct by showing stable levels of generativity. Generativity was assessed by a large number of
methods including a self-reporting scale (e.g., 'I try to pass along the knowledge
I have gained through my experiences'), generative behaviors, setting generative
goals for daily life, and themes of generativity in narrative accounts of important
autobiographical episodes (McAdams, Hart, & Maruna, 1998). The convergence
of this personal characteristic with various assessment methods demonstrates its
coherent nature. Moreover, and as suggested by Erikson, highly generative individuals were also high in self-esteem, happiness, and psychological and social

well-being (de St. Aubin & McAdams, 1995; Peterson, Smirles, & Wentworth, 1997; Keyes and Ryff, 1998; McAdams et al., 1998).

As a general overarching psychosocial stance, generativity is expected to be present in various domains, including family and friendship relations, community activities, and society at large. Erikson viewed all these investments as reflecting the same general concern. However, accepting the view that one motivational system of generativity governs all its manifestations including parenting is not straightforward. Caring as part of parenting is conceived as having evolved through strong evolutionary mechanisms related to reproductive success and inclusive fitness. What, then, might be the selective evolutionary mechanisms associated with adult generativity in such roles such as mentors for youth, community leaders, or Little League coaches? Are these all manifestations of the same overarching system? McAdams (2000), an eminent researcher of generativity, suggests that the empathy and responsibility for future generations shares deep conceptual links with the caregiving in parent-child relationships among highly generative adults; he summarizes this point (p. 119) by stating that "Generativity may not spring directly out of caregiving, and caregiving may involve different psychological mechanisms than, say, serving on the local school board. But the two concepts would appear to share more than a phenotypic similarity." In line with this suggestion and the perception of generativity as an overarching developmental achievement, a number of studies have demonstrated that these different domains are indeed related among generative adults and that generative individuals show an "expanded radius of care," which involves parenting, community involvement, and prosocial acts with strangers (Peterson & Klohnen, 1995, p. 20). The extant research on generativity thus demonstrates that individual differences in generativity are related to the quality of parenting, predict a range of social involvements, and are positively associated with psychological well-being (McAdams & Logan, 2004). Parents who are high on generativity, for example, invest more in parenting and demonstrate better parenting skills than other parents (i.e., they are more authoritative and emphasize prosocial values) (Peterson & Klohnen, 1995; Peterson et al., 1997; Pratt, Norris, Arnold, & Gilyer, 1999; Hart, McAdams, Hirsh, & Baur, 2001). Furthermore, generativity is also associated with involvement in prosocial activities in the community and with a sense of efficacy related to community and political issues (Cole & Stewart, 1996; Peterson et al., 1997; Hart et al., 2001). These studies provide important evidence supporting the interconnection of caring within different domains, contexts, and roles and suggest that a somewhat broad motivation to care and nurture directed at the next generations is in operation.

Generativity as a developmental goal within a stage model of human development is somewhat restricted in time to midadulthood. However, an expanded version of Erikson's (1968) epigenetic chart of psychosocial development has been suggested, in which developmental tasks do not just become central at a certain period in one's life cycle (Bradley & Marcia, 1998; Pratt & Lawford, 2014). According to this model, forerunners of developmental issues to come and legacies of previously encountered issues are also current and influential alongside the primary developmental issue in a particular period (e.g., identity in adolescence). Forerunners of generativity thus appear in earlier developmental periods, and the legacy of generativity is also relevant in later adulthood and in old age (Stewart & Vandewater, 1998). I certainly concur with this approach and view the general comprehensive motivation to care as relevant across the whole life span: in childhood, adolescence, emerging adulthood, mid adulthood, late adulthood, and old age. Still, the manifestations of such a general motivation and its salience may differ at different stages of development. A variety of manifestations of generativity will be presented and discussed in the next chapter.

Prosocial behavior

The study of prosocial behavior originally reflected the focus on a somewhat different domain of caring than parenting, friendships, or romantic relations. Following the disturbing Katherine Genovese case, researchers tried to comprehend the conditions under which individuals would (or would not) provide help and care to strangers. At first, the studies focused on situations in which a stranger is unexpectedly in distress and needs help, as when a stranger collapses on a pavement (Latané & Darley, 1970). The help that was required was typically unplanned and spontaneous and the interaction between the helper and the recipient involved relatively brief encounters without prior or future contact beyond the helping incident. Over time, the research focus expanded to include help provided to known others as well as to care in close relationships, as with friends and spouses (Mikulincer & Shaver, 2010). To some researchers, in fact, the "prosocial behavior" became a general overarching category for all acts of caregiving and caring toward strangers and kin alike (Caprara & Steca, 2007 and the edited volume by Mikulincer & Shaver, 2010). The study of the development of prosocial behavior then became intertwined with the study of the development of empathy and caring in general (Eisenberg, Fabes, & Spinrad 2006; Eisenberg, 2010). Research described here pertains mostly to prosocial behavior with strangers and when other targets were studied—this will be indicated.

Within this literature, several known models were developed from the mid-1960s until the early 1980s in order to explain *when* people would help in emergency and nonemergency situations. One of them is Latané and Darley's (1970) bystander intervention model, which describes the decision processes that individuals undergo when they are faced with a situation that might call for help. Imagine that you came for an examination escorted by a female representative who ushered you to the examining room adjacent to her office, where you notice a desk and bookcases piled high with papers and filing cabinets. As you start filling out your questionnaire, you are aware of her working in the next room and then hear a loud crash and a scream as a chair collapses and she falls to the floor. "Oh, my God, my foot . . . I . . . I . . . can't move it. Oh . . . my ankle," the representative moans. "I . . . can't get this . . . thing . . . off me." She cries and moans like this for about a minute more. Would you have stopped working, entered the adjacent room, and offered help?

In one such study (Latané & Rodin, 1969), around 70% offered help within the first minute if they were alone in the room but only 40% if two participants were filling out questionnaires in the same room. This illuminates the bystander effect, where the presence of others hinders an individual from intervening in an emergency situation. The bystander intervention model suggests that the individual needs to recognize the situation as one requiring assistance, to choose to take personal responsibility, and to decide how to help. Having others around you who, like you, are not sure whether the situation is a real emergency can lead to discounting it as an event needing outside intervention and to a diffusion of responsibility that can lead bystanders to expect others to intervene. Another model, the cost-reward analysis of helping (Piliavin et al., 1981), assumes that bystanders would help if the rewards—such as feeling better about oneself and noticing that the recipient is in better shape thanks to one's intervention—outweigh the costs, such as time and money invested in the assistance. This model as well as the bystander intervention model provide a general way of looking at any prosocial behavior and examining whether the motivation to care, once aroused, will in fact be enacted and implemented; these models are therefore relevant in other situations as well (e.g., volunteering, mentoring, providing social support, caring for the elderly and sick, and even parenting).

Distal and proximal causes and developmental processes in prosocial behavior

Subsequent research tried to go one step further and attempted to understand *why* people help—that is, to understand the distal and proximal causes of help and uncover the developmental origins of prosocial behavior (see review in Dovidio, Piliavin, Schroeder, & Penner, 2006). The answers to these questions generally relied on several different levels of analysis. These included references to biological origins and evolutionary theory, such as a general agreement that humans have genetically based predispositions toward prosocial behaviors (see Chapters 3, 4, and 5). In addition, the research recognized that individuals act prosocially as a result of a combination of genetic and socialization processes and personality and situational antecedents. Acting on these convictions, developmental psychologists have examined the interplay of genetic variance and socialization in the emergence of prosocial behavior and investigated prosocial behaviors with strangers and familiar others (Eisenberg & Fabes, 1998; Eisenberg et al., 2000). The main insights of these lines of research are discussed in the section on the developmental origins of caring and individual differences (see Chapters 13 and 14). Still, a concise presentation of this research is brought out here too.

Genetic variance was often assessed via various temperamental dimensions reflecting broad emotional and behavioral predispositions that were assumed to be genetically based. For example, different temperamental aspects such as a positive emotionality (i.e., the tendency to be enthusiastic, happy, and energetic) and particularly low levels of impulsivity and high levels of regulation were found to be associated with high levels of prosocial behavior. The temperamental dimension of negative emotionality (i.e., the tendency to experience negative emotions) was also associated with prosocial responses. Negative emotionality was associated with higher levels of prosocial behavior if the specific emotion that arose was sadness rather than anger and especially related to children being taught to regulate their negative emotions in general, anxiety and distress in particular, so as to not be overwhelmed by them.

Direct socialization effects were also found to be implicated in prosocial behavior. Specifically, secure attachment relationships and having warm, comforting, empathic, and authoritative mothers who were also high on perspective taking were associated with empathy and prosocial behaviors (Grusec, 1991; Hastings, Zahn-Waxler, Robinson, Usher, & Bridges, 2000; Grusec, Davidov, & Lundell, 2002). Additionally, socialization efforts—particularly within the parent-child relationship arena—that model such care (by being empathic and caring to the child as well to others) and which help children to regulate and direct their behavior toward caring for others also contribute to prosocial behavior (see review by Grusec et al., 2002). Parenting practices that promoted prosocial behavior included clear messages regarding the value of caring and of being prosocial, parenting styles (i.e., a warm, responsive, and autonomy-promoting style; the use of inductive reasoning) that promote compliance and the adoption of parental values (Grusec & Goodnow, 1994), and the incorporation of routines that involve helping others. Socialization for prosocial behavior occurred also outside parent-child relations, as with siblings and peers. Specifically caring for younger siblings and the practice of caring in community settings or school have emerged as clear predictors of prosocial behavior.

Situational antecedents of prosocial behavior have predominantly included variables identified by the bystander intervention model. For example, the clarity of the distressed individual's need increased the likelihood of help, while a larger number of other possible helpers decreased it (see review in Dovidio et al., 2006). In addition, there were other situational facets that were more culture-bound. For example, prosocial behavior varied in relation to societal expectations and the norms governing such behaviors, such as the reciprocity norm denoting the expectation of reciprocation or the norm of social responsibility relating to the responsibility of members of a community to help others in distress (Dovidio, 1984). In cultural contexts where members of the group are deemed highly responsible for the welfare of other group members (the social responsibility norm), for example, we expect a higher degree of prosocial behavior (see review by Grusec et al., 2002).

Individuals are generally more prosocial with their in-group members than with others outside their group even when both in-group and out-group members are strangers, regardless of cultural context. Social psychologists have extensively documented the general tendency to perceive one's own social group (in-group) as better than out-groups and to favor in-group members over others (e.g., Tajfel & Turner, 1986; Devine, 1995). As discussed in Chapter 3, the division into in-group/out-group that affects such tendencies need not be a well-established one or one that reflects deep-seated core divisions such as one's cultural or ethnic group, one's religious group, or one's sorority. Such in-group favoritism appeared even when differentiations between groups were arbitrary and transient and the participants did not expect to meet the other group members again (see review in Penner, Dovidio, Piliavin, & Schroeder, 2005). Explanations for these processes were provided on several levels. From an evolutionary point of view, one's in-group is the most relevant to one's survival, meaning that helping in-group members may be advantageous in terms of inclusive fitness, both because such help will be reciprocated and because the prosperity of an individual group member depends on the prosperity of the group as a whole (see Chapter 3). At the psychological level, group favoritism sustains self-identity and self-esteem, with familiarity and similarity providing proximal cues for such membership (Tajfel & Turner, 1986).

Besides contextual factors, prosocial behavior appears also to be affected by stable personality dispositions. Such prosocial dispositions show moderate stability from childhood throughout the adult years (Eisenberg et al., 2002). This stability might reflect genetic inputs as well as internalized values and learned affect-regulation strategies. More specifically, dispositional differences in empathic tendencies and agreeableness (one of the "Big-Five" dimensions of personality) were consistently associated with prosocial behavior (see review by Penner et al., 2005).

Finally, scholars of prosocial behaviors have also tried to go beyond the behavior itself and examined why such spontaneous helping occurs by focusing specifically on helper motivations. Their findings are understandably highly relevant to the focus of this book. Generally speaking and in close similarity to the thesis advocated in this book, some researchers have proposed that prosocial behaviors reflect intrinsically altruistic and humanitarian concerns that reveal a general human capacity for empathy and caregiving as well as individual differences in its expression (e.g., Shaver, Mikulincer, & Shemesh-Iron, 2010). The high end of such individual dispositions was studied extensively and referred to as having an "altruistic personality" (e.g., Rushton, 1984; Carlo, Eisenberg, Troyer, Switzer, &

Speer, 1991). Other scholars have similarly discussed altruistic motives for help-ing others (Batson, 1989, 1990) but have also uncovered selfish concerns (boosts to self-esteem or social recognition) (Baumann, Cialdini, & Kenrick, 1981; Cialdini et al., 1987). These different motives will be discussed more thoroughly in the next section, on altruism.

Prosocial behavior was originally seen as involving situational reactions to cir-cumstances in which others are in need; research uncovered a variety of situational conditions implicated in its enactment and proposed several important concep-tual models. For the most part, researchers in this field did not speak in terms of a motivation to care but rather of a propensity to be prosocial. Furthermore, the kind of care they discussed was mostly reactive, namely caregiving provided in reaction to an observed need. Yet the study of prosocial behavior has evolved to also include more stable propensities toward helping others and sustained proso-cial behaviors. In that sense, the study of prosocial behavior identified a general human tendency toward prosociality and propelled extensive research concern-ing developmental precursors to and individual differences in the expression of this general tendency.

The identification of a general human propensity toward prosociality accords with this book's premise on the general and fundamental motivation to care. This claim appears to conflict with the competitive and selfish view of human nature. In this regard, an interesting line of studies using the conceptual frame-work of game theory has demonstrated a strong human tendency to adopt a pro-social approach even in competitive pursuits. These studies were particularly concerned with one of the best-known paradigms of competitive games—"the prisoner's dilemma," and demonstrated the frequent occurrence of a prosocial orientation in competitive games. The next section presents this intriguing line of research.

Prosocial tendency in competitive games

The prisoner's dilemma, as well as other games such as the ultimatum game, involve a situation in which individuals are asked to make a decision as part of a prearranged game situation that often pits the participants against each other. The prisoner's dilemma in particular is an example of a game that shows why two individuals might not cooperate even if it appears that it is in their best interests to do so. Think, for example, of the scenario of the prisoner's dilemma and imagine yourself participating in it. The game is usually presented as a situation involving two prisoners, A and B, who are taken into custody for a crime. The police don't have enough evidence to convict either prisoner on the principal charge. They plan to sentence both to a year in prison on a lesser charge but try to convince each to betray the other. The prisoners are then separated and approached individually. Each is given the opportunity to either betray the other by testifying that the she or he committed the crime or to cooperate with the other by remaining silent. If one testifies and the other remains silent, the betrayer goes free and the other person serves three years in prison. If both betray—they both serve two years. If both remain silent, they both serve one year. What would you do!

Because betraying one's partner is more rewarding than cooperating, purely 'rational' and self-interested prisoners were expected to betray the other prisoner. Yet many studies have demonstrated otherwise. Even those participants who had never met the other person and who never expected to meet her or him again displayed a systematic tendency, initially referred to as a "bias," towards cooperative behavior (Fehr & Fischbacher, 2003).

Using experiments based on game theory, which presented social dilemmas such as the prisoner's dilemma, a group of researchers identified what they called *major interpersonal orientations* that became apparent when people played these games (Van Lange, De Cremer, Van Dijk, & Van Vugt, 2007). These interpersonal orientations were broadly defined by them as the set of cognitions, affects, and motivations that lay at the foundations of interpersonal behavior and social interaction. These orientations include *altruism* (enhancement of outcomes for the other), *cooperation* (enhancement of joint outcomes), *egalitarianism* (enhancement of equality in outcomes), *individualism* (enhancement of outcomes for self), *competition* (enhancement of relative outcomes in favor of self), and *aggression* (reduction of outcomes for other). A large number of such studies uncovered a general "prosocial orientation" encompassing both cooperation and egalitarianism. In line with the focus of this book, this group of researchers found that most people (over 60%) tend to adopt this prosocial orientation and that the percentage of "prosocials" increases with age and could even reach 80% (Van Lange, Otten, De Bruin, & Joireman, 1997). Specifically and in a large variety of (mostly western) countries, the distribution of "prosocials," "individualists," and "competitors" was around 4:2:1 (see Van Lange, Otten, et al., 1997). Hence, they suggested that having a prosocial orientation was probably the preferred strategy, although it leaves some room for the existence of less cooperative individuals.

These findings attest to the pervasiveness of the tendency to cooperate and act prosocially even toward strangers, even within a competitive context specifically designed to arouse competitive and selfish motives. Here I am not suggesting an idyllic and naïve human tendency to be prosocial but rather a quite pervasive tendency toward being prosocial with others even in obstructing circumstances. Furthermore, the near universality of the minimum of 60% "prosocials" probably tells us something about a minimal level of caring and prosociality that must be present for the sustainability of cultures. Finally, the finding that a nonnegligible minority show orientations that are not prosocial (i.e., being "individualists" or "competitors") possibly underscores the importance of variability in human conduct and especially in human societies.

Altruism

The study of altruism incorporates a variety of definitions, semantic confusions, and heated debates. The definitions of what constitutes altruism vary quite considerably from "helping another at a cost to oneself" through "high-cost prosocial behavior," "helping with the welfare of others as the ultimate goal," to "benefiting others while reducing one's inclusive and reproductive fitness." The vast literature on altruism reflects a continuum of altruistic acts, from heroic acts that involve a high personal cost (i.e., risking one's life) to low-cost altruism that can be observed in daily life, referred to by Oliner as "conventional altruism" (e.g., giving a lift to a stranger) (Oliner, 2002).

More than almost any other part in this book, this section touches on the core of human values and the most fundamental views of humanity. Are humans good by nature—are we altruistic, benevolent and caring,—or are we bad—usually meaning egoistic, aggressive, and competitive? In this section I discuss heroic altruistic acts and highlight some of the stories of extraordinary men and women and also consider more conventional altruistic acts. It further address fundamental conceptual issues related to gender differences in altruistic care and to the question of whether we actually can be altruistic and engage in "true" altruism (i.e., have the other person's well-being and welfare as our ultimate concern). Consequently this section deals with core dilemmas related to the thesis of this book and is much longer than previous ones. I begin, however, with a discussion of evolutionary accounts of altruism.

Altruism and evolutionary accounts

Both prosocial behavior and altruism involve the provision of care and help to the benefit of others. Altruism is, therefore, a special case of prosocial behavior. In its simplest form, altruism means that the help is enacted with benefit to the recipient as the ultimate goal and without any expectation of reward or any direct benefit to the donor. In the most extreme case, the cost of this prosocial act to the donor outweighs the possible benefit that the donor might gain from this act. Therefore altruism posed an enigma to researchers who believed the motive of self-preservation to be central to human existence. Unsurprisingly, the most fervent discussions arose among evolutionary researchers, who thought that natural selection would long ago have eliminated such "suicidal" tendencies. After all, if altruistic genes have a lower probability than selfish ones of being passed on to the next generation, then altruistic genes should, in the long run, become extinct.

Batson (2010) persuasively highlights the fact that the seeming contradiction derives from confusion between two separate levels of analysis—psychological and evolutionary. The first part of the definition already given refers to the psychological realm—namely, that altruism occurs when individuals engage in caring without *expecting* rewards or direct benefits at the psychological level. This does not preclude that these same individuals, their relatives, or their social group and culture would have benefited from such acts and that eventually such acts would actually have contributed to the altruists' inclusive fitness; it would only simply mean that one's own inclusive fitness would not have been *intended*. The gene-culture coevolution models presented in Chapter 3 discuss precisely such processes, whereby "altruistic" contributions to the general good of a culture significantly contribute to the culture's survival and with it to the survival of its altruistic members and their genes, including the genes of the altruists.

Similar clarification was provided by West, Griffin, and Gardner (2007), thus disarming the perceived contradiction between altruism in the psychological sphere and evolutionary perspectives (See also Brown & Brown, 2006b). Using evolutionary conceptualizations and models, they eloquently showed that altruism—which may affect the specific individual negatively—can still be evolutionarily worthwhile in the long run because it increases the survival of the person's genes through its beneficial effects on kin, on the person's in-group, and on the person's culture. In fact a large number of evolutionary models have underscored such processes: the kin selection theory, the theory of reciprocal altruism, the group selection models, and the gene-culture coevolution models. According to all of these models, benefiting others, kin, group members, or strangers can benefit the inclusive fitness of the self despite incurring costs to the individual himself or herself.

de Waal (2008) takes these models one step further and suggests that empathy evolved as a proximate mechanism for supporting an evolutionarily beneficial altruism. He notes that not all altruistic behavior relies on emotional empathy, leading to the evolutionary development of cognitively oriented empathic processes that involve perspective taking. Examples of these include orienting others to a food source, alerting others to impending danger, or working together to accrue various benefits. These may not necessitate a mechanism of direct emotional empathy with others and often rely on perspective taking and mentalizing processes. Both types of empathic responses provide quick access to others' emotional states and needs and pave the way for coordination, cooperation, and caring, including situations where the individuals are altruistic and act prosocially with the benefit of the other as the ultimate goal and without expecting to be rewarded.

As discussed by others (e.g., Brown & Brown, 2006a), de Waal (2008) suggests that empathy-induced caring and investment in others are especially important in long-term bonds (i.e., friendships, pair bonds). In fact, de Waal (2008) suggests that in such relations partners derive benefits not only from receiving care but also from giving care because of reciprocity, even if the intention was solely for the benefit of the partner: in promoting their companion's well-being, they increase the other's ability to help them should they need it. de Waal nevertheless suggests that empathic processes are also at work in situations that can be construed as involving *nonreciprocal altruism* in the sense that they are not governed by careful accounting of who did what for whom. Such altruism may be prevalent in close relations as well as in relations with less familiar others. Together, such contexts led to the evolution of cultural norms of caring, social responsibility, benevolence, and reciprocity along with the relevant genes that support them (i.e., caring genes and genes that help us identify whom we can and cannot trust) and sustain a caring and cooperating society.

Another perspective, *competitive altruism*, has also been suggested to account for the uniquely moral altruistic tendency among humans (Van Vugt, Roberts, & Hardy, 2007). According to this theory, the need to cooperate and form coalitions with nonkin for various survival-promoting ends, as when internal and external group threats are being faced, provided advantages for people with altruistic reputations. People preferred to have an altruistic partner as a group companion and even preferred leaders who were altruistic over ones who were not. It was thus the case that altruistic acts—particularly those performed in public and especially if they were perceived as stemming from concern for the other's welfare rather than a give-and-take orientation—granted individuals a higher status both within their groups and as mating partners. This resulted in a process of natural selection for altruistic genes. Evidence from anthropological and social psychological research as well as from nonhuman studies was provided in support.

Thus despite an apparent contradiction between altruism and evolutionary accounts, central current evolutionary theorizing views altruistic care as compatible with evolutionary concerns. In all of these accounts altruistic actions involve "helping another at a cost to oneself," the cost being only in the short term or in one's *survival and reproduction success*; but such altruistic actions were conceived as beneficial in the long run and in particular in the *inclusive fitness* sense—that is, they contribute to the propagation of one's genes.

Perhaps the most remarkable and exceptional altruistic acts are those in which people risk their lives to help others who are unrelated to them. In this section and in the next ones I discuss some of the most notable examples of extraordinary acts of altruism and bravery: The righteous among the nations, heroism in emergencies, and kidney donations to strangers. I then discuss conventional altruism, which is prevalent all around us and includes daily acts of kindness and consideration that emanate from the motivation to help others and to enhance their welfare.

The righteous among the nations

The "righteous among the nations" were non-Jewish people who endangered themselves and their families by rescuing Jews who were persecuted by the Nazis during World War II. The risks associated with rescuing or attempting to rescue Jews were considerable, even for acts as trivial as providing water to a thirsty passer-by, let alone providing shelter, food, and medicine for prolonged periods of time. Those who helped Jews in any way were officially risking execution and deportation to concentration camps, especially in eastern Europe. Furthermore, the Nazis also offered monetary rewards for information on hidden Jews and their rescuers (Oliner & Oliner, 1988). Estimates suggest that thousands of rescuers were executed or died in concentration camps for trying to help Jews. Over 24,800 such rescuers have been identified since 1963, and it is estimated that many more remain unreported (Yad Vashem website, 2013). The following are two representative examples.

The Syriers family. Johannes Syrier was a fisherman in the occupied Netherlands. Both he and his wife Anna were over 50 years old when the war broke out. In the summer of 1942, when the deportation of Jews to the extermination camps in the east began, they welcomed the Goldschmidt family (two parents and a child) and three other Jews: Anna Pollack, Dr. Barend, and Augusta Luza, to their home and hid them for two years. In addition to the great danger to themselves, the rescuers were also faced with the challenge of feeding another six mouths in wartime, when food was rationed and in short supply. They were betrayed in the summer of 1944. The Syriers and the Jews they sheltered were sent to the concentration camps. All the Jews survived the war, but Johannes and his wife did not. Mr. Syrier died in the Stutthof camp, while his wife, Anna, died in the Ravensbrueck concentration camp for women.

(http://www.yadvashem.org/yv/en/righteous/stories/syrier.asp; retrieved on February 2, 2014)

The Mozūraitis and Rakevičius families. The murder of the Kovno (Kaunas) Jews began shortly after the German occupation of Lithuania at the end of June 1941. The ghetto was established in August 1941, and massacres of Jews were carried out periodically throughout its existence. The Ninth Fort near Kovno also became the execution site for tens of thousands of Jews from Germany and other countries. Jaroslavas Rakevičius, a farmer, and his family provided shelter for 20 Jewish families that managed to flee from the Kaunas ghetto. Some had been smuggled out of the ghetto by Jaroslavas Rakevičiuses himself and by his sons, who accompanied the Jews through the forests to their home in the village. This extensive rescue operation involved enormous danger, and the farmers' home was turned into a kind of fortress, with three shelters, escape routes, and observation points on the roof. When staying at their home became too dangerous for the refugees, the Rakevičiuses enlisted some of their neighbors and asked them to provide shelter. With enormous resource-fulness and with the aid of their neighbors, the Mozūraitis family, the Rakevičius family managed to keep the existence of the Jews secret until the Red Army arrived to liberate the area. Among the rescued persons was a young eight-year-old child, Aharon Barak (Brik), who later served as Israel's Attorney General (1975-1978), as a Justice of the Supreme Court in 1978, and as Chief Justice from 1995 until his retirement in 2006. He was also the one who recounted this story to Yad Vashem.

(http://www.yadvashem.org/yv/en/righteous/stories/rakevicius. asp; Retrieved on February 2, 2014)

Most of the research on these remarkable individuals sought to discover what set them apart from the majority of contemporary Europeans who did not offer help (Gushee, 1993). The most extensive study on this topic was conducted by Samuel P. Oliner and Pearl M. Oliner (1988). The Oliners interviewed over 400 rescuers who met the criteria of voluntarily helping Jews under conditions of high risk and no external rewards. The Oliners found that 80% of respondents reported deciding to help within a few minutes and consulting no one. When asked to name the main reasons for their decision, the overwhelming majority of rescuers phrased at least some of their answers in care-related terms. This included not only feeling concern for others but also taking responsibility for their wel-fare: "I could not stand idly by and observe the daily misery that was occurring"; "[if I hadn't helped], I never would have forgiven myself." Some rescuers referred to a preexisting affection for the people they helped ("they were good friends—I liked them very much"). But most expressed their motivation to care for anyone in need ("I did it out of a feeling of compassion for those who were weaker and who needed help"; "any kind of suffering must be alleviated"). And, in fact, more than 90% of rescuers reported helping at least one stranger.

Rescuers referred to equity and responsibility for others, regardless of their origin or religion, as ethical principles that compelled them to act—and spe-cifically to the need for justice and equality among human beings: "I could not comprehend that innocent persons should be persecuted just because of race"; "every person is equal; we all have the right to live." Some rescuers saw their activities as stemming from their faith. They felt that saving others was what God wanted them to do and was in fact their duty as Christians. This interpretation of Christianity was unique to the rescuers and unlike that of the nonrescuers, who were also Christians; it reflected their broad humanistic and altruistic approach. In fact, the study found no general connection between one's religious affiliation and one's inclination to help.

Several noteworthy characteristics stood out in rescuer profiles. In upbringing, rescuers tended to come from close, warm families, who used induction and expla-nation to discipline their children. Most distinctively, they came from families that inculcated humanistic and prosocial values in both word and deed. Some of the rescuers came from communities in which such values prevailed. In Denmark, for example, following the October 1, 1943, order to arrest and deport all Danish Jews and despite the great personal risk, the Danish resistance movement, with the assistance of many ordinary Danish citizens, collectively embarked on a mission that evacuated almost all the Danish Jews to nearby (and neutral) Sweden (see more information in the US Holocaust memorial museum: http://www.ushmm.org/outreach/en/article.php?ModuleId=10007740). This rescue operation and the concerted rescue efforts of the community of the village of Le Chambon-sur-Lignon and its surrounding area in France are two clear examples of such communities. (http://www.ushmm.org/wlc/en/article.php?ModuleId=10007518)

Rescuers were also distinct in their empathy and compassion and especially in their willingness to act altruistically based on these emotions. They saw no other way than responding with help: "I looked at him, in striped camp clothing, his head bare, shod in clogs . . . . And he begged, his hands joined like a prayer—that he had escaped from Majdanek and could I help him? . . . Well, how could one not have helped such a man?" (Oliner, 2002, p. 127). In terms of character, rescuers tended to be self-confident and independent-minded, showing efficacy, determination, individuality, and independence, although these qualities in themselves, did not distinguish rescuers from nonrescuers.

Rescuers also differed from nonrescuers in certain situational factors. For example, they had more social contacts that could be expected to help them care for Jews, and were reportedly asked to help (by Jews or intermediaries) much more often than nonrescuers (67% vs. 25%). However, the Oliners concluded that although such factors probably facilitated rescues, they alone did not suffice in determining whether a rescue took place. Some 32% of rescuers, for example, initiated their helping activities without being asked. Furthermore, it is possible that rescuers were asked more often because they had signaled their receptivity to such requests (Varese & Yaish, 2000) or that nonrescuers were reluctant to admit that they had been asked but refused the request (Gushee, 1993).

Empathy, self-confidence, a supportive community, and being asked to help were all relevant contributors, and it is clear that the altruistic rescuing of Jews during the Holocaust was multiply determined. Yet there was another dimension that became increasingly apparent with the appearance of more and more studies conducted by researchers from a variety of disciplines and points of view (Baron, 1992; Block, & Drucker, 1992; Fogelman, 1995; Hallie, 1979/1994; Monroe, 1996; Oliner & Oliner, 1988). Among the hundreds of rescuers interviewed, researchers identified a very similar core humanistic and altruistic moral worldview embedded within each rescuer's personality and functioning; this appeared to be the main vehicle driving the rescuer's heroic altruistic behavior.

For example, and as described previously, the Oliners noted that rescuers were highly conspicuous in having a strong and coherent feeling of responsibility for the welfare of others, including those outside their familial and communal circles. The Oliners termed this quality "extensivity" in a clear reference to the extension of empathy and care to all humanity. Other researchers reached very similar conclusions. Monroe, Barton, and Klingemann (1990), for example, referred to an overarching perception of a connection to all humankind that characterized the rescuers: "You help people because you are human and [because] you see that there is a need . . . . There are things in this life you have to do and you do them" (Monroe et al., 1990, p. 118). The ongoing nature of this altruism was sustained by a strong humanistic conviction that "all human beings belong to one . . . family" (two separate quotes from two different rescuers in Monroe et al., 1990). Monroe and her colleagues have suggested that this feeling, belief, and moral attitude was so ingrained in the rescuers' being that it could be described as a core part of their identity reflecting their upbringing and conduct prior to the Holocaust. Because it was so central to their 'being' and 'doing' in the world, their altruistic help had an instinctive and spontaneous quality, which was reflected in the rescuers' insistence that they had done nothing praiseworthy or extraordinary. See, for example, this quotation from Johtje Vos, a Dutch woman rescuer, in the Oliners' book (1988, p. 228):

> We are now called "Righteous Gentiles" or even sometimes "heroes." We very much object to this title, and I can tell you why. One day there was an air raid on the German barracks near our house, some five kilometers away. My husband happened to be there. . . . When it was over, the barracks were very badly hit. A German soldier came running out with his head practically destroyed. He was bleeding heavily and was obviously in shock. He was running in panic. My husband saw that within minutes he would fall down and bleed to death. So my husband put him on his bicycle—without thinking about it—and brought him to the commandant's house. He put him on the step, rang the bell, waited to see the door open, and left. Later some of our friends and people who were hiding with us heard about it and said: "You are a traitor because you helped the enemy." My husband replied: "No, the moment the man was badly wounded, he was not an enemy anymore but simply a human being in need." As little as we could accept the title of "traitor," so little can we accept the title of "hero" for things we did to help Jewish people. We just helped people who were in need.

When they see a person in distress, rescuers see a human being in need, and they feel empathy, compassion, and a personal responsibility to help. This rests on the moral conviction that human beings are basically the same, that the differences between them are to be respected, and that our life in the world involves a common bond of humanity that entails kindness, compassion, and responsibility toward others. The Oliners referred to this constellation as "the altruistic personality."

Heroism in emergencies

The study of the Holocaust teaches us that "'ordinary people'" are capable of heroic altruistic acts where they risk their lives to save others who are not family members and are often total strangers. But the Holocaust and the Nazi regime in Europe were a very exceptional case in human history. Do we have evidence for altruistic acts in more normative circumstances? Actually we do. There are formal records of thousands and thousands of such heroic altruistic acts throughout history. Some of these acts were performed as part of the person's duty (i.e., a policeman or a firefighter), but most often these extraordinary deeds went well beyond the call of duty and reflected an intrinsic voluntary and courageous act on the rescuer's part. Consider the case of Scott E. Teuscher and Jason R. Ivey, who received a Carnegie Hero medal for rescuing Amy L. Stapleton-Horn from a burning car in Grass Valley, California, on July 12, 2012.

> Unconscious, Stapleton-Horn, 37, remained in the driver's seat of her car after an accident in which the vehicle struck an oncoming tractor-trailer in the vicinity of its fuel tanks. The tanks burst into flame, setting fire to the tractor and its flatbed trailer, the car coming to rest in close proximity to the flames. Motorists, including Teuscher, 35, [a] courier, and Ivey, 41, [a] handyman and caretaker, stopped at the scene. Despite the growing and advancing flames, Teuscher went to the driver's side of Stapleton-Horn's car, opened the front door, and, leaning inside, unfastened her safety belt. As he began to pull her out, Ivey joined him and helped take her from the vehicle and carry her across the highway to safety. An explosion at the tractor-trailer sent flames to the car, and both vehicles were shortly engulfed, with flames spreading to the trees and grass along the highway. Stapleton-Horn required extensive hospitalization for treatment of serious injuries, including burns of up to third-degree. (http://carnegiehero.org/awardees/#5 retrieved February 1, 2014.)

Even children perform such altruistic heroic deeds. See, for example, the case of Robert F. Barton, a Carnegie Hero awardee who was 12 years old when he saved Germaine, 14, and Beatrice, 13, from drowning in icy water in Providence, Rhode Island on January 11, 1931:

> While Robert, two older boys, Germaine, and Beatrice were skating in a line abreast on Roger Williams Park Lake, they broke through the ice, which was one inch thick, and went into water five to seven feet deep.

The hole in the ice was more than 25 feet long and was five to six feet wide. It was dark, and the water was very cold. Robert, who was the nearest to the bank, touched bottom and then broke the ice for eight or nine feet to the bank. The girls went under the surface briefly in deep water and then grasped one of the older boys, who could not swim. Robert waded from the bank and then swam three feet to Germaine. He grasped her, swam three feet to wadable water, and took her to the bank. He then worked himself close to Beatrice by holding to the ice and swam a few feet to her. Towing her, he swam five feet to wadable water. The other boys pulled themselves to wadable water by holding to the ice. (http://carnegiehero. org/awardees, retrieved February 1, 2014.)

A large number of institutions and organizations that honor heroism are operating in the world, as attested by the Lt. J. Frank Murphy Medal of Valor, the Californian Good Samaritan Law of 1966, the Toronto Civilian Citations, the Canadian Medal of Bravery, the Caring Canadian Award, as well as many other such establishments worldwide. Perhaps, the oldest one that is still operating is the Carnegie Hero Fund Commission, which was established by Andrew Carnegie in 1904 and has since awarded more than 9,600 medals to heroes whose heroic acts took place in the United States or Canada. Approximately 20% of these were awarded posthumously, ordinarily because the honoree died while performing her or his heroic act. The Carnegie Hero Fund Commission awards medals and grants to men and women who knowingly and voluntarily "risk their own lives to an extraordinary degree while saving or attempting to save the life of another person." (http://carnegiehero.org/about-the-fund/history/ retrieved February 1, 2014.)

The Carnegie Hero Fund has honored and assisted rescuers who were involved in world-famous disasters such as the San Francisco earthquake of 1906, the sinking of the *Titanic* in 1912, the 1982 crash of Air Florida Flight 90 in the Potomac River, and the terrorist attacks of September 11, 2001. However, the large majority of awardees risked their lives in situations that did not attract such a lot of media attention. These "'ordinary'" emergencies included burning buildings, vehicle fires, drownings, assaults, electrocutions, avalanches, and other adversities.

What can we learn from these extraordinary acts of heroism and altruism? Why men like Scott Teuscher and Jason Ivey knowingly and spontaneously risked their lives to save Amy Stapleton-Horn from burning in her car? Rescuers usually felt efficacious and confident, were often eyewitnesses to the events in question and were often related in some way to the victims (shared the boat trip with them, were neighbors, swam close by). Yet what set them apart from some of the others in the vicinity of the emergency who did not intervene was a clear and almost automatic feeling of responsibility to help. Most heroic acts are enacted spontaneously upon noticing a need and without much contemplation. Although empathy is aroused, it is often a cognitive realization of the danger and the need rather than a strong emotional reaction.

"I didn't have time to think, I just wanted to get her out of there" recounted a man who rescued a woman from a burning car (McCann, 2002, Section 2, p. 3). As with Holocaust rescuers, heroes in emergency situations often experience a strong sense of personal responsibility to help the endangered person or persons. Taylor (2002) has observed that heroes are often embarrassed when they are celebrated as such: "I did what any ordinary person would do in my place," perhaps reflecting their ingrained moral responsibility. It appears that in a manner akin to Holocaust rescuers, a sense of responsibility described as an "inability" to stand by while someone else was in real danger, along with a sense of efficacy, prompted a quick, spontaneous, life-threatening act of rescue (Wooster, 2000). Rescuers tended to refer to their upbringing and to religiosity as instilling this moral sense of responsibility and duty.

It appears that both kinds of heroism, in emergency situations and during the Holocaust, reflect a similar profile. This profile included a deep concern for the welfare of others, a strongly embedded sense of personal responsibility, inner capacity, and efficacy all probably affected by the rescuers' upbringing.

A similar profile of rescuers in emergencies emerged in a study by Huston, Geis, and Wright (1976). They conducted a study of 32 random recipients of the Good Samaritan Award who were injured while intervening to prevent criminal events such as muggings, bank holdups, and armed robberies in California. The participants were mostly men, taller and heavier than average, with some emergency training and with what would currently be referred to as anger-management problems. Furthermore, these men were familiar with crime in their neighborhood and had firm beliefs about the necessity of law and order and their responsibility to stand by victims and protect them. This profile probably reflects some general qualities shared by a large number of those involved in heroic acts in emergencies, such as having a personal sense of responsibility to help others and a sense of competence and capacity to do so. Yet, this profile also probably includes characteristics that are specific to the kind of altruistic act involved—that is, saving the victims of crime from the perpetrators. Other heroic acts such as those involving fires or potential drownings do not involve crimes and do not require standing against others, although they obviously necessitate quick responses, physical prowess, and agility, qualities often characteristic of men. Interestingly, among those awarded the Carnegie Hero medals in North America, over 90% were men (Johnson, 1996; Becker & Eagly, 2004). This begs the question of gender differences in the display of heroism and altruism.

Men's and women's heroism and altruism

The large majority of heroes in emergency situations are men. Addressing this finding, Becker and Eagly (2004) have suggested that two behavioral tendencies are crucial to heroism—taking physical risks and manifesting empathy and compassion with regard to the well-being of others. The first accords with a male gender role while the second accords with a female gender role. Thus the male gender role fosters helping that is heroic and chivalrous, whereas the female gender role fosters helping that is nurturant and caring. Taylor (2002) further suggests that the kind of heroism that emerges in high-risk emergency circumstances accords with the neurocircuity for aggression and dominance, whereas altruistic caregiving that derives from compassion and the tending instinct (which characterizes more women than men and emerges from the neurocircuities of caregiving and bonding) is where female heroism is to be found.

Heroism in the Holocaust also involved great risk to the rescuers' lives yet was less physically driven, more prolonged, and often involved actions that departed from the social norm of others in the rescuer's social environment. According to the logic of gender differences discussed earlier, we would expect men and women to be equally involved in such heroism. Becker and Eagly (2004) examined the gender composition of recipients of the Righteous Among Nations citation, taking the wartime gender distribution in different parts of Europe into account. They found an almost equal proportion of men and women, with a large number being active as couples in the rescue efforts. Examining the rescuer sample without taking couples into account revealed a slightly higher proportion of women.

In light of this gendered depiction of altruistic acts, the use of different definitions of altruistic acts that deserve recognition appears to make a difference in terms of gender composition. Canada, for example, awards distinct types of medals. The Medal of Bravery recognizes civilians who risked their lives to save others in the face of considerable danger, and most of its recipients are men. The Caring Canadian Award recognizes volunteers who have demonstrated an extraordinary and long-term commitment to providing care to others or to supporting community service or humanitarian causes, and the gender composition of its recipients is roughly equal. In a study examining 50 medalists from both groups and a comparison group of 50 individuals and using extensive interviews and questionnaires, Walker, Frimer, and Dunlop (2010) identified three distinct routes leading individuals to engage in intensive, high-cost caring for others: (1) through relatedness, nurturance, communion and empathy, which are more feminine; (2) through a deep-seated holistic and principled moral identity, which appears to be gender-neutral; and (3) through being receptive to environmental circumstances (e.g., emergencies) that call for help, which appears to be more masculine. Thus it appears that heroic altruism is variable and that its manifestations interact with gender roles and genderized capacities.

Kidney donations to strangers

In this section I would like to zoom in on a very special case of altruism that unlike rescuers in emergencies involves a proactive and preplanned altruistic act that can offer us more insight into human altruism. Kidney donations present a special case of a high-cost prosocial act that is preplanned and proactive and involves a considerable physical risk, albeit one with a minor likelihood of death. Kidney donations are needed for individuals suffering from kidney failure and thus requiring continual dialysis. Those patients who must undergo daily or almost daily dialysis experience poor physical and psychological welfare and face high chances of mortality. A large number of kidney donations come from the recipients' family members. However, there are also donations from strangers who volunteer to undergo the procedure and donate a kidney without even knowing the recipient's identity. In the medical community, these cases are known as living anonymous donors. Although a person can function with only one kidney, the operation is still highly invasive and donors typically report major pain following the operation and an average recovery period of two to three months. The overall rate of minor and major complications is 8%, and if donors ever have kidney problems themselves, they are in real trouble. Furthermore, and from a medical point of view, the "first, do no harm" bioethical principle is violated with respect to the donor, because performing such an operation on a donor inflicts ostensibly needless harm at no benefit to the donor. This is why living anonymous donation was not extensively embraced by the medical community at first. In fact, individuals who wanted to donate a kidney to a stranger were deemed to be psychologically unstable.

Yet a number of international surveys have indicated that a sizable percentage of individuals (reports range from 11% to 54%) would be willing to donate a kidney to a stranger (Henderson et al., 2003). There is obviously a big difference between such an indication and the act itself, but these findings show that individuals view this altruistic act as plausible. In the course of the past decade, more and more medical centers have begun to accept such donations (Matas, Garvey, Jacobs, & Kahn, 2000) and carried out research in order to develop screening tests to determine who can qualify to become a donor and to understand the donors' psychological makeup.

Studies conducted in different countries (e.g., Canada, the United States, Germany, Australia, and the United Kingdom) have come up with strikingly similar findings (e.g., Henderson et al., 2003; Jacobs, Roman, Garvey, Kahn, & Matas, 2004; Clarke, Mitchell, & Abraham, 2014). The motivation to donate a kidney was very clearly intrinsic. The studies' samples were based on lists of unsolicited individuals who proactively contacted the medical center asking to donate a kidney, registering as potential donors, and often being persistent and clear about their wishes despite being initially refused. Furthermore, they were willing to undergo extensive assessments and often traveled significant distances to the medical center at substantial personal costs for lengthy interview sessions. Among these unsolicited volunteers, between a quarter to half were eventually identified as qualified donors (both medically and psychologically).

The medical centers employed somewhat different methods for examining psychological suitability and used somewhat different criteria but found similar psychological differences between the accepted and the rejected donors. The individuals who registered as donors but were screened out had various contraindications, both medical and psychological. At the psychological level, these contraindications involved such mental problems as depression, active grief, and low self-esteem. Additionally, candidates were ruled out if they had psychosocial issues or motivations that could increase their vulnerability and make it difficult for them to withstand potential donor-related stresses—for example, wanting to donate as a statement against their families, seeking praise and publicity, or intending to bolster their self-image. In addition, volunteers were not chosen as candidates for donation if they tended to downplay the donation's impact on their lives.

Those eventually selected as potential anonymous donors revealed a distinct psychological profile. They considered their donation as a natural extension of giving in lives already rich with philanthropy and social responsibility. All had also made other donations, such as blood, ovaries, and stem cells, they were also on the bone marrow donor registry or had already signed donor cards. In all cases, giving constituted an integral part of their identity. In other words, their wish to donate a kidney merely reflected preexisting plans and identities. One interviewee in Clarke, Mitchell, and Abraham's (2014, p. 398) study, for example, stated that "I always try and maximize people's happiness and welfare. It's not like I don't value myself or my own health, it's just I only value it as much as I value someone else, all other things being equal."

A large number of them were motivated by a spiritual belief system and felt that donating was an act of living out their faith and their spiritual dedication to serving others. One participant in the study of Henderson et al. (2003, p. 207) said, for example: "I don't care who gets my kidney—family, friend, or stranger. . . . God doesn't have a club. God's works are for everyone." Potential anonymous kidney donors felt that such a donation was an acceptable price to pay for dramatically improving another person's life. These donors described themselves as being "'rich in health" and saw the kidney donation as a way of sharing their good fortune with others: "So it seemed to me that I could give away a certain amount of money but not a great deal, but I do have a kidney that I don't need, so it seemed to me I'm rich in kidneys" (Clarke, Mitchell, & Abraham, 2014, p. 399). They described their lifestyles as fulfilling and active and said they wanted to help others experience the same level of enjoyment in their lives. In fact, they were not merely appropriate psychologically but emerged also as exceptional and extraordinary individuals who were moved to take an active role in making the world a better place.

Unlike altruistic acts during the Holocaust or in emergencies, these donors took time to think about this act and chose it in a voluntary and fully conscious manner. They were quite realistic about the process's hardships and difficulties. They took time and exerted effort to obtain information about the process and made the necessary family and work arrangements. They did not minimize the difficulties involved but were quite clear and certain, human and humble in their desire to help another. In their other-oriented motivations they showed what appears to be premeditated, planned, "'pure'" altruism.

Yet they were not "saints" in the sense of being immune to negative feelings (Henderson et al., 2003). These donors were concerned about others construing their motives as pathological or selfish. They often felt hurt and frustrated by the attitudes of the medical team and the suspicions that they encountered (i.e., being accused of acting out of stupidity or seeking to elicit praise and fame). Yet, just like rescuers in the Holocaust or in emergency situations being treated as heroes or extremely brave by others often made them feel embarrassed. As far as gender differences were concerned, slightly more women than men were kidney donors (the percentages are often 10% higher among women), both for strangers and for relatives (mostly spouses), even after differences in eligibility and the general incidence of end-stage renal disease were taken into account (Becker & Eagly, 2004).

Conventional altruism—The empathy-altruism hypothesis

The altruistic examples that have been presented here involve clear risks to the caregiver's welfare. But altruism may not be limited to high-cost prosocial giving. In fact, Oliner (2001, 2002) has suggested that altruism should be viewed on a continuum from heroism entailing risks to the helper's life to conventional altruism involving some sacrifice but at a significantly lower cost. Batson (1991), who studied mostly conventional altruism, has suggested a clear, coherent, and comprehensive view of altruism from a psychological point of view. According to his suggestion, psychological altruism means a motivational state with the psychological *ultimate goal* of increasing another's welfare. I emphasize the words *ultimate goal* because they capture the main point of his suggestion. In a psychological rather than evolutionary context, this term means that the relevant goal is an end in itself. In contrast, an instrumental goal is only a step on the way—a means—for attaining the ultimate goal; it is not an end in itself. If an instrumental goal cannot be reached, it will be replaced by an alternative route to the ultimate goal. As far as altruism is concerned, it means that the other person's welfare is the end goal sought and the ultimate reason for the relevant prosocial behavior. Egoism, on the other hand, is a motivational state whose ultimate goal is an increase in one's own welfare. Yet there are cases in which helping others is an instrumental goal on the way to an egoistic ultimate goal. This is the case, for example when people help because they want to be relieved from anticipated guilt or because they want others to perceive them as benevolent.

Both ultimate and instrumental goals should be distinguished from the *unintended consequences* of the action once implemented. In that sense the *intention* is the crucial element that distinguishes altruistic help. Even if a helper foresees the consequences of feeling good or of gaining a good reputation following a prosocial deed, this does not mean that the act is egoistic if its ultimate goal was another's benefit. But how can we know psychologically what another person "really" wants? How do we know if the ultimate goal was benefiting the other (an "altruistic motivation" according to Batson) or feeling that one is a good person (an "egoistic motivation" according to Batson)? From this point of view the relevant question is whether we can observe motivational states that lead to acts of helping whose ultimate goal is benefiting the other even if some of the unintended and yet possibly foreseen consequences contribute to the person's own welfare. Following a remarkable series of studies examining this issue, Batson's answer is strongly and clearly affirmative (Batson, 2010). Furthermore, his studies also reveal that such altruistic help is quite pervasive.

The empathy-altruism hypothesis that Batson advocates claims that empathic concern is a source of altruistic motivation—namely a motivation whose ultimate goal is benefiting the other, and that any self-benefits (e.g., feeling that one is a good person and gaining good reputation) are unintended consequences. According to Batson, empathic concern is an other-oriented emotional response elicited by the perceived welfare of another person in need and congruent with it; in other words, it is a sense of feeling *for* the other and includes sympathy, compassion, tenderness, and other such emotions. Batson stresses that it should not be confused with what he terms empathy, emotional contagion, or affective resonance, which involve feeling *as* another person feels. Others refer to empathic concern as sympathy (Eisenberg, 2010) or compassion (Goetz, Keltner, & Simon-Thomas, 2010). A large number of mostly laboratory-based studies have revealed empathic concern as leading people to behave prosocially toward others. In other words, people with a high degree of empathic concern toward someone in need are more prosocial toward that person than people with low empathic concern (see review by Batson, 1991).

But how do we know that peoples' motivations are altruistic? Perhaps they help because they are distressed by the other person's situation and want to relieve their own distress? Such personal distress is a prevalent outcome of witnessing another person in need and reflects the operation of empathy, emotional contagion, or affective resonance with that person, but it also involves feelings of tension and discomfort triggered by witnessing another's plight. If help is geared toward alleviating the helper's distress, benefiting the other is just a means to the end of alleviating the helper's own distress and is therefore done for egoistic reasons. But what if the helper can alleviate her or his distress in another way besides helping, as by escaping the situation or boosting his or her mood? If the ultimate goal is benefiting the other, the potential helper would still help; yet if the ultimate goal is relieving one's distress, providing a viable escape would substantially reduce the incidence of help. In one of the first studies to examine this hypothesis, Batson and colleagues (Batson, Duncan, Ackerman, Buckley, & Birch, 1981) had participants who were allegedly assigned to be observers watch another female undergraduate—the "worker"—receive two electric shocks (out of ten) as part of an experiment. The worker was very distressed by the shocks, allegedly because of a trauma in her childhood. The observers were then given a chance to help her by exchanging roles and taking the remaining shocks themselves. The level of empathic concern was manipulated by making the subjects perceive themselves to be similar (high empathic concern) or dissimilar (low empathic concern) to the female receiving the shocks. The observers were either offered an easy escape from continuing to watch the "worker" suffer by leaving the experiment if they chose not to help (easy escape condition) or no escape—meaning that they had to continue their observation and watch the "worker" suffer from electric shocks until the end of the experiment. If high empathic concern indeed led to altruistic motivation, this motivation should be observed in similar levels of readiness to help in both the "easy escape" and the "no escape" conditions in the high-empathic-concern condition. In contrast, in a low-empathic-concern condition, the incidence of help should be lower in the "easy escape" condition compared with "no escape" because the observers' distress upon viewing the "'worker's" suffering could be alleviated by escaping the situation, although the "victim" herself would continue to suffer.

The results were quite clear and have since been replicated in dozens of studies. In the high-empathic-concern conditions, with the "easy escape" and the "no escape" conditions being similar in terms of help provision, more than 80% of subjects volunteered to help and receive the "worker's" electric shocks instead. In the low-empathic-concern conditions, help was higher in the "no escape" condition (more than 60%) than in the "easy escape" condition (less than 20%). Since then, researchers have consistently found that when empathic concern is low, helping drops dramatically if escape is easy. When empathic concern is high, however, helping remains high even when the high-empathic-concern individuals can easily reduce their distress by escaping (Toi & Batson, 1982;Fultz, Batson, Fortenbach, McCarthy, & Varney, 1986). In fact, Batson and his colleagues have shown that the relative strength of empathic concern and personal distress drives the dominant motivation. When personal distress is high, egoistic motivation tends to be predominant; however, when empathic concern is stronger than personal distress, help is propelled by altruistic motivation. This pattern of results shows that empathically aroused individuals help in order to benefit others rather than to reduce their own aversive empathic arousal.

In the same vein, Eisenberg (2010) has suggested that a high degree of empathy may not lead to altruistic help in and of itself. According to her model, empathy may lead to sympathy ("empathic concern" in Batson's terms), which would culminate in altruistic help if the personal distress that is also aroused in the face of another's predicament is not too high. When personal distress is high, it can generate a self-focused effort toward dealing with this distress, which can result in low levels of help provision and/or in help that is generated by self-focused motivations and is thus less sensitive and responsive than optimally desired. This led her to study these effects, and her studies as well as others' demonstrated, as expected, the importance of affect regulation and regulation of distress in particular in the development of prosocial behavior (see review in Eisenberg & Fabes, 1998; Eisenberg et al., 2000).

Batson and colleagues have also examined other self-focused reasons for helping. Specifically they addressed the suggestion that the prosocial motivation associated with empathy is directed toward the goal of obtaining social or self-rewards (i.e., praise, honor, and pride) or toward the goal of avoiding social or self-punishments (i.e., censure, guilt, and shame). Here too they devised laboratory experiments for examining the empathy-altruism hypothesis (Batson et al., 1988). For example, in a study where empathic concern occurred naturally, half of the helpers learned that the "worker" was relieved from the need to experience electric shocks before they had the chance to engage in a task that could have helped her to avoid these shocks. If self-enhancement motives were predominant, we would expect such relief to deprive the helpers with high empathic concern from feeling helpful and thus negatively affect their mood. In contrast, if altruistic motives are dominant for those with high empathic concern, any relief of the "worker's" distress, either because the situation had changed or because of the helper's actions, would improve the helper's mood. The findings clearly showed the expected altruistic effect for those with high empathic concern. In other experiments, the researchers examined the possibility that people help to avoid feeling guilty if they do not. Batson and colleagues (1988) devised experiments where they provided the participants with information that would justify a choice of not helping (e.g., most of their peers did not volunteer to help). Here too, individuals with high empathic concern showed similar levels of volunteering to help regardless of the justifications for not helping.

All together, this fruitful line of research regarding conventional altruism has provided strong support for the empathy-altruism hypothesis, demonstrating that when empathic concern is aroused, people tend to help altruistically, namely with the welfare of the recipient as their ultimate goal. It further demonstrated that such other-oriented helping depends on the balance between empathic concern and personal distress—both emanating from witnessing another's distress. High levels of altruistic helping can be observed when empathic concern is stronger than personal distress.

Altruism—conclusion and implications

This section addressed both high-risk altruism involving different kinds of heroism as well as low-cost conventional altruism. The research examining low-cost altruism has demonstrated that once a high level of empathic concern is aroused (whether naturally or experimentally), many individuals strive to help the recipient as the ultimate goal (showing an altruistic motivation) even though the unintended consequences of such help may make them feel good, gain a good reputation, or avoid feeling guilty. Although such positive outcomes for the helper may be forseen they were not the focus and the reason for offering the help. It should be noted that what constituted high empathic concern in these experiments was variable, that it was relative to the specific sample, and that between 50% to 90% of the participants in the "high empathic concern" condition volunteered to help. Hence the main point that should be taken from these studies is substantiation of the claim that altruistic help exists in ordinary situations when the help is not too costly and that help is altruistic to the extent that it "truly" originates from a concern with the other's benefit rather than self-focused motives. This kind of altruistic help, though not heroic, is all around us and forms a part of the fabric of our social lives. Furthermore, recent research, some of it conducted as part of the "positive psychology" paradigm, has shown that such help not only makes the recipient happy but also contributes to the helper's well-being and may enhance an organization's interpersonal climate (Grant, 2007, 2008; Dunn, Aknin, & Norton, 2008; Weinstein & Ryan, 2010; Lyubomirsky & Layous, 2013).

High-cost altruism is of course less prevalent and not all people engage in such acts. Studies in this area have identified several characteristics in those who become high-cost altruists and have even pointed to the possibility of several distinct profiles or routes toward becoming an altruistic exemplar. In summing up a lifelong study of human altruism and after examining over 1,500 people who have helped others (rescuers in the Holocaust, recipients of Congressional Medal of Honor or Victoria Cross, Carnegie Heroes, moral exemplars, and hospice volunteers), Samuel Oliner has provided a clear profile of the people who put the welfare of others alongside their own (http://www. yesmagazine.org/issues/can-love-save-the-world/ordinary-heroes, retrieved February 10, 2014). These people are deeply empathetic, with a clear capacity for love and compassion (e.g., "I was always filled with love for everyone, for every creature, for things. I am fused into every object. For me everything is alive."). They have a strong conviction that they can succeed at some tasks despite the dangers that might be involved. They had internalized the ethic of caring and social responsibility (e.g., "We had to help these people in order to save them, not because they were Jews but because they were persecuted human beings who needed help"), and often learned from their parents and significant others (e.g., "My parents taught me discipline, tolerance, and service of other people when they needed something."). For some, this social universal responsibility to others was also related to religious teachings, such as viewing all people as the children of the same God, worthy of protection and love (e.g., "Our religion says we are our brother's keeper."). Finally, as children they were likely to have been disciplined by reasoning and taught to consider the consequences of their misbehavior. Other studies have also examined a variety of altruistic exemplars and suggested that besides these common characteristics they may have somewhat different profiles of these attributes with some stronger on the caring and nurturance side (the caring type), others on the justice and moral identity side (the just type), and still others stronger on the heroic side (the brave type) (Walker & Hennig, 2004).

There are clear lessons to be learned from these descriptions and from the prevalence of low-risk altruism that should be applied in our postmodern, fragmented, yet networked society if we wish to promote empathy and caring and to develop our benevolent and spiritual natures (see Chapter 19).

Chapter conclusion

This chapter addressed generativity, prosocial behavior, and altruism. In discussing the research related to these conceptual frameworks, several insights came to the fore. First, the chapter uncovered the high prevalence of prosocial acts with strangers, which reflect a large variability in costs and investments. Second, the presentations in the chapter highlighted the prevalence of other-oriented motives, which are altruistic by nature and are even displayed with strangers in competitive contexts by the majority of people (about two thirds of the population). Third, the chapter underscored the importance of contexts and circumstances in shaping the extent and way such motivations are displayed. Finally, the different research traditions exposed a salient, clear, and stable individual propensity for prosocial acts.

10

Caring for Strangers: Examples of Caring and Nurturance

From heroic high-risk altruism to conventional altruism in daily encounters, individuals help nonkin to alleviate their pain, contribute to their survival, benefit them, and enhance their welfare. Such giving to others is a prevalent phenomenon in human experience. In fact, and as I discuss in this chapter, it is common in daily life, in volunteering, donations, mentoring at work, and other benevolent pursuits. In this chapter I would like to zoom in on three areas of caring for strangers that involve generativity, prosocial behavior, and often altruistic motives: volunteering, monetary donations, and mentoring. These domains provide us with remarkable and valuable insights on the enactment of the general caring motivation.

Volunteering

Volunteering represents a distinctive form of helping. It is defined by Warburton and Terry (2000) as "any service to the community given without payment through a group or organization" (p. 249). It might, for example, include providing companionship to the lonely, health care to the sick, counseling to the troubled, mentoring to youths at risk, helping out in sports organizations, or performing services for the homeless. It involves the provision of a service in order to help individuals and communities improve the quality of their lives and is a nonemergency helping behavior. Volunteers are proactive and often seek out opportunities to help; moreover, they carefully consider the initiation, scope, and precise nature of their involvement. Some forms of volunteering entail commitments that extend over significant periods of time and at substantial personal cost. Volunteers typically do not know in advance those whom they help, often being matched with recipients by service organizations.

Unlike the prototypical prosocial response of helping others, which is usually reactive in nature and emerges in response to a specific request or to noticing someone in need, volunteers usually search for opportunities to help in an orga-nizational context and may maintain this prosocial behavior over extended peri-ods of time (Penner, 2002). Consequently volunteering, because of its volitional, unpaid, and collectively oriented nature, represents a unique type of care distinct from ascribed and more formally obligated care involving close social ties and networks. It is considered an essential and exceptional form of social solidarity and is a central part of what is currently referred to as the "civil society." In that sense it is a proactive form of care that reflects generativity concerns.

Variety, prevalence, and gender

Volunteering involves a large number of different kinds of prosocial and benev-olent activities encompassing extremely varied roles and is enacted through hundreds of thousands of different organizations worldwide (Bussell & Forbes, 2002). These include, for example, hospice volunteers, individuals who mentor children and adolescents, AIDS volunteers, coaches for sports teams, helpers in schools or kindergartens, assistants to the elderly, carers for the sick, providers of meals for the hungry, volunteers in religious organizations, promoters of a cleaner environment, defenders of the weak, providers of guidance and companionship to prison inmates, and counselors for individuals who want to stop drinking or give up the use of drugs, to name just a few of these roles and activities.

Volunteering is a widespread phenomenon; in 1991, approximately 94.2 mil-lion American adults engaged in some form of volunteering, with 25.2 million giving five or more hours per week to volunteer service and many doing so over the course of many years (Omoto & Snyder, 1995). Volunteering rates vary con-siderably between countries, reflecting the role of cultural context in this regard. Recent surveys, for example, have found that over 40% of the population of Canada (Hall et al., 2007), the United Kingdom (Low, et. al., 2007), and Sweden (GHK, 2010) have engaged in some form of volunteer work. Looking at the American population as a whole, the Bureau of Labor Statistics found that 26% of the US population were engaged in some form of volunteer work (BLS, 2013), similar to the percentage in France (GHK, 2010) and above the percentage in Greece and Italy (10%) (GHK, 2010).

Research shows that people who volunteer tend to have various kinds of "capi-tal," including "human capital" (higher education and income, better health), "social capital" (number of children, social networks, empathy), and "cultural capital" (religious faith and benevolent values), which they wish to share with less fortunate others (Wilson & Musick, 1997).

Interestingly and unlike some of the other domains in which the caring moti-vation is expressed (i.e., caregiving for elderly or sick relatives), there is only a small and inconsistent gender effect: women, mostly in North America, demon-strated a slightly greater tendency to volunteer than males. This is not the case in Europe or in other countries, where for the most part there are no consistent gender effects in volunteering or in the number of hours volunteered (see review in Wilson, 2000). This small and inconsistent gender effect is puzzling because women report higher altruism and empathy, feel more guilty than men when they have not been benevolent, consider helping others a more valuable pursuit than do men, and believe that they are expected to care for the personal and emotional needs of others. Furthermore, many women consider their volunteer work an extension of their roles as wives and mothers, in which they provide care to those close to them. One suggested cause is that men often have more human capital and free time (see review in Wilson, 2000).

There are, however, gender differences in the kind of volunteering work that men and women do. Women volunteers are inclined toward more caring, person-to-person responsibilities and fewer public or sports activities and are less likely to be found in leadership positions in the volunteering sphere. This profile is quite universal (Wilson, 2000). Thus, and from the point of view of the caring motivation, volunteering provides men with a gender-appropriate arena for expressing their caring and fulfilling their motivation; this is unlike other domains, such as parenting, where a clear gender difference emerges, with women more invested in caring than men.

Motivations for volunteering

The act of volunteering stands out as a primary expression of core human values, such as altruism, compassion, concern for others, generosity, social responsibility, and community spirit (Wuthnow, 1991). In the words of a volunteer from Queensland, Australia: "It was something I was put on this earth to do and I don't care whoever asks me, I say it is what I love doing—to help other people in need" (Warburton & McLaughlin, 2006, p. 64). Hence it is not surprising that "altruistic motives" such as the desire to help others are the most frequently cited reasons for volunteering among diverse groups of volunteers, both older and younger (Clary et al., 1998; Okun, Barr, & Herzog, 1998; Bussell & Forbes, 2002; Greenslade & White, 2005); in fact, such motives can predict whether or not volunteers complete their expected period of service (Clary & Miller, 1986; Clary & Orenstein, 1991). According to the Marriott Seniors Volunteerism Study (Marriott Senior Living Services, 1991), for example, the motive endorsed most frequently by older volunteers as a major reason for volunteering was "to help others" (83%). Similarly, in a series of six studies, Clary et al. (1998) found that involvement in volunteer service was strongly related to the opportunities that volunteerism provided for individuals to express values related to altruistic and humanitarian concerns for others, and this reason was the most strongly endorsed across the different studies and different types of volunteering. Besides altruistic motives, volunteers view their volunteer activity also as affording them opportunities for self-actualization and growth (Anderson & Moore, 1978; Jenner, 1982). In the words of a volunteer helping people with serious mental illness: "No matter how much time, or lost sleep, or stress you feel the investment requires, the satisfaction of being intimately involved with another life in recovery is just extraordinarily self-enhancing and reinforcing" (Mccorkle, Dunn, Wan, & Gagne, 2009, p. 299).

Additional, more self-oriented motivations have also been found, such as gaining new skills, increasing one's self-esteem, and strengthening social relationships (Clary et al., 1998). The importance of such factors varied across different volunteer profiles: social aspects, for example, played a stronger role in adolescent volunteering than in adult volunteering (Haski-Leventhal et al., 2008); career-related aspects tended to be more important to younger adults than to older ones (Clary & Snyder, 1999); and feeling "useful or productive" was stronger among elderly volunteers compared with others (Marriott Senior Living Services, 1991). Thus, like any act of caring, volunteering can have diverse functions and reflects a combination of different types of motivations (Clary et al., 1998). People can and do perform the same actions in the service of different psychological functions. Furthermore, people often have distinct profiles that include several reasons for a specific activity. This view is shared by a large number of researchers who have examined diverse phenomena (Snyder & Debono, 1987) and is also espoused in this book. Yet for the most part a strong and clear motivation to help others, nurture them, and see to it that they thrive—the caring motivation—occupies a central place in these personal profiles and was almost always the strongest motive.

The intrinsic motivation to engage in volunteering and the element of choice and autonomy in selecting its object proved to be very central in volunteers' experiences. Another volunteer from Queensland, Australia, put it very clearly: "And you know, you can't force anyone to do volunteer work. You are doing it from your heart or don't do it at all" (Warburton & McLaughlin, 2006, p. 64). This is especially relevant to adolescents and college students who are often required to volunteer. Mandatory civic participation may not have a positive effect on youth and may even contribute to alienation among those originally high in altruistic motivation unless it involves a prominent measure of autonomy and choice—for example, mandatory civic activity in an organization of one's own choosing (Henderson, Brown, Pancer, & Ellis-Hale, 2007). This is related to the issues discussed extensively by Deci and Ryan (Deci & Ryan, 2000; Ryan & Deci, 2000) in their self-determination theory concerning intrinsic and extrinsic motivations and the importance of the core human need for autonomy. In volunteering, which rests on a proactive, volitional, and intrinsic caring motivation, the sense of autonomy and the choice of a setting that is meaningful to the volunteer are crucial. People volunteer because they want to help and contribute to society, but the sustenance of such a motivation demands that this contribution be aligned with their values, inclinations, predispositions, and aptitudes. This is how volunteering imbues their lives with meaning and gives them a sense of well-being that is eudaemonic (i.e., one that truly reflects their core self, or "daimon") (see Ryan & Deci, 2001, on two types of well-being). Indeed, the extent to which volunteers' experiences was found to match their motivations predicted their satisfaction and future intentions to volunteer (Clary et al., 1998).

Benefits of volunteering

Volunteering is not just good for the recipients. It is also beneficial to the volunteers, reflecting a salutary effect of volunteering. Volunteering can generate feelings of efficacy and self-worth—a feeling that one "matters"—as well as giving the volunteer a sense of purpose and meaning. See, for example, quotations from two volunteers who articulated this. The first is from a caregiver volunteering to help people living with HIV and AIDS in southern Africa: "I can say that my life has changed for the better because as a person, I grew up not worrying about another person's problem. And this (volunteer care work) has taught me to help other people, especially those that are sick, and I have learnt to be concerned about other people's problems" (Akintola, 2010, p. 5). The second is from a volunteer in a sport and youth development program:

> If you ever see a kid that throws a rock and it goes right to the button and you see the smile on their face and they are jumping up and down. It is great to see the development, it is better than getting it myself. I like their enthusiasm, it makes me feel young. I like to think that I am helping to improve young kids and get them involved in sport. (Misener, Doherty, & Hamm-Kerwin, 2010, p. 276.)

In addition, because volunteering is often performed in a social setting, it can provide social integration, support, and a sense of belonging (Thoits & Hewitt, 2001). Indeed, studies have found that volunteer work correlated with various aspects of mental well-being, such as happiness (Borgonovi, 2008), life satisfaction (Van Willigen, 2000), and a sense of purpose (Greenfield & Marks, 2004). Volunteer work may have somewhat different benefits for the volunteers depending on their characteristics (e.g., age). Among high-school and college students the benefits also lie in personal growth (Switzer, Simmons, Dew, Regalski, & Wang, 1995) and the development of pro-social attitudes and empathy for others (Atkins, Hart, & Donnelly, 2005). Among disadvantaged and at-risk students, civic engagement has also been observed to improve academic achievement and future academic and occupational goals as well as to decrease the likelihood of dropping out from school (e.g., Duckenfield & Swanson, 1992).

Older adults appear to derive more benefits from volunteering than their younger counterparts. This is possibly due to the greater role volunteering fulfills in older people's lives, probably as a reflection of generativity, which is assumed to be strongest among adults. See how succinctly and clearly Hannah, a 79 year-old "reader" for immigrant children at a neighborhood school, expressed the generative reason for her volunteering: "When you grow old, you should leave the world a better place" (Narushima, 2005, p. 575). In addition, one of the most intriguing findings in this respect is that volunteer work among adults has been found to correlate with better physical and psychological health (Thoits & Hewitt, 2001) and even lower mortality rates among older volunteers (Musick et al., 1999). Because younger people are generally in better physical health, benefits in this area might be harder to detect than in older individuals (Li & Ferraro, 2006). The correlations between volunteering and physical health or lower mortality rates may, of course, be due to self-selection; that is, those with better health would be more likely to volunteer. This is especially true for older volunteers. Some studies have therefore used longitudinal designs and various statistical methods to try and determine the causation of these correlations. They found that while better health does allow more extensive volunteering (Thoits & Hewitt, 2001), volunteering also contributes to one's physical and mental health over and above the levels measured at the outset (Van Willigen, 2000; Thoits & Hewitt, 2001; Li & Ferraro, 2006).

A recent meta-analysis of the relation between organizational volunteering by older adults (at least 55 years of age) and the risk of mortality provided a statistical summary of the results from 12 samples with around 50,000 participants who were followed for an average six years and provided strong evidence to the effect that helping others yields health benefits for the helper (Okun, Yeung, & Brown, 2013). After controlling for covariates such as age, sex, ethnicity, socioeconomic status, work status, marital status, religious faith, emotional health, health behaviors, social connection, social interaction, and physical health, the adjusted effect size predicted a 25% reduction in the risk of death for volunteers compared with nonvolunteers. Why, then, does volunteering reduce the risk of mortality? Okun, Yeung, and Brown (2013) refer to a caregiving system model (Brown et al., 2012) proposing that the perceptions of another's need combined with the ability to meet this need trigger the motivation to help. This, in turn, activates neural circuits related to parenting that release hormones such as oxytocin and progesterone. Both of these regulate stress and downregulate inflammation. In other words, these investigators suggest that the arousal of the motivation to care initiates the biological and hormonal processes associated with its activation and that these biological processes operate to downregulate stress and anxiety and introduce restorative physiological effects that contribute to mental and physical health. Consequently it is logical to expect health benefits such as lower mortality if volunteering emanates predominantly from the caring motivation rather than from other more self-oriented and utilitarian motivations.

This was empirically confirmed by a group of scholars (Konrath, Fuhrel-Forbis, Lou, & Brown, 2012). They used data from a longitudinal study that followed a

random sample of over 10,000 male and female Wisconsin high school gradu-
ates since their graduation in 1957. The authors wanted to examine the effects
of motives for volunteering on the respondents' mortality risk. In 2004, respondents were asked whether they had volunteered within the past 10 years and
if so, how regularly. In addition, respondents were asked to report the reasons
for their volunteering (or their intent to volunteer for those who had not volunteered). Four years later, when the sample's mean age was around 70, the sample
was risk-assessed for mortality. In line with earlier work, respondents who volunteered (about half of the sample) were at a lower risk for mortality, especially
those who volunteered more regularly and frequently. Specifically 4.3% of the
nonvolunteers passed away in 2008, as opposed to 2.3% of the volunteers, and
the mortality risk was only 1.8% for those who volunteered regularly. These
effects remained statistically significant even after controlling for a host of variables reflecting potential differences between volunteers and nonvolunteers that
could affect survival (e.g., age, gender, socioeconomic variables; physical, mental, and cognitive health; health risk behaviors; personality traits; and received
social support).

Yet the main point of this study was related to the effect of the *reasons for volunteering*. As in other samples, there was a mix of motives for volunteering, with altruistic and other-oriented reasons being the strongest. In fact, more than 70% of the
volunteers reported predominantly altruistic reasons (e.g., "I feel it is important to
help others"). Controlling for all the previously mentioned covariates, the authors
found that those who volunteered for self-oriented reasons (such as "volunteering
makes me feel better about myself") had a mortality risk (4.0%) similar to that of
nonvolunteers (4.3%), whereas those who volunteered for other-oriented, altruistic reasons had a significantly decreased mortality risk (1.6%). The results of this
study provide convincing corroboration of the claim that engaging in caring that
is intrinsically chosen for "altruistic" or other-oriented reasons and is therefore
an expression of the motivation to care is beneficial to the provider, whereas caring for selfish reasons may not have the same positive benefits. Volunteering may
not always be beneficial, however. For example, one study found that the benefits
of volunteer work start declining at around 100 hours per year and in fact may
turn into negative effects at more than 140 hours per year (Van Willigen, 2000).
These findings and others showing burnout effects indicate the importance of a
balanced lifestyle, where giving to others is balanced with other pursuits of the
caregiver (Hooper et. al., 2010).

In sum, the study of volunteering has exposed a moderately high prevalence of
intrinsically motivated caring for strangers that is modulated by culture. It also
uncovered a variety of motives and revealed the centrality of an "altruistic" motivation that is geared to help others and reflects the caring motivation. The expression of the caring motivation through volunteering, especially when enacted with
a sense of autonomy and volition, results in a large variety of benefits not only for

the recipients but also for the volunteers themselves; these included both hedonic (i.e., pleasure) and eudaemonic (meaning and purpose) well-being as well as psychological and physical health.

Money donations and generosity

Volunteers who donate their time are usually discussed separately from those who donate material things such as money or gifts (i.e., books, clothing, food) (Yavas & Riecken, 1985). In what follows, I would like to focus on monetary donations and generosity and illustrate the mix of a number of motivational antecedents, particularly the strength of the altruistic motivation, as well as the similarity in the underlying biological and neurological processes between generosity with strangers and caring for close others.

Prevalence of generosity

Charitable giving is a special case of prosocial behavior in that the recipient is usually absent from the context in which a donation is made. It involves the donation of money to an organization that benefits others beyond one's own family. Monetary donations are common and are made not only by rich people. Information regarding the global prevalence of charitable giving can be found in the World Giving Index (Charities Aid Foundation, 2013). This index includes data from 135 countries representing around 94% of the world's population. The survey participants constituted a representative sample of the entire civilian and noninstitutionalized population aged 15 and above of each country. On average, 28% of the respondents reported donating money during the previous month and around 20% reported volunteering. Interestingly, these average numbers showed only minor fluctuations across the five years during which the World Giving Index was calculated (a 1% to 3% change). There is, however, a large variation across countries, and percentages range from 3% to 85% in donations and 4% to 57% in volunteering.

As with volunteering, people who engage in donating tend to have human, social, and cultural capital. Education, wealth, religious faith, and belonging to an extended social network, for example, are positively associated with donating and with the amount donated (Wiepking & Maas, 2009). As far as socioeconomic status is concerned, current research reveals some interesting findings. High-income earners spend a larger amount of money on donations than lower-income earners but give proportionally less of their incomes to charity (2.7% in the United States) than their lower-income counterparts (4.2% in the United States) (Piff et al., 2010). Furthermore, in four different studies, lower-class individuals have been shown to be more generous, charitable, trusting, and helpful than their upper-class counterparts (Piff et al., 2010). The authors suggest that this reflects a greater commitment to egalitarian values and feelings of compassion among lower-class individuals because they are more dependent on others for achieving their desired life outcomes and more cognizant of others in their social environ- ment. These effects (i.e., social class, income, religious faith), along with the vari- ability across countries reflect the significance of contexts (i.e., cultural, political, economic, religious) in the ways individuals express their motivation to care.

Motivations of generosity

Several antecedents have been identified as relevant to donating (Bekkers, & Wiepking, 2011), with most reflecting what we already know of the general decision process underlying prosocial behavior—such as the awareness of a need, responding to direct solicitation, the interplay of costs and benefits, and the perception of oneself as being able to make a difference. As with volunteer- ing, several motivations to donate were identified. Some could be categorized as other-oriented or as related to altruism and humanitarian values, and others could be seen as self-oriented, because they were related to gaining reputation and psychological benefits, such as boosting one's self-esteem or relieving guilt. I provide here more detailed discussions of the various motives to illuminate how caring might be multiply determined.

At the other-oriented pole, which reflects the caring motivation, "altruism" and "values" were described as motivations, and they appear to be similar, although the second is often more abstract and reflects a general stance on the part of the donor. Altruism involves the donor's concern about the services rendered to the recipients and the focus is on empathizing with the specific care receivers' condi- tion and wanting to alleviate their distress and answer their needs. Values relate to the donors' motivation to make the world a better place according to their val- ues, which are often humanitarian and egalitarian. Through giving, the donors wish to reduce poverty, empower women, equalize the distribution of wealth, and protect animals, wildlife, or the ozone layer. This is a clear manifestation of generativity. Studies have assessed such humanitarian values using somewhat dif- ferent terms, such as *altruistic values, prosocial values, nonmaterialistic values, being spiritual, endorsing a moral principle of care, caring about social justice in society*, and *feeling responsible for society as a whole* (Bekkers, & Wiepking, 2011). These values were found to relate to a general prosocial orientation, which is often viewed as a personality disposition and is associated with a large number of prosocial behav- iors including donations. For example, both dispositional empathic concern (the empathic aspects) and the moral principle of caring about others (a moral identity aspect) were linked to 10 different helping behaviors—including donations—in a study that used data from the General Social Survey, a nationally representative random sample of the US adult population (see review in Bekkers & Wiepking, 2007, 2011). The similar yet distinct nature of these two motivational sources of generativity, both reflecting the operation of the caring motivation, may reveal two complementary routes for the activation of this motivation: an empathy-based process and one that derives from a general worldview or identity often based on one's moral standing and values. These same aspects were implicated in high-cost altruism and heroism, as discussed in the previous chapter and appear again in the study of helping, caring, and generosity (see also Chapter 13 on the development of the motivation to care).

Scholars (see review in Bekkers & Wiepking, 2007) have also discussed other salient motivations that are more self-oriented, such as gaining a good reputation through donating. People who give to charitable causes are held in high regard by their peers and receive recognition and approval from others. Conversely, not giving may damage one's reputation. This reflects the high value accorded to being generous and kind and, of course, is relevant only if the donations are known and public. Such conspicuous donations appear to enhance the donor's status and prestige because they signal a positive yet less observable quality. A public contribution may convey important and reliable information about the giver's qualities as a potential interaction partner, group member, and even sexual mate. This is related to the costly signaling perspective (Van Vugt & Hardy, 2009). According to this perspective, in a social environment where individuals can choose whom they form alliances with, they might prefer to interact with people who have a reputation for being generous and kind, as has been found in studies examining personal attraction and brain activity (Singer, Kiebel, Winston, Dolan, & Frith, 2004). Consequently individuals may want to be seen as generous and kind or, at least, more generous than others and may therefore engage in donations to gain such a reputation. Using competitive games in a laboratory setting, Van Vugt and Hardy (2009) found that where one's contributions are known and reputation building is possible, there will be more contributions as opposed to when the donor's identity would not be revealed. Yet their results also showed a strong altruistic effect, because 50% to 58% of the participants still contributed even when their identities were concealed.

Similar findings were reported by De Cremer, Snyder, and De Witte (2001), underscoring individual differences in the importance of reputation as a reason for generosity. They found that public accountability did not affect contribution among high trusters, who comprised the majority of the participants. Only people who were low on trust and who regulated their behavior according to situational circumstances contributed more when they were identifiable and hence held accountable. These findings show the effects of a mixture of motivations whereby the prosocial altruistic motivation is the most prevalent. But why was being a prosocial person evolutionarily selected to be cherished by one's community? Along with others, and in line with the claim for a general and fundamental caring motivation which was evolutionarily selected, I suggest that the importance ascribed to acquiring a reputation as a kind and prosocial person strongly reflects the inherent centrality and significance of helping, cooperating, and donating in human society and human nature, a trait that was evolutionarily selected because of its merit for survival.

Another interesting set of possible motivations is related to the donors' psychological affect-related states. These are often viewed as more self-focused. Giving may contribute to one's self-image as an altruistic, empathic, socially responsible, agreeable, effective, and significant person. In addition, giving may alleviate feelings of guilt or aversion aroused when a negative situation is perceived in others. It also satisfies a desire for showing gratitude. Consequently individuals may donate in order to boost their self-esteem and self-image, to feel good about themselves, or to refrain from feeling bad if they do not donate. All of these reflect self-focused motivations (see review in Bekkers, & Wiepking, 2007).

Taken together, prosocial donations may therefore reflect the operation of intrinsic, other-oriented altruistic motives and prosocial values as well as the operation of self-presentational needs and affective needs of the donors. Individuals might evince variable profiles and combinations of these motives, yet extant research shows that other-oriented motives are the predominant ones.

Some scholars have also underscored the importance of "empathic joy" (Batson & Shaw, 1991) or a "warm glow" that reflects the joy of giving (Andreoni, 1989). This warm glow is an automatic positive emotional reaction that is often an unintended consequence of giving rather than an end in itself. Hence its appearance does not entail it being the reason for the prosocial deed. A new line of research has indeed demonstrated that spending money on others is more rewarding than spending it on oneself (Dunn, Aknin, & Norton, 2008) and that such rewarding feelings are unintended, occur spontaneously following prosocial spending and even when participants are instructed to spend the money on others and reflect a universal phenomenon (Aknin et al., 2013). This is an affective mechanism that probably evolved to sustain cooperation and caring, which included both high- and low-cost contributions to others, both those who were known as well as strangers. The increasingly available evidence from neuropsychological studies accords with this contention and is the topic I will turn to next.

Biological aspects of generosity

Two tasks borrowed from experimental economics, the ultimatum game and the dictator game, have often been used to examine giving and generosity in the context of neural and neuroendocrine processes. In both games, one person in a dyad receives a monetary award and can split it with the other, who does not receive anything. Behavior in the ultimatum game is contingent on empathy and perspective taking because the recipient can refuse the offer, in which case both players receive nothing. Donors must therefore take the recipient's perspective into consideration in order to decide how much to offer so that the donation would not be perceived as too stingy and thus rejected. In contrast, in the unilateral one-time dictator game the recipient cannot reject the offer, meaning that the amount offered is largely dependent on the dispositional altruism of the donor.

In one such study, Harbaugh, Mayr, and Burghart (2007) used functional magnetic resonance imaging (fMRI) while participants played a dictator game. The participants received $100 and then made two decisions: whether or not to give money to a local food bank and how much to retain for themselves. They also observed mandatory tax-like transfers of their money to the food bank. Similar neural substrates serving as a reward system—the caudate, the right nucleus accumbens, and the insula—were activated during monetary payoffs to oneself, observing a charity get money through tax-like transfers, and freely donating to charity. In addition, the results showed higher activation in these areas (probably involving a greater sense of reward at the psychological level) during voluntary transfers as opposed to mandatory transfers. Moreover, the authors found that increased neural responses to mandatory contributions to the public good increased the likelihood of voluntary giving—demonstrating the operation of an altruistic disposition even in mandatory situations. These results underscore the fact that prosocial acts such as charitable giving and even mandatory donations are experienced as rewarding, probably reflecting the warm glow effect, and implicate the same common neural reward system that is activated in relation to a host of other stimuli, including food, sex, and drugs.

In line with this book's claim that a common biological and psychological structure underlies many manifestations of the caring motivation, the same oxytocin that is centrally involved in parenting and caring for romantic partners and friends (see Chapters 4 and 5) was also strongly implicated in generosity with strangers. For example, intranasal oxytocin injections, compared with a placebo, raised generosity in the ultimatum game by 80%, and this was a costly generosity because it caused the participants to leave the experiment with less money. The increased generosity was not due to greater dispositional altruism, and oxytocin's effect on generosity remained statistically significant even when altruism as a predisposition was taken into account. Taken together, oxytocin administration and dispositional altruism predicted almost half the interpersonal variation in generosity, demonstrating the somewhat different paths of dispositional altruism and the experimentally induced temporary arousal of empathic perspective taking and trust (Zak, Stanton, & Ahmadi, 2007).

Another study, which examined the neural mechanisms of charitable donations also using fMRI, sheds light on these two somewhat distinct neural routes to generosity. One route involves empathic perspective taking and oxytocin, as described by Zak, Stanton, and Ahmadi (2007); a second relates to dispositional altruism and engages mentalizing and morality (Moll et al., 2006). Participants made anonymous decisions to donate or refrain from donating to real charitable organizations linked to a wide range of societal causes, including children's rights, euthanasia, and gender equality. Reflecting the general prosocial human nature, behavioral analyses showed that all participants consistently made costly decisions, sacrificing an average of 40% of their endowment ($100). Donating to societal causes enlisted two types of reward systems in the brain. The first involves a general reward system, the ventral tegmental area (VTA)-striatum mesolimbic network, which was also involved in pure monetary rewards to the participants and is similar to the automatic reward that we have seen in the Harbaugh, Mayr, and Burghart (2007) study described earlier. It reflects the rewarding feeling (warm glow) that we get when we engage in giving and donating, which is similar to other rewarding experiences, such as consuming food. The second involves the subgenual area, which was specific for donations and was not activated when participants received monetary awards; it plays a key role in the release of the neuromodulators oxytocin and vasopressin and in social attachment; it also serves affiliative reward mechanisms in humans and other animals, probably reflecting empathic and perspective taking processes that implicate oxytocin. Finally, individual differences in self-reported engagement in real-life voluntary activities were associated with yet another area of the brain—the anterior prefrontal cortex, an area previously implicated in higher-order mentalizing such as planning and reasoning.

Taken together, these lines of evidence indicate that engaging in donations as one reflection of human altruism draws on a general mammalian neural reward system—that associated with basic motivations such as the search for food, as well as on another general mammalian neural system—that associated with emotional empathy, social attachment, and their rewards and the operation of oxytocin. Yet in the context of sustained planned philanthropy linked to moral values, human altruism is also connected to the uniquely developed human anterior prefrontal cortex, which is associated with our innate capacity for principled moral action. Empathic processes and morality have already emerged in previous discussions as central routes that engage our fundamental motivation to care. Yet the line of studies regarding volunteering and donating also exposed the rewarding aspect of such giving and its neural basis. Although volunteering and donating often rest on altruistic caring motivation, where the ultimate goal is the welfare of the recipient, a sense of reward appeared as an unintended yet almost automatic consequence of such caring. From an evolutionary perspective, these are all proximate biological mechanisms that have probably evolved to maintain a society of cooperating and caring individuals.

Mentoring

Mentoring is a special case of prosocial behavior and of volunteering because it reflects the mentor's proactive decision to form a *caring bond*. Most caring bonds that include the assumption of a responsibility to care for a person occur with kin, such as one's children, spouse, or parents, where the care is part and parcel of close relations involving several other important facets and is seen as obligatory. Mentoring is a different situation because it is not obligatory, it is proactive rather than reactive, and it involves the active choice to form a caring bond with nonkin and even total strangers. See, for example, how a volunteer in a mentoring program for at-risk high school youth in an urban setting with high rates of youth and violent crime recounts what led him to become a mentor: "Lots of kids don't have any support. They don't have an ear. They don't have anyone they can talk to. I'm glad to be that ear . . . . It sounds corny, but that's the way I really feel, not trying to change the world, but one or two people at a time" (De Anda, 2001, p. 106).

Mentorship is first and foremost a personal relationship between a mentor and a protégé, or mentee. In such as relationship, a more experienced or more knowledgeable person—the mentor—helps to guide and scaffold the development, often in the work or career domain, of a less experienced or less knowledgeable person—the protégé. This guidance relies on a connection between the two people involved, which often includes spending time together, developing trust and mutual regard, and building closeness and affection toward each other. Mentoring is often not an all-encompassing personal relation and the responsibility for the mentee's thriving is limited in scope, covering only the specific domains in which the mentor is responsible for helping and teaching the mentee. It is often limited in time, in the intensity of meetings or communications, and in the length of the relationship. This is the case, for example, when expert teachers help new teachers acquire the skills needed to successfully traverse the first year of teaching. Hence mentoring provides an illuminative example of the proactive voluntary desire to form a caring bond that is limited in time and scope.

Scholarly interest in mentoring is often attributed to Levinson's insights regarding human development in adulthood (Levinson, Darrow, Levinson, Klein, & McKee, 1978). Levinson and his colleagues investigated the development of 40 men who recounted their life experiences. In their life stories, the participants noted the importance of a relationship with a mentor who functioned as a guide, teacher, and counselor and who helped them realize their dreams. In fact, Levinson and others have noted that those who made it to the top of their profession often had such a "godfather" or "rabbi," which led Levinson to liken the mentor's importance in adulthood to that of a parent in childhood. Similar insights have been articulated with regard to youth. The importance of such mentors was especially noted with youth or children at risk, where mentors appear to play a vital role in the mentees' future resilience and success (Werner & Smith, 1982; Williams & Kornblum, 1985). Realization of the positive outcomes of mentoring for protégés served to advocate the creation of formal mentoring programs. Interestingly, most researchers and scholars have not discussed the complementary proactive motivation of potential mentors to be involved in caring and developing others through the formation of caring bonds.

Mentoring is a fairly common caring relationship and can be found among youth as well as among adults as a spontaneous informal occurrence and also as part of a formal program. Youth mentoring, for example, as a school- or community-based program in the United States engages more than 5 million mentor-protégé dyads. But mentoring is also implemented regularly in the workplace, where new employees are matched with more senior workers who are expected to help the newcomers adjust to the workplace, learn the required skills, and adjust to the social milieu. The mentors in this case often take this new role upon themselves without extra pay as part of their *organizational citizenship behavior*, which will be discussed in Chapter 12 (Allen, 2003). This often reflects the importance placed on a mentor's intrinsic motivation to enter this relationship, which attests to the essential role of the proactive caring motivation in this respect. Several professions, such as education, rely heavily on such mentoring bonds for initiating novice or preservice teachers to the school and the profession. Similarly, within the academic context, it is quite common to have an experienced faculty member guiding and mentoring graduate students or early-career members of faculty (see the review by Ehrich, Hansford, and Tennent, 2004). In what follows, I briefly discuss youth and workplace mentoring, with each exemplifying somewhat different issues related to the motivation to care. In particular I highlight the centrality of an intrinsic motivation to care in these relations, the diversity of provisions involved, and the multifaceted nature of this unique caring bond.

Youth mentoring

Mentoring relationships are among the most significant bonds that children form with nonparental nonprofessional figures (Klaw & Rhodes, 1995). Youth mentoring is naturally fairly common. For example, in national surveys of US youths, 50% to 80% report having a meaningful relationship with a nonparental adult. In national surveys of American adults, one of three surveyed reported having been a mentor at least once in their lives, mostly in a an unstructured and "natural" way, and one in seven reported being a mentor at the time of the survey (see review in DuBois & Karcher, 2005). Given that entering these relationships and staying in them is not obligatory, this amounts to saying that mentoring provides a common arena for the expression of our universal intrinsic motivation to care.

In "natural" mentoring, this valuable and beneficial relationship is embedded in the protégé's social network. However, natural mentors are not always part of the social network of youths from underprivileged or at-risk populations (Rhodes 2002). Organized mentoring programs have therefore been suggested and implemented to fill this gap. Organized, or formal, mentoring involves volunteers who are coupled with their protégés—often for a designated period of time. Their aim is to empower the protégés, promote their personal development, and compensate for their lack of role models (Keller, 2008). Research has demonstrated that such mentoring is successful. A meta-analysis of 55 evaluations of the effects of mentoring programs on youths found a modest to small benefit to participation in the program in the form of better social, emotional, and academic adjustment. Reflecting the importance of the bond in affecting the mentorship program's outcomes, the benefits for the mentees appear to increase significantly where relationships of greater intensity, duration (over one year), or quality were formed between the mentors and youths (DuBois, Holloway, Valentine, & Cooper, 2002; DuBois & Silverthorn, 2005). For example, in a study conducted in Israel's largest mentoring program (PERACH), which pairs students from disadvantaged backgrounds (mostly from elementary schools) with university student mentors for about nine months, greater closeness in the mentoring relations as reported by mentors and protégés alike predicted better social and academic functioning (Goldner & Mayseless, 2009). Similar effects were found in the United States's largest youth mentoring program—the Big Brothers, Big Sisters program—where youths who enjoyed a long duration of the bond (i.e., were mentored for more than a year) showed positive effects in levels of self-worth, perceived social acceptance, scholastic competence, parental relationship quality, school value, and level of drug and/or alcohol abuse (Grossman & Rhodes, 2002). This is not surprising given that mentoring is all about an ongoing caring relationship.

In line with the view of mentors as forging such caring relationship as an expression of their desire to care, mentors also benefit from the mentoring relationship as they experience satisfaction with their roles as mentors, a sense of self-worth, and enjoyment in sharing their expertise and gaining new personal insights (Gilles & Wilson, 2004). For college students who served as mentors, such mentoring also augmented their civic engagement, demonstrating that helping others may strengthen altruistic motives and attitudes (Weiler et al., 2013). These benefits for college students were found after controlling for age, gender, minority status, major, prior volunteer service, and preintervention level and was found even when mentoring was part of a mandatory program that still allowed for some measure of autonomy.

Researchers and practitioners have underscored the diversity and richness of the mentoring relationship as involving a mix of mutual yet asymmetrical facets and have highlighted the mentor's ability to meet a variety of the protégé's academic, work-related, personal development, and socioemotional needs. In fact, youth mentoring involves a variety of both affective (i.e., warmth, encouragement, companionship) and instrumental (i.e., teaching skills, exposing the protégé to new realms, strengthening competence) provisions (Darling, Hamilton, Toyokawa, & Matsuda, 2002). Goldner and Mayseless (2008) have suggested that the mentor-protégé relationship may involve interpersonal dynamics reflecting several roles, central among which are parent, therapist, friend, and teacher.

Goldner and Mayseless (2008) applied key concepts from attachment, social support, and social learning theories to demonstrate how mentors flexibly play these different roles to some degree without embodying any one of them in particular and suggest that the uniqueness of the mentoring role lies in its capacity to juggle these different roles. Consequently they argue that there might be different profiles of mentoring relationships and that these profiles might address different protégé needs. This diversity of provisions and the flexibility in providing them reflect the multifaceted, versatile, and sophisticated nature of the caring motivational system as it is manifested in nonobligatory and limited caring bonds.

Akin to the general findings regarding volunteering, volunteering to mentor is based on a similar profile of motivations with altruistic, other-directed motives such as "I feel it is important to help others" being the most prevalent. Yet other motives such as self-learning and understanding (i.e., "Mentoring allows me to gain a new perspective on things") also play important roles (Caldarella, Gomm, Shatzer, & Wall, 2010).

Mentoring at work

Traditionally, mentoring at work has been defined as a relationship between a more experienced (and usually older) mentor and a less experienced (usually younger) protégé for the purpose of helping and developing the protégé's career (Kram, 1985). Workplace mentorships are developmental helping relationships focused on the mentee's career and personal growth. Being mentored is often described as essential in young adults' early careers (Torrance, 1984; Kram, 1985) and is even viewed as an essential stage in anyone's career which, if successful, is seen as including four stages: apprentice, colleague, mentor, and sponsor (Dalton, Thompson, & Price, 1977). The inclusion of the mentorship role as part of one's career probably reflects the salience of generativity motives in adulthood.

A large number of studies conducted in diverse work contexts—such as academic institutions, law firms, high-tech companies, financial institutions and the military—have identified a high prevalence of mentoring, with 50% to 85% of employees recounting at least one significant mentoring relation throughout their careers in their institutions/organizations, and most reporting more than one such experience (e.g., Yoder, 1992; Allen, Poteet, Russell, & Dobbins, 1997; Steinberg & Foley, 1999). In fact, the term *developmental networks* was suggested to encompass the set of people that a protégé names as taking an active interest in him or her and acting to advance the protégé's career by providing developmental assistance (Higgins & Kram, 2001). A large number of major American corporations (e.g., MTV Networks, Lockheed-Martin, American Airlines, Bank of America, Charles Schwab, Mariott International, Sarah Lee, and Proctor and Gamble) currently have formal mentoring programs (Eddy, Tannenbaum, Alliger, D'Abate, & Givens, 2001). This high prevalence demonstrates both the need of novice workers to receive guidance and the importance of mentoring in their careers as well as the motivation of expert workers to engage in caring for others and assisting them on a regular basis and hence their wish to form sustained caring bonds in this context.

Diversity of provisions

As with youth mentoring, a diversity of provisions was noted, with two central kinds of support described as most frequent and referred to as career and psychosocial functions (Kram, 1985; Thomas, 1993). Career functions involve a range of behaviors that help protégés learn how things are done in a given organization, the "ins and outs" of the work and its social context, as well as the kinds of behavior that will help the mentee to advance within the organization. These mentoring behaviors include coaching protégés, sponsoring their advancement, increasing their positive exposure and visibility, and offering them both protection and challenging assignments. Mentors may also provide psychosocial functions based on trust, intimacy, and interpersonal bonds, which would include behaviors that enhance the protégé's professional and personal growth, identity, self-worth, and self-efficacy. In this capacity, mentors may engage in offering acceptance and confirmation and in providing counseling, friendship, and role modeling.

Reflecting the potential diversity of the provisions within the caring motivational system, career and psychosocial functions tend to have different roots and outcomes and to exhibit significant variability both within and across relationships (summarized in Ragins & Kram, 2007a). For example, career functions are mostly associated with the mentor's position and influence in the organization and directly affect protégés' compensation and advancement, whereas psychosocial functions depend to a greater degree on the quality of the emotional bond created and contribute to protégés' job and career satisfaction as well as their satisfaction from the relationship. Furthermore, the same person may mentor differently in different relationships and at different times and even within the same relationship, reflecting the versatility and flexibility involved in caregiving as part of caring bonds, even between nonkin.

Although mentoring at work is often not limited in time in advance, these bonds change and dissipate as the protégé's needs change and in response to organizational changes, including those that lead to a greater physical distance between the mentor and the protégé, which is one of the most prevalent reasons for a bond's dissipation. Thus assumption of the responsibility for care, which lies at the core of the caring bond, may not last forever. Nonetheless, some of the mentoring relations, especially those with prominent psychosocial functions, may turn into long-term intimate friendships as well (summarized in Ragins & Kram, 2007b).

Mentoring at work is generally successful in helping protégés. The results of a meta-analysis of studies examining mentoring at work indicate that mentored individuals were more satisfied with their careers, more likely to believe that they would advance in their careers, more likely to be committed to their careers, and more likely to report greater overall well-being as well as greater visibility and access to resources within their organizations. They were also more likely to attain higher salaries and a greater number of promotions than nonmentored individuals and reported a greater willingness to mentor others as their careers developed. These outcomes were associated with the extent of the mentor's provision of career and psychosocial functions (Russell & Adams, 1997; Allen et al., 2004).

As with youth mentoring, aspects relating to the quality of the relationship also appear to be central to the success of workplace mentorships. Mutuality and reciprocity, as well as relational skills such as empathetic and emotional competence, were identified as important. In addition, more instrumental and cognitive aspects—such as knowledge of the organization and industry and fluid expertise—appear to also be central according to the reports of both mentors and protégés (Allen & Poteet, 1999; Fletcher & Ragins, 2007).

Motives for mentoring others

As with other instances of caring, there are multiple possible reasons for engaging in mentoring. Employing both qualitative and quantitative methodologies on American participants, Allen and her colleagues identified a clear pattern of three central motivations (Allen, Poteet, & Burroughs, 1997; Allen, 2003). The first, "benefiting others," included other-focused motivations such as the desire to help others succeed in the organization and to benefit the organization; this was the strongest motive. The second, in terms of strength and centrality, related to "intrinsic satisfaction" and included references to the personal pride and gratification that comes from seeing the protégé grow and develop. Allen referred to this motive as self-focused, yet it is quite similar to the "warm glow" that is associated with generosity and parents' feelings of pride and joy when their child is successful. It is thus a sense of gratification from the achievements of the person that one has nurtured and helped to raise; it may be an outcome that serves as a proximate mechanism for sustaining caring rather than an actual motivation to care. The third and weakest motive was related to a self-focused extrinsic motivation of "self-enhancement" and included such aspects as "to enhance my visibility within the organization" and "to enhance my reputation in the department."

The motivation to mentor for the purpose of benefiting others—an altruistic, other-oriented motive reflecting the caring motivation—was the strongest by far and was positively and more strongly related than other motives to both career and psychosocial provisions, even after controlling for a large number of background variables such as age, gender, experience as a protégé, and prosocial dispositions. In another study conducted in a different cultural context—Singapore—altruism, assessed by the proclivity to engage in helping and altruistic behaviors, was positively associated with the willingness to mentor (Aryee, Chay, & Chew, 1996). Thus the motivational basis for mentoring behavior is most likely driven by concerns for the well-being of others and the organization, although, as with other caring pursuits, it is also motivated by self-interest.

As with prosocial behavior, engagement in actual mentoring is also related to the expected costs and benefits associated with being a mentor (Ragins & Scandura, 1999). Additionally, earlier experiences as a mentor, and prior experience as a protégé are strongly related to a future willingness to mentor. This may reflect a motivation to pass on to others what you have received as well as the importance of experience in receiving and in giving for the development of a proclivity to give to others (see Chapter 13 on the developmental course of the motivation to care). In addition, prosocial dispositions that reflect a prosocial personality facet, such as other-oriented empathy and helpfulness (Penner, Fritzsche, Craiger, & Friefield, 1995), were associated with the actual mentoring and the willingness to mentor (see summary in Allen, 2007).

Reflecting the tendency to help in-group members more than others, interpersonal similarity proved to be an important factor in mentor-protégé attraction and matching. Mentors indicated that they were attracted to protégés who reminded them of themselves earlier in their careers. Furthermore, mentors reported offering more career and psychosocial mentoring provisions to protégés who were perceived as being similar to themselves in intelligence, personality, background, ambition, education, and leisure activities (Burke, McKeen, & McKenna, 1993; Ensher & Murphy, 1997). Finally, research has also demonstrated that mentor-protégé similarity is an important element in relationship quality (Allen & Eby, 2003).

Growth-fostering motif vs. rescue-and-healing motif

Interestingly, mentoring at work was often related to a specific strand or facet of the motivation to care. In general, the overarching caring motivation involves sustaining and healing as well as helping someone grow, thrive, and prosper. The motivation to care as well as the formation of caring bonds can be enacted with any of these provisions as a goal. A great deal of the scholarship concerned with nurturing and caregiving focuses on cases that involve a person in distress or in need who summons the caregiver's empathy, compassion, and tender feelings (Brown, Brown, & Preston, 2012). In these circumstances, individuals will choose to form a caring bond in response to their aroused empathic concern stemming from the neediness, deprivation, or difficult situation of the potential care receiver. In other words, their offer of care may be characterized as reflecting a *rescue and healing motif.* In fact, it is often the case that this scenario is viewed as the characteristic caring "script" (Taylor, 2002; Shaver, Mikulincer, & Shemesh-Iron, 2010).

However, this is probably not the case in workplace mentoring relationships, where mentors often choose to form mentorships not on the basis of the neediness or the distress of the protégés. Most workplace mentors and protégés in the work environment generally have a say in the choice of their partner even in formal mentoring programs. In informal mentorships, many report that their mentoring relationship began mutually, or that it "just happened." Using interviews and quantitative methodologies, Allen and her colleagues found that mentors preferred and picked protégés who were high in ability, motivation (e.g., "willing to work hard," "has the drive to succeed"), and willingness to learn (e.g., "open mind to learning all the different ways of doing things"). Most importantly the protégé's *need* for help was not an important factor in instigating a mentorship (Allen, Poteet, & Burroughs, 1997; Allen et al., 2000, 2004).

It appears that care receivers are not chosen in workplace mentorships because they are in pain or at risk or because they are distressed or needy but because the provision of care can help them develop, grow, and thrive in their work and careers. Mentors choose those who could benefit from their care—those who show potential and are willing to learn. In other words, mentors look to form a caring bond where they can scaffold the protégé to success. Thus their choice of a protégé is not dictated by the greatest need but by who has the greatest capacity to benefit from the care they would like to bestow. Unlike the *rescue-and-healing motif*, which is often prevalent in caring acts with strangers, the main motif in workplace mentorships appears to reflect a *growth-fostering motif*, which involves furthering the thriving and growth of an already successful care receiver and helping that person move toward the realization of her or his potentials. Consequently one of the most rewarding experiences of mentors relates to rejoicing in and feeling proud of their protégé success. See, for example, how one mentor described this: "for me personally, I mean I got a good bit of satisfaction out of seeing these people succeed . . . . that was rewarding" (Eby & Lockwood, 2005, p. 449). In line with this suggestion, studies have found that mentors' other-oriented motivation to benefit their mentees and the organization was positively related to selecting protégés based on the latters' ability and their willingness to learn (Allen, 2004). This distinction may be similar to the observation in the social support literature discussed in Chapter 8 between caring to relieve distress and negative affect and caring in response to positive affective experiences.

It should thus come as no surprise that mentoring also benefits mentors. In mostly cross-sectional surveys, the mentoring of others was related to concurrent subjective career success and satisfaction as well as to tangible career benefits to the mentor, such as promotions and pay raises (Bozionelos, 2004). These benefits were found even after controlling for variances that could be attributed to demographic and human capital factors characterizing those who tend to mentor and that are often associated with career success (Allen, Lentz, & Day, 2006). Interestingly, both protégés and mentors reported learning as the most common benefit of both formal and informal mentoring (e.g., Allen, Poteet, & Burroughs, 1997; Eby & Lockwood, 2005). In mentors, this was also related to gaining a new perspective on their organizations and on themselves both personally and professionally. See, for example the following quotation from a mentor: "probably one of the biggest benefits is some self-reflection on your own leadership skills based on the things that the mentee shares with you" (Eby & Lockwood, 2005, p. 449). In that sense, the mentoring bond also helped mentors to develop and flourish as people.

Chapter conclusion

Volunteering, donating, and mentoring—all prosocial acts directed at unfamiliar others—appear to be quite widespread and, cultural diversity notwithstanding, expose a high prevalence of intrinsic giving and helping. In all three, researchers employing a variety of methodologies and terminologies have identified other-oriented motivations as the most salient and central impetus that directs individuals toward engagement in caring and helping. This research has also underscored the importance of this kind of motivation for the intervention's success as well as for its outcomes for both care receiver and caregiver. In fact, studies have demonstrated that caregivers—volunteers, donors, and mentors—accrue a variety of perhaps unintended positive benefits from their caring. This was related to tangible outcomes but most often to psychological ones (i.e., happiness, joy, warm glow, sense of meaning and mattering) and physical well-being (i.e., longevity). In addition, other studies have demonstrated the variety of provisions implicated in the expression of the caring motivation and the diversity of caring bond profiles, reflecting both a rescue-and-healing motif and a growth-fostering motif. Finally, studies have also demonstrated the multidimensionality of processes leading to caring and the similarity in the underlying biological and neurological processes between caring enacted with strangers and caring for close others. These included a strong effect exerted by a personality disposition toward helping (i.e., a prosocial or altruistic personality) as well as effects related to circumstantial empathy, prior experience both as a receiver and a giver, and processes related to values and moral identities.

11

Caring for Nonhuman Entities

Caring as a human motivation may not be limited to other humans. In fact, caring and nurturing has been both emotionally, cognitively, and behaviorally extended to animals (pets), vegetation (gardening), objects (dolls, collectibles), and even abstract entities (e.g., the environment). I believe that most people will view caring for pets as an extension of the general caring for close others and as similar to such caring in a large number of aspects. However, the other types of caring may be viewed as totally different, and some of my readers might argue that these sorts of caring behaviors do not constitute part of the general caring motivation. I chose to incorporate all these entities because I wanted to cast the largest possible net in covering the instances in which caring dynamics are at work. Adopting the "fuzzy set" notion described by Rosch (1973), I view the instances in which the motivation to care is enacted as a fuzzy set (i.e., a category with no clear boundaries but with instances that vary in their prototypicality). Some instances might be highly prototypical, such as maternal care, whereas others, such as caring for the environment, may lie at the categorical periphery. In this chapter, I would like to discuss what we currently know about these types of caring and to try and convince the skeptics that caring for humans as well as caring for nonhuman entities share a core of basic emotions, attitudes, cognitions, and behaviors that, as I will argue, reflect the general motivation to care.

As will be presented in this chapter, it appears that people form caring bonds with nonhuman entities in which they assume a responsibility to care for and ensure their well-being and thriving. Some of the manifestations of the motivation to care may constitute what appears to be a full-blown caring bond and involve intense emotions similar to those expressed toward intimate and close people. The adoption of pets and caring provided to them may sometimes involve such bonds. Other manifestations of the motivation to care may involve caring dynamics that reflect a more partial responsibility and more temperate emotions. In what follows, I will discuss four general categories of caring for nonhuman entities and helping them thrive, grow, and develop. These include caring for pets, or—as they are currently termed—companion animals, caring for plants and nurturing gardens, caring for inanimate entities (mostly objects), and even caring for nonmaterial abstract entities such as causes. These categories are differentiated by their degree of resemblance to humans. Clearly the more an entity resembles a human, the clearer and more natural the application of the motivation to care for it.

The discussion of the different instances will therefore serve to illustrate several noteworthy issues regarding the human motivation to care. First, as indicated, it will serve to highlight the breadth of the entities for which we care; Second, almost all of the instances discussed in this section clearly demonstrate the proactive nature of the motivation to care, as most involve a proactive decision by individuals or families to engage in caring and at times to form a caring bond as a result of a proactive and intrinsic search and decision. A third issue involves the growing literature demonstrating the positive outcomes for the caregiver accrued by such caring. A large part of the literature on caring for nonhuman entities has demonstrated clear health benefits for the caregiver from caring and from the formation of such intrinsic caring bonds. Although the literature on the more prototypical instances of caring is replete with discussions of the burden of care, caring for pets and gardens accrues a large number of positive benefits to the caregiver, as will be highlighted below. A fourth aspect relates to the interesting combination of motivational systems that is often present in these instances of caring. In a large number of cases, what we observe is a combination of attachment, companionship, and caring dynamics. For example, individuals care for their pets but also derive deep satisfaction from this relationship based on a sense of companionship and security. In some cases, therefore, both the giving and receiving ends of the relation are expressed and are somewhat inseparable.

Caring for pets

The profound relational significance of human-animal bonds has been documented throughout history and across cultures (Ritvo, 1987; Serpell, 1987, 1995; Franklin, 1999). The last two decades have seen a surge in research on the human bond with companion animals, demonstrating its prevalence and psychological significance as well as its benefits for health and well-being throughout life (Walsh, 2009a). Owning pets is first and foremost an act of caring, since it entails a large number of caring responsibilities (Zimolag, 2011). For example, pet owners need to provide daily food and water for their pets; they need to secure an indoor and/or outdoor living space (or enclosure), and they are responsible for their pet's health care and well-being. In the case of dogs, for example, they must also ensure that they are exercised and groomed.

Pet ownership is quite common. More than 60% of North American households own a pet (Zimolag, 2011), and over 75% of households with children care for at least one pet (Walsh, 2009a). Dogs are the most common pets, followed by cats. Almost all pet owners regard their pets as their friends (95%) and/or family members (87%). At the heart of the human-pet relationship is a unique affectionate bond (Podberscek, Paul, & Serpell, 2000). Consequently 87% of pet owners include their pets in holiday celebrations; 65% sing or dance for a pet; 52% prepare special meals for their pets, 53% take time off from work to care for a sick pet; and 36% of Americans celebrate their pets' birthdays (Wells & Perrine, 2001). This strong sense of closeness and responsibility is also manifested in monetary investments, as in costly and extensive medical treatments for illnesses and in a range of consumer products and services, from special meals and toys to ergonomic feeding tables and day spas (Walsh, 2009a).

Pets offer an opportunity to nurture others, since they are forever dependent on their owners (Gunter, 1999). Thus they may function as surrogate children for childless couples (Veevers, 1980) and for parents whose children have grown up and who wish to prolong their parental role (Gunter, 1999). The term *pet* probably originated from the French word *petit* (meaning small) and is thus related to an important aspect of a large number of pets: their small size, which arouses the motivation to care for them like babies or small children (Katcher & Beck, 1987). Katcher and Beck (1987), for example, have engaged in a lengthy discussion of how keeping a pet resembles the nurturing provided to human infants and have suggested that caring for a pet is an extension of human nurturance. Indeed, nearly all the characteristics of "motherese," the style that parents use in talking to babies and very young children, have also been found in human-animal interactions (Katcher & Beck, 1987).

Besides the caring motivation, there are other motivations, such as the need for companionship and affiliation or security, that may also underlie the desire to adopt a pet. Pets have been found to fulfill a variety of psychological needs, such as providing the opportunity to care (which is the focus of this book), providing companionship, facilitating contact with others, providing a feeling of being protected, serving as status symbols, and offering social support (Gunter, 1999). For example, dogs that are properly cared for offer love, loyalty, and a devotion that is unconditional, consistent, and nonjudgmental in return. Dogs greet their human companions enthusiastically even on their worst days; they accept their human companions as they are, forgive mistakes, and do not need to talk things through. Thus pets often provide a reliable, consistent, and "uncomplicated" bond. Some owners even view their pets as their "significant others" and "soul mates." The companionship of a pet can have compensatory qualities, as suggested by the stronger attachment to pets shown by those with relatively few social contacts (Stallones, Marx, Garrity, & Johnson, 1990) as well as by single, divorced, and widowed individuals (Albert & Bulcroft, 1988). The benefits of the human-pet relationship are so strong that even the homeless often choose to keep pets despite their cost, reporting that their companionship and affection make it worthwhile (Kidd & Kidd, 1994).

A number of behavioral systems, to use the terms of attachment researchers, are clearly involved. The affectionate bond with pets reflects attachment dynamics and specifically a sense of closeness, of being unconditionally accepted, and of feeling secure and protected throughout the relationship (Melson, 1990). The owner-pet bond also includes a companionship facet that involves having fun together and enjoying each other's company. Furthermore, and in line with the focus of this book, the affectionate bond between an owner and a pet includes a clear caregiving aspect that involves the assumption of responsibility for the pet and the indispensability of the owner for the pet's survival. The caring bond also incorporates a sense of happiness, joy, and pride at the pet's accomplishments as well as a sense of meaning in life that comes from being needed and depended on and from contributing to the thriving of another entity.

The decision to adopt a pet is a good example of a proactive search for the opportunity to care. The widespread motivation for adopting pets starts quite early. Children aged 3 to 13 years report a near universal (98% to 99%) desire for a pet (Kidd & Kidd, 1985). When this desire is realized, children rank their relationship with their pets as among their most intimate (Melson, 2001), often considering them part of the family (Beck & Katcher, 1983). They also report that having pets makes them feel good and satisfied with themselves (Juhasz, 1985). One of the reasons for this satisfaction may be the opportunity for caregiving that pet care offers. Children report providing more nurturance to their pets than to anyone else in their social networks (Furman 1989) and feel that this is an important part of their relationship with the pet (Melson, 2003). The fact that children who lack younger siblings spend more time caring for their pets supports the notion that caring for others is a basic need among children and that pet keeping may serve as one of its outlets (Melson, 2003). Pets also offer boys an opportunity to nurture in a gender-appropriate manner. Specifically, whereas children view caring for babies as a female activity, caring for animals is considered gender-neutral. Accordingly and as they grow up, girls increase and boys decrease their participation in child care but continue to nurture their pets equally (Melson, 2003). In fact, most of the research in this field did not find gender differences in pet ownership, as inferred from several wide-scale surveys of adults in the United States, Australia, and Northern Ireland. Similar findings were reported with children and adolescents, where boys and girls did not differ in the frequency of pet ownership (see review in Herzog, 2007).

A large number of studies have documented the positive health benefits of having a companion animal (see review in an edited book by McCardle, McCune, Griffin, & Maholmes, 2011, and a paper cautioning against premature optimism concerning these effects in Herzog, 2011). Specifically, relations with companion animals contribute to good health, psychosocial well-being, and recovery from a variety of serious conditions including heart disease and other health problems (Barker et al., 2003; Friedmann & Tsai, 2006; Wells, 2009). Research evidence has demonstrated associations between pet ownership and positive physiological measures, such as lower blood pressure and cholesterol levels. In addition, people who acquire pets report improved health over subsequent months compared with controls, and pet owners receiving Medicaid make fewer visits to their physicians than nonowners. Longitudinal research spanning more than two decades in nationally representative samples in Germany (N = 9,723) and Australia (N = 1,246) found that continuous pet owners were the healthiest group (Headley & Grabka, 2007), an association that remained significant after controlling for a variety of variables associated with health, such as gender, age, marital status, and income. Interestingly, the presence of a pet was found to be more effective than that of a spouse or friend in ameliorating the cardiovascular effects of stress (Allen, Blascovich, & Mendes, 2002). Following a heart attack, patients with pets also had a significantly higher one-year survival rate than those without pets, even after controlling for physiological severity, demographics, and other psychosocial factors. Dog owners (N = 87, 1 died) were significantly less likely to die within one year than those who did not own dogs (N = 282, 19 died) (Friedmann, Katcher, Lynch, & Thomas, 1980; Friedmann & Thomas, 1995).

Attenuation of stress responses—as demonstrated by decreased sympathetic arousal and higher heart rate variability—is probably among the mechanisms involved in the cardiovascular benefits of pet ownership that might be responsible for the differences in survival between pet owners (and especially dog owners) and nonowners (Friedmann, Thomas, Stein, & Kleiger, 2003). As far as the mechanisms involved in such effects are concerned, interactions with companion animals were found to increase the level of neurochemicals associated with relaxation and bonding and thus to improve the functionality of the human immune system (Charnetsky, Riggers, & Brennan, 2004). In line with the idea that the human-pet bond is a caregiving bond akin to that of mothers and infants, dog owners showed higher oxytocin levels after playing with their dogs as a function of the frequency of the dog's gaze at them (Nagasawa, Kikusui, Onaka, & Ohta, 2009). Katcher (1981) remarks that the health benefits of caring for pets relate to the inherent benefits of responsibility for the well-being of another living being and its concomitant displays of physical affection.

In the same vein, animal-assisted activities and therapies have recently become increasingly widespread and have been implemented in a variety of contexts (e.g., Walsh, 2009b; see also the edited volume by Fine, 2006). Studies of these interventions have reported positive outcomes with children, adolescents, and the elderly. For example, a well-replicated intervention program in the course of residential treatment that provided opportunities for forming a bond with an animal, taking responsibility for its care, and experiencing empathy and non-threatening affection elicited a range of prosocial behaviors, including nurturing, affection, cooperation, lower aggression, and responsibility among children and adolescents with severe conduct disorders (Katcher & Wilkins, 2000). Assuming responsibility for animals, grooming and training them, and engaging in affectionate touching with them help youths by enhancing their confidence and teaching them to relate empathically and prosocially to others. These positive effects are also clear with adult populations. For example, a recent meta-analysis of studies using animal-assisted therapy with elderly participants and people suffering from depression and schizophrenia found a very large effect size for improved social functioning and more moderate effects for decreased depression, anxiety, and behavioral disturbances.

In sum, the motivation to adopt pets is almost universal among children and having a pet is widespread among households, with more than 60% of the population being involved in caring for a pet. For the most part, caring for a pet involves an affectionate bond that reflects the dynamics of various behavioral systems, including attachment, companionship, and caring. The caring facet is clear because pets depend on their owners' care. Such proactive and intrinsically chosen care is associated with positive health benefits to the caregivers' physical as well as psychological well-being. These benefits are also related to a large number of other aspects, such as physical exercise, the opportunity to socialize with others through pet ownership and caring, companionship and fun, the opportunity for affectionate touching, the feeling of being loved and welcomed, and last but certainly not least, the sense of meaning and significance attained from caring for another living thing that is dependent on its owner and the satisfaction derived from its thriving and well-being. It is therefore hardly surprising that a growing number of studies of animal-assisted interventions and therapies provided evidence for their positive benefits.

Caring for plants and gardens

Although caring for pets appears to be a natural extension of care for children, this is less obvious in caring for plants or gardens. Such caring has not been studied extensively despite its relatively high prevalence. For example, a very high proportion of urban households lacking a private garden grow house plants ranging from a small selection of several plants to a full in-house "garden." There are also large numbers of people who take care of domestic gardens near their homes. A 2003 survey by the US National Gardening Association found that 78% of US households (84 million people) engage in lawn maintenance and garden activities (Clayton, 2007) and 35 million occupants identify themselves as gardeners (Kiesling & Manning, 2010). In the United Kingdom around 84% of the population has access to a home garden, with around 52% involved in some form of cultivation (Bhatti & Church, 2004). Another British study estimates that 67% of the population are amateur gardeners (Gross & Lane, 2007).

People also voluntarily own and tend "allotment gardens." These are small land parcels between 50 and 400 square meters in size that are concentrated in one place, typically somewhere in a city or its suburbs; plots in such gardens are assigned to individuals or families who usually form a registered association. An allotment garden is made legally available by city authorities to be used exclusively for growing vegetables, fruits, and flowers but not for residential purposes (Holmer, Clavejo, Dongus, & Drescher, 2003). Current estimates suggest that millions of people in Europe cultivate such gardens (en.wikipedia.org/wiki/Allotment [gardening], retrieved October 23, 2013). The current system of allotment gardens has its roots in 19th-century Europe, when land was given to the laboring poor for growing their own food. Today most people tend their allotment gardens as a leisure activity rather than primarily as a source of food (Hassink & Van Dijk, 2006). There are also common gardens where the entire area is collectively tended by a group of people.

The significance of gardening is also evident in other respects besides its prevalence. Gardening is a pastime on which many people spend significant amounts of time and money and that they consider to be important to their social and personal identities (Kaplan & Kaplan, 1989). These people usually invest themselves creatively, financially, physically, and emotionally in the garden, so that it becomes a significant part of their lives (Clayton, 2007). Why would people invest so much in gardening? In a survey of over 4,000 members of the American Horticultural Society, sensory aspects (colors, smells, and beauty), peacefulness, tranquility, and fascination with nature were rated as the most important benefits of gardening (Kaplan & Kaplan, 1989). Similar findings were reported in a study conducted almost 20 years later (Clayton, 2007). These findings are consistent with the predictions of the biophilia hypothesis, which suggests that humans have a genetically based predisposition to affiliate with nature (Wilson, 1984; Kellert & Wilson, 1993).

According to Wilson's biophilia hypothesis, humans possess an "innate tendency to focus on life and lifelike processes" (Wilson, 1984). Specifically they are inclined to respond positively to such natural features as have promoted human survival in the course of evolution, such as bodies of water, grasslands, and certain trees and flowers. Support for this proposal has been found in the positive effects of viewing natural scenes on physical and mental well-being (e.g., Moore, 1982; Ulrich, 1984; Ulrich et al., 1991; Parsons, Tassinary, Ulrich, Hebl, & Grossman-Alexander, 1998). Spending time in natural environments has also been found to promote relaxation and recovery from illnesses (for a review, see Kaplan & Kaplan, 1989). Wilson (1984) suggests that people's attraction to nature also causes them to wish to cherish and protect it. Similarly, Kellert (1993) argues that humans are biologically inclined to feel an emotional connection to nature and a sense of responsibility for its welfare. However, he also recognizes the (likewise innate) need to control and exploit our natural surroundings.

Fromm (1964/2011) argues that this innate emotional bond with nature involves "a reverence for life, all that enhances life, growth, unfolding" (Fromm, 1964/2011, p. 43), and that this bond generates a creative and deeply caring attitude toward nature, which is perceived by him as reflecting the heart of human nature and signifying the psychological and moral height of human striving. Similarly Weinstein, Przybylski, and Ryan (2009) suggest that immersion in nature supports autonomy, being in touch with oneself, having a sense of inner congruency and the feeling that one can express oneself or behave in ways that are self-endorsed, among them caring. In line with this depiction, they found that immersion in nature promotes more intrinsic and enjoyable pursuits, facilitates the adoption of more intrinsic prosocial values, and being more caring and generous.

In light of this human attraction to natural environments, it is not surprising that many choose to have such an environment in their homes in the form of gardens. And indeed, as indicated previously, such factors as a fascination with nature and its calming effects have been cited as major motivations for gardening (Kaplan & Kaplan 1989; Clayton, 2007). Caring for one's garden also has other, more social uses, such as reflecting personality and taste (Francis, 1990; Twigger-Ross & Uzzell, 1996; Gross & Lane, 2007), expertise (Nassauer, 1988), and social status (Jenkins, 1994). It can also be seen as caring for the neighborhood (Robbins, Polderman, & Birkenholtz, 2001) and as demonstrating conformity to its norms (Nassauer, 1988). Lawns and gardens may also serve other psychological functions, such as the human control of nature. People thus tend gardens for a number of reasons: to be close to nature, to socialize, to relax and unwind, for physical exercise, and in order to satisfy the motivation to care (Francis & Hester, 1990).

Plants are animate and thus often need care in order to survive. Caring for a garden entails personal involvement and assumption of the responsibility to take care of it. This responsibility includes a large number of caring activities, such as planning what the garden should look like, buying plants, planting them, weeding, watering, digging, pruning, using pesticides, fertilizing, and generally planning the garden's growth, maintaining its viability, and nurturing it so that it flourishes and grows as planned while protecting it from harm. In fact, gardeners often develop a strong caring relation toward their gardens (Bhatti, Church, Claremont, & Stenner, 2009).

These special caring relations were revealed in a large number of studies that examined gardeners. Bhatti, Church, Claremont and Stenner (2009), for example, reported on a qualitative study based on data drawn from the Mass Observation Archive in the United Kingdom; they found that the domestic garden was experienced as an intimate place in everyday life. People enjoyed the physical work and the touch of earth and plants. They were also enchanted by the beauty of nature. In line with the topic of this book, they found that gardening involved a strong manifestation of care and concern in which gardeners culti-vated relationships with nonhuman entities such as the plants, trees, birds, and animals in the garden.

Other studies have demonstrated that gardeners not only care for their gardens and invest instrumentally in them but are also emotionally involved with their gardens and with specific plants and trees in them. They feel proud and happy if the garden looks pretty and neat, if the flowers bloom and the trees bear fruit. Gardeners further feel alarmed and even gloomy if a beloved tree catches a disease or a storm spoils a budding flower bed (Hitchings, 2003; Gross & Lane, 2007). The resulting bond with the garden can be quite strong (Gross & Lane, 2007) and may even have compensatory qualities for those without a caregiving role, such as the elderly (Heliker, Chadwick, & O'Connell, 2000; Martin, Baldwin, & Bean, 2008). A vivid example of this can be seen in the words of an elderly lady who compared taking pictures of her flowers to taking pictures of her grandchildren, because "it kind of replaces the need when you don't get to be with your loved ones" (Heliker et al., 2000, p. 50).

Gardeners view the garden as alive and the plants as "endearing companions" in need of constant maintenance and care (Hitchings, 2003). They feel respon-sible for making sure that the garden is well kept and that all the plants, trees, and flowers get the care they need. In fact, gardeners monitor the welfare of their plants in a way that clearly resembles the care provided to animate beings and to humans (Hitchings, 2003). For example, in a study of experienced gardeners in London, one interviewee directly compared caring for his garden to pet keeping and raising children (Hitchings, 2003, p. 106):

> Peter: *I think it's almost like keeping dogs . . . you know, they are one's familiars.*
> Interviewer: *Yes?*
> Peter: *Oh yes, definitely. You know one needs to water them and feed them and to protect them from the greenfly and the snails . . . and, oh yes, it's definitely a child-substitute in some ways.*

Gardeners often consider their relationship with their garden as reciprocal, with the garden "giving back" in return for the gardener's continued efforts (Hitchings, 2003; Milligan, Gatrell & Bingley, 2004; Gross & Lane, 2007). In that sense, the garden is perceived as a special amalgamation of the vital force of nature and its beauty and the gardener's investment in care (Power, 2005). Interestingly, signs of such human care as reflected in the appearance of a cared-for garden arouse perceptions of attractiveness and beauty among onlookers (Nassauer, 1988). This might be related to the hybrid nature of a domestic garden. It is part of nature and thus arouses positive sentiments and feelings toward nature, such as those suggested by biophilia theorists, but it is also the gardener's creation and is thus also judged from an esthetic perspective (Cooper, 2006). Moreover, the garden is not a static work of art; it is a living, growing, and developing one, and the relations between gardeners and their gardens are often close care relationships with certain reciprocal elements. This special quality is related to the special role of gardening as a source of meaning.

Caring for and about gardens gives gardeners a sense of meaning and purpose in life (e.g., Kidd & Brascamp, 2004; Freeman, Dickinson, Porter, & van Heezik, 2012). In a study of 361 New Zealand gardeners, for example, Kidd and Brascamp (2004) found strong associations between gardening and feelings of autonomy, self-acceptance, positive relations with others, and purpose in life. This sense of meaning and purpose is manifested in a variety of ways. One way relates to the emotional bond with the garden which provides meaning and purpose and may function like other affectional bonds as described earlier (Hitchings, 2003). Another way is the garden's unique status as the gardener's creation on one hand but also a product of nature—a large, infinite, enchanting, and grand entity—on the other (Cooper, 2006). This cocreative aspect often constitutes a transcendental connection and evokes feelings of fascination, awe, and enchantment among gardeners, leading to such descriptions as flowers being the "essence of the soul" (Bhatti et al., 2009). In that sense, the gardeners' connection with their gardens and their acts of caring for it may represent a spiritual connection to a larger, infinite, and divine entity (Stokols, 1990). Here are some examples of how elderly gardeners have described this type of spiritual experience (Heliker, Chadwick, & O'Connell, 2000, p. 50): "'a wonderment between myself and God . . . it's as close as you can be [to God]"; "the most worthwhile thing you can do. It teaches you how to grow. Like the parable of the seed, it teaches life cycles"; "It gives you a new lease on life. I talk to the Lord when I work with flowers."

Yet another way in which gardens provide meaning and purpose is the sense of continuity and connection afforded by specific trees, flowers, smells, and activities in the garden. Gardeners have reported that their gardens connected them to childhood experiences, to important people and significant events in their lives (e.g., Bhatti et al., 2009). The living garden thus provides continuity with the past and maintains connections to experiences that constitute important aspects of one's identity. See, for example, this statement from a 72-year-old woman (Bhatti et al., 2009; p. 70):

> When my husband was alive he used to look after the plants and flowers in the house—now I treasure the plants he grew and look after them like the apple of my eye! Most of my "gardening" is done on my husband's grave, where I really do take a great deal of trouble to keep it looking lovely all the year round. My pride are some rosebushes I planted on the occasion of each of my granddaughters' births and they flower beautifully each year.

Caring for a garden can thus be seen as reflecting the proactive nature of the fundamental caring motivation and as with other manifestations of the motivation to care, it offers the gardener a sense of meaning and purpose in life.

Interestingly, and as with adopting pets, gardening has also been shown to contribute to physical and psychological well-being. A study of 863 Dutch men aged 65 to 84, for example, revealed significant correlations between gardening and healthy levels of total cholesterol, high-density lipoprotein cholesterol, and systolic blood pressure (Caspersen, Bloemberg, Saris, Merritt, & Kromhout, 1991). Evidence for the effectiveness of gardening as a means of relieving acute stress was also provided by an experimental study conducted with allotment gardeners (Van Den Berg & Custers, 2011). After being exposed to a stressful task, gardeners were randomly assigned to conditions of either caring for their own allotment or reading in their allotment shack. As expected, gardening promoted a stronger psychophysiological recovery from stress than did indoor reading. After 30 minutes of gardening, the levels of salivary cortisol and a self-reported "positive mood" had fully returned to their baseline. Reading also led to some reduction of cortisol levels, but this was weaker and not accompanied by an increase in the participants' positive mood. Unsurprisingly, relaxation and stress relief are among the most prevalent self-reported benefits of gardening (Armstrong, 2000; Dunnett & Qasim, 2000; Catanzaro & Ekanem, 2004; Clayton, 2007). This may also be related to caring for house plants. In reviewing more than 20 studies on the psychological benefits of indoor plants, Bringslimark, Hartig, and Patil (2009) concluded that these studies suggest that indoor plants can provide such psychological benefits as stress-reduction and increased pain tolerance.

Thus, and as with animal-assisted therapies, horticultural therapy and therapeutic horticulture have been developed. Horticultural therapy is "the use of plants by a trained professional as a medium through which certain clinically defined goals may be met" (Sempik et al., 2003). Therapeutic horticulture does not have a predefined goal but is geared toward well-being in general (Elings, 2006).

Horticultural therapy has reportedly been effective in the treatment of a variety of psychiatric conditions, such as anxiety (Lee et al. 2004; Stepney & Davis 2004), depression (Stepney & Davis 2004; Gonzalez et al. 2010), posttraumatic stress (Atkinson, 2009), and substance abuse (Cornille, Rohrer, Phillips, & Mosier, 1987; Benson, 1996). Gardening has also been successfully used with youths (e.g., Robinson & Zajicek, 2005), but many of these studies have been inconclusive or anecdotal and lacked the scientific rigor to substantiate the suggested benefits (see review in Phibbs & Relf, 2005). Horticultural therapy is especially suitable for the elderly and was found to improve elderly patients' psychological well-being (Heliker, Chadwick, & O'Connell, 2001) and satisfaction with life (Tse, 2010).

Clinicians and researchers have suggested a number of reasons for the positive effects of horticultural therapy and therapeutic horticulture on well-being, several of which have already been discussed (Simson & Straus, 1998). First, gardens and plants tend to elicit positive responses in humans. According to the attention restoration theory, for example, nature has a calming and restorative effect because, unlike modern stimuli, which require directed attention, nature stimulates automatic, effortless attention (Kaplan & Kaplan, 1989). Second, the physical work and exercise that are part of gardening contribute to the fitness of the gardener and provide a sense of efficacy and competence. Another beneficial aspect (Elings, 2006) that is highly pertinent to this book is that such therapies involve the nurturance of another living thing. Sustaining life in another entity can lead to a sense of accomplishment, efficacy, and control (Shapiro & Kaplan, 1998). Plants are especially suited for this purpose, as they are nonjudgmental and respond to anyone who cares for them (Lewis, 1995). Horticultural therapy and therapeutic horticulture were thus seen as valuable contexts for providing an opportunity to experience responsibility and care for "others" (Simson & Straus, 1998). These points of views accord with the proposition that caring and form-ing a caregiving bond can have positive health benefits for the caregivers (Post, 2007), especially since such care affords a sense of meaning and purpose and thus contributes to eudaemonic well-being.

Caring for inanimate objects and abstract entities

The proposition that the motivation to care is also enacted with regard to animals, plants, and objects is especially challenging with objects, because mechanisms that have evolved in relation to our involvement with the material world may dif-fer from those that have evolved in relation to our involvement with the social world or with living things. However, using some imagination and a capacity for projection, we are capable of animistic attributions and hence of imbuing objects with human-like or animate properties. We can thus care for dolls as if they were human (Caldera & Sciaraffa, 1998) and feel empathy toward digital characters in a computer game (Misselhorn, 2009). Consequently, when we apply animistic perspectives to objects, they too may be the target of our motivation to care. In what follows I will discuss caring relations and caring dynamics with objects and with abstract and nonmaterial entities.

Caring for objects—dolls

Humans are clearly capable of animistic perceptions, cognitions, and emotions. Toddlers treat dolls and other toys as if they were living things and play with them while demonstrating empathy and care. Toddlers as young as 20 months of age, for example, initiated more caregiving behaviors towards baby as opposed to clown dolls, and this preference was similar across the toddlers' gender (Caldera

& Sciaraffa, 1998). Throughout human history and in diverse cultural contexts, dolls have been used in play to enact nurturance, tending, and care. Play is a ubiquitous activity with a large number of possible purposes (Pellegrini, 2010), one of the most important of which is learning. Play socializes and prepares the young for their adult roles in humans as well as in a large number of nonhuman species (Millar, 1968; Fagen, 1981); it can serve as a training ground for many adult roles and skills. In order for an activity to be considered play, the experience must include a measure of inner control and the ability to imagine and make believe; it must reflect a facet of autonomous choice that does not have a particular outcome as its purpose (Frost, Wortham, & Reifel, 2012; Dietze & Kashin, 2011). In that sense, playing with dolls in a caregiving capacity is a reflection of a proactive desire/motivation to engage in caring.

Playing with dolls in a caregiving role requires the activation of role-playing capacities and imagination, whereby the doll is seen as requiring nurturance and care. It is part of a general make-believe capacity and pursuit that is common among children (Fein, 1981; Nielsen, 2012). For example, in what has become a classic study, observations in a preschool nursery indicated that playing family, house, and dolls was the second most frequent type of play and elicited the most complex social interactions (Parten, 1933). Playing with dolls in a caregiving role consists of tending the dolls and includes such activities as dressing and undressing them, rocking them to sleep, "feeding" them, and putting them to bed, and comforting them in clear imitation of parental roles and caregiving actions. This caregiving play becomes more sophisticated as children grow older and is particularly apparent between 2 and 7 years of age (Watson & Fischer, 1980; also see edited book by Bretherton, 1984). This activity includes episodes of solitary play as well as others of dramatic play with peers or adults. At first, the child is active and the doll is a passive recipient of the child's action. At a more advanced level, and especially toward the age of three, the child "acts out" both roles and manipulates the doll as if it were acting on its own (i.e., crying, walking, demanding care—Watson & Fischer, 1977). By four years of age children are able to "make a doll talk" as if it were a baby and to talk to the doll in the role of a parent (Sachs & Devin, 1976). Within the frequent pretend and dramatic play, the enacted caring relationship evolves and becomes an ongoing complex story or relationship script in which the child occupies the role of caregiver (Howes & Matheson, 1992).

Caring, tending, and nurturing actions toward dolls thus begin at quite an early stage as part of make-believe play, reflecting an enactment of caring for "objects" imbued with human-like needs, emotions, and cognitions through imagination and projection. Such caring can develop also into an affectionate bond with one or more specific dolls. These relations are for the most part observed with girls more than with boys. In a large number of households, children who own dolls become attached to them, give them specific names and personalities, and engage in an affectional caring relationship with them. As with pets and gardens, there are probably several motivational systems at work here. Some of these dolls also serve as transitional objects and provide a sense of security and stability, reflecting the operation of the attachment behavioral system. At the same time, the child-doll relationship also reflects the caregiving end and involves the dynamics of care, nurturance, and protection.

Being a frequent and universal phenomenon, such caring reflects the centrality of the motivation to care, the wish to play out this role, and perhaps to "train" for it in the arena of play. Although the motivation to enact such caring may rest on a variety of sources, the most obvious is the caring motivation, which is already observed by the beginning of the second year of life (Hay, 2009; Warneken & Tomasello, 2009; Brownell, 2013; see also Chapter 13). Yet, such caring can also reflect the children's motivation to imitate their parents, who serve as sources for modeling. The social learning perspective suggests that parents and others can reinforce such behaviors by various means of socialization, such as employing rewards or punishments, using explanations and persuasions, and arranging situations and circumstances that encourage the practice of care, such as buying dolls (Maccoby, 1998).

Gender effects in doll play

Social learning perspectives are also relevant when we attempt to explain the clear gender difference in playing with dolls. Playing with dolls appears to be a central category of play for girls to a greater extent than for boys, especially as part of a general category of playing "house." Gender differences in such play appear from the age of two and become more and more salient during the preschool years and in school-age children. Girls' play generally contains more nurturing themes than boys', especially insofar as dolls are concerned (Blakemore, & Centers, 2005). For example, as early as 1933, Parten's preschool observations found that the sex difference was slight in the dramatization of home and family that did not involve dolls but that doll play occurred three times as frequently with girls than with boys. In a large number of households and cultures, it is the mothers who are mostly charged with caring for infants and toddlers, and the majority of gender norms reflect different expectations for males and females insofar as engagement in caring is concerned (Wood & Eagly, 2002). Thus parents, other caregivers, and the cultural context may be seen as exerting various socialization efforts in this direction. There are a large number of studies demonstrating the biased attitudes of mothers, fathers, and the general cultural context toward buying dolls for girls rather than boys and toward encouraging girls' doll play to a greater extent than boys' doll play (Maccoby, 1998; Campenni, 1999). Moreover, the theory of and research on gender schemes suggest that an identification with and the internalization of the cultural gender scheme may lead to differential adoption of caring as an activity and a motivation by girls vs. boys (Campbell, Shirley, & Caygill, 2002).

Sex differences may also arise in part from early hormonal differences between boys and girls (Hines, 2004). More specifically, it was suggested that high concentrations of androgens, hormones typically produced in large amounts by the male fetus, lead to brain masculinization and increased male-typical behavior. Indeed, girls with a genetic condition in which the female fetus is exposed to abnormally high concentrations of androgens (congenital adrenal hyperplasia, or CAH), spend more time playing with masculine toys and less time playing with feminine toys as compared with control group girls (Berenbaum & Hines, 1992; Nordenstrom, Servin, Bohlin, Larsson, & Wedell, 2002; Meyer-Bahlburg et al., 2004; Pasterski et al., 2005). This occurs despite the finding that parents encourage feminine toy play rather than masculine toy play in CAH-positive daughters more than in other daughters (Pasterski et. al., 2005). Furthermore, a regular variability in prenatal androgen exposure was also associated with male-typical behavior (i.e., interest in real cars, trains, and airplanes, playing with swords or playing with a tool set (Hines et al., 2002; Auyeung et al., 2009). Finally, sex-typed toy preferences similar to those seen in children have also been reported in vervet and rhesus monkeys (Alexander & Hines, 2002; Hassett, Siebert, & Wallen, 2008).

This sex-typed toy preference appears quite early in humans and even before the full acquisition of gender schemes and a possible identification with the same-sex parent. Examining preferences for different toys, colors, and shapes in 12- to 24-month-old infants, Jadva, Hines, and Golombok (2010) found that girls looked at dolls significantly more than did boys and that boys looked at cars significantly more than did girls. These outcomes were also seen with younger infants; even though 12-month-old boys too looked at dolls more than they looked at cars, girls still looked at dolls longer than the boys did. Interestingly, it was the identity of the toy rather than its color or general shape that was relevant (Jadva, Hines, & Golombok, 2010). The strong gender effect with regard to doll play notwithstanding, it is clear that caring for dolls reflects a motivation to provide care and nurturance whose origin may be multidetermined and may reflect nature and nurturing effects. Chapter 15 is devoted to the discussion of gender differences in caring.

Caring for objects—artificial pets

There are other toys besides dolls that were purposefully created to enlist the motivation to care, such as the Tamagotchi keychain pet (Retrieved October 31, 2013; http://en.wikipedia.org/wiki/Tamagotchi) or the AIBO, an artificial dog (Kahn, Friedman, & Hagman, 2003). These toys and others that serve as mechanical or artificial pets provide an interesting case for examining the enactment of the caring motivation. One of the most successful toys to date in this category, the Tamagotchi, is physically unremarkable: it is a small plastic keychain egg with simple animations on a low-resolution screen. Yet people became extremely attached to it, assigning a high priority to caring for it and mourning it when it "died." The Tamagotchi was first sold in Japan in 1996; as of 2013, about 80 million have been sold worldwide.

A Tamagotchi is a keychain-sized virtual simulation game featuring simplistically designed creatures. According to their "background story," Tamagotchis are a small alien creatures who have deposited eggs on Earth to see what life is like, and it is up to the player to raise such an egg into an adult "creature." The creature goes through several stages of growth and will develop differently depending on the care the player provides, with better care resulting in an adult creature that is smarter, happier, and more independent. Hence players can care for their pets as much or as little as they choose, with the eventual outcome depending on the players' actions. Pets have a hunger meter, a happiness meter, and a discipline meter to determine how healthy and well behaved they are. Filling up the hunger meter can be achieved by feeding the pet a meal or a snack. Filling up the happiness meter can be achieved by playing minigames with the pet. The discipline meter can be filled by selecting the "scold" option when a pet calls for attention but refuses to play or be fed. The pet will also leave droppings around the screen from time to time and can become sick if they are not cleaned up. The pet can also be toilet trained. The pet can become sick for a number of reasons, such as overfeeding of snacks or its owner's failure to clean up droppings. The pet can die if its sickness is left unchecked but can also be cured. The pet goes through several distinct stages of development throughout its "life cycle" (i.e., baby, child, teen, adult). Each stage lasts for a set amount of time, with the end of each leading to changes in the pet's appearance. When first introduced, the Tamagotchi became a hit and production could not catch up with the demand. Many children started bringing them to school and engaging themselves quite intensely with their care. This became so disruptive to school life that many American schools prohibited their use on school premises.

Another artificial pet success story is AIBO, an artificial dog-puppy and one of the most popular entertainment robots ever produced. AIBO owners developed feelings toward the artificial pet, with 42% of them speaking of AIBO as possessing emotions and 26% considering it a companion (Kahn, Friedman, & Hagman, 2003). Children referred to AIBO as if it were a living dog, using "he" or "she" rather than "it" in referring to AIBO.

Donath (2004) provides a very interesting analysis of the qualities of these artificial pets, which mimic living things and hence evoke the motivation to care and engage children and adults alike in relations with a nonliving entity. These various toys appear to share several key behaviors, such as appearing to act autonomously with their own goals, feelings, and desires; depending on their owners for nurturance; and requiring frequent interaction. If the owners do not "feed" or "entertain" them, they become ill or even die. Moreover, these pets develop in response to their owners' actions and are embodied and three-dimensional rather than just images on a screen; hence they cannot be turned off and continue to "live" even if their owner does not pay attention to them.

Nurturing collections—a caring bond

An interesting case of forming what appears to be a proactive caring bond with objects is the phenomenon of nurturing collections. This is a very special case of owning objects and caring for them in which people acquire new items in order to manage their care and not because they intend to use them. Collecting has been defined as "the process of actively, selectively, and passionately acquiring and possessing things removed from ordinary use and perceived as part of a set of non-identical objects or experiences" (Belk, 1995, p. 67). This pursuit differs from most other types of consumption in the concern for a set of objects, in the passion invested in obtaining and maintaining these objects, and in the lack of ordinary uses to which these collected objects are put. Nearly all western children collect something, and boys and girls are equally likely to collect (albeit not the same things) until adolescence (e.g., Newson & Newson, 1968; Danet & Katriel, 1989; Katriel, 1988/1989; McGreevy, 1990). This is a common activity in the United States, where it is estimated that 42.9 million households and one-third of individuals engage in some form of collecting (O'Brien, 1981; Prior, 2002). Although collecting is more widespread (or better documented) in western postindustrial societies, it is also common in other cultural settings (Apostolou, 2011).

Collectors cite the will to repair, preserve, and protect items as one of the motivations for their hobby (Formanek, 1991). One collector has even compared his practice of restoring damaged manuscripts to his work as a psychiatrist (Schwartz, 2001). He notes that both patients and manuscripts undergo a "loving, corrective experience" and that while treating both targets can be a long and repetitive process, it leads to a great deal of satisfaction as results begin to appear. Collectors invest time, effort, and money in their collections and take care of them by protecting, preserving, and displaying them as well as by taking care to ensure that the collection will grow and thrive by buying and adding to it (Belk, 1995). The items in a collection must be unique and different from the others, reflecting what might be a personalized bond with each (Danet & Katriel, 1989). It can thus reflect a caring bond or a caring bond dynamic at the very least.

Collecting entails a variety of activities: looking for items, research, caring for and displaying the collection and interacting with other collectors. It is mostly the curatorial aspects of collecting—such as cataloging, displaying, and searching for and buying new items—that clearly reflect the nurturance facet. It should be noted that, in addition to its nurturing aspect, collecting also entails competitiveness and even aggression in the hunt-like acquisition of new items (Belk, 1995). These aspects have traditionally served to explain the fact that men are more likely to be collectors, although no gender effects are apparent in childhood. In addition, it has also been argued that collecting and hence the collectible items serve a signaling function for men. According to this proposition, collecting has evolved to enhance men's competitiveness by communicating to others their unobserved capacity to acquire resources (Apostolou, 2011). However, another reason for the popularity of this hobby among men may be that it provides them with socially acceptable targets for nurturance and affection (see Belk & Wallendorf, 1994). The nurturing aspect of collecting can be seen in the owners' concern for the future fate of their collections. As they age, collectors often identify an "heir" who will take care of the collection after they are gone. These heirs are often not chosen among the collectors' closest family members, as the latter tend to resent the collection and view it as a rival for the collector's affection. This "rivalry" serves as another indication of the emotional significance collections have for their owners (Belk, 1995).

As with other caring bonds, there are a variety of reasons for cultivating a collection. For example, collections may provide the collector with a hobby and a way to stand out and be special, contributing to the collector's sense of identity and uniqueness. Individuals may cultivate a collection as a way of bolstering their self-esteem and showing off (Belk et al., 1991). Furthermore, such an activity provides a social connection with like-minded individuals or organizations and thus contributes to a sense of social belongingness (Dannefer, 1980; DiMaggio, 1987). In line with the focus of this book and with the claim that cultivating a collection is a reflection of the motivation to care, the practice is often seen as an act of passion, love, and affection for the items the person collects and for the collection as a whole (Danet & Katriel, 1989; Danet & Katriel, 1990; Belk, 1995). Finally, cultivating the collection often gives the collector a strong sense of meaning in his or her life (Smith and Apter, 1977). In sum, although cultivating a collection may be driven by several possible reasons and motivations, the dynamics of care clearly play a central part. Cultivating a collection may therefore often reflect the operation of a proactive motivation to care enacted with objects.

Caring for a cause

Caring for a cause may involve a less prototypical instance of the motivation to care, yet it is often one of the expressions of such motivation. A cause can be any general outcome that is deemed significant, meaningful, and helpful to the common good. It might be an abstract value, such as justice or equality; a state of affairs that indicates a value, such as sustainability; or a desired outcome, such as clearing land mines, that implies a value—that of saving lives. Diana, Princess of Wales, for example, lent her highly visible support to the international campaign to ban land mines, a campaign that won the Nobel Peace Prize in 1997. Her interest in land mines was focused on the injuries they create, often in children, long after a conflict is over. Caring for such causes means that a person invests a great deal of effort in bringing about these outcomes, often with a sense of mission and commitment, and views this as an investment in the common good and/or in future generations. Such concern is similar to the way in which generativity was discussed by Erikson and others (McAdams & St Aubin, 1992; Also see the section on generativity in Chapter 9), meaning that caring for a cause can be conceptualized as a subcategory of generativity. In what follows, I would like to provide one prominent example, that of caring for the environment (environmentalism), and to highlight the caring dynamics involved in it.

Environmentalism is a broad ideology and social movement whose main focus is its concern for the environment, including its human and nonhuman elements. Environmentalism advocates the preservation, restoration, and/or improvement of the natural environment and involves such concerns as controlling pollution and protecting plant and animal diversity. Thus such conceptual orientations as biodiversity, ecology, and the biophilia hypothesis are central to its ideology. At its heart, it represents an attempt to balance relations between humans and the various natural systems on which they depend in such a way that all components are accorded a proper degree of sustainability. In other words, it attempts to reconcile environmental, social equity, and economic demands. It thus considers that humanity's moral and ethical duty is to preserve the planet's biological and ecological diversity and promote healthy ecosystems and environments. These aims are seen as essential to the survival and well-being of both humans and other organisms.

Such calls for caring have spurred the establishment of a large number of volunteer organizations such as Ecoworld and The Wilderness Society as well as global groups like the World Wide Fund for Nature, Friends of the Earth, and Greenpeace. In that sense caring for the environment is a special case of volunteering whereby the target is an abstract cause or a value rather than specific individuals. Why would people choose to work in such organizations for no pay? Several motivations have been identified, with the love of nature and the commitment to protect it being central, along with a sense of duty toward future generations. In fact, people caring for a specific cause often discuss generativity concerns such as "making the world a better place" as motivating their involvement. Miles, Sullivan, and Kuo (1998), for example, examined a group of volunteers (N = ~300) who were personally involved in protecting and restoring sensitive natural landscapes in the Chicago metropolitan area as part of the Volunteer Stewardship Network. In an activity spanning several decades and still in progress, these volunteers meet at a designated site every Sunday morning and work for three hours to restore the Illinois prairie. Respondents reported that meaningfulness (i.e., making life better for future generations, being of benefit to society or the community, causing good things to happen, acting in a responsible manner toward the planet Earth) and a fascination with nature (i.e., seeking out and enjoying the wonders of nature) are the strongest sources for their involvement and satisfaction.

A comparable profile of "altruistic" motivations emerges in other studies whereby nature or the environment as generalized and abstract entities served as the targets for care. Examining hundreds of volunteers from six natural resource organizations, Bruyere and Rappe (2007), for example, found that "helping the environment" emerged as the most important reason for volunteering, with second-tier motivations including "expressing their values" and "learning about the natural environment."

As with other proactive voluntary enactments of the motivation to care, such volunteering was found to be associated with unintended positive benefits for the volunteers, such as good health and less depression (Grese, Kaplan, Ryan, & Buxton, 2000; Warburton & Gooch, 2007; Pillemer, Fuller-Rowell, Reid, & Wells, 2010).

Chapter conclusion

The study of caring for pets, plants and gardens, objects, and causes under-scores several recurrent issues. First, nonhuman entities and even inanimate and abstract ones can be the targets of the caring motivation, and individuals may even form caring bonds with them. Although other motivations and reasons for engaging with these entities are in operation, the caring motivation clearly plays a dominant role. This reveals the operation of a general and encompassing caring motivation aimed at a very large array of targets, animate and inanimate, and includes a large variety of provisions. Second, and thus reflecting a voluntary, pro-active activation of the intrinsic motivation to care, these pursuits are associated with joy, satisfaction, meaning, and purpose. Third, such pursuits are also associated with positive outcomes for the caregiver in both psychological and physical well-being. These unintended yet highly positive outcomes probably relate to the downregulation of the stress reaction, the feelings of joy associated with the general reward system, and finding meaning and purpose associated with the expression of the caring motivation, particularly when it is activated in a volitional and intrinsic fashion and it is enacted in a way that makes the caregiver feel competent and efficacious.

12

Caring in Different Social Roles and Contexts

The breadth of caring in society can also be examined through the different roles and contexts in which it unfolds. In previous chapters, I have discussed the arena of close relationships (Chapter 8) and the realm of leisure activities (Chapters 10 and 11). In the chapter that follows, I refer to four other major arenas—education (caring in teaching and schools), the workplace (the helping professions and caring in organizations), leadership, and intergroup transgressions.

Caring in teaching and schools

What does care have to do with teaching and schools? Schools are presumably central societal contexts in which the acquisition of the skills and knowledge required for successfully adapting and flourishing in a specific society is expected to take place. As such they are considered an important socialization context. Such socialization has been the province of parents and other caregivers (i.e., older siblings) during most of our evolutionary history and in some respects still is. For example, Ruddick, a prominent contemporary feminist writer, has suggested three major practices that comprise the "work" of mothering: "preservative love"—preserving and protecting the child's life, "fostering growth," and "social training," which involves teaching children to become acceptable and successful members of the mother's social group (Ruddick, 1989/1995). In modern societies, the formal educational system has been imbued with the task of implementing the training and teaching aspect in order to supplement the initial parental investment in this type of care. Consequently teaching in schools comprises some of the caring functions of parenting. In this sense, every teacher is a caregiver performing one of the central functions of parenting—the socialization of the young.

Yet, the term *caring*, and the idea that teachers should care about and for their students, has been considered mainly from a different perspective by scholars of education, a perspective that places the relationship component rather than teaching at center stage. When educators discuss caring, they generally rely on the influential works of Carol Gilligan (1982) and Nel Noddings (1984/2003)— both eminent feminist philosophers. According to these scholars and others (e.g., Pianta, 1992), caring involves the formation of meaningful relationships between teachers and students in which teachers assume a commitment to helping students learn and prosper and to responding to their needs with professional integrity, responsiveness, flexibility, and sensitivity. In terms of classroom practices, this entails listening, respecting, sensitively addressing students' needs and interests, encouraging dialogue, teaching students to be caring, and creating an environment in which students feel safe, secure, and engaged in meaningful activities. An ethics of care in schools means that teaching is based on needs, relations, and specific responses rather than on universal principles that apply to all students equally (Gilligan, 1982). Noddings further stresses that an ethics of care embodies a relational view of caring and not just caring as a personal virtue (i.e., "she is a caring person"). Students needs to feel that they are being cared for. Thus if teachers feel that they care for students and about their education (and even if others observe that they do) but students feel that "nobody cares," a situation that can occur quite frequently, relational care has not been established (Noddings, 1992/2005). From the perspective of this book, the caring motivation can and does express itself through teaching, even when it is not optimal. However within the educational field, teaching in and of itself was not conceived as an act of care: within this context the term *caring* refers to very specific ways in which teachers are expected to do their work. It amounts to expecting "good teaching" that involves warmth, trust, respect, and sensitivity and that makes students feel cared for.

Indeed, students perceive teachers as caring when teachers' inculcation of skills and knowledge is conducted in a *responsive and sensitive* manner. Wentzel (1997), for example, has found that caring teachers are perceived as such if they recognize each student's uniqueness as a learner (e.g., "the teacher takes time to make sure I understand and asks if I need help"), care about teaching (i.e., makes class interesting), have open and respectful ways of communicating (e.g., pays attention, listens), and shows nurturance and positive affect (e.g., "the teacher tells me when I do a good job and praises me"). Such perceived care by middle school students accounted for the students' eighth-grade intrinsic motivation to learn, even after the effects of seventh-grade motivation and perceived motivational influences from parents and peers had been taken into account (Murdock & Miller, 2003). In her eminent writings and teaching, Noddings makes the case that caring and the ethics of care should be central in educational policy and practices. This approach has gained a growing prominence in schools and in the curriculum of preservice teacher education (Goldstein & Lake, 2000).

Attachment theory has also been applied to teacher-student relations (see Sabol & Pianta, 2012, and Pianta's 1992 edited volume). Adopting an attachment perspective on teacher-child relationships, researchers have suggested that teachers, like parents, often serve attachment functions such as the safe haven and the secure base. In the educational context, the provision of the caring function of a safe haven involves a relation in which students feel free to turn to the teacher when they are in distress or when they need to be comforted. The provision of the secure base function involves a reliance on the presence and proximity of the teacher that offers a sense of security, allowing the student to venture into academic and social exploration. The teacher-child relationship, however, is not the same as the parent-child bond. For one, it is usually not exclusive or durable, and the main caring is restricted to instruction. Hence most students do not form a full-fledged attachment bond with their teachers. Nevertheless, teacher-student relations may involve attachment and caregiving dynamics. Within such relations, the provision of the safe haven and secure base caregiving functions enables students to freely explore and learn, to form positive and adaptive social relations, and to develop their self-efficacy and self-esteem (Sabol & Pianta, 2012). Teachers' sensitivity and responsiveness in particular appear to be key practices that facilitate security as well as bold and creative exploration on the part of students.

Wentzel (2002) also likened teachers to parents and applied parent socialization models to examining teachers' influence on student adjustment in middle school. Teachers were assessed with respect to Baumrind's (1967; 1971) parenting dimensions of control, maturity demands, democratic communication, and nurturance. In a manner akin to studies exploring the effects of these parenting dimensions on children's adjustment, Wentzel showed that high expectations reflecting appropriate maturity demands and nurturance were positively associated with student motivation, social behavior, and achievement in the school context.

As in other contexts, research within educational institutions has revealed that teachers' caring makes a difference for their students and that such caring is associated with children's better functioning at school as measured by adjustment, academic outcomes, and social skills. By following a subsample of the National Institute of Child Health and Human Development's Study of Early Childcare, for example, Pianta and Stuhlman (2004) predicted social and academic performance of first-grade students from the quality of their relations with their teachers. After controlling for demographic variables and level of skills in kindergarten, the students' closeness to first-grade teachers as reported by the teachers themselves predicted better academic performance, lower scores in mother-rated internalizing behavior problems, and higher scores in trained observers' ratings of the children's social competence.

The effects of caring on the part of teachers should be most pronounced for students who are at risk, given that good relations with teachers can protect these students from a negative developmental trajectory (Wentzel & Asher, 1995; Baker, Grant, & Morlock, 2008). Meehan, Hughes, and Cavell (2003), for

example, found that third-grade teacher-reported support predicted lower levels
of aggression after second-grade aggressive behaviors had been taken into consideration. In an informative study involving 671 (53.1% male) children at academic
risk in one of three school districts in Texas, researchers found that close, warm,
and nonconflictual teacher-student relations in the first grade predicted objective
achievements in reading and mathematics in the third grade and that this effect
was mediated through the more effortful engagement (i.e., persistence, effort,
attention) of these students during second grade (Hughes, Luo, Kwok, & Loyd,
2008). This promising direction soon found its way to classroom assessments
that also involved such caring aspects and to interventions with preservice and
inservice teachers aimed at promoting their in-school caring capacities (Sabol &
Pianta, 2012).

As in other caring relations (e.g., volunteering), caring teachers also benefit
from these relations, and they provide an important source of professional satisfaction for teachers. For teachers, who often choose this profession because they
"love children" and have a strong personal commitment to caring for them, the
opportunity to be personally involved in close and caring relations with their students in addition to the "regular" teaching of skills and knowledge brings about
a deep sense of satisfaction throughout their careers (Nias, 1989; Hargreaves,
1994). In fact, teachers often comment on the reciprocal nature of these relations, which embrace loving and giving on their part and being loved and appreciated by their students and how this reciprocal affection and appreciation helps
to sustain the relationship: "Don't think I'm the one who's doing all the giving
. . . . I know that by the end of the day several people will have shown that they
love me" (Nias, 1989, p. 87).

However, a commitment to caring in the sense of being warm, sensitive, and
responsive as a teacher might also prove challenging owing to the expected obligation of caring about *every* student and showing this through caring acts that
would make each student feel cared for (Rogers & Webb, 1991). Yet children do
not always respond favorably to caring, and classes may be difficult to manage.
Moreover, the need to devote attention sensitively and responsively to more than
a few children, especially in a crowded classroom, requires efforts that may often
exceed the teacher's ability. Even under favorable circumstances, caring for students can be demanding and challenging and may lead to frustration, exhaustion,
and even professional burnout (Hargreaves, 1994). This state of affairs, which
appears to be fairly common in schools (at least in some countries) (Noddings
2005), accords with similar accounts related to other contexts that require intensive, demanding caregiving—such as providing care to a disabled spouse or in
parenting young children (see Chapter 8). This underscores the importance of
providing care in a balanced and judicial way, reflecting sensitivity to the needs
of both care receiver and caregiver. For the purpose of this book, it is indicative
that the large majority of teachers continue to care about their students' learning

by trying to make them understand and internalize what they are expected to learn; teachers also feel pride in their students' successes and disappointment at their failures. They are engaged in this way even if they may not be able to provide an optimal degree of care owing to situational or dispositional reasons (Noddings, 2005).

Caring in the workplace—caring as a profession (the helping professions)

Society has institutionalized tending and caring in various professions such as nursing, child care, clinical psychology, social work, and elder care. These professions involve taking care of others by attending to their various needs, which may be physical and involve sustaining life, as in nursing, or more psychological, as in social work. To borrow Sara Ruddick's (1989/1995) categorization of mothering goals, these needs may be tied to different goals, which include sustaining life, fostering growth, and training to become an acceptable member in society or any combination of these. It appears that the term *helping professions* was linked to caring in situations that involve distress or suffering—or, generally speaking, any negative affective state that requires alleviation, healing, or repair.

In some of these areas, particularly clinical psychology and mostly within psychoanalytic writings, caring was likened to maternal care, and the psychoanalyst or psychotherapist was described as a parental figure with respect to a host of caring functions. Winnicott (1965), for example, was the first to provide a detailed description of the maternal holding function, which involves both physical and emotional/psychological holding and is crucial to the development of the child's self. He articulated the need for the therapist to recreate a "holding environment" resembling that of the mother and her infant in the therapeutic context. In a large number of prominent writings, psychotherapists were described as alternative attachment figures who provide fundamental psychological caring that serves the same function and role as good parenting and can thus help clients overcome and compensate for difficult and insecure experiences with their parents (see a brief reviews in Farber, Lippert, & Nevas, 1995; Farber & Metzger, 2009).

Interestingly, although the helping professions are categorized as similar in professional inclinations and predispositions, they may differ markedly in the kinds of help that they offer and are thus not interchangeable from the helpers' point of view. For example, although nursing and clinical psychology are both helping professions with a high level of individualized investment in care recipients, most nurses would not trade places with psychotherapists and vice versa, because members of each profession specifically chose to engage in a specific kind of provision (to tend the body vs. the psyche), meaning that their caring motivation within the professional realm is highly specialized. Even within a specialized domain such as caring for the body, there are subspecializations, and physiotherapists, for example, would not easily change their profession to become nurses. We have seen equivalent processes in volunteering, where the intrinsic and autonomous choice of the specific organization and the kind of caring that is to be enacted was crucial and critical to the volunteers' satisfaction. This specialization teaches us something about the motivation to care—namely that despite being a general fundamental motivation, the specific kinds of provision and possibly the specific targets of care (i.e., children, adults, or elders) are quite idiosyncratic and reflect an intrinsic and personal choice, whether in one's profession or one's leisure activity. Such a choice is clear when we are concerned with nonobligatory caring relations, as in choosing a profession or an organization to volunteer in. This is not necessarily the case in obligatory caring, such as caring for children or a spouse, where the assumption of caring responsibility encompasses a large variety of needs. Still, the personal preference to care in some ways rather than others is also evident in parents' preferences and actions (e.g., one parent may like to play chess with an older child while another may prefer to bathe and dress the baby).

Some caring professions involve the creation of a limited caring bond. It is often a caring bond that is limited in time and kind of provision. This is the case, for example, in psychotherapy. In accordance with the importance of close and trustworthy relationships in caregiving bonds, several meta-analyses across dozens of studies have found that the positive outcomes of psychotherapy are mediated to a significant extent by the general quality of the relation between psychotherapist and client, referred to as the "working alliance" (e.g., Horvath & Symonds 1991). This alliance reflects the existence of mutually agreed goals and a bond involving mutual trust, acceptance, and confidence; its positive effects are similar and robust across the type of outcome assessed, the measure used to assess the working alliance, and even the type and length of treatment provided (e.g., Horvath & Symonds 1991; Martin, Garske, & Davis 2000). These remarkable findings reveal several core attributes of good caring relations—mutuality; agreed-upon goals; and warm, sensitive, responsive communication.

A large number of studies have examined the motivations for choosing a helping profession; these have focused on both candidates for these professions as well as accomplished professionals. By and large, participants cite the desire to help people as the top reason for choosing their profession (e.g., Hanson & McCullagh, 1995; Millan et al., 2005; Byrne, 2008). This was found to be true in a variety of professions (e.g., social work, clinical psychology, counseling psychology, and even medicine), in large-scale quantitative studies as well as in qualitative studies employing in-depth interviews. This clearly reflects the caring motivation.

Alongside the clear motivation to help others and heal their wounds, a large number of studies have also found a wish to understand oneself and help oneself by helping others (Farber, Manevich, Metzger, & Saypol, 2005; Norcross & Farber, 2005). This wish was especially pertinent to those who practiced psychotherapy. In fact, several interesting findings regarding the motivations of helping professionals and their origin pertain specifically to psychotherapists. A relatively large number of studies have found that psychotherapists tend to come from troubled backgrounds, having suffered some degree of emotional neglect, abuse, or trauma in childhood (e.g., Fussel & Bonney, 1990). Scholars suggest that these experiences have made such people more sensitive and empathic toward others in pain, leading to their interest in practicing psychotherapy (Farber et. al., 2005; Buchbinder, 2007). This is especially true in cases where difficulties at home led to the parentification of a child, a constellation where parent-child roles are somewhat reversed and the child is called upon to take care of at least one of the parents at an early age. This may occur because the parent is physically disabled and/or emotionally hurt or helpless to the extent of needing instrumental and/or emotional care, which is provided by the child.

Parentified children who assume this parental role vis-à-vis one of their parents learn to anticipate the needs of others in the family and are often rewarded for their caretaking behavior. Thus they develop the capacity to care for others; as a result, their self-worth and sense of competence are based on nurturing others, and this may carry over to adulthood (Jurkovic, 1997; DiCaccavo, 2002; Farber et al., 2005). Adopting an attachment perspective, researchers have suggested a dynamic in which the child's caregiving behavioral system is activated to serve her or his attachment needs for proximity and closeness (West & Keller, 1991). In children whose regular bids for proximity were not answered or were answered with threatening behaviors, the early activation of their caregiving system toward their parents might have provided them with some proximity to these attachment figures. If they succeeded in calming and comforting the parent, this may have partially satisfied their attachment-related needs for proximity and closeness (Mayseless, 1996; Mayseless, Bartholomew, Henderson, & Trinke, 2004). These children thus learned that taking care of others was their way of getting close to them, as opposed to revealing their own needs and distress and being rebuffed. This behavior might eventually become a personality predisposition (referred to as "'caretaker syndrome" by some scholars, such as Valleau, Bergner, and Horton (1995), that is later transferred to other relations in adulthood and might bring about the choice of a helping profession (see edited book by Chase, 1999, and Vincent, 1996).

In addition, people from troubled backgrounds may be drawn to psychotherapy because helping others deal with their emotional difficulties promotes their own healing. This has been referred to by some scholars as the "wounded healer" situation (Norcross & Farber, 2005). In fact, in some situations, such as alcoholism or drug abuse, it is quite customary for individuals who have experienced these problems and succeeded in overcoming them to help others in similar situations. That is, these healers feel that it is now their calling to help others as they themselves have been helped. It is also as a way of reminding themselves to stay away from harm (Zerubavel & Wright, 2012).

This depiction can help us to understand how a greater than usual motivation to care for others and even the choice of a helping profession can develop from an adverse upbringing and difficult experiences. This path is somewhat different from the one identified by Oliner and others with respect to the kind of heroic altruism that involves risking one's life to save others (see Chapter 9). In Oliner's accounts (e.g., 2002), the families of origin were for the most part described as functioning well and even as exemplary in their warmth, disciplinary style, and moral conduct. However, adverse situations can also lead individuals who have found a way of overcoming them to become compassionate and caring toward others. More spe-cifically, such experiences may lead them to want to help and heal others who are currently experiencing distress and suffering. In fact, the vast psychotherapeutic literature is replete with cases of individuals who have surmounted and success-fully coped with adversities such as loss or trauma and are now engaged in helping others surmount the same obstacles and challenges. Life stories of such individu-als are often recounted by them as "redemption stories," where they make sense of their life experience and recount a life narrative that includes a transformation from bad and affectively negative experiences to good and affectively positive ones. Such transformations are experienced by them as allowing them to find renewed mean-ing and purpose in their lives, and they often choose generative ways to express this. For them, caring offers a way to give to others what they themselves lacked and to express gratitude for their healing through such helping (McAdams, Diamond, de St. Aubin, and Mansfield, 1997; McAdams, Reynolds, Lewis, Patten, & Bowman, 2001). But not all caregivers in helping professions choose their profession follow-ing adverse childhoods or experiences; there are a variety of life experiences in the personal histories of caregivers in the helping professions, including psychotherapy.

Caregivers in the helping professions also experience negative outcomes from their caring acts. Some of the individuals involved in the helping profes-sions and particularly those involved in high-intensity helping and caring (e.g., working directly with trauma victims) experience what is referred to by some scholars as "secondary traumatic stress" or "compassion fatigue" (Figley, 1995). This is a recurrent experience among professionals working with individu-als who have experienced such traumas as rape, violence, or extreme neglect (Adams, Boscarino, & Figley, 2006). It is a situation in which the helper's com-passion and capacity for empathy decrease to such an extent that he or she feels hopelessness, stress, and anxiety, even experiencing nightmares and a nega-tive outlook on life and people. This often damages the helper's relationships with significant others and her or his sense of safety, self-esteem, control, and trust; it can culminate in a serious disruption of the helper's life. This condi-tion is related to recurrent exposures to the trauma and distress of others that overload a person's capacity to hold and process them. Research has shown that this situation can be quite common among health care workers such as emergency room nurses, ambulance paramedics, and hospice nurses (in these professions, a consistent ratio of around 25% of practitioners appear to display compassion fatigue) (Hooper et al., 2010).

Compassion fatigue is also common among caregivers for dependent people, especially if the care recipient's disability is permanent and she or he is not expected to become healthier but rather to deteriorate. The prolonged and taxing nature of consistently exhibiting compassion toward someone whose suffering is continuous and unresolvable may prove too difficult, even for caregivers with a strong intrinsic motivation to care. Obviously our capacity for compassion is not unlimited, and excessive caring or prolonged caring in extreme and intense situations places a heavy toll on our physical, psychological, and spiritual being (Oakley, Knafo, & McGrath, 2012). This underscores the importance of balance in the expression of the caring motivation, because extreme or unbalanced expressions of care can indeed backfire (see edited book by Oakley, Knafo, Madhavan, & Wilson, 2012).

Caring in the workplace—caring in organizations (organizational citizenship behaviors)

Besides professions that have formalized caring as part of their role, workplaces are replete with prosocial behaviors beyond the professional role. There are many instances where individuals in organizations perform tasks that are above and beyond their formal role requirements in order to benefit others in the organization as well as the organization itself. These extra-role prosocial acts that are not directly specified in any job description and which do not entail any direct benefit to the individual have been referred to as *organizational citizenship behaviors* (OCBs) (Organ, 1988) or prosocial behaviors. Good citizenship behavior is characterized in a variety of ways (see review by Podsakoff, MacKenzie, Paine, & Bachrach, 2000), such as helping behavior targeted to benefit others (termed altruism in the original scheme suggested by Organ), conscientiousness, organizational loyalty and compliance, sportsmanship and cooperation, and protecting the organization. In line with the focus of this book, helping behaviors are often considered the most robust and clear aspect of OCBs and involve voluntarily helping others with work-related problems or by preventing the occurrence of work-related problems. These behaviors have also been referred to as *affiliation-oriented organizational citizenship behaviors* because they involve contributions to the maintenance and enhancement of the social and psychological context that support the performance of organizational tasks.

Such helping OCBs include instructing a new employee on how to use equipment; helping a coworker catch up with a backlog of work; fetching materials that a colleague needs and cannot procure independently; communicating with people before deciding on actions that will affect them; helping to prevent, resolve, or mitigate unconstructive interpersonal conflict; and encouraging and/or reinforcing coworkers. All are clear markers of the motivation to care. Another category of OCBs reflects behaviors directed at the organization or its structure and processes, such as respect for rules and instructions, punctuality, task completion, and organizational loyalty (i.e., staying with the organization during hard times and representing the organization favorably to outsiders).

What might be the motivations behind such helping in the workplace context? As in other situations where prosocial behaviors are observed, such helping can reflect other-oriented motivations which are both voluntary and intrinsic. Indeed, most of the research on OCBs appears to have assessed such behaviors and underscored the importance of other-oriented altruistic motivations (See review by Podsakoff et al., 2000). However, as with the prosocial behaviors discussed earlier, other motivations may also be involved. These relate to feeling coerced to engage in OCBs because of perceived organizational norms that exert citizenship pressure or because of managerial expectations to engage in such behaviors. In such cases, these prosocial behaviors are seen as emanating from an obligation rather than from the worker's free will and have been referred to as *compulsory citizenship behaviors* (CCBs). CCBs and citizenship pressures have been associated with negative outcomes such as job-related stress and negligence, work-family conflict, and intentions to quit (Vigoda-Gadot, 2007; Bolino, Klotz, Turnley, & Harvey, 2013). OCBs can also be enacted for self-oriented goals, such as impression management, for the maintenance of a good reputation, or for gaining a promotion (Hui, Lam, & Law, 2000). Finally, and even if OCBs stem from intrinsic motivations, too many OCBs can interfere with one's professional and personal life (Bolino et al., 2013).

As in other instances of the expression of the motivation to care, a number of different motivations can operate at the same time in the enactment of prosocial behaviors, helping, and nurturing. Furthermore, and as with other instances of the provision of care, the helper's motivation, in particular the extent to which caring is voluntary, make a big difference with regard to the helper's feelings and the outcomes for her or him. Care that is more obligatory than voluntary tends to entail negative feelings and cause problems in adaptive functioning. Finally, and even if care is voluntarily provided, too much of a good thing is also problematic and may cause individuals to feel burnout and stress. Optimal caring must balance the needs and sensitivities of helpers and recipients alike (see review in Organ, Podsakoff, & MacKenzie, 2006).

Studies that have examined the antecedents of OCBs have found that it is related to employee characteristics as well as to contextual aspects. On the employee side, aspects that reflect a "morale" factor—such as employee satisfaction, organizational commitment, perceptions of fairness, and perceptions of leader supportiveness—were consistently associated with OCBs. These are not employee characteristics in the strict sense but a reflection of their perceptions of the organizational climate. In fact, the contextual conditions that were associated with OCBs mirrored the morale factor in the employees. More specifically, organizational contexts that fostered trust, a sense of justice, clear expectations and rules, and efficacy promoted the emergence of OCBs. Similarly, fairness (i.e., contingent reward behavior), caring and support, and positive modeling by leaders also contributed to OCBs. Interestingly, the same positive parental qualities that affected the development of a prosocial altruistic personality also promoted OCBs in employees if enacted by leaders. Transformational leadership behaviors, for example, that include providing a vision, being an appropriate model, having high performance expectations, showing individual consideration, and providing intellectual stimulation were all associated with higher levels of OCBs, particularly of the affiliation-oriented kind (i.e., help directed to individuals) (see review in Organ et al., 2006).

Several stable employee predispositions—such as conscientiousness, agreeableness, and positive affectivity—were also associated with OCBs and may be the antecedents that set a circular process in motion in the first place. These predispositions were not as clearly and consistency associated with OCBs as the morale antecedents, possibly reflecting the contingent nature of such helping. In other words, if engagement in OCBs associated with employee dispositions eventually creates or contributes to the sustenance of a cooperative, caring, and trustworthy work environment, this will feed and sustain their continuation through their effects on employee morale and job satisfaction. However, if the positive cycle is not enhanced for whatever reason (e.g. uncooperative management or downsizing) individuals with these predispositions will stop engaging in OCBs.

Although affiliation-oriented OCBs are not sanctioned by formal job descriptions, managers appreciate employees who engage in them. In cross-sectional as well as in experimental studies, the effect of engaging in OCBs was at least as great as that of in-role performance on such management decisions as performance evaluations and salary and promotion recommendations, showing the robust effect of OCBs on managers' positive evaluations. This attests to the importance that managers accord to OCBs and to the central and significant place OCBs occupy in organizational life despite being *extra*-role behaviors. (see review in Organ et al., 2006).

OCBs also contribute to organizational success. In fact, in the original introduction of the term (Organ, 1988; Organ et al., 2006), the definition of OCBs also included references to the outcomes of such behaviors, which should promote the efficient and effective functioning of the organization. Indeed, research has shown that OCBs are related to organizational performance and success as assessed by objective measures (e.g., operating efficiency and customer satisfaction) in a variety of organizational contexts, including insurance agency units, paper mill work crews, pharmaceutical sales teams, and limited-menu restaurants. Furthermore, the evidence is stronger for affiliation-oriented OCBs than for other aspects of OCBs (see review in Podsakoff et al., 2000). And these effects on persistence, performance, and productivity are enhanced the more people engage in OCBs out of autonomous and intrinsic prosocial motivation (Grant, 2008). The centrality and necessity of OCBs for organizational functioning is now acknowledged in contemporary literature on organizational behavior and current management textbooks stress their remarkable importance for organizational success (Grant, 2008).

But why do OCBs engender such outcomes? The answer should be clear. People work best in an environment that establishes relations of cooperation and trustworthiness, where they can rely on others to help them and care for them if necessary, and where they enjoy reciprocating such care (i.e., where they feel a sense of comradeship with their coworkers). People work best in such environments because they often need help, they enjoy helping others, and, for the most part, work is best done in teams rather than on one's own. Furthermore, people work best when the "relational architecture" of their jobs connects them to the impact they are having on the beneficiaries of their work. This in turn increases their motivation to make a prosocial difference, thus contributing to their sense of meaning and purpose and enhancing their eudaemonic well-being (Grant, 2007). Indeed, current descriptions of the optimal working environment stress the importance of working in cooperative teams where both the receiving and giving of care is encouraged (Grant, 2007; Grant, Dutton, & Rosso, 2008). Educational systems worldwide are now required to teach this essential skill; it appears to have been lost from the goals of such systems, which now tend to stress competitiveness and individualism (OECD teamwork competencies; http://www.oecd.org/innovation/research/1842070.pdf; retrieved February 23, 2014.)

From an evolutionary perspective, the hunter-gatherer groups that formed our ancestors' "work" environment were inherently cooperative and survived mainly because of the communal and cooperative relationships among their members. These were also the contexts in which cooperation, generosity, trust, and care for one's group evolved as part of the caring motivation. In the industrialized modern context, which tends to view workers as machine-like entities and industrial and bureaucratic work as involving prescribed and exact demands from such entities, we as a society have forgotten our inherent social, cooperative, and caring nature and thus must rediscover it.

Interestingly, gender was not associated with OCBs; this may relate to at least two issues. First, if the main sustaining and driving force has to do with a general workplace climate that involves trust, cooperation, and support (as suggested earlier), both men and women should be similarly affected. Second, from an evolutionary perspective, cooperation in small groups for a joint cause is considered evolutionarily advantageous for men and women alike.

Leadership and caring

Leadership has traditionally been associated with dominance hierarchies and issues of power. Researchers have evolutionarily tracked the emergence of leadership to processes within groups of males, especially during hunting activities, in which dominance hierarchies were naturally established, as can also be seen today in primates. In most primate groups one male—the alpha male, to use the scientific term, becomes dominant and is rewarded with various payoffs, such as easy access to a larger number of females, being groomed by others, and receiving better portions of food (see review in Van Vugt, 2006).

Interestingly, as convincingly articulated by Taylor (2002) and others (e.g., Van Vugt, 2006), leadership is actually based, even among most apes, on social skills, caring, nurturance, and altruism rather than physical strength. A leader's caring among apes includes a large number of domains. In primates, for example, alpha males protect the group from outside threats, arrange the acquisition and distribution of food such that all members of the group receive their share, and even engage as peacemakers who intervene to solve problems among group members in order to protect the group from inside turmoil. All this requires sensitivity to others' needs and a motivation to act upon this need in a way that fosters the life and development of group members. I am purposefully referring to groups of primates because if such caring is manifested by the dominant males in these groups, we should also expect it in human leaders.

My main argument here, in line with that of others (e.g., Van Vugt, 2006), is that leaders are not just those who possess the most power but rather that they, and particularly those that arise naturally within a group or a society, are first and foremost caring people in the sense that they devote themselves to managing, directing, and seeing to it that others are OK, that their needs are met, and that their welfare is maintained.

In an intriguing tentative account of the evolutionary development of leadership, Van Vugt (2006) has suggested that the hunter-gatherer societies which typified most of our evolutionary history as a species, and which included groups of between 50 to 150 individuals, probably had a rather flat dominance hierarchy. Within these groups, leaders were naturally chosen, usually through bottom-up processes, and their leadership was fluid rather than fixed and assigned by peers to whoever was recognized as adept in a specific domain depending on the group's needs and circumstances. In these groups leaders had to help protect members of the tribe, find good places to stay, arrange food distribution, and solve internal disputes. Among other attributes, these tasks required interpersonal sensitivity and a concern for others. In line with this suggestion and following a seminal ethnographic study of 48 hunter-gatherer societies, Boehm (1993) concluded that followers were not keen on having a dominant leader and preferred a more egalitarian and democratic style of leadership. Furthermore, he contended that if a dominant and authoritarian leader emerged, followers (i.e. tribe members) had various means of changing the situation by disobeying or ridiculing the leader and sometimes even by killing or by letting other tribes kill the overly dominant leader. Employing this analysis of the emergence of leaders, Van Vugt, Hogan, and Kaiser (2008) have suggested that based on these egalitarian "hunter-gatherer" standards—which we seem to have internalized throughout our evolutionary past—initiative, social intelligence, fairness, generosity, and concern for others are regarded as central attributes of good leaders, whereas dominance and self-ishness are viewed as the antithesis of leadership (Den Hartog, House, Hanges, Ruiz-Quintanilla, & Dorfman, 1999; Dirks & Ferrin, 2002; Epitropaki & Martin, 2004; Van Vugt, Jepson, Hart, & De Cremer, 2004; Nicholson, 2005). This would explain the association currently found between leadership and such qualities as empathy, perspective taking, and nonverbal sensitivity (Zaccaro, Gilbert, Thor, & Mumford, 1991; Hogan & Hogan, 2002; Kellett, Humphrey & Sleeth, 2002).

What might be the relevant basis for naturally evolving leaders? An interesting series of studies suggest that at least part of it may be related to altruism. In a series of experiments Hardy and Van Vugt (2006) showed that when members' contri-butions were public, the most altruistic members gained the highest status in their group. Furthermore, high-status members behaved more altruistically than low-status members. The authors thus suggested that group members "compete" for social status within their group by behaving altruistically. These findings accord with the claim that naturally emerging leaders in human groups are expected to have caring qualities and to be at least more altruistic than the average group mem-ber. Furthermore, for individuals to be chosen as leaders in natural circumstances, they should be perceived as both competent and benevolent. Followers want leaders who can help the group attain its goals, and through this acquire assets and capital, as well as leaders who are able and willing to share these assets with group members in a way that fosters the members' prosperity and the group's continued success. The willingness and capacity to share in a way that would be perceived as reflecting such qualities is associated with such traits as reliability, fairness, and generosity. As found in a variety of studies, these traits are deemed universally desirable leader attributes (Lord Foti, & De Vader, 1984; Den Hartog, et. al., 1999; Dirks & Ferrin, 2002; Epitropaki & Martin, 2004; Nicholson, 2005; Hardy & Van Vugt, 2006).

Lest readers think that I am ignoring a variety of leaders throughout history who were selfish, uncaring, and sometimes even cruel, I would like to stress that my intention is not to romanticize leadership. In fact, a large number of leaders display a strong need for power and a nonnegligible number of them may utilize their power for personal gain. They also tend to be the leaders that we remember as negative and, at times, highly negative examples of corrupt or cruel leadership. I nonetheless contend that one of the central motivations that propels leaders, or at least a large number of them, is to "do good," to set things right, and to help their group members or citizens to prosper. These are undoubtedly caring motives.

In fact, a new view of leadership as involving, besides gaining power, the capacity and motivation to **form nurturing** relations with followers has emerged in recent decades (Burns, 1978; Bass, 1985). This type of leadership has been called *transformational leadership*. It involves charisma, or idealized influence (i.e., acting as a role model for followers), and vision (the ability to articulateg a vision that is appealing and inspiring) but is especially distinguished by the provision of intellectual stimulation (i.e., encouraging and promoting followers to be innovative and creative) and by individual consideration (i.e., attending to followers' needs, listening to their concerns, mentoring them, and acknowledging their contributions). Transformational leaders thus transform followers and help them perform beyond their own expectations. The caring facet in transformational leaders is thus quite apparent. It is hardly surprising, therefore, that transformational leadership has been likened to good parenting (Popper & Mayseless, 2003). Both parents and transformational leaders, for example, are sensitive and responsive, show individual consideration, reinforce followers'/children's autonomy in a supportive, nonjudgmental way by actively providing opportunities, and both are positive examples of people others can identify with and look up to. Both parents and transformational leaders promote trust, self-confidence, and self-realization and a tendency of followers/children to become like them. Reflecting this similarity and supporting the claim that leaders in general and transformational leaders in particular partly act on the basis of the motivation to care, leader–follower relationships were also found to involve attachment dynamics. This is related both to the affective process connecting followers to leaders (which involves attachment dynamics on the part of the followers) (Mayseless & Popper, 2007) and to the role of attachment security in the leaders, affecting their becoming leaders and also their leadership style. For example, the results of several studies conducted in diverse contexts and within several cultures have shown that secure individuals tend to be nominated as leaders and that leaders' attachment security is associated with a prosocial leadership style and the empowerment of their followers (see review in Mayseless, 2010). These findings suggest that, selfish leadership notwithstanding, leadership in general and transformational leadership in particular is associated with prosocial tendencies and with the motivation to care.

Apology, forgiveness, and reconciliation: coping with transgressions in dyadic relations, groups, and nations

The caring motivation is relevant to processes of apology, forgiveness, and reconciliation among close others and strangers and among groups and even between nations. Specifically caring is implicated in more benevolent coping with conflicts and situations of harm, injury, maltreatment, and destruction among people. Such situations may lead to anger, antagonism, hostility, and even aggression, retaliation, and revenge. However, individuals and groups often choose other, more benevolent means to address and cope with such offenses. These include apology, forgiveness, and reconciliation, which often recruit the capacity and the motivation to care on both sides—the "perpetrator" and the "injured."

McCullough, an eminent researcher of processes of revenge and forgiveness, even assumes the existence of a forgiveness instinct (McCullough, 2008). Appealing to psychological, neurological, evolutionary, anthropological, and ethological research, he demonstrates that group-living animals, humans included of course, have an innate tendency to reconcile and forgive— rather than to retaliate and avenge—following interactions that include harm and maltreatment. From an evolutionary point of view, such an innate tendency is viewed as serving the ultimate purpose of gene survival and propagation (our inclusive fitness) among humans who rely for their survival and procreation on cooperating within groups. Keeping one's close group together instead of avenging by harming others in the group clearly serves the ultimate purpose of inclusive fitness of the individual if the doer of harm is perceived as generally safe and cooperative. Thus, within intimate and close relations such as with friends, family, good neighbors, and romantic partners, we often have the urge to forgive and reconcile after being harmed. This propensity to forgive and reconcile instead of distancing ourselves, avoiding others, or retaliating is what keeps the relationships working despite recurrent incidents where partners are hurt, and it serves to repair breaches in the relationship.

McCullough (2008) assumed that three major processes that are related to the activation of forgiveness on the part of the "injured": the capacity to view the offenders as "appropriate targets for kindness and compassion" (p. 147), seeing the other as a possible target for care, as valuable to the self, and as safe partners, namely as "being unwilling and unable to harm them again" (p. 147). Signals that communicate that the transgressor is valuable, safe, and worthy of care tend to arouse forgiveness in the "injured." These same psychological processes are also relevant to the '"transgressor's" inclination to ask for forgiveness, apologize, and seek reconciliation. Clearly the caring motivation is implicated in such processes on both sides. The motivation to care is not the only motivation that is implicated in this tendency, but it is an important one. Often people forgive because both parties care about the other person and the relationship and want the other to be happy and to thrive. Furthermore, empathic concern, which is at the basis of the caring motivation, allows "offenders" to understand that they have hurt their partners, and the motivation to care for the latter prompts reparation processes. For those who have been hurt, empathic concern allows them to understand why the other person hurt them; based on such empathic understanding, they may view reparation attempts as genuine and may tend to forgive. Thus in relationships where each partner is viewed as worthy of care and when partners are often loved, appreciated, and honored by each other, processes of apology, forgiveness, and reconciliation after conflict or interpersonal injury flow as part of the normal interactions.

This may not be the case in other types of human connections, as between different groups or nations in conflict, where closeness, trust, and care are not the default sentiments. Besides implicating the caring motivational system that prompts the view of the transgressor as worthy of care, McCullough (2008) discusses at least two other motivational systems that operate in such cases: the need to restore one's honor, social worth, and reputation which were harmed by the transgression and the need for equity and fairness where justice needs to be restored by various means, such as compensation and punishment. According to this view, for forgiving to take place in nonintimate relations, the caring motivation must be activated, at least by the inclusion of the offender in the circle of people who are worthy of care (the circle of care). Such activation of the caring motivation is also often implicated in transgressors when they appeal to be forgiven and aim at reconciliation. Some level of genuine honor and empathy toward the injured must be present in the transgressor for the injured to view the transgressor's attempts at reconciliation as authentic and trustworthy (Oliner, 2005; McCullough, 2008; Oliner & Zylicz, 2008).

Consequently the central underlying aspect of the caring motivation that is implicated in forgiveness in intimate and nonintimate relations alike is the extent to which the other party is perceived as part of the circle of care that deserves to be honored and cared for. As discussed in previous chapters, people have the tendency to draw such circles often involving in-group vs. out-group demarcations and tend to activate empathy toward members of the in-group much more than toward those of the out-group and in the extreme may even totally shut down their empathic responses toward those outside their circle of care. Yet these demarcations are flexible and malleable and can change depending on upbringing, circumstances, and internal psychological processes. Thus, even enemies who are perceived as unworthy of care and empathy may be seen as humans deserving compassion, forgiveness, and care.

Such processes of reconciliation that are based on expanding the circle of care also happen when atrocities and gross human rights violations are enacted between groups or nations. One noteworthy example is the process of reconciliation through The Truth and Reconciliation Commission (a court-like assembly) that South Africa implemented after the abolition of apartheid. Seeking restorative justice rather than retributive justice victims and perpetrators were invited to give statements and accounts of the aggression they witnessed, suffered, or perpetrated. Public hearings of such statements were held and perpetrators could ask for forgiveness and in some cases were indeed accorded amnesty. This process allowed some level of reconciliation in a nation that was torn because of inter-group atrocities.

Interestingly, within psychoanalytic thinking a need to engage in reparation was postulated to arise in infancy. Klein postulated that when infants recognize their own destructive impulses toward those they love and understand that they are separate from them, they have an urge, a strong instinctual need, to make reparation for the damage they perceive having caused both in their internal men-tal representations and in the real world (see collected works 1921–1945 Klein, 1975). Winnicott further discussed this need as it is manifested in the actual behavior of infants with their caregivers. He suggested that these reparative ges-tures need to be positively acknowledged by the mother so that internal secu-rity can be instilled, He viewed such successful reparative processes as central to the infant's mental health and to adaptive mother-infant relations (Winnicott, 1965). Both the reparative actions and their acceptance rely on love and care for the other party.

In that sense the caring motivation plays an important role in the restoration of working relationships in intimate and close relations where partners hurt each other at times as part of their daily conduct and on occasions even seriously injure each other's feelings and trust. Caring provides part of the motivation needed to seek reparation on both sides and find forgiveness. In nonintimate relations among individuals or groups, the motivation to care on the side of the perpetrator and on the side of the injured provide a necessary albeit not sufficient ingredient for remorse, apology, forgiveness, and reconciliation and is an antidote to cycles of retribution, retaliation and revenge.

Chapter conclusion

In our postmodern world and unlike the case in hunter-gatherer societies, the realms of family and close relations, the workplace, and education are sepa-rate. Yet each of these contexts features our motivation to care, which is a fun-damental part of our nature. Being a caring species (Taylor, 2002; Keltner, Marsh & Smith, 2010; Brown, Brown, & Penner, 2012), care is interwoven in the fabric of these contexts of human life. In each of these contexts, research-ers have discovered that our functioning is less optimal and in fact appears to be highly jeopardized if caring is not provided and received as part of daily life in these realms. Thus caring is not just reserved for the immature and helpless (i.e., children), the weak or disabled, or for emergencies but is part and parcel of the ongoing interchanges among people at home, in the education system, and in the workplace; it involves listening, accommodating, assisting, validat-ing, and being there for others. This caring is enacted not only by unique indi-viduals but also by all or most of us in different ways and to variable degrees.

It should therefore come as no surprise that such caring is also enacted by our leaders and is a significant characteristic of many leaders. Caring is also central to processes of reconciliation and reparation of relationships in intimate and nonintimate contexts and even among groups and nations. In fact the study of revenge and forgiveness has underscored the indispensable role of viewing others as worthy of care in dissipating anger, hate, and retaliation after transgressions, thus keeping the human fabric intact despite daily conflicts and even major injuries and atrocities.

The study of our caring motivation in these contexts has underscored its prevalence and the existence of other-oriented altruistic motives as well as the fact that these motives can be enhanced—not only through optimal backgrounds but also through overcoming adversity and trauma. In fact, those who have been helped—either during childhood by their own familial background or afterward by mentors, coaches, and psychotherapists—often want to pass this good fortune on and to engage in helping others. Finally, the study of these contexts has also exposed the importance of balance and autonomy in expressing the motivation to care. Obligatory care or overnurturance can overtax the capacity for compassion and result in burnout and in compassion fatigue.

Part II Conclusion

In Part II I presented and discussed a variety of domains and contexts as well as targets for care which have been studied using different conceptualizations and under different terms. The motivation to care, tend, nurture, and help other entities grow, thrive, heal, and develop is central in each of these manifestations of caring. These include the love and care extended to familiar and close others such as offspring, spouse, friends, and parents; the support and help provided to strangers in emergency situations; as well as altruistic heroic rescues and kind and generous deeds. These caring manifestations also cover volunteering in myriads of organizations worldwide and the formation of mentoring caring bonds with others. They involve the tending of pets, caring and cultivating gardens and plants, and caring for objects as well as abstract causes, the latter often reflecting generative concerns for future generations. Such caring is manifested in a variety of contexts: in family and neighborhood; in clubs, congregations, and societies; in the education system; at work; and even in the political sphere. Furthermore even in competitive contexts an observed propensity to exhibit caring, cooperative, and altruistic attitudes appears to characterize the majority of people (about two thirds) across a variety of cultures. Moreover, the capacity to view the other as worthy of care is central to our capacity to reconcile after being harmed by others, thus keeping the interpersonal and intergroup human fabric intact. All together, these manifestations are universal and are all around us. They are different streams of the same large river of a general, sophisticated, multifaceted, and encompassing motivational system of caring.

Several general insights can be derived from the vast literature on caring. First, a number of different motivations might be involved in caring, even during the same act of caring. These include both other-oriented motivations (e.g., to help others or to express humanitarian and altruistic values) and self-oriented ones (e.g., to refrain from feeling guilt or to enhance one's reputation). However, other-oriented motivations are by far the most prevalent and they are most often the strongest when several motivations are concurrently involved.

Second, people engage in caring because of other-oriented reasons both as a reaction to distress and need in others as well as because of an intrinsic desire to express their motivation to care. Both types of care can involve unplanned temporary helping as well as the formation of a caring bond, and such care can be provided in low- and in high-cost help situations. Third, as part of their help, people offer a variety of provisions and they often have personal inclinations toward certain kinds of help that they prefer to engage in.

Fourth, the presentation in this part of the book uncovers a variety of targets for the help and care that people may offer to others, including close friends or family, familiar others, strangers, animals, plants, objects, and abstract causes. In this respect the research has uncovered both a "rescue and heal" motif reflecting responses to others in need or in adverse circumstances and a "growth fostering" motif, which reflects caring geared to thriving and developing. As with the variety of provisions, the extant research reveals that people have preferred targets, and these as well as the inclinations for specific kinds of help relate to personal preferences as well as to cultural expectations and expose some gender differences in this regard. However, as yet we know very little about these preferences, what their origins are, how they develop, and how stable they are.

Fifth, the extant research has discovered several recurrent positive outcome for caregivers following care. These include happiness (warm glow or hedonic well being), satisfaction, meaning and purpose (eudaemonic well being), physical health, and even longevity. Some forms of help (e.g., mentoring at work, volunteering) also provided instrumental benefits, such as a good reputation. Although these different outcomes were not intended—since the ultimate goal was benefit for the recipient, not the giver—some of these outcomes could be foreseen. These positive outcomes probably act as proximate mechanisms from an evolutionary perspective. Rewarding experiences following the provision of help (hedonic pleasure), sense of meaning and purpose (eudaemonic well-being), physical health, and good reputation, for example, may all serve to sustain caring in the daily lives of humans despite its cost. At the same time research has also uncovered that in certain situations—such as parenting, engaging in the helping professions, and caring for an ailing relative—negative affective states are also very prevalent and include exhaustion, anger, frustration, guilt, and depression. In some cases, as in parenting, most accounts reveal that the affective balance is negative, reflecting what has been termed the "parenthood paradox." In Chapters 16 and 19 I get back to these issues and provide some suggestions to reconcile this paradox.

Sixth, in this respect the research has uncovered the importance of choice, autonomy, and a sense of competence in the enactment of care and the centrality of balance and equilibrium in its deployment. As with any intrinsic and fundamental motivation, excessive engagement in caring that leads to the neglect of other needs and motivations of the caregiver or caring that is not intrinsically and autonomously chosen (e.g., obligatory care) or one that is not successful result in negative outcomes, at times even dire ones for the caregiver (e.g., compassion fatigue, burnout, depression).

Seventh, research has uncovered clear individual differences in enacting care, which are similarly manifested in the diverse kinds of care with which an individual is involved. Research has also uncovered several routes that might affect individual differences in caring. These include, for example, a stable propensity to be caring that functions as a personality trait. This propensity relates, for example, to the tendency to experience empathy, the capacity to mitigate self-distress, the development of a moral identity of service and a humanitarian moral perspective, a positive experience of being cared for and being previously engaged in acts of caring, and also experiences of overcoming diversity and suffering. These qualities appear to reflect genetic and environmental effects. In addition, circumstances such as the clarity of the other's need and whether there are other potential caregivers as well as cultural norms and expectations are important in affecting how, when, and to whom caring is extended.

THE DEVELOPMENT OF CARING AND INDIVIDUAL DIFFERENCES

Part III Introduction

The enactment of the general caring motivation is observed in the wealth, richness, and multifaceted display of prosocial activities, as described in Part II of this book. This part will deal with the development of the caring motivation as well as individual differences in its enactment and their sources. I will start by delineating a general and universal developmental process—the ontogenic development of caring—and will present a tentative developmental course of this motivation from infancy to adulthood in Chapter 13. In doing so, I review research from diverse groups of researchers, who have tended to focus on one developmental period or a distinct aspect of caring and prosocial responding, so as to propose a universal developmental path of the caring motivational system. Chapter 14 will consider developmental processes relevant to the emergence of individual differences in the motivation to care and in styles or ways of caring and will propose a definition of good care and also discuss nonoptimal care and its origin. Finally, Chapter 15 will discuss a central issue that relates to individual differences in the study of caring, caregiving, and altruism that has been apparent throughout the discussions so far—the issue of gender differences in the arousal and expression of the caring motivation. In this chapter I attempt to provide a tentative resolution of the issue of gender differences in caring by integrating previous conceptualizations by eminent scholars, genetic and biological research, psychological perspectives, anthropological accounts, cultural considerations, and feminist and psychoanalytic orientations.

13

The Developmental Course
of the Motivation to Care:
Ontogenic Development of Caring

Elementary forms of the motivation to care arise quite early in human development. Studies have shown that one-year-old infants are motivated and able to comfort others in distress, assist in household tasks, and help adults, even nonfamiliar ones, by bringing or pointing to out-of-reach objects that they need (Zahn-Waxler, Radke-Yarrow, Wagner, & Chapman, 1992; Liszkowski, Carpenter, Striano, & Tomasello, 2006; Warneken & Tomasello, 2006, 2007, 2013). Although the mechanisms underlying these behaviors are not entirely understood, they reflect some understanding of others' emotions and desires and an intrinsic motivation to act on others' behalf. These caring acts have been of interest to social, developmental, psychoanalytic, and evolutionary psychologists as precursors of the human motivation to be concerned with the welfare of others and the capacity to be caring, cooperative, and altruistic with kin and nonkin (Fehr & Rockenbach, 2004; Warneken & Tomasello, 2009). This chapter is not intended as an in-depth overview of this vast literature but as a general synopsis of a possible developmental trajectory of the motivation to care and its enactment.

The early incipience of the motivation to care

Hoffman (2000), one of the pioneers of empathy studies, describes a developmental process of the motivation to care and its enactment during the first years of children's lives. This motivation originates in empathy, develops into concern for others, and culminates in actual prosocial responses. Specifically Hoffman argues that young infants may experience self-distress in response to another's distress and that this reflects a very simple precursor of empathy. As infants start differentiating between themselves and others, usually around 12 months of age, they may evince what Hoffman termed *egocentric empathic distress*, which also includes concern for the other and behavior aimed at reducing their *own* distress when exposed to others' distress besides demonstrating empathy. Around the second year of life, toddlers already show concern for others and also try to comfort others—a stage Hoffman termed *quasi-egocentric empathic distress*. It is quasiegocentric because at this stage children often provide comfort and care that does not take into account possible differences between themselves and others in what might be their needs. Hoffman suggested that toward the age of three, toddlers develop a more mature theory of mind, as reflected in becoming more aware of the differences between what they feel, think, and desire and what others feel, think, and desire; that is, they have a better grasp of the inner states of others. The three-year-olds thus become more sophisticated caregivers and start to use corrective feedback and perspective taking and can further tailor their care for others' needs. Hoffman termed this phase *veridical empathic distress*.

Elaborate research involving laboratory experiments as well as naturalistic observations has provided a rich delineation of these processes and has even suggested that they may occur earlier than depicted by Hoffman. For example, empathic contagion probably exists very early on, as observed in one-month-old infants' reactive crying after hearing the sound of another baby's cry (Simner, 1971; Geangu, Benga, Stahl, & Striano, 2010). Several months later, eight- and 10-month-old infants already show the beginning of affective and cognitive concern for others—interest and sympathy—that are very similar to such displays in older toddlers. Some researchers thus contend that infants by the end of the first year of life experience affective empathy as well as affective and cognitive concern for others on encountering distress in others (see review in Davidov, Zahn-Waxler, Roth-Hanania, & Knafo, 2013). By 14 months of age, infants already start helping—providing useful assistance in situations where the nature of the help required is particularly clear. For example, if you drop an object accidentally on the floor and try to reach for it from a desk, most infants around this age will walk over, pick it up, and return it to you (Warneken & Tomasello, 2007). This help was provided when needed (the experimenter accidentally dropped the object) but not in comparable control tasks in which helping was not necessary (the experimenter purposefully put the object out of reach).

Several months later, toddlers already help in more complex situations, as when the experimenter required help opening a cabinet because his hands were full or when the experimenter had trouble stacking books. The intrinsic and autonomous nature of the motivation to help became quite clear as toddlers even pulled themselves away from a fun activity or surmounted an array of obstacles in order to help a stranger even when a parent was not present and without directly being asked (Warneken & Tomasello, 2013). Toddlers even helped a geometric-shape agent lacking human-isomorphic body parts. When 17-month-olds observed a ball-shaped nonhuman agent trying to cross over a barrier but failing because it was blocked, 40% of them helped the agent at least once by lifting it over the barrier. They thus demonstrated concern and helping even for an inanimate toy that "behaved" as an agent (Kenward & Gredebäck, 2013). To provide this kind of help infants must both understand the other's goal and be motivated to help achieve it (Warneken & Tomasello, 2006, 2009). The available research demonstrates such understanding as well as the operation of a clear motivation to help others in toddlers during their second year of life.

Compared with instrumental help, where the other's goal may be clearer and simpler, situations that involve comforting and those that involve coordinated cooperation or sharing may be more difficult to understand and interpret (Svetlova, Nichols, & Brownell, 2010). However, by two years of age toddlers already provide such help enthusiastically. For example, laboratory experiments have shown that 24-month-olds frequently and spontaneously shared toys and food with an adult playmate who had none. They shared without being asked approximately 75% of the time and almost always when the playmates were more explicit about their need (Brownell, Iesue, Nichols, & Svetlova, 2013). In more naturalistic settings, as at home, the majority of 18- to 30-month-olds enthusiastically helped their parents and an observer with different aspects of housework and clearly articulated their helpful intentions (Hay & Rheingold, 1983).

At two years of age, more than 80% of children reacted with prosocial responding and comfort to the feigned pain of their mother (i.e., after ostensibly hurting her knee while getting up). Interestingly, although 50% demonstrated empathic concern to a stranger in a similar situation, only 10% offered her help. This may be related to their hesitation about their accuracy in reading of her needs and about approaching a stranger (Zahn-Waxler et al., 1992).

The emergence of comforting is related to growing perspective-taking capacities and understanding of others' emotions and needs. Understanding more intricate needs and others' emotions and states of mind and making out what kind of help can be offered are developmental achievements that take some time to learn. Such learning relies on cognitive and emotional maturational processes, on experience in a variety of situations, and on the couching and scaffolding of these capacities by socialization agents. In line with this depiction, toddlers' understanding of internal state words and their self-understanding (as reported by mothers) were associated with their prosocial behavior toward experimenters (Brownell, Svetlova, & Nichols, 2009). Children who helped and shared more quickly and more often, especially in tasks that required more complex emotional understanding, had parents who often asked them to label and explain the emotions depicted in books, even after controlling for age (Brownell et al., 2013).

In line with such developmental achievements, toddlers showed a more sophisticated understanding of needs and deservingness after two years of age. For example, two-year-old toddlers were more likely to express concern for and share a balloon with an adult who lost her balloon and who had been previously harmed (another adult destroyed or took away her possessions) than with someone who had not been previously harmed; 65% helped in the harmed condition compared to 37% in the no-harm condition. This happened even if the harmed individual did not express any emotion during the transgression, suggesting that children can sympathize with a victim in the absence of overt emotional cues of distress, and that they base their understanding of needs and deservingness across situations requiring perspective taking skills (Vaish, Carpenter, & Tomasello, 2009).

After their third birthday, children become even more adept at these issues and helpfulness becomes ubiquitous across different domains of helping: instrumental help, comforting, sharing, providing needed information, and cooperating. Three-year-olds, for example, are able to differentiate between justified distress (e.g., a lid closes on the experimenter's fingers) and unjustified distress (e.g., a lid closes on the experimenter's sleeve). They showed more concern and help toward the former, demonstrating perspective-taking abilities and a top-down regulation of the motivation to help (Hepach, Vaish, & Tomasello, 2012). Preschoolers demonstrated these prosocial behaviors with mothers, adult strangers, and even peers (Liszkowski, Carpenter, & Tomasello, 2008; Dunfield, Kuhlmeier, O'Connell, & Kelley, 2011). For example, in naturalistic observations at home in the presence of their peers, nearly half the toddlers who had the opportunity to respond prosocially to their peers' distress did so (Demetriou & Hay, 2004). However, toddlers and preschoolers appear to find it harder to help peers than to help adults (Caplan & Hay, 1989). The sophisticated and adaptive activation of the caring motivation and prosocial responding in the peer arena may be the developmental tasks attained in subsequent periods, most notably middle childhood and adolescence, where peers play an increasingly important role in children's social and mental worlds.

The extant research demonstrates that by preschool age children already evince distinct individual differences in their propensity to care and that these are quite stable and predictable, providing a strong basis for subsequent personality structure (Knafo et al., 2008). Eisenberg et al. (1999), for example, found that four-year-olds' spontaneous prosocial behaviors were significantly associated with subsequent other- and self-reported prosocial behavior, self-reported sympathy, actual behavior, and perspective taking assessed at several points in childhood through early adulthood. These individual differences appear to reflect a transaction of genetic and environmental effects and demonstrate that children have already had developed a moderately stable personality characteristic related to caring and prosocial responding by their midpreschool years.

Studies have also demonstrated the intrinsic nature of the motivation to help. This means that help is provided because the child "really" wants to help and because alleviating the distress or answering the need is an end in itself rather than means for gaining other rewards. Previous research with other intrinsic motivations has demonstrated that when children or adults are offered extrinsic rewards, these replace rather than supplement the intrinsic motivation. This is exactly what happened in a study by Warneken and Tomasello (2008). As in other studies, toddlers spontaneously and without encouragement or praise helped an experimenter who could not reach a required object, but when external reward was provided for their help (a desired part needed for play) this actually diminished the helping behavior in a subsequent session as in other cases of intrinsic motivation.

In fact, two-year-old toddlers almost universally help without encouragement or reward even at a cost to themselves, and they engage in this behavior enthusiastically, spontaneously, and without communicative support or scaffolding or the presence of their parents (Warneken & Tomasello, 2013). This universal intrinsic propensity is not restricted to laboratory contexts. Hay and Cook (2007) and Zann-Wexler et al. (1992), who made extensive studies in home and preschool naturalistic settings, concluded that spontaneous prosocial acts are part of almost all toddlers' behavioral repertoire.

This profile of findings demonstrates that the ontogenetic roots of the caring motivation are apparent very early in childhood. I will summarize them briefly here because of the importance of these observations to the major claim of this book. Specifically, by 12 months of age infants show clear concern and a motivation to help in some situations but are unsure of what they can do to help the other. By 14 months of age, toddlers are able to help others with simple, goal-directed actions; by 18 to 24 months, they can help in action-related situations that are more cognitively demanding, and they do so willingly and spontaneously with mothers and strangers without reward or encouragement. By 30 months of age, they show almost universal help and are able to help in emotional situations requiring more complex inferences about others' needs based on their feelings and internal states; they tend to act prosocially mostly with familiar others, although they evince empathic concern with others too. This difference with regards to comforting familiar vs. unfamiliar adults may be related to the toddlers' greater knowledge and understanding of their mothers' feelings and needs compared with those of an unfamiliar experimenter. These developments culminate in increased helping and caring behaviors on the basis of an innate motivation to help and care. Indeed, there appears to be consistent evidence for increases in the rate of prosocial behavior during infancy and toddlerhood (less than three years of age), preschool years (three to six years of age) and from early to middle childhood (see review in Eisenberg, Fabes, & Spinrad, 2006; also the meta-analysis in Eisenberg & Fabes, 1998).

Thus the extant research accords with the conclusion shared by a large number of eminent researchers that infants and toddlers evince a near-universal impulse to help, comfort, share, and cooperate (Hay, 2009; Warneken & Tomasello, 2009; Davidov, Zahn-Waxler, & de Waal, 2012; Brownell, 2013; Roth-Hanania & Knafo, 2013; but see Paulus, 2014). Most importantly, the cumulative research evidence suggests that what is acquired over the first years of life is not the motivation to help, share, care, or be sympathetic but rather the capacity to identify a variety of need situations and the means of providing help in these situations (Hay, 1994). Researchers have indicated that infants do not have to learn to care about other people; they have an inborn predisposition that appears early on, as soon as they show a rudimentary understanding of others' minds and self-other differentiation around their first birthday (e.g., Hay, 1994; Warneken & Tomasello, 2009). The existence of similar motivations among other mammals accords with the phylogenetic and early evolutionary origin of such an urge/motivation (Warneken & Tomasello, 2009; de Waal, 2012). For example, and just like human infants, semi-free ranging chimpanzees handed an out-of-reach object to an unfamiliar experimenter when he was unsuccessful in reaching for it. Rewarding was unnecessary and did not raise the rate of helping, and the chimpanzees continued to help even when their help required slightly more effort (Warneken, Hare, Melis, Hanus, & Tomasello, 2007). Furthermore, chimpanzees also helped other chimpanzees by unlocking a chain that prevented them from entering a location where they could access food. However, and unlike human infants, chimpanzees were less helpful in situations requiring food sharing.

Even nonprimate mammals such as rats demonstrate empathic prosocial behavior (Bartal, Decety, & Mason, 2011). Free rats placed in an arena with a cage mate trapped in a restrainer autonomously learned to intentionally and quickly open the restrainer and free the cage mate. Rats did so even when social contact with the freed cage mate was prevented and did not open empty or object-containing restrainers. Furthermore, when faced with the option of opening another restrainer with chocolate, the rats opened both restrainers and typically shared the chocolate. These studies and others (de Waal, 2012) provide clear evidence of the biological roots of intrinsically motivated helping behavior in at least some primates and indicate that the prosocial predisposition seen early in human ontogeny has phylogenetic roots, substantiating the claim for an innate human caring motivation.

Socialization practices build upon this motivational predisposition for altruism and care and teach children *how* and *when* to care (Hay, 2009). Children appear to learn such skills and rules in the context of home relationships, most often with their mothers, but also with their fathers and siblings and in other contexts, and they practice these scenarios in pretend play, mostly with dolls and with other toys such as teddy bears. Observations in preschools and homes have indicated that playing house or family and tending dolls in particular develops between two and seven years of age and becomes more sophisticated with age (Watson & Fischer, 1980; Howes & Matheson, 1992). Being an autonomous and deliberate activity, such play reflects the operation of the intrinsic motivation to care in a proactive manner and not only in response to the observed needs of others. Other motivations may also be implicated in such care, particularly children's powerful urge to imitate their parents. Playing with dolls in a caregiving role includes solitary play as well as dramatic play with peers or adults. This develops into a complex dramatic play in which children may act out an elaborate and nuanced relationship script, finding an outlet for the natural motivation to care and for their wish to emulate their parents and other significant adults, enabling them to practice and refine their caring skills (Howes & Matheson, 1992).

Developmental research has mostly focused on reactions to needs involving negative affectivity—distress or frustration. However, as noted by Paulus (2014) and Vaish, Carpenter, and Tomasello (2009), children sometimes offered help voluntarily even when no distress was demonstrated; they probably identified the need based on other processes besides affective empathy, as through knowledge of the meaning of certain acts (looking at an out-of-reach object that fell down by mistake and was needed to complete an action) vs. others (looking at such an object that was put down intentionally). Furthermore, the extant literature appears to neglect the development of care in affectively positive circumstances. This is the kind of care evinced when one person shares the happiness, satisfaction, delight, or awe that another person feels. For instance, think of a case when you had something good happen to you, when you just bought something you liked very much, when you attended a concert by your favorite band, or when you were hired for the position you wanted. You would probably want to share this with others and have them listen and rejoice with you. Scholars of early development did not define this as care and hence did not investigate it, and such help did not attract a great deal of scholarly attention besides research on social support in adulthood. Similar neglect is apparent in studies of empathy that did not focus on empathic reactions to positive emotions and such studies are lacking in the social support literature, which has only recently begun to examine support in affectively positive situations. Still, developmental research has demonstrated that same-sex peers' mutual (reciprocated) positive emotion, as observed in intense preschool observations, was associated with prosocial behavior and cooperation (Sallquist, DiDonato, Hanish, Martin, & Fabes, 2012).

Childhood and adolescence—the powerful role of socialization

Once the basic and universal inclination and ability to help other people emerges in the human repertoire, what might be the prospective ontogenic changes? During early and middle childhood children in a large number of cultures start spending longer periods of time with their peers. Although parent-child relations provide the first relational context in for the development of the caring motivation and prosocial responding, this context is hierarchical and hence cannot offer the necessary conditions for learning and practicing caring in an egalitarian relational context. Siblings may provide a better approximation of egalitarian conditions, but these relations include other considerations as well, such as unequal ages and maturity levels and competition for parental time and resources. Hence we would expect that one of the central developmental challenges of middle childhood and adolescence insofar as the caring motivation is concerned would be to learn how to handle helping and caring in egalitarian relations. The most significant aspects of this would probably be cooperation and sharing and the need to sustain an equitable balance between giving and receiving among peers.

Scholars have only begun to address some of these issues but, as delineated in the next sections, the extant research does indicate that issues of sharing and cooperating appear to be salient during middle childhood, while more sophisticated types of cooperation that include issues of forming coalitions, and hence allegiance to friends and ingroups, and caring reactions related to social exclusion become more salient in adolescence. For example, cooperation in noncompetitive contexts starts to be universal at the beginning of early childhood and is similar with respect to both friends and nonfriends. With age, such cooperation increases and equality concerns become salient (Berndt, 1985). Reflecting this developmental process, in a meta-analysis conducted more than a decade ago, Eisenberg and Fabes (1998) found significant increases in prosocial behavior from preschool to adolescence, although there was little evidence of a change in the mean levels of prosocial behavior throughout adolescence. Yet, this general increase was not found in all types of prosocial behaviors. Between middle childhood (7 to 12 years of age) to adolescence (13 to 17 years of age) increases were apparent in only sharing/donating, but not in instrumental helping or comforting.

Besides specific challenges and new caring skills related to the peer group (equity, cooperation), childhood and adolescence encompass three general developmental processes that are postulated to co-occur and affect the developmental trajectories of the expression of the motivation to care. These relate to sociocognitive, socioemotional, and sociocultural processes, with each involving the transaction of socialization processes and cognitive, emotional, and cultural aspects respectively.

Sociocognitive, socioemotional, and sociocultural processes

Sociocognitive developmental processes reflect advances in a variety of social cognitive capacities. These include perspective-taking skills that involve an understanding of others' minds, feelings, emotions, and desires as well as an understanding of increasingly more sophisticated interpersonal interactions. Such information on others' (as well as one's own) internal states can be obtained by imagining oneself in another's position and through a sophisticated and elaborate knowledge of social scripts and "theories" about how people feel, think, and interact. These advances are often described as reflecting mentalizing or theory-of-mind capacities, which are also augmented by the more sophisticated use of language to describe our inner mental life (Brownell & Carriger, 1990; Zahn-Waxler et al., 1992; Hoffman, 2000; Brownell, Ramani & Zerwas, 2006).

With the development of language, children become increasingly able to empathize and sympathize with a wider range of emotions. Furthermore, they also become more capable of reflecting and imagining such states in others across distances and differences, while younger children's empathic responses are restricted to another's immediate or situation-specific needs. Think, for example, of the capacity of young children to feel sorry for and wanting to help the persons who were struck by typhoon Haiyan in the Philippines although they themselves have never experienced or seen such an event. This capacity increases the potential for arousing the motivation to care through a top-down route of cognitive empathy and understanding without the presence of an actual person in need. Such advances reflect maturational processes, the accumulation of experiences in a variety of social interactions, and the scaffolding of such capacities by socialization. These lead to greater sophistication in discerning others' needs, even less salient ones (Weller & Lagattuta, 2014), and to a greater incidence of prosocial acts. In addition, prosocial behavior may now involve increasingly more elaborate, sophisticated, sensitive, and responsive acts and may grow not only in quantity but also in quality.

Similarly, *emotional regulation and the maturation of executive functions* develop throughout early childhood and adolescence. These affect the capacity to regulate one's responses to the needs of others, as by effectively dealing with one's own distress while observing another's and attending others' needs in a sensitive, responsive, and adequate manner. Furthermore, empathic processes and helping may become more regulated and governed by top-down evaluative responses that also include mentalizing rather than bottom-up visceral emotional responses. Decety and Michalska (2010) have provided a nice demonstration of such developmental processes at the neural level in a functional magnetic resonance imaging (fMRI) study in which participants ranging from 7 to 40 years of age were exposed to people in pain or being harmed by another individual. The researchers found, for example, that the older the participants, the less strongly the amygdala and posterior insula (primitive emotional processing regions) were recruited upon watching painful accidental situations. At the same time, the participants' subjective ratings of the painful situations decreased with age and were significantly correlated with the activation of the medial prefrontal cortex (mPFC), an area that is often associated with the top-down modulation of visceral emotional responses.

A large number of studies have demonstrated the contributions of affect regulation to prosocial responding. Eisenberg and her colleagues, for example (Eisenberg et al., 1996) found that teacher- and parent-reported regulation was positively associated with children's sympathy (the empathic concern or compassion aspect that reflects the motivation to care) among second graders. Moreover, regulation appears to maximize the potential of children with a predisposition to high emotionality toward prosocial behaviors. Unregulated children were low in sympathy regardless of their level of general temperament-based emotional intensity. In contrast, the level of sympathy (i.e., caring) increased along with the level of general emotional intensity when children had at least moderate levels of regulation. In other words, when children are regulated, their temperamental emotional sensitivity to others translates into increased helping. Similarly, higher regulation and empathy were associated with a higher prevalence of prosocial behaviors in adolescence (Padilla-Walker & Christensen, 2011).

At the *sociocultural level* we see stronger effects of socialization on caring with age. From early childhood onward, societal norms and expectations as well as moral mores become increasingly more salient and begin to affect the arousal and the implementation of the caring motivation. Societal and familial expectations and norms often guide decisions regarding the *"who, when, what,* and *how"* of prosocial behaviors. Sociocultural considerations affect the targets to whom care should or should not be directed (i.e., "we help only those from our community"), the contexts and conditions that should or should not instigate care (e.g., "in preschool, it's the teacher's responsibility to help children in trouble"), the provisions that could or could not be given (e.g., "don't give your toys to strangers"), and the manner in which they are provided (e.g., "when you share your food with others—smile and say please"). These processes may even affect the motivation itself by denouncing certain situations or targets and viewing them as unsuitable for arousing the motivation to care. These norms, expectations, and regulations are not synonymous with morality because they often reflect conventions or habits and do not directly rely on moral principles. Issues related to moral aspects are discussed in a subsequent section.

Hay and her colleagues have argued that prosocial behavior becomes more selective in early childhood (i.e., directed to friends and relatives, not to everyone), and is increasingly governed by display rules and social norms through the acquired capacity for self-regulation (Hay & Cook, 2007). Thus these authors suggest that what might have started as indiscriminate altruism becomes more selective as children grow older (Hay, 2004, 2007, 2009). Warneken and Tomasello (2008) suggest that this selectivity reflects the evolutionary need for limiting prosociality so as to avoid rewarding free riders and cheaters. Without such constraints an indiscriminate propensity to help others could be exploited, thus depleting one's resources and becoming evolutionarily extinct. Consequently, and in order to maintain a general human prosocial disposition, we as a species need to learn how to be selective in the deployment of prosociality.

This process starts in preschool and continues thereafter. Interviews with preschoolers and observations of their play have revealed a knowledge of adult norms that govern help, such as responsibility, deservingness, and reciprocity (Rheingold & Emery, 1986). For example, preschoolers tend to think that it is not their personal responsibility to help distressed peers when competent adult caregivers are present. They appear to learn this rule because preschool teachers are more likely to reward helpfulness in pretend play than in children's real interactions with classmates (Caplan & Hay, 1989). Furthermore, preschoolers tend to offer less help to an experimenter who does not "deserve" it, although she may evince the same need as another. Specifically, they offered an experimenter less help because in a previous session she was unwilling rather than unable to give them a toy (Dunfield & Kuhlmeier, 2010) or because she caused—or intended to cause—others harm (Vaish, Carpenter, & Tomasello, 2010). Middle childhood also proves to be an important developmental period where such norms and rules are learned and enacted, in particular rules that relate to attenuation of a general motivation to help that is costly as well as rules about sharing and cooperation, governing relations with equals.

For example, three- to eight-year-old children develop inequality aversion and prefer resource allocations that remove inequality, as opposed to purely altruistic allocations (i.e., giving others a share larger than theirs, which could characterize their transactions earlier) (Fehr, Bernhard, & Rockenbach, 2008). In addition and as they get older, children learn specific rules regarding sharing and cooperation that reflect their cultural norms. A study of three- to fourteen-year-old children and adults across six societies—including foragers, herders, horticulturalists, and urban dwellers across the Americas, Oceania, and Africa—found general developmental processes as well as culturally dependent ones in tasks that involved sharing. When prosocial acts did not require personal sacrifices, prosocial responses increased steadily as children matured, with little variation in behavior across societies. However, when sharing was personally costly, rates of prosocial behavior dropped across all societies as children approached middle childhood, probably reflecting a general progression in their understanding of the meaning and significance of these costs and in becoming more self-oriented. From middle childhood onward the rates of prosociality diverged as children moved toward the behavior of adults in their own societies, demonstrating the importance of acquired cultural norms in shaping costly forms of cooperation that involve sharing (House et al., 2013).

Furthermore, with age children learn to direct their helping selectively to close others (e.g., family or friends) rather than strangers or to prefer their in-group. For example, six-year-old children prefer an equitable division of resources with friends but treat nonfriends less well (Moore, 2009). In response to pictorial characters, five- to thirteen-year-old European American children predicted that these characters would feel happier self-sacrificing to help an unfamiliar child from their racial in-group vs. helping a child from an out-group (African American), and that the characters would feel a greater sense of obligation to help a child from the racial in-group as opposed to a child from an out-group (Weller & Lagattuta, 2013). This in-group bias in representations was also mirrored in behavior. From three to eight years of age, children exhibit a greater sharing of resources with in-group members (peers from their own school) vs. out-group members (children from a different social group) (Fehr, Bernhard, & Rockenbach, 2008). Together, these findings reflect the growing influence of culture, which steers the ubiquitous caring motivation in culturally congruent ways.

The internalization of morality

Sociocultural processes also initiate the internalization of moral expectations and principles. These have been depicted as reflecting two major aspects of interpersonal relations: *harm/care* and *fairness/justice*. The moral principles governing how one should act when others are vulnerable or need protection relate to altruism, the provision of care, and refraining from harming others—the harm/care aspect. The moral principles governing how one should act when people have rights to certain resources or kinds of treatment, on the other hand, relate to issues of fairness, reciprocity, and justice—the fairness/justice aspect. In a remarkable and significant paper in *Science*, Haidt (2007) suggests that these two topics (which he terms harm/care, fairness/reciprocity) might reflect the gene-culture coevolution of neural mechanisms and cultural principles that match two evolutionary mechanisms. The first is kin selection, or the preference to help and protect kin and thus propagate the genes that they share with us. This evolutionary mechanism can work when we are sensitive to the suffering and needs of close kin, leading to the coevolution of genetic propensities as well as moral mores that support such sensitivity. The second evolutionary mechanism is reciprocal altruism, whereby we increase our inclusive fitness if we enter relations where help and goods are reliably reciprocated. This evolutionary mechanism is supported by being especially sensitive to who deserves what; through the coevolution of relevant genes and social and moral rules, it presumably led us to be cooperative with those who reciprocate our help and to punish those who exploit us.

Haidt (2007) further suggests that although research often focused on moral reasoning and the primacy of directed, conscious cognition, morality involves two systems at the neural level: an ancient, automatic, and very fast affective system and a phylogenetically newer, slower, and motivationally weaker cognitive system. As such, the early building blocks of human morality are in fact fast affect-laden *moral intuitions* (e.g., sympathy and concern in response to suffering, anger at nonreciprocators, affection for kin and allies) that have primacy over slower cognitive processes. This claim amounts to suggesting that the caring motivation, whether in comforting and protecting others or in cooperating and sharing with them, is innate, affect-laden, and intuitive as well as cognitively based and backed by a coevolved cultural structure of morality. Research appears to substantiate these suggestions and demonstrates that prosocial responding may sometimes reflect processes that are fast and intuitive. For example, responding quickly in an economic game—naturally occuring or following such request—resulted in greater cooperation and generosity than when responding more slowly (Rand et al., 2012).

Haidt further suggests that this depiction of morality as a set of cultural practices and moral principles that coevolved at the neural and cultural levels is not only about how to treat other individuals; it also relates to being part of a group and particularly a group that is competing with other groups. He claims that alongside the harm/care and fairness/reciprocity foundations there are also widespread moral affect-laden intuitions and social principles about in-group/outgroup dynamics and the importance of loyalty, about authority and the importance of respect and obedience, and about bodily and spiritual purity and the importance of living in a sanctified rather than a carnal way. He suggests that in some cultures these issues are also considered as moral issues.

Although a rudimentary moral structure probably starts to develop early on, it is during early and middle childhood, as children learn social rules and moral expectations, that they internalize a prosocial moral structure. According to Hoffman (2000), this structure includes principles and behavioral norms concerning right and wrong, scenarios that reflect them, and associated moral emotions: feeling proud, happy, or good when abiding by a moral rule, or feeling guilty, sad, or bad otherwise. These rules are internalized through socialization, with parental induction (explaining why a certain behavior is expected and discussing how this behavior or refraining from acting affects others), as well as modeling appearing to be the best ways of achieving this goal. Moral internalization occurs when the child feels obligated to abide by its principles regardless of external punishments or rewards.

Such internalizations can be experienced as involving a sense of internal *coercion* through feelings of guilt or shame if the moral rules and expectations are not observed and because one's self-worth is contingent on acting morally. In these cases moral action is not an end in itself but means to gain self-worth or avoid feeling guilty; hence it is extrinsically governed. Yet, such internalizations can also become part of a person's self and identity, and in this case morally sanctioned actions are intrinsically governed and reflect an autonomous decision rather than a sense of coercion by internalized guilt or a need to be perceived as good by others (Deci & Ryan, 2000, in their theory of intrinsic motivation). The heroic acts described in the chapter on altruism, for example, by gentiles who saved Jews during the Holocaust (Chapter 10) were often linked to an internalized and autonomous motivation embedded in a moral self to help others. Both routes, a fully internalized moral identity that is intrinsically endorsed and internalized sanctions and rewards that are still felt as coercive may culminate in moral and prosocial behavior along with other routes to such care, as through emotional or cognitive (perspective taking) empathy. A study that investigated sharing among children aged four to twelve, for example, identified two compensatory emotional pathways to sharing that appear to exhibit two of these routes: via sympathy and via negatively valenced moral emotions such as guilt (Ongley & Malti, 2014). Children's self-reported sympathy as an intrinsic motivational component emerged as a significant predictor of sharing. However, in children with low levels of sympathy, sharing was also predicted by negatively valenced moral emotions following the failure to perform prosocial actions, reflecting an extrinsic source for prosocial behavior.

These sociocultural effects also reflect the operation of the sociocognitive and socioemotional processes described earlier, which allow a better regulation of one's emotions, attributions, and actions and hence a better tailoring of aid to the needs of the other *and* to social and moral expectations. Taken together, several routes thus emerge for the arousal of the caring motivation: (1) the emotional empathy bottom-up path, where empathic processes are activated by the observation of another's need; (2) the cognitive empathy top-down path, which originates in mentalizing, imagining, perspective taking, and thinking about the other's needs or predicaments; and (3) the social moral sanctioning of caring and help top-down path which can be enacted autonomously as part of one's value system or extrinsically in order to avoid guilt or to seek internal (feeling good) or external (gaining good reputation) rewards.

Proactive helping

Most of the studies described thus far discuss reactive helping, or helping as a reaction to others' needs. However, from three years of age, there are also indications for the proactive arousal of such motivations as children express their desire to take care of others (younger siblings, pets) and to assume responsibility for others' care on a more continual basis and not only as a reaction to an apparent need. The almost universal motivation of children from three to thirteen years of age to adopt a pet, for example (Kidd & Kidd, 1985), may reflect a proactive search for an opportunity to care. Indeed, most households with children (75%) have pets (Walsh, 2009a). Children report that they provide more nurturance to their pets than to anyone else in their networks (Furman, 1989; Bonas, McNicholas, & Collis, 2000) and accord this caring high significance as part of the bond with the pet (Melson, 2003). Furthermore, children without younger siblings spend more time caring for their pets than children who have younger siblings.

Children in early and middle childhood also tend to help with caretaking activities involving their younger siblings (if they have any), and such help relies on direct requests or expectations from parents but also on what appear to be intrinsic, spontaneous, and intentional overtures by the older sibling. For example, in a study conducted in the first months following the birth of a sibling, almost all the older siblings (most between two and three years of age) intrinsically attempted to help, at least occasionally, the mother in caring for the baby without being asked, and about 75% showed affectionate physical interest; also, more than half entertained the baby without being asked (Dunn, 1981). Furthermore, in a "strange situation" in the lab (like the one used to assess parent-infant attachment) involving preschoolers and their baby siblings, 52% of the older siblings reassured and comforted their younger siblings in the mother's absence (Stewart, 1983).

Such nurturance has also been observed in naturalistic settings. Several studies that included natural observations in various cultural communities (in Kenya, India, Liberia, Okinawa, the Philippines, Mexico, and the United States, for example) observed children in middle childhood taking care of infants on average approximately 10% of the time (see review in Edwards, 1993). On average, around 40% of this time included clear nurturance activities (offering comfort, physical contact, help, information, approval, food, or material goods). There were also large cross-cultural differences ranging from 5% to 26% in the time devoted to caring during the observations and also clear gender differences, with girls evincing higher involvement in caring for younger siblings than boys. These attest to the importance of the socialization context.

Often researchers discussing such caring allude to the role of culture in *demanding* such care from children, especially girls. But culture may also affect children's care by curtailing their autonomous motivation to care. In a series of studies examining children's reactions to an unfamiliar infant, Berman and her colleagues (1986) found strong sex differences appearing at around the age of five, where American boys became generally passive toward babies unless the babies needed direct instrumental help, whereas girls became highly interactive and nurturant. Berman suggests that this age-related change reflects social restrictions on engaging in feminine types of care, thus directing boys to find other avenues for exercising their motivation to care, such as taking care of pets. Consequently the motivational origin of the involvement in sibling care is probably multidetermined and reflects, among other things, intrinsic motivation, compliance with social expectations, and the internalization of specific parental expectations. Still, the relatively pervasive prevalence of such nurturance across different cultures accords with the claim that children (and especially girls) may find caring for infants a welcome outlet for their proactive motivation to care.

Gender differences

By the end of the preschool years and the beginning of early and middle childhood, reports by mothers and teachers also reveal the genesis of gender differences in empathy, sympathy, and prosocial responding, with higher levels ascribed to girls, although no gender effects were apparent in earlier periods (see review in Eisenberg et. al., 2006; Malti, Gummerman, Keller, &

Buchmann, 2009). Although researchers suggest that these effects may be attributed to socialization (Fogel & Melson, 1986), many issues remain undecided. Gender differences in toy preferences (e.g., dolls vs. trucks) that were associated with hormonal differences, specifically androgens, which are typically produced by the male fetus (Hines, 2003, 2004), suggest the existence of certain biological antecedents to gender differences in caring. With the almost universal formation of same-sex peer groups during middle childhood, these gender effects become more salient than in earlier stages (see review in Rose & Rudolph, 2006).

Participation in same-sex peer groups contributes to the development of sex-typed peer relationship processes, including prosocial responding. These separate peer groups function as significant acculturating contexts that are distinct from the socialization influences of adults (Harris, 1995). For example, from six years of age and increasingly in adolescence, boys tend to play in larger groups than girls, and these groups function as dense social networks that develop well-defined dominance hierarchies. Furthermore, boys engage in more rough-and-tumble play, sports and competitive games than girls. Girls engage in more extended dyadic interactions that involve greater self-disclosure and verbal communication, especially as part of friendships, and in more prosocial behavior and especially emotional provisions. These differences in peer cultures are also reflected in clear gender differences that increase during middle childhood and adolescence and show a higher degree of prosocial responding among girls vs. boys. Specifically, girls tend to care and invest more in dyadic friendships and to receive and give more emotional provisions; they tend to adopt prosocial and relationship goals in peer contexts and to feel more empathy for others, whereas boys focus on more agentic goals, including their own dominance in the peer group, and are keen in cooperative exchanges in competitive contexts. Unlike girls, who tend to talk things over to buffer stress, boys tend to use humor. It is interesting to note that although girls appear to have more prosocial interchanges than boys in their peer groups, boys and girls are similarly satisfied with their friendships (Rose & Rudolph, 2006).

Overall, it appears that by the end of childhood prosocial behavior becomes intentional and self-regulated, rule-governed and selective, supported by domain-specific knowledge, morally informed, gender appropriate, and part of one's individual character. In addition, a top-down mentalizing route is also available by the end of childhood, as is a morally informed one that is as yet less developed alongside the intuitive empathic reaction, which appears to be prevalent in toddlerhood and during the preschool years. Furthermore, children are now capable of engaging in diverse and quite complex types of care, some of which, such as sharing and reciprocity, are mostly acquired in childhood as part of peer-group interactions, and children are also now capable of practicing a sustained assumption of responsibility to care.

Adolescence—puberty, loyalty in peer groups, caring bonds, and caring in romantic relations and across differences

Adolescence is characterized by hormonal changes, which increase emotional reactivity (e.g., Spear, 2009), and puberty, which opens the doors for adolescents to become parents. Both are expected to affect caring. Puberty in particular is expected to augment adolescents' and mostly adolescent girls' interest in infants and their care (George & Solomon, 2008). The extant research accords with only some of these expectations. Puberty is associated with increases in emotionality in both empathic concern and personal distress (Masten, Eisenberger, Pfeifer, Colich, & Dapretto, 2013). Pubertal changes between the ages of 10 and 13 were associated with increases in empathic concern—the caring motivation—during observed peer exclusion at age 13, which was in turn reflected in a higher activation of mentalizing areas (mPFC brain activity) (Masten et al., 2013). Puberty has also been linked to an increased interest in babies, especially among girls (Fullard & Reiling, 1976). However, this effect, which was found almost four decades ago, was not replicated in other studies, and its robustness is unclear (Maestripieri & Pelka, 2002). Furthermore, although girls evince more interest in babies than boys and demonstrate a more nuanced perception of their cuteness, these behaviors do not demonstrate a clear developmental trajectory during adolescence, and findings do not tie such manifestations to pubertal changes per se (Fogel, & Melson, 1986; Sanefuji, Ohgami & Hashiya, 2007; Glocker et al., 2009; Lehmann, Veld & Vingerhoets, 2013). Thus some biological processes relating to preparedness for parenting may operate during adolescence but they do not appear in a clear and universal manner.

Adolescence is also marked by a strong reorientation of social behavior toward peers and romantic/sexual contexts. The pubertal rise in reproductive hormones as well as other maturational processes activate appetitive motivations to attract friends and romantic partners and to attain social status and other social goals and rewards (Steinberg, 2008; Forbes & Dahl, 2010). These are expected to be reflected in the development of the motivation to care and its enactment. For example, we would expect the peer context to become a central arena for the display of prosocial acts and the formation of caring bonds; we would also expect specific issues and skills related to the operation of groups and to competition among groups to become more salient in the expression of the caring motivation.

Indeed, research on friendships and peer relations throws light on interesting care-related developments during adolescence that involve new skills and provisions as well as the growing size of the groups of friends, cliques (moderately cohesive groups of 2 to 12 friends), or crowds (reputation-based larger groups). For example, besides the domains previously observed in prosocial behaviors—such as instrumental help, comforting, sharing, and cooperating— prosocial responding in the same-sex peer arena becomes associated with issues of friendship exclusivity, status maintenance, and in-group allegiance. Adolescents describe distinct forms of prosocial behaviors that include standing up for others, encouraging others, helping others to develop skills, and including others who are left out (Bergin, Talley, & Hamer, 2003). Furthermore, compared with earlier developmental periods, loyalty to friends and social groups—cliques and crowds—becomes a more salient domain. In addition, adolescence serves as a significant developmental context for learning how to cooperate and help others without compromising one's status and independence as part of a clique.

In this respect a somewhat new form of caring comes to the fore within non-romantic peer relations—that of practicing a caring bond and, more specifically, a mutual caring bond, whereby friends in a dyadic relation as well as friends as part of a clique assume a responsibility to take care of and protect one another (Corsaro & Eder, 1990). Close friendships that are also caring bonds and where caring is often mutually provided are quite prevalent in adolescence. Although such relationships appear earlier in childhood, adolescence reveals a significant and even qualitative change in the intensity and importance of such dyadic and group connections. Before adolescence, sustained caring and protective bonds are much less frequent and appear mostly with regard to siblings and pets. Furthermore, these preadolescent protective bonds are less intense and protection is often partial and intermittent, as other guardians are often the primary caregivers. In this sense, adolescence may serve as a significant developmental context for learning and practicing mutual caring bonds, where partners assume a proactive responsibility to take care of one another's safety and reputation and to ensure their fair treatment by the peer group (Corsaro, 1997; Giordano, 2003). In line with this depiction, prosocial behavior toward friends increases over time from 11 to 14 years of age, while prosocial behavior towards one's family is generally stable or decreases (Padilla-Walker et al., 2013). Furthermore, reflecting the arousal of the saliency of equality concerns among friends during adolescence, in competitive contexts mutual friends show higher levels of cooperation and helpfulness compared with nonfriends, only by eighth grade but not before.

Another new arena for care, that of romantic relations, also becomes salient in adolescence, and adolescents are required to learn new ways to express their motivation to care within such relations. The study of romantic relations in adolescence demonstrates that they grow in prevalence, depth, and commitment from early to late adolescence; although most are not stable, they still act as learning grounds for subsequent romantic bonds where intimacy, mutuality, and caring are expected. A large number of cultures feature spontaneous and natural gender segregation in friendship groups during middle childhood. Furthermore, the caring-related norms held and skills practiced in girls' and boys' separate friendships and groups differ in many respects. This means that when young people

enter upon heterosexual romantic relations, the two different "cultures" of prosocial responses must be reconciled. Furthermore, different societies have distinct
rules and norms on how caring is to be expressed in romantic relations, which also
include distinct roles for men and women. Consequently part of the adolescent
developmental process insofar as the motivation to care is concerned is to learn
how to care in a romantic relationship; research demonstrates that adolescents do
indeed engage in such learning.

A number of researchers have documented the development of romantic relations in adolescence in the United States and identified several stages. These start
in simple interchanges and with discussing and fantasizing in same-sex groups
about the other sex; adolescents then move to mixed-gender groups and perhaps
casual dating. Later development involves the creation of more stable romantic
relationships where learning how to express affection and develop intimacy and
trust, including caring, is exercised, and this eventually culminates in the formation of bonding and committed relationships (Furman & Wehner, 1994; Brown,
1999; Connolly & Goldberg 1999). Consequently, by late adolescence, romantic relations involve greater commitment, closeness, mutual help, and confiding
than existed earlier, resembling the mature couple relationships of adulthood
(Shulman, 2003; Collins, Welsh, & Furman, 2009; Connolly & McIsaac, 2011).

Late adolescence also marks another major achievement related to the development of the caring motivation. The maturation of capacities for formal thought
and processes of identity exploration result in the consolidation of a moral structure, which becomes more coherent, stable, and internalized than in earlier periods. In early adolescence, children start using reasoning based on abstract moral
principles and internalized moral emotions; they express self-reflective sympathy based on mentalizing and perspective taking (Eisenberg et al., 1995). With
age, they are able to articulate and act upon more sophisticated modes of moral
reasoning and show caring across differences and distances. Based on internalized moral principles of equality, justice, care, and responsibility and through the
development of a moral identity that is rooted in caring, adolescents engage in
voluntary sustained help to strangers (e.g., by volunteering) or in contributing to
abstract causes (e.g., environmentalism or justice and equality) (Hart & Fegley,
1995; Eisenberg et al., 1995, 2013; Lawford, Pratt, Hunsberger & Pancer, 2005).
Furthermore, these internalizations allow adolescents to somewhat overcome the
process of selectively narrower caring (i.e., to kin or ingroups) that develops from
preschool onward.

Such a structure counteracts the characteristic adolescent tendencies of being
focused on the self and involves a sense of proactive responsibility toward giving
to others who are not part of one's inner circle (family, friends). It thus directs the
adolescents toward larger contexts, such as one's school, community, and country, and even toward future generations. Studies of the prevalence of prosocial
behaviors in adolescence aggregated across a variety of types of such behavior

show an unclear pattern; some even demonstrate that prosocial behavior declines in adolescence and starts to rebound only in late adolescence or early adulthood. However, and in line with the development of the capacity to care across differences and distances, adolescent volunteering shows a clear increase (Eisenberg & Fabes, 1998).

This achievement is related to another process that is central to adolescence—that of forging an identity through exploration and contemplation, which includes significant processes of meaning generation and a search for life purpose (McLean, Breen, & Fournier, 2010). Adolescents attempt to imbue their lives with meaning, try to determine their worldviews and values, and seek to pursue them in work and love, thus giving meaning to their existence (Mayseless & Keren, 2014). Connecting to wider systems of meaning and engaging in helping other people outside one's inner circle starts to be salient in late adolescence, and such engagement is associated with subsequent generativity in adulthood (Lawford, Pratt, Hunsberger, & Pancer, 2005). After all, connecting with others and helping them to grow and thrive are the central ways in which we as a species find meaning in our lives (Little, 1998; Wong, 1998; Emmons, 1999; Schnell, 2011). Such giving across distances and/or differences, which is significant in adolescence, marks the foundation for activism in the operation of the caring motivation. The caring motivation is no longer mostly reactive but involves a proactive search for contexts and relationships in which it can be exercised.

Furthermore, and in line with these processes of consolidation, what starts as individual differences in the propensity to care and provide help and comfort during the preschool years culminates in a highly stable personality characteristic often termed a *prosocial personality* in late adolescence (Penner et al. 1995). Eisenberg and her colleagues (2002) appraised prosocial propensities very broadly and included empathy, helpfulness, and moral reasoning assessed by different methods (i.e., questionnaires, in-depth interviews) and reporters (self, mothers, friends) in a longitudinal study spanning more than two decades from the preschool years to emergent adulthood. The assessments in adolescence converged and demonstrated the existence of a coherent and interconnected internal structure of prosocial predisposition that was associated with childhood markers of prosociality and showed high stability throughout emerging adulthood, almost as high as the stability of IQ. These results thus clearly demonstrate the consolidation of a prosocial personality in adolescence.

Adulthood—primacy of caring bonds and generativity

These processes of consolidation, as well as other developmental achievements, such as the capacity for mutuality and cooperation in the peer group and engagement in sustained and long-term close relations with peers, set the stage for the central developmental milestones of the caring motivation in adulthood. Adulthood marks the significant achievement of two of the most important caring bonds that most individuals will ever hold in their lives—the committed romantic relationship, which involves mutual care, and parenting, which is non-mutual and is probably the most intense and comprehensive caring bond of all. These are mostly achieved in emerging or early adulthood. Not all adults enter such relations, but in a variety of cultural groups and historical times and even in our current postmodern world, the large majority of adults do: over 90% enter one and/or two of these caring bonds. By midadulthood but often earlier, generative concerns targeted toward caring for the next generation become salient and culminate in a variety of prosocial behaviors that address these concerns in wider circles.

From a sociopsychological point of view, adulthood is a developmental period of commitment—to an identity, to a profession, to a place of living and community, to a romantic partner, and to raising children. It is also associated with becoming an established member of society. At the neural level, the maturation of the cognitive control system in the prefrontal cortex and the connections across cortical areas and between cortical and subcortical regions during late adolescence and emerging adulthood strengthen individuals' abilities to engage in longer-term planning; these developments inhibit impulsive behavior and facilitate the coordination of cognition and affect (Steinberg, 2008). These maturational processes set the stage for a long-term, stable investment in caring that is both good enough and sustainable.

Forming a committed romantic relationship entails the assumption of a potentially lifelong commitment to caring for the partner. This is associated with heightened sensitivity, coordination, and synchronicity with the partner and with sustained vigilance to responding to the other's needs. Although equity considerations and mutuality are still as important, as they were with friends, communal rather than exchange orientations become more central. More specifically, the basis of caring becomes the love of the other and concern for the other's welfare rather than a quid-pro-quo exchange meant to incur or repay an obligation. A caring bond that reflects what Brown and Brown (2006) (Chapter 3) termed "costly long-term investment" with fitness-interdependent others is thus created. As presented and discussed in Chapter 8, such a bond often starts with the activation of other behavioral systems, such as the sexual and affiliative ones, but with time may develop to include attachment and caregiving dynamics. In time some of these relations develop to include a committed bond with its synchronous exchanges of care (see Feldman, 2012; also Chapter 5) that result in a similarity between the partners in styles and ways of caring and involve the creation of a coevolved dyadic "dance" related to the activation and operation of caring. This investment might come at a cost for caring in other close relations, such as with parents, siblings, and friends (Keren & Mayseless, 2013). Research has demonstrated that earlier engagements in mutual care with friends, as well as caring in close relations with parents, which involve more mutual exchanges in late adolescence and early adulthood, set the stage for this caring bond (Scharf & Mayseless, 2001; Seiffge-Krenke, 2003).

The transition to parenting often involves an extensive and significant transformation in the caregiving motivational system. The emotional, cognitive, and behavioral investments and commitments are vast, unlike those of any other caring bond. The distinctiveness in this caring bond is associated with the infant's total dependency on the parent, the time devoted to caring, the length of this bond, the monetary expenditures, and the vast amount of new information and skills needed for taking proper care of the new infant and subsequently the growing child. George and Solomon (2008), who were pioneers in focusing on the *parental* caregiving behavioral system from an attachment perspective (see Chapter 6), view this system as involved in a narrow aspect of the parent-child caring bond and specifically the provision of protection to the young. They refer to earlier caregiving examples as immature and nonfunctional, and suggest that the parental caregiving behavioral system begins its transformation only toward maturity in puberty. They further suggest that another critical phase involves processes related to the transition to parenthood, such as pregnancy and birth, and their associated hormonal changes, and to the baby itself. All of these transformations evoke maturational processes in the caregiving behavioral system. The investigators mostly describe these processes in mothers, and indeed clinicians and researchers have overwhelmingly suggested that women do not experience this transformation in the same way as men. At the proximal level, this is related to the biological and hormonal changes that biological mothers undergo during pregnancy, birth, and breast feeding and to the sociological and psychological processes that "prepare" girls and women for motherhood; however, these observations are less relevant to expectations regarding men's fathering (see Chapter 6 on feminist orientations, Chapter 15 on gender differences, and earlier sections of the present chapter).

Attachment researchers (e.g., Ainsworth, et. al., 1978; Feldman, 2012) and psychoanalytic writers (e.g., Winnicott, 1965; Ruddick, 1989/1995; Stern, 1995; Hollway, 2006) viewed the parental bond as highly inclusive and involving a large number of other aspects besides protection. These scholars provide insightful observations on the processes that mothers undergo as they become mothers for the first time. While I cannot do justice with these thoughtful and nuanced insights in the context of this chapter, I would still like to highlight some of the aspects they discuss. Stern (1995), for example, a psychoanalytic researcher and therapist, provides nuanced in-depth accounts of the "motherhood constellation," a new mind set that starts emerging during pregnancy and lasts in an intensive form for more than a year and even longer after childbirth. The mother becomes preoccupied with the protection of her child, with herself as a mother, with her relations with the infant, and with the relations with her own mother. This preoccupation with internal dialogues helps the new mother to rework past relations with her own mother as well as to develop her own mother-infant bond and maternal identity. This process thus culminates in substantial changes to her own caring motivational structure; it necessitates help and "holding" from her own mother and other maternal figures as well as help and "holding" from the child's father.

Because caring for an infant and later for a child can be quite overwhelming, scholars have discussed the challenges facing a parent (with a special focus on mothers) in providing attuned, sensitive, thoughtful care (see Chapters 7 and 8). Winnicott (1958) coined the term *good enough mothering* to refer to the expectation of moderately good rather than ideal mothering, and psychoanalytic scholars have stressed the importance of regulating strong, unavoidable negative emotions, accepting their inevitability and acknowledging that a parent is human rather than omnipotent (Benjamin, 1994).

Although these processes in mothers were described as strongly tied to biological processes related to pregnancy, birth, and perhaps breast feeding, very similar experiences and developmental processes are reported by first-time mothers who adopt babies. Their care for the adopted infant arouses similar concerns and even similar emotional turmoil. In fact, research has demonstrated that oxytocin levels in biological mothers and adoptive mothers (as well as in fathers, for that matter) are similar and that the biobehavioral synchrony and similarity between parent and infant is comparable in the different cases—biological mothers, adopting mothers, and fathers (reviewed in Feldman, 2012).

What about fathers, then? Scholars have generally devoted much less effort to understanding and highlighting the processes that men undergo when they become fathers, and we thus know much less about these changes (Cabrera, Tamis-LeMonda, Bradley, Hofferth, & Lamb, 2000; but see Benedek, 1970; Herzog, 1982; and Diamond, 1998; also the recent edited book by Lamb, 2010). Psychoanalytic writers have underscored several such internal processes including a sense of widening the self and the coupled relationship along with perceiving the new baby as a rival. These need to be resolved to allow the new father to provide important caring tasks such as serving as a holding environment for the mother and baby and facilitating the separation and individuation of the child at a later stage (Diamond, 1998). The caring provided by their own fathers and mothers supplies fathers with models to emulate or to rework, and they also rely on the child's mother to introduce them to this role (Henwood & Procter, 2003; Bretherton, Lambert, & Golby, 2006; Maurer & Pleck, 2006).

Throughout history, fathers have been more concerned with disciplining their offspring, teaching them about morality and values, and introducing them, especially boys, to the work sphere and the larger social context rather than with the kind of nurturing or physical care characterizing maternal care. Fathers' care for their progeny is strongly shaped by cultural expectations and norms and is variable across cultures and historical periods (Lamb, 2010). These range from a very low involvement in direct care and strong expectations for providing a safety network of physical and economic security to the new family to fully fledged physical caring and nursing, which is similar to the care given by mothers. It thus appears that the male caring motivation in the context of caring for offspring is versatile and adaptable and that present-day men are working their way toward constructing and reworking their paternal identity and the way in which their caring is to be expressed in this role (See edited book by Lamb, 2010).

Changes during the transition to parenthood are not the end of the transformations that the caring motivation and the caregiving motivational system undergo through parenting. With age, new challenges emerge and parents are faced with the need to learn new skills and make new adjustments in their operation of this motivational system. These include such transitions and challenges as sibling rivalry, child entering the formal education system, child puberty, empty-nest phase and more. Several books, such as the five volumes of the handbook of parenting edited by Bornstein (2002), describe such processes across the life span in great detail, and include also less normative challenges (e.g., parenting children with disabilities) and I will not describe them here. Changes throughout one's life are further expected as people mature and face new life challenges and opportunities. For example, changes in caring with the transition to grandparenting are also reported. It appears that grandparenting gives grandparents a different way of expressing the caring motivation than when they themselves were parents and promotes further personal growth related to changes in life's priorities and finding growing meaning and purpose by caring for adult offspring and grandchildren (King & Elder, 1997; Landry-Meyer & Newman, 2004; Taubman–Ben-Ari, Findler, & Ben Shlomo, 2013). Maturation as well as life transitions and different phases or stages in one's life provide a variety of changing different ways to express the caring motivation and affect the way in which caring is expressed and experienced, including major changes in the drive or need to care.

Related to this need to care, adulthood involves a more salient emergence of generativity. Generativity is expressed in the concern for future generations and has been described as the developmental task of midadulthood by Erikson (1963). It can be expressed through parenting and through a large number of other activities that involve caring for future generations, such as community service, volunteering, or mentoring. Although generativity pertains to midadulthood (see Chapter 9), precursors of such a motivation are observed earlier and mostly begin in adolescence. What is unique about generativity are two of its aspects—namely the proactive nature of such giving and its nonmutual character. Generativity-based caring means that the adult is autonomously searching for opportunities to give and help in the caregiver role in sustained or casual relations and often not as part of reciprocal relations of giving and receiving. Such generative acts mostly connect people to something larger than themselves and reflect a sense of being connected in time and with other entities (people, animals, plants, and nature). Indeed, cross-sectional research spanning respondents aged 19 to 60 found that altruism increases during adulthood (Rushton, Fulker, Neale, Nias, & Eysenck, 1986). When we consider all the manifestations of generativity in adulthood—parenting, volunteering, mentoring, donations, and engaging in activities that promote a cause—it becomes clear how universally widespread they are, and the altruistic and kind side of our human nature comes alive.

Chapter conclusion

We appear to begin the developmental trajectory of the motivation to care with a basic innate "feeling with" others which is already present in the first months of infant life. This develops during the second year of life to encompass an innate feeling *for* the other (empathic concern) and a motivation, the caring motivation, to engage prosocially with others. Contingent on the capacity to identify another's needs and to learn what can be done to answer this need, this motivation is implemented in more situations and domains and with growing categories of others during toddlerhood and the preschool years, encompassing such provisions as instrumental help, comforting, and providing information and sharing. It is universal, intrinsic, and autonomous.

When an child enters formal education, there are already clear individual differences and a moderate stability in empathic concern and prosocial behavior; there is also the beginning of gender differences. Sociocognitive, socioemotional, and sociocultural processes that involve the transaction of maturational and environmental effects are active during middle childhood and adolescence. The higher sophistication in discerning others' needs and the growth of helping capacities and skills that ensues may lead to a higher incidence of prosocial acts and to a higher sensitivity and adequacy of helping. However, greater sensitivity to and knowledge of cultural and familial expectations and social conventions leads the display of the caring motivation to be more selective, morally sanctioned, and rule-governed during childhood. Additionally, culture becomes central in aligning caring with societal norms and expectations and fostering demarcation between ingroup and outgroup.

Different paths that activate the caring motivation emerge with the development of mentalizing, theories of mind, and the internalization of morality. These include bottom-up processes starting from emotional or motor empathy, top-down processes starting from imagining and representing the needs of others, and morally sanctioned helping that relies on moral emotions and is centered in one's identity. Throughout this time externally governed helping is also exhibited, involving external rewards or costs for being caring and helpful (e.g., gaining or losing reputation) as well as help that is extrinsically provided, which stems from internalized yet "coercive" affective mechanisms such as guilt or contingent self-worth (e.g., helping one to avoid feeling guilty or to feel worthy). Furthermore, proactive caring, the sustained assumption of the responsibility to care as well as the formation of caring bonds—mostly with peers—also emerge.

During middle childhood and especially adolescence new caring situations become salient and new prosocial skills are learned in the context of moderately egalitarian peer relations: cooperation, coalition formation, dyadic and group loyalty, and concerns with fairness, justice, and equality. For some individuals, late adolescence involves the initiation of romantic relations and the salience of a moral identity that sets the stage for caring as involving something greater than oneself alongside processes related to the search for meaning and purpose in life. By late adolescence, prosocial personality dispositions become stable and robust. Adulthood marks the primacy of caring bonds with a romantic partner and off-spring. At this stage caring is also extended to larger circles and to future generations in particular and is often enacted across distances.

|| 14 ||

Individual Differences in Caring

Alongside the general and universal emergence of the motivation to care and its enactment as already described, research has also identified distinct individual differences in caring and prosocial behaviors. These differences were observed in the strength of the motivation to care, in the domains in which it was enacted, and in the ways or styles of helping.

Individuals manifest variable levels of intensity and strength in the caring motivation. These individual differences can be observed in the tendency to experience empathic concern, the immediacy and intensity of its arousal, the centrality of humanistic values in the person's identity, the capacity for perspective taking, and of course the prevalence of prosocial acts. At the extreme ends of the scale, one can see remarkable acts of altruism (such as those discussed in Chapter 9), as well as nonoptimal care, as when care is excessively or very marginally provided.

Individual differences also surface in the types and kinds of provisions or of caring bonds that people prefer. The research on volunteering and on the helping professions is especially revealing with regard to this dimension of individual differences, as people are very unique as to the kind of help in which they want to engage; these preferences characterize them and their personalities. One person, for example, may like to comfort others in dyadic relations, another thrives in organizing cooperative endeavors among different parties, and a third loves helping instrumentally by aiding the needy. We currently know very little about the developmental precursors of such preferences. Similarly, people differ with respect to their preferred caring targets (e.g., young children, the elderly, pets, nature). Finally, people also differ in their styles of caring. Some, for example, care in a sensitive and responsive manner, whereas others may be more dominant and controlling.

I would like to stress that the existence of such individual differences does not detract from the universality of the caring motivation and its innate and biological nature. In fact, similar individual differences can be seen in other innate motivations, such as hunger or sleep. For example, some people like to eat sweet foods, whereas others cannot do without spicy ones; for some, eating and food are more central and important in their lives than they are for others, and such people invest more time and psychological energy in eating. Furthermore, biological motivations may also become pathological, as with anorexia nervosa or extreme and life-threatening obesity.

Of course needs like hunger or sleep, which are described in Maslow's hierarchy of needs as more basic and as "deficiency needs," differ in many respects from the motivation to care, which reflects a higher-order "being need" (Maslow, 1953). The point I am making is that if such basic needs show diverse individual differences in their expression, including pathological cases, we would all the more expect similar individual differences in the caring motivation. In fact the variability in manifestations of various fundamental human motivations attests to the flexibility and malleability of human nature. This flexibility and plasticity is often conceived as one of the most important evolved characteristics of our nature, which has contributed to human survival and thriving throughout our evolutionary history (e.g., Scheiner, 1993; Price, Qvarnström, & Irwin, 2003).

This chapter provides a general overview of the developmental processes that produce such individual differences, describes the emergence of prosocial personality dispositions as stable personality traits, and considers the issue of the multidimensionality of caring and its relevance to developmental precursors. In addition, I also discuss individual differences in caring styles and conceptualizations of optimal, nonoptimal, and pathological care and end with a suggestion for a general definition of good care across the diverse manifestations of the caring motivation.

The development of individual differences in caring

As with other human motivations, individual differences in the expression of the motivation to care originate in a combination of genetic and environmental influences, and these sources often reflect transactional processes. A person's genetic background can influence environmental and contextual inputs. For example a child's sociable and emotionally positive genetic makeup tends to evoke sympathy and warmth in others, which in turn augments the child's caring. Similarly, environmental effects can modulate how a certain genetic potential will materialize. For example, a person's vulnerability to distress can be regulated in a warm and validating family environment and may, in such a context, lead to a stronger capacity to engage in caring and a higher prevalence of prosocial behaviors than in others who do not have such a genetic predisposition.

Genetic background

Individual differences in the motivation to care and its expression are noticeably based on genetic endowments. Individuals differ genetically in their tendency to experience empathy and in their warmth and expressiveness. They also differ genetically in their tendency to be anxious and fearful and in their capacity to regulate these emotions. All of these aspects are implicated in the strength of the caring motivation and its enactment. As discussed in the introduction to this chapter, this genetic variability does not, however, distract from the centrality, significance, and universality of the caring motivation. Similar individual genetic differences are also apparent in other biologically based motivations and needs. For example, individuals show a high degree of genetic variability in strength and in the frequency of their desire for food, sleep (needing very few hours of sleep vs. many hours), and sex.

Several large adult twin studies have demonstrated substantial levels of heritability in self-reports, with genetic factors typically accounting for 40% to 60% of the variance in altruism, empathy, and nurturance (see Knafo & Israel, 2010, for a review). Similar though somewhat smaller genetic effects were found with children. For example, in a large sample of 168 four-year-old twin pairs, genetic effects accounted for 34% to 53% of the variance in prosocial behavior, depending on the measure, with 43% genetic effects for a set of three self-initiated prosocial behaviors (Knafo, Israel, & Ebstein, 2011). Finally, greater genetic effects were found with age in longitudinal as well as cross-sectional studies (Knafo et al., 2008; see review in Knafo & Uzefovsky, 2013, on empathy). This increase may relate to novel genetic effects that emerge with age owing to greater maturity, such as perspective-taking skills, affect and behavior regulation, and/or evocative effects, wherein children's genetically determined behavior affects the input they receive from others, such as a higher inborn empathy leading to more scaffolding of mentalizing by caregivers (Scarr & McCartney, 1983). All in all, these studies demonstrate a substantial genetic heritability of individual differences in empathy, altruism, and nurturance as assessed by different measures and in various cultures.

Scholars have also examined some of the possible psychological qualities that drive these genetic effects, specifically inborn temperamental qualities (see review in Eisenberg, Fabes, & Spinrad, 2006). Temperament relates to individual differences in reactivity and self-regulation that manifest in the domains of emotion, activity, and attention. Although not all innate temperamental qualities appear at birth, they do arise from one's genetic endowment and affect and are partly modified by experience. The temperament-environment transactional developmental process serves as the basis for one's personality, including the personal propensity to be altruistic and prosocial. Several temperamental qualities have been implicated in the development of individual differences in prosocial responding. For example, reactivity or emotionality relates to the innate propensity to be positively and/or negatively aroused. Positive emotionality, for example (the tendency to happy, active, and to seek stimulation), has been associated with higher levels of empathy and prosocial responding. In contrast, the effects of negative emotionality (the tendency to feel sadness, anxiety, or frustration) were mostly negative but have also depended on another temperamental quality—effortful control, which is related to the capacity for self-regulation (see review in Eisenberg, Fabes, & Spinrad, 2006).

Temperamental effortful control refers to cognitive (e.g., attention shifting and focusing) and behavioral (e.g., inhibitory control, activation) regulatory processes; individuals show diverse levels of such capacities. Self-regulatory abilities, which develop on the basis of these innate temperamental qualities, and socialization effects have been strongly and positively related to empathy and prosocial behavior. In addition, self-regulation may moderate the links between negative emotional arousal and responding. High negative arousal, possibly leading to high empathy *and* high personal distress, can result in a higher degree of prosocial responding if a child has good self-regulatory skills, which help regulate the personal distress that arises and direct the child toward focusing on the caring motivation and on the activation of prosocial responding. Finally, sociability and shyness also appear to affect a child's tendency to assist others. Children who are sociable and low in shyness, social anxiety, or social inhibition have higher tendencies toward empathy and are more likely to help than other children. This is especially apparent in situations that require social initiatives in unfamiliar circumstances. Interestingly, studies of twins that examined the heritability of empathy, altruism, and prosocial behavior have shown that most of the remaining variance was accounted for by environmental effects, which twins do not share; thus these results underscore the importance of each twin's unique experiences (see Knafo & Israel, 2010, for a review).

Environmental antecedents

Environmental effects relate to a large number of contexts. These include parent-child relationships, sibling relationships, school contexts, peer contexts, nonacademic contexts such as the neighborhood or the religious community, the media, and the general cultural context. I will now refer briefly to some of these contexts but want mostly to provide examples rather than to thoroughly review existing research. Early relationships with parents (mostly mothers) are among the most significant arenas in which infants and children learn to care (Hollway, 2006; Solomon & George, 2008). In this respect, a notable psychoanalytic perspective is Hollway's (2006) standpoint, which asserts that humans are not born with a *capacity* to care. Rather, they develop their potential capacity to care through the experience of primary care, gender development, and, later, parenting. She accords a special place to the intersubjective experiences that form part of early parent-child relations in the development of the capacity to care. Intersubjectivity reflects interrelationships that involve sensitivity, empathy, and feeling with and for another person. It relates to shared cognition and consensus as well as shared feelings and states of mind among people, which unconsciously flow from one to another and constantly modify the participants. During the first months of life and through an experience of sensitive and responsive care and containment, the infant's self emerges and becomes more differentiated and integrated. The infant is then able to internalize and resonate the caring emotions and states of mind that she or he experiences and is thus able to introjecting such care toward her or his own self and toward parents and others, evincing the elementary capacity to care. Accordingly, we first learn about care in the context of receiving care as infants and children. This experience is crucial in the emergence of our capacity to care for ourselves and for others.

Feldman and her colleagues provide illuminating empirical evidence of such processes. Using observational measures, they coded the biobehavioral synchrony between parents and infants during social contact. They examined minute social behaviors in the gaze, vocal, affective, and touch modalities and how they dynamically integrate to create dyad-specific affiliations. Furthermore, they assessed the levels of oxytocin—which is assumed to provide the neurohormonal substrate for close bonds involving attachment and caring in humans—in each of the participants. In line with the intersubjectivity notion, the children's levels of oxytocin correlated with those of the parents and were predicted by the level of synchrony the child experienced in the first months of life. In addition, three-year-old children who experienced more synchronous parenting in infancy and more sensitive and responsive concurrent interactions with their parents transferred these positive internalized relationships to their best friends and showed greater reciprocity and concern for the friends' needs (see review in Feldman, 2012). The importance of experiencing maternal care is also clearly seen in other animals. Rhesus macaques that were separated from their mothers during their first year of life, for example, do not practice the kind of maternal play as others and display highly unadaptive forms of mothering in maturity (Pryce, 1995).

A large number of other studies demonstrate the importance of the family context and parent-child relations in particular to the development of empathy, the caring motivation, and prosocial behaviors (see review in Eisenberg, Fabes, & Spinrad, 2006). Among the various parenting variables I would like to underscore the importance of five domains that contribute to caring. First, the development of empathy, sympathy (empathic concern or compassion), and prosocial behavior is enhanced by practices in which the parent models caring, such as warmth, sensitivity to the child's distress, and closeness; these often culminate in the child's attachment security. Second, parental use of *inductive discipline* —a distinct style of parental control and discipline—has also been closely associated with caring. Induction includes verbal discipline in which the parent provides explanations or reasons for requiring the child to change her or his behavior (Hoffman, 1970). Hoffman (2000) has argued that induction is likely to promote moral development because it induces an optimal level of arousal for learning (i.e., it elicits the child's attention but is unlikely to cause overarousal and anxiety, which interfere with learning). Moreover, induction focuses children's attention on the consequences of their behavior for others, thereby promoting perspective taking and empathy. Induction is thus not felt as coercive and tends to be internalized. In contrast, power-assertive and punitive discipline is negatively associated with prosocial behavior and empathy. Third, participation in prosocial activities at home—such as helping with household chores, taking care of younger siblings, and other parent-sanctioned contexts on a regular basis—is also associated with higher levels of prosocial responding. Fourth, the investment in responding to and teaching about emotions, mental states, and relationships has also been related to children's caring motivation and prosocial behaviors. Fifth, the parental modeling of prosocial responding, as well as the discussion and active promotion of prosocial values (if done in a noncoercive manner), is also associated with higher prosocial responding. Finally, older and younger siblings can learn and practice prosocial capacities through engagement in positively valenced sibling relationships; these effects exceed the contributions of the parent-child relationship context (e.g., Padilla-Walker, Harper, & Jensen, 2010; Harper, Padilla-Walker, & Jensen, 2014).

Children learn about prosocial responding in other contexts too (see review in Eisenberg, Fabes, & Spinrad, 2006). Besides parents, teachers are also significant socializing agents, and teacher closeness and warmth has been found to promote prosocial responding. Organized opportunities, sanctioned and promoted by adults for the purpose of practicing caring for others, contribute to children's internalization of moral perspectives that endorse a person's responsibility for helping others; they also augment the capacity for empathy. Such opportunities include community service programs in schools, religious institutions, or youth organizations and other school-based programs designed to enhance prosocial values, behaviors, and attitudes in children (Durlak, Weissberg, Dymnicki, Taylor, & Schellinger, 2011). In addition, exposure to media (TV, video games) that promote prosocial responding is also effective in promoting empathy, care, and prosocial responding; research has shown that some of the mediating factors for this may lie in prosocial cognition (Greitemeyer & Osswald, 2011).

Finally, the peer context is of central importance. It provides unique situations for learning and practicing caring, nurturance, and cooperation with one's equals as well as for learning and practicing fairness, justice, and loyalty (see review in Smetana, Campione-Barr, & Metzger, 2006). It is only in a peer context that children learn to cooperate in egalitarian dyadic relationships and in groups of same- and different-sex others. Hence cooperation and sharing, equity, and fairness as well as the coordination of the balance between being a caregiver and a care receiver—such that the dignity, independence, and individuality of self and other are maintained without compromising interconnection and mutual helpfulness—are mostly learned within this context. There is a transactional relation between having prosocial friends and having higher prosocial tendencies because children both affect and are affected by their peers and friendships (see review in Eisenberg, Fabes, & Spinrad, 2006).

The cultural context appears to have a significant effect on the provision of care and the norms governing the target of the motivation to care, the strength of this motivation, and whether children and adults would act upon it. This is related to emotional and instrumental responding as well as to cooperation and sharing. As discussed in the previous chapter, sociocultural effects modulate and shape empathic and prosocial responding, and studies that have examined the operation of the caring motivation show clear cross-cultural differences. In one of the earliest studies involving observational data, for example, some cultures (such as those of Kenya, Mexico, and the Philippines) had higher rates of prosocial behaviors (e.g., offering food, toys, information, and support) than others (such as those of Okinawa, India, and the United States). Whiting and Whiting (1975) found that people in prosocial cultures tended to be more traditional and to live together in extended families. Additional aspects of these cultures included women making major economic contributions to the family, a less centralized government, and the assignment of chores and responsibilities to children at an early age. Similarly, when the research focused on cooperation and sharing, children from traditional rural cultures tended to be more cooperative with peers on low-cost tasks compared with children from urban or westernized cultures (see Eisenberg & Fabes, 1998). However in a study of adults in 23 countries, participants from cultures that regarded the family or extended in-group as the key social unit were *less* likely to provide low-cost helping to strangers than participants from cultures that considered the autonomous person as the key social unit (Knafo, Schwartz, & Levine, 2009). Thus close-knit extended families may promote prosocial responding with familiar others but not with strangers. Accordingly, cultures appear to differ in the types of prosocial behaviors that they value most and in their beliefs about the worthy targets of help and caring.

In sum, and as with other complex human behaviors, it is currently commonly understood that individual differences in caring and prosocial responding arise as a transactional effect of internal states and external circumstances. In addition, the research efforts of a large number of devoted and creative researchers have identified a clear profile of antecedents for good care, meaning that today we know a great deal about how to foster the capacity to provide good care in a variety of situations. This has clear implications for education, child welfare, and public policy. Finally, the similarity in the developmental antecedents of the capacity to enact good care (i.e., temperamental positive expressivity, warm and secure family relations, and experience in caring in extrafamilial contexts that is expressed across diverse targets, contexts, and circumstances) underscores the existence of a common core of caring in the context of this variety (but see the discussion in the section on multidimensionality of prosocial behavior in this chapter).

Prosocial personality disposition

A moderately stable personality characteristic of empathic and prosocial responding emerges as early as in the preschool years (Knafo & Plomin, 2006). By adolescence, this propensity becomes quite coherent and stable and has been described as reflecting a prosocial personality structure. Generally speaking, prosocial individuals tend to experience high levels of empathy, to feel responsible for the welfare of others, and to adopt other-oriented moral reasoning. These internal processes are most likely to result in actual prosocial behavior among those who feel competent and in control, who tend to be socially dominant and assertive (Penner & Orom, 2010). In line with this depiction, prosocial individuals are expected to display conspicuous internal processes and behavioral inclinations. Based on a comprehensive examination of the existing literature, Penner and his colleagues (Penner, Fritzsche, Craiger, & Freifeld, 1995) have developed a measure that captures a prosocial personality structure that includes the cognitive, emotional, and behavioral manifestations of such a stable propensity. The other-oriented empathy factor taps primarily prosocial thoughts and feelings and addresses being empathetic and feeling responsibility and concern for the welfare of others. It also appears to tap the generalized motivation to care. The helpfulness factors concern prosocial actions and reflect a history of being helpful and being unlikely to experience self-oriented discomfort in response to others' distress (Penner et al., 1995).

These two aspects are moderately correlated, yet they clearly tap conceptually and empirically different aspects. As with any other motivation, the arousal and enactment of the caring motivation are related yet distinct and are often linked to distinct concurrent antecedents and developmental history trajectories (Penner & Orom, 2010). Scores on the other-oriented empathy dimension, for example, strongly correlate with measures of personality attributes such as agreeableness and nurturance and with affective and cognitive responses to distress, but scores on the helpfulness dimension do not. Conversely, scores on the helpfulness dimension, which taps behavior rather than motivation, correlate strongly with measures of dominance and assertiveness, but scores on the other-oriented empathy dimension do not (Penner & Fritzsche, 1993; Penner et al., 1995). Taken together, these aspects have been associated with helping and caring in a variety of situations and domains, such as speed of response in simulated emergencies; the frequency of mundane, everyday acts of helping; the caring responses of parents helping their child cope with invasive treatments for pediatric cancer; the willingness to mentor coworkers; organizational citizenship behaviors; volunteering;

and the willingness to serve as an organ donor. Thus there is strong evidence to support the existence of a general personality-stable propensity to help across domains, targets, and types of prosocial responding.

Similar findings arise from the study of generative adults—those high in generativity—who exemplify the motivation to invest in future generations. As described in Chapter 9, generativity is seen as a personal characteristic by midadulthood, demonstrating stable individual differences (McAdams et al., 1998). Those high in generativity demonstrate high levels of self-esteem, happiness, and psychological and social well-being and show an "expanded radius of care" that reflects caring investments in a variety of domains (e.g., parenting, community service, volunteering, and prosocial acts with strangers) (Peterson & Klohnen, 1995, p. 20).

A different angle on the prosocial personality comes from research on moral and prosocial exemplars. One of the most famous examples concerns Colby and Damon's study of 23 American exemplars who had shown "a sustained commitment to moral ideals or principles" throughout their lives (1992). The study culminated in their book *Some Do Care*, which presents an in-depth discussion of five such individuals. Among them are Suzie Valadez, who spent years providing food, clothing, and medical care to thousands of poor Mexicans, and Virginia Durr, a civil rights activist in the South. The authors identified a number of qualities that were consistent across the entire group of exemplars. These include a sense of conviction about their core moral beliefs, which reflects a strong integration of their moral values into their sense of self. These convictions involve setting high standards for themselves as well as considering charity and service to others as very important values constituting the compass for their lives. They also stand out in their receptivity and openness to new ideas and goals, reflecting a lifelong capacity for moral growth, a manner of conduct that encourages collaborative activities with others, and a conspicuously clear perspective of positivity, optimism, and hopefulness.

A somewhat similar profile was identified by King and her colleagues (King, Clardy, & Ramos, 2014) in a study of young spiritual exemplars. The participants were 30 adolescents aged 12 to 21, representing eight religions and six countries from around the world. These individuals were noted for living with a profound spirituality within their own cultures. As would be expected in such a sample, all the participants reported that transcendence in the sense of being deeply aware of or connected to something greater than themselves was prevalent in their experiences and, interestingly, almost all of them also described such transcendence in relation to others around them and humanity in general. In addition, they also exhibited a fidelity involving a commitment to beliefs, worldviews, and values that reflected a strong sense of morality, devotion, and purpose along with an openness to and respect for other belief systems. These convictions were manifested in an expressed commitment to caring for others and serving others less fortunate than themselves and in behavior that involved intentionally making a contribution through acts of service or leadership.

Although research on exemplars and prosocial personality dispositions as well as on generative adults (see also Chapter 9 on altruism) has used different methodologies and even defined the research domain somewhat differently (i.e., addressing prosocial responding, morality, or spirituality), these studies have uncovered a very similar profile reflecting strong prosocial convictions that are morally embedded in connections with social circles beyond the in-group; an open, optimistic, and kind outlook; and both being altruistic—which involves personal values, sentiments, and empathy—and doing prosocial acts. Furthermore, research has found that these individuals (exemplars, generative adults, and those high on prosocial personality attributes) tended to be prosocial in a variety of domains and with a variety of targets, demonstrating a convergence in the expression of the caring motivation and underscoring its common core across diverse manifestations.

Multidimensionality of prosocial behavior

The interplay of the various genetic and environmental effects is not observed only in the quantity or prevalence of prosocial responding. In fact, and as discussed in Part II, there are many ways in which the motivation to care is enacted, and this diversity is manifested along a variety of dimensions. The research conducted thus far within the prosocial tradition, and particularly the research examining the development of prosocial responding, has tended not to focus on this variety and often lumped different kinds of prosocial responding together. Yet prosocial acts can vary along a number of dimensions.

For example, and as we have seen in Part II, the *recipients or targets of care* can vary to a great extent. As far as the motivation to care and its development are concerned, the important distinctions among targets involve categories that may relate to distinct developmental processes. One such categorization differentiates between helping family members, helping friends, and helping strangers. For example, recent studies have found that family-oriented prosocial behavior was generally stable or decreased over time during adolescence, whereas prosocial behavior toward friends increased over time (Padilla-Walker et al., 2015). Furthermore, a person's culture may have different expectations and norms with regard to helping one's inner circle as opposed to helping strangers. This relates to another important differentiation: that between helping in-groups vs. out-groups. When children start to understand the notion of in-group and out-group, probably around four or five years of age, they begin to develop a preference toward helping the former (Weller & Lagattuta, 2013; 2014). Yet, with age, such a preference may attenuate, and perspective-taking abilities, moral convictions, and generativity concerns in particular open the way for wider prosocial sentiments and responsibility.

In relating to *kinds or types of help*, one of the obvious distinctions is between the degrees of the help's cost, as between low-cost help (providing directions, telling the time), medium-cost help (babysitting a neighbors' infant for a day), and very high-cost help (risking one's life to save a drowning person). Low-cost help (sharing), for example, was found to be quite similar in various cultures and appears to increase throughout childhood, whereas high-cost sharing reflected culture-specific norms (House et al., 2013). It makes sense that the universal autonomous inclination to help, reflecting the operation of the caring motivation, would be freely exercised as it is aroused in low-cost conditions. However, when a high cost is at stake, cultural norms would intervene to direct prosocial responding in a way that would maximize the cultural group's benefits. Cultures differ in how they govern and direct the major basic, innate, and biologically based motivations such as hunger and sex, and this is also the case with the innate caring motivation.

Another significant difference among the types of help relates to distinctions already observed in infancy and toddlerhood. Several distinct domains of helping and caring have been identified in toddlerhood and the preschool years: the provision of instrumental help to aid someone attain her or his goal, emotional comforting, sharing, the provision of information, and cooperation. These provisions show somewhat different developmental trajectories. In infancy and the preschool years, for example, there is little correlation between the prevalence of different provisions; these appear to require skills that mature at different times. In addition, there is an increase in sharing/donating from middle childhood to adolescence but no change in instrumental help or comforting (Eisenberg, Fabes, & Spinrad, 2006). In a pioneering study different neurophysiological activation patterns in EEG during resting state in 14-months-old infants' were associated with the emergence of instrumental helping and comforing several months later (Paulus, Kühn-Popp, Licata, Sodian, & Meinhardt, 2013). Still, to date there is little research on the developmental trajectories of different kinds of provisions. Researchers have pointed out the diversity in instances of prosocial behavior (see review in Eisenberg, Fabes, & Spinrad, 2006; also Paulus, 2014); some have suggested that they might be governed by different mechanisms and therefore exhibit different ontogenetic developmental trajectories (Paulus, 2014).

Furthermore, individuals may differ in the provisions that they prefer to give, and such differences may reflect the interplay of genetic and environmental influences. For example, some individuals may be better at comforting and psychologically soothing others (i.e., listening, talking things over, hugging) and also more inclined to provide such care, whereas others may be great at instrumental care (i.e., fixing things, carrying stuff, lending money) and be motivated to offer such help. We currently know very little about these individual differences and about how they develop (but see research on the antecedents of choosing a helping profession, Chapter 12). A recent call to explore the multidimensionality of prosocial behavior culminated in an edited book by Padilla-Walker and Carlo (2014), in which the different chapters attempt to capture the multidimensional nature of prosocial development. The editors claim that alongside the success of extant research in elucidating empathic and prosocial developmental processes in general there might be unique correlates for the different forms of such behavior. They suggest that the adoption of such a multidimensional perspective can furnish a more nuanced, sophisticated, and useful, and—I would add—a more valid understanding of prosocial responding. I concur with this view and discuss this issue in more detail in Part IV.

Individual differences in how people care—caring styles

The study of individual differences in how people care is a very broad research domain. The vast research on parenting alone discusses more than a hundred aspects, styles, or dimensions of individual differences in parental care. Researchers have identified many more distinct styles in other realms, such as volunteering, social support, caregiving to the elderly, donations, and mentoring. Although some of these individual differences are described as general styles or attitudes that characterize individuals, there is great flexibility in their enactment, which means that the specific enactment of caring is also highly dependent on the identity of the care recipients, their relative power in relation to the caregiver, their common history, the specific context, the cultural climate, and a host of other variables. Different research modalities have identified a somewhat different set of styles or dimensions of individual differences. In what follows, I will not review this considerable literature but will focus on two issues. I succinctly present some of the more prevalent conceptualizations and discuss what constitutes "optimal care." I then discuss the negative side of caring—specifically what it looks like when it goes awry and even becomes pathological. I will end by attempting to provide an overarching characterization of good care.

Conceptions of optimal care

Several major dimensions of caregiving have been discussed within the parenting domain. One of the best-known schemes of parenting styles was suggested in the early 1960s by Baumrind (1967/1971). Using naturalistic observation, parental interviews, and other research methods, she identified four important aspects of *parenting practices*: disciplinary strategies, warmth and nurturance, communication styles, and expectations of maturity and control. By investigating these parenting practices, Baumrind identified three different overarching parenting styles, while further research by Maccoby and Martin (1983) added a fourth.

These styles can generally be seen as exemplifying the intersection of two dimensions of parenting practices: responsiveness and demandingness.

Parenting that is high on responsiveness and demandingness—authoritative parenting—is depicted as optimal. Authoritative parents are nurturant and responsive to children's needs (high responsiveness), and they establish rules and guidelines that their children are expected to follow (high demandingness). When their children want to discuss these norms and regulations, these parents are responsive to their children and willing to listen to their questions. When children fail to meet these parents' expectations, the parents are assertive but not intrusive and supportive rather than punitive. In contrast, authoritarian parents are often demanding, but in a restrictive manner and are low on responsiveness. They fail to explain the reasoning behind their rules, expect obedience, and may use coercive and punitive methods. Permissive or indulgent parents are high on responsiveness and nurturance but make few demands for maturity and self-control; they rarely discipline their children. Finally, uninvolved or neglectful parents have low responsiveness and communication with the child and make few demands; they appear to be detached from their child's life although they fulfill some of the child's basic needs. In extreme cases, they are also neglectful of their children's needs.

The research that followed these pioneering insights similarly distinguished between practices related to closeness, warmth, sensitivity, and responsiveness—the affective domain—and practices related to the domain of socialization, which involve setting high expectations and standards and providing guidance, control, and scaffolding to promote their attainment. Although there are important distinctions between the different practices within each domain, good parental care is generally characterized by (1) providing warm, sensitive, responsive, and secure parenting along with thoughtful socialization practices; (2) setting high but achievable standards, where autonomy and competence are promoted through scaffolding; and (3) establishing limits and rules where control is not too rigid, is respectful of children's individuality, and is promoted through induction (Grusec, Goodnow, & Kuczynski, 2000; Steinberg, 2001).

In discussing parenting, Grusec and Davidov (2010) have suggested that what constitutes good care is domain-specific. They distinguish between five socialization domains in parent-child relations and suggest that each may require a different kind of care. Protection is expected to engender a sense of security, and feeling protected and requires adequate responsiveness to distress and threat. The second— reciprocity— is expected to induce bonding as well as cooperation and requires mutual exchanges or sharing of favors, positive affect, and coordinated play. The third—control — involves interactions wherein the goals of children and caregivers conflict and should be geared to allow the internalization of children's moral and principled behavior. Good care in such a domain reflects the parents' capacity to make use of the power imbalance inherent in the relation in ways which are sufficient for producing the desired behavior but, at the same time, are not too forceful or autonomy-threatening. The fourth— guided learning—involves learning of the cognitive, physical, vocational, social, and emotional knowledge and skills needed to function adaptively in social contexts and requires the support and scaffolding of children's learning by the parents. The fifth—group participation—involves children's participation in cultural practices as part of their daily lives and requires the promotion of such participation by the parents and modeling this heritage of social customs and cultural norms.

Similarly, Ruddick—an eminent feminist writer—has discussed three major provisions or practices that mothers are engaged in and provided detailed descriptions of how each of these provisions may challenge mothers in different ways and hence may demand somewhat different care to be considered good enough (1989). The first is protection, or preserving the child's life, which she termed *preservative love*. The second, which she termed *nurturance*, involves fostering the child's emotional and intellectual growth and reflects mothers' attentiveness to the child's potential as a human being and a distinct individual. The third, which she termed *training*, reflects the mother's role as socializing agent because it reflects caring that is geared to train and teach the child how to become an accepted member of society.

A somewhat different way of assessing individual differences in parenting focuses on *parenting representations*, not their practices. These representations involve the parents' own thoughts, emotions, beliefs, and attitudes as well as defense mechanisms. From an attachment perspective, these representations reflect the parents' internal working model of caregiving, which comprises their internalized understanding of the child's needs, their role as parents, and their sense of how to enact it (Mayseless, 2006b). Based on the insightful categorization of attachment states of mind suggested by Main and colleagues (1985) using the Adult Attachment Interview (see review in Hesse, 2008), researchers have proposed several ways of conceiving individual differences in the internal working model of caregiving. For example, in assessing the parents of infants, Zeanah and Benoit (1995) have suggested three overarching categories of representations: balanced, disengaged, and distorted. Balanced representations, reflecting optimal functioning, are characterized by moderate to high coherence, high levels of involvement and acceptance, and sensitive caregiving. Disengaged representations are characterized by coolness, emotional distance, and indifference. Distorted representations reflect an internal inconsistency with intense feelings, both positive and negative, and the parent may be confused, angry or anxious, self-involved, and insensitive and may have unrealistic expectations of the child.

Examining older children and relying on an elaborate theoretical model, Solomon and George (1996) have suggested four parenting strategies for providing protection, which resemble those suggested by Zeanah and Benoit: flexible protection (the equivalent of balanced representations), distant care (the equivalent of disengaged representations), close care (the equivalent of the distorted representations), and partial or full abdication of the protective role (Solomon, George, & De Jong, 1995). Finally, Mayseless and Scharf (2006), studying adolescents' parents, categorized parenting representations similarly as balanced (optimal), restricted (similar to disengaged or distant), or flooded (similar to distorted or close) protection. In fact, the three schemes of categorizing parenting representations appear to view the flexible and balanced enactment of sensitivity and responsiveness as key aspects of positive and optimal parenting, with an extreme distance or an extreme closeness disrupting this balance, conceived as less optimal, and finally an abdication of the parental role, which involves difficulties in providing protection, often related to an unresolved trauma or loss, seen as pathological.

There are other caring relations that often involve some power inequality. These include relations between teachers and students, doctors and patients, mentors and mentees, clergymen and parishioners. In these relations some element of guidance and expectation setting, at times even control, may be appropriate and reflective of good care. Yet unlike in parenting, the scope of power and responsibility in such relations is much less comprehensive and pervasive. Caring in such relations must therefore be more accommodating to the care receiver's will so as not to provide unwanted care or use undue control.

Similar dimensions were identified in examining processes of social support or caregiving within the more egalitarian romantic relations and friendships. In these relations among equals, a socialization function is less relevant. This means that rules and limit setting, control or induction are not expected to be part of the caring relations. The affective dimension, however, remains fundamental. For example, *proximity*, reflecting the tendency to approach and contact the care receiver, and *sensitivity*, which reflects being attentive and responsive to a partner's signals and requests for help, have been offered as aspects of optimal care in romantic relations (Kunce & Shaver, 1994). In addition, within these relations and unlike parenting, moderately equal power and dominance should prevail. This means that concern and respect for both partners' autonomy and mutuality in being both a giver and a receiver are crucial. Consequently good care in relations among equals is care that reflects warmth, sensitivity, and responsiveness and respects others' need for autonomy and competence, honoring one another's dignity and will and refraining from overprotection or from providing help when it is not needed or welcomed.

This brief overview should hopefully demonstrate that caring practices reflecting good care may differ according to the provisions offered. Caring that is geared toward alleviating distress may not be characterized by the same aspects as caring geared toward teaching someone manners and societal norms. Yet we can still come up with a general description of optimal care that might be relevant to all of these relations. For example, the attachment literature has amply used two major terms to describe good care in parent-child, friend, and romantic relations: *sensitivity* and *responsiveness*. Reis and Shaver (1988) have explained that sensitivity is related to attentiveness to each individual's cues to being in tune with the other and to offering the type and amount of support wanted or needed. Responsiveness involves giving support in a prompt manner and in a way that makes the other person feel understood, validated, and cared for. These two qualities are general in that they do not differentiate among the various provisions. In that sense they provide a general measure for examining optimal care on one hand and discussing nonoptimal and even pathological care on the other.

Nonoptimal caring

There are many ways in which caring can go awry, and some have been described as reflecting nonoptimal care, as they are often negative mirror images of optimal care. I briefly discuss some of these nonoptimal care manifestations. Within the parental domain, a large number of styles or practices are deemed nonoptimal; some of these are highly detrimental to the child, the parent, and their relationship. In the affective domain the extreme lower levels may involve cold, distant and rejectful parenting, and the extreme higher levels may involve enmeshed and anxious parenting that does not differentiate emotionally between the child and the parent. In the socialization or demandingness domain, the extreme lower levels may reflect uninvolved and neglectful parenting, and the extreme higher levels may involve coercive and punitive control, guilt induction, and psychological control all disrespect and devalue the child in general and the child's autonomy in particular (Barber et al., 2012). There are, of course, other negative parenting behaviors, and some involve a certain measure of abdication of the parental protective role, as in engaging in physical or psychological abuse, role reversal (parentification), or spousification (relating to the child as a romantic partner).

Abuse can take many forms, including physical, sexual, or emotional mistreatment or neglect of the child (Garbarino, Eckenrode, & Barry, 1997). In that sense some of the parenting practices described earlier including punitive and physically coercise control, neglect and psychological control when extreme can be considered abusive.

Parentification, or role reversal, occurs when parent-child roles are somewhat reversed and the child is called upon to take care of at least one of the parents early on. This caring can include emotional and instrumental care, companionship, and taking care of the household; it tends to occur when the parent is helpless, frightened, and frightening or when the parent partially or fully abdicates the parental protective role. Role reversal is more prevalent following divorce, in families with a history of parental alcohol abuse, or when parents are depressed or seriously ill, as with HIV-infected parents (Jurkovic, 1997; Stein, Riedel, & Rotheram-Borus, 1999; Jurkovic, Thirkield, & Morrell, 2001). This situation does not always result in negative consequences for the child. In fact, if the caretaking burden does not exceed the child's capacities and if the child feels competent and positively validated in these endeavors, such a situation may lead to a sense of accomplishment, to the internalization of a caretaker identity, and sometimes to the choice of a helping profession (Valleau, Bergner, & Horton, 1995; Mayseless, Bartholomew, Henderson, & Trinke, 2004).

Spousification reflects a situation where a parent treats the child as a spouse, often with sexual nuances and expectations, thus failing to protect the child from harm and in fact becoming a harmful agent. In all of these conditions (abuse, neglect, parentification, and spousification) the parent appears to at least partially abdicate the crucial parental role of protection; at times, especially in abusive relations and spousification, the parent seriously jeopardizes the child's physical and psychological welfare, with possible dire consequences for the child (Garbarino, Eckenrode, & Barry, 1997; Norman et al., 2012). Thus abuse, spousification and neglect can sometimes represent very maladaptive forms of care.

Parents who abuse, disrespect or neglect their children do not always understand how harmful it can be and may think that this is the right way to discipline the child or to show that they care. At other times they may find it difficult to control their anger, frustration, depression, or distress and express these feelings through abuse or neglect. Research into the antecedents of child abuse underscores the debilitating experiences of abusive parents when they were children, their poor capacity for emotional and behavioral regulation, their faulty beliefs about how to raise children, and concurrent circumstances that often involve an accumulation of risk factors such as poverty, violent neighborhoods, and a lack of social support (Garbarino, Eckenrode, & Barry, 1997; Barber et al., 2012; Norman et al., 2012).

Within the realm of romantic relations, a *controlling* style, which reflects the degree to which caregivers are controlling in their attempts to help their partners solve problems, and *compulsive caregiving*, which is related to the extent to which caregivers become overinvolved in their partners' problems, were considered the two major manifestations of nonoptimal caring (Kunce & Shaver, 1994).

A different, more systematic, and more conceptual way of looking at suboptimal caring has been suggested by Shaver, Mikulincer, and Shemesh-Iron (2010). They refer to the deactivation and hyperactivation of the caregiving behavioral system and view these propensities as reflecting personality dispositions in adulthood that are related to caring in a variety of domains. Both dispositions involve problems at the motivation and enactment levels. Hyperactivating reflects an unnecessary overinvolvement in caring. This includes a hypervigilance in identifying needs, even when they do not exist, and help geared to satisfying the help provider's own desire to feel needed and worthy, thus involving less consideration of the other's needs. Care is often insensitive, intrusive, and coercive, yet caregivers feel that they give too much and may be distressed or exhausted. In contrast, deactivation reflects a decreased involvement in caregiving. Thus cues for the activation of caring tend to be ignored or dismissed, and when caring is provided, it is done with insufficient empathy and often in a nonresponsive and insensitive manner that is not truly helpful. Shaver, Mikulincer, and Shemesh-Iron (2010) have provided evidence indicating that these individual differences are manifested in different domains and with different targets, whether between parents and children, between romantic partners, or between strangers. Furthermore, this delineation of two major nonoptimal "styles"—a compulsive, excessive care born of anxiety and insufficient care that is cold, distant, and controlling—closely resembles other depictions in the literature on caring. Within the family therapy field, for example, one of the known distinctions between optimal and nonoptimal family functioning relates to the dimension of cohesiveness, whereby enmeshment—the overly intrusive style—and disengagement—the deactivation strategy—reflect two negative poles; their midway point characterizes balanced families (Olson, 2000).

An important difference between good and problematic care that is directly tied to the major issues discussed in this book relates to the underlying reasons or motivations for care. It involves the distinction between other-focused concern, which reflects the caring motivation, and self-focused help, which is problematic in that it is ultimately geared toward helping the caregiver. It can result from guilt from failing to engage in help, distress due to empathic processes the caregiver wants to alleviate, the need to uphold a reputation as a good and kind person, the wish to feel needed, group or authority figure pressure, and more. Such care is often less attuned to the needs of the care receiver and tends to have detrimental effects on both sides (Crocker & Canevello, 2008; Kappes & Shrout, 2011; Konrath et al., 2012).

Collins et al. (2006) have discussed factors that hamper optimal caregiving in the context of romantic relations, but their categorization is relevant to other domains too and to the examples of problematic caring provided here and can be viewed as a preliminary conceptual framework for understanding how caring in general can go awry. Collins et al. (2006) have discussed two factors relating to the *motivational aspect*: (1) a lack of motivation and (2) motivation directed by concern for the self rather than concern for the other, as well as two factors that relate to *difficulties in enactment*: (3) moderately permanent difficulties (social skill deficits, faulty belief-system) and (4) transient difficulties in enactment (depletion of psychological resources). Most if not all of the nonoptimal yet somewhat normative instances of care described here fit this general and succinct delineation. Yet there are some extreme situations of mistreatment that appear to cross the line and have been called pathological (Oakley, Knafo, Madhavan, & Wilson, 2012).

Pathological care

Pathologies of the caring motivation can be seen in the absence of care, when people ignore clear and overwhelming signs of distress and need and do not respond with some measure of empathy and concern. Psychopathy, which involves a lack of empathy to distress in others, can culminate in cruelty and is the most prominent disorder of this kind; it has been associated with distinct developmental antecedents and a genetic vulnerability. In particular, biological and genetic precursors that are related to underactivation of the fear/anxiety system have been identified as accounting for a lack of empathy that can result in indifference to others' suffering and cruelty and may culminate in psychopathic predispositions (Blair, Mitchell, & Blair, 2005). But caring can be pathological also when it is excessively and nonjudiciously enacted.

A recent edited book by Oakley, Knafo, Madhavan, and Wilson (2012) discusses pathological altruism, or the many ways in which what appear to be altruistic motives can culminate in harmful and even destructive outcomes. This relates to situations in which caregivers sincerely engage in what they intend to be altruistic acts but that result in harm to the care receiver, the caregiver, or other people and groups involved; thus these well-intentioned efforts worsen the very situation they were meant to resolve. These include cases of pathogenic guilt, as may develop among survivors of the death of close relatives or in the aftermath of a military trauma involving the deaths of a survivor's comrades in arms. Such guilt leads to unwarranted, unneeded, and excessive self-sacrifice in the service of caring for others (O'Conner, Berry, Lewis, & Stiver, 2012). Self-sacrifice is also apparent in cases of compulsive caregiving, when the caregiver places herself or himself second to the interests and desires of others, making excessive attempts to please them and accepting deprivations, victimization, and even abuse (Wildiger & Presnall, 2012). In these cases of self-sacrifice, help is often provided not because of other-oriented reasons (though it may be presented as such) but to alleviate the caregiver's guilt, to receive recognition and approval, or to experience some contact and connection with others. Such pathological altruism may also develop in codependent relations, where one person enables another's highly dysfunctional behavior and in fact "helps" the other to harm herself or himself. This can happen, for example, in cases of alcoholism, when a spouse provides the alcoholic partner with more alcoholic beverages and thus exacerbates his or her condition yet feel that the spouse has been helped (McGrath & Oakley, 2012). Finally, altruism as expressed in the acts of suicide bombers may appear to benefit the group that sent them to their fate but it is also considered pathological altruism because of its intended indiscriminate destructiveness of both the suicide bomber and her or his innocent victims (Oakley et al., 2012).

These situations, as well as other extreme forms of pathological care, bring to the fore a fundamental question related to the present volume's core claims. If the caring motivation is indeed as basic, innate, and biologically and genetically based as I maintain, how can it become so pathological? How can spouses care by providing alcohol to alcoholic partners and suicide bombers believe that they are rescuing humanity?

In this context we need to make a conceptual distinction between caring that becomes pathological and acts that reflect other sides in human nature—aggression, selfishness, and even cruelty. Part IV of the present volume deals with alternative conceptions of human nature and presents my own take on the intriguing issue of human nature (i.e., are we good or bad, selfish or benevolent?). Pathological care is another matter, because the caring motivation is at stake, the caregiver is motivated, at least partially, by the goal of protecting the other and helping her or him to heal, thrive, and prosper, yet the caregiver acts in a way that clearly jeopardizes the care receiver's welfare. How can such a contradiction be accounted for? This question can be answered on several levels.

First, the apparent contradiction rests on the implicit supposition that any innate and evolutionarily based motivation should *always* be enacted in an optimal way. This is clearly not the case. At the conceptual level we would not expect innate motivations to *always* be optimally expressed but only that they be expressed in *a good enough manner in the majority of situations*. In fact, at the evolutionary level, variability in the deployment of human qualities is a survival asset and hence evolutionarily chosen because it allows for a better capacity for flexible coping in diverse environments and contexts. Such flexibility is important both within and between individuals. Variability in the expression of a certain quality within the same person—within- individual variability—is considered an important asset that allows flexibility in adjusting to a variety of environments and situations. In the case of caring this amounts to flexibility in being more or less empathic, kind, and benevolent on different occasions. Additionally, variability in the expression of human nature among individuals within cultures (i.e., where individuals differ in their expression of care) is also an asset as it allows the society similar levels of coping flexibility. A nice empirical illustration of such an advantage comes from a study on variability in attachment styles. Although attachment security is deemed the optimal strategy for this innate and fundamental motivation, it is displayed by only about two thirds of the population. In accordance with the claimed advantage of between-individuals variability, groups that included participants with variable attachment orientations were more effective in dealing with dangerous situations than were more homogeneous groups, even when the latter included mostly secure participants (Ein-Dor et al., 2010).

At the empirical level, these kinds of flexibility (within and between individuals) are observed in relation to very basic human needs, including those that are phylogenetically old and mandatory for our survival, such as hunger, thirst, attachment, the need for sleep and for sex. Despite having inborn action sequences and clear biological strata to support them, their enactment can be highly variable and flexible and can also include pathological expressions. In other words, phenotypical variability and plasticity is evolutionarily chosen even for our most fundamental motivations and also incorporates extremes that we conceive of as pathological (see discussion in Price, Qvarnström, & Irwin, 2003). Consequently the possibility of pathological enactment of caring, though reflecting an extreme case, may still be part of this general human flexibility. At the proximal level, hereditary and environmental effects as well as concurrent precursors might interact to bring about pathological caring.

Furthermore what is eventually expressed as pathological care often builds upon affordances of the caring motivation that are part of the "normative" repertoire. For example, we as a species have the potential to downregulate empathic responses even at the intuitive preconscious emotional empathy level, and we feel less empathy in certain situations or toward certain targets. This was the case when the activity of physicians' brains did not show the common bottom-up processing of the perception of pain when they observed others being pricked by a needle (Decety, Yang, & Cheng, 2010). Similarly, we have the potential to subject someone we love to pain as an expression of our care—for example, when parents see to it that their cancer-stricken child will undergo the required treatments even when they are painful. In addition, when we believe that someone has not been honest with us or has cheated, a concomitant of the caring motivation is the tendency to punish that person or at least gloat at her or his misfortune. Oxytocin, the same neurotransmitter implicated in caring, is also involved in this response (Singer et al., 2006).

At the phenomenological level, we have all probably experienced instances in which we were insensitive helpers because we did not really care about the recipient or because we did not know what to do. We can probably even recall situations in which we provided care but were angry that we had to do so and were thus impatient, unkind, and perhaps even mean. There may also be cases in which we were so sure about what needed to be done that we urged the other to do it against her or his overt and covert will. There are probably many other occasions in which another's clear and even urgent need may be ignored. I am certainly not suggesting that these reactions reflect pathological care but only that our caring repertoire already includes a large number of options that may serve us well in regular or normative circumstances but which can transform into pathological care. What we see in pathological care is probably the co-opting of these (and other) "normative" processes and their use in a very extreme and maladaptive way.

Finally, in some situations of pathological care, other motivations, such as attachment needs, the need to belong, or sexual needs are superimposed on the caring motivation. In these situations, the caregiver acts in a caregiving capacity but his or her other needs are the ones that take precedence, whether knowingly or unintentionally. Pathological care is nonetheless not destiny and is responsive to therapy (e.g., MacMillan et al., 2009), thus demonstrating the importance of concurrent circumstances and the flexibility and malleability of the caring motivational system even when it is pathologically expressed.

Definition of good care

The discussions thus far can help us understand what good care looks like. Good caregiving is care that emanates from a concern for the other's welfare and happiness and needs to involve synchronization and coordination between caregiver and recipient. To this end, a balance needs to be achieved between distance and closeness and between dominance and submission. Too much distance restricts the caregiver's capacity to decipher and validly identify the other person's needs and to be responsive; it does not provide the closeness required for the recipient to feel held and appreciated. On the other hand, too much closeness may lead the caregiver to be overinvolved and to answer his or her own needs for reassurance in a manner that does not validate the recipient and does not provide the necessary support. Excessive dominance on the caregiver's part may include help that is insensitive and disrespectful. Excessive submissiveness on the caregiver's part may lead to self-sacrifices often associated with covert anger and resentment in the caregiver and may even lead to abuse and exploitation by the recipient.

Taken together, the extant research on good care in different domains and relationships and the study of nonoptimal and even pathological care set the stage for the possibility of coming up with a generalized way of defining good care. For this purpose and as a heuristic approach, I adopt the conceptual framework of self-determination theory (Deci & Ryan, 2000a; Ryan & Deci, 2000). Self-determination theory posits three basic psychological needs or concerns that are central to human experience: competence, relatedness, and autonomy. Competence involves feeling effective in one's efforts and capable of achieving desired outcomes. Relatedness involves being connected to and understood by others as well as experiencing caring for others. Autonomy involves feeling volitional in one's actions, being the causal agent of actions and decisions, and acting in accordance with internalized values and an integrated self. The satisfaction of these three needs has been shown to be closely related to self-fulfillment and to finding meaning in life (Ryan & Deci, 2000; Weinstein, Ryan & Deci, 2012). Each of these general concerns is obviously multifaceted, and other models of human thriving may suggest additional core concerns/motivations, such as our will for meaning (Frankl, 1988), or they may conceptualize these concerns in a different way (Kenrick et al., 2010). I employ this perspective as a heuristic tool.

I suggest that *good care* is care that addresses the overt as well as the covert specific needs of the recipient/target in a responsive and sensitive manner *at the same time as it respects* the three major concerns—relatedness, autonomy, and competence (and/or other concerns deemed central in human experience, such as meaning or self fulfillment)—in both the caregiver *and* the care receiver. Specifically, I contend that even if help is functional and beneficial in addressing the focal distress or need, such help may not fully qualify as good caring if it violates the care receiver's or caregiver's fundamental concerns.

Such violations may often lead to negative outcomes for both caregiver and care receiver and adversely affect their relations. This general definition holds true for caring directed at different targets, at different levels of power balance or imbalance, and in different domains or provisions. It can thus function as a general description of good care emanating from our comprehensive and fundamental motivation to care.

Chapter conclusion

The rich variety of the manifestations of care in different domains exposes a wide range of conceptualizations about and expressions of individual differences in caring. These differences reflect the transactions between genetic, environmental, and contextual effects and demonstrate a common core of how caring is expressed and what affects it as well as a high degree of flexibility in the way it is expressed across domains and targets. Such flexibility reflects the general human capacity to adjust to a variety of contexts and circumstances and the versatility of human motivation. Such flexibility is also reflected in the existence of optimal, nonoptimal, and even pathological caring in the different domains, yet several clear characteristics of good care could be uncovered that are similar across the variety of domains, targets, and circumstances (e.g., responsiveness and sensitivity, respecting the core concerns of caregiver and care receiver). This similarity in what constitutes good care underscores the existence of a common core underlying these different expressions of the general caring motivation.

Likewise, the emergence of similar genetic, contextual, and environmental antecedents for prosocial responding and good care in the different domains highlights the common origin of these expressions (e.g., unique temperamental qualities, parental warmth, and parents' use of inductive disciplinary methods, as well as opportunities to practice being prosocial). Finally, the emergence of a stable altruistic and prosocial personality disposition, which is similarly manifested across domains and targets, is another indication for the existence of such a common core. Consequently the study of individual differences and their development provides strong indication for the existence of a core motivation to care, which can be flexibly enacted in a multitude of contexts and toward a multitude of recipients.

|| 15 ||

Sex/Gender Differences in Caregiving

Gender differences in caregiving are perhaps the strongest and most salient aspect related to its variability. This is most conspicuous in care for infants and toddlers, which is performed by far more women than men (Lamb, 2000; Taylor, 2002). For example, studies in western industrialized countries have demonstrated that in two-parent families in which mothers are not otherwise employed, fathers assume almost no responsibility for their children's daily care, and the average father spends about 20% to 25% as much time as the mother does in direct interaction or engagement with his children and about 33% as much time being accessible to his children. In two-parent families where both parents are similarly employed (over 30 hours a week), direct interaction and passive accessibility average 44% and 66%, respectively, owing primarily to a decrease in the mother's involvement, not an increase in the father's; yet, even when fully employed, mothers remain almost the sole parent with direct responsibility for arranging and supervising the children's daily care (See review in Lamb, 2000).

This gender difference is also apparent in areas other than parenting, where mothers or other women were and still are the most frequent caregivers worldwide, as in caring for elderly parents or for sick spouses, or as grandparents in a principal caregiver role substituting for parents (Eagly, 2009). This state of affairs raises several questions: What is the nature of this strong gender difference? Are men really less caring than women or do they show their caring in other domains? Is this gender difference rooted in biology or in socialization? Do men care differently than women? In what follows, I discuss some of the relevant findings as well as present some of the explanations offered to account for this strong gender effect: I try to address some of these questions and to come up with a suggested resolution.

Evolutionary and biological accounts

Evolutionary accounts suggest that the birth of infants that are helpless to survive on their own, the rather long lactation period, and the added long dependency period until puberty or maturity have required a heavy investment on the mother's part in caring for the young in the environment of evolutionary adaptedness—the environment where natural selection of our ancestors developed. In addition, the evolution of a long developmental immaturity (neoteny) in humans required help in caregiving tasks and in the protection of both mother and offspring. In such conditions, paternal investment in offspring and in mates probably enhanced the physical well-being of their children and their own social competitiveness, making such investment a candidate for natural selection processes. In addition, the concealed ovulation of human females meant that human males could not be sure that they had fathered the offspring unless they chose to remain close to the mother and to be her sole mate, at least until she became pregnant. Mothers, however, could rely on other supports, such as other related women. Furthermore, men could adopt different procreational strategies, such as valuing quantity over quality (i.e., impregnating a large number of women without investing in fathering) (Geary, 2000). According to this perspective, maternal caring is viewed as evolutionarily ancient and strongly selected through evolutionary processes, while paternal care for offspring and mates (e.g., by forming pair bonds) is conceptualized as more tentative and less strongly wired in.

Consequently maternal and paternal care have been discussed as reflecting quite distinct evolutionary developments. Indeed, maternal caregiving is much more prevalent, has a much earlier onset in the phylogenetic development of the species, and—in mammals—is considered obligatory for the survival of the young. For example, maternal care is prevalent among 300 species of nonhuman primates, but only 5% show also paternal care (Clutton-Brock, 1991; Maestripieri & Roney 2006). Furthermore, research with mammals has clearly identified the genetic and biological onset of caring and caregiving in mothers but much less so in fathers. Maternal behavior appears to be under relatively strong genetic control (including uterine hormonal influences) and is proximally regulated by a combination of hormonal changes and offspring stimuli (Maestripieri & Roney 2006). In mammals with a short life span (e.g., mice and rats), for example, first-time mothers without any prior experience with pups show the full range of required maternal caregiving from the moment their pups are born and successfully raise their offspring to maturity (Fleming & Orpens, 1986).

In mammals with longer life spans than rodents (e.g., Old World monkeys, apes, and humans) mothering is also strongly affected by previous experiences (Pryce, 1996). These include new mothers' interactions with their own mothers in their infancy and juvenile years, the observation of caregiving provided by their own mothers and others, and direct interaction and provisioning of care—for example, to siblings—before becoming mothers themselves. Nonhuman primate mothers who were separated from their mothers after birth or were reared by their biological mothers but in environments where opportunities to interact with infants or others were limited, for example, tended to neglect or abandon their firstborn offspring and generally exhibited clear deficiencies in their mothering (Suomi, 1978). Still, even in primates, a strong and clear sex difference in the development of caring can be attributed to genetic and biological differences.

One of the indicators of adaptive mothering in mammals and humans is the interest in infants in juvenile years and the motivation to play with them and care for them. In a review paper, Maestripieri and Roney (2006) present an accumulation of comparative evidence from *nonhuman primates* that supports the claim that an early interest by young females in infants in nonhuman and human primates is a developmental adaptation based on genetic and biological processes in primates more than a product of *human* culture and socialization. For example, despite experiencing highly similar treatment by their mothers, young rhesus macaque females display a much stronger interest in infants than young males by the end of their first year, and this strong sex difference persists from then on; it is a strong predictor of their mothering quality. Similar gender effects whereby females show a stronger interest in and preference for infants compared with males have also been observed in humans and appear around the end of the preschool years—at around age five and onward (Berman & Goddman, 1984; Maestripieri & Pelka, 2001). Preference for doll play to playing with trucks or other masculine toys requiring physical manipulation (i.e., vehicles, robots, weapons) begins to appear even earlier, usually during the second year of life (Jadva, Hines, & Golombok, 2010). Such a preference is related in part to prenatal androgen exposure and is seen also in nonhuman primates. For example, despite parental encouragement for playing with feminine toys, girls with congenital adrenal hyperplasia (CAH), a genetic condition in which the female fetus is exposed to abnormally high concentrations of androgens, spent more time playing with masculine toys and less time playing with feminine toys compared with control group girls (Berenbaum & Hines, 1992; Nordenström, Servin, Bohlin, Larsson, & Wedell, 2002; Pasterski et al., 2005). Normal prenatal variability in androgen exposure also relates to male-typical childhood behavior (Auyeung et al., 2009). Sex-typed toy preferences similar to those seen in children have also been reported in two species of nonhuman primates (Alexander & Hines, 2002). All together, these findings support the claim of an innate biological basis for females' proclivity to mother, which starts early on.

In contrast, paternal care appears to have evolved quite differently and is much less frequent. In fact, in the majority of mammal fathers do not care for their off-spring (Fraley, Brumbaugh, & Marks, 2005). Interestingly, although paternal investment is infrequent among mammals, it is found in many species of birds and fish (Geary, 2000). Pertinent to these differences is a distinction between obligatory and facultative fathering. Evolutionary scientists differentiate between obligate investment, which means that male care is necessary for the survival of offspring, as is the case in many bird species, and facultative investment, which is not an ultimate necessity for the survival of offspring and can usually vary with proximate conditions, as is the case with humans (Westneat & Sherman, 1993). In humans, maternal parenting was seen as obligate, but paternal investment was conceived as facultative and contingent on personal, social, and ecological conditions.

From an evolutionary perspective, an important proximate condition for paternal investment is that such an investment procures an improvement in the survival rate of offspring. This is clearly the case among many birds. For example, in an analysis across 31 bird species, Møller and Cuervo (2000) determined that 34% of the variability in offspring survival was due to paternal investment. Another important condition for paternal investment is the certainty of fatherhood. When avian males, for example, suspect that they are not fathers, they reduce their level of paternal investment and often do so in direct relation to the magnitude of the risk of fatherhood (Ewen & Armstrong, 2000; Møller & Cuervo, 2000). Besides paternal certainty and potential benefits to offspring, the availability of other female mates is also relevant to the fathers' facultative tendency to invest in raising offspring. Generally speaking, if the certainty of paternity is high, an investment in fathering improves offspring survival or quality, and if the benefits associated with this investment outweigh its costs, fathers will tend to invest in parenting.

According to evolutionary analyses, similar proximal conditions are relevant to fathers' investment in *human* parenting as well (Geary, 2000). Human paternal investment is related to reductions in infant and child mortality rates and to improvements in children's social competitiveness (see review in Geary, 2000). Furthermore, paternal investment is higher when paternal certainty is higher and when mating alternatives are not as frequent or as easy to get, as when women are selective regarding casual sex or when society places strong constraints on infidelity and a high value on monogamous relations.

Although human paternal investment is viewed in this manner, several studies have documented biological processes related to paternal care that are similar to those that have been observed in mothers. For example, both maternal and paternal cortisol levels were correlated in a similar way with the sensitive parenting of babies (Corter & Fleming, 1995; Stallings, Fleming, Corter, Worthman, & Steiner, 2001). Men whose romantic partners were pregnant and who responded to an unfamiliar infant's distress cues with concern and a desire to comfort the infant had higher prolactin levels and lower testosterone levels than other men (Storey, Walsh, Quinton, & Wynne-Edwards, 2000).

In a series of studies with fathers and mothers, Feldman and her colleagues identified similar biobehavioral synchrony in the mothers and fathers of infants. For example, comparable levels of baseline plasma oxcytocin (OT) were found in both fathers and mothers one month and six months postpartum, and both mothers and fathers showed higher levels of OT compared with nonattached singles. Furthermore, maternal and paternal OT levels were interrelated in both cases. In addition, both maternal and paternal OT levels were significantly associated with their respective observed caring (Gordon et al., 2010a). Feldman further showed that salivary OT increased in both mothers and fathers who provided high levels of their typical respective type of play and touch for 15 minutes as compared with mothers and fathers who provided low levels of such touch and play (Feldman et al., 2010). Unlike mothers, in whom we expect oxytocin levels to be high and associated with mothering because they are biologically triggered by birth and lactation, the biobehavioral processes for fathers are less obvious. Yet these findings provide clear evidence for the implication of biological and hormonal processes in fatherhood also.

In one twin study, modest genetic contributions to two facets of parental investment, care (e.g., sensitivity to emotional state) and protection (e.g., keeping the child close) (Pérusse, Neale, Heath, & Eaves, 1994), were found in both mothers and fathers. Genetic models have explained similar levels of variance in individual differences in these aspects for fathers (18% to 25%) and mothers (23% to 39%). Still, there are distinct sex differences in the operation of various hormones in male and female care. For example, prolactin and vasopressin may play a more prominent role than oxytocin in inducing male parental investment (Wynne-Edwards, 2001; see review in Feldman, 2012).

"Fight or flight" vs. "tend and befriend" approaches to stress

A notable and remarkable perspective on gender differences in caring has been suggested by Taylor (Taylor et al., 2000; Taylor, 2002). She has presented a persuasive case suggesting women react differently to stress than do men. Whereas men tend to resort to the known reaction of fight or flight (attack or flee), women are predisposed to tend and befriend in reaction to stress. Taylor defines these two tendencies as follows: "Tending involves nurturant activities designed to protect the self and offspring that promote safety and reduce distress; befriending is the creation and maintenance of social networks that may aid in this process" (Taylor et al., 2000; p. 411). She argues that when facing stress, women tend to activate their caring either for their young (if they have offspring) or for close others, such as family and friends. Furthermore, befriending others is described as a central female strategy for resisting stress and danger and for reducing women's vulnerability. It involves joining social groups and contributing to the development and sustenance of such groups, particularly with other women, for the mutual exchange of resources and responsibilities.

Taylor (2002) presents considerable empirical evidence to support her claims. For example, one of the most intriguing series of studies in this regard (Repetti, 1989) shows that on stressful workdays fathers are more likely to be interpersonally conflictual or withdrawn in the home after work (as reported by them and their children). In contrast, women in the same situation are more nurturant, loving, and caring toward their children (as reported by them and their children). Some ceiling effects were also noted, inasmuch as chronically stressed mothers are somewhat more likely to show withdrawal behavior on stressed days rather than increases in affection (Repetti & Wood, 1997). With regard to befriending under stress and in accordance with Taylor's claim, robust gender differences in seeking and using social support have been noted (Belle, 1987; Luckow et al. 1998), and the greater tendency of women to seek and mobilize social support was found to be particularly salient with regard to other women, female relatives, and female friends. In difficult circumstances, female networks (and mostly female kin networks) for child care and the exchange of resources often emerge to provide the necessary support and maintenance (see a review by Belle, 1987).

Taylor et al. (2000; Taylor, 2002) have presented results from animal and human studies that provide neuroendocrine evidence implicating the attachment-caregiving system as underlying the tend-and-befriend reaction. This evidence suggests that oxytocin, as well as other hormones and endogenous opioid peptide mechanisms, are involved in these processes. An interesting demonstration of the variant male and female reactions to befriending in groups under stress comes from a study with rodents. As assessed by corticosteroid levels, spatial crowding was observed as stressing males but as calming females (Brown & Grunberg, 1995).

Discussing our natural instincts to comfort and support one another, Taylor (2002) amasses impressive evidence demonstrating that women are the most prevalent and typical human caregivers in their various roles as mothers, daughters, friends, wives, and grandmothers and that they provide care as part of routine caregiving activities as well as in response to special needs, as in caring for disabled children, aging parents, ill spouses, or grandchildren whose parents are divorced. According to Taylor (2002), this sex difference, evinced in behavior as well as in biological processes that support and sustain it, is related to evolutionarily evolved mechanisms whereby men mostly fought for status and access to women while women tended the young. In her book, Taylor (2002) notes both the benefits of such a general tendency for caring for the women themselves and for society and its costs. However, she unequivocally states that evolutionary underpinnings are not destiny and that, especially in humans, processes of caring are highly flexible and a result of complex and intricate interactions between genetics, environments, cultures, and changing ecological conditions.

Feminist and psychoanalytic approaches

Feminist approaches discuss sexual differences in social power and in the arenas where each sex was expected to invest. According to these accounts (elaborated in Chapter 7), women were and still are the world's major caregivers. Caregiving was socially constructed as a woman's duty as well as a woman's central joy, as it was seen to reflect women's caring nature, and women were not allowed to pursue other activities or interests. Furthermore, this caring was not appreciated or accorded the high status it deserved. In most of these writings, scholars did not come up with a well-thought-out suggestion regarding the distinct role of men in caring. Some scholars have called for a drastic change whereby males would be required to be involved in the arduous caring almost exclusively carried out by women (Rich, 1976; Ruddick, 1985, 1989). Others placed less emphasis on such a possibility, and writers mostly called for changes in the way society viewed women's caring. In particular, the freedom to decide whether or not to care and in what capacity was espoused, as was the freedom of women to pursue other activities. Most prominently, these scholars espoused the urgent need to accord caring and caregiving a higher status (Gilligan, 1982).

Psychoanalytic approaches have accorded mothers and fathers distinctive roles in caring for children and have extensively discussed these issues. Here I provide only a very brief delineation of major tenets of this perspective. Mothers were originally seen as forming a symbiotic connection with their infants that served to hold and protect that infant's body and psyche. Current relational theorizing describes an intersubjective space in which the mother holds the baby and interacts with her or him, fostering the psychological birth of the child and the creation of mutual recognition and a quality of mutual mental space—often termed "thirdness" (Benjamin, 2004). Later on, fathers were expected to mediate the child's transition away from this intersubjective yet fusional relationship with the mother, enabling the introduction of the child to the social world beyond the dyadic space with the mother (Benedeck, 1970; Diamond, 1986; Benjamin, 1992). Fathers were also seen as providing the support needed for mothers to engage in such comprehensive immersion (Stern, 1995). Fathers were also expected to serve as the other third and as role models as children passed through the oedipal phase and needed to establish their sexual identity (Diamond, 1998). Thus, despite the primacy and primeval nature of mother's care, fathers too were conceived as having distinct caring roles, albeit much less intensive ones than mothers.'

Anthropological and cross-cultural perspectives

Most of the comparative study of societies and cultures is based on the exceptional work of Murdock and his colleagues. They amassed ethnographic records
based on the work of anthropologists who visited the societies and recorded their
observations. These records have been archived and coded for various aspects
and these codes were based on established common criteria and made available for research. These records include the *Ethnographic Atlas* of 1,264 societies (Murdock, 1967) and the *Atlas of World Cultures* of 563 societies (Murdock,
1981). Furthermore, and along with White, Murdock compiled the Standard
Cross-Cultural Sample, a set of 186 societies selected as representative of the distribution of societies across the world and documented by sufficient ethnographic
records (Murdock & White, 1969), which became the most widely used ethnographic resource for cross-cultural research.

Anthropological accounts that are based on these sources and involve a variety
of nonindustrial cultures, as well as ones that resemble ancient hunter-gatherer
societies, converge on four major tenets regarding gender differences in caring
(Murdock & Provost, 1973; also see review in Wood & Eagly, 2002). First, gender
differences were quite prevalent, and only a minority of tasks were interchangeably performed by both sexes within the same culture. Second, in some distinct
caring tasks there was a strong resemblance across cultures. Specifically, some
caring tasks appeared to be predominantly masculine across all cultures, with
over 90% exclusivity for males (e.g., tasks requiring physical strength and the
mobilization of brief bursts of high energy). These included hunting big game to
provide food and engaging in warfare to protect the family or tribe or to obtain
new resources needed for survival.

Other caring tasks appear as predominantly feminine, again with over 90%
exclusivity for females across all cultures. These included taking care of infants
and toddlers and the preparation of vegetal food. Finally, some caring-related
undertakings—such as befriending, supporting, and cooperating with other
adults in daily exchanges—tended to be similarly enacted across cultures by both
men and women within their gender groups. Third, notwithstanding this similarity across cultures in sex-typed caring, a substantive proportion of tasks involved
"swing activities," which were performed by men *or* women depending on the culture and historical period (e.g., crop planting and harvesting, burden carrying).
Fourth, this variation could be predicted by specific conditions related to differences in ecological contexts and alternatives to subsistence. Fifth, even within
similar ecological niches, societies could develop different cultural "solutions" for
a variety of subsistence and procreation challenges related to caring.

Most ethnographic accounts of gender differences in caring have focused on
caring for offspring, and in the next few paragraphs I would like to provide a more

detailed discussion of this domain of care from both ethnographic and cross-cultural perspectives. Caring for infants and toddlers, predominated by women, was often shared among different caregivers. In about half of the cultures, mothers were the exclusive or near-exclusive caregiver in infancy, and in the other half other females, such as older siblings or maternal relatives (sister, grandmother), as well as other women from the tribe also played important roles. By preschool age, mothers were no longer exclusive caregivers, and fathers often contributed substantially, albeit much less than mothers in directing child care, most often to sons and frequently as disciplinarians and initiators to the larger social context (See review in Wood & Eagly, 2002).

The universal caring for infants and toddlers by women was understood in light of biological necessities related to women's pregnancy and nursing of infants. Most women in nonindustrial societies appear to have borne children and lactated throughout their reproductive years. These same biological capacities appear to limit women's ability to perform tasks that require speed, uninterrupted periods of activity, or long-distance travel away from home. These became the province of men and possibly led to the evolutionary selection of some of the biological attributes of men, such as men's greater average size, oxygen-carrying capacity, and capacity for activities involving speed and upper-body strength (See review in Wood & Eagly, 2002). We need to understand fathers' involvement in care for the offspring in this light.

Hewlett (1991, 2000) has provided a comprehensive description of fathers' involvement in caring in various cultures spanning human history. He notes that throughout the history of humankind and across a variety of cultures, we have evidence that fathers contributed to their children in a variety of ways. Furthermore, he shows that this variability was not arbitrary and reflected the effects of different ecologies and modes of production. Along with evolutionary biologists, he claims that looking only at involvement in direct care as reflecting fathers' caring is erroneous and suggests using the term *investment*. Fathers' investment (or caring, using my preferred term) reflects all the ways in which fathers contribute to their children and help them to survive and thrive. In that sense, such investment is clearly related to the caring motivation as defined in this book. This includes direct forms of investment, such as daily caregiving, nurturance, protection, knowledge transmission or teaching, as well as providing food, shelter, and other necessary resources, and indirect forms of investment that target others but benefit the young and may be intentionally executed to enhance the offspring's success and well-being (e.g., emotional support of the mother, maintenance of kin resources). According to this view, all of these provisions can be conceived of as different forms of caring provided that they were activated by the caring motivation with the welfare, survival, and thriving of the offspring in mind.

Specifically, among foragers (hunter-gatherers) more than 20,000 years ago, paternal caring was mostly enacted by being the provider of food and shelter, by transmitting knowledge (primarily to sons), and by investing resources in a kin group. At this period, the defense of the family or kin group was also significant, but defending became much more important as humans became simple farmers about 10,000 years ago and started to stock food and material resources—wealth that needed to be protected. During the simple farming period, farming became central in supplying the resources for subsistence, and the activity took place near a more stable dwelling. Hunting, which often took place away from the dwelling and could last for long periods of time, proved difficult for women carrying babies to participate in. But women could more easily take part in farming near their dwellings, and indeed men and women tended to share farming tasks. Consequently the importance of a father's provision of food and shelter declined and men became more involved in direct caring for the young.

With the advent of intensive farming and industrialization—5,000 years ago—the provision of food and shelter again became a very important task of fathers because of the new sophistication and technical level of these provisions, which led men as opposed to women to specialize in them, since women were busy with child-care. The importance of the kin group declined, and personal, often inherited wealth became important. Whereas caring for young children was somewhat important for fathers before the advent of intensive farming and industrialization, it declined in importance and remained thus for 5,000 years, until the last century. During the last century, fathers' roles as defenders and educators have declined because these responsibilities have been taken over by modern states. Yet during that period fathers were still considered the breadwinners, and their wealth and material resources were considered very important in providing for their families and offspring. Consequently support of the kin group has often not been a substantial issue. Currently direct caregiving appears to be rising as source of caring and is similar to the levels seen among foragers some 20,000 years ago and in surviving groups of foragers such as the Aka tribe.

Lamb, a pioneering and eminent researcher on fatherhood in western industrialized countries, recounts the changing focus of societal expectations and the construal of good fathering for the past hundred years through the lens of research on fatherhood (Lamb, 2000, 2004). He notes that over the course of the 20th century the ways in which fatherhood has been viewed and defined have shifted considerably. Specifically he highlights the change over time in the dominant or defining motif from a father's role in moral guidance, to breadwinning, and then to sex-role modeling (especially for his sons) and the provision of marital support so that the mother could engage in optimal mothering, and finally to today's nurturance of the young (Lamb, 2000, 2004). In line with this broad depiction of paternal caring, he suggests that the currently restricted focus on paternal nurturance and the direct involvement in child care misses other central functions or aspects of paternal caring, such as providing economically to the stability and security of the family.

Taken together, these cross-cultural and historical accounts demonstrate a clear picture and suggest that caring appears to be multiply determined. For example, women's pregnancy and nursing of infants is biologically determined and indeed leads to the universal predominance of women as caregivers for infants and toddlers. Men's larger size and competence in activities involving speed and upper-body strength made them better candidates for protecting the family and tribe from predators and enemies. Yet even such biological tendencies can be variably exhibited. For example, in societies where mothers are significantly involved in production tasks, supplemental foods are introduced to infants early in life to free their mothers from nursing, and when women are more involved in contributing to subsistence, men become more involved in direct care for the young. Thus cultures engage in strong sex-typed socialization which—in the case of women—have almost invariably directed them toward caring for children; in the case of men, this was more variable (see review in Wood & Eagly, 2002). Male care appears to have involved a diverse set of roles reflecting the necessary provisions at a certain historical time and ecological niche; it included such roles as breadwinner, defender, and provider of support (whether directly or through the amassing and maintenance of a group of cooperative relatives), teacher, disciplinarian, and nurturing agent. What becomes apparent in the extant literature, therefore, is the high level of flexibility and cultural ingenuity in these provisions of care and support by fathers as a function of changing contexts and circumstances.

What can we make of men's and women's caring? A proposed resolution

The discussion of women's and men's caring has undergone several changes as research has attempted to uncover the origin of these sex differences and their manifestations. Generally, and within the different paradigms addressing issues of sex differences in caring, it is possible to distinguish between three major accounts of male and female caring. The first views men's lower levels of care as mostly reflecting issues of socialization and expectations. The main point stressed is that despite the sexual differences in biological and neurological mechanisms, men are in principle as capable of giving care as women and can provide good, nurturant, sensitive care to the same extent as women. Men have simply not been socialized to provide care and to assume caregiving roles to the same extent as women, and the current social norms that still view caring and caregiving as having a lower status than other activities and professions—and which tie these activities and professions to women—do not attract men to take them upon themselves. Because women engage in practicing such skills and are more motivated to use them, they are more adept at caring for their children and other close relations than men, who lack the relevant experience and may thus be less sensitive and attuned to their children and to others and less confident in their caring abilities.

According to this view, men can "mother" as much as women can. For example, meta-analyses of studies on gender differences in empathy among children and adolescents found that females' greater empathy reflects mostly self-reports and does not appear in physiological or unobtrusive observations of nonverbal reactions to another's emotional state (Eisenberg & Lennon, 1983). Similarly, meta-analysis of laboratory studies with adults found that women's greater empathy reflects a greater motivation rather than differential ability, because instructions and incentives that directed men and women to pay attention to such cues wiped out this gender difference (Ickes, Gesn, & Graham, 2000). Furthermore, studies have indeed demonstrated that there are no inherent differences in competence between mothers and fathers that cannot be undone by increased motivation, practice, and learning and that parenting skills as well as other caring skills—such as comforting or caring for elders—can be acquired through practice by both men and women (see edited volume on fathers' roles Lamb, 2010).

The current political appeals by homosexual couples for the right to have and raise children in such families reflect this point of view. In fact, the growing (albeit still insufficient) research on children growing up in such families suggests that children develop normally and adequately in such arrangements and that male partners tend to share caregiving in an egalitarian manner (Johnson & O'Connor, 2002; Mallon, 2004; Schacher et al., 2005; Amato, 2012). Similarly, the growing number of studies (mostly on homosexual males) that describe male partners' care for their HIV-positive companions or friends include descriptions of sensitive, committed care (Park & Folkman, 1997), demonstrating the plausibility of males' care being similar in quality and investment to women's care. Still, these initial findings are based on research involving homosexuals, and it is currently unclear how heterosexual men fare in undertaking the "mothering" role.

The second possibility, which is currently less popular at least in western countries, is that there is a clear sex difference between males and females and that females are far more geared toward caregiving than males. Various accounts converge in supporting this somewhat less "politically correct" position. Biologically, through their neuroendocrine affiliative circuitry (Taylor, 2002) and their distinct and unique relations with their mothers, whom they learn to emulate through conscious and unconscious processes (Chodorow, 1978/1999), women have a much greater capacity *and* propensity to care than men and construe their world through this perspective (Gilligan, 1982). Sons, in contrast, probably would not be able to have this kind of unique and intimate relation with their mothers. A large gender difference ($d = 0.93$) found in a meta-analysis of data based on 47 inventories indicates that women are more interested in people whereas men are more interested in things, and accords with the former claim

(Su, Rounds, & Armstrong, 2009). The finding of such differences as early as toddlerhood in relation to toy preferences provides further substantiation (Jadva, Hines, & Golombok, 2010). Scholars who appear to advocate such a position (e.g., Chodorow, 1978/1999; Gilligan, 1982, Taylor, 2002) do not say so explicitly and, although they provide ample evidence and persuasive assertions supporting this view, they still maintain that biology or psychoanalytic processes of socialization are not destiny. Their writings can therefore be interpreted as suggesting that society needs to change the way it values caring and caregiving, especially as it is performed by women. They suggest that society should accord these activities and roles a higher status and, furthermore, that men should nevertheless try to partake in these caring actions and caregiving roles and share them with women.

The third possibility discussed with regard to sex differences in caring involves the contention that both sexes care and have inborn biological caring motivations, capacities, and propensities that play out in different ways. These different ways may reflect the distinct evolutionary adaptation of men and women, although there is still room for flexibility and variability (e.g., Taylor, 2002; Eagly, 2009; Van Vugt, De Cremer, & Janssen, 2007; Feldman, 2012). Specifically and according to these accounts, male caring mostly evolved as a response to the need to cooperate in small to moderate-sized groups and to defend those groups against predators and other groups. In contrast, female caring evolved in response to the need to care for and raise children to sexual maturity, to cooperate with a small and close-knit group of females in child care as well as in gathering food, and to care for one's mate so as to attract the mate to stay and invest in the female's offspring. Accordingly, the coevolved social gender roles comprise distinct expectations of care: the male gender role fosters helping that is heroic and chivalrous, and the female gender role fosters helping that is nurturant and caring. In the same vein, Baumeister and Sommer (1997) suggest that the male need to belong is better satisfied by a broader social structure emphasizing hierarchies of status and power, whereas the female need to belong is better satisfied through interpersonal dyadic bonds.

In line with these suggestions, women appear to be the preferred caregivers within close relationships. The research literature provides ample evidence supporting the primacy of women in caring for their children, for each other, and for their romantic partners (Taylor, 2002) (see Chapter 8). As reported in Eagly (2009), women also outweigh men in caring for older family members and friends (75% of these caregivers in the United States are women) and in living with and caring for grandchildren (62% of such grandparents are women). Women are also predominant among caring professionals such as preschool and kindergarten teachers (98% in the United States), registered nurses (92%), and social workers (79%). Women are even somewhat more predominant than men in being living donors of all organs including kidneys (58% in the United States). These tendencies are already apparent during childhood and adolescence, when children almost universally tend to play and socialize in same-sex groups. Within these groups, girls engage more in prosocial responding involving empathy, self-disclosure, and comforting, whereas boys engage more in cooperative (and competitive) games in larger groups (Rose & Rudolph, 2006).

Different meta-analyses that have examined help and care and concomitant qualities provide further support for such sex differences. For example, meta-analyses have demonstrated a moderate effect size ($d = 0.37$) favoring females in prosocial responding (Fabes & Eisenberg, 1998). Similar moderate to large effects in the personality disposition of nurturance (alternatively referred to as tender-mindedness) and altruism were also apparent (Feingold, 2004) and recently replicated with regard to compassion (Weisberg, DeYoung, & Hirsh, 2011), though effects varied substantially as a function of culture (Costa, Terracciano, & McCrae, 2001; Weisberg et al., 2011).

There are certain caring domains where men clearly outweigh women in number; these reflect what we would have expected on the basis of the coevolution of distinct caring realms for men and women. Whereas women tend to engage in help that includes emotional work, comforting, and nurturance (especially with close others), men are more likely than women to engage in more heroic, chivalrous, risky, and physically demanding forms of helping (Becker & Eagly, 2004) as well as in cooperation and help with in-group members, especially during intergroup conflict (Van Vugt, De Cremer, & Janssen, 2007). For example, whereas women's cooperation in their group did not change as a function of intergroup threat (in general women's cooperation was higher than men's), men increased their cooperation with their group members under similar conditions (Van Vugt, De Cremer, & Janssen, 2007). Additionally, men displayed greater levels of ingroup favoritism in same-sex groups (Yamagishi & Mifune, 2009) and greater levels of cooperation in same-sex dyads than women (Balliet, Li, Macfarlan, & Van Vugt, 2011).

In addition, when high-risk altruistic and especially heroic actions are considered, such as the heroic rescue acts of the Carnegie Hero Fund Commission medalists (see Chapter 9), the proportion of men overwhelmingly outweighed that of women (Becker & Eagly, 2004). Specifically, the Carnegie medalists were 91% male; in a similar Canadian endeavor, termed the Medal of Bravery, 85% were male. Men also volunteer much more often than women to serve their country and fellow men in the military and commonly serve among firefighters (95% male) and police officers (85% male) in protecting and rescuing professions. Furthermore, in field and laboratory experiments on helping behaviors, where a stranger appeared to be distressed or endangered (e.g., helping a man who fell in the subway) or in need of assistance (e.g., having dropped packages), men helped more than women. A meta-analysis of these studies found a moderate effect size ($d = 0.34$) (Eagly & Crowley, 1986). This effect size was even larger when helpers had to take the initiative ($d = 0.55$) rather than simply respond to a request. In the latter case, the effect size dropped significantly ($d = 0.07$).

Similarly, using a questionnaire that addressed a large number of altruistic acts with strangers or distant acquaintances, Johnson and colleagues (1989) found that men reported giving more help than women across different types of altruism and across diverse cultures and that male-female differences were greatest in help provision when the help involved physical effort, pain, or physical or psychological harm. Furthermore, when helping demands the kinds of skills that men are expected to have (e.g., changing a flat tire), men are much more likely that women to offer help.

Finally, other domains of caring that are not as charged with emotional comforting and dyadic care or with heroic or risky helping with strangers do not show clear gender differences in terms of the prevalence of one sex or the other. These include community volunteering and organizational citizenship behaviors as well as owning and caring for pets (see Chapters 10, 11, and 12).

Contemporary accounts of sex differences in how caring is actually enacted in the parenting domain also accord with the view that each sex has distinct expertise and ways of caring. Observational and survey data suggest that mothers and fathers engage in different types of interactions with their children (see review in Lamb, 2004, 2010). Maternal interactions are dominated by caretaking and the provision of nurturance and protection, whereas fathers engage in interactions that induce high positive arousal, exploratory focus, and rough-and tumble contact (Parke, 1996; Lamb, 2004). Differences emerge as early as infancy. As summarized in Paquette (2004), fathers tend to engage infants in interactions that are physical and stimulating and also initiate unpredictable or idiosyncratic play, whereas mothers tend to be more didactic and verbal with infants and engage primarily in visual object–centered play.

Integrating a large number of findings regarding mothering and fathering and their distinct characteristics in western developed countries, Paquette (2004) offers an intriguing conceptualization regarding fathers' distinct role. He suggests that fathers play a particularly important role in the development of children's openness to the world. Fathers excite, surprise, and momentarily destabilize children. While providing a sense of safety and security, they also tend to encourage children to take risks, scaffolding them to be braver in unfamiliar situations and to stand up for themselves. This relationship is termed *the father-child activation relationship* (in contrast to the mother-child attachment relationship, which is aimed at calming and comforting children in times of stress) and is implicated in distinct ways in children's development (see a special issue of Early Child Development and Care in 2013 devoted to this subject and Dumont & Paquette, 2013).

Feldman (2012) similarly suggests that mothers establish a sense of predictability and safety while fathers prepare children for novelty and excitement and that both components are necessary for optimal development. Her research on infants' and toddlers' synchronous interactions with both their fathers and mothers indeed reveal distinct differences. Mother-infant synchrony is rhythmic and socially focused, whereas father-infant synchrony is outward-oriented, and contains quick and unpredictable peaks of positive arousal. In line with these depictions of distinct provisions by mothers and fathers, maternal oxytocin levels correlated with the social affective repertoire, including maternal gaze, affect, vocalizations, and affectionate touch, whereas paternal oxytocin was associated with object-oriented stimulatory play, consisting of positive arousal, object exploration, and stimulatory touch (Gordon et al., 2010a). Furthermore, an increase in salivary oxytocin following a 15-minute play period was seen in mothers who engaged in maternal affectionate touch and in fathers who engaged in a father-specific pattern of paternal care—stimulatory contact (Feldman et. al., 2010a).

Taken together, these accounts accord with the view that males and females have distinct care specializations that are expressed in distinct contexts (small close-knit groups vs. larger groups), distinct kinds of provisions (emotional care/comforting vs. chivalrous, risky, and instrumental care), and distinct targets (close others vs. acquaintances/strangers). These differences in behavior reflect predispositions that have coevolved at the biological and genetic levels as well as at the cultural and contextual levels. The biology or socialization view is thus incorrect, since both sources shape our caring.

Most of the gender effects identified in meta-analyses with regard to the caring motivation have been moderate in size and explain 10% to 25% of the variance. Furthermore, cross-cultural research as well as changing contextual and personal circumstances demonstrate that men and women can be quite flexible in their care. Although I have referred up to now only to men taking on women's types of care, the other direction is also a viable and indeed implemented possibility. For example, during World War II, when a large number of men were off fighting (e.g., in the United States and England), women engaged in many caring tasks that are typically the province of men; think about "Rosie the Riveter" as a cultural icon in the US duting that time (Milkman, 1987) (e.g., breadwinning, fixing around the house, working in factories). Furthermore, currently many more women are engaged in professions and in workplaces that require cooperation and managing coalitions in the context of large groups that include nonintimate relationships, and women now enter professions that demand bravery and the exertion of physical strength, including the military and engaging in combat (Barnett & Hyde, 2001; Powell & Greenhaus, 2010). Thus both sexes show a definite potential for engaging in a variety of types of care and hence may engage in quite similar care if circumstances or contexts require it. This capacity reflects our evolved genetic predisposition to be flexible and sensitive to context, culture, and circumstances and to adapt our behavior accordingly. In other words, despite observed gender differences in caring, when our *caring motivation* and *potential caring qualities* and capacities are considered, males and females are very much alike. This relates to the gender similarities hypothesis proposed by Hyde (2005), which asserts that when we consider a diverse array of important behaviors and personality attributes, "males and females are similar on most, but not all, psychological variables." (Hyde, 2007, p. 259)

Chapter conclusion

During the last decade, several conceptualizations coming from different research paradigms (e.g., biology, evolution, brain research, anthrophony, developmental and social psychology, psychoanalysis, feminism) have converged in suggesting that men and women have developed specialized forms and kinds of care. Such specialization reflects the coevolution of culture and genes at the ultimate level and the joint operation of biological/hormonal antecedents, cultural expectations and norms, and personality dispositions as proximal determinants of caring. Various scholars have used somewhat different terms but refer to very similar dimensions that underlie sexual differences in caring, as reflected in adult relations and in parenting.

In her award-winning address to the American Psychological Association, Eagly (2009) suggested that the defining difference in men's and women's caring is the male focus on agency and the female focus on communion. In line with the claim advocated in this book regarding an overarching and multifaceted caring motivation, Eagly suggests that women and men are similar in engaging in extensive prosocial behavior but different in the kinds of prosocial responding they specialize in. Female prosocial behaviors are more focused on communal, expressive, and relational aspects whereas men focus on prosocial behaviors that are more agentic and collectively oriented as well as strength-intensive. Not surprisingly, widely shared gender roles reflect this differentiation. Similar distinctions refer to instrumental roles, which reflect an orientation toward the external world, vs. expressive roles, which refer to nurturance and affective aspects. Both proficiencies are needed for the adequate functioning of relationships and society, yet they reflect distinct specializations. Eagly further suggests that at its core, this distinction reflects a biosocial interaction between male and female physical attributes and social contexts, including gendered social roles and the division of labor. Consequently, although male and female caring is distinct and partly rooted in biology, culture and socialization, as well as personal dispositions (which are both genetically and socially determined) may occasionally make male and female care quite similar.

In this sense, it is important to underscore Hyde's (2005) contention that we have overinflated claims of gender differences by focusing on distinctions and discussing them at length while ignoring the vast similarities among males and females. This results in an underestimation of how similar the sexes are in most human concerns, capacities, and experiences. I would like to add to Eagly and Hyde by underscoring one of the salient aspects revealed by the discussions on gender differences in caring presented in this chapter. The delineations of male and female caring throughout history and along the lines of cultural diversity highlights the variability of our functioning in diverse contexts and circumstances and thus reflects the remarkable flexibility and creativity of human functioning and adaptation as well as our resourceful, multifaceted, and vibrant nature. These qualities are also reflected in our fundamental, general, and multifaceted caring motivational system.

Part III Conclusion

The presentations and discussions in this part provide two complementary perspectives on the caring motivational system: one relates to what appears to be a universal process of development—an ontogenic perspective—and the other deals with the variations in how such caring in developed and displayed and their origins. Because the study of caring has been dispersed among a variety of disciplines (Berscheid & Collins, 2000), scholars who have studied developmental processes of caring often addressed distinct issues or developmental periods (but see Eisenberg, Fabes, & Spinrad, 2006). The presentation in Chapter 13, which targets the developmental course of the caring motivation and discusses the uniqueness of each developmental period and how development in each period builds on its predecessor, provides a broad overview that offers us a better understanding of this motivational system. Several insights can be gained from this review. First, the caring motivation appears quite early in human development and is intrinsic and universal. Second, each developmental period involves unique new challenges and new arenas for the expression of the caring motivation and hence invites the learning of new capacities and skills. Third, some of these challenges appear to be universal, such as the importance of caring skills relevant to the same-gender egalitarian peer arena in childhood or the learning and training in forming caring bonds in adolescence and early adulthood.

Fourth, with age and the addition of new skills, new arenas, and new ways of expressing the motivation, the universal caring motivational system grows in complexity and sophistication and encompasses a variety of targets, kinds of care, and rules of display. Fifth, with age, two complementary processes that streamline the caring motivation appear to operate: constraint and expansion. Biological, cognitive, emotional, and sociocultural processes work both to constrain and limit the arousal and expression of care (e.g., toward in-group and not out-group members) as well as to open up new routes to arouse it (e.g., morality) and express it (e.g., across distances and differences).

Individual differences in the caring motivational system appear to be multiply determined through an intricate transaction of genetic endowment, biological processes, family context, and a host of other social settings (i.e., education, neigh-borhood), culture, and circumstances. These are manifested in the multifaceted expressions of caring. Yet several fundamental similarities emerge across the varieties of domains and targets in what constitutes good or optimal care, thus highlighting the central core of the diverse manifestations. Consequently a general definition of what constitutes good care across the different manifestations and domains of care was offered. The study of individual differences also exposes nonoptimal expressions of care, which are multiply determined and also reflect our capacity to be flexible and versatile in the expression of caring and other fundamental motivations.

The study of gender differences exposes the variety of provisions that we as a species have evolved to include in our caring repertoire and our reliance on all of them for survival and thriving, including those that are viewed as less characteristically caring, such as breadwinning or heroism. The research further underscores the tendency of men and women to specialize in somewhat distinct types of care (agency and the external world vs. expressive facets and the close relational world respectively) and the creative flexibility and malleability that we have to engage in all sorts of expressions of caring, including those that may be less biologically, socially, or culturally sanctioned for our gender.

Together this part contributed to our understanding of the common and probably universal aspects of the operation of the caring motivational system and its development as well as to its multiplicity, versatility, and flexibility.

A CONCEPTUAL MODEL OF CARING AS A MOTIVATION

Part IV Introduction

In this final part of the book I discuss in more detail my claim that human beings as a species have an evolved fundamental, general, and overarching caring motivation to nurture, care, tend, and help others, both human and nonhuman, and that this motivation entails the desire to help sustain (preserve) an entity and to help it heal, grow, thrive, and prosper. Building on the extant research and theoretical models presented in this book, I suggest a comprehensive conceptual model regarding this motivation in which I address the diverse caring phenomena discussed in this book. Specifically I discuss the composition and universal components and mechanisms of the operation of the caring motivational system and address the issue of its being innate and fundamental as well as general, encompassing, sophisticated, and flexible. I also provide an overview of ultimate and proximate mechanisms for its operation. Finally, I present and discuss the significance of this conceptual model and its ramifications to our view of human nature, underscore several major research questions that emanate from the model and briefly discuss applied applications.

Specifically, in Chapter 16 I build on the evidence from the previous parts of the book and discuss how this motivation is *fundamental* in our nature and describe it as including historical layers of evolutionary development that culminate today in a multifaceted and multidimensional *caring motivational system*. I further discuss its *composition* and *major aspects of its workings*. Specifically I address the distinction between a caring bond, a caring state, caring behaviors, and caring relationships as well as caring as a reaction and caring as a drive and their interrelations (kinds of involvement in caring). I also discuss the centrality of autonomy in enacting the caring motivation and stress the importance of conscious decisions and unconscious instinctual processes in the expression and enactment of the caring motivation. Additionally, I relate these observations to the interplay between the caring motivational system and other motivational systems. I also reflect on issues of satiation in the enactment of the caring motivation, the existence of a personal optimal level of caring, and the importance of balance and judiciousness in its deployment. In this respect I revisit the definition of good care suggested in Chapter 14 and discuss the variety of cultural, biological, and psychological mechanisms that have evolved to sustain such care. Finally I discuss the model for the universal developmental course of the caring motivation presented in Chapter 13 and underscore some major insights as well as the need for further research on these issues.

In Chapter 17 I underscore the *general, encompassing, diverse,* and *flexible* nature of the caring motivational system and discuss the indications for the existence of *one overarching motivational system* that is *multifaceted and flexible.* I further describe the varied and different care recipients (plants, children, elderly people, dogs, the environment) and their organization as a fuzzy set in the general category of caring. Notwithstanding the similarity among the different manifestations of the general caring motivational system, I also underscore the distinctions among the different manifestations of caring. Specifically I discuss the diversity of provisions and distinctions among caring relations, including gender differences. I also consider a prevailing phenomenon of within-individual coherence but also underscore within-individual diversity and flexibility, including processes of compensation and interference among different caring manifestations. Finally, I deal with the emergence of a prosocial majority in the diverse research literatures reviewed in this book, which appear to comprise at least two thirds of the population and reflect on the advantage of interindividual diversity in the display of caring in the context of this prosocial majority.

In Chapter 18 I discuss the proposed *model of operation* of the caring motivational system with its ultimate and proximal causes and how they operate on a variety of levels, evolutionary, biological, social, and psychological. I discuss these processes with regard to caring behaviors in general and to caring bonds, and differentiating between egalitarian and hierarchical caring bonds. I refer to several routes that activate caring, specifically empathy, perspective taking, morality, and search for life meaning and self-actualization. I also discuss sustaining mechanisms of bonding, such as warmth and exclusivity. Finally I discuss unintended consequences of caring, such as the "warm glow" and hedonic pleasure, health benefits, sense of meaning and eudaemonic well-being, self-worth, and good reputation, which also sustain and reinforce caring.

In Chapter 19, I discuss the implications of my argument for the existence of a general, encompassing, fundamental, and innate caring motivational system. In particular I consider its implications for our view of the world, the human condition, and the nature of our species. I discuss my claim that it is a significant endeavor that imparts meaning to our life and is a primary path to self-actualization. I further show that it is mostly related to our eudaemonic rather than our hedonic well-being. In particular I suggest that caring is fundamental in our nature because it reflects our *daimon*—our true self—and is a reflection of our inner spiritual core. I then briefly discuss this spiritual core and the manner in which it is associated with caring.

I was not sure how to present my view of the centrality of the spiritual in our caring in this book. This hesitation was related to my concern that for some people the inclusion of this perspective may detract from the veracity and reliability of the solid scientific foundation that I have amassed and discussed throughout this volume. I therefore decided to discuss my take on the spiritual core and its relevance to caring in this chapter, where I consider the ramifications of the existence of a fundamental and encompassing caring motivational system to our view of human nature.

Hence I make a distinction between issues that have been examined scientifically and are presented throughout the book and organized into a conceptual model in chapters 16, 17, and 18—such as the pervasiveness of care, its innate nature, and its connection to our meaning and purpose of life and to our self fulfillment and eudaemonic well-being—and aspects that have not been demonstrated scientifically, such as the existence of a spiritual core, which is discussed in a separate section in this chapter. I do ask readers who do not endorse my spiritual beliefs or who view this as inherently irrelevant to the presentations in this volume to separate the two and judge the scientific evidence that I have presented and discussed at its face value. If, by any chance, you find the view that I present regarding the spiritual and its association with caring interesting, that its great. And if not, that is great too.

I end this part by discussing and illuminating new research questions as well as applied implications.

At the end of this volume, in Chapter 20, titled "Summary and Major Contributions," I provide a succinct summary of the comprehensive conceptual model of the caring motivational system as well as highlight the main new understandings that this model offers.

16

The "Caring Motivational System": Fundamental, Innate, Complex, and Sophisticated (Composition and Operation)

In his famous book on human motivation, McClelland (1987) offered the following conclusion:

> On the other hand, a natural incentive to nurture may not exist. It is impossible to know on the basis of present evidence, despite the large number of studies of helping behavior. Little work has been done on measuring a motive like the need for nurturance which might arise out of such a natural incentives as the joy-happiness-pleasure that comes from holding and helping babies. (p. 161)

In a way, this sentence reflects the general viewpoint of a large number of human motivation scholars at the time. Now, over 25 years later, I argue that we have plenty of research evidence to support the claim that human beings as a species have an evolved general, overarching, and innate motivation to nurture, care, tend, and help others, both human and nonhuman. This motivation entails the desire to help sustain (preserve) an entity, whether animate or inanimate, and to help it heal, grow, thrive, and prosper. This is my definition of the caring motivation.

Caring as fundamental

The caring motivation as expressed within the fabric of human life is central to human existence in the different realms and contexts in which it is manifested.

The fact that a vast number of models and theories have been suggested to account for it in a large number of contexts and relations attests to its prevalence and ubiquity. In fact, one of the remarkable features of studying the caring motivation is the multitude of often independent approaches and contexts in which it was investigated. Think, for example, of the host of grand and midlevel theories and models that arose within evolutionary science alone to account for each of the realms where caring was observed and could not be ignored or was brushed aside. A similar plethora of thought is evident in the diversity of research fields that have examined topics in this category, such as parenting, social support to family and friends, caregiving to the elderly and sick, altruism to strangers, and prosocial behavior. The fact that different fields have employed somewhat divergent nomenclature has tended to obscure the similarity between them. What all these cases share regardless of terminology, is the existence of a motivation to sustain, heal, and help an entity thrive and develop.

Such widespread prevalence is not surprising given that without the caring motivation, we as a species would not have survived, be it because we rely on the caring of our parents (both mothers and fathers), of romantic partners, of friends, of our group members, or of strangers in times of danger or distress and even for mundane needs. Thus it is not surprising that caring is all around us and is quite general and comprehensive. Its centrality makes clear evolutionary sense, as conceptualized by a large number of outstanding scholars. Furthermore, being such a vital and essential motivation, it is genetically and biologically governed. We currently have solid beginnings of research and theory regarding the genetic, biological, and neuroendocrinological basis of the general caring motivation, all of which are similarly implicated in the diverse manifestations of caring.

But the importance of this general caring motivation lies not only in its centrality to our survival but also in its being a core characteristic of our nature and a defining cornerstone of our sense of meaning in life (Baumeister et. al., 2013). In line with its centrality, engagement in caring and tending represents a high level of human potential and is strongly tied to our sense of self-fulfillment and self actualization, which is also deemed a core aspect of human experience (Maslow, 1973, 1968/2013).

As we have seen throughout this book, such a motivation is manifest in different ways and in a large variety of relationships and contexts. Some of these caring contexts might be more crucial to survival than others, yet together they furnish a web of caring that seems to flow naturally from an inner source, sustaining us as a species and defining our nature. Consequently the distinct relationships and contexts in which caring is revealed are all seen as *instances of a general category of caring* and as *manifestations of the general caring motivation* despite their differences.

The nature of the caring motivation as a complex and sophisticated motivational system

In accounts of caring within various contexts and relationships, caring or caregiving has been depicted as reflecting the operation of a behavioral system (Bowlby, 1969/1982, 1988; George & Solomon, 2008), as an emotion (Bell & Richard's connection theoretical orientation, 2000a), as a drive-like system that sustains "costly long-term investments" (Brown & Brown, 2006a), as an innate spiritual capacity (Ashlag, with commentary by Laitman, 2005), and as a thinking-based undertaking (Ruddick, 1989/1995). Let me start by saying right away that I believe it is all of the above, meaning that caring is conceived as involving the operation of a sophisticated and multifaceted *motivational system* that is not only behavioral in essence but also involves cognitions, emotions, affectional caring bonds, values and morality, as well as a spiritual core.

Next, allow me to elaborate on this complexity by referring to evolutionary accounts that address the plausible processes that have shaped care. It is quite reasonable to assume that the evolutionary origin of the caring motivational system resides in the emergence of mammals and in the need for fairly extensive care (maternal care) for the young. As depicted by Bell (2001) and described in Chapter 3, this motivational system evolved from very crude ways of caring that involved nursing and rudimentary forms of protection to a complex system of maternal care. In humans, this system included the potential to acquire the behavioral repertoire needed for care, the mechanism to form a caring bond, the empathic processes needed to provide care in an adequate and sensitive manner, and the mechanism for sustaining the caring bond once it was created—along with the relevant underlying biological, hormonal, and neurophysiological processes. Along with others (e.g., Hrdy, 1999; Taylor, 2002), I assume that other forms of caring evolved as the biological, emotional, cognitive, and behavioral foundations/strata of this motivational system were generalized, with adaptations to other relationships and situations, such as romantic relations and cooperation with group members, first in hominids and then in *Homo sapiens*. During this process, the system changed in order to accommodate other types of relations and their distinct nature, and the general motivational system of caring became more complex, compound, and flexible, allowing for a larger number of adaptations.

As described by Decety (2010) with regard to the development of empathic processes, new evolutionary additions and adaptations do not discard old structures and processes but coexists with them as interacting layers, sharing a core of similar structures and processes as well as unique adaptations that inform each other. In fact, new and unique adaptations, such as that of trust in group cooperation, may have come to play significant roles in evolutionarily older domains such as mothering. This is exemplified, for example, in the goal-corrected partnership between parents and children in the preschool years, which requires joint volitional cooperation and accommodations where both child and parent need to trust each other. This means that the *older* system of maternal care may be viewed as the bedrock for the development of other types and functions of care. However, newer adaptations to other relationships and domains were not just added on top of an already fully developed maternal caring system. Rather, maternal as well as other caring processes coevolved on the basis of the early and less sophisticated maternal care system. It is thus the case that the operation of the caring system in the various relationships and domains, although distinct, still reflects similar processes and involves very similar biological agents and mechanisms.

The result that we see today is a broad *motivational system of caring*, which is quite flexible, sophisticated, and adaptable and incorporates a large number of caring goals (e.g., caring to ensure physical survival, to promote well-being, to develop autonomy and efficacy, to make someone happy), a large number of cared-for "entities" (e.g., one's children, friends, romantic partner, group members, future generations, pets), a large repertoire of ways and styles in which this caring can be enacted, and a variety of caring dynamics.

Caring is therefore a more complex and sophisticated system than attachment, which is focused on the receipt of one central provision—protection—and is enacted very early in one's life and hence is governed to a greater extent by innate and instinctive mechanisms. Although certain instinctive and biological components are clearly implicated in the operation of caring, it is much more dependent than attachment on the learning history of the caregiver and the immediate cultural context. Thus personal history, the current context, and culture all play a major role in the provision of care, both in where, when, and to whom it is revealed and in the ways in which it is provided. This creates highly complex transactions between the various factors that affect caring: we all engage in extensive caring in a variety of domains throughout our lives, but its expressions vary depending on culture, genetic influences, and upbringing.

I refer to this complex system as a *caring motivational system* that comprises a large number of the characteristics of behavioral systems as described by attachment researchers (see Chapter 6) but is more complex and multifaceted. For example, besides being activated by cues, the caring motivational system also involves enduring caring bonds and a voluntary drive-like search for occasions that call for caring. Although I have alluded to these processes elsewhere in this book, I will now proceed to discuss in greater detail the different types of caring included in the caring motivational system.

Kinds of involvement and care

The caring motivational system involves a variety of constellations and procedures in the way it operates, reflecting its complexity. I distinguish here between *caring bonds, caring relationships, caring states,* and *caring behaviors.* As depicted at the beginning of Part II, a *caring bond* is "an enduring affectional bond between a caregiver and an entity or an object where the caregiver assumes a committed responsibility to take care of the entity and to concern herself or himself with that entity's survival and welfare." An affectional bond is an enduring emotionally significant relationship with another person who is not interchangeable with another. In such a relationship one party wishes to maintain proximity and contact with the other and would feel distress and anguish upon involuntary separation (Ainsworth, 1989).

A caring affectional bond adds the committed assumption of a *responsibility* to care for the other's welfare. The characteristic examples of such a bond are the parental caring bond, caring bonds between romantic partners and between friends, and caring bonds between mentors and mentees. The scope of this responsibility may differ across different caring bonds and fluctuate during the lifetime of a bond as conditions and needs change (the child becomes more autonomous and leaves the parental home, the spouse becomes ill). Furthermore, specific caring responsibilities can be shared with others; hence responsibility can become limited in scope and time. However, a caring bond always entails a committed responsibility for the welfare of another entity. Furthermore, a caring bond involves distinct affective, cognitive, and biological processes. Insel (1997), for example, reports different biological mechanisms for the formation of the maternal dyadic bond and for its maintenance in female rats. Some of these processes may be similar in all affectional bonds, but caring bonds also have distinct affective, cognitive, and biological characteristics related to the caring component. Such a bond is often formed based on a conscious and deliberate decision, but the process is occasionally inconspicuous and people may "formally" commit themselves to such a bond after they have actually become emotionally tied to the object of care (e.g., feeding a stray cat by putting food outside the door without thinking to adopt it and eventually developing a caring commitment to it).

Unlike caring acts or the temporary assumption of a caring state, a caring bond requires a considerable and significant investment on the caregiver's part, even if not much actual caring is always required. The major investment is in the commitment to monitor the well-being and thriving of the cared-for entity and particularly in the commitment to be there for the cared-for entity in times of need. Caring bonds may differ in the provisions they encompass. For example, parental caring bonds include physical care, which is often less salient in caring bonds with friends and romantic partners. Furthermore, some caring bonds involve hierarchical relations between the participants, as in parenting and men-toring, while others are more equal, egalitarian, and reciprocal, as with friends and romantic partners. Finally, caring bonds may be heterogeneous in terms of their length and duration. Parenting is often a lifelong commitment; this can be seen even after the child has become independent and has left the parental home. An example of such a case is when an adult child is hospitalized because of a major illness (e.g., cancer) or undergoes difficult life experiences (such as a divorce) and the parents reassume active caregiving (Da Vanzo & Goldscheider, 1990; Sage & Johnson, 2012). Despite being affectional bonds that involve emotional invest-ment, caring bonds may also dissolve and dissipate, as may occur in mentorships, friendships and romantic relations. (See further discussion of the dynamics of care bonds and their antecedents in Chapter 18.)

People may have *caring relationships* that include more than one-time inciden-tal helping but do not imvolve caring *bonds*. Affectional bonds of any kind take time to develop. For example, even attachment bonds between an infant and an adult take about a year to become established, and there are indications that romantic bonds take even longer to fully develop (about two years) (Hazan & Zeifman, 1994). Furthermore, not all caring relationships (e.g., between doctors and patients) develop into caring affectional bonds. Put differently, there are rela-tionships where caring dynamics have developed but that do not include an affec-tional committed investment in the other and its concomitant uniqueness for the parties involved. The dynamics of caring in caring relationships may involve dif-ferent provisions and can be hierarchical, as in a senior person helping a novice at work, or egalitarian, as between coworkers or neighbors.

A *caring state* is a state of readiness to take care, which includes an assumption of responsibility for the entity for which one cares. A caring bond always entails such readiness. However, individuals may assume a temporary caring state with-out forming a caring bond, as when asked to guard another person's pet for a weekend or even in the case of such mundane occasions as feeling responsible to guard someone's belongings left on a nearby restaurant table while their owner is paying her or his bill in a different location at the restaurant.

Although no observable caring behavior may be detected, a caring state involves vigilance on the part of the caregiver and the allocation of attention for the purpose of discerning if and when care is necessary. Thus cues that would have been overlooked or ignored by other people are picked up by the assumed caregiver. A case in point is the tendency of a baby's "designated caregivers" to hear the baby's cry at night and wake up when they are on call but to sleep well without waking up when this is their night off. Furthermore, once responsibil-ity is assumed and even when no caring behavior has yet been provided, the potential caregiver becomes much more attuned to the potential care receiver and hence receptive to emotional contagion and empathy. For example, when the care receiver is distressed, the caregiver feels it more intensely than other people around her or him, and when the care receiver is happy, the caregiver feels a stronger sense of happiness and joy than if she or he were not the caregiver. Similarly, when the care receiver achieves mastery over a certain task, the feelings of pride and accomplishment are experienced by both care receiver and caregiver. Similar processes of emotional sharing with the care receiver are observed in parenting, among romantic couples, in mentoring, in friendships, and in teacher-student relations, albeit at varying intensities.

Caring behaviors encompass any specific behavior aimed at helping the care receiver survive, develop, heal, and thrive. Such behaviors can be enacted as a reaction to a cue with or without having a caring bond or caring relationship (e.g., giving a seat in a bus to a needy adult or rescuing an unfamiliar drowning child).

Another important distinction is between *caring as a reaction* to the "demands" of the care receiver (Ruddick, 1989) and caring as a result of an intrinsic *proactive motivation to care*, which I refer to as a *drive*. In the first case, the assumption of a caring state is supposedly brought about from the outside, as by the existence of a certain condition in the care receiver (e.g., distress), by situational circumstances (e.g., outside danger), or by cultural and social expectations (e.g., the norm stating that a child under eight years of age should not cross the street alone). This is the most prevalent or prototypical portrayal of caring. The caregiving behavioral system as depicted by attachment researchers, for example, was expected to be activated by such cues. Similarly, research on empathic processes has underscored how a person offers help as a *reaction* to perceiving a need in another. And research on moral development highlights how societal expectations and values activate the wish and the obligation to help others who are in need.

This situation is contrasted with cases of an intrinsic proactive urge or need to care—a *caring drive*. This is an inner need that a person feels an urge to satisfy. Such a person actively looks for situations in which she or he could provide care, either temporarily or as part of a caring bond, and will feel dissatisfied if no such occasions can be found. This drive may be enacted as part of a series of temporary assumptions of caring states, as by someone working as part of an ambulance team. In this case, the drive may include a need to give care but not a need to form an enduring caring bond. However, in other instances, we may witness a drive to not only give care but also to form a caring bond. In such cases, the caring drive will be enacted by actively searching for and developing one or more active caring bonds. Should the caring bond become inactive (i.e., the cared-for person no longer requires much care) the caregiver may feel dissatisfied and may look for other caregiving situations or other caring bonds (e.g., decide to adopt a pet or to have another baby). This need to care, described here as a drive, is sometimes depicted in the literature on parenthood as "baby fever" (Brase & Brase, 2012). Indeed, in the age of effective birth control measures, this drive may be one of the major reasons (as a proximate cause) for why people have children and for why they want to take care of them.

In some individuals, this caring drive may be directed toward others who are not one's progeny, such as students, protegees, and pets. The description of generativity, the urge to care for next generations, as a developmental task of adulthood accords with the delineation of caring as reflecting a proactive drive. Although often egalitarian caring relations as with friends and romantic partners start on the basis of other motivations besides caring, the caring drive might also be directed toward friends and romantic partners. In such cases the caring bond reflects a proactive search for a relation in which caring can be enacted. I use the term *drive*, which is often associated with instinctual needs, to underscore the insistence of such a need to care and its spontaneous emergence from within. Interestingly, Taylor (2002) used similar terminology but preferred the term *instinct* to underscore the insistent nature of the "tending *instinct*," as did Keltner, Marsh, and Smith (2010), who referred to the compassionate *instinct*.

One should not confuse the nature of caregiving (i.e., reactive caring or drive-like proactive caring) and the type of caring relationship (e.g., incidental caring relationship or caring bond). For example, a person may have a caring bond that involves a committed responsibility to the welfare of another, such as a romantic caring bond, and will be vigilant in order to be able to detect cues signaling a need on the partner's part, and—if the need arises—will indeed engage in reactive care, sometimes quite extensively, but will not proactively look for opportunities to care within this relationship. In other caring bonds, most often hierarchical, as between parents and children, mentors and mentees, and in pet adoption, a drive-like caring that satisfies the caregiver's inherent and proactive need to give care may be expressed. In such cases caregivers look proactively for opportunities to provide care. In fact, the desire to provide care is often the impetus to form such bonds in the first place. Similarly, people may assume a temporary caring state either as a reaction (e.g., the spontaneous rescuing of a victim of fire) or owing to their need (drive) to care (e.g., the decision to become a teacher for children with special needs). In fact, several professions (e.g., the helping professions) and social activities (e.g., volunteering, donations) may be described as cultural arenas that allow and even welcome the expression of such a need or urge to care. This is not to say that all caring acts within such arenas reflect the operation of drive-like caring. For example, even within bonds that were formed on the basis of the caring drive (e.g., the adoption of pets) some specific caring behaviors may be reactive (e.g., tending the dog during illness). A large number of cases, thus, especially as part of caring bonds, rather involve a combination of reactive caring and proactive caring.

All together, the complex, multidimensional, and broad nature of the caring motivational system is revealed in a variety of aspects: (1) *kinds of involvement and care*—the distinction between a caring bond and a caring state, as well as between caring as a reaction and caring as a drive; (2) *care recipients*—the diverse and different kinds of "objects" or "entities" (plants, children, old people, dogs, the environment) for which we care; (3) *provisions*—the variety and different kinds of provisions or goals that caring may include; and (4) *caring styles*—ways of expressing care. Finally, people may evince distinct caring profiles and feature a large number of combinations of these aspects in different arenas of life, reflecting what I term different *caring dynamics*.

Intrinsic motivation and autonomous vs. controlled regulation as part of the caring motivation

The caring motivation is an *inherently innate* desire to help, nurture, and heal another entity. Such a desire arises in different circumstances and reflects diverse levels of autonomous regulation, ranging from intrinsic motivation to externally regulated motivation. Ryan and Deci (2000) have comprehensively discussed self-determination theory (SDT) and investigated this range of motivations. An act is considered fully intrinsically activated when it is naturally enacted solely because of the interest, pleasure, joy, and satisfaction associated with the activity itself. Hence it reflects an autonomous choice. However, human conduct can and does reflect the operation of autonomous motivations that, unlike intrinsic motivations, are not enacted for their inherent enjoyment value but for other reasons that are still autonomously chosen.

SDT scholars have suggested that *nonintrinsic motivations* vary greatly in the extent to which their regulation is autonomous—that is, the extent to which they relate to feelings of volition and choice as contrasted with feelings of compulsion or coercion, whether external or internal. SDT theory describes two distinct situations of nonintrinsic yet autonomous motivation—integration and identification. *Integrated regulation* is considered the most autonomous nonintrinsic motivation. In such cases, people integrate their behavior preferences with deeply held values that form a harmonious whole; such individuals are autonomously motivated to exhibit these personally valued behaviors. In the caring motivation domain, this relates, for example, to caring based on an internalized and self-congruent morality that is embedded in one's identity. In *identified regulation*, people realize the personal importance of a behavior that is not inherently satisfying and endorse this behavior as their own. However, they may not see the behavior itself as very important and as an integral part of their identity but rather as serving another central value in their lives. Intrinsic motivation, identification, and integration are considered instances of the autonomous caring motivation because all are characterized by feelings of choice, personal agency, and volition, though to somewhat different degrees.

SDT further suggests that controlled motivation involves situations in which people feel compelled, pressured, and forced to engage in a particular behavior with low levels of autonomy. *Externally regulated motivation,* for example, involves compliance with an external regulation of rewards and punishments and is considered the most controlled kind of motivation, while *introjected regulated motivation* is regulated by internalized forms of external constraints and leads to behaviors performed in order to avoid guilt or anxiety or in order to attain ego enhancements such as pride or self-esteem. In both cases, people feel coerced and pressured rather than autonomous in their actions. Caring enacted for these reasons has been depicted in previous chapters as reflecting self-centered as opposed to other-centered motives for caring.

SDT researchers have extensively discussed and studied these different motivations and demonstrated that the extent to which a motivation is autonomously regulated is pivotal with regard to how it is enacted and with regard to its outcomes (Ryan & Deci, 2000). Following their suggestion that autonomy, relatedness, and competence constitute three basic psychological human needs, they expect more autonomous pursuits that satisfy such basic needs to be associated with better outcomes. Specifically—and in a variety of domains such as education, work, and health care—they have found that more autonomous motivations are associated with more engagement and effort, more interest and enjoyment, an enhanced sense of subjective well-being, more positive coping styles, and better performance.

Similar positive outcomes with more autonomous motivations have also emerged in caring. These were observed in authority-based hierarchical caring relationships (e.g., parent-child or teacher-student) and in egalitarian intimate caring relationships characterized by mutuality (e.g., close friendships and romantic partners) (Blais, Sabourin, Boucher, & Vallerand, 1990; Deci, La Guardia, Moller, Scheiner, & Ryan, 2006; Assor, Kaplan, & Roth, 2002; Kanat-Maymon & Assor, 2010) as well as in prosocial behaviors in general enacted with acquaintances (Weinstein & Ryan, 2010). In interpersonal relationships, researchers have distinguished between motivations and reasons for *being in a caring relationship* and motivations for specific *caring acts,* thus reflecting their recognition of the differences between the caring bonds and caring behaviors discussed and underscored in this book. In both cases, we expect that more autonomous motivations would be associated with more effective help, a closer engagement between helper and recipient, and better outcomes for both the helpers whose need for autonomy is satisfied *and* for the recipients.

Specifically helpers who experience a greater sense of personal volition are expected to put greater effort into helping and to be more enthusiastic. Thus they are expected to respond in a more congruent way to the recipient's wishes. Recipients were therefore also expected to benefit from autonomously regulated care because it is more effective and more conducive to relatedness between the helper and recipient.

Extant research accords with these depictions. In romantic relationships, for example, being motivated to maintain the relationship for intrinsic or more self-determined reasons has been associated with couples' more adaptive behaviors and with their greater happiness. Furthermore, the more each partner endorsed autonomous reasons for being in the relationship, the more positive their self-reported and observed responses to conflict. At the level of specific behaviors within a dyadic romantic bond, the extent to which people were autonomous vs. controlled with regard to social support, instrumental support, support for their partner's spiritual life, and support for their partner's life aspirations was positively related to their commitment, satisfaction, intimacy, and vitality within the relationship, and these effects were exhibited beyond the effects of the overall autonomy of their general motivation to be in the relationship. (See reviews of these studies in La Guardia & Patrick, 2008.)

In prosocial behavior with unfamiliar others, an autonomous motivation for helping that included, for example, playing the dictator game and volunteering to help with an experiment yielded higher levels of helping and benefits for both helper and recipient (e.g., better well-being, a more positive affect, and greater self-esteem). As expected, greater satisfaction of the needs for autonomy, competence, and relatedness had also partially mediated these effects (La Guardia & Patrick, 2008).

I would like to underscore here the importance of the caregiver's *subjective experience*. In the hundreds of studies carried out by SDT researchers, the participants' *self-reports* on their reasons and motivations for engaging in a behavior were the key predictors of the different outcomes, which included observations, reports by others, and hard data such as school achievements as well as self-reports. In other words, what matters is what caregivers *feel* and *think* about the reasons for their care. With regard to the main focus of this book, to the extent that caregivers *experience* autonomous volition—as contrasted with being controlled or coerced by external or internal mores—*their care is viewed as reflecting our innate motivation to care.*

The distinction between autonomously regulated caring and more controlled types of motivation to care highlights an important issue when caring is enacted as part of a caring bond. This is related to the difference between volitional choice to form a relationship and to be in a relationship and volitional and autonomous engagement in specific caring behaviors. Caring bonds involve a commitment to the welfare of the other that is often voluntary and often reflects an autonomous motivation to care. However, specific instances of care may involve caring that is reactive and *obligatory*. In other words, the caregiver who engages in such care may not have chosen to engage in the specific caring, to carry it out at the specific time that caring was needed or requested, or for the specific length of time or at the intensity expected. In such cases, the *specific caring acts* may not always reflect the same level of autonomous or intrinsic volition even though their performer may have volitionaly committed to the caring bond.

This is most clearly observable in parenting. A large number of parents probably chose to have children for intrinsic reasons; that is, they chose to form a parental caring bond for the inherent joy and satisfaction associated with such bond or because it is a central part of their identity and aligns with central values in their lives. Consequently parents may experience joy and satisfaction as a result of having an affectional caring bond with their child and of engaging in some of the caring activities in which they have autonomously chosen to engage. However, other caring activities may be less autonomously chosen and thus may arouse negative feelings. A large part of the provisions that parents offer are reactive in nature and hence may not have been "freely" and volitionally chosen. Parents feed their infants "on demand," dress them in the morning when already pressed for time, engage them in order to prevent a tantrum, and discipline them to avoid embarrassment in public places. They often cannot choose the caring activity that they will engage in, nor can they determine its intensity and timing. This is related to their sense of autonomy in *enacting* the caring that they may have autonomously committed to and may have clear ramifications in terms of lowering their well-being. These distinctions, suggested here, bear strongly on the enigma of the "parenthood paradox" (Baumeister, 1991), wherein despite being volitionally chosen and very important and significant in the parents' life, parenting is associated with negative affective outcomes (see Chapter 8). I return to this issue in Chapters 18 and 19.

The importance of conscious decisions and unconscious instinctual processes

I would like to stress the importance of both conscious and planned processes as well as unconscious or preconscious processes in the caring motivational system. As described in a previous section, caring involves a readiness to care either as part of a caring bond or temporarily. This requires a decision to care and to take responsibility for the welfare and survival of another. We can easily ignore such pleas for care, as we often do when we sift the cues and stimuli that we receive to decide which ones to answer and which ones to overlook. Hence caring is first and foremost a decision. Such a decision may include extensive processes of contemplation and considerations such as those involved in the decision to marry, but it may also occur quickly, as recounted by a large number of the Carnegie Hero Fund medalists who risked their lives to save others in danger.

Moreover, caring also involves internal conscious deliberations and planned actions. In this respect, caring behaviors are considered "goal-corrected" (Bowlby, 1969/1982). This means that their overall goal may be constant (e.g., teaching a child to read) but that the techniques and means for reaching it are flexible and involve a process of correction as a function of feedback. This process involves thinking, deliberating, deciding and reevaluating, as powerfully described by Ruddick (1989) in her book on maternal thinking.

At the same time, however, caring is also based on a large number of preconscious automatic action patterns and instincts as well as on unconscious decision processes. In caring, the perception of cues, their processing, and the choice of responding and enactment must often be done quickly and without much hesitation or contemplation, as the survival of another entity might be at stake. This relates to the quick and unconscious *empathic processes* extensively described in Chapter 4, which include both bottom-up and top-down processes. Such processes also involve *instinctive moral judgments* that affect our caring (Haidt, 2007) (see discussion in Chapter 13). It also relates to the somewhat *automatic procedural processes* in the ongoing operation of caring, involving behavioral action sequences that are automatically enacted without conscious deliberation (Bowlby, 1969/1982; Crittenden, 2006). Crittenden skillfully discusses such automatic and unconscious action tendencies and describes them as preconscious, precortical dispositional representations that are the outcome of the mental processing of information which disposes us to behave in particular ways (Crittenden, 2006). She suggests that they tend to appear in situations perceived as emergencies and that on these occasions they reflect an almost automatic response pattern. Interestingly, both Bowlby and Crittenden discuss them in relation to parenting, but Taylor (2002) makes a similar argument concerning altruistic acts. In such situations, Taylor contends, people often say that they acted without thinking and somewhat automatically and even suggest that anyone would have acted in the same way. Recently a study that examined brain activity while participants made decisions about allocating their money found clear indications for both processes—a very quick and instinctive decision culminating in generosity under instructions to act intuitively and a slower process that involved contemplation under instructions to be reflective and ostensibly included inhibition of the quick generous act before it occurred (e.g., Carlson, Aknin, & Litti, 2015).

This depiction of the centrality of both conscious and unconscious processes in the operation of the caring motivational system accords with current views of human functioning that posit a dual-process or dual-system view (see review in Evans, 2008). Automatic and unconscious processes that generate impressions, tentative judgments, and action sequences reflect the operation of the first system, which is fast, automatic, and unconscious and is responsible for most of our daily actions. The second system involves controlled, deliberate, more conscious, and slower processes. Similarly, caring involves highly sophisticated, cognitively based plans that include controlled and deliberate evaluations and programs of action that reflect the operation of the second system as well as preconscious and almost automatic perceptions, evaluations, and action patterns reflecting the first one.

The interplay between the caring motivational system and other motivational systems

The caring motivational system functions alongside a large number of other motivations, which interact in a variety of ways. First, the different motivations compete in terms of attention and investment, meaning that individuals need to consciously or subconsciously prioritize them. Second, some motivations, and attachment in particular, have direct effects on the functioning of the caring motivational system (see Chapter 6). Specifically, when they are feeling either dispositional or situational security, individuals are freer to engage in caring, and the caring provided may be more optimal than that provided under conditions of insecurity. Third, individuals may engage the caring motivational structure in the service of other motivations. For example, childhood parentification probably reflects a situation in which children engage in role reversal and take care of their parents in order to satisfy their own attachment needs and feel closer to their attachment figures.

Finally, the different and diverse prosocial *behaviors* can be enacted for other reasons beside the caring motivation. People can engage in caring and helping because they are forced to do so, because they get paid for doing so, because of guilt and self-esteem considerations, or in order to procure good reputation. This is also related to the distinction between autonomous and controlled (nonautonomous) motivations to care and help, as discussed in a previous section of this chapter. The discussions in previous chapters provide ample evidence that a variety of motivations, including self-serving ones, can motivate prosocial behaviors. In fact, since human behavior is a complex and multifaceted phenomena, it is often the case that a variety of motivations (including the innate caring motivation) are involved in a specific observed behavior. For example, individuals may comfort their spouses because they care about them (an autonomous motivation to care), because this is socially expected, and because they feel that they owe it to them. A woman may mentor because she wants to help others realize their potential (an autonomous motivation to care) and also because this reflects well on her and boosts her status in the workplace. The caring motivation can be coupled with other considerations and motives and a behavior can be multiply determined by a combination of various motivations. This, too, adds to the multidimensionality of caring dynamics. In order to consider an activity as reflecting the caring motivation, therefore, this motivation need *not* be the sole reason for that activity, but the prosocial activity needs to be enacted *also* because the helper wants to contribute to sustaining and preserving an entity and/or contribute to its growth and thriving.

The importance of balanced and judicious enactment of care

A central insight regarding the operation of the caring motivational system is that the practice of caring, as with other biologically based innate systems (e.g., hunger, curiosity), works best when it is *balanced*. Activations that surpass the optimal level are problematic and result in a depletion of resources, exhaustion, and at times even breakdowns because the person has reached the point of satiation. Hence people who engage in caring in which they have reached their *personal* optimal level will probably have less motivation to continue to engage in caring, and if they express their care they most often will enact it less optimally than is usual for them. The experience of compassion fatigue, for example, provides one such example. This optimal level is highly personal (i.e., there is high variability in what constitutes the optimal level for different individuals) and in addition depends on the kind of care and provisions enacted, context, and circumstances.

In general, as depicted in Chapter 14, good and optimal care involves addressing the overt as well as the covert specific needs of the recipient/target in a responsive and sensitive manner at the same time as it respects the major concerns (such as relatedness, autonomy, and competence) in both the caregiver and the care receiver. Even if help is functional and beneficial in addressing the focal distress or need, help that violates the care receiver's or caregiver's fundamental concerns or exceeds the resources of the caregiver may often lead to a negative outcomes for both. This appears to hold true for the variety of caring acts.

Biological, psychological, and cultural mechanisms have coevolved as part of the development of the caring motivational system in order to sustain the caring motivation through a variety of checks and balances and contribute to its well-adjusted, balanced operation such that people will not reach a breakdown point. At the psychological level, these mechanisms include the capacity to downregulate and even "shut down" the activation of empathy and compassion. This also relates to our capacity to spot people who betray our trust, identify such interpersonal situations, and attempt to resolve them by various means such as talking, leaving the relationship, and/or punishing that person. At the biological level, this is probably related to the operation of brain areas that allow for the top-down regulation of empathic responses and the balancing of oxytocin secretion. At the social and cultural level these checks and balances are revealed through cultural norms and expectations that address when and to whom people are expected to provide care and the situations in which they are expected to refrain from giving care or at least to express judiciousness in their giving.

The universal path of development of the caring motivation

Being a fundamental, innate, and universal motivation, the caring motivational system unfolds in a universal developmental path in the lives of individuals. In Chapter 13 I provide a detailed delineation of this developmental process. Here I would like to underscore several major aspects of this process. First, the study of the development of caring and prosocial responding has uncovered that the propensity and motivation to care and help emerges very early in life (around one year of age) and appears to reflect a universal phenomenon. Second, a review of the research from different domains suggests the existence of distinct developmental milestones that are central in different age periods. These include, for example, the capacity to identify needs in others and the innate urge to respond by helping that appears in toddlerhood, learning to streamline the innate caring motivation according to societal expectations during the preschool years and early childhood, learning how to cooperate in an egalitarian context in middle childhood, or learning how to engage in caring bonds with peers during adolescence and young adulthood. Third, these age-related developmental achievements appear to build on each other, and some of these processes appear to be quite universal; yet more research is needed to understand these ontogenic processes. Fourth, research has uncovered the importance of socialization and context in streamlining these innate predispositions and underscored that socialization both curtails some of these expressions of care and also cultivates new capacities and venues for its expression. Fifth, as with other universal developmental paths, maturation and context and their joint interactions appear to affect the expression of the caring motivation. Sixth, a review of the extant research has uncovered the emergence of clear individual differences in this developmental path already in the preschool years. These appear to crystalize during late adolescence. Finally, a review of the extant research points to the need for further research on this developmental process.

Chapter conclusion

The caring motivation emerges as a highly sophisticated and complex motivational system that is a fundamental and core characteristic of our nature. It is all around us and is central to our survival. It has biological, neural, and genetic underpinnings that support its enactment and it functions as a major cornerstone of our sense of meaning in life. It includes various types of involvement and care (e.g., caring bonds and caring behaviors, reactive and proactive drive-like care) and reflects the coevolution of a variety of care recipients and provisions, including mothering, which is probably the oldest evolutionary structure, and cooperation in groups, which evolved later. As an intricate and highly developed motivational system, it comprises unconscious instinctual processes that serve us well in situations that need very quick responding and also conscious slower processes that reflect our free will. Thus autonomous expression of this innate motivation and feelings of choice, personal agency, and volition appear to be critical to its optimal operation. Additionally, its operation is always in the context of other motivations and often the same prosocial responding may reflect equifinality, or the operation of several reasons and antecedents.

As in the case of other vital and innate motivations, people have personal optimal levels of engaging in care (i.e., they can reach satiation in caring, which at times leads to exhaustion and breakdown). This level also depends on the kinds of care and provisions enacted, context, and circumstances. Furthermore, good care is care that addresses the needs of the care-receiver in a sensitive and responsive manner but at the same time also respects other concerns of both caregiver and receiver (e.g., concerns for relatedness, autonomy, and competence). Hence the caring motivational system works best when it is balanced and is judiciously expressed.

Finally, the caring motivational system shows a universal developmental course that starts very early in life—around one year of age. It involves developmental milestones that characterize each age period, where each appears to build on the other. As in other developmental processes, maturation, culture, social context, and circumstances interact to affect its expression. A review of extant research indicates that more research is needed to fully understand the developmental course of the caring motivational system.

17

The "Caring Motivational System": General, Encompassing, Diverse, and Flexible (Similarity and Diversity)

The expression of the caring motivation is highly varied and multidimensional. Yet all the different manifestations flow from the same motivational system with relevant adaptations of course. This chapter discusses this issue and ties together insights from the different chapters of the book to substantiate this claim and discuss its ramifications. In addition, this chapter underscores the diversity within this general motivation and discusses some of the most prevalent distinctions among care recipients and types of caring relations and provisions; it also illuminates possible interrelations among the different manifestations of caring in the same person as well as the importance of within- and interindividual flexibility and balance in its operation.

Caring as a general motivation—similarity across different domains and targets

Throughout this book I maintain that despite the caring motivation's enactments in a variety of domains with different targets and as a part of different kinds of relationships, all are manifestations of a general motivation to care. Although each may involve specific adaptations, they all reflect similar core processes.

For one, different strands of research assessing the expression of the caring motivation in different domains and with various targets have implicated similar internal psychological mechanisms. These relate, for example, to empathic responding, perspective taking and mentalizing, the internalization of morality as part of the self and one's identity, and the capacity for self-regulation at the emotional and behavioral levels. These psychological mechanisms, often acting as direct causes associated with the caring motivation, are implicated across targets, domains, and circumstances, demonstrating the similarity in psychological mechanisms in a variety of caring manifestations, such as caring for a child, lending a hand to a stranger, contributing to charity, and mentoring a young colleague.

There is also strong evidence for the existence of stable individual differences in caring that are similar across different domains and situations of care. This is apparent in the variety of ways that were used to assess such individual differences. Studies by attachment researchers examining caring sensitivity, compulsive caregiving, and the hyperactivation and deactivation of caregiving, for example, have demonstrated similar individual differences across diverse domains, such as parenting, romantic relations, and caring for strangers. Cross-domain similarity was also amply demonstrated in the developmental research tradition concerned with generativity and in the research paradigms within personality and social psychology that investigated prosocial personality dispositions. In both cases individuals rating high on generativity or on prosocial personality dispositions showed a greater number of caring manifestations across domains and targets. Furthermore, the investigation of moral and spiritual exemplars as well as kidney donors has demonstrated a profile of consistent benevolence, kindness, and generosity. Finally, research on the heredibility of prosocial responding has also shown moderate levels of genetic effects consistent across different methods of assessment and has demonstrated longitudinal stability across domains and relationships. Taken together, these different strands of research demonstrate that people show similar levels of prosocial behavior and caring motivations across contexts, targets, and circumstances, corroborating the claim for a general encompassing motivation.

In addition, what constitutes good care appears to be quite similar across domains and targets. As Taylor phrased it (Taylor, 2002, p. 30): "Across various relationships, modes and types there are several similar attributes of good care. These include attentiveness, nurturance and warmth." As I suggest in Chapter 13, *good care* is care that answers the overt as well as the covert specific needs of the recipient/target in a responsive and sensitive manner *while respecting* the three major concerns of relatedness, autonomy, and competence (and/or other concerns deemed central in human experience) in both the caregiver *and* the care receiver. Notwithstanding specific adaptations in different relationships, such care appears to be universally good regardless of the targets, contexts, or domains related to its manifestation.

At the biological level too, it is possible to note a similarity across domains, targets, and provisions. For example, similar brain areas are implicated in empathic processes with kin and nonkin, as part of caring bonds, and with strangers in physical and psychological pain. In addition, oxytocin and other related neuropeptides are distinctly implicated in caring in a variety of situations and targets: with one's child, spouse, and friends as well as in cooperation with unfamiliar others and in expressing generosity and kindness toward strangers. Similar genetic markers, such as the GG allele in *OXTR* rs53576, were also implicated in prosocial behaviors broadly defined to include kin and nonkin and in comforting, generosity, and cooperation.

In sum, there are indications for similar neuroendocrinologal and genetic processes in different contexts and with different targets. Furthermore, in the different domains we observe similar characteristic of what constitutes good care, similar underlying psychological processes, and the expression of similar dimensions of individual differences. What we see is a surge of a variety of distinct ways in which a central flow of motivation bears itself out. We might call each flow by a different name, but the fact that we see so many of them expressed in so many ways and contexts, all reflecting care, attests to the centrality of the caring motivation and its nature as a fundamental core of our existence.

Caregiving targets organized as a fuzzy set

Throughout this book, I maintain that the caring motivation is general, broad, and encompassing and that it includes diverse endeavors such as parenting, caring for the elderly, helping a friend, teaching, altruistic heroism, leadership, mentoring, caring for a pet, gardening, cultivating a collection, and working to bring peace to the world or to preserve the environment. It is clear why caring for others, kin, friends, or strangers is subsumed under this general definition. It might also be clear why caring for a pet is a manifestation of a caring motivation. In all of these instances, the cared-for entity is animate, as is the potential for its preservation and for the furtherance of its thriving and growth as a living being. However, I also argue that caring for plants, objects, and causes might reflect the operation of a caring motivation. Specifically I suggest that whenever this caring entails the preservation of the existence or "life" of an entity and its potential for growth and thriving, it may be an expression of the caring motivation. It might therefore be apparent why gardening can be construed as a manifestation of the caring motivation. Here, the reasoning is easier because we are discussing things that are alive and grow and in that sense can react to our care by growing and thriving.

But this might also be the case with objects. When a collection of model airplanes is perceived by the collector as something in need of preservation, that can potentially grow and thrive, and when that individual indeed intends to make efforts in that direction, we can talk about a caring motivation. People have been known to invest resources, both material and psychological, in their collections, and to devote themselves to their growth and improvement. Caring for causes and promoting values are similar. Most or all of these values (care for the environment, care for justice and equality in one's country, saving the whales, caring for better education in a school district) can be easily construed as a reflection of generativity (i.e. as caring for the next generations in an attempt to foster a better world).

The reader might ask why I am trying so hard to include such extreme instances in the caring motivation. First, because I indeed think that they all reflect the operation of the general caring motivation as demonstrated in the clear caring dynamics expressed as part of these diverse endeavors. Second, such view can provide us with much better understanding of processes of care within individuals (e.g., the adoption of a pet as a form of practicing caring among young childless or child-free couples; the investment in gardening as an outlet to care for lonely adults) and within society, thus underscoring the variability of caring manifestations and giving people viable and valued opportunities to engage in them. Third, such view opens up a variety of significant research questions at various levels—theological, philosophical, biological, and psychological. For example, researchers may target similar biological mechanisms underlying all these instances of care or address the interplay among the different caring domains in individuals' lives.

Prototype theory, first suggested by Rosch in the 1970s to explain the organization of natural and cultural categories (Rosch, 1973; Rosch & Mervis, 1975) can help us describe how the variety of caring targets and contexts can be considered when subsumed within one overarching category of care. According to this theory, which has been corroborated across many types of categories and cultures (Rosch, 1999), categories are not organized in a strict manner of inclusion vs. exclusion based on necessary and sufficient conditions but rather according to a graded centrality, where some members of a category are more central than others. For example, when asked to give an example of the concept *furniture*, *chair* is more frequently cited and hence perceived as more central and prototypical than, say, *stool*. Similarly, a *robin* is a more prototypical *bird* than, say, a *penguin*, yet this, of course, is dependent on culture. Accordingly we find the least prototypical members of the category at its extreme end, and these may or may not be perceived as belonging to that category depending on changing circumstances and perceivers. For example, in the case of the furniture category, some individuals viewed shelves, mirrors, or pillows as furniture, albeit with fairly low levels of prototypicality, while others did not. In other words, categories were viewed as fuzzy sets—categories with fuzzy rather than clear-cut borders.

The category of instances or situations that reflect the operation of the caring motivation is similarly construed as a fuzzy set in which some instances are more prototypical and central to the category (e.g., mothering) while others are less characteristic (e.g., caring for objects). The different instances can therefore be ordered according to the extent to which they are characteristic of the category (Rosch, 1973). Others, like Noddings (1984/2003), have preferred to discuss a somewhat narrower category of caring and to define clearer borders, suggesting a demarcation between caring for living things and other pursuits. An empirical examination of how these different caring endeavors evoke similar dynamics and how they are construed by people from different cultures and backgrounds might be illuminating.

Diversity, flexibility, and multidimensionality—distinctions among the different manifestations of caring

Throughout this book I underscore the *similarity* across diverse domains and contexts in which caring is displayed. However, the caring motivational system is also characterized by its *diversity, multidimensionality,* and *flexibility.* For example, caring differs greatly in how costly it is and how much is invested in it. Some caring responsibilities are very broad, with caring being recurrent and persistent, such as parenting, while in other cases caring may be narrow in scope and incidental. Furthermore, some cases of caring may involve little risk, whereas helpers risk their lives in others instances. Some caring relations, such as parenting and romantic relations, are very central in the lives of the people involved, and their existence is pivotal to the meaning of their lives. Yet other relations, such as those with coworkers or neighbors, may be less central and important. In addition, caring relations differ in length. Caring may involve short-term provisions, as when a person offers to help a tourist by showing her how to get to the train, or when a person risks her life to save a drowning man. It can, of course, last across an extended period of time, as is the case with military camaraderie. Nonetheless, even extended caring may be limited in duration, as with a schoolteacher and her students, which is expected to end as the school year concludes. Alternatively, it can also be (theoretically) unlimited in duration, as with parents and children, spouses, or friends.

In this section, I would like to highlight this diversity and discuss some of the most prevalent *distinctions* within the general caring motivational system. I do not intend to provide an exhaustive discussion of the various aspects that distinguish between the different kinds and types of caring but to briefly underscore a number of them. In Chapter 16, I discussed differences that relate to *types of involvement and care*—the distinction between a caring bond, a caring state, caring relations, and caring behaviors as well as caring as a reaction and caring as a drive. Another important distinction relates to *what* is provided—the variety and different kinds of provisions or goals that caring may include.

Diversity of provisions

Caring as enacted in different contexts and relations involves a large number of *provisions and goals*, which may differ depending on a variety of factors, such as the cared-for object or entity, the context, and the caregiver's assumed responsibility. In some relations, such as parenting, caring is quite broad and involves a very large number of goals and provisions. Ruddick (1989/1975), for example, has suggested three main goals for parenting: (1) preservation of the child's life, which is similar to protection; (2) fostering and nurturing the child's emotional and intellectual growth; and (3) training the child to be an acceptable member of society. In other cases, caring involves a more specific set of goals and provisions. For example, caregiving provided to terminally ill friends or parents may focus on physical and mental preservation, if possible, and often on easing the process of leaving this life but without the capacity to contribute to the person's growth and thriving. This might be one of the reasons why such care is often less satisfying and perceived as more arduous. A similar narrowing of focus occurs in other caring contexts. Teacher-student relations, for example, mostly involve teaching skills and knowledge and are less preoccupied with preservation and survival (if at all). Others, such as nursing, are geared to enhancing physical survival and are less focused on contributing to growth and thriving through teaching cognitive abilities. For mentors who form caring bonds with their protégées, the promotion of the protégé's efficacy and ability to manage successfully and autonomously in the world may be the most salient goal.

The developmental literature discusses different provisions—such as comforting, sharing, cooperating, instrumental help and informational help—and highlights the possibility of different developmental trajectories for them, as each may require different skills that may develop and mature at different ages and in different contexts (see Chapter 13). For example, comforting relies on the capacity to represent and understand what others are feeling in a variety of circumstances, while cooperation also necessitates the capacity to balance the actions and needs of at least two partners and an understanding of reciprocity, mutuality, and equality. Whereas comforting can be developed within hierarchical relationships, as between parents and children, mutuality in cooperation is more easily developed within an interpersonal context of partners with moderately equal power. Furthermore, people often develop their caring preferences through different provisions. Some like to help instrumentally in mechanical aspects, others like to listen and provide psychological advice, while still others like to provide physical care. This may have to do with hereditary traits as well as with environmental influences. Part of the multidimensionality of the caring motivational system thus involves the acquisition of a variety of skills and preferences, and this happens in the context of hereditary individual differences, maturational processes, and a variety of social contexts. (See edited volume devoted to multidimentionality in prosocial development, Padilla-Walker & Carlo, 2014).

Evolutionary accounts as well as behavioral research underscore one of the most central distinctions among types of care: care and nurturance expressed mostly within close relations that appear to characterize feminine care, and care, help, and cooperation in groups that appear to characterize masculine care. These general categories of care, themselves very broad and multifaceted, appear to reflect a somewhat different process of evolutionary development. The feminine type of care developed from basic forms of empathy-based nurturance in mother-offspring dyadic and intimate relations and already appears in rudimentary forms in reptiles (a much older species than humans). These caring qualities probably predate the development of aspects of trust and cooperation in larger groups mostly with peers—the care depicted as more masculine. Because both coevolved during a nonnegligible developmental period; they are very similar in many respects. Both are similar in the biological strata that they rely on (e.g., the use of oxytocin), both rely on empathic processes, and for both there are morally sanctioned norms and intuitions, observed in the operation of the automatic, fast, and affective system (Haidt, 2007). In addition, and as discussed in the chapter on gender differences (Chapter 15), men and women evince high levels of flexibility and plasticity, and—in general—both genders can and do engage in both kinds of help and care. Thus what might have started in our distant evolutionary past as somewhat different caring specializations have long been combined into a much more sophisticated and multifaceted caring motivational system that is highly flexible and has a variety of possibilities for individual differences and specializations that have some genetic base but are also strongly related to the caregiver's individual upbringing and concurrent conditions.

Distinctions among caring relations

Caring relations can be distinguished along a variety of dimensions, and I will discuss some of them. One of the most salient dimensions, and one that has attracted a great deal of research interest, relates to *differences in closeness and similarity* and particularly to the distinction between helping close others, helping acquaintances, and helping total strangers. Specifically the help and care provided to strangers has baffled evolutionary researchers and others who subscribe to the egoistic or self-centered view of humankind. As we have seen throughout this book, such help and care is quite prevalent, and some core processes—such as the operation of empathy and morality, biological and neuroendocrine processes, the involvement of conscious and unconscious processes, and the reactive and proactive nature of care—are quite similar across these different relations. Nevertheless several different adaptations are involved. Culture has exerted a strong influence on normative expectations concerning the kind of care and help that should or should not be provided to people on the basis of their closeness/distance from the helper and has set demarcations between in-groups and out-groups.

Naturally people would tend to care for and help others who are closer to their circle of intimacy and who reflect the greater importance of those people in their lives. Yet people also risk their lives and health helping total strangers or furthering abstract causes in remote places with unfamiliar others (e.g., fighting for freedom in another country). In addition, issues of equity and mutuality are often not applicable to the help provided to strangers, whereas they may be quite salient in egalitarian relations with intimate or casual relations. Furthermore, equity concerns in close and casual relations may be governed by different relational dynamics. Exchange orientations, where partners keep count of what they give and what they get, may be more salient in casual relations, while communal orientations—in which giving, helping, and caring are not contingent on what one receives from the other but on need—are more characteristic and salient in close relations.

This issue of equity is also related to another important distinction—that which exists between *hierarchical* and *egalitarian caring relations*. A clear power imbalance and hierarchy between the caregiver and the cared-for entity exists in a variety of caring relationships—such as teacher-student, mentor-protégée, and owner-pet—as well as in the parent-child bond. In such relations the caregiver is deemed wiser and/or more able than the care receiver. This discrepancy is part of the underlying motivation for forming a caring bond: one person extends help, care, protection, and empowerment to another who is less able and is therefore in need. However, people also form egalitarian caring relations, such as those that exist between friends and between romantic partners. In these instances both sides engage in giving and receiving help and care. At times one partner is in need of comforting, reassurance, or a boost to her or his sense of worth, while at others it is the other person who is in need. Partners may also simultaneously engage in caring, either by providing similar provisions or by providing different provisions concurrently. This constant change of perspectives requires fairly sophisticated caring capacities as well as mutual coordination. Consequently it appears that children learn to provide care to young siblings or pets in a hierarchical caring relationship more easily than to their same-status friends. The kinds of caring provisions within egalitarian and hierarchical relations also differ. For example, disciplining or teaching are the more salient and probably more frequent types of care in hierarchical relations than in egalitarian relations, where sharing and protecting the partner's reputation may be more common.

In addition, the caring dynamics may also be distinct. Caring in hierarchical caring bonds is often a key aspect of the relationship and, in fact, the bond is often created as the fulfillment of one side's proactive need (drive) to care. This may not be the case in egalitarian caring relations, where other motivational systems—such as companionship in friendship or sexuality in romantic relations—also exist and are often more pivotal to the formation of the relationship (at least in the beginning). Consequently, caring relations that people form with their friends and romantic partners tend to be based on caring as a reaction rather than on fulfilling the caring drive.

Finally, issues of reciprocity, mutuality, and equity play out differently in hierarchical and egalitarian caring relationships. In hierarchical caring relations—as in parenting, mentorship, or pet ownership—the inequality among partners is built in and is part and parcel of the relations and in fact may have been the reason that such relationships were formed in the first place. As far as the caregiver is concerned, the well-being and happiness of the other are themselves the reward and there is little expectation of getting help or caring in return, although other positive responses—such as acknowledgment and gratitude, as well as the expression of joy and happiness in the company of the caregiver—are expected. Although some forms of equity considerations operate in these relationships, grossly uneven distributions of costs and benefits are probably taken for granted. Thus, giving is mostly provided by one side and concerns with mutuality are not salient. However, in egalitarian caring, people may have equity considerations related to how much they give and how much they get in the relationship (e.g., Kenrick, 2006). Clear deviations from equitable exchanges can trigger emotional reactions associated with injustice. In relations with friends and even with romantic partners, they may also lead to the termination of the relationship (Fagundes & Schindler, 2012; Bagwell & Schmidt, 2013). Yet in some romantic relationships or friendships there is a clear imbalance of power. In such relationships we may witness the same drive-like involvement in caring as in hierarchical relationships, where one person largely acts as the caregiver and the other largely acts as the care receiver, meaning that equity and mutuality considerations become less salient.

There are other clear differences among the various caring relations, and even in those with intimate others in *egalitarian relationships*. For example, besides the obvious sexual considerations, issues of exclusivity and jealousy are more salient in romantic relations than in friendships. Sexual considerations and in particular compatibility in these matters as well as fidelity are central to romantic relations and affect issues relevant to caring as well. Similarly, friendship, romantic love, and parenting, all intimate relations, are associated with different developmental periods and developmental tasks, meaning that caring in these relations reflects somewhat different capacities and provisions and different needs. For example, in both parenting and romantic bonds, the assumption of responsibility to care for the other is very broad. However, the actual enactment of care in romantic caring bonds is often much less intense than in parenting. This may be related to the partners being independent adults with developed capacities to manage in the world and solve problems on their own and to their possession of a network of others (e.g., friends, colleagues, neighbors, parents, and siblings) on whom they can fall back for help and support.

Interrelations among the different manifestations of caring in the same person (within-individual diversity and flexibility)

One of the interesting questions resulting from the contention that we have a general motivational system of caring concerns the interrelations among the different manifestations of caring within individuals. Is our caring motivation limited and hence is caring in one context or one relationship enacted at the expense of other contexts and relationships? For example, does caring as part of an individual's profession deplete the caring motivation such that he or she does not have the need or the motivation to take care of his or her children when coming home? Reflecting the compartmentalization of caring into different domains and research communities, there is not much research on these issues. Generally speaking, we can observe two interrelated processes that are relevant to this issue: (1) within-individual *coherence* in caring across caring contexts and caring situations and (2) within-individual *flexibility* in the enactment of caring across targets, domains, and circumstances, which exposes processes of compensation and interference.

As described in Chapter 14, people differ in their caring, and this difference is reflected in many aspects, such as the strength of their general motivation to care, the capacity to be empathic and sensitive, the domains in which they like to care, and their caring styles. A nonnegligible part of these differences is genetic, but a comparable share is related to a person's developmental history (Knafo & Israel, 2010). By adulthood, individual differences in the caring motivation become a personal attribute and reflect personal predispositions that are generalized and are often similarly displayed across situations, contexts, and targets. Individual differences in generativity, for example, are similarly manifested in the quality of parenting, in social support, and in a variety of social and political involvements such that more generative persons at the trait level are more involved in caring in a variety of contexts, and their care is qualitatively more sensitive, responsive, and adaptive (McAdams & Logan, 2004).

Likewise, research on moral and on spiritual exemplars demonstrates that they display high levels of benevolence, compassion, and prosocial behaviors concurrently and in a variety of situations (e.g., Colby & Damon, 1992; King, Clardy, & Ramos, 2014). Similarly, individual differences in caring as assessed within the attachment theory paradigm, such as the hyperactivation and deactivation strategies of the caregiving behavioral system, were similarly implicated in parenting, in romantic relations, and in relations with strangers, attesting to the generalization of the caregiving system's activation across targets (Shaver, Mikulincer, & Shemesh-Iron, 2010). It thus appears that individual differences in the strength of the general motivation to care, the capacity to be empathic and sensitive, and people's caring styles or strategies show within-individual coherence and gen-eralize across domains, targets, and situations. People also tend to specialize in distinct provisions and often show coherence in their preferences for such caring across situations (e.g., preferences to care by listening and advising rather than by physical help). However, the study of this aspect of within-individual coherence is only at its beginning (see a recent review by Eisenberg, Spinrad, & Knafo, 2015).

Along the prevalent within-individual coherence people are also flexible in their enactment of caring and can tailor their care to changing needs and circum-stances. Within-individual flexibility is beneficial for the individuals themselves, as it allows them to cope and adapt to diverse circumstances and promotes their resourcefulness and resilience as well as letting them express their care in a bal-anced and judicious way. When needed (e.g., in an emergency situation with strangers or when someone dear to them is in serious crisis) they can summon caring capacities and exertions that they normally do not exhibit. At other times they can refrain from extending help and care, and this can have both positive and negative connotations in terms of moral, evolutionary, or functional points of view. For example, people tend to compartmentalize their care; in particular, people use demarcations between in-groups and out-groups to constrain their circle of care. This can be conceived of as morally negative, yet it can also be seen as functionally advantageous when it is done to preserve balance in one's caring exertions. At other times people can extend their circle of care and forgive and reconcile with their enemies. Hence we can sometimes observe significant differ-ences in whether and how caring is enacted with different targets or in different situations by the same person.

Furthermore, it appears that caring in one domain can at times compensate for failure to caring in another. For example, the caring of an elder for her garden was described by her as compensating for not being able to care for her grandchil-dren who live far from her (Heliker, Chadwick, & O'Connell, 2000). Similarly, caring for pets was more intense for children without younger siblings (Melson, 2003). These are mostly anecdotal demonstrations and more research is needed in this area.

Sometimes caring in one domain interferes with caring in another. This situa-tion is particularly apparent when caring taxes people's physiological and psycho-logical resources and thwarts their basic psychological needs (e.g., relatedness, autonomy, competence, and meaningfulness) or when they exceed their optimal level of care and reach a point of satiation. For instance, research has documented experiences of compassion fatigue and caregiving burnout among individu-als who are exposed to the intensive and extensive needs of others (e.g., Adams et al., 2006; Hooper et al., 2010). In such cases caregivers feel less motivated and less adept at caring in other domains or with other targets. In a study of adoles-cents, for example, Little (1998) has observed that engagement in one domain of connectedness and giving tended to go along with less engagement in another, as if domains compensated for each other or interfered with each other. These instances show that like many other innate motivations, caring can reach a point of satiation; this observation highlights the importance of a balanced and judicious enactment of caring (see Chapter 16).

Prevalence of prosocial predispositions and the advantage of interindividual diversity

One of the most interesting and recurrent finding across the variety of domains is that the majority of individuals (around two thirds of the population) show salient prosocial predispositions, which appear to be dominant in their conduct. This was apparent, for example, in prosocial interpersonal orientations in competitive games (Van Lange et al., 1997), in the prevalence of secure state of mind in parenting (van IJzendoorn, 1995), in the prevalence of altruistic motives among volunteers (Clary et al., 1998), and in the frequency of those showing altruistic care in everyday situations in laboratory settings (See review in Batson, 2010). Together, these findings attest to the pervasiveness and dominance of a prosocial, trusting, and caring predisposition in our conduct with kin in intimate relations and with strangers. The near universality of the minimum of 60% of the population having a dominant prosocial and trusting predisposition may indicate a minimal level of caring and prosociality that needs to be present within cultures for their sustainability.

The nonnegligible minority also engage in caregiving, yet they tend to provide it in less optimal ways. For example, they are controlling or self-centered in the way they provide care or have a dominant orientation that is less trusting and prosocial. The existence of this nonnegligible minority begs for an explanation. If caring is so good for us, how come not all of us have a dominant prosocial predisposition? I suggest that the existence of less prosocial predispositions, though as a minority, tells us something about the benefits of diversity and the flexibility it allows, and that it underscores the importance of variability in human conduct.

From an evolutionary point of view, phenotypical variability and plasticity in the expression of human qualities is a survival asset because it allows higher flexibility in coping in diverse environments and contexts (see discussion in Price, Qvarnström, & Irwin, 2003). This is relevant at the individual level (i.e., within-individual variance in the expression of care), which was discussed in the previous subsection, but also at the cultural level (i.e., between-individual variance in the expression of care). An interesting indication of such benefit at the group level was demonstrated in a study wherein groups were expected to cope with an emergency situation (detection of smoke in their rooms). Groups that were composed of participants with diverse attachment orientations, which included members with different coping styles, were more successful in coping than groups composed only of secure members (Ein-Dor et al., 2010). For example, the researchers suggest that hypervigilance in an emergency situation may be instrumental in identifying the situation as one needing intervention and is therefore advantageous. The extension of these findings to caring and prosocial responding indicates that individual differences in caring (e.g., diversity in preferences for certain provisions), including the existence of less optimal caring, may be beneficial for human societies in a context where the majority are "prosocials." Together, flexibility and diversity within and between individuals appear to be adaptive and advantageous.

Chapter conclusion

The caring motivational system involves high similarity in processes and dynamics across the very varied types and domains in which it is expressed as well as rich and prolific diversity in its targets and manifestations. Together these seemingly contradictory characteristics form a rich tapestry of human caring that demonstrates how we share a similar core yet have a variety of ways to express it in unique and special ways. I conceive of the multitude of targets and domains as reflecting a fuzzy-set constellation where some targets and domains are more characteristic and prototypical (e.g., parenthood, social support) than others (e.g., gardening). The diversity reflects a variety of provisions (e.g., comforting, instrumental help, cooperating) as well as a varied array of caring relations (e.g., hierarchical and egalitarian) where each demonstrates unique characteristics and adaptations and may have a somewhat distinct developmental course. In this respect I note that although men tend to be more prevalent in some domains of care and women in others, all also evince high levels of flexibility.

Summarizing across different lines of research, I show that research has demonstrated a moderately high level of within-individual coherence in the tendency to be caring and in styles of caring across these diverse provisions and contexts. Yet individuals also demonstrate within-individual flexibility, as is evident in the demarcation between in-groups and out-groups. Individuals also demonstrate processes reflecting compensation and interference among different domains of care, thus underscoring the importance of the balanced and judicious expression of the caring motivation.

Considering a variety of research perspectives, I highlight the fact that the study of between-individuals variability has exposed a majority of people (around two thirds of the population) who show salient and dominant prosocial predispositions across a variety of domains. My discussion underscores the significant role of the large minority who are still caring yet exhibit less benevolent approaches, and it highlights the benefits of diversity and the flexibility and adaptability it allows in human conduct. Finally, the presentations and discussions in this chapter have uncovered many areas that as yet we know very little about, owing in part to the compartmentalization in the study of caring. These discussions have also underscored the importance of the research that is yet to be done.

18

Tying the Diverse Conceptual Perspectives Together: Ultimate and Proximate Causes

Throughout this book I have discussed a variety of conceptual frameworks that have been used to study and explain the various manifestations and experiences of caring. These explanations are provided at different levels—evolutionary, biological, psychological and cultural. I conceive of these as complementary perspectives that address different levels or facets of the caring motivation and its expression (see similar arguments by Sharabany & Bar-Tal, 1982). This chapter is an attempt to tie these different perspectives together. The familiar distinction between the ultimate and proximate causes of a behavior will serve me in elucidating these perspectives' answers to two major questions: *why the caring motivation exists in the first place and how it is activated and sustained in the variety of its manifestations.*

The Nobel laureate Niko Tinbergen has discussed these two levels of causation in animal behavior, arguing that they are complementary rather than mutually exclusive (Tinbergen, 1963). From an evolutionary perspective, ultimate explanations examine the survival value of a behavior, or—in more general terms that are also relevant in other conceptual frameworks—ultimate explanations relate to "what for" questions. Proximate explanations are concerned with the mechanisms that underlie the manifestation of a behavior. In other words, they relate to direct causation, or to the issue of what in the "daily" functioning of the organism leads to a specific behavior.

Ultimate causation—"what for" questions

The most obvious theoretical perspective that has included a discussion of ultimate causation is the evolutionary perspective. As considered at length in Chapter 3, a number of evolutionary models and theories have been proposed to account for the diverse phenomena of caring in human societies. The traditional evolutionary model (direct fitness) provided an ultimate evolutionary explanation for caring for offspring. "Inclusive fitness" theory explains why it is evolutionarily advantageous to care for genetic relatives. "Reciprocal altruism" or "competitive altruism" theories explain why it is evolutionarily advantageous to cooperate and care for a person's small group or tribe if reciprocation is expected and enforced by punishing cheaters or those who do not reciprocate and try to exploit others. Finally, "gene-culture coevolution" theories explain the evolutionary advantage inherent in caring and cooperating with strangers in large groups, where direct reciprocation may not be expected, and this approach has even explained the evolutionary advantage of engaging in high-cost altruism, where an individual may sacrifice her or his life while providing care for unfamiliar others.

Taken together, these models provide explanations at the ultimate level and explain why it is evolutionarily advantageous to care and to provide care in a host of situations and with a variety of targets, kin and nonkin, familiar others and strangers, and even to engage in what appear to be altruistic acts with unclear proximate benefits. The main point arising from these models is that caring of all sorts generally enhances the survival of those possessing such caring genes and gives them an edge in survival across generations compared with those possessing uncaring genes. Scholars of evolution nonetheless restrict this general assertion by claiming that this broad depiction of caring is advantageous and stable as a human characteristic only when genes and cultural norms that help us identify and punish free riders have evolved, making such exploitation disadvantageous in the long run. This explanation generally underscores the functionality and utility of the caring motivation to our survival as a species and to the survival of caring genes. This functionality and utility are often not present in the experience and phenomenology of people's care where other causal agents, such as one's emotional connection to the other person or a sense of an intrinsic moral necessity and conviction are in operation and are therefore seen as direct (proximate) causes.

Another, perhaps less obvious ultimate explanation can be found in theology. Although not viewed as a scientific endeavor, theological concerns and explanations feature as central meaning systems in the lives of the large majority of individuals (Li & Bond, 2010). Hence I consider and relate to these explanations in my discussions of the ultimate cause of caring. As discussed in Chapter 2, a large number of theological perspectives from Christianity, Buddhism, Jewish mysticism (Kabbalah), and contemporary spiritualities converge in viewing the core nature of human beings as having the potential to be benevolent and caring. Furthermore, many of them converge in viewing the ultimate and highest potential of humans as reflecting the actualization of this inner capacity for giving and compassionate conduct and in that capacity to become one with the divine that exemplify these qualities. In that sense humans have both the innate capacity and the innate motivation to be compassionate, loving, and kind to others and to care and help others and the whole universe. In addition, many theological perspectives maintain that the human race's teleological destiny is to become fully caring and giving, overcoming aggression, indifference, and egoism and thus fulfilling its ultimate purpose of becoming divine. The development toward becoming fully giving and caring is not automatic and entails engagement in various practices, such as contemplation, observing religious commandments, working on the self, and other endeavors, which can be undertaken by only humans acting of their own free will. Different religious and spiritual traditions may describe this state of benevolence, kindness, grace, and caring in different ways and may advocate diverse ways to achieve it. Yet the ultimate goal and purpose of individuals as well as the human race at large is often viewed as becoming divine by maximizing their inherent capacity for goodness and caring. In that sense, the ultimate explanation for our caring human nature and for the existence of the general caring motivation resides in our ultimate purpose here on earth, which is fulfilling this potential and developing spiritually in order to become both fully and authentically caring beings.

Are these two ultimate explanations contradictory? Not necessarily. Proponents of the theological view could conceive of the evolutionary explanation as reflecting the earthly mechanism of a spiritual destiny. Proponents of the evolutionary view could conceive of the spiritual-theological explanation as reflecting a belief system that evolved as a cultural adaptation serving as a cultural mechanism or proximate cause, which leads people to adopt caring attitudes and to aspire to behave prosocially, and hence to care about and for others. Thus either perspective is capable of viewing the other as a mechanism rather than a teleological purpose. In this respect it is illuminating to quote Darwin himself in the last paragraph of his groundbreaking book *The Origin of Species*, where he alludes to the existence of a grand scheme that initiated the grand process of evolution:

> There is grandeur in this view of life, with its several powers, having been *originally breathed* into a few forms or into one; [italics mine] and that, whilst this planet has gone cycling on according to the fixed law of gravity, from so simple a beginning endless forms most beautiful and most wonderful have been, and are being, evolved. (p. 425)

Proximal or direct causes for providing care—an overview

Different but complementary direct causes or reasons for caring have been discussed throughout this book. The caring motivation can be proximally explained by reference to biological and neuronal levels, by adopting sociological and cultural perspectives, and through an explication of psychological mechanisms and processes (to name the three most central perspectives). These perspectives are here conceived as complementary with each addressing a unique facet of our existence which cannot be reduced to another.

At the biological and neuroendocrinal levels, the existence of certain genes (i.e., variations in *OXTR*), the activation of certain brain areas associated with bottom-up and top-down empathic responses (i.e., the dorsal anterior cingulate cortex and insula), and the natural as well as administered levels of oxytocin and some other neuropeptides in the blood and brain associated with an activation of the motivation to care. This was observed in a large number of studies within caring bonds with offspring and with romantic partners as well as with strangers and in contexts of pain or distress as well as in contexts of cooperation and trust (see Chapters 4 and 5).

At the cultural level, norms, expectations, and roles that govern different kinds of caring are quite prevalent across cultures and societies. Cultural contexts that value collectivism or are characterized by higher economic interdependence, for example, give rise to higher levels of prosocial actions (see review in Keltner, Kogan, Piff, & Saturn, 2014). In fact, and as described in the chapter related to the development of the caring motivation (Chapter 13), the cultural context exerts a strong influence on when, toward whom, and how the caring motivation is enacted. In studying the development of prosocial behaviors, this was often examined with regard to cooperation and especially in relation to in-group vs. out-group caring. However, society exerts strong effects in other domains too (see Chapters 7, 8, and 10) and channels the expression of our caring motivation in culturally congruent ways through norms, habits, expectations, and moral internalizations. A Gallup survey, a World Poll initiative that included representative samples from 135 countries representing 94% of the world's population, for example, indicated a high degree of variability in volunteering, donations, and help provided to strangers who needed help in the preceding month: 3% to 85% in donations, 4% to 57% in volunteering, and 21% to 77% in helping a stranger (Charities Aid Foundation, 2013). This demonstrates the importance of cultural context in the prevalence of different ways of expressing the motivation to care. Culture also has a large effect on the expected caring to be provided by men and women by virtue of their respective sex roles; hence it exerts a significant effect on the involvement of men and women in what is often deemed feminine (i.e., care of young children, care of the sick and needy) or masculine care (i.e., providing economic stability and housing to family, defending family and country) (Wood & Eagly, 2002).

The psychological research on caring has identified a number of causal processes that are relevant to the activation/arousal of the caring motivation and to its sustenance. In what follows, I will discuss in greater detail the psychological realm as it resonates most with our phenomenological experiences and hence with our understanding of proximal and *direct* reasons to engage in caring. I specifically refer to four distinct yet interrelated routes to activate caring and discuss in greater detail what instigates the formation of caring bonds, hierarchical and egalitarian; I also focus on what sustains these bonds. I then present several unintended consequences of caring that serve to sustain and enhance it.

Different routes to arousing care: empathy, perspective taking, morality, and meaning/purpose

Research has demonstrated the existence of somewhat distinct routes to the activation of the caring motivation in the psychological realm and has also identified a concomitant neuroendocrine basis for most. Although I describe these routes separately, most caring is multiply determined and hence a variety of routes for activating the caring motivation may be involved in each caring situation, although one route may occasionally be more dominant than others. These routes all reflect other-oriented caring, namely caring with the ultimate goal of helping others. These are differentiated from self-oriented caring, such as caring because of felt guilt, the need to augment self-esteem, or the desire to gain good reputation and recognition by others. Still it is important to note that caring is often multidetermined by a variety of reasons—self-oriented and other-oriented.

Possibly the most prototypical antecedent of other-oriented caring involves emotional empathy and concern, which may culminate in motivated care emanating from emotional sharing. This process is somewhat automatic and preconscious and alerts us to others' physiological and emotional situations. It is often the case that when people recount prototypical caring situations they describe the emotionally based activation of the motivation to care: "I saw this puppy and it was so cute and helpless—I had to pick it up." Or "I noticed how distressed she was, and this was alarming, so I decided not to go to the party and stay with her." Empathy is often cited with respect to a negative affective state in the other. But we also emotionally empathize with positive emotional states, and they too can arouse our caring motivation. As discussed in the chapter on social support (Chapter 8), caring also involves being there for the other in situations of positive affect, such as feeling pride for the other's success and achievement and listening and empathizing when a friend shares a precious and exciting moment.

Another route relates to mentalizing processes and to perspective taking, in which we cognitively imagine the state of mind of the other, understand his or her needs, and hence want to help. This is also considered an empathic process, albeit one that is more cognitively based and reflects a top-down process whereby imagining, mentalizing, or perspective taking evokes emotional processes of empathy. Ruddick (1989/1975) discusses such processes at length when she focuses on maternal caring as thinking and offers many examples where mothers rely on perspective taking rather than emotional empathy in order to understand their babies and contemplate their best interests.

In addition, mentalizing and perspective taking do not need to involve a reaction to a perceived need. Mentalizing and perspective taking may start as a proactive, planned or unplanned contemplation of other people's situations, of the future of our planet, or of what could make others happy and content. The proactive side of caring, for example, includes situations in which a caregiver wants to make someone happy as a proactive act of kindness, love, and generosity. In such cases, perspective taking is activated to envision and imagine how the other person would feel, but this often takes place only after the motivation has already arisen or in conjunction with its arousal. Think, for example, of being in a mall and deciding to make your friend happy by buying something that you think your friend would like; such proactive mentalizing is also relevant to kind deeds toward strangers.

A third route relates to beliefs and values, and to a person's moral self in general. It involves a principle-driven caring motivation. By relying on moral principles and core beliefs, individuals may want to rectify situations that are unjust, immoral, or cause agony and suffering. These situations may reflect the operation of the caring motivation. This is another process that relies heavily on cognitive processes and yet is based on moral convictions rather than on empathic identification with a certain person. Such a process based on moral convictions may lead to caring acts (e.g., recycling, money donations, kidney donation, rescuing) based on generalized formal and abstract notions that came to be internalized as core values and as an inherent part of a person's identity; in that sense these are not only abstract principles but also very concrete guidelines that translate into actions.

A fourth route relates to our sense of meaning in life and to our need to feel that we are involved in something greater than ourselves—that is, to make a difference by contributing to others and/or to future generations (Baumeister et al., 2013). Our search for meaning is considered a core characteristic of humanity and is strongly associated with the caring motivation, because a meaningful life is often achieved through caring (e.g., Frankl, 1988; Emmons, 2005; Schnell, 2011). Such caring may be quite diverse in its targets and manifestations and could, for example, include caring for children, caring for the needy—both kin and nonkin—caring for future generations, caring for a pet, and caring for a garden or for nature in general. In fact, caring constitutes a central if not pivotal way of expressing purpose and meaning in life, and people choose to care as a way of expressing such concerns. Caring is thus strongly associated with one's eudaemonic well-being (Baumeister et al., 2013) (i.e., the well-being associated with living and acting in accordance with one's deep-seated values and self-actualization processes). In this respect, generativity has been established as the most powerful predictor of meaningfulness (Schnell, 2011). As discussed quite extensively throughout this book, people engage autonomously in care as an expression of self-fulfillment, which gives them a strong sense of meaning in life.

Our morality, values, and search for meaning in life are often implicated in our proactive and preplanned activations of the caring motivation. In wanting to live a worthy and meaningful life that matters, people often actively search for roles and situations in which care is required in order to be able to extend themselves to others and to offer them such care. Volunteering and donating are often based on this kind of autonomous, intrinsic prosocial source, as are a host of other kind and generous acts that do not involve formal volunteering, such as those workplace behaviors known as organizational citizenship behaviors.

Psychological processes relevant to the formation and maintenance of caring bonds

The formation and maintenance of caring bonds involves several additional proximal psychological causes, and different psychological mechanisms may operate in different types of involvements, such as hierarchical and egalitarian caring bonds.

The creation of hierarchical caring bonds

The process of forming caring bonds may be different depending on their type. Some bonds, such as the parent-child caring bond, are established from the outset with caring as a central motivation and are often based on a conscious decision to form a bond. Such are parent-child relationships, but also less comprehensive and intensive hierarchical caring bonds, such as those that exist between pet owners and pets as well as between mentors and mentees. In such cases, a proactive intention to form a caring bond starts an interactive process which may or may not culminate in an affectional bond. The creation of an affectional bond often takes time and specifically involves spending time together, as well as interpersonal transactions that build the relationship within its intersubjective space. This requires communication, synchronicity, mutual alignment, and trust as well as positively rewarding exchanges. Thus, although people may start a relationship with the intention to forming a caring affectional bond, such intentions may not always be realized. Dog owners may find that they do not enjoy the company of the dog they have adopted, mentors may discover that they do not like their mentees and cannot find anything that they have in common, and even parents may sometimes find it difficult to bond with their child for a host of reasons, such as depression (e.g., Sluckin, 1998).

Very little is currently known about what leads people to form a hierarchical caring bond in general and why people choose to form it with a particular "entity."

One of the most acknowledged cues that activate the motivation to assume the responsibility of taking care and often also the desire to form a caring bond relates to what ethologist Konrad Lorenz has termed the "baby schema." A baby schema includes a set of infantile physical characteristics, such as small size, a round face, a helpless look, and big eyes. These were assumed to be perceived as cute and to motivate caretaking behaviors, thus enhancing the chances of babies to receive care and to survive. Indeed, photographs of infants high in baby schema features were rated as cuter and elicited a stronger motivation for caretaking than photographs of infants low in these features. Such pictures also elicited the activation of a key brain structure, the nucleus accumbens, which modulates reward processing and appetitive (approach) motivation in nulliparous women (Glocker, et al., 2009a,b). Similar reactions of a heightened tendency to assume caring responsibility are activated by the same cues if they are displayed by animals, and children and adults alike have similar reactions of caring toward a small puppy or a kitten (Sanefuji, Ohgami, & Hashiya, 2007; Lehmann, Huis in't Veld, & Vingerhoets, 2013).

But such cues cannot explain why and under what conditions people choose one baby over others with which to form a caring bond. In parenting (and grandparenting), the knowledge that a child is one's offspring acts as a very strong motivator. Since there was no direct proof that could have been used in our ancestral history for this genetic link, there were probably other mechanisms based on this link that contributed to the readiness to provide care and to the assumption of a committed responsibility to engage in care. Part of the higher readiness of mothers compared with fathers to become primary caregivers, for example, may be explained on this basis. The mother knows for sure (if the baby stayed with her after birth) that it is her baby, whereas the father has only a less direct way of ascertaining that the infant is his. In the absence of a better means of ascertaining a genetic link, the child's perceived similarity to the mother/father would work as a substitute to gene inspection. This would explain the human tendency to try to observe family resemblances in the baby and to insist on finding such similarities even if they are hard to find (Daly & Wilson, 1982).

In general we expect the bond between parents and children to be asymmetrical, in that children form an attachment bond mostly driven by their attachment needs and parents form with their children a caring bond driven by their caring motivational system. However, as early as two years of age, toddlers demonstrate empathy and caring toward their parents, and these capacities develop even further and at times can become a full-blown caring bond whereby the child feels responsibility to take care of the parent. Within the literature examining these processes this is often termed *parentification* or *role reversal*, which is regarded as interfering with the child's capacity to develop properly and is considered a negative situation, requiring clinical intervention (Jurkovic, 1997). Research has nevertheless shown that parentification may also have positive effects (e.g., when the child's contributions are acknowledged and valued and the demands do not exceed the child's capacities). For the child, it may culminate in the adoption of a helping profession (Chase, 1999). In adulthood and as the adult child matures and develops a more egalitarian stance with the parent, mutual caring and confiding, friendship, and other aspects can become more prominent in the relationship (Nydegger, 1991). When the parent grows older and may require more assistance, what had started as an attachment bond may evolve to include also a caring bond, whereby the adult child assumes responsibility to take care of the parent and also minds the parent's physical and emotional well-being. Of course such responsibility and the development of a full-fledged caring bond between an adult child and his or her parent becomes more prevalent if the parent has a disability or becomes sick.

The formation of egalitarian caring bonds

Indicators of lower status (e.g., small size, helplessness) seem to serve as cues to forming a hierarchical caring bond and to elicit caring responses. Indeed, they may be among the most significant characteristics that draw people to adopt a caring stance or to form a hierarchical caring bond with a cared-for entity. However, what leads people to form a caring bond in mostly egalitarian situations is less clear. Why would either of the partners develop a caring bond with the other? This may have to do with that partner's importance to the individual, an importance that is based on other considerations, such as affiliation, sexual desire, and attachment. Because the partner is important to the individual, her or his welfare and well-being are important, and the individual may want to ensure that the partner survives and is happy and thriving.

The extant research on the formation of romantic affectional bonds in western cultures, for example, often implicates sexual attraction as the first instigating factor, with other aspects, such as social norms, as additional determinants governing potential partner's suitability. Other aspects related to companionship and affiliation—such as a similarity in various qualities and interests, a mutuality of attraction, and enjoying time together—are also often quite salient at the early stages of the relationship. In contrast, the development of trust and intimacy involving attachment and caregiving dynamics often becomes salient at a later stage of the relationship's development. Furthermore, the mutual commitments to remaining together that forge the central elements of a romantic *bond* often take some time to emerge. Current research suggests that a full-blown romantic affectional bond that reflects both attachment and caring dynamics takes time to develop and may appear only after several years together, with some studies identifying two years as the characteristic length of time required to this end (Hazan & Zeifman, 1994; Fagundes & Schindler, 2012).

Such affectional bonds, which include an essential caring part, are described in Brown and Brown's (2006a) evolutionary model as "costly long-term investments." These authors discuss the evolutionarily benefit of such bonds when individuals attain mutual reproductive dependence or, in their terms, "fitness interdependence," which indicates that the survival and reproduction of one individual is enhanced by the survival and reproduction of another. In such cases, caring for another person with whom one shares fitness interdependence leads to a reproductive benefit to oneself. The affectional bond that includes an evolved emotional regulatory mechanism activates emotions associated with concern for others, and caring was seen as the proximate motivational mechanism that evolved to sustain such "costly long-term investments." Such bonding was said to be based on joint synchronized interactions involving a high degree of emotional arousal and reflecting fitness interdependence. According to this depiction, the development of a mutual caring bond between romantic partners serves to sustain the relationship to both partners' benefit as well as to the benefit of their survival and reproductive fitness. In such cases the partners both receive and give care. They may take turns in these roles in different situations, simultaneously receiving solace and comfort from the other within the same encounter, and they may also specialize in distinct provisions. This is a very sophisticated interconnected dance, and research has often found that among the majority of well-functioning couples both giving and receiving are indeed strongly related (Crowell et al., 2002).

A somewhat similar process occurs with caring bonds within friendships. Here the first instigating motivation may be the affiliative motivational system that relates to companionship and to sharing a pleasurable time together (Shulman, Elicker, & Sroufe, 1994). However, the formation of a specific friendship with a distinct individual also involves the reciprocal giving and receiving of care. The relevant provisions may, for example, involve providing instrumental help and advice, cooperating in achieving a desired outcome, protecting the friend's reputation and status, comforting, listening, capitalizing, and validating (Sharabany, Gershoni, & Hofman, 1981). Although all friendships involve some form of caring, not all friendships involve affectional caring *bonds*, and some friendships do not last very long. In elementary and middle schools in the United States, for example, between 30% and 50% of friendships do not last from one school year to the next (Berndt & Hoyle, 1985; Hruschka, 2010). We do not yet know enough about the physiological, psychological, and interpersonal mechanisms that mediate the unfolding of friendships and the creation of an affectional bond with friends in particular. However, like other affectional bonds, friendship caring bonds take time to develop and require distinct kinds of interactions. These generally appear to include jointly rewarding experiences, a similarity of interests, and the building of trust and mutuality in care and affection such that the relationship is no longer based on a strict reciprocation but on the premise that the other is committed to the welfare of her or his friend and would stand by her or him if necessary—a communal orientation.

The importance of uniqueness and exclusivity in the caring bond

One of the defining features of a caring bond is the uniqueness of the relationship meaning that the other person is not interchangeable with another. In the mother-infant bond, for example, it means that the infant prefers the mother over others and specifically smiles for her and that the mother prefers her infant over others and uniquely invests in her or him. The reason for this preference might be related to the ultimate evolutionary function of protection. At face value, such a strategy does not appear to be a good policy since this is like putting all the eggs in one proverbial basket. Why would an infant focus her or his efforts on only one person to the exclusion of others? Findings from the research literature on prosocial behavior may give us a clue as to why this may be the best policy. As reviewed in the chapter on prosocial behavior (Chapter 9), a counterintuitive "bystander" effect has been identified by Latané and Darley (1970), in which the more people are present when someone is in distress, the less help will be provided. People tend to diffuse responsibility and to be afraid of embarrassment if they incorrectly identify a nonalarming situation as a crisis, so they tend to take more time to notice an occurrence, to label it an emergency, and to decide to assume responsibility and to help, if they help at all, when they are in groups. When only one person is in the vicinity of the distressed individual or when one person is clearly in charge of the situation, there is a greater probability that help will be provided, and that it will be provided sooner rather than later.

Taking this human tendency into consideration, the infant's (and older person's too) preference for a small and select group of attachment figures organized in a hierarchy of importance may be better suited for the infant's protection than a more diffuse social network. Children's strong and exclusive reliance on their preferred attachment figure, for example, sends a signal to that figure indicating that he or she is responsible and that there is no one else. This dependency and exclusivity may thus serve to secure the bond between child and parent and provides higher probability that the infant's needs will be promptly met.

That the child wants his or her parents, needs them, and prefers them over others in times of trouble and also prefers to share joyful moments with them is often very rewarding for parents. This serves as a strong reinforcing cue for the parents to be attentive to the child and to devote themselves to the child's care. This parental attentiveness clearly serves in a protective capacity. By being attentive to the infant, parents, most often mothers, make sure that they will notice and not miss any sign of discomfort or danger and thus will do better in securing the child's safety. In other words, both sides of the bond need to show an exclusive preference toward the partner (both child to parent and parent to child) in order to optimally attain the goals of keeping the child safe and secure and furthering her or his survival and thriving.

If an exclusive preference on both sides of the relationship is instrumental in achieving these goals, it becomes rewarding in itself as a way to keep it going. Thus for the infant to be his mother's delight and center of attention is rewarding (Kohut, 1977/2009), and for the mother to be needed exclusively and preferred by the infant is also highly rewarding. This reflects a strong realization that she matters, and it contributes to her sense of connectedness and meaningfulness. Because parenting in particular appears to be associated with a large number of negative affective states and with a decline in well-being, this exclusive preference may provide one of the vehicles necessary for sustaining and maintaining the commitment and investment even when positive reinforcements such as a sense of joy, pride, fun, or pleasure are less prevalent.

We also witness the importance of uniqueness and exclusivity in other kinds of relationships. This is most obvious in romantic relations. As eloquently described by Hazan and Shaver (1987), the romantic couple are highly engrossed in each other, at least during the formative time of the relationship. They talk their own language, engage in long periods of mutual gazing, and expect exclusivity. Such exclusivity becomes a cornerstone for the relation's existence and a central reason for breakups if it is not honored. Other mechanisms besides the importance of caring-bond exclusivity are obviously involved here, such as issues of sexual fidelity, yet emotional infidelity is also perceived as a major threat to the relationship (e.g., Shackelford, LeBlanc, & Drass, 2000). All together, it might be the case that different mechanisms (such as those related to caring and those related to sexuality) have co-opted to forge a similar preference for uniqueness and exclusivity in romantic affectional bonds.

Other caring bonds may also evince such a focus on uniqueness and exclusivity. In various mentoring programs such as the Big Brothers and Big Sisters in the United States as well as PERACH, Israel's largest mentoring program, the uniqueness of the mentor for the mentee proved important in fostering positive outcomes (e.g., Goldner & Mayseless, 2009). It appears that the sense that they are special and unique in their role in the child's life provides mentors with a strong incentive to commit themselves and invest in their relationship with the mentee. A somewhat similar profile emerges in friendships, where people may assume caring states or engage in caring behavior but do not usually develop an exclusive caring bond. However, when a caring bond is developed, as within friendships in times of strife or within friendships in adolescence and adulthood, it is also possible to observe similar processes that underscore the importance of uniqueness and exclusivity, including jealousy and anger when the boundaries of the exclusive relation are jeopardized (Bagwell & Schmidt, 2013). Thus the knowledge that someone depends solely or entirely on the caregiver (reflecting uniqueness) and the realization that the care-receiver prefers the caregiver over others (reflecting exclusivity) appear to contribute strongly to the assumption of a caring state and also to the creation of a caring bond and its sustenance.

Warmth as a strengthening mechanism in caring relations

Another major aspect that helps to sustain a caring bond has to do with its rewarding nature. Besides protection and the promotion of thriving, caring bonds may involve the wish to enhance the cared-for party's happiness and contentment. This caring goal is associated with the affiliative/warmth system, which regulates positive feelings of affection, and specifically feelings of happiness and pleasure through social interactions. As described in Chapter 6, MacDonald (1992) conceptualized warmth as distinct from attachment security, which was seen as related to another caring goal—the provision of protection and comfort in times of distress and danger. Warmth has been conceived as a human affectional system meant to enhance cohesive and close relationships and to cement affectional bonds through joint positive experiences that are strongly rewarding.

In the parent-child bond early in the infant's life, the provision of this goal may manifest itself in attempts to make the infant smile and laugh. Later in life, people may hug, play together, prepare favorite foods, and bring presents (among many other things) in order to make the cared-for person happy. The time, money, and effort caregivers expend in making the child happy and the enormous joy they feel when they succeed attest to the importance of warmth as a joint rewarding experience that binds people together. Success in establishing positive interchanges helps to sustain a relationship and ensure that it will survive more difficult times, increasing the probability that the parent will be ready to provide care in cases of distress or emergency and even when she or he is tired, angry, or otherwise less attuned to the child (Bowlby (1969/1982). The bond between the partners (parent and infant) is thus strengthened by having this rewarding time together.

Warmth has similar functions in the romantic bond (MacDonald, 1992) and in caring bonds among friends. The sharing of positive and pleasant experiences together, the mutual enjoyment from each other's company, and shared moments of affection and fun all help in "gluing" the relationship together. This accords, for example, with the findings suggesting that among romantic couples the ratio between positive and negative interactions, rather than the mere frequency of negative interactions, is a potent predictor of positive long-term relationship outcomes and the continuation or cessation of the relationship in particular (Gottman, 1994).

Unintended consequences of caring
that may sustain caring

An engagement in caring carries a variety of unintended consequences, some of which have distinct rewarding qualities (see review in Batson, 2010). These are unintended consequences in the sense that the caring person does not engage in helping to accrue these "rewards" and does not experience them as reasons for engaging in caring. Though unintended, these consequences are not redundant or superfluous and probably serve to sustain caring in the long run. In what follows, I will refer to several such unintended consequences of caring and discuss their role in caring dynamics.

Positive affect and happiness—hedonic well-being

The first category of unintended consequences that I would like to highlight relates to the positive affect and rewarding feelings that are often associated with caring and helping, especially if they are successful. This relates to what research-ers have called the "warm glow" effect and involves a rewarding feeling, a sense of satisfaction, happiness, and joy (Ferguson, Atsma, de Kort, & Veldhuizen, 2012). It is often not exhilarating or exciting in its intensity but is very fulfilling and hence the term *warm glow* is probably a better descriptorn than *elation* or *joy*. Engaging in caring acts, even small ones, and even toward strangers, augments one's happiness and has been advocated by positive psychologists as a way to boost one's day-to-day happiness (Kurtz & Lyubomirsky, 2008). Furthermore, spending money on others provided more happiness than spending it on oneself. This was demonstrated in a variety of research designs: in a nationally representa-tive survey, in a longitudinal field study of windfall spending, and by assigning participants randomly to either spend money on others or on themselves (Dunn, Aknin, & Norton, 2008, 2014).

At the neurobiological level the positive affect and happiness associated with expressing the caring motivation is probably related to the connection of caring neural structures and processes, in particular the oxytocin neural system with two other known brain systems. The oxytocin neural system is consistently implicated in a large number of caring feelings, cognitions, and behaviors and is assumed to be one of the central neuroendocrine systems to govern at the neu-ral level the motivation to care (see Chapter 5). This system is connected to the dopaminergic system, which is involved in reward centers in the brain. As sum-marized by Feldman (2012), oxytocin neurons are reciprocally connected with mesolimbic dopaminergic neurons, and this interconnection serves an important role in caring bonds, as with romantic partners and offspring. Such a connection associates the activation of caring with a sense of reward, and hence increases the incentive value of giving. In the case of caring bonds where care is recurrent and sustained, this association attaches an intuitive and powerful positive reinforcement to the care receiver (i.e., infant or spouse), which may underlie the process of psychological bonding at the biological level.

The oxytocin system is also connected to the hypothalamic pituitary adrenal (HPA) axis, which mediates stress and calming responses. These systems (oxytocin and HPA) are probably mutually regulated. Oxytocin, for example, is associated with significant reductions in anxiety and antistress effects and thus induces a feeling of safety and calm. All together, the neuropeptide oxytocin system is implicated in giving and caring as part of a one-time act of cooperation or generosity to strangers as well as in intense caring bonds as with a person's spouse or offspring. This system is associated with general rewarding experiences through its connection to the dopamingeric reward system and to a sense of security and calm through its mutual regulation with the HPA system, which mediates stress and anxiety. Although individuals do not give to others and care for them to achieve these inner states, the mutual connections between caring and rewarding and caring, security, and calm (also referred to as anxiolytic and antistress effects) reinforce caring and promote the creation of caring bonds.

Health benefits

The anxiolytic and antistress effects of oxytocin are probably also related to one of the more surprising and less expected effects of caring. Caring, giving, and helping are associated with health benefits at both the psychological and physical levels. Volunteering and pet ownership, for example, were associated with longevity and psychological well-being after accounting for a large variety of relevant factors. The downregulation of stress reactions as well as the upregulation of positive affectivity and rewards described previously, both associated with caring, may function as central biological mechanisms that could mediate such connections (e.g., Brown, Brown, Schiavone, & Smith, 2007). In an edited volume dedicated to altruism and health, Post (2007) amasses an impressive group of scholars who provide a conceptual and empirical basis for the claim that altruism and caring (if judiciously cultivated) enhance well-being, health, and even longevity. In Post's book, such effects were addressed by discussing volunteerism at different ages and with different populations, pet ownership, and caregiving provided to sick others, such as caring for AIDS patients by caregivers who were also infected or support provided to patients with multiple sclerosis (MS) by peers who also had MS.

This is not to say that caring is always associated with positive consequences to the caregiver (Post, 2007). In fact, caring might also be associated with frustration, compassion fatigue, and burnout. What, then, might differentiate between cases that contribute to the caregiver's health and welfare and those that hinder them? One important aspect that appears to modulate these opposing outcomes has to do with the extent to which the helping and/or caring are done in a way that also respects the caregiver's needs and is therefore balanced and conducted in a judicious way. In discussing what constitutes good care, I underscored the importance of respecting the caregiver's basic psychological needs and specifically used self-determination theory to underscore three major psychological needs: the need for relatedness, the need for competence, and the need for autonomy (see Chapter 14).

I suggest that caring may be associated with positive health benefits when it is associated with a sense of relatedness, competence, and autonomy. Indeed, the domains in which positive effects were particularly noted and observed are often those where caring is voluntary, autonomously chosen, and not obligatory—namely those that do not involve an internalized compelling expectation to help. These include volunteering, mentoring, donating, caring for pets, and tending gardens, and research has already documented that engaging in care in these domains is associated with positive effects in health, well-being, and longevity. In contrast, there are situations where caring is fundamentally obligatory even when it is voluntarily chosen. This is the case with parenting, for example, where a large number of caring behaviors may not be chosen by the parent but are still enacted because they are needed for sustaining the child. This is also the case with caring for a sick relative or friend and even with caring for others as part of one's profession. Such obligatory caring has at times been associated with compassion fatigue, burnout, and an emotional and physical burden. What, then, is unique about these situations? In most of them the caregiver's assumption of a responsibility to care is voluntary and hence autonomous, but the intensity, timing, and type of care needed is often dictated by the care receiver and may not be on a par with the caregiver's needs and desires. In such cases, the caregiver's autonomous conduct is thwarted and the task of caring may feel overwhelming. Rather than "altruistic flourishing," therefore, we may observe an "altruistic burden" (Post, p. 4).

The positive effects of caring may also be moderated by a sense of efficacy and competence in alleviating the care receiver's distress, pain, or need. As indicated by Brown et al. (2007), such a sense of competence may not be at work in caring for a loved one who is experiencing cognitive or physical decline. Caring in such situations may thus also be painful, taxing, and stressful for the caregiver. However, in many cases, care is given voluntarily and with a sense of autonomy, competence, and success such that the caregiver enjoys the unintendedly positive physical and psychological health benefits of caring as well as the rewarding warm glow of giving and helping.

Meaningfulness, mattering, and eudaemonic well-being

The engagement in caring, especially if successful, is strongly associated with a sense of self-fulfillment and meaning in life. Such a sense of meaning and purpose also serves as a sustaining and rewarding experience because it provides eudae-monic well-being—the kind of well-being that result from a life worth living. Thus the meaning derived from being involved in something greater than oneself is both a rewarding experience that reinforces future caring and giving and a pre-cursor of caring that is often involved in proactive caring (see discussion of this issue in this chapter in a previous section on different routes to arousing care). The rewarding quality of eudaemonic well-being is clearly apparent in caring situ-ations that are affectively positive and pleasant (i.e., that involve hedonic well-being), such as volunteering, as well as in caring situations where the affective balance may be more compound, as in parenting or caregiving provided to ailing others, and is often an unintended consequence of caring. In other words, people may help and give as a result of empathy, perspective taking, or morality and then experience a strong sense of meaningfulness and eudaemonic well-being after engaging in caring. These processes often work through a sense of mattering, which involves our realization that we are a significant part of the world around us. In fact, giving and helping others was found to be one of three central ways through which we discover that we matter, and a sense of mattering was found to be central in finding meaning and happiness in life (Elliott, Kao, & Grant, 2004). In line with this depiction, mattering has been shown to mediate the link between volunteering and well-being (Piliavin & Siegl, 2007). The status of meaningful-ness and the association between caring and a sense of purpose in life is very fun-damental and will be discussed at length in the next chapter.

Individuals' worth—reputation and self-esteem

Another important and often unintended consequence of caring and helping has to do with the caregiver's worth—external worth (e.g., social standing, reputation) and internal worth (e.g., self-esteem). All cultures value individuals who care and who are giving, generous, and benevolent, although cultures differ in the rules and norms governing the enactment and exhibition of such care and often have differ-ent expectations from men and women in this regard. Thus engaging in caring and helping while adhering to such cultural norms and expectations often results in a more positive reputation and in a better social standing. Such a valued social stand-ing has beneficial ramifications for our survival and inclusive fitness because others will want to cooperate with us and will help us too, and we would thus have better prospects also in joining valuable coalitions and in mate selection. Although unin-tended, such gains in self worth may therefore work to sustain care when we con-sider such processes from both evolutionary and psychological perspectives.

Helping and engaging in caring also reflects on our self-worth and enhances our self-esteem. This may relate to our reputation, the sense of accomplishment, or our sense of mattering and meaningfulness. Very relevant in this regard is the finding that compassion and caring were found to boost self-esteem to a greater extent than direct attempts to enhance it, which actually appear to hinder it (Crocker, 2011). High self-esteem in its turn has been associated with a host of positive outcomes, including happiness (Baumeister, Campbell, Krueger, & Vohs, 2003). Thus, though unintended, higher self-esteem following care may help sustain and enhance caring.

How these unintended consequences sustain caring

All together, and although most people do not engage in caring to accrue these benefits (i.e., the warm glow of giving, psychological and physical health benefits, higher social standing, meaning and mattering), all serve as unintended incentives that enhance and sustain caring and hence may be described as *sustaining and enhancing incentives*. The sustaining and enhancing effects may involve an unconscious association between caring and these positive incentives, which lead people to engage in more helping. Furthermore at the evolutionary level these consequences contribute to individuals' inclusive fitness. A person who is psychologically and physically healthier, who enjoys good reputation and greater sense of competence, has better success in propagating these caring genes as well as these caring behaviors to future generations.

However, there is also another route. Healthier, happier, and more socially connected people (regardless of cause) tend to be more benevolent, generous, and helpful. In an influential theory termed "broaden-and-build," Fredrickson (2001) claimed and demonstrated by a large number of studies that the cultivation of particular positive feelings such as joy, interest, pride, and contentment increases the tendency of people to be benevolent and prosocial through broaden-and-build processes that widen the array of their thoughts and actions (see also Haidt, 2003a,b). Thus, in a spiral reinforcing process, caring makes people happier, healthier, more self-assured, and more connected, and these in turn enhance their inclination to engage in caring (Luhmann, Lucas, Eid, & Diener, 2013).

Finally, some people may be aware of the connection between caring and these positive outcomes and therefore engage in caring intentionally to achieve these benefits. In such cases, of course, they are intended rather than unintended consequences. In my discussion of the variety of proximal causes I did not suggest a structural or a dynamic model for their joint operation. A recent proposal of such a model— a "framework of core psychological processes that give rise to prosocial behavior" —is a very promising step in this direction (Keltner et al., 2014, p. 428).

The parenthood paradox revisited

I have reviewed the variety of proximal incentives as well as other unintended consequences of care which, together with other insights discussed in Chapters 8 and 16, can help us untangle one of the most puzzling issues in caring: how is it that caring, and especially parenting, which is so central to our survival, is not clearly associated with positive affect? How is it that caring also involves strong negative affective experiences? The conceptual model regarding the caring motivation advocated in this book addresses this "parenthood paradox" by suggesting four interrelated explications: (1) at the proximal level caring is governed by hedonic and eudaemonic incentives as well as by a variety of other unintended yet positive outcomes, such as self-worth, good reputation, and health; (2) whereas choosing to parent or to take care of an ailing relative are most often autonomously chosen and hence have positive valence, the specific provisions, their timing, and intensity are often less autonomously regulated, hence they are more affectively negative, resulting in a combination of positive and negative affectivity; (3) in fact, although caring is often associated with strong positive and negative affective states, the net result shows very modest effects, either positive or negative, probably reflecting the balance between these two opposing affects; (4) current social and cultural contexts are not conducive to supporting care and are dissimilar to the collective and supportive context where such caring evolved.

Together, these explications offer explanations at evolutionary, cultural, and psychological levels and help to clarify the parenthood paradox.

Chapter conclusion

This chapter exposes the variety of mechanisms that operate to activate and sustain caring in all its diversity. In this chapter I have tried to answer two major questions: why the caring motivation exists in the first place (ultimate causation) and how it is activated and sustained in the variety of its manifestations (proximal causation). Two distinct ultimate explanations have been discussed—evolutionary reasoning and theological perspectives. I contend that these two perspectives do not necessarily negate each other but that each can be viewed as means when the other one is the ends.

At the proximal level I suggest that the main different perspectives presented in this book—biological, psychological, and cultural—can be seen as complementary levels of explanation without a reduction of one to the others. At the biological level we already see the beginning of sound research demonstrating distinct brain areas and neurohormonal circuitry that are causally implicated in the caring motivational system; at the cultural level we discover large variability in the expression of caring, especially with regard to issues of who, when, to whom, and how. With regard to psychological processes, four proximal antecedents that have been discussed in previous chapters are summarized and presented: empathy, perspective taking, morality, and seeking meaning/purpose.

The formation of caring bonds and their sustenance may implicate several unique causative mechanisms, and some may be specifically relevant to hierarchical or to egalitarian caring bonds. We currently know very little on how these work. Nevertheless I provide some suggestions and in particular underscore the importance of the 'baby schema' in arousing care in hierarchical relations, the importance of uniqueness and exclusivity and the significance of warmth or the affiliative system even in hierarchical caring relations. I then discuss unintended consequences of caring that may sustain caring, such as hedonic pleasure, eudaemonic well-being and meaningfulness, physical health, self-worth and good reputation. I end by revisiting the enigma of the "parenthood paradox" and suggest explications at the evolutionary, cultural, and psychological levels that help to clarify it.

Perhaps the most salient insights that arise from this chapter relate to the clear combination of innate (e.g., empathy) and acquired (e.g., morality) processes in the operation of this multifaceted motivational system and the strong involvement of both hedonic (e.g., "warm glow" and health benefits) and eudaemonic (e.g., life meaning, mattering, and self-fulfillment) concerns as well as the paucity of research on central mechanisms regarding the activation and sustenance of caring as part of the complex and sophisticated caring motivational system.

19

The Nature of the Human Species: Conceptual and Applied Implications

The core contention presented in this book with regard to the general innate caring motivation has clear ramifications for the nature of our species and on our destiny. In what follows, I would like to highlight these implications and state my own take on human nature.

My first and central point is that we as a species have an innate motivation to care, and that this motivation is central to our nature and associated with our core existence. Engaging in caring and realizing this potential therefore provides us with a vital and fundamental sense of meaning, purpose, and self-fulfillment. I further contend that caring is so strongly associated with our self-actualization and the concomitant sense of life's meaning because it is a central expression of our spiritual core.

There is an important distinction between caring as discussed here and other similar notions—such as connectedness, the need to belong, affiliation, or warmth—which relate mostly to the receiving side or do not conceptually deal with the differences between giving and receiving. My discussion of caring involves only the giving side—the motivation to help sustain (preserve) an entity and help it heal, grow, and thrive.

Although I assume that this motivation is inherent, I do not presume that the expressed capacity is solely innate. In fact, and although manifestations of the caring capacity can be observed very early in life, a highly sophisticated process of both conscious and unconscious learning needs to take place for us to become caring, and especially if we are to engage in good caring. The caring motivational system is thus highly flexible, and this flexibility is apparent in its highly diverse manifestations and in the importance of context and developmental experience in shaping its eventual form and expression.

One reason for focusing on the caring side of human nature (as I do) could be to offset the former strong focus on the other poles, such as selfishness, cruelty, and individuation. A similar practice can be identified among those feminist scholars who have strongly advocated women's voice of relatedness as a counterweight to the view of human nature as autonomous or individualistic (de Beauvoir, 1949; Gilligan, 1982). In my case, I do not focus on caring in order to balance the focus on autonomy and individuation. In fact, feminist writers (e.g., de Beauvoir, 1949/1973; Gilligan, 1982; Miller, 1976/1982) and others (e.g., Bowlby, 1969/1982; MacDonald, 1992) have already done a great job in demonstrating that connections and relationships are fundamental to our nature and experience. One of the reasons for my intense focus on the caring end, however, is counterbalancing the strong focus on the receiving end.

Most contemporary psychological discourses on human nature strongly underscore the need for warmth, acknowledgment, positive regard, safe haven, and being loved (Macdonald, 1992; Baumeister, & Leary, 1995; Mikulincer & Shaver, 2010). This focus on the receiving end is so strong that discussions of caring almost invariably turn to the recipient and to what she or he gains from such care (but see, for example, Keltner, Marsh, & Smith, 2010, and Post, 2007). This can be clearly seen in the outstanding work by Taylor (2002), where she powerfully demonstrates how care and tending in a host of contexts and relationships are very helpful to the recipients and beneficial to their well-being and longevity. She marshals her evidence to very clearly and strongly show that the extent to which we rely on care in different contexts is enormous and has not been appreciated as such. This indeed supports the importance and centrality of care, but only through a discussion of its effects on the recipient. In my view, caring is not merely an antidote to the selfish, cruel, or disengaged side of human experience but an expression of the centrality of the wish to give (apart from the wish to receive) as a fundamental human motivation. Caring is not something that "somehow" happens all around us because people need to be tended; rather, it is expected and predictable because we intrinsically *want* to give, foster growth, and help.

The shift in *zeitgeist* regarding the centrality of care and the wish to give

The want of discussions and research on caring as a central human capacity and as a fundamental human motivation has not gone unnoticed. Feminist writers (e.g., de Beauvoir, 1949/1973; Gilligan, 1982; Miller, 1976/1982), as well as others (Taylor, 2002), for example, have discussed the excessive focus on autonomy and individuation and the disregard for the importance of relationships, close ones in particular, to our development. Such patriarchal portrayals of human development mostly ignored caring and considered it the province of women, and thus a less developed emotional and manual activity than more "masculine" activities. This division further led to a situation in which the various caring and caregiving activities provided by women were taken for granted or deemed natural and expected, and were thus not considered work that needed to be appreciated through various social mechanisms, including pay. Even when it did exist, professional caregiving was considered a low-status profession and paid accordingly.

Taylor (2002) also underscores the western capitalist tendency to focus on individualism and the generally accepted view of the human species as selfish, individualistic, and competitive. Several different approaches have thus converged to accord caring and caregiving a lower and neglected status in western society. First, tending, caring, and providing support—especially within close relationships such as caring for children or spouses—were seen as needed *but* as instinctual and almost automatic. They thus remained unrecognized insofar as their voluntary nature, their centrality and importance and the extent to which society needed to value and accord them high status were concerned. Second, despite studies attesting to the centrality of support and care in the lives of individuals even in adulthood, this impact on human development and human conduct, especially as far as psychological as well as health outcomes were concerned, was depreciated and demeaned. This was particularly true when contrasted with nonpsychological means of helping others, such as providing money to alleviate the ill effects of lower economic status or drugs to alleviate illnesses. Third, cooperation, volunteering, and altruistic acts were viewed with suspicion and were often conceived as mostly reflecting self-interest. Taken together, these attitudes converged in according caring in general and caregiving professions in particular a lower status, especially if performed by women (Taylor, 2002).

In the last two decades, however, a clear change can be observed in the general world views advocated by the social sciences, most notably psychology, sociology, management studies, political science, and economics. Rather than focusing solely on the autonomous, individuated, rational, selfish, and separate human being, they have come to appreciate the connected, interdependent bioemotional and caring facets of human existence. This can be seen in the surge of research published on these issues, including several wonderful and fascinating accounts of caring and its centrality to human experience and motivation whose conceptual and empirical contributions were discussed throughout the present volume (e.g., Murdock, 1971; Noddings, 1984; Oliner & Oliner, 1995; Post, Underwood, Schloss, & Hurlbut, 2002; Taylor, 2002; Dovidio, Piliavin, Schroeder, & Penner, 2006; Dugatkin, 2006; Hollway, 2006; Post, 2007; de Waal, 2009; Keltner, 2009; Hrdy, 2009; Mikulincer & Shaver, 2010; Brown, Brown, & Penner, 2012; Grant, 2013; Keltner et al., 2014; and many more).

This general focus on connections and relationships as opposed to separation and individualism, and on the positive and benevolent side of human development, is closely associated with a somewhat new and promising conceptual framework termed *positive psychology* (Seligman & Csikszentmihalyi, 2000). This is the scientific study of positive human functioning, which focuses on strengths and virtues rather than on weaknesses and suffering to promote and enable thriving and flourishing in individuals and communities. The viewpoint that underlies this new and surging branch of psychology is that we need to focus on the positive side of human existence if we wish to cultivate what is best in ourselves. Adherents of this view consider it as a complement to rather than a replacement of the current psychological focus on illnesses and problems. For the past decade or so a large number of studies have demonstrated that positive feelings, emotions, and states of mind—such as optimism, awe, forgiveness, and flow, including those related to caring, such as benevolence, compassion and kindness—can be investigated through the use of rigorous measures and research designs. These studies further demonstrate the benefits of thinking positively and engaging in kind acts with others to a person's own and others' well-being (Sin & Lyubomirsky, 2009; also see the edited volume by Lopez & Snyder, 2009). All together, these pioneering and remarkable achievements by many scholars have shifted the *zeitgeist* toward viewing human nature as more connected, positive, and benevolent. I personally share their view of caring as a virtue and as a central, innate, positive, and fundamental core capacity of human nature.

The caring motivational system in the context of major human dichotomies

Several dichotomies come to mind in discussing the implications of these new perspectives on human nature. One, usually highlighted by feminist writers, refers to the dichotomy between autonomy/individuality and connectedness. Another is related to the sensual, irrational, and affectional vs. the rational and transcendental. A third involves a highly known dichotomy between good (referring to benevolence, kindness, and compassion) and evil (referring to cruelty, viciousness, and destruction). A fourth refers to selfishness and self-centeredness vs. being other-oriented and altruistic. These dichotomies are obviously partially equivalent, and some writers use them interchangeably or as adjectives describing the same pole (i.e., selfish and independent vs. altruistic and connected). They all correspond to different dimensions in human experience and all four are related to caring. Among the four, caring is probably more specifically related to the connected, benevolent, and altruistic sides and is somewhere in the middle regarding rationality and affectivity. Among these, my own position on human beings as a caring species might appear surprising.

I generally subscribe to the contention that the either-or staging is false. I rather suggest that each of these aspects is part of our nature and hence can and probably will surface in human experience. We are not one but all of the above—namely good, caring, cruel, other-oriented, affective, selfish, benevolent, autonomous, rational, and connected.

In fact, some of these dichotomies obscure important syntheses among these so-called opposites. For example, recent discussions of the intersubjectivity needed to forge caring relations underscore the need to be both individuated and connected in order to be able to form an intersubjective space between the care receiver and the caregiver. This is done through projections and introjections that promote identification and culminate in a connection that respects both partners' individuality (Hollway, 2006).

Similar contentions regarding our complex nature have been raised by positive psychology scholars. Within this paradigm, the focus on the positive emotions, strengths, virtues, and thriving of individuals, relationships, and communities may appear to neglect a holistic view of people and their unavoidable faults, aggressiveness, difficulties, and sufferings. Investigators have cautioned against such a simplistic and potentially biased view and suggested that "to meet the challenge of complexity, positive psychology must move beyond the description of main effects (optimism, humor, forgiveness, and curiosity are good) and begin to look more closely at the complex interactions that are the hallmark of most of psychology, as well as of medicine" (Gable & Haidt, 2005, p. 108).

In fact, a relatively recent conceptual and empirical paper published in *American Psychologist* by McNulty and Fincham (2012) reviews data from four longitudinal studies of marriage and demonstrates that forgiveness, optimism, positive attributions, and kindness can either benefit or hamper well-being. More specifically, in moderately healthy marriages with less hostility and less severe marital problems, these processes predicted a better relationship and better well-being among spouses over time. In contrast, in more troubled marriages, these ostensibly positive processes predicted a worse relationship and worse well-being. These findings underscore the fact that human experience is multifaceted and that too much of a good thing that is not balanced by other concerns may not be optimal to our survival and well-being. More specifically, characterizing "good" qualities or behaviors such as caring in absolute terms without considering context and other aspects of our being may not reflect our true nature, which involves a degree of flexibility and balance between our "good" and "bad" sides, both selfish and benevolent, caring and harsh, individuated and connected.

Where, then, does the caring motivational system reside in this context? In most cases caring is obviously treated as a highly positive and virtuous quality. In fact, some of the virtues studied as exemplars by positive psychologists are compassion, empathy, and kindness. Yet caring can and often is also associated with negative emotions, difficulties, and exhaustion. Furthermore, we have seen that the benefits of caring to the caregiver, the recipient, their social context and society at large are moderated by many factors such as how caring is enacted, under what circumstances, by whom, and with whom. In that sense, it is a virtue and a fundamental human motivation, but, as with any other motivations or predispositions, its effects are contingent on many other factors.

In fact, the caring motivational system itself includes a variety of mechanisms for fostering its balanced expression. Like other biologically based innate systems, the caring motivational system is optimal when balanced, when giving and caring is coupled with self-care, and when helping does not deplete the caregiver's capacities for empathy and giving (Oakley, Knafo, Madhavan, & Wilson, 2012). In line with this view, evolutionary scholars, for example, have suggested that the punishment of others who betray our trust or the trust of our group, or who exploit benevolent individuals, evolved along with the development of the caring motivation in order to sustain caring and cooperation in the long run. Interestingly the same neuroendocrine circuitry of empathy and caring appears to govern such "punitive" responses too, probably because they help to sustain caring within our social groups and interpersonal relations.

Moreover, caring may involve *behaviors* that are harsh and even aggressive. Think, for example, of caring for your children or loved ones by defending them against offensive or aggressive people, or soldiers protecting and defending their country in combat. Furthermore, it may be the case that the protection and care of your children requires you to be strict with them, cause them frustration (e.g., not allow them to play with things that are dangerous although they really want to) and discipline them (e.g., insist that they stop hitting the neighbors' child and even stop such behavior by using force). Thus caring is not a mere rose-colored sweetness that involves nurturance, softheartedness, and tenderness, which is often the characteristic depiction of feminine empathic and nurturant care. It also includes the capacity to be punitive and sometimes even harsh when needed. These "negative" acts are also part of the caring motivational system to the extent that they are carried out in the service of the innate caring motivation and in order to help sustain entities both human and nonhuman and help them to heal, grow, thrive, and prosper.

Optimal caring in such situations is thus quite complex and difficult to master. A parent may "force" certain behavior on a child (e.g., to stop hitting her friend) but would optimally do so with empathy and respect. Such an optimal intervention will allow the child some autonomy and teach her or him alternative ways to behave while also defending and respecting the others involved in the incident. Optimal caring has to balance the variety of needs of the care receiver and to respect her or his integrity and autonomy while considering the needs of the caregiver and also the needs of others around them. It must thus be enacted in a *judicious, respectful,* and *thoughtful way.*

At this point, some of my readers may have become confused and puzzled. Statements such as the foregoing appear to obscure the "pure" goodness of caring and present a muddied picture of this motivational system. Readers may wonder: "So, the caring motivational system is morally 'good' in the sense of being enacted to further positive and hence morally good outcomes in others, such as thriving, and well-being or enhancing such qualities in society at large, and yet its enactment may involve causing 'harm' to others? Is this what you really mean?" Indeed, I would say that in optimal circumstances such "harm" may be enacted only when needed and in a judicious, thoughtful, and balanced way that respects the other. At times, however, it can also become disrespectful and aggressive to the caregivers, the care receivers, and others around them. As indicated in the thought-provoking edited volume by Oakley, Knafo, and McGrath (2012), altruism can become pathological and atrocities have been committed with the intention of helping companions or one's own in-group (e.g., suicide martyrdom, genocide). The point I am making is that we are multifaceted and complex beings, making some borderlines far from clear. These portrayals thus reflect what I see as four distinct inherent and fundamental qualities of our human nature. We are *multifaceted and holistic and hence possess opposing innate predispositions, we are flexible in our capacity to enact these potentials, we have some measure of free will and hence can choose, and we can correct our mistakes.*

Had we been mostly cruel or selfish or automatically and effortlessly caring and compassionate, we would probably not have held these philosophical and psychological debates but would have solved this enigma long ago. Similarly, were it the case that some people embody one side (e.g., individualistic and selfish, or cruel and competitive) whereas others embody the other pole (e.g., connected and caring or compassionate and cooperative), we would long ago have solved this dilemma and acted accordingly. The fact that the debate goes on attests to something unique about human nature: as a species, we have the capacity to express *all* these attributes and we grow up in environments that allow us some leeway for our own choices. Thus we can be both selfish and caring, rational and affective, or good and evil depending on a large number of things, internal and external, conscious and unconscious, easily controlled or not. The same caring and attuned mother can become a suicide bomber; the same aloof, cold father can be very affectionate with his dog; and the same self-centered millionaire can donate a fortune to hungry children in underdeveloped countries. We all have these many wonderful capacities withine us—the remarkable capacity to be flexible and to choose, to be judicious and balanced in the enactment of our choices, and to try to redress and rectify our mistakes. Some measure of free will and choice then reflect a central aspect in our nature and implicates our responsibility and accountability (Frankl, 1959/1985; Kane, 2005).

Caring as a reflection of our *daimon*

The astute reader may be correct in noting that I appear to contradict myself. If all of this is in our nature, how is the caring motivation a central, significant, and core aspect of this nature? According to this depiction, it is but another possibility that we can choose among others. This is true. My response to this reflects my conviction that we do have a large number of possibilities when we conduct ourselves in the world and with each other, and some of these possibilities are morally better than others. More importantly, some of these possibilities are more *central to our nature—they occupy a more fundamental core or hub of our existence, meaning that their enactment is imbued with a strong sense of life meaning, self-fulfillment, and self-actualization.* More specifically, I suggest that the caring motivation, unlike other possible voluntary endeavors, both reflects and manifests a deep-seated facet of our "true" nature as human beings.

In this sense I concur with Erikson (1963), who viewed generativity as key universal developmental milestone for people during middle adulthood. However, unlike Erikson (1963), I do not limit this motivation to a specific period in one's life and to future generations. The caring motivation is displayed throughout our lives and is manifested in a variety of contexts and relationships, some clearly relevant to the future generations (e.g., our own children, the global warming of our planet) and others not so (e.g., caring for our ailing older relatives, cooperating with friends). It starts emerging from very early on, during the first year of life, at the same time that one's self begins to form and one's first intimate intersubjective space develops. It is thus both central and fundamental in a much larger sense than Erikson's notion of generativity.

What then makes it so central to our nature? My answer to this is clear. The caring motivation is central in our lives because it is associated with our *daimon*, "spirit," or "true self" as a species. Furthermore when we express this *daimon*, this realization provides us with a strong sense of meaning in life. This depiction is closely related to the distinction between eudaemonic and hedonic types of happiness or well-being (Ryan & Deci, 2001; Ryff & Singer, 2006) and to current discussions on meanings of life and their manifestations in life goals (Schmuck & Sheldon, 2001; Sheldon, 2001). This term (*daimon*), and *eudaemonia* (happiness in the sense of flourishing), in particular, were discussed in Hellenic philosophy and particularly in Aristotle's *Nicomachean Ethics*, but they were also later elaborated by other philosophers (see discussion by Waterman, 1990). The *daimon* refers to the potentials that represent the greatest fulfillment in life that we are capable of. Realizing these potentials or advancing in our efforts to realize them prompts a sense of *eudaemonia*.

Caring and our sense of life's meaning and purpose

During the past two decades a new delineation of what constitutes well-being has emerged with the discussion of two types of happiness (Deci & Ryan, 2000). Happiness based on hedonic pleasure is related to maximizing positive affective experiences and minimizing negative ones. Eudaemonic well-being appears to be more comprehensive and involves realizing a person's own full potential and is associated with a sense of purpose in life, meaning and self-fulfillment.

These two types of happiness appear to signal two somewhat distinct goals or attainments in life, with eudaemonic pleasure signifying successful progress toward goals associated with life's meaning and purpose. These two types are highly related (Waterman, 1993) because (among other things) progress in attaining goals that provide meaning to life and self-actualization according to a person's "true self" is hedonically rewarding. However, not all such efforts are positive, and eudaemonic exertions may also be associated with negative affect, as in parenting. Consequently each type of well-being is distinct (e.g., Compton, Smith, Cornish, & Qualls, 1996) despite being highly correlated and is associated differently with a variety of experiences (Waterman, 1993), and even with different profiles of brain activation (Urry et al., 2004). For example, in line with the different roles of these two types of well-being, eudaemonic well-being is more strongly associated with feeling challenged and competent, investing a great deal of effort, having a high level of concentration and assertiveness, having clear goals, and knowing how well one is doing, whereas hedonic well-being is more strongly associated with feeling relaxed, excited, content, happy, losing track of time, and forgetting one's personal problems (Waterman, 1993).

The study of eudaemonia is part of a larger discussion within behavioral science that involves a surging new interest in issues of meaning in life, in the pursuit of meaningful life goals, and in self-actualization. This discourse contends that the pursuit of meaning, and the pursuit of meaningful goals in particular, is fundamental and essential and appears to distinguish us as a species (Baumeister, 1991; Emmons, 2005). A very large body of research, described and summarized skillfully and eloquently by Baumeister (1991), attests to the centrality of our striving for meaning. Baumeister suggests that a central part of this striving includes the satisfaction of four aspects: purpose, value, efficacy, and self-worth. To attain a sense of meaning in life we embrace a purpose that we deem valuable and which we feel that we can successfully accomplish; this provides us with a sense of self-worth. In fact, striving to find a meaning to life has been suggested as the primary and most powerful motivating and driving force in humans (Frankl, 1985/1959; 1988).

Following three years in concentration camps during the Holocaust, the Austrian neurologist and psychiatrist Victor Frankl identified the "will to meaning" as the most fundamental in our existence, more than our will to have pleasure or to have power, the latter two having been advocated by Sigmund Freud and Alfred Adler respectively. In *Man's Search for Meaning*, his highly influential, groundbreaking book, Frankl, the founder of logotherapy (a system of psychotherapy based on Frankl's ideas), suggests that we can discover this crucial meaning in a variety of ways: by creating a work or doing a deed, by experiencing something or encountering someone, and by the attitude we take toward unavoidable suffering. He further suggests that people have their own distinctive life meanings and yet that such meaning, which he termed ultimate meaning, is always directed toward something or someone other than the self. Over the past two decades issues concerned with the creation and search for meaning have increasingly become the focus of behavioral science research (Wong & Fry, 1998). In this line of research meaningfulness was found to be associated with positive adjustment, life satisfaction, and happiness (French & Joseph, 1999; Robak & Griffin, 2000), while a lack of meaning was associated with depression, psychological distress, and pathology (Wong & Fry, 1998).

This begs the question of what might constitute a meaningful life goal. It should come as no surprise that I contend that caring plays a key part in it. We see it in donors who despite "having everything they desire" opt to give to others, in adults who have human companions but still adopt a pet, in individuals who choose to parent, and in those who volunteer to help unfamiliar others. All these deeds, often intrinsically chosen, tell us something about human nature and about the intrinsic and fulfilling sense of meaning we accrue through these caring deeds. In fact, research has shown that caring in its diverse manifestations is the most central domain in the pursuit of meaning in life.

Specifically, different accounts using a variety of samples, cultures, and age groups—as well as a variety of research methods—have converged on a few major domains implicated in people's lives that accord them a sense of purpose and meaning (Ebersole, 1998; Little, 1998; Wong, 1998 ; Bar-Tur, Savaya, & Prager, 2001; Emmons, 1999, 2005). Three of these have appeared in all studies and cultures. One involves caring for known others as part of close relationships and includes having intimate connections with others, trusting them, and being altruistic and helpful to them. Another involves caring for the community or for future generations, termed "service" or "self-transcendence" in the sense of transcending self-interest. Both were most central to all accounts and were thus suggested as principal anchors with regard to the meaning of people's lives. The third was related to religion, spirituality, a connection with divinity, and the importance of living according to clear values. Another major domain refers to work and achievement and includes being committed to one's work, believing in its worth, and liking challenges, but it did not appear in all accounts and was less consistently associated with well-being.

Clearly, then, caring in intimate or large circles is emerging as one of a few central domains of meaning in life and in fact as the central one across different age groups and cultures. Unsurprisingly, spirituality and religion also emerge as central domains in these spheres, since caring within intimate relations, service, and caring in less intimate circles and spirituality are interconnected and share a similar core of one's *daimon*. In all three *we extend ourselves beyond our personal selves to something greaters—the intimate intersubjective space, the community or universe at large, and the transcendent.*

The strong sense of meaningfulness associated with caring may play several roles in the caring motivational system. In acknowledging this connection, people may choose caring as a way to express their search for a meaningful life and for meaningful life goals. Furthermore, the sense of meaningfulness associated with caring is also a strong sustaining incentive. Why am I not assuming pleasure or hedonic happiness to be the only or major sustaining incentive of caring (to use McClelland's words)? Caring is associated with highly positive and exhilarating feelings such as joy, elation, love, being proud and having a sense of accomplishment, and these rewarding experiences may indeed serve as sustaining and enhancing incentives as described in the previous chapter. Yet most accounts of caring comprise a combination of both positive and negative affective responses. Despite its significance and centrality in human life, caring is not necessarily associated with hedonic pleasure. In fact, a large number of studies, some of which have been concisely summarized in previous chapters, have shown that caring may be associated with burdens, difficulties, and exertions. This has been most clearly discussed in several domains of caring, parenting in particular, by a number of researchers (see Chapter 8) (Lyubomirsky & Boehm, 2010; Hansen, 2012; Nelson et al., 2013; Nelson, Kushlev & Lyubomirsky, 2014). These scholars have argued that unlike other fundamental human motives, such as physiological needs, affiliation, self-worth, or romantic love, parenting does not always demonstrate the expected association with hedonic happiness but is paradoxically often associated with decrements in hedonic well-being. Caring cannot therefore be psychologically sustained only by hedonia, or a rewarding positive affect.

This led Baumeister (1991) to discuss what he termed the *parenthood paradox*, which involves most people's strong desire to have children, including the extremes to which people will go to achieve this goal, along with parenting's demonstrated association with a decreased sense of hedonic well-being. Baumeister (1991) has further suggested that among the various goals that people adopt parenting in particular is strongly associated with a sense of meaning, and that this might be the primary reason for choosing to parent in the first place. In his words: "Having children makes life much more meaningful even if it does diminish happiness" (Baumeister, 1991, p. 396).

Similar accounts of the central place of meaning in life in the choice to help, care, and tend and in the continued sustenance of such caring have been discussed throughout this book with regard to diverse types of caregiving besides parenting, such as care for sick or elderly relatives and friends, volunteering, and caring for gardens. Similarly, the centrality of a sense of mission and meaning has been amply expressed in caring for a general cause, and similar accounts were salient in studies examining generativity. Thus the eudaemonic well-being that results from autonomous and successful caring and which expresses our innate search for a meaningful life serves to sustain caring and probably provides a strong proximate incentive to continue even when care is difficult and demanding. From an *evolutionary* point of view, therefore, the sense of meaning in life and the self-fulfillment resulting from successful caring as well as the underlying motivational energy that these represent are central *proximal* mechanisms for sustaining caring.

Caring as self-actualization

The strong association of caring with our sense of meaning is not a coincidence. I maintain that caring provides us with eudaemonic pleasure because it allows us to live life by realizing our full potential as human beings. An engagement in caring and tending appears to be strongly tied to a sense of self-fulfillment deemed to be a core aspect of human experience. Abraham Maslow (1953, 1970) is the scholar most commonly associated with the view of self-actualization as the epitome of human development and the highest state to which we can aspire. In one of the best-known models of human development, Maslow suggested a hierarchical pyramid of human needs extending from lower and more basic needs, such as physiological needs and the need for affiliation, to the highest need, the need for self-actualization. Maslow suggested a gradual progression from lower and more basic needs to self-actualization and proposed that a minimum level of satisfaction of more basic needs is required before other and higher needs can be attended to.

A revision of this hierarchy informed by evolutionary accounts and life-history perspectives in particular has recently been suggested (Kenrick, Griskevicius, Neuberg, & Schaller, 2010). In this revision, parenting is suggested as residing at the top of the hierarchy. The accordance of a special and privileged place for parenting in this hierarchical model of human development reflects the central place that current evolutionary accounts accord these caring and tending capacities and goals. Self-actualization was removed from the hierarchy entirely because—according to the authors—it does not appear to have a corresponding evolutionary explanation. They claim that current evolutionary analyses have not yet identified the proximal or functional goal of meaning in life, authenticity, and self-actualization. Kenrick and his colleagues (2010) nevertheless struggled with this decision because, as they maintain, it appears that a large number of human accounts attest to the centrality of endeavors for self-actualization, such as those carried out through artistic endeavors. Still, one of the ways they employed to support their decision was alluding to the fact that self-actualization focuses on the self while current research, or so they contend, suggests that people shift toward a growing concern for others' welfare over time (Krebs & Van Hesteren, 1994; Van Lange, Otten, DeBruin, & Joireman, 1997). According to their analyses, the top of the hierarchy should be defined by taking care of others and not by pursuing idiosyncratic and self-focused pleasure.

My own reading of these accounts is that the two perspectives, both Maslow's focus on self-actualization and Kenrick et al.'s (2010) focus on evolution, relationships, and a growing concern with age for others' welfare are actually quite compatible. I suggest that *parenting, as well as other manifestations of the caring motivation (e.g., generativity), constitute central paths toward the attainment of self actualization.* This might be one of the main reasons for the strong sense of meaning in life that is attached to such endeavors.

I am not suggesting that the caring motivation is the only way to achieve self-actualization but that it is one of the central and most frequent ways, as it characterizes each and every one of us and does not necessarily require a special and unique gift, such as an artistic talent. I suggest that specifically because caring is in our nature, its diverse actualizations—whether parenting, volunteering, devoting oneself to charitable endeavors, or working to improve the world for the next generation—not only provide us with a sense of *self-fulfillment* but also with a concomitant strong sense of *life meaning. We actualize our true selves when we help others thrive and help make the world a better place, but through such engagement we also thrive and find a deep meaning and purpose to our own lives.*

In this view, self-actualization does not mean self-indulgence or self-focus but a realization of the central, authentic nature of our selves which involves, among other things, extending beyond the self and caring. I maintain that a central defining feature of our true nature is that we are a caring species and therefore desire to give and to facilitate thriving in the world. Hence, actualizing and fulfilling this caring nature is a core manifestation of self-actualization. *Paradoxically, therefore, it is through a benevolent involvement in something other and greater than ourselves that we appear to express the self in a most authentic and profound way.* My personal conviction ties this central motivation in our nature to our spiritual origins and brings me to the spiritual realm and to its association with the caring motivation.

Caring as reflecting our spiritual core

Spiritual traditions worldwide view the divine as reflecting or embodying the ultimate care; they expect humans to live their lives by bringing this aspect of spiritual nature shared with the divine to the fore and radiating it to others. In line with this approach I would like to go one step further in my discussion of human nature and suggest that the capacity and motivation to connect and extend across distances and differences to help an entity survive, grow, and thrive is so central in our self-actualization pursuits because it reflects a central aspect of our spiritual origin and nature. In fact, our "need" for self-actualization itself is seen as a manifestation of the internal urge to unwrap, express, and realize the spiritual in us in a variety of ways including caring. By "spiritual," I mean the aspect in us that is divine, that gives us life as we know it, and through which we know ourselves as humans; it is that sphere which we share with all other things in the universe and with the cosmos itself. In discussing this point, I will allude to the perspectives of transpersonal psychology and to the work of scholars who have studied and discussed spirituality and spiritual development.

The advocated connection between self-actualization, caring, and the spiritual is related to a lesser known part of Maslow's legacy. As one of the founders of humanistic psychology, Maslow was also the founder of transpersonal psychology. During his final years he became interested in what lay beyond self-actualization. In a posthumous book titled *The Farther Reaches of Human Nature* (1971), which Maslow did not finish because of his sudden death, he suggests that there are developmental possibilities beyond self-actualization. He describes a developmental level that he termed *transpersonal*—one that involves transcendence beyond the expression of self-identity—that "self" which is the personality or ego-self, and which develops through one's interactions with others and with the environment. Transpersonal approaches hold that this ego-self is not the same as one's deep nature or essence and that self-transcendence opens us to experiencing this deeper nature. Such self-transcendence refers to an experience of a fundamental connection, harmony, or unity within and with others and the world. In self-transcendence, the sense of self dissolves into an awareness of a greater unity and individuals have a deep sense of peacefulness or tranquility; they feel in tune, in harmony, or at one with the universe and with all that exists, and experience a deep or profound understanding along with strong and deep sense of compassion (Walsh & Vaughan, 1993). The transpersonal developmental process includes such "peak experiences" but may also be expressed in somewhat stable "plateau experiences." These are profoundly spiritual and sacred experiences, although they can and do occur both inside and outside of institutionalized religion. Maslow had only begun to explore these processes, but others who built upon his groundbreaking ideas developed them further as part of a new branch of psychology termed transpersonal psychology (Mann, 1984; Tart, 1975/1992; Grof & Bennett, 1992; Rothberg, Kelly, & Kelly, 1998; Wilber, 2000; Koltko-Rivera, 2006).

According to this view, self-transcendence involves connecting at higher *and* deeper levels and entails unity and harmony within and with the universe as well as a deep sense of compassion. Self-transcendence is thus reflected in an extension and expansion of the self and involves a benevolent state of mind, where people are "involved in a cause outside their own skin" (Maslow, 1971, p. 43). Caring and compassion emanate from the deep responsibility for all that exists that such connectedness entails. Subsequent research has indeed found that self-transcendence is associated with being generous, empathic, and altruistic (e.g., Mayseless & Russo-Netzer, 2012). Furthermore, and in a very large international study of youths, Benson, Scales, Syvertsen, and Roehlkepartain (2012) have observed that spiritual development includes the search for connectedness, meaning, purpose, and contribution both inside and outside institutional religions. Furthermore, together with others they have observed that this can be construed as a universal developmental process.

Current approaches to and definitions of spiritual development tend to incorporate several common themes, which are very similar to the ones identified by transpersonal researchers. These themes include references to a transcendence reflecting a cognitive and experiential realization that "there exists a broader paradigm for understanding existence that transcends the immediacy of our own individual consciousness and that binds all things into a more unitive harmony" (Piedmont, 1999, p. 988). Another central theme relates to ultimate questions about the nature, purpose, and meaning of life, leading to the construction of a relationship to the sacred (e.g., Kiesling, Sorell, Montgomery, & Colwell, 2006). One of the most common definitions that refers to both themes thus defines spiritual development as the "process of growing the intrinsic human capacity for self-transcendence, in which the self is embedded in something greater than the self, including the sacred. It is the developmental 'engine' that propels the search for connectedness, meaning, purpose, and contribution." (Benson, Roehlkepartain, & Rude, 2003, pp. 205–206). The development of spirituality along these lines is reflected in a person's life orientation, way of living, and conduct in the world. The development of such a capacity often involves an inner and outer journey of discovery and awareness along with the desire and capacity to experience this transcendence and unity *and act accordingly* (Lerner, Roeser, & Phelps, 2008). This involves a prosocial connection and responsibility to others, to nature, and to the whole universe (Benson et al., 2013).

In describing how spirituality is played out in human experience, scholars using diverse psychological perspectives have used diverse sets of notions to describe three interconnected facets that can be represented by spatial metaphors: *down within, up and beyond,* and *sideways and interconnected* (see handbooks edited by Miller, 2012, and Pargament, 2013). Coming from a philosophical perspective and identifying very similar facets of spirituality in philosophical writings, Alexander (2001) has termed them *subjective, objective,* and *collective* spirituality, respectively. The "down within" facet relates to our capacity to act in a harmonious and balanced way and often resembles what others have described as emotional maturity, integrity, and fidelity. The "up and beyond" facet relates to our capacity to connect our physical and personal existence to the ideal, the ultimate, the sacred, the eternal, and the divine or transcendent in a sphere that lies outside the confines of space and time. The third, "sideways and interconnected," relates to our spiritual capacity to experience our interconnectedness to all that exists. All three capacities and in particular the synergy among them are associated with caring. Caring and compassion emanate from the deep responsibility for all that exists—the wish to be part of creation and to contribute by actively engaging in healing and the promotion of thriving that such connectedness within the self, with the universe, and with the transcendent entails.

Spiritual development involves increasing each of these capacities and expanding the synchronicity among them (Benson et al., 2013). Caring can be enacted at any level of such spiritual development, but our capacity and predisposition for it develops along with our spirit. The more we are balanced and integrated within, the more we connect to the ideal, the eternal, and the divine, and the more we perceive and experience the universe and us as emanations of the same divine source the stronger our compassion and our capacity to care in the way that *best reflects our unique individual nature*. Experiencing self-transcendence and being interconnected does not mean that we all become alike. Each of us is a unique spirit (*daimon*) that manifests its unique life meaning as part and as a reflection of the ultimate meaning (Frankl, 1997). When we develop spiritually our unique individual and spiritual nature can be best fulfilled and hence our caring too manifests itself in reflecting this unique quality.

In essence, therefore, caring is one of the manifestations and expressions of our spiritual and divine core. It is certainly not the sole one but a central one (Hart, 2014). *In compassion and caring we are "divine" because through care we extend ourselves beyond our distinct and limited existence and we create—we give and sustain life and help it heal, grow, and thrive.* We contribute to the ongoing force of life with its beauty, abundance, and multitude of emanations. The enactment of care is therefore a fulfillment and an actualization of a central aspect of our *daimon*; thus its successful enactment provides us with a deep and profound sense of satisfaction and meaning, indicating our mysterious and unique realization of the divine within us.

Implications for research

The research discussed in this book and the conceptual model of the general and comprehensive caring motivational system presented in this part of the book in particular exposes many new and challenging questions. Here I will not discuss this large number of specific questions but rather highlight several general issues or domains, each covering many specific issues that might be addressed in future research.

The first domain relates to the multidimensionality of caring. Despite clear similarities, the different kinds of care show distinct manifestations and adaptations (e.g., the importance of equity in reciprocal and egalitarian vs. nonreciprocal and hierarchical caring). An important research question thus relates to identifying the most relevant and significant distinctions between the different kinds of care and to uncovering interrelations between different types of caring.

For example, future studies can examine how caring in one domain (e.g., as part of one's profession) affects others (e.g., parenting) as well as the moderating conditions involved in such situations. Related to this multidimensionality are questions concerned with the developmental trajectory of different types of care; for example, the ways in which their developmental trajectory is similar and the ways in which they diverge; the role of genetics in different kinds of caring; the factors that lead people to prefer one type or kind of care over others; the developmental trajectory for helping nonkin as opposed to that for helping family members; the developmental trajectory of providing physical as opposed to that of providing psychological care, and more.

Another central domain relates to the evolutionary development of such an innate motivation. Following others, I have suggested that the evolutionary origin of the caring motivational system resides in the need for fairly extensive maternal care for the young, and that this provided the basis for the development of other types of care. However, the evolutionary development of the current complex and multifaceted caring motivational system on the basis of this ancient maternal care system is unclear. For example, the evolutionary development of warmth, the capacity to socialize others and to teach, bonding with mates and friends, and cooperation in groups are not yet spelled out (but see Thornton & Raihani, 2008). The evolutionary development of the different caring types should therefore be traced, as should the timing and method of their emergence in evolutionary history.

Another major research area relates to the role of meaning and self-fulfillment as proximate causes. A central proximal mechanism for sustaining caring is postulated to be our sense of meaning and self-actualization. Thus its role in care should be investigated, as should the manner of its development. Specifically, researchers may try to uncover when and how such a sense of meaning begins, what aspects are similar across individuals and how diversity develops, what is the contribution of socialization, and how it interacts with individuals' predispositions. Researchers may also target its relation to spiritual experiences and to self-transcendence and its evolutionary origin.

Additional area for research relates to the different kinds of care. While reactive care has been studied quite extensively, we know much less about proactive caring, its antecedents, how and when it is aroused, and how it interacts with reactive care instances in the same person. Similarly we currently know very little about what leads people to form hierarchical caring relations and how these relations start and evolve. In particular we do not know how and why people choose to form such relation with a particular entity. Similar lacunae are apparent in these processes with regard to egalitarian caring relationships, as with friends. How are these relations created? At what stage and how does caring enter the picture? What leads to the dissolution of caring relationships and how? Furthermore, despite the clear distinctions between caring relations and between caring bonds and caring behaviors, so far we do not understand the biological and neural processes that accompany and underlie such distinct phenomena. In addition and unlike the developmental trajectory of women's caring, there are still many things we do not know about men's caring and "the birth of a father"; future studies would do well to examine this in greater detail.

Finally, the study of the biological, genetic, neural, and hormonal basis of the caring motivational system is advancing at a rapid pace. However, research has just begun to unravel these mysteries and much remains to be studied. For example, we do not yet know the ways in which different types of care and gender differences in caring (e.g., toy preferences; preference for dyadic and intimate contexts vs. larger groups) are implicated in neural processes and in the endocrine system. Furthermore, the role of various genes in affecting caring processes and the exact associations between genes, hormones, and brain processes has yet to be uncovered. In addition, research has yet to uncover the biological mechanisms that underlie the intriguing association between caring and physical health and longevity. These issues would need to be explored in future research.

Applied implications

Our innate motivation to care is morally and instrumentally good; it expresses our spiritual nature and provides us with life meaning and self-fulfillment. In addition, socialization, cultural context, and immediate circumstances play central roles in the molding and enactment of this innate caring motivation. Hence the most obvious applied implication of the conceptual model presented in this book is the importance of promoting and scaffolding balanced caring; this can be achieved through socialization and the creation of contexts that encourage caring. A large number of scholars have provided detailed and inspiring accounts on how caring can be promoted in different realms: in parenting, in schools, in organizations, in psychotherapy, at the community level, in society at large, as part of intergroup relations, and particularly with regard to those mired in intractable conflicts (e.g., Eisenberg & Valiente, 2002; Nadler, Malloy, & Fisher, 2008; Noddings, 2005; Oliner & Oliner, 2005; Bronfman & Solomon, 2012; Keltner et al., 2014; and many more). I will not be able to do justice to these accounts by summarizing them here; the reader is advised to consult them in full. Nonetheless these various accounts can be generally seen as addressing four major aspects: teaching caring skills, imparting caring values, creating a caring community, and broadening the circle of care.

Teaching caring skills includes such activities as teaching youths how to regulate their emotions as well as to understand and consider the emotions and feelings of others and their own effects on them. In addition such teaching includes scaffolding in diverse situations and providing informative and caring feedback to enhance such learning using induction and warmth. Similarly, the provision of opportunities for children and youths to be engaged in caring and helping offers them contexts (the family, school, youth organizations, community centers) in which to practice caring skills.

Imparting caring values relates, for example, to socializing agents who must be explicit about the values that guide them, including references to humanitarian and caring perspectives in a sustained and recurrent manner and in a variety of situations and contexts. In addition, setting an example through their own conduct is also a very effective way for socializing agents or leaders to impart values through emulation rather than preaching.

In order to create a *caring community*, as in schools or in other organizational contexts, bonding at the dyadic and community levels needs to be promoted so that people will feel that they matter to each other. In addition, and in order to promote care, the community would need to set norms and be organized in a way that furthers its members' capacity to engage in caring (e.g., reinforce norms of reciprocity and compassion; Keltner et al., 2014). Leaders in such a community need to exhibit authentic caring themselves. When we try to *broaden the circle of care*, we encourage what Oliner and Oliner (1988) have referred to as "extensivity" in their study of the Righteous Among the Nations (gentiles who rescued Jews during the Holocaust). This relates to our innate capacity to extend the lines that demarcate between "us" and "them" or between in-groups and out-groups, and to consider very different others and at times even enemies as part of the circle of empathy and care. This can be done, for example, by getting to know and appreciate others who are different from us through direct interactions and networking and through the promotion of respect, which refers to a broad humanistic tendency to value each person as a worthy human being and only then to supplement this by promoting empathy (Mayseless & Scharf, 2010).

There are, however, several dilemmas surrounding such scaffoldings that I would like to highlight. My main concern relates to the intrinsic and autonomous nature of the caring motivation and to its authenticity. We need to beware of the commodification of care and prosocial acting or of relating to it as merchandise to be sold and marketed. Caring, as a reflection of our spiritual core and self-realization, should be based on an autonomous volition that reflects a self-conscious choice rather than an attempt to please others, to be seen as a good person, or to gain fame and status. It should be a reflection of our inner authentic desire. As described elsewhere in this book (e.g., Chapter 14), there are large individual differences in how much people want to engage in caring as well as in how and where, and these differences should be deeply and truly respected.

Furthermore, people want to give and to provide care, and this intrinsic desire begins very early in life. Too often adults brush off children's attempts to help and comfort them and view these caring acts as improper role-reversals reflecting a breach in adults' care. However, if we view these caring acts as reflecting the children's inner desire to care, we would probably act differently. In our different spheres of life we can accommodate children's and adults' gifts of care and accept, acknowledge, and respect them. The biblical tale of Cain demonstrates how painful it is to have your gift rejected and how devastating the results of this rejection can be. Fairbairn, an eminent pioneer of object relations theory, expresses this very eloquently with regard to children's needs not only to receive but also to give: "The greatest need of a child is to obtain conclusive assurance (a) that he is genuinely loved as a person by his parents, (b) that his parents genuinely accept his love" (Fairbairn, 1952, p. 39)

Finally, authentic caring resides in our striving to self-actualize and find meaning in our lives; hence *a deep self-understanding* and *compassion and love for one's self* are often crucial for the best kind of caring. Such self-awareness can and must be promoted in a variety of contexts, the most important of which is the formal education system. In this sense, it is when the three core processes of spirituality—(1) attending and minding our true self, deep within; (2) reaching out and connecting to a sacred and ultimate sphere, up and beyond; and (3) connecting with all that exists—are in harmony that our caring flows and radiates in the best possible ways.

Chapter conclusion

In this chapter I have presented my own take on the implications of the conceptual model of the caring motivational system presented in Chapters 16, 17, and 18 for our human nature. Caring emerged as a fundamental, innate, general, encompassing, sophisticated, and flexible motivational system. The focus on the caring motivation in this book is part of a larger change in views of human nature that has moved from being seen as individualistic, autonomous, self-centered, and competitive to a view that underscores our connected and relational nature. Many scholars have already done a great job of demonstrating that connections and relationships are fundamental to our nature and experience. However, most have focused on the receiving end—that is, our needs for warmth, acknowledgment, positive regard, safe haven, and being loved. Thus one of the reasons for my intense focus on the caring motivation is the importance of counterbalancing the strong focus on the need to receive. Both are central in our existence.

Several dichotomies regarding human nature are relevant to the model of the caring motivational system presented in this book: autonomy/individuality vs. connectedness; the sensual, irrational, and affective vs. the rational and transcendental; the good (benevolence, kindness, and compassion) vs. evil (cruelty, viciousness, and destruction); and selfishness and self-centeredness vs. being other-oriented and altruistic. Caring is probably more specifically related to the connected, benevolent, and altruistic sides and is somewhere in the middle regarding rationality and affectivity.

However, each of the aspects reflected in these dichotomies is part of our nature and hence can and probably will surface in human experience. Furthermore, caring may be conceived as a virtue, but the caring motivational system itself is not only rose-colored nurturance. It includes a variety of mechanisms for fostering its balanced expression that reflect other aspects as well. For example, the caring motivational system includes the capacity to punish others who betray our trust or cheat, the use of harsh behaviors if necessary (defending one's family), and the tendency to balance care for others with self-care and self-interest. We are multifaceted and holistic and hence possess opposing innate predispositions, good and bad, benevolent and aggressive. We are flexible in our capacity to enact these potentials; we can choose and we can correct our mistakes.

Yet, caring does occupy a unique position among the alternative aspects (e.g., being selfish, being cruel) because it is strongly associated with our sense of life's meaning. In fact, in many studies, caring in intimate relations, service in society at large (often termed self-transcendence), and spirituality and religion emerge as central domains of meaning in life across different age groups and cultures. In all three people extend themselves beyond the personal self to something that is greater than the individual—the intimate intersubjective space, the community or universe at large, and the transcendent.

The strong association of caring with our sense of meaning is not fortuitous. Caring provides us with eudaemonic pleasure because it allows us to live life by realizing our own full potential as human beings. I suggest that the caring motivation, unlike other possible voluntary endeavors, both reflects and manifests a deep-seated facet of our "true" nature as human beings—our *daimon* and *spirit*. Caring is one central way of fulfillment of such a "true self"; hence its enactment provides us with a sense of meaning and purpose and an intense experience of *eudaemonic* happiness.

My personal conviction ties this central motivation in our nature to our spiritual origins. In compassion and caring we are "divine," because through care we "create"—we give and sustain life and help it heal, grow, and thrive. Following advocates of transpersonal psychology and other scholars studying spirituality and spiritual development, I discuss spirituality as involving a search for connectedness, ultimate meaning, purpose, and contribution. Our spirituality is viewed as involving a connection to our deeper and true spiritual core (deep within facet), an expansion and connection with the ultimate through self-transcendence (up and beyond facet) and experiencing our interconnectedness to all that exists (the sideways and interconnected facet). Caring and compassion thus emanate from the deep responsibility for all that exists, which such connectedness within the self, with the universe, and with the transcendent entails.

The conceptual model of the caring motivational system suggested in this volume opens up a large number of research questions. I highlight five broad domains. The first relates to the multidimensionality of caring and the search for similarities, distinct adaptations as well as interrelations among the variety of kinds of research. Another central issue relates to the evolutionary development of such an innate and multifaceted motivation. A third research area relates to the role of meaning and self fulfillment as proximate causes and their development as well as individual differences in this realm. The fourth domain deals with the explication of how the different kinds of care (e.g., caring bonds with friends) develop and operate. Finally, the fifth domain relates to the study of the biological, genetic, neural, and hormonal basis of the multifaceted caring motivational system including similarities and distinctions in the different kinds of care.

Finally I briefly addressed the applied implications through the prism of four major aspects: teaching caring skills, imparting caring values, creating a caring community, and broadening the circle of care. Readers are referred to central sources that provide detailed suggestions yet the discussion underscores the importance of balanced care and the need to allow others, even as children, to express their care.

20

Summary and Major Contributions

The aim of this volume has been to try and unravel the mystery of the human motivation to care, the caring motivation, and to review what has been scientifically written and conceptualized on this issue so as to be able to come up with a suggestion of a general conceptual model of caring as a motivation. Throughout this book a large number of insights regarding the caring motivation and how it functions and operates have emerged and were spelled out. Some of them were quite specific to the domain that I reviewed and others were more general and were elaborated and discussed in the suggested conceptual model presented in Part IV.

In this section I provide a succinct summary of the main tenets of the conceptual model of the caring motivational system and discuss the major unique advances to our understanding of the caring motivation that this model accords.

Summary of the main tenets of my conceptual perspective on caring

I decided to organize this summary in a bulleted format so as to contribute to its readability, and I arranged it by themes.

General organization and contents

1. Caring is all around us and is essential to our survival and fundamental in our nature.
2. We have an innate, evolutionarily selected, biologically governed intrinsic motivation to care that is naturally and volitionally enacted and includes instinctual, unconscious, and conscious processes.
3. The caring motivation is multifaceted and diverse and is organized as a complex and sophisticated caring motivational system that includes cognitions, emotions, procedures, and behaviors. It involves a variety of care dynamics

including caring behaviors, assumption of caring states, caring relations, and caring bonds and is enacted both reactively and proactively.

4. The caring motivational system also encompasses diverse provisions (e.g., comforting, defending, instrumental aid) that involve different levels of investment and costs (e.g., sustained parental care, heroic rescue).

5. The caring motivational system also encompasses a variety of targets, intimate and unfamiliar, human and nonhuman. Targets and domains of care are organized as a fuzzy set, with some more characteristic of caring than others.

6. The caring motivational system is thus multilayered, complex, multifaceted, and sophisticated and includes core processes that are expressed in all of its diverse manifestations as well as distinct adaptations for specific domains and kinds of care.

7. These distinct adaptations reflect different layers of evolutionary development that coevolved (e.g., mothering, cooperation in groups) and serve a variety of survival goals.

Variety and individual differences

8. The general, encompassing, and multidimensional caring motivational system involves salient and significant individual differences expressed in the extents, targets and manners in which people engage in caring.

9. Research has revealed a moderately high level of within-individual coherence in the tendency to be caring and in caring styles; these propensities emerge as stable in late adolescence.

10. Research has exposed similarity across all manifestations of care in what constitutes optimal care.

11. Research has revealed a clear human tendency to act cooperatively and prosocially among the majority of individuals (about two thirds of the population) in diverse cultures and using diverse research paradigms.

12. Yet human conduct in this respect shows also flexibility and malleability, both within and between individuals. This flexibility also characterizes the salient gender differences in caring.

13. Such variability and flexibility are advantageous for individuals and societies because they contribute to our resilience and capacity to deal with diverse contexts and challenges.

Developmental course

14. The caring motivational system starts developing early on (in the first year of life) and demonstrates systematic universal processes of development with age.

15. Though innate and intrinsic, socialization, culture, and concurrent context have strong effects on the development of the caring motivation and its enactment; they affect how, when, with whom, and to what extent people engage in caring.

Causal paths

16. At the ultimate level evolutionary accounts show that caring is highly critical and beneficial to our survival; theological accounts also provide explanations as to why this caring motivation exists – as a central manifestation of our divine potential.
17. At the proximal level the caring motivational system is governed by the interplay of biological, psychological, cultural, and contextual processes that are conceived as complementary perspectives.
18. Among the proximal psychological processes we have empathy, perspective taking, morality, and the search for meaning and purpose.
19. Often prosocial responding reflects the operation of several antecedents and reasons.
20. Autonomous expression of the innate caring motivation is central to its optimal operation.
21. The enactment of caring provides us with a sense of meaning and purpose and constitutes one of the central paths to self-fulfillment and self-actualization.
22. This eudaemonic sense of meaning and fulfillment serves to sustain caring intrinsically even when it is arduous and less hedonically satisfying, as with parenting.
23. Caring benefits not only the care receiver and society but also the caregiver and accords the caregiver pleasure and joy, better health and longevity, self worth, good reputation, and social connections. Though unintended, these benefits still sustain and enhance care.
24. However, caring can also become nonoptimal (e.g., when it reaches a point of satiation or when needs for autonomy of caregiver or receiver are not respected) and even pathological, as happens with other innate motivations such as hunger.
25. Although caring is both morally good and good for the caregiver and society, its provision should not be limitless, and optimal caring should be balanced (taking into considerations needs of the provider and the recipient) and judiciously and autonomously enacted as a reflection of our free spirit.

Human nature

26. Being a caring species does not invalidate other (sometimes opposing) facets of our nature, such as selfishness, competitiveness, and the need for power.

Our nature includes all of the above, but we have some measure of free will, we can choose among alternatives and we can correct our mistakes.

27. In fact, the caring motivational system itself includes "harsh" aspects, as in defending close friends or relations against aggression and in sustaining care as a norm and practice by punishing those who betray our trust.

28. Caring is still more central and fundamental in our nature than some of the other facets because it reflects a central way of self-fulfilment and self-actualization and is strongly associated with our life meaning.

Caring and our spiritual core

29. I contend that caring is so central in our self-actualization because it is a central defining feature of our "true" nature, our *daimon*, which reflects our spiritual core.

30. Caring and compassion emanate from the deep responsibility for all that exists and the wish to be part of creation and to contribute by actively engaging in healing and the promotion of thriving that are entailed by inner and outer connectedness and self-transcendence.

The main contributions of this volume and the suggested conceptual model

In exploring and studying the extant literatures on caring for this volume, I consulted a large number of perspectives to examine caring from a variety of angles and disciplines so as to be able to provide a comprehensive, multi-faceted, and hopefully nuanced understanding of this motivational system. Within each domain I reviewed dozens of studies, often organizing their results in a way that illustrates their distinct contributions and underscores new insights. Many of these insights can be found in the specific chapters throughout this volume. In addition, each of the summary points presented in the preceding paragraphs provides new understanding regarding caring as a motivation. In this section I would like to underscore what I see as the *main* new and significant insights that provide unique advances to our understanding of caring as a motivation, which are embedded in the suggested conceptual model and throughout the volume.

Fundamental motivation

The first main contribution rests on the extensive evidence that I have reviewed demonstrating that our caring motivation is fundamental. It is innate and has biological strata to support it; it is essential for our survival and is all around us; hence it is a very central facet of our existence. Previous accounts have often focused on parenting as the most obvious caring endeavor and neglected other caring pursuits (e.g., Kenrick, Griskevicius, Neuberg, & Schaller, 2010) or underscored the importance of caring through discussions of its significant role for the care receiver (e.g., Taylor, 2002). The perspective advocated and substantiated in this volume gives caring as a motivation a most central and significant place in the fabric of human motivation and pursuits not only in its manifestation in parenting or as part of a general human need for connectedness and relatedness but as a broad cardinal motivational system of care in its own right. Furthermore, resolving some of the debates in the literature regarding whether caring is a behavioral system, an emotion, or whether it involves mostly cognitions, the suggested model includes all of these aspects in the caring motivational system.

Encompassing and comprehensive motivational system

The second main contribution of the perspective underscored here and substantiated by research evidence is that caring is a multifaceted, multidimensional, and sophisticated motivational system that includes diverse kinds and domains of caring. Despite this diversity, all these caring pursuits reflect a core motivation which is biologically and evolutionarily based. The diverse manifestations coevolved into this grand complex system and share a common biological and psychological core and yet also show distinct adaptations. Building on previous calls for such perspective (Berscheid & Collins, 2000) this novel and pioneering view opens up exciting new arenas for research and highlights the centrality and comprehensiveness of the care all around us.

Proactive care—care as a drive and desire

Most previous theories regarding caring have discussed its reactive nature (George & Solomon, 1999; Taylor, 2002). However, caring as a motivation is not only *activated* in response to contextual or outside demands but also functions as an inner drive or desire. Although we currently know much less than we might about this proactive manifestation and how it operates, the reviews and discussions in this volume clearly uncovered many caring pursuits that start from within, such as volunteering. This view changes the way we understand caring and underscores the intrinsic need or desire to care and help an entity heal and thrive.

Distinctions among a variety of care dynamics

The distinctions among caring relations, caring bonds, caring states, and caring behaviors in the operation of the caring motivational system as well as other distinctions—such as between hierarchical and egalitarian caring bonds and among a variety of provisions—help untangle the confusion in the research literature that discusses and investigates caring. These distinctions help to clarify and understand a variety of caring dynamics and thus to study their similarity and their distinctiveness. For example, these distinctions have made it possible to identify the importance of uniqueness in caring bonds and the suggested differentiation between the "growth-fostering motif" and the "rescue and healing motif" in caring endeavors.

The operation of the caring motivational system

The model presented here has unraveled several alternative psychological routes that can instigate the arousal of caring (empathy, perspective taking, morality and values, seeking meaning and purpose) as well as a number of unintended consequences that sustain and enhance care. Each of these mechanisms has been suggested previously by different scholars, often using different terms to describe similar processes. However the suggested conceptual model first provides an integrative organization of these mechanisms as different routes that lead to other-oriented (altruistic) giving and underscores their distinction from self-oriented motives such as guilt, self-esteem, or gaining reputation. Furthermore, the suggested model highlights the fact that often a variety of causes and reasons interact, hence showing equifinality in the enactment of care. Together, these observations provide new important insights regarding the operation of the caring motivation in the psychological realm.

Coherent and stable and yet flexible and sophisticated—individual (and gender) differences

The conceptual model presented here underscores two complementary processes. On the one hand research on caring has uncovered within-individual stability and coherence in the enactment of care as well as a pervasive tendency to be prosocial even in competitive contexts. On the other hand research has also uncovered sophistication, variability, and flexibility in caring pursuits. These are reflected in within-individual variability, such as the capacity to differentiate between in-group and out-group and care only for the former and the opposing capacity to extend the circle of care even to enemies. This flexibility as well as the between-individuals variability (e.g., some people engage in instrumental care and others prefer emotional comforting; some engage in a lot of care and others are only minimally caring) contribute to our versatility and resilience as individuals and as societies. Such flexibility and malleability also explain and provide at least partial resolution to the hot debate regarding gender differences in caring, as psychological, cross-cultural, and historical accounts have demonstrated that although each sex tends to have a characteristic preference for certain provisions, people can and do engage in care that characterizes mostly the other sex.

The importance of life meaning and purpose and autonomous regulation

The review of research on caring in a variety of domains uncovered that caring is strongly tied to our sense of life meaning and purpose and our self-fulfillment and underscored that it is both hedonically and eudaemonically governed. Furthermore, the conceptual model underscored the centrality of autonomous self-directed regulation of caring. These are important discernments because they help us understand one of the most baffling issues in caring: how is it that caring and especially parenting, which is so central to our survival, are not clearly associated with positive affect? How is it that caring also involves strong negative affective experiences? The suggested conceptual model untangles this "parenthood paradox" by suggesting several explanations related to the importance of eudaemonia in sustaining care and the centrality of autonomy in our conduct in being hedonically pleased.

Suggested ontogenic developmental model

One of the most central contributions of the conceptual model proposed here is the introduction of a developmental model for the ontogenic, universal development of the caring motivational system (see Chapter 13). This is a preliminary model, yet the first one that attempts to tackle such a task and to provide a developmental scheme that covers different age periods from infancy to adulthood, different caring domains, and a variety of caring dynamics. Consequently it points only to *optional* developmental paths. Most of it opens up the field for further research and conceptualizations and invites researchers and scholars to engage with this issue and perhaps refine, adapt, or contest this developmental model.

Caring is not only rose-colored limitless benevolence and sweetness

The conceptual model clarified a very significant issue that has been mostly implicit in discussions and investigations of caring. The caring motivational system does not include only sweetness and benevolence. To be caring people may need at times to be harsh, punitive, and even aggressive. To protect their progeny (a caring act that sustains life) they may need to fight aggressors. To make sure a child does not harm himself or herself, they may forcefully intervene. To evolutionarily sustain care so that it will not be exploited by selfish others, people may need to punish those who betray their trust or even those who have such a reputation. These "caring" acts must be judiciously enacted to be considered as reflecting optimal care. Furthermore, optimal care is not limitless caring. Everyday care that can be sustained without dangerously harming the caregiver, and hence can allow these caring genes to pass to the next generation, is care that respects the optimal level of exertion of the caregiver and the caregiver's and care receiver's salient central needs. Thus the caring motivational system itself includes checks and balances for judicious and balanced expressions and mechanisms for its sustenance.

Final concluding remarks

The vast research and conceptual perspectives discussed in this book have unraveled how central caring is in our lives and nature and how much we personally thrive—physically, psychologically, spiritually, and socially—by giving. The perspective presented in this book underscores the centrality of caring in human experience and human development and helps it both gain visibility and acquire the pivotal place it deserves among contemporary theories of human nature and human motivation. Furthermore, the suggested conceptual model opens up a large number of new research questions that have remained unexplored owing to the dispersion of research in a variety of research paradigms. It also opens the way for applied implications relating to our conduct in a variety of circles and social contexts.

This view has clear ramifications with regard to the conception of our species as innately prosocial. This is an optimistic perspective on human nature because it views human nature as innately caring and because there is a lot that we can do to change things if we want to. I hope that this volume will help accord the caring motivation its central and indispensable place in our current views of human nature and the human potential to be good and thrive by spreading goodness. Hopefully these ideas will help to pave the way for scholars and researchers to explore these potentials.

REFERENCES

Acevedo, B. P., Aron, A., Fisher, H. E., & Brown, L. L. (2012). Neural correlates of long-term intense romantic love. *Social Cognitive and Affective Neuroscience, 7*(2), 145–159.

Adams, R. E., Boscarino, J. A., & Figley, C. R. (2006). Compassion fatigue and psychological distress among social workers: A validation study. *American Journal of Orthopsychiatry, 76*(1), 103–108.

Agrillo, C., & Nelini, C. (2008). Childfree by choice: a review. *Journal of Cultural Geography, 25*(3), 347–363

Ainsworth, M. D. S. (1967). *Infancy in Uganda: Infant care and the growth of love.* Baltimore, MD: Johns Hopkins University Press.

Ainsworth, M. D. S. (1989). Attachments beyond infancy. *American Psychologist, 44,* 709–716.

Ainsworth, M. D. S., Blehar, M. C., Waters, E., & Wall, S. (1978). *Patterns of attachment: A psychological study of the strange situation.* Oxford, UK: Lawrence Erlbaum.

Aknin, L. B., Barrington-Leigh, C. P., Dunn, E. W., Helliwell, J. F., Burns, J., Biswas-Diener, R., . . . & Norton, M. I. (2013). Prosocial spending and well-being: Cross-cultural evidence for a psychological universal. *Journal of Personality and Social Psychology, 104*(4), 635–652.

Akintola, O. (2010). Perceptions of rewards among volunteer caregivers of people living with AIDS working in faith-based organizations in South Africa: A qualitative study. *Journal of the International AIDS Society, 13*(1), 22.

Albert, A., & Bulcroft, K. (1988). Pets, families, and the life course. *Journal of Marriage and Family, 50*(2), 543–552.

Alexander, G. M., & Hines, M. (2002). Sex differences in response to children's toys in non-human primates (Cercopithecus aethiops sabaeus). *Evolution and Human Behavior, 23*(6), 467–479.

Alexander, H. A. (2001). *Reclaiming goodness: Education and the spiritual quest.* Notre Dame, IN: University of Notre Dame Press.

Allen, K., Blascovich, J., & Mendes, W. B. (2002). Cardiovascular reactivity and the presence of pets, friends, and spouses: The truth about cats and dogs. *Psychosomatic Medicine, 64*(5), 727–739.

Allen, T. D. (2003).Mentoring others: A dispositional and motivational approach. *Journal of Vocational Behavior, 62,* 134–154.

Allen, T. D. (2004). Protégé selection by mentors: Contributing individual and organizational factors. *Journal of Vocational Behavior, 65,* 469–483.

Allen, T. D. (2007), Mentoring relationships: From the perspective of the mentor. In B. R. Ragins & K. E. Kram, K. E. (Eds.), *The handbook of mentoring at work* (pp. 123–147). Thousand Oaks, CA: Sage.

Allen, T. D., & Eby, L. T. (2003). Relationship effectiveness for mentors: Factors associated with learning and quality. *Journal of Management, 29,* 469–486.

Allen, T. D., Eby, L. T., Poteet, M. L., Lentz, E., & Lima, L. (2004). Career benefits associated with mentoring for proteges: A meta-analysis. *Journal of Applied Psychology, 89,* 127–136.

Allen, T. D., Lentz, E., & Day, R. (2006). Career success outcomes associated with mentoring others: A comparison of mentors and nonmentors. *Journal of Career Development, 32,* 272–285.

Allen, T. D., & Poteet, M. L. (1999), Developing effective mentoring relationships: Strategies from the mentor's viewpoint. *The Career Development Quarterly, 48,* 59–73.

Allen, T. D., Poteet, M. L., & Burroughs, S. (1997). The mentor's perspective: A qualitative inquiry and agenda for future research. *Journal of Vocational Behavior, 51,* 70–89.

Allen, T. D., Poteet, M. L., & Russell, J. E. A. (2000). Protégé selection by mentors: What makes the difference? *Journal of Organizational Behavior, 21,* 271–282.

Allen, T. D., Poteet, M. L., Russell, J. E. A., & Dobbins, G. H. (1997). A field study of factors related to willingness to mentor others. *Journal of Vocational Behavior, 50,* 1–22.

Anderson, J. C., & Moore, L. F. (1978). The motivation to volunteer. *Nonprofit and Voluntary Sector Quarterly, 7*(3), 120–129.

Andreoni, J. (1989). Giving with impure altruism: Applications to charity and ricardian equivalence. *Journal of Political Economy, 97,* 1447–1458.

Apostolou, M. (2011). Why men collect things? A case study of fossilised dinosaur eggs. *Journal of Economic Psychology, 32* (3), 410–417.

Apter-Levi, Y., Zagoory-Sharon, O., & Feldman, R. (2014). Oxytocin and vasopressin support distinct configurations of social synchrony. *Brain research, 1580,* 124–132.

Armstrong, D. (2000). A survey of community gardens in upstate New York: Implications for health promotion and community development. *Health and Place, 6* (4), 319–327.

Aron, A., Norman, C. C., Aron, E. N., McKenna, C., & Heyman, R. E. (2000). Couples' shared participation in novel and arousing activities and experienced relationship quality. *Journal of Personality and Social Psychology, 78*(2), 273–284.

Aryee, S., Chay, Y. W., & Chew, J. (1996). The motivation to mentor among managerial employees. *Group & Organization Management, 21,* 261–277.

Ashlag, Y., with commentary by Laitman, M. (2005). *Introduction to the book of Zohar.* Toronto, Ontario, Canada: Laitman Kabbalah Publishers.

Assor, A., Kaplan, H., & Roth, G. (2002). Choice is good, but relevance is excellent: Autonomy-enhancing and suppressing teacher behaviours predicting students' engagement in schoolwork. *British Journal of Educational Psychology, 72*(2), 261–278.

Atkins, R., Hart, D., & Donnelly, T. M. (2005). The association of childhood personality type with volunteering during adolescence. *Merrill-Palmer Quarterly, 51*(2), 145–162.

Atkinson, J. (2009). *An evaluation of the Gardening Leave project for ex-military personnel with PTSD and other combat related mental health problems.* Retrieved from http://www.gardeningleave. org/wp-content/uploads/2009/06/completeglsummary.pdf

Auyeung, B., Baron-Cohen, S., Ashwin, E., Knickmeyer, R., Taylor, K., Hackett, G., & Hines, M. (2009). Fetal testosterone predicts sexually differentiated childhood behavior in girls and in boys. *Psychological Science, 20*(2), 144–148.

Axelrod, R., & Hamilton, W. D. (1981). The evolution of cooperation. *Science, 211*(4489), 1390–1396.

Badinter, E. (1981). *Mother love: Myth and reality: Motherhood in modern history.* New York, NY: Macmillan.

Bagwell, C. L., & Schmidt, M. E. (2013). *Friendships in childhood and adolescence.* New York, NY: Guilford Press.

Bakan, D. (1966). *The duality of human existence: An essay on psychology and religion.* Chicago, IL: Rand McNally.

Baker, J. A., Grant, S., & Morlock, L. (2008). The teacher-student relationship as a developmental context for children with internalizing or externalizing behavior problems. *School Psychology Quarterly, 23*(1), 3–15.

Bakermans-Kranenburg, M. J., & van IJzendoorn, M. H. (2008). Oxytocin receptor (OXTR) and serotonin transporter (5-HTT) genes associated with observed parenting. *Social Cognitive and Affective Neuroscience, 3,*128–134.

Balliet, D., Li, N. P., Macfarlan, S. J., & Van Vugt, M. (2011). Sex differences in cooperation: a meta-analytic review of social dilemmas. *Psychological Bulletin, 137*(6), 881–909.

Barber, B. K., Xia, M., Olsen, J. A., McNeely, C. A., & Bose, K. (2012). Feeling disrespected by parents: Refining the measurement and understanding of psychological control. *Journal of Adolescence, 35*(2), 273–287.

Bar-David, G. (1999). Three phase development of caring capacity in primary caregivers for relatives with Alzheimer's disease. *Journal of Aging Studies, 13,* 177–197.

Barker, S. B., Rogers, C. S., Turner, J. W., Karpf, A. S., & Suthers-McCabe, H. M. (2003). Benefits of interacting with companion animals: A bibliography of articles published in refereed journals during the past 5 years. *American Behavioral Scientist, 47*(1), 94–99.

Baron, L. (1992). The Dutchness of Dutch rescuers: The national dimension of altruism. In P. M. Oliner et al. (Eds.), *Embracing the other: Philosophical, psychological, and historical perspectives on altruism* (pp. 317–322). New York, NY: New York University Press.

Barraza, J. A., & Zak, P. J. (2009). Empathy toward strangers triggers oxytocin release and subsequent generosity. *Annals of the New York Academy of Sciences, 1167*(1), 182–189.

Bartal, I. B. A., Decety, J., & Mason, P. (2011). Empathy and pro-social behavior in rats. *Science, 334*(6061), 1427–1430.

Bar-Tur, L., Savaya, R., & Prager, E. (2001). Sources of meaning in life for young and old Israeli Jews and Arabs. *Journal of Aging Studies, 15*(3), 253–269.

Bartz, J. A., Zaki, J., Bolger, N., & Ochsner, K. N. (2011). Social effects of oxytocin in humans: Context and person matter. *Trends in Cognitive Sciences, 15*(7), 301–309.

Bass, B. M. (1985). *Leadership and performance beyond expectations.* New York, NY: Free Press.

Batson, C. D. (1989). Personal values, moral principles, and a three-path model of prosocial motivation. In N. Eisenberg et al. (Eds.), *Social and moral values: Individual and societal perspectives* (pp. 213–228). Hillsdale, NJ: Erlbaum.

Batson, C. D. (1990). How social an animal? The human capacity for caring. *American Psychologist, 45,* 336–346.

Batson, C. D. (1991). *The altruism question: Toward a social–psychological answer.* Hillsdale, NJ: Erlbaum.

Batson, C. D. (2010). Empathy-induced altruistic motivation. In M. Mikulincer & P. R. Shaver (Eds.), *Prosocial motives, emotions, and behavior: The better angels of our nature* (pp. 15–34). Washington, DC: American Psychological Association.

Batson, C. D., Duncan, B. D., Ackerman, P., Buckley, T., & Birch, K. (1981). Is empathic emotion a source of altruistic motivation? *Journal of Personality and Social Psychology, 40,* 290–302.

Batson, C. D., Dyck, J. L., Brandt, J. R., Batson, J. G., Powell, A. L., McMaster, M. R., & Griffitt, C. (1988). Five studies testing two new egoistic alternatives to the empathy–altruism hypothesis. *Journal of Personality and Social Psychology, 55,* 52–77.

Batson, C. D., Fultz, J., Schoenrade, P. A., & Paduano, A. (1987). Critical self-reflection and self-perceived altruism: when self-reward fails. *Journal of personality and social psychology, 53*(3), 594–602.

Batson, C. D., & Shaw, L. L. (1991). Evidence for altruism: Toward a pluralism of prosocial motives. *Psychological Inquiry, 2,* 107–122.

Baumann, D. J., Cialdini, R. B., & Kenrick, D. T. (1981). Altruism as hedonism: Helping and self-gratification as equivalent responses. *Journal of Personality and Social Psychology, 40,* 1039–1046.

Baumeister, R. F. (1991). *Meanings of life.* New York, NY: Guilford Press.

Baumeister, R. F., Campbell, J. D., Krueger, J. I., & Vohs, K. D. (2003). Does high self-esteem cause better performance, interpersonal success, happiness, or healthier lifestyles? *Psychological Science in the Public Interest, 4*(1), 1–44.

Baumeister, R. F., & Leary, M. R. (1995). The need to belong: Desire for interpersonal attachments as a fundamental human motivation. *Psychological Bulletin, 117*, 497–529.

Baumeister, R. F., & Sommer, K. L. (1997). What do men want? Gender differences and two spheres of belongingness: Comment on Cross and Madson (1997). *Psychological Bulletin, 122*, 38–44

Baumeister, R. F., Vohs, K. D., Aaker, J. L., & Garbinsky, E. N. (2013) Some key differences between a happy life and a meaningful life. *The Journal of Positive Psychology, 8*(6), 505–516.

Baumgartner, T., Heinrichs, M., Vonlanthen, A., Fischbacher, U., & Fehr, E. (2008). Oxytocin shapes the neural circuitry of trust and trust adaptation in humans. *Neuron, 58*(4), 639–650.

Baumrind, D. (1967). Child care practices anteceding three patterns of preschool behavior. *Genetic Psychology Monographs, 75*, 43–88.

Baumrind, D. (1971). Current patterns of parental authority. *Developmental Psychology Monographs, 4*(1), 1–103.

Beck, A., & Katcher, A. H. (1983). *Between pets and people: The importance of animal companionship.* New York, NY: Perigee Books.

Becker, S. W., & Eagly, A. H. (2004). The heroism of women and men. *American Psychologist, 59*, 163–178.

Bekkers, R., & Wiepking, P. (2007). *Generosity and philanthropy: A literature review.* Retrieved from http://ssrn.com/abstract=1015507

Bekkers, R., & Wiepking, P. (2011). A literature review of empirical studies of philanthropy: Eight mechanisms that drive charitable giving. *Nonprofit and Voluntary Sector Quarterly, 40*, 924–973.

Belk, R. W. (1995). *Collecting in a consumer society.* London, England: Routledge.

Belk, R. W., & Wallendorf, M. (1994). Of mice and men: gender identity in collecting. In S. M. Pearce (Ed.) *Interpreting objects and collections* (pp. 240–253). New York: NY: Routledge.

Belk, R. W., M. Wallendorf, M, Sherry, J. F. Jr., & Holbrook M. B. (1991). Collecting in consumer culture, In R. Belk (Ed.), *Highways and buyways: Naturalistic research from the consumer behavior odyssey* (pp. 178–215). Provo, UT: Association for Consumer Research.

Bell, D. C. (2001). Evolution of parental caregiving. *Personality and Social Psychology Review, 5*, 216–229.

Bell, D. C., & Richard, A. J. (2000a). Caregiving: The forgotten element in attachment. *Psychological Inquiry, 11*, 69–83.

Bell, D. C., & Richard, A. J. (2000b). The search for a caregiving motivation (authors' response). *Psychological Inquiry, 11*, 124–128.

Belle, D. (1987). Gender differences in the social moderators of stress. In R. C. Barnett, L. Biener, & G. K. Baruch (Eds.), *Gender and stress* (pp. 257–277). New York, NY: Free Press.

Belsky, J., Steinberg, L., & Draper, P. (1991). Childhood experience, interpersonal development, and reproductive strategy: An evolutionary theory of socialization. *Child Development, 62*, 647–670.

Benedek, T. (1970). Fatherhood and providing. In E. J. Anthony & T. Benedek (Eds.), *Parenthood: Its psychology and psychopathology* (pp. 167–184). Boston, MA: Little, Brown.

Benjamin, J. (1988). *The bonds of love: Psychoanalysis, feminism and the problem of domination.* New York, NY: Pantheon Books.

Benjamin, J. (1992). Recognition and destruction: An outline of intersubjectivity. In N. J. Skolnick & S. Warshaw (Eds.), *Relational perspectives in psychoanalysis* (pp. 43–60). Hillsdale, NJ: Analytic Press.

Benson, P. L., Roehlkepartain, E. C., & Rude, S. P. (2003). Spiritual development in childhood and adolescence: Toward a field of inquiry. *Applied Developmental Science, 7*, 205–213.

Benson, P. L., Scales, P. C., Syvertsen, A. K., & Roehlkepartain, E. C. (2012). Is youth spiritual development a universal developmental process? An international exploration. *The Journal of Positive Psychology, 7*(6), 453–470.

Benson, R. (1996). What's a nice guy like me doing in a place like this? A landscape architect and recovering alcoholic's thoughts on designing therapeutic landscapes. *Journal of Therapeutic Horticulture, 8,* 88–91.

Berenbaum, S. A., & Hines, M. (1992). Early androgens are related to childhood sex-typed toy preferences. *Psychological Science, 3*(3), 203–206.

Bergin, C., Talley, S., & Hamer, L. (2003). Prosocial behaviours of young adolescents: a focus group study. *Journal of Adolescence, 26*(1), 13–32.

Berman, P., & Goodman, V. (1984). Age and sex differences in children's responses to babies: Effects of adults' caretaking requests and instructions. *Child Development, 55,* 1071–1077.

Berndt, T. J. (1985). Prosocial behavior between friends in middle childhood and early adolescence. *The Journal of Early Adolescence, 5*(3), 307–317.

Berndt, T. J., & Hoyle, S. G. (1985). Stability and change in childhood and adolescent friendships. *Developmental Psychology, 21*(6), 1007–1015.

Berscheid, E., & Collins, W. A. (2000). Who cares? For whom and when, how, and why? *Psychological Inquiry, 11,* 107–109.

Bhatti, M., & Church, A. (2004). Home, the culture of nature and meanings of gardens in late modernity. *Housing Studies, 19*(1), 37–51.

Bhatti, M., Church, A., Claremont, A., & Stenner, P. (2009). "I love being in the garden": enchanting encounters in everyday life. *Social & Cultural Geography, 10*(1), 61–76.

Bick, J., Dozier, M., Bernard, K., Grasso, D., & Simons, R. (2013). Foster mother–infant bonding: Associations between foster mothers' oxytocin production, electrophysiological brain activity, feelings of commitment, and caregiving quality. *Child Development, 84,* 826–840.

Blais, M. R., Sabourin, S., Boucher, C., & Vallerand, R. J. (1990). Toward a motivational model of couple happiness. *Journal of Personality and Social Psychology, 59*(5), 1021–1031.

Blakemore, J. E. O., & Centers, R. E. (2005). Characteristics of boys' and girls' toys. *Sex Roles, 53*(9–10), 619–633.

Blatt, S. J. (2008). *Polarities of experience: Relatedness and self-definition in personality development, psychopathology, and the therapeutic process.* Washington, DC: American Psychological Association.

Block, G. and Drucker, M. (1992). *Rescuers: Portraits of moral courage in the Holocaust.* New York, NY: Holmes and Meier Publishers.

Bloom, D. E., & Trussell, J. (1984). What are the determinants of delayed childbearing and permanent childlessness in the United States? *Demography, 21*(4), 591–611.

Boehm, C. (1993). Egalitarian society and reverse dominance hierarchy. *Current Anthropology, 34,* 227–254.

Bolger, N., Zuckerman, A., & Kessler, R. C. (2000). Invisible support and adjustment to stress. *Journal of Personality and Social Psychology, 79*(6), 953–961.

Bolino, M. C., Klotz, A. C., Turnley, W. H., & Harvey, J. (2013). Exploring the dark side of organizational citizenship behavior. *Journal of Organizational Behavior, 34*(4), 542–559.

Bonas, S., McNicholas, J., & Collis, G. M. (2000). Pets in the network of family relationships: An empirical study. In A. L. Podberscek, E. S. Paul, J. A. Serpell (Eds.), *Companion animals and us: Exploring the relationships between people and pets* (pp. 209–236). New York, NY: Cambridge University Press.

Bonnie, K. E., & de Waal, F. B. (2006). Affiliation promotes the transmission of a social custom: Handclasp grooming among captive chimpanzees. *Primates, 47*(1), 27–34.

Borgonovi, F. (2008). Doing well by doing good: The relationship between formal volunteering and self-reported health and happiness. *Social Science and Medicine, 66,* 2321–2334.

Bornstein, M. H. (Ed.) (2002). *Handbook of parenting* (Vols. 1–5, 2nd ed.). Mahwah, NJ: Erlbaum.

Bowlby, J. (1980). *Attachment and loss: Vol. 3. Loss, sadness and depression.* New York, NY: Basic Books.

Bowlby, J. (1982). *Attachment and loss: Vol. 1. Attachment.* New York, NY: Basic Books. (Original work published 1969).

Bowlby, J. (1988). *A secure base. Clinical applications of attachment theory.* London, England: Routledge.

Bozionelos, N. (2004). Mentoring provided: Relation to mentor's career success, personality, and mentoring received. *Journal of Vocational Behavior,64*(1), 24–46.

Bradley, C. L., & Marcia, J. E. (1998). Generativity-stagnation: A five-category model. *Journal of Personality, 66*(1), 39–64.

Brase, G. L., & Brase, S. L. (2012). Emotional regulation of fertility decision making: What is the nature and structure of "baby fever"? *Emotion, 12*(5), 1141–1154.

Bretherton, I. (1984). *Symbolic play.* San Diego, CA: Academic Press.

Bretherton, I., Lambert, J. D., & Golby, B. (2006). Modeling and reworking childhood experiences: Involved fathers' representations of being parented and of parenting a preschool child. In O. Mayseless (Ed.), *Parenting representations: Theory, research, and clinical implications* (pp. 177–207). Cambridge, England: Cambridge University Press.

Bretherton, I., & Munholland, K. A. (2008). Internal working models in attachment relationships: Elaborating a central construct in attachment theory. In J. Cassidy & P. R. Shaver (Eds.), *Handbook of attachment: Theory, research, and clinical applications* (2nd ed., pp. 102–127). New York, NY: Guilford Press.

Brewer, M. B., & Caporael, L. R. (1990). Selfish genes versus selfish people: Sociobiology as origin myth. *Motivation and Emotion, 14,* 237–243.

Bringslimark, T., Hartig, T., & Patil, G. G. (2009). The psychological benefits of indoor plants: A critical review of the experimental literature. *Journal of Environmental Psychology, 29*(4), 422–433.

Bronfman, C., & Solomon, J. (2012). *The art of doing good: Where passion meets action.* San Francisco, CA: Jossey-Bass.

Brown, B. B. (1999). "You're going out with who?": Peer group influences on adolescent romantic relationships. In W. Furman, B. B. Brown, & C. Feiring (Eds.), *The development of romantic relationships in adolescence* (pp. 291–329). New York, NY: Cambridge University Press.

Brown, S. L., & Brown, R. M. (2006a). Selective investment theory: Recasting the functional significance of close relationships. *Psychological Inquiry, 17,* 1–29.

Brown R. M., & Brown, S. L. (2006b). AUTHORS' RESPONSE: SIT Stands and Delivers: A Reply to the Commentaries. *Psychological Inquiry, 17,* 60–74, DOI: 10.1207/s15327965pli1701_03

Brown, S. L., Brown, R. M., & Penner, L. A. (Eds.). (2012). *Moving beyond self-interest: Perspectives from evolutionary biology, neuroscience, and the social sciences.* New York, NY: Oxford University Press.

Brown, S. L., Brown, R. M., & Preston, S. (2012). The human caregiving system: A neuroscience model of compassionate motivation and behavior. In S. Brown, R. Brown, & L. Penner (Eds.), *Moving beyond self-interest: Perspectives from evolutionary biology, neuroscience, and the social sciences* (pp. 75–88). New York, NY: Oxford University Press.

Brown, S. L., Brown, R. M., Schiavone, A., & Smith, D. M. (2007). Close relationships and health through the lens of selective investment theory. In S. G. Post (Ed.), *Altruism and health: Perspectives from empirical research* (pp. 299–313). New York, NY: Oxford University Press.

Brownell, C. A. (2013). Early development of prosocial behavior: Current perspectives. *Infancy, 18*(1), 1–9.

Brownell, C. A., & Carriger, M. S. (1990). Changes in cooperation and self-other differentiation during the second year. *Child Development, 61*(4), 1164–1174.

Brownell, C. A., Iesue, S. S., Nichols, S. R., & Svetlova, M. (2013). Mine or yours? Development of sharing in toddlers in relation to ownership understanding. *Child Development, 84*(3), 906–920.

Brownell, C. A., Ramani, G. B., & Zerwas, S. (2006). Becoming a social partner with peers: cooperation and social understanding in one-and two-year-olds. *Child Development, 77*(4), 803–821.

Brownell, C. A., Svetlova, M., Anderson, R., Nichols, S. R., & Drummond, J. (2013). Socialization of early prosocial behavior: Parents' talk about emotions is associated with sharing and helping in toddlers. *Infancy, 18*(1), 91–119.

Brownell, C. A., Svetlova, M., & Nichols, S. (2009). To share or not to share: when do toddlers respond to another's needs? *Infancy, 14*(1), 117–130.

Bruyere, B., & Rappe, S. (2007). Identifying the motivations of environmental volunteers. *Journal of Environmental Planning and Management, 50*, 503–516.

Buchbinder, E. (2007). Being a social worker as an existential commitment: From vulnerability to meaningful purpose. *The Humanistic Psychologist, 35*(2), 161–174.

Burke, R. J., McKeen, C. A., & McKenna, C. (1993). Correlates of mentoring in organizations: The mentor's perspective. *Psychological Reports, 72*, 883–896

Burns, J. M. (1978). *Leadership*. New York, NY: Harper and Row.

Bussell, H., & Forbes, D. (2002). Understanding the volunteer market: the what, where, who and why of volunteering. *International Journal of Nonprofit and Voluntary Sector Marketing, 7*, 244–257.

Byrne, N. (2008). Differences in types and levels of altruism based on gender and program. *Journal of Allied Health, 37*(1), 22–29.

Cabrera, N., Tamis-LeMonda, C. S., Bradley, R. H., Hofferth, S., & Lamb, M. E. (2000). Fatherhood in the twenty-first century. *Child Development, 71*(1), 127–136.

Caldarella, P., Gomm, R. J., Shatzer, R. H., & Wall, D. G. (2010). School-based mentoring: A study of volunteer motivation and benefits. *International Electronic Journal of Elementary Education, 2*, 200–216.

Caldera, Y., & Sciaraffa, M. (1998). Parent-toddler interactions with feminine sex-typed toys. *Sex Roles, 39*, 657–668.

Callahan, D. (1985). What do children owe elderly parents? *Hastings Report, 15*(2), 32–37.

Callan, V. J., Kloskf, B., Kashima, Y., & Hennessey, J. F. (1988). Toward understanding women's decisions to continue or stop in vitro fertilization: The role of social, psychological, and background factors. *Journal of In Vitro Fertilization and Embryo Transfer, 5*(6), 363–369.

Campbell, A., Shirley, L., & Caygill, L. (2002). Sex-typed preferences in three domains: Do two-year-olds need cognitive variables?. *British Journal of Psychology, 93*(2), 203–217.

Campenni, C. E. (1999). Gender stereotyping of children's toys: A comparison of parents and nonparents. *Sex Roles, 40*(1–2), 121–138.

Canevello, A., & Crocker, J. (2010). Creating good relationships: responsiveness, relationship quality, and interpersonal goals. *Journal of Personality and Social Psychology, 99*(1), 78–106.

Caplan, M. Z., & Hay, D. F. (1989). Preschoolers' responses to peers' distress and beliefs about bystander intervention. *Journal of Child Psychology and Psychiatry, 30*, 231–243.

Caporael, L. R. (1997). The evolution of truly social cognition: The core configurations model. *Personality and Social Psychology Review, 1*(4), 276–298.

Caprara, G. V., & Steca, P. (2007). Prosocial agency: The contribution of values and self-efficacy beliefs to prosocial behavior across ages. *Journal of Social and Clinical Psychology, 26*, 218–239.

Carlo, G., Eisenberg, N., Troyer, D., Switzer, G., & Speer, A. L. (1991). The altruistic personality: In what contexts is it apparent? *Journal of Personality and Social Psychology, 61*, 450–458.

Carlson, R. W., Aknin, L. B., & Liotti, M. (2015). When is giving an impulse? An ERP investigation of intuitive prosocial behavior. *Social Cognitive and Affective Neuroscience.* Advance online publication. doi: 10.1093/scan/nsv077.

Carnelley, K. B., Pietromonaco, P. R., & Jaffe, K. (1996). Attachment, caregiving, and relationship functioning in couples: Effects of self and partner. *Personal Relationships, 3,* 257–278.

Carr, L., Iacoboni, M., Dubeau, M. C., Mazziotta, J. C., Lenzi, G. L. (2003). Neural mechanisms of empathy in humans: A relay from neural systems for imitation to limbic areas. *Proceedings of the National Academy of Sciences of the U.S.A., 100,* 5497–5502.

Carter, C. S. (1998). Neuroendocrine perspectives on social attachment and love. *Psychoneuroendocrinology, 23,* 779–818.

Carter, C. S. (2007). Neuropeptides and the protective effects of social bonds. In E. Harmon-Jones & P. Winkielman (Eds.), *Social neuroscience: Integrating biological and psychological explanations of social behavior* (pp. 425–438). New York, NY: Guilford Press.

Carter, C. S., Ahnert, L., Grossmann, K. E., Hrdy, S. B., Lamb, M. E., Porges, S. W., & Sachser, N. (Eds.) (2005). *Attachment and bonding: A new synthesis.* Cambridge, MA: MIT Press.

Caspersen, C. J., Bloemberg, B. P., Saris, W. H., Merritt, R. K., & Kromhout, D. (1991). The prevalence of selected physical activities and their relation with coronary heart disease risk factors in elderly men: The Zutphen Study, 1985. *American Journal of Epidemiology, 133*(11), 1078–1092.

Cassidy, J. (2008). The nature of the child's ties. In J. Cassidy & P. R. Shaver (Eds.), *Handbook of attachment: Theory, research, and clinical applications* (pp. 3–22). New York, NY: Guilford Press.

Cassidy, J., & Shaver, P. R. (Eds.), (2008). *Handbook of attachment: Theory, research, and clinical applications* (2nd ed.). New York, NY: Guilford Press

Catanzaro, C., & Ekanem, E. (2004). Home gardeners value stress reduction and interaction with nature. *Acta Horticulturae, 639,* 269–275

Chachamovich, J. R., Chachamovich, E., Ezer, H., Fleck, M. P., Knauth, D., & Passos, E. P. (2010). Investigating quality of life and health-related quality of life in infertility: a systematic review. *Journal of Psychosomatic Obstetrics & Gynecology, 31*(2), 101–110.

Charities Aid Foundation. (2013).*World giving index 2013: A global view of giving trends.* Retrieved from https://www.cafonline.org/PDF/WorldGivingIndex2013_1374AWEB.pdf

Charnetsky, C. J., Riggers, S., & Brennan, F. (2004). Effect of petting a dog on immune system functioning. *Psychological Reports, 3*(2), 1087–1091.

Charnov, E. L. (2003). Cohort-size/body-size scaling rules for stationary populations. *Evolutionary ecology research, 5*(7), 1111–1112.

Chase, N. D. (Ed.). (1999). *Burdened children: Theory, research, and treatment of parentification.* Thousand Oaks, CA: Sage.

Chisholm, J. S. (1996). The evolutionary ecology of attachment organization. *Human Nature, 7*(1), 1–37.

Chodorow, N. J. (1999). *The reproduction of mothering: Psychoanalysis and the sociology of gender.* Berkeley and Los Angeles, CA: University of California Press. (Original work published 1978.)

Cialdini, R. B., Schaller, M., Houlihan, D., Arps, K., Fultz, J., & Beaman, A. L. (1987). Empathy-based helping: Is it selflessly or selfishly motivated? *Journal of Personality and Social Psychology, 52,* 749–758.

Cicirelli, V. G. (1993). Attachment and obligation as daughters' motives for caregiving behavior and subsequent effect on subjective burden. *Psychology and Aging, 8,* 144–155.

Clarke, A., Mitchell, A., & Abraham, C. (2014). Understanding donation experiences of unspecified (altruistic) kidney donors. *British Journal of Health Psychology, 19*(2), 393–408.

Clary, E. G., & Miller, J. (1986). Socialization and situational influences on sustained altruism. *Child Development, 57,* 1358–1369.

Clary, E. G., & Orenstein, L. (1991). The amount and effectiveness of help: The relationship of motives and abilities to helping behavior. *Personality and Social Psychology Bulletin, 17*(1), 58–64.

Clary, E. G., & Snyder, M. (1999). The motivations to volunteer. *Current Directions in Psychological Science, 8,* 156–159.

Clary, E. G., Snyder, M., Ridge, R. D., Copeland, J., Stukas, A. A., Haugen, J., & Miene, P. (1998). Understanding and assessing the motivations of volunteers: A functional approach. *Journal of Personality and Social Psychology, 74*, 1516–1530.

Clayton, S. (2007). Domesticated nature: Motivations for gardening and perceptions of environmental impact. *Journal of Environmental Psychology, 27*, 215–224.

Clutton-Brock, T. H. (1991). *The evolution of parental care.* Princeton, NJ: Princeton University Press.

Clutton-Brock, T. H., & Godfray, C. (1991). Parental investment. In J. R. Krebs & N. B. Davies (Eds.), *Behavioural ecology: An evolutionary approach* (3rd ed., pp. 234–262). Oxford, England: Blackwell Scientific.

Colby, A., & Damon, W. (1992). *Some do care: Contemporary lives of moral commitment.* New York, NY: Free Press.

Cole, E. R., & Stewart, A. J. (1996). Meanings of political participation among Black and White women: Political identity and social responsibility. *Journal of Personality and Social Psychology, 71*(1), 130–140.

Collins, N. L., & Feeney, B. C. (2000). A safe haven: an attachment theory perspective on support seeking and caregiving in intimate relationships. *Journal of Personality and Social Psychology, 78*(6), 1053–1073.

Collins, N. L., & Ford, M. B. (2010). Responding to the needs of others: The caregiving behavioral system in intimate relationships. *Journal of Social and Personal Relationships, 27*(2), 235–244.

Collins, N. L., Ford, M. B., Guichard, A. C., Kane, H. S., & Feeney, B. C. (2010). Responding to need in intimate relationships: Social support and caregiving processes in couples. In M. Mikulincer & P. R. Shaver (Eds.), *Prosocial motives, emotions, and behavior* (pp. 367–389). Washington, DC: American Psychological Association.

Collins, N. L., Guichard, A. C., Ford, M. B., & Feeney, B. C. (2006). Responding to need in intimate relationships: Normative processes and individual differences. In M. Mikulincer & G. S. Goodman (Eds.), *Dynamics of romantic love: Attachment, caregiving, and sex* (pp. 149–189). New York, NY: Guilford Press.

Collins, W. A., Welsh, D. P., & Furman, W. (2009). Adolescent romantic relationships. *Annual Review of Psychology, 60*, 631–652.

Compton, W. C., Smith, M. L., Cornish, K. A., & Qualls, D. L. (1996). Factor structure of mental health measures. *Journal of Personality and Social Psychology, 71*, 406–413.

Connolly, J., & McIsaac, C. (2011). Romantic relationships in adolescence. In M. K. Underwood & L. H. Rosen (Eds.), *Social development: Relationships in infancy, childhood, and adolescence* (pp. 180–206.) New York, NY: Guilford Press.

Cooper, D. E. (2006). *The philosophy of gardens.* Oxford, England: Oxford University Press.

Cornille, T., Rohrer, G., Phillips, S., & Mosier, J. (1987). Horticultural therapy in substance abuse treatment. *Journal of Therapeutic Horticulture, 2*, 3–8.

Corter, C. M., & Fleming, A. S. (1995). Psychobiology of maternal behavior in human beings. In M. H. Bornstein (Ed.), *Handbook of parenting: Vol. 2. Biology and ecology of parenting* (pp. 87–116). Mahwah, NJ: Erlbaum.

Crittenden, P. M. (2006). Why do inadequate parents do what they do? In O. Mayseless (Ed.), *Parenting representations: Theory, research, and clinical implications.* New York, NY: Cambridge University Press.

Crocker, J. (2011). Presidential address self-Image and compassionate goals and construction of the social self: Implications for social and personality psychology. *Personality and Social Psychology Review, 15*(4), 394–407.

Crocker, J., & Canevello, A. (2008). Creating and undermining social support in communal relationships: The role of compassionate and self-image goals. *Journal of Personality & Social Psychology, 95*, 555–575.

Crowell, J. A., Treboux, D., Gao, Y., Fyffe, C., Pan, H., & Waters, E. (2002). Secure base behavior in adulthood: Measurement, links to adult attachment representations, and relations to couples' communication and self reports. *Developmental Psychology, 38*, 679–693.

Da Vanzo, J., & Goldscheider, F. K. (1990). Coming home again: Returns to the parental home of young adults. *Population Studies, 44*(2), 241–255.

Dalton, G. W., Thompson, P. H., & Price, R. L. (1977). The four stages of professional careers—A new look at performance by professionals. *Organizational Dynamics,6*, 19–42.

Daly, M., & Wilson, M. (1983). *Sex, evolution, and behavior* (2nd ed.). Boston, MA: Willard Grant Press.

Daly, M., & Wilson, M. I. (1982). Whom are newborn babies said to resemble?.*Ethology and Sociobiology, 3*(2), 69–78.

Danet, B., & Katriel, T. (1989). No two alike: Play and aesthetics in collecting. *Play and Culture, 2*, 253–277.

Danet, B., & Katriel, T. (1990). *Glorious obsessions, passionate lovers, and hidden treasures: collecting, metaphor, and the romantic ethic.* Paper presented at the International Conference on the Socio-Semiotics of Objects: The Role of Artifacts in Social Symbolic Processes, Toronto, Alberta, Canada, June.

Dannefer, D., 1980. Rationality and passion in private experience: Modern consciousness and the social world of old-car collectors. *Social Problems, 27*, 392–412.

Darling, N. Hamilton, S., Toyokawa, T., & Matsuda, S. (2002). Naturally occurring mentoring in Japan and the United States: Social roles and correlates. *American Journal of Community Psychology, 30*, 245–270.

Darwin, C. (1870). *The origin of species.* New York, NY: D. Appleton &Company.

Davidov, M., Zahn-Waxler, C., Roth-Hanania, R., & Knafo, A. (2013). Concern for others in the first year of life: Theory, evidence, and avenues for research. *Child Development Perspectives, 7*(2), 126–131.

Dawkins, R. (2006). *The selfish gene* (30th anniversary ed.). New York, NY: Oxford University Press. (Original work published 1976.)

De Anda, D. (2001). A qualitative evaluation of a mentor program for at-risk youth: The participants' perspective. *Child and Adolescent Social Work Journal, 18*(2), 97–117.

de Beauvoir, S. (1973). *The second sex* (H. M. Parshley, Trans.). Harmondsworth, England: Penguin Books. (Original work published 1949.)

De Cremer, D., Snyder, M., & De Witte, S. (2001). The less I trust the less I contribute (or not)? *European Journal of Social Psychology, 31*, 93–107.

de St. Aubin, E., & McAdams, D. P. (1995). The relations of generative concern and generative action to personality traits, satisfaction/happiness with life, and ego development. *Journal of Adult Development, 2*, 99–112.

De Vignemont, F., & Singer, T. (2006). The empathic brain: how, when and why? *Trends in Cognitive Sciences, 10*(10), 435–441.

de Waal, F. B. M. (2008). Putting the altruism back into altruism: The evolution of empathy. *Annual Review of Psychology, 59*, 279–300.

de Waal, F. B. M. (2009). *The age of empathy: Nature's lessons for a kinder society.* New York, NY: Three Rivers Press/Random House.

de Waal, F. B. M. (2012). The antiquity of empathy. *Science, 336*(6083), 874–876.

Decety, J. (2010). The neurodevelopment of empathy in humans. *Developmental Neuroscience, 32*(4), 257–267.

Decety, J. (2012). Neuroscience of empathic responding. In S. L. Brown, R. M. Brown & L. A. Penner (Eds.), *Moving beyond self interest: Perspectives from evolutionary biology, neuroscience, and the social sciences* (pp. 109–132). New York, NY: Oxford University Press.

Decety, J., & Jackson, P. L. (2004). The functional architecture of human empathy. *Behavioral and Cognitive Neuroscience Reviews, 3*(2), 71–100.

Decety, J., & Jackson, P. L. (2006). A social-neuroscience perspective on empathy. *Current Directions in Psychological Science, 15*(2), 54–58.

Decety, J., & Michalska, K. J. (2010). Neurodevelopmental changes in the circuits underlying empathy and sympathy from childhood to adulthood. *Developmental Science, 13*(6), 886–899.

Decety, J., Norman, G. J., Berntson, G. G., & Cacioppo, J. T. (2012). A neurobehavioral evolutionary perspective on the mechanisms underlying empathy. *Progress in Neurobiology, 98*(1), 38–48.

Decety, J., Yang, C.-Y., Cheng, Y. (2010). Physicians down-regulate their pain empathy response: An event-related brain potential study. *NeuroImage, 50*, 1676–1682.

Deci, E. L., La Guardia, J. G., Moller, A. C., Scheiner, M. C., & Ryan, R. M. (2006). On the benefits of giving as well as receiving autonomy support: Mutuality in close friendships. *Personality and Social Psychology Bulletin, 32*, 313–327.

Deci, E. L., & Ryan, R. M. (2000). The "what" and "why" of goal pursuits: Human needs and the self-determination of behavior. *Psychological Inquiry, 11*, 227–268.

Demetriou, H., Hay, D. F. (2004). Toddlers' reactions to the distress of familiar peers: The importance of context. *Infancy, 6*, 299–319.

Den Hartog, D. N., House, R. J., Hanges, P. J., Ruiz-Quintanilla, S. A., & Dorfman, P. W. (1999). Culture specific and cross-culturally generalizable implicit leadership theories: Are attributes of charismatic/transformational leadership universally endorsed? *The Leadership Quarterly, 10*(2), 219–256.

Devine, P. (1995). Prejudice and out-group perception. In A. Tesser (Ed.), *Advanced social psychology* (pp. 466–524). New York, NY: McGraw-Hill.

Diamond, M. J. (1986). Becoming a father: A psychoanalytic perspective on the forgotten parent. *The Psychoanalytic Review, 73*(4), 445–468.

Diamond, M. J. (1998). Fathers with sons: Psychoanalytic perspectives on "good enough" fathering throughout the life cycle. *Gender and Psychoanalysis, 3*, 243–300.

DiCaccavo, A. (2002). Investigating individuals' motivations to become counselling psychologists: The influence of early caretaking roles within the family. *Psychology and Psychotherapy: Theory, research and practice, 75*(4), 463–472.

Dickerson, S., & Zoccola, P. (2009). Towards a biology of social support. In S. Lopez & C. R. Snyder (Eds.), *Oxford handbook of positive psychology* (2nd ed., pp. 519–526). New York, NY: Oxford University Press.

Dietze, B., & Kashin, D. (2011). *Playing and learning in early childhood education.* Toronto, Alberta, Canada: Pearson Education.

DiMaggio, P., 1987. Classification in art. *American Sociological Review, 52*, 440–455.

Dirks, K. T., & Ferrin, D. L. (2002). Trust in leadership: meta-analytic findings and implications for research and practice. *Journal of Applied Psychology, 87*(4), 611–628.

Ditzen, B., Schaer, M., Gabriel, B., Bodenmann, G., Ehlert, U., & Heinrichs, M. (2009). Intranasal oxytocin increases positive communication and reduces cortisol levels during couple conflict. *Biological Psychiatry, 65*(9), 728–731.

Donath, J. (2004). Artificial pets: Simple behaviors elicit complex attachments. In M. Bekoff (Ed.), *The encyclopedia of animal behaviour* (Vol. 3, pp. 955–957). Westport, CT: Greenwood Press.

Dovidio, J. F. (1984). Helping behavior and altruism: An empirical and conceptual overview. In L. Berkowitz (Ed.), *Advances in experimental social psychology* (Vol. 17, pp. 361–427). New York, NY: Academic Press.

Dovidio, J. F., & Penner, L. A. (2001). Helping and altruism. In G. Fletcher & M. S. Clark (Eds.), *Blackwell handbook of social psychology: Interpersonal processes* (pp. 162–195). Oxford, England: Blackwell.

Dovidio, J. F., Piliavin, J. A., Schroeder, D. A., & Penner, L. (2006). *The social psychology of prosocial behaviour.* Mahwah, NJ: Erlbaum.

DuBois, D. L., Holloway, B. E., Valentine, J. C., & Cooper, H. (2002). Effectiveness of mentoring programs for youth: A meta-analytic review. *American Journal of Community Psychology, 30,* 157–197.

DuBois, D. L., & Karcher, M. J. (2005). Youth mentoring: Theory, research, and practice. In D. L. DuBois & M. J. Karcher (Eds.), *Handbook of youth mentoring* (pp. 2–11). Thousand Oaks, CA: Sage.

DuBois, D. L., & Silverthorn, N. (2005). Natural mentoring relationships and adolescent health: Evidence from a national study. *American Journal of Public Health, 95,* 518–524.

Duckenfield, M., & Swanson, L. (1992). *Service learning: Meeting the needs of youth at risk.* A drop-out prevention research report. Retrieved http://files.eric.ed.gov/fulltext/ED348622.pdf

Dugatkin, L. (2006). *The altruism equation: Seven scientists search for the origin of goodness.* Princeton, NJ: Princeton University Press.

Dumont, C., & Paquette, D. (2013). What about the child's tie to the father? A new insight into fathering, father–child attachment, children's socio-emotional development and the activation relationship theory. *Early Child Development and Care, 183*(3–4), 430–446.

Dunbar, R. (1996). Determinants of group size in primates: A general model. In J. Maynard Smith, G. Runciman, & R. Dunbar (Eds.), *Evolution of culture and language in primates and humans* (pp. 33–57). Oxford, England: Oxford University Press

Dunfield, K. A., & Kuhlmeier, V. A. (2010). Intention-mediated selective helping in infancy. *Psychological Science, 21*(4), 523–527.

Dunfield, K. A., Kuhlmeier, V. A., O'Connell, L., & Kelley, E. (2011). Examining the diversity of prosocial behavior: Helping, sharing, and comforting in infancy. *Infancy, 16*(3), 227–247.

Dunn, E. W., Aknin, L. B., & Norton, M. I. (2008). Spending money on others promotes happiness. *Science, 319*(5870), 1687–1688.

Dunn, E. W., Aknin, L. B., & Norton, M. I. (2014). Prosocial spending and happiness using money to benefit others pays off. *Current Directions in Psychological Science, 23*(1), 41–47.

Dunn, J. (1981). The reaction of first-born children to the birth of a sibling: Mothers' reports. *Journal of Child Psychology and Psychiatry and Allied Disciplines, 22,* 1–18.

Dunnett, N., & Qasim, M. (2000). Perceived benefits to human well-being of urban gardens. *HortTechnology, 10*(1), 40–45.

Durlak, J. A., Weissberg, R. P., Dymnicki, A. B., Taylor, R. D., & Schellinger, K. B. (2011). The impact of enhancing students' social and emotional learning: A meta-analysis of school-based universal interventions. *Child Development, 82*(1), 405–432.

Dwyer, J. W., & Coward, R. T. (1991). A multivariate comparison of the involvement of adult sons versus daughters in the care of impaired parents. *Journals of Gerontology, 46,* 259–269.

Eagly, A. H. (2009). The his and hers of prosocial behavior: an examination of the social psychology of gender. *American Psychologist, 64*(8), 644–663.

Eagly, A. H., & Crowley, M. (1986). Gender and helping behavior: A meta-analytic review of the social psychological literature. *Psychological Bulletin, 100,* 283–308.

Ebersole, P. (1998). Types and depth of written life meanings. In P. T. P. Wong & P. S. Fry (Eds.), *The human quest for meaning: A handbook of research and clinical applications* (pp. 179–191). Mahwah, NJ: Erlbaum.

Ebstein, R. P., Israel, S., Chew, S. H., Zhong, S., Knafo, A. (2010). Genetics of human social behavior. *Neuron, 65,* 831–844.

Eby, L. T., & Lockwood, A. (2005). Protégés' and mentors' reactions to participating in formal mentoring programs: A qualitative investigation. *Journal of Vocational Behavior, 67*(3), 441–458

Eddy, L. T., Tannenbaum, S., Alliger, G., D'Abate, C., & Givens, S. (2001). *Mentoring in industry: The top 10 issues when building and supporting a mentoring program.* Technical report prepared for the Naval Air Warfare Center Training Systems Division (Contract No. N61339-99-D-0012).

Edwards, C. P. (1993). Behavioral sex differences in children of diverse cultures: The case of nurturance to infants. In M. E. Pereira, & L. A. Fairbanks (Eds.), *Juvenile primates: Life history, development, and behavior* (pp. 327–338). New York, NY: Oxford University Press.

Ehrich, L., C., Hansford, B., & Tennent, L. (2004). Formal mentoring programs in education and other professions: A review of the literature. *Educational Administration Quarterly, 40*, 518–540.

Eibl-Eibesfeldt, I. (1989). *Human ethology.* New York, NY: Aldine de Gruyter.

Ein-Dor, T., Mikulincer, M., Doron, G., & Shaver, P. R. (2010). The attachment paradox: How can so many of us (the insecure ones) have no adaptive advantages?. *Perspectives on Psychological Science, 5*(2), 123–141.

Eisenberg, N. (2010). Empathy-related responding: Links with self-regulation, moral judgment, and moral behavior. In M. Mikulincer & P. R. Shaver (Eds.), *Prosocial motives, emotions, and behavior: The better angels of our nature* (pp. 129–148). Washington, DC: American Psychological Association.

Eisenberg, N., & Fabes, R. A. (1998). Prosocial development. In W. Damon (Series Ed.) & N. Eisenberg (Vol. Ed.), *Handbook of child psychology:Vol. 3. Social, emotional, and personality development* (5th ed., pp. 701–778). Hoboken, NJ: Wiley.

Eisenberg, N., Fabes, R. A., Guthrie, I. K., & Reiser, M. (2000). Dispositional emotionality and regulation: their role in predicting quality of social functioning. *Journal of personality and social psychology, 78*(1), 136–157.

Eisenberg, N., Fabes, R. A., Murphy, B., Karbon, M., Maszk, P., Smith, M., . . . & Suh, K. (1994). The relations of emotionality and regulation to dispositional and situational empathy-related responding. *Journal of Personality and Social Psychology, 66*(4), 776–797.

Eisenberg, N., Fabes, R. A., Murphy, B., Karbon, M., Smith, M., & Maszk, P. (1996). The relations of children's dispositional empathy-related responding to their emotionality, regulation, and social functioning. *Developmental Psychology, 32*(2), 195–209.

Eisenberg, N., Fabes, R. A., Murphy, B., Maszk, P., Smith, M., & Karbon, M. (1995). The role of emotionality and regulation in children's social functioning: A longitudinal study. *Child Development, 66*(5), 1360–1384.

Eisenberg, N., Fabes, R., & Spinrad, T. L. (2006). Prosocial development. In N. Eisenberg & W. Damon (Eds.), *Handbook of child psychology: Vol. 3. Social, emotional, and personality development* (6th ed., pp. 646–718). Hoboken, NJ: Wiley.

Eisenberg, N., Guthrie, I. K., Cumberland, A., Murphy, B. C., Shepard, S. A., Zhou, Q., & Carlo, G. (2002). Prosocial development in early adulthood: A longitudinal study. *Journal of Personality and Social Psychology, 82*(6), 993.

Eisenberg, N., Guthrie, I. K., Murphy, B. C., Shepard, S. A., Cumberland, A., & Carlo, G. (1999). Consistency and development of prosocial dispositions: A longitudinal study. *Child Development, 70*, 1360–1372.

Eisenberg, N., Hofer, C., Sulik, M. J., & Liew, J. (2013). The development of prosocial moral reasoning and a prosocial orientation in young adulthood: Concurrent and longitudinal correlates. *Developmetal Psychology, 50*, 58–70.

Eisenberg, N., & Lennon, R. (1983). Sex differences in empathy and related capacities. *Psychological Bulletin, 94*(1), 100–131.

Eisenberg, N., Spinrad, T. L., & Knafo, A. (2015). Prosocial development. In M. E. Lamb (Volume Ed.) & R. M. Lerner (Series Ed.), *Handbook of child psychology and developmental science: Vol. 3. Social emotional and personality development* (7th ed., pp. 610–656). Hoboken, NJ: Wiley.

Eisenberg, N., Spinrad, T. L., & Sadovsky, A. (2006). Empathy-related responding in children. In M. Killen & J. G. Smetana (Eds.), *Handbook of moral development* (pp. 517–549). Mahwah, NJ: Erlbaum

Eisenberg, N., & Valiente, C. (2002). Parenting and children's prosocial and moral development. In M. H. Bornstein (Ed.), *Handbook of parenting: Vol. 5. Practical issues in parenting* (2nd ed., pp. 111–142). Mahwah, NJ: Erlbaum.

Eisler, R., & Levine, D. S. (2002). Nurture, nature, and caring: We are not prisoners of our genes. *Brain and Mind, 3*(1), 9–52.

Elings, M. (2006). People-plant interaction: The physiological, psychological and sociological effects of plants on people. In J. Hassink & M. van Dijk (Eds.), *Farming for health: Green-care farming across Europe and the United States of America* (pp. 43–55). Dordrecht, the Netherlands: Springer.

Elliott, G., Kao, S., & Grant, A. M. (2004). Mattering: Empirical validation of a social-psychological concept. *Self and Identity, 3*(4), 339–354.

Emmons, R. A. (1999). *The psychology of ultimate concerns: Motivation and spirituality in personality.* New York, NY: Guilford Press.

Emmons, R. A. (2005). Striving for the sacred: Personal goals, life meaning, and religion. *Journal of Social Issues, 61*, 731–745.

Ensher, E. A., & Murphy, S. E. (1997). Effects of race, gender, perceived similarity, and contact on mentor relationships. *Journal of Vocational Behavior, 50*(3), 460–481.

Epitropaki, O., & Martin, R. (2004). Implicit leadership theories in applied settings: factor structure, generalizability, and stability over time. *Journal of Applied Psychology, 89*(2), 293–310.

Erikson, E. H. (1963). *Childhood and Society* (2nd ed.). New York, NY: Norton.

Erikson, E. H. (1968). *Identity: Youth and crisis.* New York, NY: Norton

Evans, J. S. B. (2008). Dual-processing accounts of reasoning, judgment, and social cognition. *Annual Review of Psychology, 59*, 255–278.

Ewen, J. G., & Armstrong, D. P. (2000). Male provisioning is negatively correlated with attempted extrapair copulation frequency in the stitchbird (or hihi). *Animal Behaviour, 60*(4), 429–433.

Fabes, R. A., & Eisenberg, N. (1998). Meta-analyses of age and sex differences in children's and adolescents' prosocial behavior. Working paper, Arizona State University. Retrieved from www.public.asu.edu/~rafabes/meta.pdf.

Fagen, R. (1981). *Animal play behavior.* New York, NY: Oxford University Press.

Fagundes, C. P., & Schindler, I. (2012). Making of romantic attachment bonds: Longitudinal trajectories and implications for relationship stability. *Personal Relationships, 19*(4), 723–742.

Fairbairn, W. R. D. (1952). *Psychoanalytic studies of the personality.* London, England: Tavistock.

Fan, Y., Duncan, N. W., de Greck, M., & Northoff, G. (2011). Is there a core neural network in empathy? An fMRI based quantitative meta-analysis. *Neuroscience and Biobehavioral Reviews, 35*, 903–911.

Fan, Y., & Han, S. (2008). Temporal dynamic of neural mechanisms involved in empathy for pain: An event-related brain potential study. *Neuropsychologia, 46*, 160–173.

Farber, B. A., Lippert, R. A., Nevas, D. B. (1995). The therapist as attachment figure. *Psychotherapy: Theory, Research, Practice, Training, 32*(2), 204–212.

Farber, B. A., & Metzger, J. (2009). The therapist as secure base. In J. H. Obegi & E. Berant (Eds), *Attachment theory and research in clinical work with adults* (pp. 46–70). New York, NY: Guilford Press.

Farber, B. A., Manevich, I., Metzger, J., & Saypol, E. (2005). Choosing psychotherapy as a career: Why did we cross that road? *Journal of Clinical Psychology, 61*(8), 1009–1031.

Feingold, A. (1994). Gender differences in personality: a meta-analysis. *Psychological Bulletin, 116*, 429–456.

Feeney, B. C. (2004). A secure base: responsive support of goal strivings and exploration in adult intimate relationships. *Journal of Personality and Social Psychology, 87*(5), 631–648.

Feeney, B. C., & Collins, N. L. (2001). Predictors of caregiving in adult intimate relationships: An attachment theoretical perspective. *Journal of Personality and Social Psychology, 80*, 972–994.

Feeney, B. C., & Collins, N. L. (2003). Motivations for caregiving in adult intimate relationships: Influences on caregiving behavior and relationship functioning. *Personality and Social Psychology Bulletin, 29*, 950–968.

Feeney, B. C., & Collins, N. L. (2004). Interpersonal safe haven and secure base caregiving processes in adulthood. In J. Simpson & W. S. Rholes (Eds.), *Adult attachment: New directions and emerging issues* (pp. 300–338). New York, NY: Guilford Press.

Feeney, B. C., Collins, N. L., Van Vleet, M., & Tomlinson, J. M. (2013) Motivations for providing a secure base: links with attachment orientation and secure base support behavior. *Attachment & Human Development, 15*, 261–280.

Feeney, B. C., & Thrush, R. L. (2010). Relationship influences on exploration in adulthood: The characteristics and function of a secure base. *Journal of Personality and Social Psychology, 98*, 57–76.

Feeney, J. A. (1996). Attachment, caregiving, and marital satisfaction. *Personal Relationships, 3*, 401–416.

Fehr, E., Bernhard, H., & Rockenbach, B. (2008). Egalitarianism in young children. *Nature, 454*, 1079–1083.

Fehr, E., & Fischbacher, U. (2003). The nature of human altruism. *Nature, 425*, 785–791.

Fehr, E., & Rockenbach, B. (2004). Human altruism: Economic, neural, and evolutionary perspectives. *Current Opinion in Neurobiology, 14*(6), 784–790.

Fein, G. G. (1981). Pretend play in childhood: An integrative review. *Child Development, 52*, 1095–1118.

Feldman, R. (2012). Parent–infant synchrony: A biobehavioral model of mutual influences in the formation of affiliative bonds. *Monographs of the Society for Research in Child Development, 77*(2), 42–51.

Feldman, R., Gordon, I., Influs, M., Gutbir, T., & Ebstein, R. P. (2013). Parental oxytocin and early caregiving jointly shape children's oxytocin response and social reciprocity. *Neuropsychopharmacology, 38*(7), 1154–1162.

Feldman, R., Gordon, I., & Zagoory-Sharon, O. (2010). The cross-generation transmission of oxytocin in humans. *Hormones and Behavior, 58*, 669–676.

Feldman, R., Gordon, I., & Zagoory-Sharon, O. (2011). Maternal and paternal plasma, salivary, and urinary oxytocin and parent-infant synchrony: Considering stress and affiliation components of human bonding. *Developmental Science, 14*(4), 752–761.

Feldman, R., Weller, A., Zagoory-Sharon, O., & Levine, A. (2007). Evidence for a neuroendocrinological foundation of human affiliation: Plasma oxytocin levels across pregnancy and the postpartum period predict mother-infant bonding. *Psychological Science, 18*, 965–970.

Feldman, R., Zagoory-Sharon, O., Weisman, O., Schneiderman, I., Gordon, I., Maoz, R., . . . Ebstein, R. P. (2012). Sensitive parenting is associated with plasma oxytocin and polymorphisms in the OXTR and CD38 genes. *Biological Psychiatry, 72*, 175–181.

Ferguson, E., Atsma, F., de Kort, W., & Veldhuizen, I. (2012). Exploring the pattern of blood donor beliefs in first-time, novice, and experienced donors: Differentiating reluctant altruism, pure altruism, impure altruism, and warm glow. *Transfusion, 52*, 343–355.

Figley, C. R. (1995). Compassion fatigue as secondary stress disorder: An overview. In C. R. Figley (Ed.), *Compassion fatigue: Secondary traumatic stress disorders from treating the traumatized* (pp. 1–20). New York, NY: Brunner/Mazel.

Fine, A. H. (Ed.) (2006). Animal-*assisted therapy: Theoretical foundations and guidelines for practice* (2nd ed.). San Diego, CA: Academic Press.

Fischer-Shofty, M., Levkovitz, Y., & Shamay-Tsoory, S. G. (2013). Oxytocin facilitates accurate perception of competition in men and kinship in women. *Social Cognitive and Affective Neuroscience, 8*(3), 313–317.

Fiske, A. P. (1992). The four elementary forms of sociality: Framework for a united theory of social relations. *Psychological Review, 99*, 689–723.

Fleming, A. S., & Orpen, G. (1986). Psychobiology of maternal behavior in rats, selected other species and humans. In A. Fogel & G. F. Geison, (Eds.), *Origins of nurturance* (pp. 141–208). London, England: Erlbaum.

Fletcher, J. K., & Ragins, B. R. (2007). Stone Center relational cultural theory: A window on relational mentoring. In B. R. Ragins & K. E. Kram (Eds.), *The handbook of mentoring at work* (pp. 373–399). Thousand Oaks, CA: Sage.

Fogelman, E. (1995). *Conscience and courage: Rescuers of Jews during the Holocaust.* London, England: Cassell Wellington House.

Forbes, E. E., & Dahl, R. E. (2010). Pubertal development and behavior: Hormonal activation of social and motivational tendencies. *Brain and cognition, 72*(1), 66–72.

Formanek, R. (1991). Why they collect: Collectors reveal their motivations. *Journal of Social Behaviour and Personality, 6* (6), 275–286.

Francis, M. (1990). The everyday and the personal: Six garden stories. In M. Francis & R. T. Hester Jr. (Eds.), *The meaning of gardens* (pp. 206–215). Cambridge, MA: MIT Press.

Francis, M., & Hester, R. T. (1990). *The meaning of gardens.* Cambridge, MA: MIT Press.

Frankl, V. E. (1985/1959). *Man's search for meaning: An introduction to logotherapy.* Boston, MA: Beacon Press.

Frankl, V. E. (1997). *Man's search for ultimate meaning.* New York: Plenum Press.

Frankl, V. E. (1988). *The will to meaning. Foundations and applications of logotherapy. Meridian.* New York, NY: Penguin.

Franklin, A. (1999). *Animals and modern cultures: A sociology of human-animal relations in modernity.* London, England: Sage.

Fraley, R. C., Brumbaugh, C. C., & Marks, M. J. (2005). The evolution and function of adult attachment: a comparative and phylogenetic analysis. *Journal of Personality and Social Psychology, 89*(5), 731–746.

Fredrickson, B. L. (2001). The role of positive emotions in positive psychology: The broaden-and-build theory of positive emotions. *American Psychologist, 56*(3), 218–226.

Freeman C., Dickinson, K. J., Porter, S., & van Heezik, Y. (2012). My garden is an expression of me: Exploring householders' relationships with their gardens. *Journal of Environmental Psychology, 32*(2):135–143.

French, S., & Joseph, S. (1999). Religiosity and its association with happiness, purpose in life, and self-actualisation. *Mental Health, Religion & Culture, 2*(2), 117–120.

Friedman, D., Hechter, M., & Kanazawa, S. (1994). A theory of the value of children. *Demography, 31*(3), 375–401.

Friedmann, E. and Tsai, C. C. (2006). The animal–human bond: Health and wellness. In A. H. Fine (Ed.), *Handbook on animal-assisted therapy* (pp. 95–117). San Diego, CA: Elsevier.

Friedmann, E., & Thomas, S. A. (1995). Pet ownership, social support, and one-year survival after acute myocardial infarction in the Cardiac Arrhythmia Suppression Trial (CAST). *The American Journal of Cardiology, 76*(17), 1213–1217.

Friedmann, E., Katcher, A. H, Lynch, J. J., & Thomas, S. A. (1980). Animal companions and one year survival of patients after discharge from a coronary care unit. *Public Health Reports, 95,* 307–312.

Friedmann, E., Thomas, S. A., Stein, P. K., & Kleiger, R. E. (2003). Relation between pet ownership and heart rate variability in patients with healed myocardial infarcts. *The American Journal of Cardiology, 91*(6), 718–721.

Fromm, E. (2011). *The heart of man.* Riverdale, NY: American Mental Health Foundation.

Frost, J. L., Wortham, S. C., & Reifel, R. S. (2012). *Play and child development* (4th ed.). Upper Saddle River, N.J.: Pearson/Merrill Prentice Hall.

Fultz, J., Batson, C. D., Fortenbach, V. A., McCarthy, P. M., & Varney, L. L. (1986). Social evaluation and the empathy-altruism hypothesis. *Journal of Personality and Social Psychology, 50*(4), 761–769.

Furman, W. (1989). The development of children's social networks. In D. Belle (Ed.), *children's social networks and social supports* (pp. 151–172). Hoboken, NJ: Wiley.

Furman, W., & Wehner, E. A. (1994). *Romantic views: Toward a theory of adolescent romantic relationships.* In R. Montemayor, G. R. Adams, & G. P. Gullota (Eds.), *Advances in adolescent development: Vol. 6, Relationships during adolescence* (pp. 168–195). Thousand Oaks, CA: Sage.

Gable, S. L., Gosnell, C. L., Maisel, N. C., & Strachman, A. (2012). Safely testing the alarm: Close others' responses to personal positive events. *Journal of Personality and Social Psychology, 103*, 963–981.

Gable, S., & Haidt, J. (2005). What (and why) is positive psychology? *Review of General Psychology, 9*, 103–110.

Garbarino, J., Eckenrode, J., & Barry, F. D. (1997). *Understanding abusive families: An ecological approach to theory and practice.* San Francisco, CA: Jossey-Bass.

Gangestad, S. W., & Simpson, J. A. (2000). The evolution of human mating: Trade-offs and strategic pluralism. *Behavioral and Brain Sciences, 23*(4), 573–587.

Geangu, E., Benga, O., Stahl, D., & Striano, T. (2010). Contagious crying beyond the first days of life. *Infant Behavior and Development, 33*(3), 279–288.

Geary, D. C. (2000). Evolution and proximate expression of human paternal investment. *Psychological Bulletin, 126*, 55–77.

George, C., & Solomon, J. (1989). Internal working models of caregiving and security of attachment at age six. *Infant Mental Health Journal, 10*, 222–237.

George, C., & Solomon, J. (1996), Representational models of relationships: Links between caregiving and attachment. *Infant Mental Health Journal, 17*, 198–216.

George, C., & Solomon, J. (1999), Attachment and caregiving: The caregiving behavioral system. In J. Cassidy & P. Shaver. (Eds.), *Handbook of attachment* (pp. 649–670). New York, NY: Guilford Press.

George, C., & Solomon, J. (2008). The caregiving system: a behavioral systems approach to parenting. In J. Cassidy & P. R. Shaver (Eds.), *Handbook of attachment: Theory, research, and clinical applications* (2nd ed., pp. 833–856). New York, NY: Guilford Press.

GHK. (2010). *Volunteering in the European Union—final report.* Study on behalf of the European Commission (Directorate-General for Education and Culture). Retrieved from http://ec.europa.eu/citizenship/pdf/doc1018_en.pdf

Gilles, C., & Wilson, J. (2004). Receiving as well as giving: Mentors' perceptions of their professional development in one teacher induction program. *Mentoring and Tutoring, 12*, 88–106.

Gilligan, C. (1982). *In a different voice: Psychological theory and women's development.* Cambridge, MA: Harvard University Press.

Giordano, P. C. (2003). Relationships in adolescence. *Annual Review of Sociology, 29*, 257–281.

Gintis, H., Bowles, S., Boyd, R., & Fehr, E. (2003). Explaining altruistic behavior in humans. *Evolution and Human Behavior, 24*(3), 153–172.

Glocker, M. L., Langleben, D. D., Ruparel, K., Loughead, J. W., Gur, R. C., & Sachser, N. (2009a). Baby schema in infant faces induces cuteness perception and motivation for caretaking in adults. *Ethology, 115*, 257–263.

Glocker, M. L., Langleben, D. D., Ruparel, K., Loughead, J. W., Valdez, J. N., Griffin, M. D., . . . & Gur, R. C. (2009b). Baby schema modulates the brain reward system in nulliparous women. *Proceedings of the National Academy of Sciences, 106*(22), 9115–9119.

Goetz, J. L., Keltner, D., & Simon-Thomas, E. (2010). Compassion: An evolutionary analysis and empirical review. *Psychological Bulletin, 136*, 351–374.

Goldner, L., & Mayseless, O. (2008). Juggling the roles of parents, therapists, friends and teachers—A working model for an integrative conception of mentoring. *Mentoring & Tutoring: Partnership in Learning, 16*, 412–428.

Goldner, L., & Mayseless, O. (2009). The quality of mentoring relationships and mentoring success. *Journal of Youth and Adolescence, 38*(10), 1339–1350.

Goldstein, L. S., & Lake,V. E. (2000). Love, love, and more love for children: Exploring preservice teachers' understandings of caring. *Teaching and Teacher Education, 16*, 861–872.

Gonzalez, M. T., Hartig, T., Patil, G. G., Martinsen, E. W., & Kirkevold, M. (2010). Therapeutic
horticulture in clinical depression: a prospective study of active components. *Journal of
Advanced Nursing, 66*(9), 2002–2013.

Gonzalez-Liencres, C., Shamay-Tsoory, S. G., & Brüne, M. (2013). Towards a neuroscience
of empathy: Ontogeny, phylogeny, brain mechanisms, context and psychopathology.
Neuroscience & Biobehavioral Reviews, 37, 1537–1548.

Gordon, I., Zagoory-Sharon, O., Leckman, J. F., & Feldman, R. (2010a). Oxytocin and the development of parenting in humans. *Biological Psychiatry, 68*, 377–382.

Gordon, I., Zagoory-Sharon, O., Leckman, J. F., Feldman, R., (2010b). Parental oxytocin and
triadic family interactions. *Physiology & Behavior, 101*(5), 679–684.

Gottman, J. M. (1994). *What predicts divorce? The relationship between marital processes and marital
outcomes.* Hillsdale, NJ: Erlbaum.

Gould, S. J. (2002). *The structure of evolutionary theory.* Cambridge, MA: Belknap Press of Harvard
University Press.

Grant, A. (2013). *Give and take: A revolutionary approach to success.* New York, NY: Penguin Group.

Grant, A. M. (2007). Relational job design and the motivation to make a prosocial difference.
Academy of Management Review, 32(2), 393–417.

Grant, A. M. (2008). Does intrinsic motivation fuel the prosocial fire? Motivational synergy
in predicting persistence, performance, and productivity. *Journal of Applied Psychology,
93*(1), 48–58.

Grant, A. M., Dutton, J. E., & Rosso, B. D. (2008). Giving commitment: Employee support
programs and the prosocial sensemaking process. *Academy of Management Journal, 51*(5),
898–918.

Greenfield, E. A., & Marks, N. F. (2004). Formal volunteering as a protective factor for older
adults' psychological well-being. *Journal of Gerontology, 59B*, S258–S264.

Greenslade, J. H. and White, K. M. (2005) The prediction of above regular participation in volunteerism: A test of the theory of planned behaviour and the volunteers functions inven-
tory. *Journal of Social Psychology 145*, 155–172.

Greil, A. L. (1997). Infertility and psychological distress: A critical review of the literature. *Social
Science & Medicine, 45*(11), 1679–1704.

Greitemeyer, T., & Osswald, S. (2011). Playing prosocial video games increases the accessibility
of prosocial thoughts. *The Journal of Social Psychology, 151*(2), 121–128.

Grese, R. E., Kaplan, R., Ryan, R. L., & Buxton, J. (2000). Psychological benefits of volunteering in stewardship programs. In, P. H. Gobster & R. B. Hul (Eds.), *Restoring
nature: Perspectives from the social sciences and humanities* (pp. 265–280). Washington,
DC: Island Press.

Grewen, K. M., Girdler, S. S., Amico, J., & Light, K. C. (2005). Effects of partner support on resting oxytocin, cortisol, norepinephrine, and blood pressure before and after warm partner
contact. *Psychosomatic Medicine, 67*(4), 531–538.

Grof, S., & Bennett, H. L. (1992). *The holotropic mind: The three levels of consciousness and how they
shape our lives.* New York, NY: Harper.

Gross, H., & Lane, N. (2007). Landscapes of the lifespan: Exploring accounts of own gardens
and gardening. *Journal of Environmental Psychology, 37*, 225–241.

Grossman, J. B., & Rhodes, J. E. (2002). The test of time: Predictors and effects of duration in
youth mentoring relationships. *American Journal of Community Psychology, 30*, 199–219.

Grusec, J. E. (1991). The socialization of empathy. In M. S. Clark (Ed.), *Review of personality and
social psychology: Vol 12. Prosocial behavior* (pp. 9–33). Newbury Park, CA: Sage.

Grusec, J. E., Goodnow, J. J., & Kuczynski, L. (2000). New directions in analyses of parenting
contributions to children's acquisition of values. *Child Development, 71*(1), 205–211.

Grusec, J. E., Davidov, M., & Lundell, L. (2002). Prosocial and helping behavior. In P. K. Smith & C. H. Hart (Eds.), *Blackwell handbook of childhood social development* (pp. 457–474). Malden, MA: Blackwell.

Grusec, J. E., & Goodnow, J. J. (1994). Impact of parental discipline methods on the child's internalization of values: A reconceptualization of current points of view. *Developmental Psychology, 30*, 4–19.

Guisinger, S., & Blatt, S. J. (1994). Individuality and relatedness: Evolution of a fundamental dialectic. *American Psychologist, 49*, 104–111.

Gunter, B. (1999), *Pets and people: The psychology of pet ownership.* London: Whurr Publishers.

Gushee, D. P. (1993). Many paths to righteousness: An assessment of research on why righteous Gentiles helped Jews. *Holocaust and Genocie Studies, 7*, 372–401.

Haber, M. G., Cohen, J. L., Lucas, T, & Baltes, B. B. (2007). The relationship between self-reported received and perceived social support: A meta-analytic review. *American Journal of Community Psychology, 39*, 133–144.

Haidt, J. (2003a). Elevation and the positive psychology of morality. In C. L. M. Keyes & J. Haidt (Eds.), *Flourishing: Positive psychology and the life well-lived* (pp. 275–289). Washington, DC: American Psychological Association.

Haidt, J. (2003b). The moral emotions. In R. J. Davidson, K. R. Scherer, & H. H. Goldsmith (Eds.), *Handbook of affective sciences* (pp. 852–870). Oxford, England: Oxford University Press.

Haidt, J. (2007). The new synthesis in moral psychology. *Science 316*(5827), 998–1002.

Hall, M., Lasby, D., Ayer, S., & Gibbons, W. D. (2007). *Caring Canadians, involved Canadians: Highlights from the Canada survey of giving, volunteering and participating.* Ottawa, Ontario, Canada: Statistics Canada.

Hallie, P. (1994). *Lest innocent blood be shed: The story of the village of Le Chambon and how goodness happened there.* New York, NY: Harper Perennial. (Original work published 1979.)

Hamilton, W. D. (1964). The genetical evolution of social behavior, I & II. *Journal of Theoretical Biology, 7*, 1–52.

Hanegraaff, W. J. (1998). *New Age religion and western culture: Esotericism in the mirror of secular thought.* Albany, NY: SUNY Press.

Hansen, T. (2012). Parenthood and happiness: A review of folk theories versus empirical evidence. *Social Indicators Research, 108*(1), 29–64.

Hanson, J. G., & McCullagh, J. G. (1995). Career choice factors for BSW students: A 10-year perspective. *Journal of Social Work Education, 31*(1), 28–37.

Harbaugh, W. T., Mayr, U., & Burghart, D. R. (2007). Neural responses to taxation and voluntary giving reveal motives for charitable donations. *Science, 316*, 1622–1624.

Hardy, C., & Van Vugt, M. (2006). Nice guys finish first: The competitive altruism hypothesis. *Personality and Social Psychology Bulletin, 32*, 1402–1413.

Hargreaves, A. (1994). *Changing teachers, changing times.* London, England: Cassell.

Harper, J. M., Padilla-Walker, L. M., & Jensen, A. C. (2014). Do siblings matter independent of both parents and friends? Sympathy as a mediator between sibling relationship quality and adolescent outcomes. *Journal of Research on Adolescence.* Advance online publication. doi: 10.1111/jora.12174

Harris, J. R. (1995). Where is the child's environment? A group socialization theory of development. *Psychological Review, 102*(3), 458–489.

Hart, H., McAdams, D. P., Hirsch, B. J., & Bauer, J. J. (2001). Generativity and social involvements among African Americans and white adults. *Journal of Research in Personality, 35*, 208–230.

Hart, T. (2014). *The four virtues.* New York, NY: Simon & Schuster.

Haski-Leventhal, D., Ronel, N., York, A. S., Ben David B. M. (2008). Youth volunteering for youth: Who are they serving? How are they being served? *Children and Youth Services Review, 30*, 834–846.

Hassett, J. M., Siebert, E. R., & Wallen, K. (2008). Sex differences in rhesus monkey toy preferences parallel those of children. *Hormones and Behavior,54*(3), 359–364.

Hassink, J., & Van Dijk, M. (Eds.). (2006). *Farming for health: Green-care farming across Europe and the United States of America.* Wageningen UR Frontis Series. Vol. *13.* Dordrecht: Springer.

Hastings, P. D., Zahn-Waxler, C., Robinson, J., Usher, B., & Bridges, D. (2000). The development of concern for others in children with behavior problems. *Developmental Psychology, 36,* 531–546.

Hay, D. F. (1994). Prosocial development. *Journal of Child Psychology and Psychiatry, 35*(1), 29–71.

Hay, D. F. (2009). The roots and branches of human altruism. *British Journal of Psychology, 100*(3), 473–479.

Hay, D. F., & Cook, K. V. (2007). The transformation of prosocial behavior from infancy to childhood. In C. Brownell, & C. B. Kopp (Eds.), *Socioemotional development in the toddler years: Transitions and transformations* (pp. 100–131). New York, NY: Guilford Press.

Hay, D., & Rheingold, H. (1983). The early appearance of some valued social behaviors. In D. Bridgeman (Ed.), *The nature of prosocial development: Interdisciplinary theories and strategies* (pp. 73–94). New York, NY: Academic Press.

Hazan, C., & Shaver, P. (1987). Romantic love conceptualized as an attachment process. *Journal of Personality and Social Psychology, 52*(3), 511–524.

Hazan, C., & Shaver, P. R. (1994). Attachment as an organizational framework for research on close relationships. *Psychological Inquiry, 5*(1), 1–22.

Hazan, C., & Zeifman, D. (1994). Sex and the psychological tether. In K. Bartholomew & D. Perlman (Eds.), *Advances in personal relationships* (Vol. 5, pp. 151–178). London: Jessica Kingsley.

Headley, B., & Grabka, M. (2007). Pets and human health in Germany and Australia: National longitudinal results. *Social Indicators Research, 80*(2), 297–311.

Heard, D., & Lake, B. (1997). *The challenge of attachment for caregiving.* London, England: Routledge.

Heelas, P. (1996). *The New Age movement: The celebration of the self and the sacralization of modernity.* Oxford, England: Blackwell.

Hein, G., Silani, G., Preuschoff, K., Batson, C. D., & Singer, T. (2010). Neural responses to ingroup and outgroup members' suffering predict individual differences in costly helping. *Neuron, 68*(1), 149–160.

Heliker, D., Chadwick, A., & O'Connell, T. (2000). The meaning of gardening and the effects on perceived well being of a gardening project on diverse populations of elders. *Activities, Adaptation & Aging, 24* (3), 35–56.

Henderson, A., Brown, S. D., Pancer, S. M., & Ellis-Hale, K. (2007). Mandated community service in high school and subsequent civic engagement: The case of the "double cohort" in Ontario, Canada. *Journal of Youth and Adolescence, 36*(7), 849–860.

Henderson, A. J. Z., Landolt, M. A., McDonald, M. F., Barrable, W. M., Soos, J. G., Gourlay, W., . . . Landsberg, D. N. (2003). The living anonymous kidney donor: Lunatic or saint? *American Journal of Transplantation, 3,* 203–213.

Henwood, K., & Procter, J. (2003). The "good father": Reading men's accounts of paternal involvement during the transition to first-time fatherhood. *British Journal of Social Psychology, 42,* 337–355.

Hepach, R., Vaish, A., & Tomasello, M. (2012). Young children are intrinsically motivated to see others helped. *Psychological Science, 23*(9), 967–972.

Herzog, H. A. (2007). Gender differences in human–animal interactions: A review. *Anthrozoos, 20*(1), 7–21.

Herzog, H. (2011). The impact of pets on human health and psychological well-being: Fact, fiction, or hypothesis. *Current Directions in Psychological Science, 20,* 236–239.

Hesse, E. (2008). The Adult Attachment Interview: Protocol, method of analysis, and empirical studies. In J. Cassidy, & P. R. Shaver (Eds), *Handbook of attachment: Theory, research, and clinical applications* (2nd ed.). (pp. 552–598). New York, NY: Guilford.

Hewlett, B. S. (1991). *Intimate fathers: The nature and context of Aka Pygmy paternal infant care*. Ann Arbor, MI: University of Michigan Press.

Higgins, M. C., & Kram, K. E. (2001). Reconceptualizing mentoring at work: A developmental network perspective. *The Academy of Management Review, 26*, 264–288.

Hines, M. (2003). Sex Steroids and human behavior: Prenatal androgen exposure and sex-typical play behavior in children. *Annals of the New York Academy of Sciences, 1007*(1), 272–282.

Hines, M. (2004). *Brain gender*. New York, NY: Oxford University Press.

Hines, M., Golombok, S., Rust, J., Johnston, K. J., Golding, J., & Parents and Children Study Team. (2002). Testosterone during pregnancy and gender role behavior of preschool children: a longitudinal, population study. *Child Development, 73*(6), 1678–1687.

Hitchings, R. (2003). People, plants and performance: On actor network theory and the material pleasures of the private garden. *Social & Cultural Geography, 4*, 99–113.

Hoffman, M. L. (1970). Moral development. In P. H. Mussen (Ed.), *Carmichael's handbook of child psychology* (Vol. 2). Hoboken, NJ: Wiley.

Hoffman, M. L. (2000). *Empathy and moral development: Implications for caring and justice*. New York, NY: Cambridge University Press.

Hogan, R., & Hogan, J. (2002). Leadership and socio-political intelligence. In R. E. Riggio, S. E. Murphy, & F. J. Pirozzolo (Eds.), *Multiple intelligences and leadership* (pp. 75–88). Mahwah, NJ: Erlbaum.

Hollway, W. (2006). *The capacity to care: Gender and ethical subjectivity*. New York, NY: Routledge.

Holmer, R. J., Clavejo, M. T., Dongus, S., and Drescher, A. (2003). Allotment gardens for Philippine cities. *Urban Agriculture Magazine, 11*, 29–31.

Holt-Lunstad, J., Birmingham, W. A., & Light, K. C. (2008). Influence of a "warm touch" support enhancement intervention among married couples on ambulatory blood pressure, oxytocin, alpha amylase, and cortisol. *Psychosomatic Medicine, 70*(9), 976–985.

Hooper, C., Craig, J., Janvrin, D. R., Wetsel, M. A., & Reimels, E. (2010). Compassion satisfaction, burnout, and compassion fatigue among emergency nurses compared with nurses in other selected inpatient specialties. *Journal of Emergency Nursing, 36*(5), 420–427.

Horvath, A. O., & Symonds, B. D. (1991). Relation between working alliance and outcome in psychotherapy: A meta-analysis. *Journal of Counseling Psychology, 38*(2), 139–149

House, B. R., Silk, J. B., Henrich, J., Barrett, H. C., Scelza, B. A., Boyette, A. H., . . . & Laurence, S. (2013). Ontogeny of prosocial behavior across diverse societies. *Proceedings of the National Academy of Sciences, 110*(36), 14586–14591.

Howes, C., & Matheson, C. C. (1992). Sequences in the development of competent play with peers: Social and social pretend play. *Developmental Psychology, 28*(5), 961–974.

Hrdy, S. B. (1981). *The woman that never evolved*. Cambridge, MA: Harvard University Press.

Hrdy, S. B. (1999). *Mother nature: A history of mothers, infants, and natural selection*. New York, NY: Pantheon Books.

Hrdy, S. B. (2009). *Mothers and others: The evolutionary origins of mutual understanding*. Cambridge, MA: Belknap Press of Harvard University Press.

Hruschka, D. J. (2010). *Friendship: development, ecology, and evolution of a relationship* (Vol. 5). Berkeley and Los Angeles, CA: University of California Press.

Hughes, J. N., Luo, W., Kwok, O.-M., & Loyd, L. K. (2008). Teacher-student support, effortful engagement, and achievement: A 3-year longitudinal study. *Journal of Educational Psychology, 100*(1), 1–14.

Hui, C., Lam, S. S. K., & Law, K. K. S. (2000). Instrumental values of organizational citizenship behavior for promotion: A field quasi-experiment. *Journal of Applied Psychology, 85*, 822–828.

Hurleman, R., Patin, A., Onur, O. A., Cohen, M. X., Baumgartner, T., Metzler, S., . . . Kendrick, K. M. (2010). Oxytocin enhances amygdala-dependent, socially reinforced learning and emotional empathy in humans. *Journal of Neuroscience, 30*, 4999–5007.

Huston, T., Geis. G., & Wright, R. (1976). The angry Samaritans. *Psychology Today, 10*(1), 61–62, 64, 85.

Hyde, J. S. (2005). The gender similarities hypothesis. *American psychologist, 60*(6), 581–592.

Hyde, J. S. (2007). New directions in the study of gender similarities and differences. *Current Directions in Psychological Science, 16*(5), 259–263.

Ickes, W., Gesn, P. R., & Graham, T. (2000). Gender differences in empathic accuracy: Differential ability or differential motivation?. *Personal Relationships, 7*(1), 95–109.

Insel, T. R. (1997). A neurobiological basis of social attachment. *American Journal of Psychiatry, 154*, 726–735.

Insel, T. R. (2010). The challenge of translation in social neuroscience: A review of oxytocin, vasopressin, and affiliative behavior. *Neuron, 65*(6), 768–779.

Israel, S., Lerer, E., Shalev, I., Uzefovsky, F., Riebold, M., Laiba, E., . . . Ebstein, R. P. (2009). The oxytocin receptor (OXTR) contributes to prosocial fund allocations in the Dictator Game and the Social Value Orientations Task. *PLoS ONE 4*(5): e5535.

Israel, S., Weisel, O., Ebstein, R. P., & Bornstein, G. (2012). Oxytocin, but not vasopressin, increases both parochial and universal altruism. *Psychoneuroendocrinology, 37*, 1341–1344.

Jacobs, C. L., Roman, D., Garvey, C., Kahn, J., & Matas, A. J. (2004). Twenty-two nondirected kidney donors: An update on a single center's experience. *American Journal of Transplantation, 4*, 1110–1116.

Jadva, V., Hines, M., & Golombok, S. (2010). Infants' preferences for toys, colors, and shapes: Sex differences and similarities. *Archives of sexual behavior, 39*(6), 1261–1273.

Jenkins, V. S. (1994). *The lawn: History of an American obsession.* Washington, DC: Smithsonian Institution Press.

Jenner, J. R. (1982). Participation, leadership, and the role of vollinteerism among selected women volunteers. *Nonprofit and Voluntary Sector Quarterly,11*(4), 27–38.

Johnson, R. C. (1996). Attributes of Carnegie medalists performing acts of heroism and of the recipients of these acts. *Ethology and Sociobiology, 17*, 355–362.

Johnson, R. C., Danko, G. P., Darvill, T. J., Bochner, S., Bowers, J. K., Huang, Y. H., Park, J. Y., . . . Pennington, D. (1989). Cross-cultural assessment of altruism and its correlates. *Personality and Individual Differences, 10*, 855–868.

Josselson, R. (1996). *The space between us: Exploring the dimensions of human relationships.* Thousand Oaks, CA: Sage.

Jurkovic, G. J. (1997). *Lost childhoods: The plight of the parentified child.* Philadelphia, PA: Brunner/ Mazel.

Kahn P. H. Jr., Friedman, B., Hagman, J. (2003). Hardware companions? What online AIBO discussion forums reveal about the human–robotic relationship. *Conference Proceedings of CHI 2003* (pp. 273–280). New York, NY: Association for Computing Machinery.

Kanat-Maymon, M., & Assor, A. (2010). Perceived maternal control and responsiveness to distress as predictors of young adults' empathic responses. *Personality and Social Psychology Bulletin, 36*(1), 33–46.

Kane, R. (2005). *A contemporary introduction to free will.* New York, NY: Oxford University Press.

Kaplan, R., & Kaplan, S. (1989). *The experience of nature: A psychological perspective.* Cambridge, England: Cambridge University Press.

Kappes, H. B., & Shrout, P. E. (2011). When goal sharing produces support that is not caring. *Personality and Social Psychology Bulletin, 37*(5), 662–673.

Katcher, A. H. (1981). Interactions between people and their pets: Form and function. In B. Fogle (Ed.), *Interrelations between people and pets* (pp. 41–67). Springfield, IL: Charles C. Thomas.

Katcher, A. H., & Beck, A. M. (1987). Health and caring for living things. *Anthrozoos, 1*, 175–183.

Katcher, A. H., & Wilkins, G. G. (2000). The centaur's lessons: Therapeutic education through care of animals and nature study. In A. H. Fine (Ed.), *Handbook on animal-assisted therapy* (pp. 153–177). New York, NY: Elsevier.

Katriel, T. (1988/89). "Haxlafot": Rules and strategies in children's swapping exchanges. *Research on Language and Social Interaction, 22,* 157–178.

Katz, R., Gur-Yaish, N., & Lowenstein, A. (2010). Motivation to provide help to older parents in Norway, Spain, and Israel. *The International Journal of Aging Human Development, 71,* 283–303.

Keller, T. E. (2008). Youth mentoring: Theoretical and methodological issues. In T. D. Allen & L. T. Eby (Eds.), *Blackwell handbook of mentoring: A multiple perspectives approach* (p. 23–47). Chichester, England: Wiley.

Kellert, S. R. (1993). The biological basis for human values of nature. In S. R. Kellert & E. O. Wilson (Eds.), *The biophilia hypothesis* (pp. 42–69). Washington, DC: Island Press.

Kellert, S., & Wilson, E. O. (Eds.). (1993). *The biophilia hypothesis.* Washington, DC: Island Press.

Kellett, J. B., Humphrey, R. H., & Sleeth, R. G. (2002). Empathy and complex task performance: Two routes to leadership. *The Leadership Quarterly, 13*(5), 523–544.

Keltner, D. (2009). *Born to be good. The science of a meaningful life.* New York. NY: W. W. Norton.

Keltner, D., Kogan, A., Piff, P. K., & Saturn, S. R. (2014). The sociocultural appraisals, values, and emotions (SAVE) framework of prosociality: Core processes from gene to meme. *Annual Review of Psychology, 65,* 425–460.

Keltner, D., Marsh, J., & Smith, J. A. (Eds.). (2010). *The compassionate instinct: The science of human goodness.* New York: NY: WW Norton.

Kendrick, K. M., Keverne, E. B., & Baldwin, B. A. (1987). Intracerebroventricular oxytocin stimulates maternal behaviour in the sheep. *Neuroendocrinology,46*(1), 56–61.

Kenrick, D. T. (2006). A dynamical evolutionary view of love. In R. J. Sternberg, & K. Weis (Eds.), *Psychology of Love* (2nd ed. pp. 15–34). New Haven, CT: Yale University Press.

Kenrick, D. T., Griskevicius, V., Neuberg, S. L., & Schaller, M. (2010). Renovating the pyramid of needs: Contemporary extensions built upon ancient foundations. *Perspectives on Psychological Science, 5,* 292–314.

Kenward, B., & Gredebäck, G. (2013). Infants help a non-human agent. *PloS one, 8*(9), e75130.

Keren, E., & Mayseless, O. (2013). The freedom to choose secure attachment relationships in adulthood. *The Journal of Genetic Psychology, 174*(3), 271–290.

Keyes, C. L. M., & Ryff, C. D. (1998). Generativity in adult lives: Social structural contours and quality of life consequences. In D. P. McAdams & E. de St. Aubin (Eds.), *Generativity and adult development: How and why we care for the next generation* (pp. 227–263). Washington, D.C.: American Psychological Association.

Khan, C. M., Iida, M., Stephens, M. A. P., Fekete, E. M., Druley, J. A., & Greene, K. A. (2009). Spousal support following knee surgery: roles of self-efficacy and perceived emotional responsiveness. *Rehabilitation Psychology, 54*(1), 28–32.

Kidd, A. H., & Kidd, R. M. (1985). Children's attitudes toward their pets. *Psychological Reports, 57*(1), 15–31.

Kidd, A. H., & Kidd, R. M. (1994). Benefits and liabilities of pets for the homeless. *Psychological Reports, 74*(3), 715–722.

Kidd, J. L., & Brascamp, W. (2004). Benefits of gardening and the well being of New-Zealand gardeners. In D. Relf, B. H. Kwack, & P. Hicklenton (Eds.), Proceedings of the XXVI International Horticulture Congress: Expanding roles for horticulture in improving human well-being and life quality. *Acta Horticultura, 639,* 27–36.

Kiesling, C., Sorell, G. T., Montgomery, M. J., & Colwell, R. K. (2006). Identity and spirituality: a psychosocial exploration of the sense of spiritual self. *Developmental psychology, 42*(6), 1269–1277.

Kiesling, F. M., & Manning, C. M. (2010). How green is your thumb? Environmental gardening identity and ecological gardening practices. *Journal of Environmental Psychology, 30,* 315–327.

King, P. E., Clardy, C. E., & Ramos, J. S. (2014). Adolescent spiritual exemplars: Exploring spirituality in the lives of diverse youth. *Journal of Adolescent Research, 29*(2), 186–212.

Klaw, E. L., & Rhodes, J. E. (1995). Mentor relationships and the career development of pregnant and parenting African-American teenagers. *Psychology of Women Quarterly, 19*(4), 551–562.

Klein, M. (1975). *Love, guilt and reparation and other works 1921–1945.* New York, NY: The free Press a division of Simon & Schuster.

Knafo, A., & Israel, S. (2010). Genetic and environmental influences on prosocial behavior. In M. Mikulincer & P. R. Shaver (Eds.), *Prosocial motives, emotions, and behavior: The better angels of our nature* (pp. 149–167). Washington, DC: American Psychological Association.

Knafo, A., Israel, S., & Ebstein, R. P. (2011). Heritability of children's prosocial behavior and differential susceptibility to parenting by variation in the dopamine receptor D4 gene. *Development and Psychopathology, 23*(01), 53–67.

Knafo, A., & Plomin, R. (2006). Prosocial behavior from early to middle childhood: genetic and environmental influences on stability and change. *Developmental Psychology, 42*(5), 771–786.

Knafo, A., Schwartz, S. H., & Levine, R. V. (2009). Helping strangers is lower in embedded cultures. *Journal of Cross-Cultural Psychology, 40*(5), 875–879.

Knafo, A., & Uzefovsky, F. (2013). Variation in empathy: The interplay of genetic and environmental factors. In M. Legerstee, D. W. Haley, & M. H. Bornstein (Eds.), *The infant mind: Origins of the social brain* (pp. 97–122). New York, NY: Guilford Press.

Knafo, A., Zahn-Waxler, C., Van Hulle, C., Robinson, J. L., & Rhee, S. H. (2008). The developmental origins of a disposition toward empathy: Genetic and environmental contributions. *Emotion, 8*(6), 737–752.

Kohut, H. (1977/2009). *The restoration of the self.* Chicago, IL: University of Chicago Press.

Koltko-Rivera, M. E. (2006). Rediscovering the later version of Maslow's hierarchy of needs: Self-transcendence and opportunities for theory, research, and unification. *Review of General Psychology, 10*(4), 302–317.

Konrath, S., Fuhrel-Forbis, A., Lou, A., & Brown, S. (2012). Motives for volunteering are associated with mortality risk in older adults. *Health Psychology, 31*, 87–96.

Kosfeld, M., Heinrichs, M., Zak, P. J., Fischbacher, U., & Fehr, E. (2005). Oxytocin increases trust in humans. *Nature, 435*, 673–676.

Kram, K. E. (1985). *Mentoring at work: Developmental relationships in organizational life.* Glenview, IL: Scott, Foresman.

Krebs, D. L., & van Hesteren, F. (1994). The development of altruism: Towards an integrative model. *Developmental Review, 14*, 103–158.

Krebs, J. R., & Davies, N. B. (Eds.). (1991). *Behavioural ecology: An evolutionary approach* (3rd ed.). Oxford, England: Blackwell Scientific.

Kunce, L. J., & Shaver, P. R. (1994). An attachment-theoretical approach to caregiving in romantic relationships. In K. Bartholomew & D. Perlman (Eds.), *Advances in personal relationships* (Vol. 5, pp. 205–237). London: Kingsley.

Kurtz, J. L., & Lyubomirsky, S. (2008). Towards a durable happiness. In S. J. Lopez & J. G. Rettew (Eds.), *The positive psychology perspective series: Vol. 4* (pp. 21–36). Westport, CT: Greenwood Publishing Group.

La Guardia, J. G., & Patrick, H. (2008). Self-determination theory as a fundamental theory of close relationships. *Canadian Psychology, 49*(3), 201–209.

Lamb, M. E. (2000). The history of research on father involvement: An overview. *Marriage and Family Review, 29*(2–3), 23–42.

Lamb, M. E. (2004). (Ed.) *The role of the father in child development,* 4th ed. Hoboken, NJ: Wiley.

Lamb, M. E. (2010). (Ed.) *The role of the father in child development,* 5th ed. Hoboken, NJ: Wiley.

Landry-Meyer, L., & Newman, B. M. (2004). An exploration of the grandparent caregiver role. *Journal of Family Issues, 25*(8), 1005–1025.

Latane, B., & Darley, J. M. (1970). *The unresponsive bystander: Why doesn't he help?.* New York: NY : Appleton-Century-Crofts.

Latane, B., & Rodin, J. (1969). A lady in distress: Inhibiting effects of friends and strangers on bystander intervention. *Journal of Experimental Social Psychology, 5*(2), 189–202.

Lawford, H., Pratt, M. W., Hunsberger, B., & Pancer, S. M. (2005). Adolescent generativity: A longitudinal study of two possible contexts for learning concern for future generations. *Journal of Research on Adolescence, 15*(3), 261–273.

Lee, Y. H., Ro, M. R., & Lee, Y. S. (2004). Effects of horticultural activities on anxiety reduction of female high school students. *Acta Horticulturae, 639*, 249–253.

Lehmann, V., Huis in't Veld, E. M., & Vingerhoets, A. J. (2013). The human and animal baby schema effect: Correlates of individual differences. *Behavioural Processes, 94*, 99–108.

Lerner, R. M., Roeser, R. W., & Phelps, E. (2008). Positive development, spirituality, and generosity in youth: An introduction to the issues. In R. M. Lerner, R. W. Roeser, & E. Phelps (Eds.), *Positive youth development and spirituality* (pp. 3–24). West Conshohocken, PA: Templeton Foundation Press.

Levine, A., Zagoory-Sharon, O., Feldman, R., Weller, A. (2007). Oxytocin during pregnancy and early postpartum: Individual patterns and maternal-fetal attachment. *Peptides, 28* (6), 1162–1169.

Levinson, D. J., Darrow, D, Levinson, M., Klein, E. B., & McKee, B. (1978). *The seasons' of a man's life*. New York, NY: Knopf.

Lewis, C. A. (1995). Human health and well-being: the psychological, physiological, and sociological effects of plants on people. In E. Matsuo & P. D. Relf (Eds.), *Horticulture in human life, culture and environment: ISHS international symposium*. August 22, 1994. Leuven, Belgium. ISHS Acta Horticulturae, 391, 31–39.

Li, L. M. W., & Bond, M. H. (2010). Analyzing national change in citizen secularism across four time periods in the World Values Survey. *World Values Research, 3*(2), 19–32.

Li, Y., & Ferraro, K. F. (2006). Volunteering in middle and later life: Is health a benefit, barrier or both? *Social Forces, 85*, 497–519.

Liszkowski, U., Carpenter, M., Striano, T., & Tomasello, M. (2006). Twelve- and 18-month-olds point to provide information for others. *Journal of Cognition and Development, 7*, 173–187.

Liszkowski, U., Carpenter, M., & Tomasello, M. (2008). Twelve-month-olds communicate helpfully and appropriately for knowledgeable and ignorant partners. *Cognition, 108*, 732–739.

Little, B. R. (1998). Personal project pursuit: Dimensions and dynamics of personal meaning. In P. T. P. Wong & P. S. Fry (Eds.), *The human quest for meaning: A handbook of research and clinical applications* (pp. 193–212). Mahwah, NJ: Erlbaum.

Lopez, S. J., & Snyder, C. R. (2009). *Oxford handbook of positive psychology*. New York, NY: Oxford University Press.

Lord, R. G., Foti, R. J., & De Vader, C. L. (1984). A test of leadership categorization theory: Internal structure, information processing, and leadership perceptions. *Organizational Behavior and Human Performance, 34*(3), 343–378.

Lovejoy, C. O. (1981). The origin of man. *Science, 211*, 341–350.

Low, N., Butt, S., Ellis, P., & Davis Smith, J. (2007). *Helping out: A national survey of volunteering and charitable giving*. London, England: Cabinet Office.

Luckow, A., Reifman, A., & McIntosh, D. N. (1998, August). *Gender differences in coping: A meta-analysis*. Poster session presented at the 106th Annual Convention of the American Psychological Association, San Francisco, CA.

Luhmann, M., Lucas, R. E., Eid, M., & Diener, E. (2013). The prospective effect of life satisfaction on life events. *Social Psychological and Personality Science, 4*, 39–45.

Lyubomirsky, S., & Boehm, J. K. (2010). Human motives, happiness, and the puzzle of parenthood: Commentary on Kenrick et al. (2010). *Perspectives on Psychological Science, 5*, 327–334.

Lyubomirsky, S., & Layous, K. (2013). How do simple positive activities increase well-being? *Current Directions in Psychological Science, 22*(1), 57–62.

Maccoby, E. E. (1998). *The two sexes: Growing up apart, coming together*. Cambridge, MA: Harvard University Press.

Maccoby, E. E., & Martin, J. (1983). Socialization in the context of the family: Parent-child interaction. In P. H. Mussen (Series Ed.) & E. M. Hetherington (Vol. Ed.), *Handbook of child psychology: Vol. 4. Socialization, personality, and social development* (pp. 1–101). Hoboken, NJ: Wiley.

MacDonald, K. (1992). Warmth as a developmental construct: An evolutionary analysis. *Child Development, 63,* 753–773.

Macdonald, K., & Macdonald, T. M (2010). The peptide that binds: A systematic review of oxytocin and its prosocial effects in humans. *Harvard Review of Psychiatry, 18*(1), 1–21.

MacLean, P. D. (1990). *The triune brain in evolution: Role in paleocerebral functions.* New York, NY: Plenum Press.

MacMillan, H. L., Wathen, C. N., Barlow, J., Fergusson, D. M., Leventhal, J. M., & Taussig, H. N. (2009). Interventions to prevent child maltreatment and associated impairment. *The Lancet, 373*(9659), 250–266.

Maestripieri, D., & Pelka, S. (2002). Sex differences in interest in infants across the lifespan. *Human Nature, 13*(3), 327–344.

Maestripieri, D., & Roney, J. R. (2006). Evolutionary developmental psychology: Contributions from comparative research with nonhuman primates. *Developmental Review, 26*(2), 120–137.

Main, M. (1991). Metacognitive knowledge, metacognitive monitoring, and singular (coherent) versus multiple (incoherent) models of attachment. In C. M. Parkes, J. Stevenson-Hinde, & P. Marris (Eds.), *Attachment across the life cycle* (pp. 127–159). London, England: Routledge.

Main, M., Kaplan, N., & Cassidy, J. (1985). Security in infancy, childhood, and adulthood: A move to the level of representation. *Monographs for the Society for Research in Child Development, 50*(1–2, Serial no. 2019), 66–104.

Main, M., & Solomon, J. (1990). Procedures for identifying infants as disorganized/disoriented during the Ainsworth Strange Situation. In M. T. Greenbert, D. Cicchetti, & E. M. Cummings, *Attachment in the preschool years* (pp. 121–160). Chicago, IL: University of Chicago Press.

Maisel, N. C., & Gable, S. L. (2009). The paradox of received social support: The importance of responsiveness. *Psychological Science, 20,* 928–932.

Malti, T., Gummerman, M., Keller, M., & Buchmann, M. (2009). Children's moral motivation, sympathy, and prosocial behavior. *Child Development, 80,* 442–460.

Mann, R. D. (1984). *The light of consciousness: Explorations in transpersonal psychology.* Albany, NY: SUNY Press.

Manne, S., & Glassman, M. (2000). Perceived control, coping efficacy, and avoidance coping as mediators between spouses' unsupportive behaviors and cancer patients' psychological distress. *Health Psychology, 19*(2), 155–164.

Marks, N. F., Lambert, J. D., & Choi, H. (2002). Transitions to caregiving, gender, and psychological well-being: A prospective US national study. *Journal of Marriage and Family, 64,* 657–667.

Marriot Senior Living Services (1991). *Marriot seniors volunteerism study.* Washington, DC: Marriot Senior Living Services and U.S. Administration on Aging.

Martin, D. J., Garske, J. P., & Davis, M. K. (2000). Relation of the therapeutic alliance with outcome and other variables: A meta-analytic review. *Journal of Consulting and Clinical Psychology, 68*(3), 438–450.

Martin, L., Baldwin, M., & Bean, M. (2008). An exploration of spousal separation and adaptation to long-term disability: Six elderly couples engaged in a horticultural programme. *Occupational Therapy International, 15*(1), 45–55.

Maslow, A. (1953). *Toward a psychology of being.* New York, NY: Van Nostrand.

Maslow, A. (1970). *Motivation and personality* (2nd ed.). New York, NY: Harper & Row.

Maslow, A. (1971). *The farther reaches of human nature.* NEW York, NY: Viking.

Masten, C. L., Eisenberger, N. I., Pfeifer, J. H., Colich, N. L., & Dapretto, M. (2013). Associations among pubertal development, empathic ability, and neural responses while witnessing peer rejection in adolescence. *Child Development, 84*(4), 1338–1354.

Masten, C. L., Morelli, S. A., & Eisenberger, N. I. (2011). An fMRI investigation of empathy for "social pain" and subsequent prosocial behavior. *Neuroimage, 55*(1), 381–388.

Matas, A. J., Garvey, C. A., Jacobs, C. L., Kahn, J. P. (2000). Nondirected living kidney donation. *New England Journal of Medicine, 343*, 433–436.

Maurer, T. W., & Pleck, J. H. (2006). Fathers' caregiving and breadwinning: A gender congruence analysis. *Psychology of Men & Masculinity, 7*(2), 101–112.

Mayseless, O. (1996). Attachment patterns and their outcomes. *Human Development, 39*, 206–223.

Mayseless, O. (2006a). (Ed.). *Parenting representations: Theory, research, and clinical implications* (pp. 3–40). New York, NY: Cambridge University Press.

Mayseless, O. (2006b). Studying parenting representations as a window to parents' internal working model of caregiving. In O. Mayseless (Ed.). *Parenting representations: Theory, research, and clinical implications* (pp. 3–40). New York, NY: Cambridge University Press.

Mayseless, O. (2010). Attachment and the leader-follower relationship. *Journal of Social and Personal Relationships, 27*, 271–280.

Mayseless, O., Bartholomew, K., Henderson, A., & Trinke, S. (2004). "I was more her mom than she was mine": Role reversal in a community sample. *Family Relations, 53*, 78–86.

Mayseless, O., & Keren, E. (2014). Finding a meaningful life as a developmental task in emerging adulthood the domains of love and work across cultures. *Emerging Adulthood, 2*, 63–73.

Mayseless, O., & Popper, M. (2007). Reliance on leaders and social institutions: An attachment perspective. *Attachment and Human Development, 9*, 73–93.

Mayseless, O., Russo-Netzer, P. (2012). The interplay of self-transcendence and psychological maturity among Israeli college students. In A. E. A., Warren, R. M. Lerner, & E. Phelps (Eds.), *Thriving and spirituality among youth: Research perspectives and future possibilities* (pp. 289–307). Hoboken, NJ: Wiley.

Mayseless, O., & Scharf, M. (2006). Maternal representations of parenting in adolescence and psychosocial functioning of mothers and adolescents. In O. Mayseless (Ed.), *Parenting representations: Theory, research, and clinical implications* (pp. 208–238). New York, NY: Cambridge University Press.

Mayseless, O., & Scharf, M. (2010). Respecting others and being respected can reduce aggression in parent-child relations and schools. In P. R. Shaver & M. Mikulincer (Eds.), *Human aggression and violence: Causes, manifestations, and consequences* (pp. 277–294). Washington, DC: American Psychological Association.

McAdams, D. P. (1980). A thematic coding system for the intimacy motive. *Journal of Research in Personality, 14*(4), 413–432.

McAdams, D. P. (1982). Experiences of intimacy and power: Relationships between social motives and autobiographical memory. *Journal of Personality and Social Psychology, 42*, 292–302.

McAdams, D. P. (2000). Attachment, intimacy, and generativity. *Psychological Inquiry, 11*, 117–120.

McAdams, D. P. (2001). Generativity in midlife. In M. Lachman (Ed.), *Handbook of midlife development* (pp. 395–443). Hoboken, NJ: Wiley.

McAdams, D. P., & De St Aubin, E. (1992). A theory of generativity and its assessment through self-report, behavioral acts, and narrative themes in autobiography. *Journal of Personality and Social Psychology, 62*(6), 1003–1015.

McAdams, D. P., Diamond, A., de St Aubin, E., & Mansfield, E. (1997). Stories of commitment: The psychosocial construction of generative lives. *Journal of Personality and Social Psychology, 72*(3), 678–694.

McAdams, D. P., Hart, H. M., & Maruna, S. (1998). The anatomy of generativity. In D. P. McAdams and E. de St. Aubin (Eds.), *Generativity and adult development: How and why we care for the next generation* (pp. 7–43). Washington, DC: American Psychological Association Press.

McAdams, D. P., Hoffman, B. J., Day, R., & Mansfield, E. D. (2006). Themes of agency and communion in significant autobiographical scenes. *Journal of Personality, 64,* 339–377.

McAdams, D. P., & Logan, R. L. (2004). What is generativity? In E. de St. Aubin, D. P. McAdams, & T. C. Kim (Eds.), *The generative society: Caring for future generations* (pp. 15–31). Washington, DC: American Psychological Association.

McAdams, D. P., Reynolds, J., Lewis, M., Patten, A. H., & Bowman, P. J. (2001). When bad things turn good and good things turn bad: Sequences of redemption and contamination in life narrative and their relation to psychosocial adaptation in midlife adults and in students. *Personality and Social Psychology Bulletin, 27*(4), 474–485.

McAndrew, F. T. (2002). New evolutionary perspectives on altruism: Multilevel-selection and costly-signaling theories. *Current Directions in Psychological Science, 11*(2), 79–82.

McCann, T. (2002, November 25). Man who rescued woman called hero. *Chicago Tribune,* Section 2, p. 3.

McCardle, P., McCune S., Griffin, J. A., & Maholmes V. (Eds.) (2011). *How animals affect us: Examining the influence of human-animal interaction on child development and human health.* Washington, D.C.: American Psychological Association.

McCarthy, M. M., Bare, J. E., & Vom Saal, F. S. (1986). Infanticide and parental behavior in wild female house mice: Effects of ovariectomy, adrenalectomy and administration of oxytocin and prostaglandin F2a. *Physiology & Behavior, 36*(1), 17–23.

McClelland, D. (1987). *Human motivation.* Cambridge, NY: Cambridge University Press.

McClelland, D. C. (1980). Motive dispositions: The merits of operant and respondent measures. In L. Wheeler (Ed.), *Review of personality and social psychology* (Vol. 1, pp. 10–41). Beverly Hills, CA: Sage.

Mccorkle, B. H., Dunn, E. C., Wan, Y. M., & Gagne, C. (2009). Compeer friends: A qualitative study of a volunteer friendship programme for people with serious mental illness. *International Journal of Social Psychiatry, 55*(4), 291–305.

McCullough, M. (2008). *Beyond revenge: The evolution of the forgiveness instinct.* Hoboken, NJ: Wiley.

McGrath, M. G., & Oakley, B. A. (2012). Codependency and pathological altruism. In B. Oakley, A. Knafo, G. Madhavan, & D. Wilson (Eds.), *Pathological altruism* (pp. 49–74). New York, NY: Oxford University Press.

McGreevy, A. (1990). Treasures of children: Collections then and now or Treasures of children revisited. *Early Child Development and Care, 63,* 33–36.

McLean, K. C., Breen, A. V., & Fournier, M. A. (2010). Constructing the self in early, middle, and late adolescent boys: Narrative identity, individuation, and well-being. *Journal of Research on Adolescence, 20*(1), 166–187.

McNulty, J. K., & Fincham, F. D. (2012). Beyond positive psychology? Toward a contextual view of psychological processes and well-being. *American Psychologist, 67,* 101–110.

Meehan, B. T., Hughes, J. N., & Cavell, T. A. (2003). Teacher–student relationships as compensatory resources for aggressive children. *Child Development, 74*(4), 1145–1157.

Melson, G. F. (1990). Studying children's attachment to their pets: A conceptual and methodological review. *Anthrozoos, 4,* 91–99.

Melson, G. F. (2001). *Why the wild things are: Animals in the lives of children.* Cambridge, MA: Harvard University Press.

Melson, G. F. (2003). Child development and the human-companion animal bond. *Animal Behavioral Scientist, 47*(1): 31–39.

Shamay-Tsoory, S. G, Aharon-Peretz, J., & Perry, D. (2009). Two systems for empathy: A double dissociation between emotional and cognitive empathy in inferior frontal gyrus versus ventromedial prefrontal lesions. *Brain, 132*, 617–27.

Shamay-Tsoory, S. G., Fischer, M., Dvash, J., Harari, H., Perach-Bloom, N., & Levkovitz, Y. (2009). Intranasal administration of oxytocin increases envy and schadenfreude (gloating). *Biological Psychiatry, 66*(9), 864–870.

Shapiro, B. A., & Kaplan M. J. (1998). Mental illness and horticultural therapy practice. In Simpson, S. P. & Strauss, M. C. (Eds.), *Horticulture as therapy: Principles and practice* (pp. 157–197). New York, NY: Hawthorn Press.

Sharabany, R., & Bar-Tal, D. (1982). Theories of the development of altruism: Review, comparison and integration. *International Journal of Behavioral Development, 5*(1), 49–80.

Sharabany, R., Gershoni, R., & Hofman, J. E. (1981). Girlfriend, boyfriend: Age and sex differences in intimate friendship. *Developmental Psychology, 17*(6), 800–808.

Shaver, P. R., Hazan, C., & Bradshaw, D. (1988). Love as attachment: The integration of three behavioral systems. In R. J. Sternberg & M. L. Barnes (Eds.), *The psychology of love* (pp. 68–99). New Haven, CT: Yale University Press.

Shaver, P. R., Mikulincer, M., & Shemesh-Iron, M. (2010). A behavioral systems perspective on prosocial behavior. In M. Mikulincer & P. R. Shaver (Eds.), *Prosocial motives, emotions, and behavior* (pp. 73–92). Washington, DC: American Psychological Association.

Sheldon, K. M. (2001). The self-concordance model of healthy goal-striving: Implications for well-being and personality development. In P. Schmuck & K. Sheldon (Eds.), *Life goals and well-being: Towards a positive psychology of human striving* (pp. 17–35). Seattle, WA: Hogrefe & Huber.

Sherif, M. (1967). *Group conflict and co-operation.* London, England: Routledge.

Shulman, S. (2003). Conflict and negotiation in adolescent romantic relationships. In P. Florsheim (Ed.), *Adolescent romantic relations and sexual behavior: Theory, research, and practical implications* (pp. 109–135). Mahwah, NJ: Lawrence Erlbaum.

Shulman, S., Elicker, J., & Sroufe, L. A. (1994). Stages of friendship growth in preadolescence as related to attachment history. *Journal of Social and Personal Relationships, 11*(3), 341–361.

Simner, M. L. (1971). Newborn's response to the cry of another infant. *Developmental Psychology, 5*, 136–150.

Simpson, J. A., & Beckes, L. (2010). Evolutionary perspectives on prosocial behavior. In M. Mikulincer, & P. R. Shaver (Eds.), *Prosocial motives, emotions, and behavior: The better angels of our nature* (pp. 35–53). Washington, DC: American Psychological Association.

Simpson J. A., & Belsky, J. (2008). Attachment theory within a modern evolutionary framework. In P. R. Shaver & J. Cassidy (Eds.), *Handbook of attachment: Theory, research, and clinical applications* (2nd ed., pp. 131–157). New York, NY: Guilford.

Simpson, J. A., Rholes, W. S., & Nelligan, J. S. (1992). Support seeking and support giving within couples in an anxiety-provoking situation: The role of attachment styles. *Journal of Personality and Social Psychology, 62*, 434–446.

Simpson, J. A., Rholes, W. S., Oriña, M. M., & Grich, J. (2002). Working models of attachment, support giving, and support seeking in a stressful situation. *Personality and Social Psychology Bulletin, 28*, 598–608.

Simson, S. P., & Straus, M. C. (Eds.) (1998). *Horticulture as therapy: Principles and Practice.* New York, NY: Food Products Press.

Sin, N. L., & Lyubomirsky, S. (2009). Enhancing well-being and alleviating depressive symptoms with positive psychology interventions: A practice-friendly meta-analysis. *Journal of Clinical Psychology, 65*, 467–487.

Singer, T., Kiebel, S. J., Winston, J. S., Dolan, R. J., & Frith, C. D. (2004). Brain responses to the acquired moral status of faces. *Neuron, 41*, 653–662.

Singer, T., & Lamm, C. (2009). The social neuroscience of empathy. *Annals of the New York Academy of Sciences, 1156*, 81–96.

Singer, T., Seymour, B., O'Doherty, J., Kaube, H., Dolan, R. J., & Frith, C. D. (2004). Empathy for pain involves the affective but not sensory components of pain. *Science*, *303*, 1157–1162.

Singer, T., Seymour, B., O'Doherty, J. P., Stephan, K. E., Dolan, R. J., & Frith, C. D. (2006). Empathic neural responses are modulated by the perceived fairness of others. *Nature*, *439*(7075), 466–469.

Sluckin, A. (1998). Bonding failure:I don't know this baby, she's nothing to do with me'. *Clinical Child Psychology and Psychiatry*, *3*(1), 11–24.

Smetana, J. G., Campione-Barr, N., & Metzger, A. (2006). Adolescent development in interpersonal and societal contexts. *Annual Review of Psychology*, *57*, 255–284.

Smith, A. (2006). Cognitive empathy and emotional empathy in human behavior and evolution. *Psychological Record*, *56*, 3–21.

Smith, K. C. P., & Apter, M. J. (1977). Collecting antiques: A psychological interpretation. *Antique Collector*, *48*(7), 64–66.

Snyder, M., & DeBono, K. G. (1987). A functional approach to attitudes and persuasion. In M. P. Zanna, J. M. Olson, & C. P. Herman (Eds.), *Social influence: The Ontario symposium* (Vol. 5). Hillsdale, NJ: Erlbaum.

Sober, E., & Wilson, D. S. (1998). *Unto others: The evolution and psychology of unselfish behavior*. Cambridge, MA: Harvard University Press.

Solomon, J., & George, C. (1996). Defining the caregiving system: Toward a theory of caregiving. *Infant Mental Health Journal*, *17*, 183–197.

Solomon, J., George, C., & De Jong, A. (1995). Children classified as controlling at age six: Evidence of disorganized representational strategies and aggression at home and school. *Development and Psychopathology*, *7*, 447–464.

Spear, L. (2009). Heightened stress reactivity and emotional reactivity during pubertal maturation: Implications for psychopathology. *Development and Psychopathology*, *21*, 87–97.

Spitze, G., & Logan, J. (1990). Sons, daughters, and intergenerational social support. *Journal of Marriage and the Family*, *52*(2), 420–430.

Stallones, L., Marx, M. B., Garrity, T. F., & Johnson, T. P. (1990). Pet ownership and attachment in relation to the health of US adults, 21 to 64 years of age. *Anthrozoos*, *4*(2), 100–112.

Stapleton, L. R. T., Schetter, C. D., Westling, E., Rini, C., Glynn, L. M., Hobel, C. J., & Sandman, C. A. (2012). Perceived partner support in pregnancy predicts lower maternal and infant distress. *Journal of Family Psychology*, *26*(3), 453–463.

Stearns, S. C. (1976). Life-history tactics: a review of the ideas. *The Quarterly Review of Biology*, *51*(1), 3–47.

Stein, J. A., Riedel, M., & Rotheram-Borus, M. J. (1999). Parentification and its impact on adolescent children of parents with AIDS. *Family Process*, *38*(2), 193–208.

Steinberg, A. G., & Foley, D. M. (1999). Mentoring in the Army: From buzzword to practice. *Military Psychology*, *11*(4), 365–379.

Steinberg, D. R., & Pianta, R. C. (2006). Maternal representations of relationships: assessing multiple parenting dimensions. In O. Mayseless (Ed.). *Parenting representations: Theory, research, and clinical implications* (pp 41–78). New York, NY: Cambridge University Press.

Steinberg, L. (2001). We know some things: Parent-adolescent relationships in retrospect and prospect. *Journal of Research on Adolescence*, *11*(1), 1–19.

Steinberg, L. (2008). A social neuroscience perspective on adolescent risk-taking. *Developmental Review*, *28*(1), 78–106.

Stepney, P., & Davis, P. (2004). Mental health, social inclusion and the green agenda: An evaluation of a land based rehabilitation project designed to promote occupational access and inclusion of service users in North Somerset, UK. *Social Work in Health Care*, *39*(3–4), 375–397.

Stern, N. D. (1995). *The motherhood constellation: A unified view of parent-infant psychotherapy*. New York, NY: Basic books.

Stewart, A. J., & Vandewater, E. A. (1998). The course of generativity. In D. P. McAdams & E. de St. Aubin (Eds.), *Generativity and adult development: How and why we care for the next genera-tion* (pp. 75–100). Washington, DC: American Psychological Association.

Stewart, R. B. (1983). Sibling attachment relationships: Child–infant interaction in the strange situation. *Developmental Psychology, 19*(2), 192–199.

Stokols, D. (1990). Instrumental and spiritual views of people-environment relations. *American Psychologist, 45*(5), 641–646.

Su, R., Rounds, J., & Armstrong, P. I. (2009). Men and things, women and people: a meta-analysis of sex differences in interests. *Psychological Bulletin, 135*(6), 859–884.

Suomi, S. J. (1978). Maternal behavior by socially incompetent monkeys: Neglect and abuse of offspring. *Journal of Pediatric Psychology, 3*(1), 28–34.

Svetlova, M., Nichols, S. R., & Brownell, C. A. (2010). Toddlers' prosocial behavior: From instrumental to empathic to altruistic helping. *Child Development, 81*(6), 1814–1827.

Switzer, G. E., Simmons, R. G., Dew, M. A., Regalski, J. M., & Wang, C. H. (1995). The effect of a school-based helper program on adolescent self-image, attitudes, and behavior. *The Journal of Early Adolescence, 15*(4), 429–455.

Tajfel, H. (1970). Experiments in intergroup discrimination. *Scientific American, 223*, 96–102.

Tajfel, H. (Ed.). (1978). *Differentiation between social groups: Studies in the social psychology of inter-group relations*. London, England: Academic Press.

Tajfel, H., & Turner, J. C. (1986). The social identity theory of intergroup behavior. In S. Worchel & W. G. Austin (Eds.), *The social psychology of intergroup relations* (pp. 7–24). Chicago, IL: Nelson-Hall.

Tart, C. T. (1975/1992). *Transpersonal psychologies: Perspectives on the mind from seven great spiritual traditions*. New York, NY: Harper & Row.

Taubman–Ben-Ari, O., Findler, L., & Ben Shlomo, S. B. (2013). When couples become grandpar-ents: Factors associated with the growth of each spouse. *Social Work Research, 37*(1), 26–36.

Taylor, S. (2002). *The tending instinct: Women, men, and the biology of relationships*. New York, NY: Henry Holt.

Taylor, S. E., Klein, L. C., Lewis, B. P., Gruenewald, T. L., Gurung, R. A. R., & Updegraff, J. A. (2000). Biobehavioral responses to stress in females: Tend-and-befriend, not fight-or-flight. *Psychological Review, 107*, 411–429.

Theodoridou, A., Rowe, A. C., Penton-Voak, I. S., & Rogers, P. J. (2009). Oxytocin and social perception: Oxytocin increases perceived facial trustworthiness and attractiveness. *Hormones and Behavior, 56*(1), 128–132.

Thoits, P. A., & Hewitt, L. N. (2001). Volunteer work and well being. *Journal of Health and Social Behavior, 42*, 115–131.

Thomas, D. A. (1993). Racial dynamics in cross-race developmental relationships. *Administrative Science Quarterly, 38*(2), 169–194.

Thornton, A., & Raihani, N. J. (2008). The evolution of teaching. *Animal Behaviour, 75*(6), 1823–1836.

Tinbergen, N. (1963). On aims and methods of ethology. *Zeitschrift für Tierpsychologie, 20*, 410–433.

Toi, M., & Batson, C. D. (1982). More evidence that empathy is a source of altruistic motivation. *Journal of Personality and Social Psychology, 43*, 281–292.

Torrance, E. P. (1984). *Mentor relationships: How they aid creative achievement, endure, change, and die*. New York: Bearly Limited.

Trivers, R. L. (1971). The evolution of reciprocal altruism. *Quarterly review of Biology, 46*, 35–57.

Trivers, R. L. (1972). Parental investment and sexual selection. In B. Campbell (Ed.), *Sexual selection and the descent of man, 1871–1971* (pp. 136–179). Chicago, IL: Aldine.

Trivers, R. L. (1974). Parent-offspring conflict. *American Zoologist, 14*, 249–264.

Tse, M. M. Y. (2010). Therapeutic effects of an indoor gardening programme for older people living in nursing homes. *Journal of clinical nursing, 19*(7–8), 949–958.

Twigger-Ross, C. L., & Uzzell, D. L. (1996). Place and identity processes. *Journal of Environmental Psychology, 16,* 205–220.

Ulrich, R. S. (1984).View through a window may influence recovery from surgery. *Science, 224,* 420–421.

Ulrich, R. S., Simons, R. F., Losito, B. D., Fiorito, E., Miles, M. A., & Zelson, M. (1991). Stress recovery during exposure to natural and urban environments. *Journal of Environmental Psychology, 11* (3), 201–230.

Umberson, D., & Gove, W. R. (1989). Parenthood and psychological well-being theory, measurement, and stage in the family life course. *Journal of Family Issues, 10*(4), 440–462.

Urry, H. L., Nitschke, J. B., Dolski, I., Jackson, D. C., Dalton, K. M., Mueller, C. J., . . . Davidson, R. J. (2004). Making a life worth living: Neural correlates of well-being. *Psychological Science, 15,* 367–372.

Uvnäs-Moberg, K. (1998) Oxytocin may mediate the benefits of positive social interaction and emotions. *Psychoneuroendocrinology, 23,* 819–835.

Vaish, A., Carpenter, M., & Tomasello, M. (2009). Sympathy through affective perspective taking and its relation to prosocial behavior in toddlers. *Developmental psychology, 45*(2), 534–543.

Vaish, A., Carpenter, M., & Tomasello, M. (2010). Young children selectively avoid helping people with harmful intentions. *Child development, 81*(6), 1661–1669.

Valleau, M. P., Bergner, R. M., & Horton, C. B. (1995). Parentification and caretaker syndrome: An empirical investigation. *Family Therapy, 22,* 157–164.

Van den Berg, A. E., & Custers, M. H. G. (2011). Gardening promotes euroendocrine and affective restoration from stress. *Journal of Health Psychology, 16,* 3–11.

Van IJzendoorn, M. (1995). Adult attachment representations, parental responsiveness, and infant attachment: A meta-analysis on the predictive validity of the Adult Attachment Interview. *Psychological Bulletin, 117,* 387–403.

Van IJzendoorn, M. H., Bakermans-Kranenburg, M. J. (2012). A sniff of trust: Meta-analysis of the effects of intranasal oxytocin administration on face recognition, trust to in-group, and trust to out-group. *Psychoneuroendocrinology, 37,* 438–443.

Van Lange, P. A. M., De Cremer, D., & Van Dijk, E., & Van Vugt, M. (2007). From aggression to altruism: Basic principles of social interaction. In E. T. Higgins & A. W. Kruglanski (Eds.), *Social psychology: Handbook of basic principles* (pp. 540–561). New York, NY: Guilford Press.

Van Lange, P. A. M., Otten, W., De Bruin, E. M. N., & Joireman, J. A. (1997). Development of prosocial, individualistic, and competitive orientations: Theory and preliminary evidence. *Journal of Personality and Social Psychology, 73,* 733–746.

Van Vugt, M. (2006). Evolutionary origins of leadership and followership. *Personality and Social Psychology Review, 10,* 354–371.

Van Vugt, M., De Cremer, D., & Janssen, D. P. (2007). Gender differences in cooperation and competition the Male-Warrior hypothesis. *Psychological science, 18*(1), 19–23.

Van Vugt, M., & Hardy, C. L. (2009). Cooperation for reputation: Wasteful contributions as costly signals in public goods. *Group Processes & Intergroup Relations, 13,* 101–111.

Van Vugt, M., Hogan, R., & Kaiser, R. B. (2008). Leadership, followership, and evolution: some lessons from the past. *American Psychologist, 63*(3), 182–196.

Van Vugt, M., Jepson, S. F., Hart, C. M., & De Cremer, D. (2004). Autocratic leadership in social dilemmas: A threat to group stability. *Journal of Experimental Social Psychology, 40*(1), 1–13.

Van Vugt, M., & Park, J. H. (2009). The tribal instinct hypothesis: Evolution and the psychology of intergroup relations. In S. Stürmer & M. Snyder (Eds.), *The psychology of prosocial behavior: Group processes, intergroup relations, and helping* (pp. 13–32). Oxford, UK: Wiley-Blackwell.

Van Vugt, M., Roberts, G., & Hardy, C. (2007). Competitive altruism: Development of reputation-based cooperation in groups. In R. Dunbar & L. Barrett (Eds.), *Handbook of evolutionary psychology* (pp. 531–540). Oxford, England: Oxford University Press.

Van Vugt, M., & Schaller, M. (2008). Evolutionary approaches to group dynamics: An introduction. *Group Dynamics: Theory, Research, and Practice, 12*(1), 1–6.

Van Willigen, M. (2000). Differential benefits of volunteering across the life course. *Journals of Gerontology Series B: Psychological Sciences and Social Sciences, 55B, S308–S318.*

Vangelisti, A. L. (2009). Challenges in conceptualizing social support. *Journal of Social and Personal Relationships, 26*(1), 39–51.

Varese, F. and Yaish, M. (2000). The importance of being asked: The rescue of Jews in Nazi Europe. *Rationality and Society, 12* (3), 307–334.

Veening, J. G., & Olivier, B. (2013). Intranasal administration of oxytocin: Behavioral and clinical effects, a review. *Neuroscience & Biobehavioral Reviews, 37*(8), 1445–1465

Veevers, J. (1980). *Childless by choice.* Toronto, Canada: Butterworths.

Vigoda-Gadot, E. (2007). Redrawing the boundaries of OCB? An empirical examination of compulsory extra-role behavior in the workplace. *Journal of Business and Psychology, 21*(3), 377–405.

Vincent, J. (1996). Why ever do we do it? Unconscious motivation in choosing social work as a career. *Journal of Social Work Practice, 10*(1), 63–69.

Vitaliano, P. P., Zhang, J., & Scanlan, J. M. (2003). Is caregiving hazardous to one's physical health? A meta-analysis. *Psychological Bulletin, 129,* 946–972.

Walker, A. J., Pratt, C. C., Shin, H. Y., & Jones, L. (1989). Why daughters care: Perspectives of mothers and daughters in a caregiving situation. In J. Mancini (Ed.), *Aging parents and adult children* (pp. 199–210). Lexington, MA: Lexington Books.

Walker, A. J., Pratt, C. C., Shin, H. Y., & Jones, L. (1990). Motives for parental caregiving and relationship quality, *Family Relations, 39,* 51–56.

Walker, L. J., Frimer, J. A., & Dunlop, W. L. (2010). Varieties of moral personality: Beyond the banality of heroism. *Journal of personality, 78*(3), 907–942.

Walker, L. J., & Hennig, K. H. (2004). Differing conceptions of moral exemplarity: Just, brave, and caring. *Journal of Personality and Social Psychology, 86*(4), 629–647.

Walsh, F. (2009a). Human-animal bonds I: The relational significance of companion animals. *Family Process, 48*(4), 462–480.

Walsh, F. (2009b). Human-animal bonds II: The role of pets in family systems and family therapy. *Family Process, 48*(4): 481–499.

Walsh, R., & Vaughan, F. (1993). On transpersonal definitions. *Journal of Transpersonal Psychology, 25,* 125–182.

Walter, H. (2012). Social cognitive neuroscience of empathy: Concepts, circuits, and genes. *Emotion Review, 4*(1), 9–17.

Wang, Z. X., Liu, Y., Young, L. J., & Insel, T. R. (2000). Hypothalamic vasopressin gene expression increases in both males and females postpartum in a biparental rodent. *Journal of neuroendocrinology, 12*(2), 111–120.

Warburton, J., & Gooch, M. (2007). Stewardship volunteering by older Australians: The generative response. *Local Environment, 12*(1), 43–55.

Warburton, J., & McLaughlin, D. (2006). Doing it from your heart: the role of older women as informal volunteers. *Journal of Women & Aging, 18*(2), 55–72.

Warburton, J., & Terry, D. J. (2000). Volunteer decision making by older people: A test of a revised theory of planned behavior. *Basic and Applied Social Psychology, 22,* 245–257.

Warneken, F., Hare, B., Melis, A. P., Hanus, D., & Tomasello, M. (2007). Spontaneous altruism by chimpanzees and young children. *PLoS Biology, 5*(7), 1414–1420.

Warneken, F., & Tomasello, M. (2006). Altruistic helping in human infants and young chimpanzees. *Science, 311*(5765), 1301–1303.

Warneken, F., & Tomasello, M. (2007). Helping and cooperation at 14 months of age. *Infancy, 11,* 271–294.

Warneken, F., & Tomasello, M. (2008). Extrinsic rewards undermine altruistic tendencies in 20-month-olds. *Developmental Psychology, 44,* 1785–1788.

Warneken, F., & Tomasello, M. (2009). The roots of human altruism. *British Journal of Psychology*, *100*(3), 455–471.

Warneken, F., & Tomasello, M. (2013). Parental presence and encouragement do not influence helping in young children. *Infancy*, *18*, 345–368.

Waterman, A. S. (1990). The relevance of Aristotle's conception of eudaimonia for the psychological study of happiness. *Journal of Theoretical and Philosophical Psychology*, *10*(1), 39–44.

Waterman, A. S. (1993). Two conceptions of happiness: Contrasts of personal expressiveness (eudaimonia) and hedonic enjoyment. *Journal of Personality and Social Psychology*, *64*, 678–691.

Watkins, S. C. (1984). Spinsters. *Journal of Family History*, *9*(4), 310–325.

Watson, M. W., & Fischer, K. W. (1977). A developmental sequence of agent use in late infancy. *Child Development*, *48*, 828–836.

Watson, M. W., & Fischer, K. W. (1980). Development of social roles in elicited and spontaneous behavior during the preschool years. *Developmental Psychology*, *16*(5), 483–494.

Weiler, L., Haddock, S., Zimmerman, T. S., Krafchick, J., Henry, K., Rudisill, S. (2013). Benefits derived by college students from mentoring at-risk youth in a service-learning course. *American Journal of Community Psychology*, *52*, 236–248.

Weinstein, N., Przybylski, A. K., & Ryan, R. M. (2009). Can nature make us more caring? Effects of immersion in nature on intrinsic aspirations and generosity. *Personality and Social Psychology Bulletin*, *35*(10), 1315–1329.

Weinstein, N., & Ryan, R. M. (2010). When helping helps: Autonomous motivation for prosocial behavior and its influence on well-being for the helper and recipient. *Journal of Personality and Social Psychology*, *98*(2), 222.

Weir, D. R. (1984). Rather never than late: Celibacy and age at marriage in English cohort fertility, 1541–1871. *Journal of Family History*, *9*, 340–354.

Weisberg, Y. J., DeYoung, C. G., & Hirsh, J. B. (2011). Gender differences in personality across the ten aspects of the Big Five. *Frontiers in Psychology*, *2*, 178–178.

Weiss, R. S. (1974). The provisions of social relationships. In Z. Rubin (Ed.), *Doing unto others* (pp. 17–26). Englewood Cliffs, NJ: Prentice-Hall.

Weller, D., & Lagattuta, H. K. (2013). Helping the in-group feels better: Children's judgments and emotion attributions in response to prosocial dilemmas. *Child Development*, *84*, 253–268.

Weller, D., & Lagattuta, H. K., (2014). Children's judgments about prosocial decisions and emotions: Gender of the helper and recipient matters. *Child Development*, *85*, 2011–2028

Wells, D. L. (2009). The effects of animals on human health and well-being. *Journal of Social Issues*, *65*(3), 523–543.

Wells, M., & Perrine, R. (2001). Pets go to college: The influence of pets on students' perceptions of faculty and their offices. *Anthrozoos*, *14*(3), 161–168.

Wentzel, K. R. (1997). Student motivation in middle school: The role of perceived pedagogical caring. *Journal of Educational Psychology*, *89*, 411–417.

Wentzel, K. R. (2002). Are effective teachers like good parents? Teaching styles and student adjustment in early adolescence. *Child Development*, *73*, 287–301.

Wentzel, K. R., & Asher, S. R. (1995). Academic lives of neglected, rejected, popular, and controversial children. *Child Development*, *66*, 754–763.

Werner E. E., & Smith, E. S. (1982).*Vulnerable but invincible: A study of resilient children*. New York, NY: McGraw Hill.

West, M. L., & Keller, A. E. (1991). Parentification of the child: A case study of Bowlby's compulsive care-giving attachment pattern. *American Journal of Psychotherapy*, *45*(3), 425–431.

West, S. A., Griffin, A. S., & Gardner, A. (2007). Social semantics: Altruism, cooperation, mutualism, strong reciprocity and group selection. *Journal of Evolutionary Biology*, *20*, 415–432.

Westneat, D. F., & Sherman, P. W. (1993). Parentage and the evolution of parental behavior. *Behavioral Ecology*, *4*, 66–77.

White, M. P., & Dolan, P. (2009). Accounting for the richness of daily activities. *Psychological Science, 20*(8), 1000–1008.

Whiting, B. B., & Whiting, J. W. M. (1975). *Children of 6 cultures: A psychocultural analysis.* Cambridge, MA: Harvard University Press

Wiepking, P., & Maas, I. (2009). Resources that make you generous: Effects of social and human resources on charitable giving. *Social Forces, 87,* 1973–1995.

Wilber, K. A. (2000). *Integral psychology: Consciousness, spirit, psychology, therapy.* Boston, MA: Shambhala Publications.

Wildiger, T. A., & Presnall, J. R. (2012). Pathological altruism and personality disorders. In B. Oakley, A. Knafo, G. Madhavan, & D. Wilson (Eds.), *Pathological altruism* (pp. 85–93). New York, NY: Oxford University Press.

Williams, G. C. (1966). Natural selection, the costs of reproduction, and a refinement of Lack's principle. *American Naturalist, 100*(916), 687–690.

Williams, T., & Kornblum, W. (1985). *Growing up poor.* Lexington, MA: Lexington Books.

Wilson, D. S., & Sober, E. (1994). Reintroducing group selection to the human behavioral sciences. *Behavioral and Brain Sciences, 17*(04), 585–608.

Wilson, E. O. (1984). Biophilia: The human bond with other species. Cambridge, MA: Harvard University Press.

Wilson, J. (2000). Volunteering. *Annual Review of Sociology, 26,* 215–240.

Wilson, J., & Musick, M. (1997). Who cares? Toward an integrated theory of volunteer work. *American Sociological Review, 62,* 694–713.

Winnicott, D. W. (1965). *Maturational processes and the facilitating environment: Studies in the theory of emotional development.* London, England: Hogarth Press.

Wirtberg, I., Möller, A., Hogström, L., Tronstad, S. E., & Lalos, A. (2007). Life 20 years after unsuccessful infertility treatment. *Human Reproduction, 22*(2), 598–604.

Wong, P. T. P. (1998). Meaning-centered counseling. In P. T. P. Wong & P. S. Fry (Eds.), *The human quest for meaning: A handbook of research and clinical applications* (pp. 395–435). Mahwah, NJ: Erlbaum.

Wong, P. T. P., & Fry, P. S. (Eds.). (1998). *The human quest for meaning: A handbook of research and clinical applications.* Mahwah, NJ: Erlbaum.

Wood, W., & Eagly, A. H. (2002). A cross-cultural analysis of the behavior of women and men: Implications for the origins of sex differences. *Psychological Bulletin, 128,* 699–727.

Wooster, M. M. (2000, September). Ordinary people, extraordinary rescues. *American Enterprise, 11,* 18–21.

Wu, N., Li, Z., Su, Y. (2012) The association between oxytocin receptor gene polymorphism (OXTR) and trait empathy. *Journal of Affective Disorders, 138,* 468–472.

Wuthnow, R. (1991). *Acts of compassion: Caring for others and helping ourselves.* Princeton, NJ: Princeton University Press.

Wynne-Edwards, V. C. (1962). *Animal dispersion in relation to social behaviour.* Edinburgh: Oliver & Boyd Ltd

Xu, X., Zuo, X., Wang, X., & Han, S. (2009). Do you feel my pain? Racial group membership modulates empathic neural responses. *The Journal of Neuroscience, 29*(26), 8525–8529.

Yamasue, H., Yee, J. R., Hurlemann, R., Rilling, J. K., Chen, F. S., Meyer-Lindenberg, A., & Tost, H. (2012).Integrative approaches utilizing oxytocin to Enhance prosocial behavior: From animal and human social behavior to autistic social dysfunction. *The Journal of Neuroscience, 32*(41), 14109–14117.

Yavas, U., & Riecken, G. (1985). Can volunteers be targeted? *Journal of the Academy of Marketing Science, 13,* 218–28.

Yoder, L. H. (1992). A descriptive study of mentoring relationships experienced by Army nurses in head nurse or nursing supervisor roles. *Military Medicine, 157*(10), 518–523.

Young, L. J., & Flanagan-Cato, L. M. (2012). Editorial comment: oxytocin, vasopressin and social behavior. *Hormones and behavior, 61*(3), 227–229.

Zaccaro, S. J., Gilbert, J. A., Thor, K. K., & Mumford, M. D. (1991). Leadership and social intelligence: Linking social perspectiveness and behavioral flexibility to leader effectiveness. *The Leadership Quarterly, 2*(4), 317–342.

Zahn-Waxler, C., Radke-Yarrow, M., Wagner, E., & Chapman, M. (1992). Development of concern for others. *Developmental Psychology, 28,* 126–136.

Zahn-Waxler, C., Robinson, J. L., & Emde, R. N. (1992). The development of empathy in twins. *Developmental Psychology, 28*(6), 1038–1047.

Zak, P. J., Kurzban, R., & Matzner, W. T. (2005). Oxytocin is associated with human trustworthiness. *Hormones and Behavior, 48*(5), 522–527.

Zak, P. J., Stanton, A. A., & Ahmadi, S. (2007). Oxytocin increases generosity in humans. *PLoS One, 2*(11), e1128.

Zeanah, C. H., & Benoit, D. (1995). Clinical applications of a parent perception interview in infant mental health. *Child and Adolescent Psychiatric Clinics of North America, 4,* 539–554.

Zerubavel, N., & Wright, M. O'D. (2012). The dilemma of the wounded healer. *Psychotherapy: Theory, Research, Practice, Training, 49*(4), 482–491.

Zimolag, U. (2011). An evolutionary concept analysis of caring for a pet as an everyday occupation. *Journal of Occupational Science, 18,* 237–253.

ABOUT THE AUTHOR

Ofra Mayseless, PhD, is a professor of developmental psychology at the Faculty of Education, University of Haifa, Israel, and a certified clinical psychologist. She served as Dean of the Faculty of Education, University of Haifa, and as Head of the National Pedagogical Secretariat at the Ministry of Education, Israel. Her research spans over 80 published articles and chapters and two edited books focused on close relationships and children's, adolescents', and adults' attachment manifestations. She has also studied caring processes in parenting, leadership, mentoring, and role reversal and investigated the transition to adulthood in the Israeli context using longitudinal studies and multimethod, multireporter, and mixed methods research designs. Her current research focuses on the caregiving/nurturing motivational system and on spiritual development.

INDEX

The Caring Motivation

Meyer, M. L., Masten, C. L., Ma, Y., Wang, C., Shi, Z., Eisenberger, N. I., & Han, S. (2013). Empathy for the social suffering of friends and strangers recruits distinct patterns of brain activation. *Social Cognitive and Affective Neuroscience, 8*(4), 446–454.

Meyer-Bahlburg, H. F., Dolezal, C., Baker, S. W., Carlson, A. D., Obeid, J. S. & New, M. I. (2004). Prenatal androgenization affects gender-related behavior but not gender identity in 5–12-year-old girls with congenital adrenal hyperplasia. *Archives of Sexual Behavior, 33*(2), 97–104.

Mikolajczak, M., Gross, J. J., Lane, A., Corneille, O., de Timary, P., & Luminet, O. (2010). Oxytocin makes people trusting, not gullible. *Psychological Science, 21*(8), 1072–1074.

Mikolajczak, M., Pinon, N., Lane, A., de Timary, P., & Luminet, O. (2010). Oxytocin not only increases trust when money is at stake, but also when confidential information is in the balance. *Biological Psychology, 85*(1), 182–184.

Mikulincer, M., Gillath, O., Halevy, V., Avihou, N., Avidan, S., & Eshkoli, N. (2001). Attachment theory and reactions to others' needs: Evidence that activation of the sense of attachment security promotes empathic responses. *Journal of Personality and Social Psychology, 81,* 1205–1224.

Mikulincer, M., Gillath, O., Sapir-Lavid, Y., Yaakobi, E., Arias, K.,Tal-Aloni, L., & Bor, G. (2003). Attachment theory and concern for others' welfare: Evidence that activation of the sense of secure base promotes endorsement of self-transcendence values. *Basic and Applied Social Psychology, 25,* 299–312.

Mikulincer, M., & Shaver, P. R. (2001). Attachment theory and intergroup bias: Evidence that priming the secure base schema attenuates negative reactions to out-groups. *Journal of Personality and Social Psychology, 81,* 97–115.

Mikulincer, M., & Shaver, P. R. (2007a). *Attachment in adulthood: Structure, dynamics, and change.* New York, NY: Guilford Press.

Mikulincer, M., & Shaver, P. R. (2007b). Boosting attachment security to promote mental health, prosocial values, and inter-group tolerance. *Psychological Inquiry, 18,* 139–156.

Mikulincer, M., & Shaver P. R. (Eds.) (2010). *Prosocial motives, emotions, and behavior: The better angels of our nature.* Washington, DC: American Psychological Association.

Mikulincer, M., Shaver, P. R., Gillath, O., & Nitzberg, R. A. (2005). Attachment, caregiving, and altruism: Boosting attachment security increases compassion and helping. *Journal of Personality and Social Psychology, 89,* 817–839.

Mikulincer, M., Shaver, P. R., Sahdra, B. K., & Bar-On, N. (2013). Can security-enhancing interventions overcome psychological barriers to responsiveness in couple relationships? *Attachment & Human Development, 15,* 246–260.

Miles, I., Sullivan, W. C., & Kuo, F. E. (1998). Ecological restoration volunteers: The benefits of participation. *Urban Ecosystems, 2,* 27–41.

Milkman, R. (1987). *Gender at work: The dynamics of job segregation by sex during World War II.* Urbana: University of Illinois Press.

Millan, L. R., Azevedo, R. S., Rossi, E., De Marco, O. L. N., Millan, M. P. B., & Arruda, P. C. V. D. (2005). What is behind a student's choice for becoming a doctor? *Clinics, 60*(2), 143–150.

Millar, S. (1968). *The psychology of play.* New York, NY: Penguin Books.

Miller, J. B. (1982). *Toward a new psychology of women.* Boston, MA: Beacon Press. (Original work published 1976.)

Miller, L. J. (Ed.). (2012). *The Oxford handbook of psychology and spirituality.* New York, NY: Oxford University Press.

Milligan, C., Gatrell, A., & Bingley, A. (2004). "Cultivating health": Therapeutic landscapes and older people in northern England. *Social Science & Medicine, 58,* 1781–1793.

Mills, J., & Clark, M. S. (1982). Exchange and communal relationships. *Review of Personality and Social Psychology, 3,* 121–144.

Misener, K., Doherty, A., & Hamm-Kerwin, S. (2010). Learning from the experiences of older adult volunteers in sport: A serious leisure perspective. *Journal of Leisure Research, 42*(2), 267–289.

Misselhorn, C. (2009). Empathy with inanimate objects and the uncanny valley. *Minds and Machines, 19*(3), 345–359.

Moen, P., Robison, J., & Fields, V. (1994). Women's work and caregiving roles: A life course approach. *Journal of Gerontology, 49*, 176–186.

Moll, J., Krueger, F., Zahn, R., Pardini, M., de Oliveira-Souza, R., & Grafman, J. (2006). Human fronto-mesolimbic networks guide decisions about charitable donation. *Proceedings of the National Academy of Sciences of the United States of America, 103*, 15623–15628.

Møller, A. P., & Cuervo, J. J. (2000). The evolution of paternity and paternal care in birds. *Behavioral Ecology, 11*(5), 472–485.

Monroe, K. R. (1996). *The heart of altruism: Perceptions of a common humanity.* Princeton, NJ: Princeton University Press.

Monroe, K. R., Barton, M. C., & Klingemann, U. (1990). Altruism and the theory of natural action: Rescuers of Jews in Nazi Europe. *Ethics, 101*, 103–122.

Moore, C. (2009). Fairness in children's resource allocation depends on the recipient. *Psychological Science, 20*(8), 944–948.

Moore, E. O. (1982). A prison environment's effect on health care service demands. *Journal of Environmental Systems, 11*, 17–34.

Murdoch, I. (1971). *The sovereignty of good over other concepts.* New York, NY: Schocken.

Murdock, G. P. (1967). Ethnographic atlas: A summary. *Ethnology, 6*, 109–236.

Murdock, G. P. (1981). *Atlas of world cultures.* Pittsburgh, PA: University of Pittsburgh Press.

Murdock, G. P., & Provost, C. (1973). Measurement of cultural complexity. *Ethnology, 12*, 379–392.

Murdock, G. P., & White, D. R. (1969). Standard cross-cultural sample. *Ethnology, 8*, 329–369.

Murdock, T. B., & Miller, A. (2003). Teachers as sources of middle school students' motivational identity: Variable-centered and person-centered analytic approaches. *The Elementary School Journal, 103*, 383–399.

Musick, M. A., Herzog, A. R., & House, J. S. (1999). Volunteering and mortality among older adults: Findings from a national sample. *Journals of Gerontology Series B: Psychological Sciences and Social Sciences, 54*, S173–S180.

Naber, F., van IJzendoorn, M. H., Deschamps, P., van Engeland, H., & Bakermans-Kranenburg, M. J. (2010). Intranasal oxytocin increases fathers' observed responsiveness during play with their children: a double-blind within-subject experiment. *Psychoneuroendocrinology, 35*(10), 1583–1586.

Nadler, A., Malloy, T., & Fisher, J. D. (Eds.). (2008). *The social psychology of inter group reconciliation.* New York, NY: Oxford University Press.

Nagasawa, M., Kikusui, T., Onaka, T., & Ohta, M. (2009). Dog's gaze at its owner increases owner's urinary oxytocin during social interaction. *Hormones and Behavior, 55*, 434–441.

Narushima, M. (2005). "Payback time": community volunteering among older adults as a trans-formative mechanism. *Ageing and Society, 25*, 567–584.

Nassauer, J. I. (1988). The aesthetics of horticulture: Neatness as a form of care. *HortScience, 23*, 973–977.

Nelson, S. K., Kushlev, K., English, T., Dunn, E. W., & Lyubomirsky, S. (2013). In defense of parenthood: Children are associated with more joy than misery. *Psychological Science, 24*(1), 3–10.

Nelson, S. K., Kushlev, K., & Lyubomirsky, S. (2014). The pains and pleasures of parenting: When, why, and how is parenthood associated with more or less well-being? *Psychological Bulletin, 140*, 846–895.

Newson, J., & Newson, E. (1968). *Four years old in an urban community.* Harmondsworth, England: Penguin.

Nias, J. (1989). *Primary teachers talking: A study of teaching as work.* London, England: Routledge.

Nicholson, N. (2005). Objections to evolutionary psychology: Reflections, implications and the leadership exemplar. *Human Relations, 58*(3), 393–409.

Nielsen, M. (2012). Imitation, pretend play, and childhood. Essential elements in the evolution of human culture? *Journal of Comparative Psychology, 126*(2), 170–181.

Noddings, N. (2003). *Caring: A feminine approach to ethics and moral education* (2nd ed.). Berkeley, CA: University of California Press. (Original work published 1984.)

Noddings, N. (2005). *The challenge to care in schools: An alternative approach to education* (2nd ed.). New York, NY: Teachers College Press. (Original work published 1992.)

Norcross, J. C., & Farber, B. A. (2005). Choosing psychotherapy as a career: Beyond "I want to help people". *Journal of Clinical Psychology, 61*(8), 939–943.

Nordenström, A., Servin, A., Bohlin, G., Larsson, A., & Wedell, A. (2002). Sex-typed toy play behavior correlates with the degree of prenatal androgen exposure assessed by CYP21 genotype in girls with congenital adrenal hyperplasia. *The Journal of Clinical Endocrinology & Metabolism, 87*(11), 5119–5124.

Norman, R. E., Byambaa, M., De, R., Butchart, A., Scott, J., & Vos, T. (2012). The long-term health consequences of child physical abuse, emotional abuse, and neglect: a systematic review and meta-analysis. *PLoS Medicine, 98*(11), e1001349–1.

Nydegger, C. N. (1991). The development of parental and filial maturity. In K. Pillemer & K. McCartney (Eds.), *Parent-child relation throughout life* (pp. 93–112). Hillsdale, NJ: Erlbaum.

Oakley, B., Knafo, A., Madhavan, G., & Wilson, D. S. (Eds.). (2012). *Pathological altruism.* New York, NY: Oxford University Press.

Oakley, B., Knafo, A., & McGrath, M. (2012). Pathological altruism—an introduction. In B. Oakley, A. Knafo, G. Madhavan, & D. Wilson (Eds.), *Pathological altruism* (pp. 3–9). New York, NY: Oxford University Press.

O'Brien, G. (1981). Living with collections. *New York Times Magazine,* April 26, Part 2, 25–42.

O'Connor, L. E., Berry, J. W., Lewis, T. B., & Stiver, D. J. (2012). Empathy-based pathogenic guilt, pathological altruism, and psychopathology. In B. Oakley, A. Knafo, G. Madhavan, & D. Wilson (Eds.), *Pathological altruism* (pp. 10–30). New York, NY: Oxford University Press.

Okun, M. A., Barr, A., & Herzog, A. R. (1998). Motivation to volunteer by older adults: A test of competing measurement models. *Psychology and Aging, 13,* 608–621.

Okun, M. A., Yeung, E. W., & Brown, S. (2013). Volunteering by older adults and risk of mortality: A meta-analysis. *Psychology and Aging, 28,* 564–577.

Oliner, P. M., & Oliner, S. P. (1995). *Toward a caring society: Ideas into action.* Westport, CT: Praeger.

Oliner, S. P. (2001). Heroic altruism: Heroic and moral behavior in a variety of settings. In *Remembering for the future 2000: Papers and proceedings: Vol. 2. Ethics and religion* (pp. 319–333). London, England: Palgrave.

Oliner, S. P. (2002). Extraordinary acts of ordinary people: Faces of heroism and altruism. In S. G. Post, L. G. Underwood, J. P. Schloss, & W. B. Hurlbut (Eds.), *Altruism and altruistic love: Science, philosophy and religion in dialogue* (pp. 123–139). New York, NY: Oxford University Press.

Oliner, S. P. (2005). Altruism, forgiveness, empathy, and intergroup apology. *Humboldt Journal of Social Relations, 29*(2), 8–39.

Oliner, S. P., & Zylicz, P. O. (2008). *Altruism, intergroup apology, forgiveness, and reconciliation.* St. Paul, MN: Paragon House.

Oliner, S. P., & Oliner, P. M. (1988). *The altruistic personality: Rescuers of Jews in Nazi Europe.* New York, NY: Free Press.

Omoto, A., & Snyder, M. (1995). Sustained helping without obligation: Motivation, longevity of service, and perceived attitude change among AIDS volunteers. *Journal of Personality and Social Psychology, 68,* 671–686.

Ongley, S. F., & Malti, T. (2014). The role of moral emotions in the development of children's sharing behavior. *Developmental Psychology, 50*(4), 1148–1159.

Organ, D. W. (1988). *Organizational citizenship behavior: The good soldier syndrome.* Lexington, MA: Lexington Books.

Organ, D. W., Podsakoff, P. M., & MacKenzie, S. B. (2006). *Organizational citizenship behavior: Its nature, antecedents, and consequences.* Beverly Hills, CA: Sage.

Padilla-Walker L. M., & Carlo, G. (Eds.), (2014). Prosocial development: A multidimensional approach. New York, NY: Oxford University Press.

Padilla-Walker, L. M., & Christensen, K. J. (2011). Empathy and self-regulation as mediators between parenting and adolescents' prosocial behavior toward strangers, friends, and family. *Journal of Research on Adolescence, 21*(3), 545–551.

Padilla-Walker, L. M., Dyer, W. J., Yorgason, J. B., Fraser, A. M., & Coyne, S. M. (2015). Adolescents' prosocial behavior toward family, friends, and strangers: A person-centered approach. *Journal of Research on Adolescence, 25*(1), 135–150.

Padilla-Walker, L. M., Harper, J. M., & Jensen, A. C. (2010). Self-Regulation as a mediator between sibling relationship quality and early adolescents' positive and negative outcomes. *Journal of Family Psychology, 24,* 419–428.

Paquette, D. (2004). Theorizing the father-child relationship: Mechanisms and developmental outcomes. *Human Development, 47,* 193–219.

Pargament, K. I. (Editor in chief), (2013). *APA handbook of psychology, religion, and spirituality* (Vol.1 and Vol. 2). Washington DC: American Psychological Association

Park, C. L., & Folkman, S. (1997). Stability and change in psychosocial resources during caregiving and bereavement in partners of men with AIDS. *Journal of Personality, 65,* 421–447.

Parke, R. D. (1996). *Fatherhood.* Cambridge, MA: Harvard University Press.

Parker, R. (1995). *Mother love/mother hate: The power of maternal ambivalence.* New York, NY: Basic Books.

Parsons, R., Tassinary, L. G., Ulrich, R. S., Hebl, M. R., & Grossman-Alexander, M. (1998) The view from the road: implications for stress recovery and immunization. *Journal of Environmental Psychology, 18,* 113–140.

Parten, M. (1933). Social play among preschool children. *Journal of Abnormal and Social Psychology, 28,* 136–147.

Pasterski, V. L., Geffner, M. E., Brain, C., Hindmarsh, P., Brook, C., & Hines, M., (2005). Prenatal hormones and postnatal socialization by parents as determinants of male-typical toy play in girls with congenital adrenal hyperplasia. *Child Develoment, 76,* 264–278.

Paulus, M. (2014). The emergence of prosocial behavior: why do infants and toddlers help, comfort, and share?. *Child Development Perspectives, 8*(2), 77–81.

Paulus, M., Kühn-Popp, N., Licata, M., Sodian, B., & Meinhardt, J. (2013). Neural correlates of prosocial behavior in infancy: different neurophysiological mechanisms support the emergence of helping and comforting. *Neuroimage, 66,* 522–530.

Pedersen, C. A. (1997). Oxytocin control of maternal behavior regulation by sex steroids and offspring stimulia. *Annals of the New York Academy of Sciences,807*(1), 126–145.

Pellegrini, A. D. (Ed.). (2010). *The Oxford handbook of the development of play.* New York, NY: Oxford University Press.

Penner, L. A. (2002). Dispositional and organizational influences on sustained volunteerism: An interactionist perspective. *Journal of Social Issues, 58,* 447–467.

Penner, L. A., Dovidio, J. E., Piliavin, J. A., & Schroeder, D. A. (2005). Prosocial behavior: Multilevel perspectives. *Annual Review of Psychology, 56,* 365–392.

Penner, L. A., & Fritzsche, B. A. (1993). *Measuring the prosocial personality: Four construct validity studies.* Toronto, Ontario, Canada: American Psychological Association.

Penner, L. A., Fritzsche, B. A., Craiger, J. P., & Freifeld, T. R. (1995). Measuring the prosocial personality. In J. Butcher & C. D. Spielberger (Eds.), *Advances in personality assessment.* (Vol. 10, pp. 147–163). Hillsdale, NJ: Erlbaum.

Penner, L. A., & Orom, H. (2010). Enduring goodness: A person by situation perspective on prosocial behavior. In M. Mikulincer, &. P. Shaver (Eds.), *Prosocial motives, emotions, and behaviors: The better angels of our nature* (pp. 55–72). Washington, DC: American Psychological Association.

Pérusse, D., Neale, M. C., Heath, A. C., & Eaves, L. J. (1994). Human parental behavior: Evidence for genetic influence and potential implication for gene-culture transmission. *Behavior Genetics, 24,* 327–335.

Peterson, B. E., & Klohnen, E. C. (1995). Realization of generativity in two samples of women at midlife. *Psychology and Aging, 10,* 20–29.

Peterson B. E., Smirles K. A., Wentworth P. A. (1997). Generativity and authoritarianism: Implications for personality, political involvement, and parenting. *Journal of Personality and Social Psychology, 72,* 1202–1216.

Phibbs, E. J., & Relf, D. (2005). Improving research on youth gardening. *HortTechnology, 15*(3), 425–428.

Pianta, R. C. (Ed.) (1992). *New directions for child development: Vol. 57. Beyond the parent: The role of other adults in children's lives.* San Francisco, CA: Jossey Bass.

Pianta, R. C., & Stuhlman, M. W. (2004). Teacher-child relationships and children's success in the first years of school. *School Psychology Review, 33*(3), pp. 444–458

Piedmont, R. L. (1999). Does spirituality represent the sixth factor of personality? Spiritual transcendence and the five-factor model. *Journal of Personality, 67,* 985–1013.

Piff, P. K., Kraus, M. W., Côté, S., Cheng, B. H., & Keltner, D. (2010). Having less, giving more: The influence of social class on prosocial behavior. *Journal of Personality and Social Psychology, 99*(5), 771–784.

Piliavin, J. A., Dovidio, J. F., Gaertner, S. L., & Clark, R. D., III. (1981). *Emergency intervention.* New York, NY: Academic Press.

Piliavin, J. A., & Siegl, E. (2007). Health benefits of volunteering in the Wisconsin longitudinal study. *Journal of Health and Social Behavior, 48*(4), 450–464.

Pillemer, K., Fuller-Rowell, T. E., Reid, M. C., & Wells, N. M. (2010). Environmental volunteering and health outcomes over a 20-year period. *Gerontologist, 50*(5), 594–602.

Pinquart, M., & Sörensen, S. (2003). Differences between caregivers and noncaregivers in psychological health and physical health: a meta-analysis. *Psychology and Aging, 18*(2), 250–267.

Podbersek, A. L., Paul, E. S., & Serpell, J. A. (Eds.). (2000). *Companion animals and us: Exploring the relationships between people and pets.* Cambridge, England: Cambridge University Press.

Podsakoff, P. M., MacKenzie, S. B., Paine, J. B., & Bachrach, D. G. (2000). Organizational citizenship behaviors: A critical review of the theoretical and empirical literature and suggestions for future research. *Journal of Management, 26*(3), 513–563.

Popper, M., & Mayseless, O. (2003). Back to basics: Applying a parenting perspective to transformational leadership. *The Leadership Quarterly, 14,* 41–65.

Post, S. G. (2007). *Altruism and health: Perspectives from empirical research.* New York, NY: Oxford University Press.

Post, S. G., Underwood, L. G., Schloss, J. P., & Hurlbut, W. B. (2002). *Altruism and altruistic love: Science, philosophy, and religion in dialogue.* New York, NY: Oxford University Press.

Poulin, M. J., Brown, S. L., Ubel, P. A., Smith, D. M., Jankovic, A., & Langa, K. M. (2010). Does a helping hand mean a heavy heart? Helping behavior and well-being among spouse caregivers. *Psychology and Aging, 25,* 108–117.

Prati, G., & Pietrantoni, L. (2009). Optimism, social support, and coping strategies as factors contributing to posttraumatic growth: A meta-analysis. *Journal of Loss and Trauma, 14*(5), 364–388.

Pratt, M. W., & Lawford, H. L. (2014). Early generativity and types of civic engagement in adolescence and emerging adulthood. In L. M. Padilla-Walker & G. Carlo (Eds.), *Prosocial development: A multidimensional approach* (pp. 410–436). New York, NY: Oxford University Press.

Pratt, M. W., Norris, J. E., Arnold, M. L., & Filyer, R. (1999). Generativity and moral development as predictors of value-socialization narratives for young persons across the adult life span: From lessons learned to stories shared. *Psychology and Aging, 14,* 414–426.

Preston, S. D., & De Waal, F. (2002). Empathy: Its ultimate and proximate bases. *Behavioral and Brain Sciences, 25*(01), 1–20.

Price, T. D., Qvarnström, A., & Irwin, D. E. (2003). The role of phenotypic plasticity in driving genetic evolution. *Proceedings of the Royal Society of London. Series B: Biological Sciences, 270*(1523), 1433–1440.

Prior, M. (2002). Nostalgia renews collectibles long-lost spotlight status. *DSN Retailing Today, 41*, 25.

Pryce, C. R. (1995). Determinants of motherhood in human and nonhuman primates: A biosocial model. In C. R. Pryce, R. D. Martin, & D. Skuse (Eds.), *Motherhood in human and nonhuman primates* (pp. 1–15). Basel: Karger.

Pryce, C. R. (1996). Socialization, hormones, and the regulation of maternal behavior in nonhuman simian primates. *Advances in the Study of Behaviour, 25*, 423–476.

Ragins, B. R., & Kram, K. E. (Eds.) (2007a). *The handbook of mentoring at work: Theory, research, and practice.* Thousand Oaks, CA: Sage.

Ragins, B. R., & Kram, K. E. (2007b). The roots and meaning of mentoring. In B. R. Ragins & K. E. Kram (Eds.), *The handbook of mentoring at work: Theory, research, and practice* (pp. 3–15). Thousand Oaks, CA: Sage.

Ragins, B. R., & Scandura, T. A. (1999). Burden or blessing? Expected costs and benefits of being a mentor. *Journal of Organizational Behavior, 20*, 493–509.

Rand, D. G., Greene, J. D., Nowak, M. A. (2012). Spontaneous giving and calculated greed. *Nature, 489*, 427–430.

Reis, H. T. (2000). Caregiving, attachment, and relationships. *Psychological Inquiry, 11*, 120–123.

Reis, H. T., Clark, M. S., & Holmes, J. G. (2004). Perceived partner responsiveness as an organizing construct in the study of intimacy and closeness. In D. Mashek & A. Aron (Eds.), *The handbook of closeness and intimacy* (pp. 201–225). Mahwah, NJ: Erlbaum.

Reis, H. T., Smith, S. M., Carmichael, C. L., Caprariello, P. A., Tsai, F. F., Rodrigues, A., & Maniaci, M. R. (2010). Are you happy for me? How sharing positive events with others provides personal and interpersonal benefits. *Journal of Personality and Social Psychology, 99*(2), 311–329.

Reis, H. T., & Shaver, P. R. (1988). Intimacy as an interpersonal process. In S. Duck (Ed.), *Handbook of research in personal relationships* (pp. 367–389). Chichester, England: Wiley.

Repetti, R. L. (1989). Effects of daily workload on subsequent behaviour during marital interactions: The role of social withdrawal and spouse support. *Journal of Personality and Social Psychology, 57*, 651–659.

Repetti, R. L., & Wood, J. (1997). Effects of daily stress at work on mothers' interactions with preschoolers. *Journal of Family Psychology, 11*, 90–108

Rheingold, H. L., & Emery, G. N. (1986). The nurturant acts of very young children. In D. Otweus, J. Block, & M. Radke-Yarrow (Eds.), *The development of anti- and prosocial behavior* (pp. 75–96). New York, NY: Academic Press.

Rhodes, J. E. (2002). *Stand by me: The risks and rewards of mentoring today's youth.* Cambridge, MA: Harvard University Press.

Rholes, W. S., Simpson, J. A., Campbell, L., & Grich, J. (2001). Adult attachment and the transition to parenthood. *Journal of Personality and Social Psychology, 81*(3), 421–435.

Rholes, W. S., Simpson, J. A., & Orina, M. M. (1999). Attachment and anger in an anxiety-provoking situation. *Journal of Personality and Social Psychology, 76*, 940–957.

Rich, A. (1976). *Of woman born: Motherhood as experience and institution.* New York, NY: W.W. Norton.

Richerson, P. J., & Boyd, R. (2005). *Not by genes alone: How culture transformed human evolution.* Chicago, Illinois: University of Chicago Press.

Riem, M. M., Bakermans-Kranenburg, M. J., Pieper, S., Tops, M., Boksem, M. A., Vermeiren, R. R., . . . Rombouts, S. A. (2011). Oxytocin modulates amygdala, insula, and inferior frontal gyrus responses to infant crying: A randomized controlled trial. *Biological Psychiatry*, 70, 291–297.

Rilling, J. K., DeMarco, A. C., Hackett, P. D., Chen, X., Gautam, P., Stair, S., . . . & Pagnoni, G. (2014). Sex differences in the neural and behavioral response to intranasal oxytocin and vasopressin during human social interaction. *Psychoneuroendocrinology*, 39, 237–248.

Rilling, J. K., DeMarco, A. C., Hackett, P. D., Thompson, R., Ditzen, B., Patel, R., & Pagnoni, G. (2012). Effects of intranasal oxytocin and vasopressin on cooperative behavior and associated brain activity in men. *Psychoneuroendocrinology*, 37(4), 447–461.

Rilling, J. K., Gutman, D. A., Zeh, T. R., Pagnoni, G., Berns, G. S., & Kilts, C. D. (2002). A neural basis for social cooperation. *Neuron*, 35, 395–405.

Ritvo, H. (1987). The emergence of modern pet-keeping. *Anthrozoos*, 1, 158–165.

Rizzolatti, G., & Craighero, L. (2004). The mirror-neuron system. *Annual Review of Neuroscience*, 27, 169–192.

Robak, R. W., & Griffin, P. W. (2000). Purpose in life: What is its relationship to happiness, depression, and grieving?. *North American Journal of Psychology*, 2, 113–119.

Robbins, P., Polderman, A., & Birkenholtz, T. (2001). Lawns and toxins: an ecology of the city. *Cities*, 18(6), 369–380.

Robinson, C. W., & Zajicek, J. M. (2005). Growing minds: The effects of a one-year school garden program on six constructs of life skills of elementary school children. *HortTechnology*, 15(3), 453–457.

Rodrigues, S. M., Saslow, L. R., Garcia, N., John, O. P., Keltner, D., (2009). Oxytocin receptor genetic variation relates to empathy and stress reactivity in humans. *Proceedings of the National Academy of Sciences of the U. S. A.*, 106(50), 21437–21441.

Rogers, D. L., & Webb, J. (1991). The ethic of caring in teacher education. *Journal of Teacher Education*, 42(3), 173–181

Rook, K. S. (1989). Strains in older adults' friendships. In R. G. Adams & R. Blieszner (Eds), *Older adult friendships: Structure and processes* (pp. 164–194). Newbury Park, CA: Sage.

Rosch, E. (1973), 'Natural categories', *Cognitive Psychology*, 4, 328–350.

Rosch, E. (1999). Reclaiming concepts. *Journal of Consciousness Studies*, 6(11–12), 61–77.

Rosch, E. and Mervis, C. B. (1975). Family resemblances: Studies in the internal structure of categories. *Cognitive Psychology*, 7, 573–605.

Rose, A. J., & Rudolph, K. D. (2006). A review of sex differences in peer relationship processes: Potential trade-offs for the emotional and behavioral development of girls and boys. *Psychological bulletin*, 132(1), 98–131.

Rose, S. (2005). *Transforming the world: Bringing the new age into focus*. Bern: Peter Lang.

Rothberg, D. J., Kelly, S. M., & Kelly, S. (Eds.). (1998). *Ken Wilber in dialogue: Conversations with leading transpersonal thinkers*. Wheaton, IL: Quest Books.

Ruddick, S. (1995). *Maternal thinking*. New York, NY: Beacon Press. (Original work published 1989)

Rushton, J. P. (1984). The altruistic personality: Evidence from laboratory, naturalistic, and self-report perspectives. In E. Staub, D. Bar-Tal, J. Karylowski, & J. Reykowski (Eds.), *Development and maintenance of prosocial behavior* (pp. 271–290). New York, NY: Plenum Press.

Rushton, J. P., Fulker, D. W., Neale, M. C., Nias, D. K. B., & Eysenck, H. J. (1986). Altruism and aggression: The heritability of individual differences. *Journal of Personality and Social Psychology*, 50(6), 1192–1198.

Russell, J. E. A., & Adams, D. M. (1997). The changing nature of mentoring in organizations: An introduction to the special issue on mentoring in organizations. *Journal of Vocational Behavior*, 51, 1–14.

Ryan, R. M., & Deci, E. L. (2000). Self-determination theory and the facilitation of intrinsic motivation, social development, and well-being. *American Psychologist*, 55, 68–78.

Ryan, R. M., & Deci, E. L. (2001). On happiness and human potentials: A review of research on hedonic and eudaimonic well-being. *Annual Review of Psychology*, 52, 141–166.

Ryff, C. D., & Singer, B. H. (2006). Best news yet on the six-factor model of well-being. *Social Science Research*, 35, 1103–1119.

Sabol, T. J., & Pianta, R. C. (2012). Recent trends in research on teacher–child relationships. *Attachment & Human Development*, 14, 213–231.

Sachs, J., & Devin, J. (1976). Young children's use of age-appropriate speech styles in social interaction and role-playing. *Journal of Child Language*, 3, 81–98.

Sage, R. A., & Johnson, M. K. (2012). Extending and expanding parenthood: Parental support to young adult children. *Sociology Compass*, 6(3), 256–270.

Sallquist, J., DiDonato, M. D., Hanish, L. D., Martin, C. L., & Fabes, R. A. (2012). The importance of mutual positive expressivity in social adjustment: Understanding the role of peers and gender. *Emotion*, 12(2), 304–313.

Sanefuji, W., Ohgami, H., & Hashiya, K. (2007). Development of preference for baby faces across species in humans (Homo sapiens). *Journal of Ethology*, 25, 249–254.

Saroglou, V., Delpierre, V., & Dernelle, R. (2004). Values and religiosity: A meta-analysis of studies using Schwartz's model. *Personality and Individual Differences*, 37(4), 721–734.

Scarr, S., & McCartney, K. (1983). How people make their own environments: A theory of genotype→ environment effects. *Child Development*, 54(2), 424–435.

Scharf, M., & Mayseless, O. (2001). The capacity for romantic intimacy: Exploring the contribution of best friend and marital and parental relationships. *Journal of Adolescence*, 24, 379–399.

Schino, G., Geminiani, S., Rosati, L., & Aureli, F. (2004). Behavioral and emotional response of Japanese Macaque (Macaca fuscata) mothers after their offspring receive an aggression. *Journal of Comparative Psychology*, 118(3), 340–346.

Schmuck, P., & Sheldon, K. (Eds.). (2001). *Life goals and well-being: Towards a positive psychology of human striving*. Kirkland, WA: Hogrefe & Huber.

Schneiderman, I., Kanat-Maymon, Y., Ebstein, R. P., & Feldman, R. (2013). Cumulative risk on the oxytocin receptor gene (OXTR) underpins empathic communication difficulties at the first stages of romantic love. *Social Cognitive and Affective Neuroscience*, 9(10), 1524–1529.

Scheiner, S. M. (1993). Genetics and evolution of phenotypic plasticity. *Annual Review of Ecology and Systematics*, 24, 35–68.

Schnell, T. (2011). Individual differences in meaning-making: Considering the variety of sources of meaning, their density and diversity. *Personality and Individual Differences*, 51(5), 667–673.

Schwartz, S. C. (2001). Narcissism in collecting art and antiques. *Journal of the American Academy of Psychoanalysis and Dynamic Psychiatry*, 29(4), 633–647.

Seiffge-Krenke, I. (2003). Testing theories of romantic development from adolescence to young adulthood: Evidence of a developmental sequence. *International Journal of Behavioral Development*, 27(6), 519–531.

Seligman, M. E. P., & Csikszentmihalyi, M. (2000). Positive psychology: An introduction. *American Psychologist*, 55, 5–14.

Sempik, J., Aldridge, J., & Becker, S. (2003). *Social and therapeutic horticulture: Evidence and messages from research*. Reading, England: Thrive with the Centre for Child and Family Research, Loughborough University.

Serpell, J. A. (1987). Pet-keeping in non-western societies. *Anthrozoos*, 1, 166–174.

Serpell, J. A. (1995). From paragon to pariah: Some reflections on human attitudes to dogs. In J. A. Serpell (Ed.), *The domestic dog: Its evolution, behaviour & interactions with people* (pp. 245–256). Cambridge, England: Cambridge University Press.

Shackelford, T. K., LeBlanc, G. J., & Drass, E. (2000). Emotional reactions to infidelity. *Cognition & Emotion*, 14(5), 643–659.

Shamay-Tsoory, S. G., Abu-Akel, A., Palgi, S., Sulieman, R., Fischer-Shofty, M., Levkovitz, Y., & Decety, J. (2013). Giving peace a chance: Oxytocin increases empathy to pain in the context of the Israeli–Palestinian conflict. *Psychoneuroendocrinology*, 38(12), 3139–3144.